UK Directory
of Property Developers,
Investors and Financiers

UK Directory of Property Developers, Investors and Financiers

Seventh edition

Edited by
Building Economics Bureau
5 Carlton Chambers
Station Road
Shortlands, Bromley
Kent BR2 0EY

E & FN SPON
An Imprint of Chapman & Hall
London · Glasgow · New York · Tokyo · Melbourne · Madras

**Published by E & FN Spon, an imprint of Chapman & Hall,
2–6 Boundary Row, London SE1 8HN, UK**

Chapman & Hall, 2–6 Boundary Row, London SE1 8HN, UK

Blackie Academic & Professional, Wester Cleddens Road,
Bishopbriggs, Glasgow G64 2NZ, UK

Chapman & Hall Inc., One Penn Plaza, 41st Floor, New York NY10119, USA

Chapman & Hall Japan, Thomson Publishing Japan, Hirakawacho
Nemoto Building, 6F, 1-7-11 Hirakawa-cho, Chiyoda-ku, Tokyo 102, Japan

Chapman & Hall Australia, Thomas Nelson Australia, 102 Dodds Street,
South Melbourne, Victoria 3205, Australia

Chapman & Hall India, R. Seshadri, 32 Second Main Road, CIT East,
Madras 600 035, India

First edition 1984, second edition 1986, third edition 1987,
fourth edition 1988, fifth edition 1990, sixth edition 1991

Seventh edition 1994

Printed in Great Britain by The Alden Press, Oxford

ISBN 0-419-18280-2

A catalogue record for this book is available from the British Library

∞ Printed on permanent acid-free text paper, manufactured in accordance with ANSI/NISO Z 39.48-1992 and ANSI/NISO Z39.48-1984 (Permanence of Paper).

Preface

This is the seventh edition of the UK Directory of Property Developers. Investors and Financiers which has proved to be an invaluable source of information in the property world. The first chapter comprises a commentary on property ownership and its aspects of finance and taxation by Geoffrey Parsons MSc BSc ARICS IRRV AILAM, Principal Lecturer, School of Land and Construction Management, University of Greenwich. This has been updated and expanded from its first appearance in the 1987/88 Directory to provide an authoritative view of this area of the property market as it stands today.

Chapters 2 – 8 are compiled from the editor's own research and questionnaire returns. Information shown is the latest provided at the time of compilation and, where applicable, dates are included.

All entries are listed free of charge and we would like to take this opportunity to thank all those companies and organisations who kindly provided information for inclusion.

Every care has been taken to make the lists as accurate as possible, but we cannot accept responsibility for errors or omissions. There will inevitably have been changes made in the information included since going to press; we would therefore welcome notification of any amendments concerning the listed companies.

“If you cannot find the information you require, or if you are aware of any discrepancies or important omissions, please telephone the BEB Helpline.”

BEB HELPLINE: 081-460 1111

OBTAINING GREATER VALUE IN EUROPEAN CONSTRUCTION

Building and Development Economics in the EC by Bernard Williams Associates
Financial Times Business Enterprises

At a time when costs are central to product specification and the building, construction and property development industries are being squeezed on margins more than ever, greater attention is being paid to the discipline of building economics.

Building and Development Economics in the EC, a timely new report from Financial Times, looks at the current state of the building, construction and development industries in each of the member countries of the EC in an impressive amount of detail. A glance at the comprehensive index shows that the authors, Bernard Williams Associates, have left no stone unturned in their thorough review of national economic policies and construction costs in each state. There is a whole chapter devoted to EC Development Activity, picking out areas where grants are most common and another concentrating on the different approaches to procurement. Other sections focus on the development budget with useful comparisons on construction costs, rents and yields.

The report culminates in a rigorous comparison of the factors influencing construction costs throughout the EC. This leads to thought-provoking conclusions about the relative efficiency of the industry in each state which will make grim reading for the British contingent amongst others.

Building and Development Economics in the EC will be useful to all those involved in building construction and property development in Europe. At last available in one volume - and the first to give equal weight to both sides of the industry - this report provides the necessary information to alert contractors, suppliers, specifiers and end-users to opportunities and pitfalls as they affect them directly.

Contents

Chapter 1

Property Ownership, Development, Taxation and Finance

Contents

INTRODUCTION

The first chapter of the Directory reviews some topics germane to property ownership, development process, investment, property taxation and finance. In the space available it does not seek to be comprehensive; merely exploratory and directive, i.e. in the sense that leads are given to some matters and to other sources of information.

Section 1 looks at the nature of property ownership in terms of status and objectives and touches upon direct and indirect property ownership, particularly by a reference to the so-called 'financial intermediaries'.

Section 2 looks at the property development process and property management.

Section 3 looks at aspects of property ownership in terms of investment policy and the factors affecting the quality of assets held in a portfolio.

Section 4 gathers together aspects of the general nature of national and local taxation as it affects property ownership, touching upon the changes to VAT and to rating. (Other aspects of taxation are also reviewed in later sections).

Section 5 highlights some of the basics of property funding, making a general distinction between corporate finance and project finance.

In sections 6 to 13 various 'corporate forms' for indirect investment are briefly considered and there is a commentary on the roles of such bodies as insurance companies, investment trusts, pension funds, property companies (both investment and dealing companies) and unit trusts including property unit trusts.

Sections 14 to 16 briefly examine bodies which are offering services (rather than beinginvolved in direct ownership), such as banks, building societies and finance houses.

The sections on property units (17) and the securities market (18) are offered in the ongoing and changing scene these topics portray. Finally, section 19 touches upon aspects of the protection of investors and others.

Legislation has required many changes of detail, particularly the legislation on capital allowances, VAT, and rating. However, many changes in practice and developments in the property markets cannot be examined within the scope of this part of the Directory. It cannot be stressed too strongly, therefore, that the need for proper professional and technical advice in property matters should be satisfied at the inception stages of any proposals.

1 PROPERTY OWNERSHIP AND THE MARKET

1.1 Objectives of direct property ownership

Generally, direct property ownership in the private sector falls into four groups: investment, dealing, business occupation and residential occupation. Any owner may be a developer in the sense that land is acquired and one or more buildings are built on it. Therefore, the objectives of ownership are apparent in holding the property and letting (as an investor); selling the property perhaps after letting (as a dealer); or occupying the buildings (for business, residential or leisure purposes). Moreover, the occupier may be either the owner of the freehold or a lessee (who holds an equity in the property). Apart from financial or economic targets, such as profit from dealing or return from investment, those holding property may have cultural, ethical or social objectives as well.

In the public sector, property ownership is 'functional', e.g. a sewerage works and railways, or 'objective'. e.g. schools, colleges, clinics, hospitals and similar uses. (Of course, schools, hospitals and so on are also 'business' property in the private sector.

The distinctions made above are particularly important for reasons of taxation.

1.2 Status

Direct ownership in one of these ways (or perhaps a mix of them) may be undertaken by an individual or some other legal 'person', e.g. a company, a trust or a charity. It is always important to be sure of status since it prescribes what can or cannot be done in respect of property. For instance, in general, charities are unable to deal in property. Also, status among other factors may be an important matter affecting liability to taxation.

1.3 Indirect property ownership

Persons with surplus funds may achieve indirect involvement in land and buildings in three general ways, one of which is to use a 'financial intermediary'. Thus a person may:

1. share in the ownership by financial devices, for instance, by investing in the shares of an investment company which buys property or develops land for long term holding;

2. invest by holding units in a unit trust, by owning property bonds or by holding a pension policy (or life insurance policy) in a pension fund (or life insurance company) which has a proportion of its assets in property: such assets may be either by direct holdings or indirectly in some other vehicle, such as shares in a property company; and

3. lend funds to another by mortgage or other device without the involvement of a financial intermediary, but this use of mortgages is probably not attractive to many investors.

Of course, individuals or companies who are dealers derive their income from the profits obtained from buying and selling property, or from buying land, building and selling. Others may share in any profit from such operations by investing in the shares of companies which trade in this way, e.g. volume house building companies which are quoted on the International Stock Exchange.

Other avenues for indirect investment in the field of property lie in such devices as company debenture stock or preference shares, some of which may be convertible to equities.

Similarly, mortgage bonds (when available), units in property (when they become available) and other devices, or variations of the above, afford opportunities for related investments.

1.4 *Kinds of owner*

Owners in the market for land and buildings fall into the four broad categories given in section 1.1, but a more specific division would include the following:

1. property investment companies (see section 11);
2. businesses, such as retailers, farmers and industrialists;
3. property dealing companies (see section 10);
4. pension funds (see section 8);
5. insurance companies (see section 6); and
6. property bonds (see section 9).

Wishing to get involved in property development, these and others may enter into various forms of 'partnership', such as joint venture companies, straight partnerships, side by side leasing arrangements, forward funding or project management arrangements. Sharing the equity in the project is a prime issue in such ventures.

1.5 *Financial intermediaries*

Some of those listed above have another function as 'financial intermediaries' in that the pension funds and insurance companies together with the building societies, the banks and finance houses are sources of funds which enable others to purchase existing property, to develop land or to refurbish or improve buildings.

These so-called financial intermediaries have the function of gathering together savings and other funds which are surplus for the time being and allocating some of them to borrowers. (They may, of course, develop land themselves). In society some considerable advantages accrue from the processes by which the financial intermediaries operate. For instance, they enable:

1. the development of expertise in structuring opportunities for savers to invest in ways which suit their particular requirements;
2. the switching by savers of funds from current investments into other investments when the need arises;
3. the structuring of opportunities to borrow funds or to participate in mixed borrowing and investment projects, e.g. by partnership arrangements; and
4. a distancing between savers and borrowers which removes or reduces the prospects of conflict and dissonance between them.

This is not to suggest that financial intermediaries do not create problems. Thus, in property development, their investment criteria for new projects may not entirely suit the needs of users. Similarly, their prudent investment policy may delay or squash the advent of innovation in the property market.

Similarly, a general shift of policy on investment allocations between sectors, say from property to equities, may depress the property market and alter the fund-seekers' routes to suppliers.

1.6 The 'property market'

It may be seen that in one sense the 'property market' is comprised of property owners on the one hand, and savers who provide funds on the others. The funds are, however, provided either directly or through a complex system of financial intermediaries. The financial intermediaries have a role of providing funds but some of them invest in property as well.

The other sense in which 'property market' is used pertains to the type of property in which interest is expressed, e.g. the office market, the industrial property market and so on. It is outside the scope of this section to review the property market (or markets).

Generally, the players in the market cluster into specific sectors. Thus, developers tend to specialise in one of house-building, developing industrial property, office development, leisure development and so on. On the other hand, investors, e.g. insurance companies, tend to spread their holdings in their portfolios into a number of market sectors so as to have a spread of offices, shops and industrial property. Nevertheless some specialise in a specific sector, e.g. some property unit trusts are 'in' agricultural property or 'in' industrial property in enterprise zones (in this instance, so as to catch the taxation reliefs which are available). Section 3 (below) highlights some of the issues which may influence developers, investors and others who are in the property market.

A dynamic aspect of the property market is spotting trends in one or other of its sectors. These may result from the needs of users, e.g. hi-tech requirements, or from other factors, e.g. taxation reliefs generating investment in enterprise zones to pick up the capital allowances and rates exemption.

1.7 Property research

Considerable research is undertaken into aspects of property, such as development, funding and investment. National and local government research is undertaken in-house or commissioned to consultancies or academic institutions. Also, many private research agencies have been created in recent years to look at a wide range problems for clients. Similarly, the larger real estate consultancies have created consultancy and research departments to undertake specific research projects for clients or to underpin other professional work undertaken in the business. Finally, the financial institutions, the professional bodies and other professional firms concerned with property matters undertake, commission or support with grants much property related research.

1.8 Information about companies

Information about companies is kept at the companies registration offices in Cardiff, Edinburgh and London.

2 ASPECTS OF PROPERTY OWNERSHIP

2.1 Property ownership, development and management

2.1.1 Introduction

On the one hand, the owner or prospective owner of one or more properties who intends to hold the estate for a long period, e.g. as an investor, is faced with a number of activities which must be undertaken if the wealth sunk into the property is to be maintained or enhanced. In planning for these activities there may, however, be conflict between what is good long-term management and stewardship of an estate and what is evidence of good short-term performance.

On the other hand, dealers are likely to have a relatively short-term viewpoint as far as individual properties are concerned. Nevertheless, the dealer may be expected to undertake many of the activities described below.

2.1.2 Property owner's objectives and documentation

The nature of property objectives was explored in section 1. Identification of requirements to meet measured or measurable objectives (in such matters as cost, time and quality) is needed, as well as careful corporate documentation to ensure that they are achieved. For instance, a company intent upon pursuing a number of objectives probably requires several corporate vehicles in a group to attain its intentions. Also, involvement in 'partnership' or joint ventures may require an appropriate 'vehicle' for this purpose.

2.1.3 Property development

Property development requires several activities to be undertaken. In this section they are only given in a general sequential order: in practice they are not likely to be so regular! Given the objectives and vehicle, the activities might include:

1. marketing research to evaluate the appropriate market segments in a particular property sector;

2. the formulation of the 'mix', once the segments have been identified, to satisfy their requirements;

3. search for land, effecting options, and the acquisition of interests in property for dealing, investment or occupation, i.e. once appropriate planning enquiries have been made and any necessary consents obtained;

4. management of acquired land, obtaining possession, demolition, fencing and clearance;

5. the procurement of new buildings using one of the many approaches, e.g. 'design and build', 'traditional', and 'project management';

6. raising funds, either by a 'corporate approach' or by 'project funding' (see section 5);

7. promotion and agency, either to let or sell the completed building or to commission for owner-occupation; and

8. evaluating taxation consequences of proposed transactions, development, funding or other activities.

The objectives of the land owner may influence the approach adopted in terms of joint venture projects or partnership arrangements (see section 1.4).

2.1.4 Property management

Once the buildings have been completed and occupied a new phase of their life begins. Property management is required on a planned basis to ensure that they meet occupiers' requirements and maintain their worth to the owner (who may be an investor or the owner-occupier). The management will involve both day to day activities and deeper study and action. The latter is sometimes referred to as 'active management' and requires the estate manager to spot opportunities for, say, redevelopment; major refurbishment; or acquisition of adjoining property, perhaps to realise marriage value. Generally, property management includes:

1. maintenance and repair of buildings, plant and machinery, and fixtures, fittings and furniture in buildings;
2. insurance against numerous perils affecting buildings, occupiers and other persons, including fire insurance, consequential loss of rent, and employer's compulsory insurance;
3. assessment of rent on letting, on review or on renewal of leases;
4. obtaining possession from tenants for the purposes of redevelopment or for other reasons, including the settlement of compensation claims for disturbance and any improvements, if appropriate;
5. management of vacant property prior to re-letting, or demolition for redevelopment;
6. re-letting, or breaking of leases;
7. evaluations for improvements, redevelopment or disposal;
8. disposal by sales, assignments, or grants of leases, by gifts, or by other means;
9. funding acquisitions, repairs, maintenance, refurbishment and development projects; and
10. planning to avoid or mitigate tax burdens and to take advantage of particular tax incentives, e.g. capital allowances (see section 4).

Property management requires a comprehensive property records system to include: rent roll; estate terrier; caution system; minor and major works programmes; storage arrangements for deeds, agreements and plans; and a library. Taxation records need to be kept, particularly for service charges and capital allowances.

2.2 Pre-occupations and objectives

What the owner does with the estate is derived from needs and pre-occupations which give rise to the policies adopted in carrying out the activities listed in section 2.1. Essentially these relate to motivations leading to investment, dealing or owner-occupation, although non-financial, cultural, ethical or social motivations will usually be apparent as well. It is outside the scope of this review to seek explanations of property ownership which are of a psychological nature.

From a practical perspective these 'motivations' lead to objectives which require the formulation of plans and budgets. Once the operations commence there is a requirement to monitor performance continuously against the standards laid down from time to time. Also, there is a need to monitor changes in the estate's local, regional and national environments.

2.3 *Performance appraisal*

Estate or portfolio standards are likely to require re-appraisal and this function requires knowledge of the environment in which the estate exists and the knowledge and skills to appraise the activities listed above.

At a different level of conceptualisation, continued investment in the estate may be compared with other opportunities to invest, e.g. in equities or gilts, Similarly, where individual properties in the portfolio are not performing in a way commensurate with the risk involved, rationalisation of the holdings will be effected and new investments sought. In particular, this would appear to be the process undertaken by the financial institutions, e.g. the pension funds in making any relative shift from property to other investment sectors, or vice versa.

Of course, not all owners have the resources to appraise their estates as fully as may be suggested above, but the function is one which the financial institutions in particular have been concerned to develop and progress. It follows that an owner's criteria for investment should be fully established and appraised.

As far as valuations of property assets belonging to institutions and companies are concerned, the 1970s and later development of accounting standards was and is linked with the development of valuation and standards practice. Thus, the Assets Valuation Standards Committee of the Royal Institution of Chartered Surveyors has produced numerous Guidance Notes Background Papers on the subject.

2.4 *Ownership and professional advice*

The activities of development and management of property are usually technically, economically and legally complex and therefore require a host of individuals with relevant knowledge, skills and experience to undertake them. The professions represented in a large scheme of development or refurbishment might include accountants, architects, insurers, builders, building surveyors, environmental services engineers, estate agents, land surveyors, landscape architects, lawyers, project managers, property managers, quantity surveyors, structural engineers, taxation consultants and valuation surveyors.

Similarly, funding a property scheme is likely to include several of the following: accountants, commercial and merchant bankers, finance brokers, fund managers, insurers, lawyers, stockbrokers, taxation consultants and valuers.

3 INVESTMENT POLICY

3.1 Property investment criteria

The traditional criteria for investment are sufficient to indicate the general range of relative considerations which must be made in selecting a field or sector of investment as well as a particular property. Thus, the investor will have the following in mind:

1. the prospect of capital being enhanced or at least maintained in real terms;
2. the prospect that income will be regularly received and will grow or be maintained in real terms;
3. management will be relatively inexpensive and the burden of outgoings may be shifted to tenants;
4. any national or local taxation incentives, exemptions, reliefs, and concessions are enjoyed to the full;
5. recognising that property is relatively illiquid, the capital may be readily realised at a reasonable expected cost;
6. opportunities for redevelopment or at least improvement will be achievable in due course;
7. the size in capital terms of any single property is suitable for a balanced portfolio;
8. the duration or lead-time to the effectiveness of decisions, e.g. development decisions, may need several years before fruit is borne, or disposal may take several months before net proceeds are received;
9. the spread of the investment both geographically and by sector (property or otherwise);
10. the availability of short, medium or long-term funds for purchase or for development having regard to the risk and the size of the property; and
11. the degree to which risks can be minimised or shifted to others, e.g. by taking out insurance policies against the happening of particular perils.

Professional property evaluation and management requires a wide and deep range of knowledge and skills in legal, financial, economic, technical and other areas. To the extent that individuals and other persons wish to invest indirectly in property the quality of advice and its application by those who manage the estate are of considerable importance.

An indication of the range of services available from professional consultants, agents and others is given in section 2.4 above.

3.2 Factors influencing property investment

It is not only the general quality of the investment which should be considered by investors in property, but also the environment or society in which it exists. At an international level, broad issues of a country's stability, e.g. political, economic and social, require attention. In this context restraints on ownership of property by foreigners to the home country and relative currency fluctuations may be important.

Within a national boundary, location is paramount so that a review is made and judgement is formed on such factors as:

1. population: size, socio-economic composition, age structure, mobility, health and morale;

2. workforce: composition, size, knowledge and skills, availability and mobility;

3. transport and communications infrastructure: road, rail, air and waterways, ports and airports, various utilities and their aggregate disposition;

4. planning fiscal and other 'governmental' policies: structure and local planning policies, scope for implementation, Enterprise Zones, assisted area status, and so on;

5. amenities and attractions: range and quality of housing, shopping, educational and training facilities, leisure and tourist facilities, art, entertainment and other cultural resources;

6. accommodation: business, cultural, tourist and residential, particularly its composition, quality and quantity;

7. state of the property market: values (capital and rental), cost of development and the quality of its processes, e.g. political, planning and financial;

8. the effect of national, regional and local policies for economic development, planning and other governmental provision;

9. the level of recent, past, current and planned capital investment in the area;

10. any predominance of employment opportunities which may be threatened by long-term structural changes in the economy; and

11. the quality of the image and identity of the area.

3.3 Quality of a property portfolio

The quality of a property portfolio will be reflected in the following:

1. the age of its buildings, their cost-in-use, condition and quality to meet the needs of occupiers and the investment criteria of the owners;

2. the spread of holdings in different sectors, i.e. industrial, offices, shops, agricultural, forestry, leisure and others;

3. the geographical spread either internationally or within the United Kingdom;

4. the pattern of tenures, e.g. freeholds, long leases and short leases;

5. the ease of management, e.g. good security arrangements, rent reviews and full repairing insuring leases;

6. the abilities of the tenants in terms of paying the rent and meeting their obligations under their leases;

7. the financial acumen of management and the financial resources in hand or on call to meet immediate needs for repair and maintenance, and in the longer term, for expansion and rationalisation;

8. the gearing of the portfolio's underlying financial resources, i.e. as a measure of vulnerability to adverse income or capital changes; and

9. the quality of the operations undertaken by management and professional advisers to improve the long-term standing of the estate with an achievable plan of operations.

Where the current performance of the portfolio is being measured short-term considerations may outweigh a longer-term perspective.

4 PROPERTY TAXATION

4.1 Introduction

4.1.1 Professional context

Property ownership is inseparable from property taxation and the importance of taxation and property cannot be over-stressed. Before implementing any proposal for a transaction or a development, an evaluation should be made of the prospective tax burden arising from investment in property; from construction of certain buildings and structures; and from certain ways of disposal or occupation of property. This section gives a broad overview of the main taxes affecting property. Other aspects of taxation may be found in subsequent sections, particularly where status, the property itself or other factors influence the burden of tax.

Generally, and at the risk of over simplification, a person may arrange affairs to take advantage of the tax exemptions and reliefs which are available. However, statutory provisions which seek to counter avoidance of tax do exist, e.g. section 776 of the Income and Corporation Taxes Act 1988; also, case law has moved against avoidance of tax.

It follows that property taxation is an area where professional advice should be obtained before transactions or works are commenced. In the context of property this usually requires joint consideration by the accountant, lawyer and surveyor.

4.1.2 Government policy

Government policy over nearly two centuries has laid down the broad structure of national taxation, with increasing detail since 1945. The annual Budget and consequential Finance Act provides incremental changes each year, sometimes with wide ranging effects. From time to time the legislation is consolidated, as follows:

(a) the Capital Allowances Act 1990;

(b) the Taxation of Chargeable Gains Act 1992;

(c) the Value Added Tax Act 1983;

(d) the Inheritance Tax Act 1984; and

(e) the Income and Corporation Taxes Act 1988.

Thus, there are three principal groups of taxes: income taxation, capital taxation and consumption taxation:

1. income taxation covers income tax and corporation tax;

2. capital taxation covers capital gains tax and inheritance tax; and

3. consumption taxation (for the purposes of this section) covers rates, value added tax and stamp duty.

4.2 Income taxation

4.2.1 Introduction

The Income and Corporation Taxes Act 1988, as amended, provides for incomes to be taxed on an annual basis.

Generally, income taxation falls into two broad categories;

1. income tax which is charged on the taxable incomes which individuals have each year. The rates range from 20% to 40% under the Finance Acts.

2. corporation tax on the taxable income and gains of large companies. The basic rate tax is 33%. (Smaller companies suffer tax at 25% with marginal relief – see section 13 of the Income and Corporation Taxes Act 1988).

The government's policy in recent years has been a general lowering of both income tax and corporation tax rates.

4.2.2 Schedule A

Rents from leases in the United Kingdom and premiums on short leases (50 years or less) and certain other items are assessed under Schedule A. (Certain premiums and deemed premiums on the grant of short leases may also suffer capital gains tax.)

The assessment of rents to income taxation is based on the gross rent receivable less permitted deductions. The chargeable amount of a premium is the premium reduced by 2% of the premium for each year of the lease except the first. Where a lease is let at a 'full rent' there are rules governing the right to carry forward losses during the currency of the lease or to offset in the same year a loss on one property against the profit from another (the so-called pooling arrangements).

4.2.3 Schedule B

Woodlands occupied and managed on a commercial basis with a view to making a profit were in the first instance assessed under Schedule B (assessment under Schedule D Case I could also be elected). The assessment under Schedule B was 1/3 of the annual value of the land in its natural and unimproved state. When profits were made such an assessment was likely to be very low. Election to Schedule D Case I would result in taxation as if the enterprise were a trade. In such cases any losses would have been absorbed and capital allowances may have been available for capital expenditure on forestry buildings (see section 4.4). As a result of Schedule 6 of the Finance Act 1988, forestry is being phased out of this beneficial tax regime (which will come to an end in 1993 after transitional provisions), i.e. Schedule B is no longer available. The election is only available until 6 April 1993 for certain taxpayers.

4.2.4 Schedule D Case I

Dealing in property, e.g. house-building, is assessed under Schedule D Case I of the Income and Corporation Taxes Act 1988, i.e. on annual profit. Where a person is trading, expenditure on land and buildings or on the erection of buildings is treated as revenue expenditure and, where wholly and exclusively incurred for the purposes of trade, is brought into the computation of profit. Section 74 of the 1988 Act sets down the limitations on revenue expenditure (see section 10).

4.2.5 Schedule D Case VI

Schedule D Case VI covers numerous sources of income. Three are dealt with here.

Rents from furnished lettings are assessed to gross rent received less allowable deductions. Provision is made for election to allow the taxpayer to take the net income from the accommodation to Schedule A for pooling purposes, i.e. for offsetting losses. (The rent for the furniture remains in Schedule D Case VI.) Rents from holiday lettings are assessed under the Schedule, but if the taxpayer meets the criteria given in sections 503 and 504 of the Income and Corporation Taxes Act 1988, a holiday letting will be dressed with the advantages of being treated as trade.

Section 776 of the Income and Corporation Taxes Act 1988 provides a pitfall for those seeking to avoid tax in certain kinds of land transactions. Cases pertinent to section 776 include: *Yuill* v *Wilson* (1980); *Page* v *Lowther and Another* (1983) and *Sugarwhite* v *Budd* (1988).

4.2.6 Schedule F

Dividends from shares in property companies are assessed under Schedule F. The basic rate of income tax is deducted at source from dividends received by shareholders. It is then allowed as advanced corporation tax (ACT) against any liability the company has to pay that tax.

4.2.7 Conclusion

The list is by no means exhaustive and belies the technical minefield of taxation confronting the investor, dealer or business. It may be borne in mind that numerous exemptions, reliefs and concessions exist. For instance, capital allowances under the Capital Allowances Act 1990, as amended, may be available to the taxpayer whereby the cost of construction of a building or of plant and machinery may be set against rental income or business profits to arrive at taxable income. (See section 4.4 below.)

4.3 *Expenditure on property*

It is important to identify expenditure on property as either capital expenditure or revenue expenditure. It will then be allocated to the correct assessment for the purposes of taxation. For instance, investors tend to hold property for long periods and expenditure by the landlord on such matters as repairs, maintenance, insurance, management and services are generally set against gross income to find the profit or loss under Schedule A or Schedule D Case VI. A similar approach is adopted in determining the profit of trades, professions or vocations under Schedule D Cases I or II, e.g. for retailers, farmers and architects.

Generally, investor landlords (or businesses owning and occupying buildings) will find that the expenditure on acquiring them and on improving them will be treated as capital expenditure. Capital expenditure is not normally allowed against income as a revenue deduction, but may be allowable for capital gains tax.

The only depreciation of capital assets allowed to landlord investors or businesses for income taxation purposes is that given as 'capital allowances' by the Capital Allowances Act 1990 and various Finance Acts. Thus, for certain types of building and for qualifying plant and machinery, capital expenditure is deductible under the regime for capital allowances. Large sums may arise and it may be prudent to review all development projects where no claims have been made previously.

It should be borne in mind, however, that the cost of buying stock-in-trade of dealers in land, e.g. house-building companies, is revenue expenditure. Thus, the cost of land, the expenditure on construction of buildings and associated costs, e.g. advertising and sales costs, will be used against turnover to ascertain profits under Schedule D Case I. On other hand, the cost of land and buildings occupied by farmers, retailers, industrialists is expenditure on capital assets and may feature in future capital gains tax computations on disposals, subject to roll-over relief or retirement relief.

4.4 Capital allowances

4.4.1 Government policy

From time to time governments have introduced capital allowances as a means of recognising the consumption of assets by a business or more pertinently to encourage particular forms of investment, e.g. thermal insulation in industrial buildings, safety at sports stadia, small workshops and development in Enterprise Zones.

The general reduction in the scope of such allowances in recent years probably signals the government's ability to bring finer tuning into the economic policy; this remains to be seen, e.g. the proposed changes at the end of 1992.

4.4.2 Nature and amounts of capital allowances

The capital allowances are as follows:

(a) an initial allowance, where the whole or a relatively large proportion of the expenditure is set against taxable income – generally, initial allowances have been abolished, except in Enterprise Zones and the new proposals at the end of 1992;

(b) a writing down allowance, where a relatively small percentage is given against taxable income – they are either 'straight line', i.e. a fixed percentage of the original cost, or 'reducing balance', i.e. a fixed percentage reduction of the last calculated written down value; and

(c) a balancing allowance which arises when on a disposal, the written down value is greater than the consideration attributable to the asset (or vice versa for a balancing charge).

For buildings, the eligible expenditure includes site clearance, cost of construction and associated professional fees. Care has to be taken that the building qualifies under the relevant statutes, i.e. the Capital Allowances Act 1990 as amended by provisions in later statutes. Also, a substantial body of case law has developed to interpret the Acts, particularly on the different types of qualification for buildings and on qualifying plant and machinery, e.g. the latter must be 'functional' rather than part of the 'setting'.

Outside of the Enterprise Zones capital allowances are writing down allowances at 4%, e.g. on industrial buildings, on hotels and on agricultural,subject to the proposals at the end of 1992 for initial allowances. Plant and machinery enjoys a writing down allowance on a reducing balance basis at 25%. Capital allowances are particularly important in Enterprise Zones where 100% of the cost of construction of industrial, retail and certain other buildings, but not residential buildings, is allowable against otherwise taxable income. In an Enterprise Zone plant and machinery enjoys capital allowances by an extra-statutory concession.

4.5 *Capital gains tax*

4.5.1 Introduction

Capital gains tax was introduced in 1965 but the legislation is found in the Taxation of Chargeable Gains Act 1992 and relevant Finance Acts. Essentially, all pay capital gains tax on any capital gain accruing on a disposal which relates to a period of ownership since 1982 (hitherto 1965), i.e. there has been a 'rebasing' of the tax.

Of course, the tax is not charged on persons who are dealing or who are eligible for some exemption or relief. For instance, exempt persons include local authorities and charities.

The tax is charged on net gains in the year at standard or higher income tax rates on chargeable gains made by individuals and at corporation tax rate on those made by companies, other than companies with low profits. Individuals enjoy an exempt slice of gain.

It is outside the scope of this section to look at the computations for tax. However, it may be noted that ownership from before 6 April 1965 requires particular calculations but this has been changed by the rebasing, although calculations may still be appropriate. Similarly, special calculations are needed for part disposals, e.g. the grant of a short lease at a premium; and the disposal of wasting assets, e.g. a short lease.

Until 1982 there was no specific provision for inflation under capital gains tax. However, as a result of the Finance Acts 1982 and 1985 two forms of 'indexation allowance' were given, reducing the taxation of 'inflation gains' for gains made prior to the 1988 Budget.

As a result of the Finance Act 1988, the gains were to be assessed from 1982 as the base year, i.e. rebasing introduces the use of the market value of the asset as at 31 March 1982. Of course, rebasing does not apply to property acquired after that date although indexation for inflation will apply. These provisions continued on consolidation of the legislation in 1992.

4.5.2 Exemptions and reliefs

The principal property exemptions and reliefs from capital gains tax include:

(a) an individual's sole or main residence, provided conditions are met;

(b) 'roll-over', i.e. where the proceeds of disposal are used to acquire assets for business, subject to qualification;

(c) 'retirement relief', a gain of up to £150,000 is exempt on retirement under prescribed circumstances together with 50% of the capital gain between £150,000 and £600,000;

(d) 'roll-over' on compulsory purchase, i.e. sales under actual or prospective compulsory purchase of non-business land which is not the claimant's sole or main residence;

(e) on the death of an individual, no liability to capital gains tax arises.

4.6 *Inheritance tax*

4.6.1 The Inheritance Tax Act 1984 provides a consolidation of legislation for what is now inheritance tax, although subsequent Acts amend the 1984 Act

The Act provides that an individual's estate is liable to inheritance tax on his or her death. The tax also covers gifts made in the seven years prior to death, in that they are aggregated with the estate at death, although 'tapering' relief may be available.

4.6.2 Exemptions and reliefs

The exemptions and reliefs under inheritance tax are too numerous to cover adequately in this section. However, the following may be noted:

(a) gifts to one's spouse are free of tax;

(b) gifts to charities, to certain heritage bodies, for public benefit, to political parties and to others are exempt subject to certain conditions; and,

(c) particular relief is given to woodlands, agricultural property, heritage buildings, certain business assets and certain government stock.

4.7 *Rating*

4.7.1 Community charge

The Local Government Finance Act 1988 provided for adult residents to pay a local 'community charge' in respect of expenditures by local authorities. There were exemptions and reliefs for certain categories of persons, e.g. students. However, the community charged is replaced by the council tax from 1 April 1993 (see section 4.7.3).

4.7.2 National non-domestic rate

A national revaluation of non-domestic hereditaments was undertaken by the Inland Revenue and the new rating lists were published by 31st December 1989. The effective revaluation date was 1st April 1988 and the new rating system operated from 1st April 1990. A period of 6 months from 1st April 1990 was set for proposals to amend the assessments.

As from that date the government determines the business rates payable by non-domestic ratepayers by setting a uniform business rate for the country.

4.7.3 Council tax

From the 1st April 1993, residential occupiers will be liable to pay a property-based council tax instead of the person-based community charge. Residential properties are banded by capital values into bands A to H.

The local rating authorities will be making, demanding and collecting the council tax from individual ratepayers. The rate of charge will very with the band.

4.8 *Value added tax (VAT)*

4.8.1 Scope of VAT

At the standard rate, value added tax is a 17½% ad valorem tax on expenditure on certain goods and services. Generally, repairs and maintenance to buildings suffer the tax. Similarly, fees for professional services result in the tax.

4.8.2 European policy

As a result of European policy on VAT, enforced by action in the European Court of Justice at Luxembourg, the Value Added Tax Act 1983 as amended by the Finance Act 1989 seeks to impose the tax on new non-domestic buildings. As a result, those who supply new industrial, commercial, agricultural and forestry buildings are charged the tax. However, domestic and relevant residential and charity property are not covered by the new provisions to charge VAT.

4.8.3 Nature of VAT

The tax was introduced in 1973 and the principal statute is the Value Added Tax Act 1983, as amended.

A supply is 'exempt', 'partially exempt', 'standard rated' or 'zero-rated'. If a supply is exempt the supplier does not charge VAT on output to customers and cannot recover any VAT on supplies purchased, i.e. input. A zero-rated supply is one on which the supplier does not charge VAT but may recover the VAT paid on supplies purchased. On standard-rated supplies the supplier charges VAT and recovers the VAT already paid on input supplies. For the taxable person who is partially exempt, some VAT input tax is recoverable. Where output tax exceeds input tax the taxable person must remit the difference to the Customs & Excise (or vice versa).

4.8.4 Property, construction and VAT

VAT on property is complex and is generally outside the scope of this section. Generally, grants of interests in, rights over or licences to occupy land are exempt supplies but there are exceptions given in Schedule 6 Group 1 of the 1983 Act. Also, a landlord (or vendor) may opt to tax a tenant (purchaser) in certain instances.

Generally, the construction of commercial and other non-domestic new building is now standard-rated. Also, conversions, alterations, reconstructions, enlargements and certain extensions are standard-rated. However, new dwellings and relevant residential or charity buildings are zero-rated under Schedule 6A of the 1983 Act. Professional fees, repair and maintenance and certain other services are standard rated. Also, demolition in the course of construction is generally standard-rated, except for dwellings and relevant residential or charity buildings.

4.9 *Stamp duty*

Under the Stamp Act 1981 and other statutes, stamp duty is a charge, by way of a stamp, on documents. Although the rates are relatively low, the import may be a substantial proportion of the incidental costs of acquisition of property or other investments.

For tax savings purposes on the grant of a lease, care should be taken to ensure the term of years does not exceed a point on the scale so increasing the tax burden unduly. Similarly, on the disposal of property where it has been agreed chattels are included in the transaction, a proper apportionment of the sale price should be made, since duty is not payable on the value attributable to the chattels.

From time to time, calls to ease or abolish one or more of the various stamp duties have been made.

4.10 Management of taxation

Statutes lay down government policy as law which is applied and managed by the Board of Inland Revenue and the Board of Customs and Excise.

Assessments to income taxation are made by Inspectors of Taxes, demands for payment and collection are made by Collectors of Taxes and the District Valuer deals with much of the work of property valuation (or Valuation Officer for rating).

Of course, value added tax is dealt with by the Commissioners of Customs and Excise.

4.11 Appeals

Appeals of various kinds are heard by the General or Special Commissioners of Inland Revenue with appeals to the hierarchy of courts, i.e. the High Court, the court of Appeal and the House of Lords. The Lands Tribunal deals with valuation appeals in most instances, but there is a local valuation court system to handle rating matters prior to the Lands Tribunal.

5 PROPERTY FUNDING

5.1 Introduction

5.1.1 Equity and debt

The scope for property funding is growing and it is likely that innovative means to meet novel funding problems will continue to emerge. The subject is too wide to be dealt with adequately in this section, which gives a general overview of 'corporate' and 'project' funding. Later sections examine aspects of some of the approaches touched upon below.

It may be noted that an important distinction in funding is that of 'debt' and 'equity' funds, the latter implying ownership in enterprise. Thus, equity is the use of one's own funds to buy and develop for investment, dealing or owner-occupation, by owning shares or units in some business, property or intermediary. Debt funding involves borrowing, e.g. by mortgage or by issuing interest bearing bonds. The relationship between the proportions of equity and debt, i.e. 'gearing', which underpin the ownership of property may have important implications on obtaining the next tranche of monies. The gearing will also affect the returns to the equity portion in times of changing rental levels or interest rates or both.

Also, it may be noted that the various ways and means of funding have different taxation implications. In any appraisal, taxation is likely to be a material factor affecting the outcome of the proposal being considered.

5.1.2 Types of funding

Funding for property acquisition, development or rehabilitation may be grouped into the following:

(a) corporate funding; and

(b) project funding

The status of the 'person' seeking funds may influence the outcome of the search. Thus, corporate bodies may seek both corporate or project related funds. On the other hand an individual intent on maintaining control may seek project funding. However, the individual wanting to plan for taxation, say inheritance tax, may wish to create a company for future property holding or dealing.

Similarly, the 'objective' of a landowner as an investor will tend to long-term funding (similarly for business ownership), whereas a dealer will tend to short-term finance. Of course, both may operate in corporate guise.

Thus, corporate funding seeks to provide or raise funds through a corporate vehicle, such as a company, a charity or a trust. Devices or means of such financing cover:

(a) creation of a private company;

(b) the flotation of a company on the International Stock Exchange (see sections 5.2.1 and 18);

(c) the issue of debenture stock (see section 5.2.4);

(d) the issue of preference shares, which are, perhaps, convertible to equity capital (see section 5.2.3);

(e) the issue of paper scrip; and

(f) the issue of bonds of some particular type, e.g. a Eurobond or a deep discounted bond (see sections 3.5 and 9.6).

On the other hand, project funding seeks to raise funds by virtue of the project itself. In practice it is likely that the use of project funding would have an impact on the capital structure of the fund user. Examples of project funding include:

(a) mortgage;

(b) sale and leaseback; and

(c) forward funding.

The essence of project finance by borrowing is the repayment of the loan from salaries, income from the business to be conducted or rental income. This will enable funds to be repaid over a period of medium duration.

It may be noted that joint ventures or 'partnership' arrangements (see section 1.4) may be regarded as vehicles for funding development projects.

5.1.3 Private sector sources of funds

A host of private sector funding sources may be identified; many are considered in later sections. They include:

(a) the clearing banks for overdraft and other short-term facilities and for mortgages;

(b) the merchant banks for short-term funds;

(c) the finance houses for equipment leasing arrangements;

(d) the insurance companies for sale and leaseback arrangements, mortgages, forward funding arrangements with ultimate purchase;

(e) the building societies for mortgages for house purchase; and

(f) mortgage houses.

5.1.4 Public sector sources of funds

In the public sector numerous local, regional and national bodies are sources of grants or loans or both. Some such bodies may be seen as underpinning development with powers of land acquisition, planning powers, provision of infrastructure and, perhaps as a catalyst, providing grants and loans in prescribed policy areas. In some instances, the authority involvement with public cash generates a substantial injection of private sector funds, of the order of, say, 1 to 4.

Although public bodies tend to be project oriented funders with their grants or loans, they may have powers in a given instance to enter into 'partnership' either as lessor, e.g. of a ground lease for a development site, or as a shareholder in a corporate body.

The European Investment Bank of the European Community may make loans or guarantee loans for private or public projects involving development.

5.1.5 Duration of funding arrangements

Generally, the duration of funding is described as 'short', 'medium' or 'long-term'.

Those who require short-term funds, e.g. funding a development which will be sold (such as house building for owner-occupation), may only need funds to cover the construction and disposal period. The sources include overdrafts from banks, trade credit from suppliers, and stage payment arrangements with the purchaser's mortgagees, and loans from contractors employed to carry out the work.

Loans from banks, the building societies and similar bodies which are made available for periods which range from, say, 5 to 10 years are regarded as medium period. They may or may not be secured on property. The kinds of borrowers will be those wanting to buy or improve property, e.g. dwellings; proprietors or owners intent on running a small hotel, guest house, restaurant and the like. Also, dealers in property may seek such funds, sometimes on a 'flexible' or 'revolving' basis.

Long-term project funds are upwards of 10 years and may be as long as 60 years, e.g. for agricultural property, but 20 or 30 years is common.

Mortgages for house purchase are traditionally long term, say 25 years. Similarly large projects may need funding for this duration and mortgages suit this need. However, in these cases the relative risks the parties face tend to result in different forms of funding, i.e. other than the mortgage. Leases, sale and leaseback and other devices are used in this context.

5.2 Corporate finance

5.2.1 Flotation of a company

The flotation of a company requires several months of intense work for its directors and senior staff. In a sense every issue of shares is a test of the board and management of a company in the eyes of the public. It is also a test of the advisers to the issue in that they must prepare the board and senior management in the presentation made in the prospectus. The matters likely to require detailed consideration are:

(a) the taxation position of existing shareholders;

(b) the taxation position of future shareholders, e.g. should a BES approach be adopted;

(c) control of the new company;

(d) the disposal of surplus assets;

(e) the settling of debts and taxation liabilities;

(f) board representation on the company; and

(g) the status of any occupational pension scheme.

The kind of issue selected is important. It may involve a quote on the International Stock Exchange (see section 18). On the other hand it may involve a Business Expansion Scheme.

Various approaches to the flotation may be considered including an 'offer for sale', an 'offer for sale by tender', a 'placing' or a 'share introduction'. A number of criteria are used, such as:

(a) the cost of the issue in money terms and in terms of management involvement;

(b) the loyalty of shareholders in terms of holding the shares;

(c) practical support of the shareholders in providing further funds;

(d) the degree of control given up by the existing proprietors or shareholders; and,

(e) the support of shareholders in times of difficulties.

5.2.2 Rights issues

For any existing company, another way of raising funds is an approach to existing shareholders with a rights issue in equity or stock.

The advantage to the issuing company is that the company's gearing is reduced, as no extra borrowing is incurred. Some dilution of earnings may follow and this may result in a drop in the value of shares, much to the consternation of the shareholders.

5.2.3 Preference shares

Preference shares rank ahead of other equities for dividends, taking a fixed dividend. They are, therefore, relatively less risky than ordinary shares but do not usually take further profits/dividends.

They come in several forms, including participating, cumulative or non-cumulative preference shares. The dividends paid on preference shares are not tax deductible, unlike debenture interest

5.2.4 Debentures

A debenture is a type of long-term corporate borrowing which may take one of several forms, e.g. mortgage debentures and convertible debentures. Interest is normally paid on the capital of the loan (which may be secured as a fixed or a floating charge). A particular advantage of debentures is that the interest, like mortgage interest, is allowed against profits for corporation tax purposes; in contrast, dividends are not allowed, since they are a distribution of profits subject to tax.

Debentures 'gear' a company's financial structure and almost all are redeemable (unlike equity shares). Debentures have featured in property company financing in the 1980s.

5.3 Project finance

5.3.1 Leasing

A lease enables the lessee to acquire and use a capital asset without immediate outlay (unless a premium is paid to the landlord or a capital sum is paid for an assignment of the lease). The landlord's capital asset is used by the tenant; the rent being paid represents the return to the lessor, and in effect interest to the lessee. The terms and conditions upon which the grant of a lease are made will partly determine the capital worth of the asset to the lessor. Where premiums are taken the net-of-tax outcome may need to be evaluated, including any relief to the tenant.

5.3.2 Sale and leaseback

In a sale and leaseback an owner of property sells the freehold or a long lease and the purchaser grants a lease to the vendor at a rent and on terms and conditions which are mutually acceptable. Care should be taken to evaluate the taxation consequences, if any, of such a transaction.

5.3.3 Mortgages

The nomenclature of mortgages, like most property finance areas, has developed with such expressions as 'term mortgage', 'droplock mortgage', 'bullet mortgage', and 'participating mortgage'. Basically, the mortgagor offers the mortgagee the property as security for a longish term loan. The loan may be repaid during the term as an annuity (interest and capital) or at the end of the term (interest only being paid during that period).

A mortgagee's 'measurement' of the mortgagor to cover the security of the investment is likely to include:

(a) references from bank or trade suppliers;

(b) accounts of business;

(c) level of earnings or joint earnings;

(d) collateral offered by the mortgagor or others;

(e) published information, e.g. Dunn and Bradstreet;

(f) deposit or equity share held by mortgagor; and

(g) profession or occupation.

The mortgagee will have the property valued at the mortgagor's expense. The valuer will provide a report on its suitability for a loan, and, perhaps, some aspects of the terms and conditions upon which the loan might be made (as a matter of policy for the mortgagee to determine).

It is likely that the mortgage agreement will be subject to most if not all of the following:

(a) period of loan;

(b) rate of interest, variable or fixed;

(c) insurance of the property;

(d) mortgage protection or endowment provisions for the life of the mortgagor;

(e) putting the property into good condition;

(f) maintaining the good condition of the property;

(g) repayment of the loan by instalments, or at the end of the loan period

Where property is used as a security for a loan, SAVP17 of the RICS Statement of Asset Valuation Practice and Guidance Notes, 3rd edition, covers aspects of valuation practice.

5.4 *Funding by contractors*

Building contractors employed on development projects sometimes provide funds for a client developer as part of the contract for the scheme. The loans may, for instance, be on deferred payment terms and secured by mortgage arrangements.

5.5 *Franchise*

A growing sector of business enterprise is the franchise. A successful entrepreneur with a suitable type of business, largely retail, but not exclusively, becomes a 'franchiser'. In essence the franchisee buys a package which enables him or her to run an already proven business. The franchiser is able to build up a network of businesses each generating initial acquisition capital and a stream of 'royalties' and sales in the provision of supplies. An added advantage for the franchiser is the likely keenness of self-motivated entrepreneurs who carry the business risk in the venture. The franchiser offers a marketing mix which may include many of the following: the name, house-style, specification for premises, detailed manuals on trading systems and operations, advice on the selection and fitting out of premises, supplies of stock and equipment, promotional services and advice, access to funding arrangements, and training of staff.

The impact of franchise operations has become apparent, especially in town centres. Already, names such as Sketchley, Thorntons and Tie Rack are seen in numerous locations and the trend is likely to grow in the next few years. In a sense, the franchisees indirectly fund the growth of the franchised business through those who offer financial support to them.

The cost of a franchise to the prospective franchisee could be from, say, £3,000 to over £500,000. Several of the clearing banks have created specialist departments to deal with applications for loans with which to fund the acquisition of a franchise and to proffer advice in this respect, e.g. by providing information packages.

The British Franchise Association represents this growing field of business where employment has grown rapidly.

6 INSURANCE COMPANIES

6.1 Investment role

The nature of the business of an insurance company will affect the general strategy for investment. If the company is an endowment assurance a steadily growing fund may be expected. If annuities are its main business, the fund is established and earns income but the payment of annuities will gradually diminish it over the years. Finally, a whole life fund will gradually grow, peak and eventually decline.

Several kinds of insurance companies exist but the important property related type is the life insurance company, which insures individuals who take up policies on their expectation of survival. The premiums are geared to calculated rates of mortality for males or females and it is the aggregate of the premiums, together with the proceeds of disposals and investment income, which is available for long-term investment at any time (after meeting claims and management expenses).

Like the pension funds, the life insurance companies spread their investments to include equities, gilts, mortgages and property. In recent years mortgages, being inflation prone, have lost favour; nevertheless companies still offer mortgages, perhaps as an adjunct to obtaining insurance business but this does not usually amount to a substantial part of their business. Gilts and other interest-bearing dated stock provide a measure of certainty in meeting actuarial estimations of future liabilities and obligations to clients.

On the other hand, direct and indirect investment in property is substantial reflecting, perhaps, a somewhat more bold policy than pension funds in that the larger companies have grown into direct development and redevelopment of land and buildings in recent years. Thus, the emphasis on investment seems to be in new building, with divestment of older properties.

The spread of investments reflects all the property sectors, i.e. shops, offices, industrial and agricultural; residential property tends not to be favoured because of statutory controls on rents below certain rateable value limits. Similarly, the marked drop in agricultural land values in recent years suggests that the rural sector is less favoured in the current climate.

Innovation in investment policy tends to develop slowly, reluctance to recognise the early retail warehouses having been cited as an example. Also, concern about exacting standards for investments in new developments, particularly in the industrial sector, reflected a view that buildings may be unnecessarily expensive or reflect design which does not fully meet the needs of occupiers.

6.2 Role as a financial intermediary

The insurance companies have an important role as providers of funds to developers and investors. As mentioned above, mortgages are sometimes available, perhaps as a package, with the prospect of offering insurance business to the recipient. Much more substantially, the insurance companies provide funds by way of equity participation in companies, either existing or on new issues, and in the field of sale and leasebacks and similar devices. Of course, their role as financial intermediaries is always linked to their investment objectives unless they are investing directly in property on their own behalf.

6.3 Statutory control

6.3.1 Statutes

The Financial Services Act 1986 provides for the insurance sector to be supervised by its own Self-Regulatory Organisation (SRO) under the auspices of the Securities and Investments Board (SIB). Insurance companies are governed by several statutes including the Insurance Companies Acts. The Department of Trade and Industry has regulatory powers, many of which will be in the hands of the SIB and hence the SRO.

6.3.2 Valuations

Every year a valuation of an insurance company's property assets is required under the Acts and the Insurance Companies Regulations 1981, SI 1981 No. 1654. The valuer should be guided by prudent professional practice and the SAVP19, produced by the Assets Valuation Standards Committee of the Royal Institution of Chartered Surveyors.

6.4 Personal Insurance Arbitration Service

The Personal Insurance Arbitration Service, provided by the Chartered Institute of Arbitrators, seeks to settle disputes between customers and certain member companies.

6.5 Insurance Ombudsman

A customer may take some kinds of complaint about insurance to the Insurance Ombudsman, but only after the complainant has sought a remedy of the insurance company concerned. The Insurance Ombudsman is independent of the industry and works for the Council of the Insurance Ombudsman Bureau, which was set up in 1981. He has power to award up to £100,000 but can only deal with cases concerning company members of the scheme.

7 INVESTMENT TRUSTS

7.1 True status

The shares of investment trusts are bought and sold on the Stock Exchange with the usual fees, charges and taxes. Thus, despite their name, investment trusts are not trusts but limited liability companies in which individuals and others may invest in the shares of the company, receiving dividends net of income taxation under Schedule F. (There are, however, many investment trust 'products', e.g. PEPs and warranties.)

The 'approved' investment trust is defined in section 842 of the Income and Corporation Taxes Act 1988. Briefly, it is a company which is not a close company and which is approved by the Department of Trade and Industry, but it will not be approved for the purposes of the Act unless:

1. The company is resident in the United Kingdom;

2. Its income is derived wholly or mainly from shares or securities;

3. No holding is of greater proportion of value of the portfolio than 15% (unless the holding is in another investment trust);

4. Its shares are quoted on a recognised stock exchange in the United Kingdom;

5. The memorandum of association prohibits the distribution of capital surpluses from the disposal of assets; and

6. Not more than 15% of its income is retained in any one accounting period, i.e. 85% of the company's income must be distributed to the shareholders.

Generally, the companies invest in equities either in a specialist sector or with other explicit policies. In effect their shareholders invest indirectly in property to the extent that the investment trust holds any shares in property investment or dealing companies.

Generally, investment trusts may obtain funds by borrowing, e.g. debentures, and by issuing preference shares.

7.2 Objectives

The principal aim is to spread the risk for the shareholders who receive dividends and may sell their holdings on the Stock Exchange in the usual way, the price being determined by the market.

One feature of the investment trust is the 'discount' the shares frequently have, i.e. the aggregate worth of the shares is usually less than the net asset value of the shares held.

Some investment trusts are set up on a limited life basis with either a fixed termination date or a determinable date. Once the date has arrived, and the shareholders so decide, the company realises its assets and the net proceeds are distributed to the shareholders. If the shares were purchased at a discount such a distribution has obvious advantages to the shareholders.

7.3 *Taxation*

7.3.1 Capital gains tax

An approved investment trust is not liable to pay capital gains tax on its capital gains by virtue of section 100(1) of the Taxation of Capital Gains Act 1992.

Of course, a shareholder who disposes of shares may be liable to capital gains tax after any exemptions and reliefs, e.g. the annual relief for investors.

7.3.2 Income and corporation taxes

Whereas franked income received by an investment trust from its investments does not suffer tax in its hands, other income is subject to corporation tax after allowing any working expenses and other allowable disbursements.

Dividends received from an investment trust are liable to income tax at the basic rate. If a shareholder does not pay tax he or she may reclaim the tax from the Inland Revenue using the tax credit obtained from the investment trust.

7.4 *Investment policy*

An investment trust may invest in property and assets other than listed equities, e.g. unquoted shares, although the majority are in the investment field of equities which are quoted. Borrowing of funds is permitted so they are able to 'gear' their investment portfolio with loans.

7.5 *Management*

Management of an investment trust is in the hands of the directors and their staff. Generally, the costs of management are of the order of 0.5% of the share value. Thus, at the outset of a trust, a quotation is obtained on the Stock Exchange and the share capital is fixed, unlike unit trusts which are 'open-ended'. It follows that the management are 'independent' of the market for their shares in the sense that they do not have to realise assets when a shareholder wishes to sell a holding.

8 PENSION FUNDS

8.1 Role

The pension funds, like the life assurance offices, hold a somewhat privileged position in society, e.g. in taxation matters. They invest as a financial intermediary on behalf of a large proportion of the employed and self-employed population. There are nearly 1,100 pension funds and they cover the funded schemes of the public sector, superannuation schemes in the private sector and the local authority schemes.

The role of pension funds as one of several kinds of 'financial institution' is the accumulation of pension contributions from individuals and employers. A capital fund producing income is created over a long term with the view to meeting pension rights at a later date. This obligation must, of course, be regarded as imperative to the role.

The pension fund has a particular and privileged status as a trust. The activities of the trustees are governed by the trust deed and any relevant statutes which protect the interests of the contributors and beneficiaries. Also, in 1980 the National Association of Pension Funds formulated a code of behaviour to which its members commit themselves.

8.2 Statutory and other controls

Regulation of the pension fund is formally overseen by the Department of Trade and Industry and the Board of Inland Revenue. Informal regulation is by the pension fund's membership of the National Association of Pension Funds. Returns must be made to the DTI every year.

The statutes which set the parameters for the pension fund include the Social Security Pensions Act 1975; the Income and Corporation Taxes Act 1988, as amended by subsequent Finance Acts; and the taxation of Chargeable Gains Act 1992, as amended. The taxation statutes exempt the income of pension funds from corporation tax and from capital gains tax. Other statutes govern investment policy, management and administration.

8.3 Investment policy and management

As far as investment policy is concerned the pension funds' range of longer-term investments include equities, gilt edge stocks, mortgages (to a very limited extent), and direct property for the larger pension funds. The smaller funds tend not to invest directly in property but use the avenues of property company equities and, in particular, the property unit trust, a vehicle which has been 'designed' for small pension funds and charities (see section 11). The property unit trust enables the pension fund to spread the risk of property investment over a range of properties depending upon the policy adopted by the unit trust managers.

Given the imperative obligation mentioned above, the trustees must seek a degree of risk which will not fault it.

Pension fund managements should be properly conscious of selecting quality investments and safeguarding that quality subsequently. Apart from a few who have in-house estate management those that invest in property will seek the services of professional real estate consultants for acquisitions, management and disposals. Since 1986 the pension funds have reduced markedly the rate of investment in property compared with previous years.

Portfolio evaluation and management has developed in recent years as an important adjunct to the traditional range of services offered by professional surveying firms.

8.4 *Valuation practice*

Regular independent valuations are required of the pension fund trustees. Firms of professional surveyors offer this service and the Royal Institution of Chartered Surveyors has published Statements of Asset Valuation Practice and Guidance Notes under the auspices of its Assets Valuation Standards Committee; in particular, SAVP22 covers thevaluation of pension fund property assets within four categories, namely: investments, properties in the course of development, properties for development and owner-occupied assets.

8.5 *Pension fund surpluses*

Legislation which came into force on the 6th April 1987 provides for occupational pension schemes which have a surplus of assets over liabilities to take action to reduce the surplus to a margin of up to 5%. Several courses of action are available to the trustees and it remains to be seen what the full extent of changes will be in individual instances. It is conceivable that there will be a moratorium on investment by some pension funds and enhanced disposals by others. Of course, some trustees may decide to increase benefits to recipients, reduce contributions from the parties to the pension fund or a mix of these. A requirement to make refunds is not amiss.

Other aspects of the treatment of these surpluses include the impact on future property investment intentions where moratoria are invoked, and the general worth of equities in companies where ongoing costs of pension payments are reduced considerably.

8.6 *Taxation*

The approved pension funds are examples of 'gross funds' which are generally afforded a privileged position under the taxation regimes; thus sections 438 and 592 of the Income and Corporation Taxes Act 1988 provide exemption from corporation tax on certain incomes and gains.

9 BONDS

9.1 Introduction

A bond enables the investor of relatively small means to make a single payment in a fund which is invested in a spread of investments. The 'property bond' is an example of this kind of single premium bond, the other is the managed fund.

The purchaser buys a 'bond' for, say, £1,000 or £5,000 and the managers invest the aggregate of bond sale net proceeds directly into property and a life policy for each individual purchaser.

9.2 Property bond

A property bond is a form of insurance policy where the payments made by an investor are invested directly into a spread of property sectors or a particular sector, e.g. agricultural property. They came into existence in the 1960s and enable individuals and others to invest indirectly in property together with the benefit of life insurance, although the latter is not an important feature of the package.

Two basic styles of property bond are available, namely:

1. 'Ordinary' or 'accumulative' funds, where the income generated by the portfolio is re-invested; and
2. 'Pension' or 'capital' where the income is distributed.

9.3 Managed fund

A managed fund is a similar device but is not exclusive to property; its spread may also include equities, gilts and other securities. The management may switch from one investment to another to take advantage of any relative changes in the investment sectors.

9.4 Taxation

A bond is taxed to corporation tax on income and on any capital gain made from the disposal of an asset within the fund. The position is more complicated for the bondholder. Briefly, if capital is withdrawn at a given average rate of 5% or less over 20 years, no tax is payable. On disposal of a bond the taxpayer who pays income tax at a rate which is higher than the standard rate must pay tax on any surplus. This is based on a 'top-slicing' calculation to find the marginal rate of tax.

9.5 International bonds

9.5.1 Introduction

An international bond, e.g. a Eurobond, is a means by which governments, international companies and others may raise funds on the international market, much of it centred in London and other major cities. A company issuing a bond usually does so to raise funds for an overseas project or the acquisition of a foreign business. The cost of such funds depends on the prevailing interest rates for the currency required by the company, and the relative strength of that currency in terms of supply and demand which is affected by such factors as the political, economic and social stability of the 'home' country.
A bond may be issued in one of several currencies including sterling, the dollar, the yen, and the deutschmark. The European Currency Unit (ECU) is also used.

Some bonds are convertible into the issuing company's equities, which has the effect of bypassing the traditional way of issuing shares by the Stock Exchange.

Prospectuses as such are not issued but the bonds are dealt with by licensed bond dealers, e.g. a merchant bank. Generally, dealers are regulated by the Securities and Futures Authority with powers to suspend, reprimand or expel members.

9.5.2 Market

The market for international bonds has been mainly institutional but building societies have used bonds as a way of funding. Similarly, some other players in the property market have issued such bonds.

9.5.3 Taxation

Subject to certain conditions, quoted bonds are tax efficient; thus section 124 of the Income and Corporation Taxes Act 1988 permits the payment of interest by companies on a gross of tax basis. The income so paid is deductible against the issuing company's profits.

The conditions are:

(a) payment of the interest is made by or through an overseas agent; or

(b) payment is by or through a person in the United Kingdom, provided the owner is non-resident or the bond is held in a 'recognised clearing system'.

9.6 Deep discount and deep gain bonds

9.6.1 Nature

A device which some property development companies and others have used in recent years is the 'deep discount bond'. Schedule 4 of the Income and Corporation Taxes Act 1988 defines such a bond as a security which is issued at a discount of more than ½% for each year of the life of the bond or more than 15% of the amount payable on redemption. A 'deep gain bond' is one where these measures are exceeded.

9.6.2 Taxation

At the time of disposal, income taxation under Schedule D arises whereby the 'gain' is taxed. At the same time the capital gains tax is reduced. There are, however, variations and exceptions to this form of charge.

10 PROPERTY DEVELOPMENT AND DEALING

10.1 Trade

An individual or other 'person' who buys and sells land and buildings as a way of trade is broadly similar in function (for taxation purposes at least) to one who trades by buying land, building on the land and selling the completed properties. Both may act as landlords or even occupy the premises during the period of ownership; nevertheless the intention is trade and the 'badges to trade' will be apparent in most instances, leading to taxation under Schedule D Case I, whereby income tax or corporation tax is charged on profits under the Income and Corporation Taxes Act 1988.

10.2 Funding requirements

As the prime purpose is trading or dealing, the duration of borrowing the funds required for this purpose is likely to be both short-term and medium-term.

10.2.1 Housebuilders

Builders of residential property for sale fall into this group. On the one hand they frequently need funds to cover a short period of deficit in their cash flow; on the other hand a body with a large land bank may need long-term funds to sustain the ownership until the land can be brought on stream for development. Of course, in some instances the annual cash flow will, no doubt, cover both requirements.

'Housebuilders' (not contractors as such) are frequently funded by their bank by overdraft or short to medium-term loans. Some, albeit rarely, may establish a link with a building society who will fund the purchase of the house or flat for the new owner-occupier arranging for stage payments to the builders up to the incremental completion of each dwelling.

Another means of raising capital will be by Stock Exchange quotation. In such instances, the builder requires the advice and contacts offered by the merchant banks and other financial advisers who are arranging the quotation.

10.2.2 Commercial, industrial and other developers

Other developers, i.e. for shops, offices and industrial premises, who intend to sell are likely to use short-term borrowing for the duration of construction, obtaining funds from merchant banks, joint stock banks and other 'short-term' providers of funds. Whilst agreeing such finance, long-term arrangements will be explored so that repayment may be at the end of the development period. This may be by way of outright sale of the freehold or headlease held by the developer.

Sometimes one of several forms of sale and leaseback may be arranged, so enabling the developer to retain an interest for a longer period; but this implies an investment policy rather than dealing.

10.3 Taxation

10.3.1 Badges of trade

For taxation, it is usually clear when a person is trading and hence liable under Schedule D Case I but in some instances recourse to law will require a review of the 'badges of trade' to determine the objectives of the taxpayer. It is outside the scope of this work to examine the subject in detail. It may be noted that case law provides guidance on the nature of dealers and others – investors, house-owners, and so on.

The badges of trade are:

1. Re-iteration:
   A series of repeated operations by a person may provide sufficient evidence that trade is being carried on. However, it is conceivable that a number of investments are being realised.
2. Intention:
   Intention either to trade or to invest is an important ingredient in determining the nature of the activity. Of course, intention to carry on a business or to reside in property is an indication.
3. Duration of ownership:
   The longer the duration of ownership the more likely the activity carried on is not trading in property.
4. Knowledge of processes:
   Professional or trade knowledge is sometimes a key to determining a trading operation.
5. Circumstances of acquisition:
   Receipt of a gift or an inheritance is not suggestive of trading intent.
6. Circumstances of disposal:
   Compulsory acquisition is an example of circumstances of disposal which is not indicative of trading, but there may be exceptions.
7. Use of property:
   Use of property for business, residential or for letting is not likely to suggest trade, but exceptions may arise.
8. Works to property:
   Carrying out works prior to disposal may suggest trade, but works to make property more suitable for business or residence point away from trade.
9. Financial arrangements:
   The trader tends to borrow on a short-term basis and may not be concerned about a short period when interest payments exceed rental income, if any. On the other hand business owners and house buyers tend to borrow on a long-term basis.
10. Documentation:
    Documents and correspondence may reveal the true nature of transactions, perhaps at variance with what the parties claim or their formal documentation suggests.
11. Nature of the asset:
    Some assets do not lend themselves to investment so indicating trade.

For trading companies interest on short-term loans is allowed as expenditure of trade, if wholly and exclusively so devoted.

10.3.2 Section 776 contrasted

As a result of section 776 of the Income and Corporation Taxes Act 1988, some circumstances may give rise to an income taxation assessment under Schedule D Case VI. Three interesting cases may be considered in this context, namely *Yuill v Wilson* (1980), *Page* v *Lowther and Another* (1983) and *Sugarwhite* v *Budd* (1988). Although the background to the cases do not seem to suggest the taxpayers were dealing as such, 'a just and reasonable assessment' probably resulted in computations reflecting trading-like operations.

10.3.3 Capital gains tax

A dealer does not pay capital gains tax on the disposal of land which is stock-in-trade; any profits will be caught under Schedule D Case I. However, any capital asset, e.g. the premises from which the business is run, may give rise to capital gains tax, although roll-over or retirement relief may be available – see section 4.5.2

11 PROPERTY DEVELOPMENT AND INVESTMENT

11.1 Operations

An individual or other body may buy land, develop it, and hold the completed building as an investment for letting. There are numerous ways in which funds may be made available for this operation.

11.2 Funding requirements

11.2.1 Corporate funding

In the main direct property investment outside the institutional sector has been by property investment companies with shareholders' funds sometimes being relatively highly geared by debentures and loans. Sometimes in the past the institutions would lend on a long-term basis but this has not generally been the case in the last twenty years, with equity participation tending to supplant such loans.

Of course, rights issues to existing shareholders have proved a fruitful source of funds for these companies, and they have also used debenture and preference share issues to generate funds for projects or general purposes.

11.2.2 Project funding

In the past, the property investment companies have also adopted project funding arrangements by mortgages or by sale and leaseback arrangements of various kinds. In more recent times bank lending, debentures or rights issues have become prevalent, particularly as the institutions have tended to move into direct development.

Generally, the traditional mortgage and sale and leaseback may be described as means of funding for long-term retention of the property. The attraction of each to the seeker of funds will be the views held on the relative advantages and disadvantages of these methods. The former, subject to interest rates, may seem more attractive in times of inflation but the latter enables the retention of realised capital (once short-term borrowing for the construction period has been repaid), provided the extent of the loss of profit rent equity is appreciated.

11.2.3 Business Expansion Scheme (BES)

The Finance Act 1988 provides a new form of BES for companies intent on investment in assured tenancy housing to rent. Up to £5 million may be raised for this purpose unlike £0.75 million generally allowed (see Section 18.2).

11.3 Valuation practice

Valuation practice for the assets of property companies is given in SAVP 10 *et al.* of the RICS Guidance Notes on the Valuation of Assets, 2nd edition. (See also SAVP 13 and 14; but others may be relevant in particular circumstances, e.g. SAVP 23 regarding property of BES companies.)

11.4 Taxation

11.4.1 Income taxation

A property investment's net income is taxed under one of several taxation schedules of the Income and Corporation Taxes Act 1988. Thus, rents under leases which are unfurnished are caught under Schedule A whilst furnished lettings are charged under Schedule D Case VI. However, the taxpayer may elect to be charged in respect of the rent for the property under Schedule A. Holiday lettings are assessed in the first instance under Schedule D Case VI but if they come within the provisions of section 503 and 504 of the Income and Corporation Taxes Act 1988 they will be treated as if they are a trade under Schedule D Case I.

Section 75 of the Income and Corporation Taxes Act 1988 provides that expenditure on management of an investment company is allowable for corporation tax purposes. Also, the taxpayer may be able to offset against taxable income interest on loans provided there is a 'qualifying purpose', e.g. the purchase of land, or improving or developing land or building on the land. Generally, interest on debenture stock is deducted against profit.

For a company, dividends paid to shareholders are not tax deductible. However, the dividends are paid net of the basic rate of income tax under Schedule F of the Income and Corporation Taxes Act 1988 and the company pays the tax under the advanced corporation tax system.

11.4.2 Capital gains tax

Disposal of an asset results in liability to capital gains tax, subject to any exemptions or reliefs which may be available. The charge is the current corporation tax rate applied to the chargeable gain as far as companies are concerned, unless the company is a small one. Individuals pay capital gains tax at standard and top rate income tax as appropriate, but an annual relief is available.

12 UNIT TRUSTS

12.1 Role

There are about 1300 unit trusts in the United Kingdom. They have the role of enabling the person who buys units to spread the risks of investment. The receipts from applications to buy units are used by the managers to acquire equities or some other investment vehicle; this has to be in accord with the trust instrument and relevant legislation, e.g. the Financial Services Act 1986.

The holders of units may recover their capital by selling units back to the management of the unit trusts. Unit trusts are popular with individuals and certain bodies who wish to invest in a relatively small way. Generally, the unit trusts are able to invest indirectly in property through the purchase of equities of property companies. Some are deterred from investing directly in property but this is not the case with property unit trusts, a rather special investment vehicle (see section 13).

12.2 Structure and organisation

Ownership of the assets of a unit trust vests in trustees, usually a bank or an insurance company. The trustees collect the dividends and make disbursements to unit holders who wish to sell.

On a day to day basis management of the unit trust is in the hands of the managers, most of whom are members of the Unit Trust Association. They recommend the acquisition and disposal of assets, advertise the unit trust, and handle the applications to purchase and sell units. The cost of management for the unit holder is divided into a joining fee of about 5% of unit worth and an annual management charge, up to about 1.25%. A trust deed may provide for this to be increased after due notice to the unit holders.

Two kinds of unit are available: those that provide income distributions to the unit holders, i.e. 'income units', and those which accumulate the income, i.e. 'accumulation units'.

12.3 Authorised or unauthorised

It should be appreciated that unit trusts are defined as 'authorised' or 'unauthorised' and some are 'exempt' and others 'non-exempt'. The Department of Trade and Industry authorises a unit trust if it meets the prescribed criteria.

A unit trust which is authorised is not permitted to invest directly in property but may advertise for buyers of units; they may, however, invest in equities of property companies, both dealing and investment companies. On the other hand, unauthorised unit trusts are not able to advertise, except in a limited way, but they may invest directly in property (see section 13).

12.4 Taxation

12.4.1 Unit holders

Unit holders may pay income tax on distributions of income or on accumulated income. Also, a liability to capital gains tax may arise on disposal of units.

12.4.2 Authorised unit trusts

Authorised unit trusts are exempt from capital gains tax on their disposals by virtue of section 100(1) of the Taxation of Chargeable Gains Act 1992, although the unit holder may be liable when disposing of units.

12.4.3 Unauthorised unit trust

Under Section 99 of the Taxation of Chargeable Gains Act 1992, unauthorised unit trusts are liable to capital gains tax on chargeable gains arising from the disposal of property. (But see section 13 regarding position for unauthorised unit trusts set up for gross funds.) In this respect they are similar to property investment companies.

12.5 Professional and regulatory framework

12.5.1 Unit Trust Ombudsman

The Unit Trust Ombudsman was appointed in 1988 to deal with unit holders' complaints against the managers of unit trusts. He has power to award up to £100,000 but only in cases involving a manager within the scheme.

12.5.2 Unit Trust Association

Membership of the Unit Trust Association is open to the 160 or so corporate managers of unit trusts. It aims to promote unit trusts and develop good practice.

12.5.3 Regulatory bodies

The unit trust managers are regulated by the Investment Management Regulatory Organisation or the Life Assurance and Unit Trust Regulatory Organisation.

13 PROPERTY UNIT TRUSTS

13.1 Role

A 'property unit trust' is a means by which charities and small pension funds may invest indirectly in property. It is an example of an unauthorised unit trust. The manager's powers to advertise are limited to charities and pension funds. At the same time, because of the special status of the members of the trust as gross tax bodies (see below), the property unit trusts have 'exempt' status under the Income and Corporation Taxes Act 1988 and other taxation statutes.

Unit trusts are 'opened-ended' in the sense that units are purchased from and sold to the managers. It follows that sales by unit holders may cause liquidity problems for the managers. Thus, because of the relative difficulty of disposing of property assets, property unit trusts hold a fair proportion of assets in quickly realisable assets, say 25%, and require notice of a unit holder's intention to dispose of units to the management; three months' notice may be appropriate.

Generally, property unit trusts provide relatively more information about themselves than, say, pension funds. This promotional policy seeks to assure prospective purchasing trustees of the quality of the portfolio and, of course, the management and their professional advisers.

13.2 Kinds of property unit trust

Two kinds of units are available, i.e. capital units and accumulation units. The former retain capital but distribute the income, after deductions, to the unit holders. The accumulation units retain net income so that the unit holders' capital holding in the unit trust may grow.

13.3 Valuation

The prices of the units for sale and 'repurchase' are based upon the worth of the property assets held in the portfolio. An independent professional valuation is, therefore, required at monthly intervals and this is done, bearing in mind the guidance proffered by the Royal Institution of Chartered Surveyors. Generally, only a proportion of the properties may be valued each time so as to save cost, say 1/12 per month. The effect of such an approach is to even out possible fluctuations in the value of the units. However, if severe movements in property market values occurred a more comprehensive approach to the valuation of the portfolio might be recommended.

13.4 Taxation

If it is 'exempt', the property unit trust does not pay corporation tax under the Income and Corporation Tax Act 1988. Similarly the Taxation of Chargeable Gains Act 1992 lifts the obligation to pay capital gains tax on the disposal of assets. Exemptions do not extend to either value added tax or stamp duty.

Prospective unit holders must be able to invest in unauthorised investments as defined in the Trustees Investments Act 1961 and will be restricted by other legislation unless they are:

1. those pension funds which are exempt under schemes approved under the Income and Corporation Taxes Act 1988;

2. superannuation funds which are treated as eligible to hold units by the Commissioners of Inland Revenue; and

3. charities which are exempt from corporation tax by virtue of section 505 of the Income and Corporation Taxes Act 1988 and section 256 of the Taxation of Chargeable Gains Act 1992.

It may be noted that the property unit trust itself will be charged income tax on net rent receivable under Schedule A and on investment income under Schedule D Case III. This is recoverable from the unit holders who will receive their income net of the income tax. However, being exempt bodies they will be able to recover the income tax on a claim to the Inland Revenue.

When a unit holder ceases to be eligible for tax exemption, it is usual for the Inland Revenue to notify the property unit trust so that the necessary expulsion from membership may be effected.

14 BANKS

14.1 Definition

The Banking Act 1987 defines a 'bank' in general terms and provides for the Bank of England to recognise a body as a bank. It may be of interest to note that upon becoming a public limited company the former building society, Abbey National, became a bank, having shed its mutual status.

Certain other bodies may offer banking services but such a body is only recognised as a 'licensed' deposit-taking institution, or a finance house (see section 16).

14.2 Types of banks

It is important to distinguish between the principal types of banks in terms of their broad role as financial intermediaries and advisers. To some extent there is an overlap in the roles which is outside the scope of this general review, e.g. clearing banks with subsidiaries which are merchant banks and the extensive representation of foreign banks.

14.2.1 Clearing banks

The clearing banks' principal funding role is to allocate the funds from current and deposit accounts to commercial, industrial and domestic borrowers using a range of devices, such as overdraft and mortgage facilities. The 'retail' banks operate with extensive networks of branches, offering face to face services to their personal and business customers.

Another dimension of the clearing banks directly related to property is the strategic diversification into estate agency, e.g. Lloyds Bank under the Black Horse logo.

14.2.2 Merchant banks

The merchant banks offer funds on both short and long-term lending but also act as advisers in the money markets and in placing equity issues and other facilities. Their clients are more than likely to be larger businesses and the institutions.

14.3 Services

The clearing banks offer a range of services which may include:

1. the provision of medium-term funds by mortgage;
2. bridging finance;
3. topping-up lending;
4. overdraft and other short-term lending;
5. insurance; and
6. estate agency.

The merchant banks offer a range of services which include:

1. short-term finance to cover the construction period;
2. the placing of equities on the Stock Exchange;

3. the arranging of commercial paper programmes, debenture and preference stock and other funding;

4. advice on and management of pension funds or investment funds and other kinds of assets; and,

5. corporate finance other than the above, e.g. mergers and takeovers.

A principal feature of the merchant bank which distinguishes it from the clearing bank is the lack of branch networks for retail banking purposes.

14.4 Loans

14.4.1 House purchase

The maximum principal for residential property purchase is usually based on a multiplier of income, something like two and three quarters or three times income being common. Some banks will add a multiplier of a second income. Maximum and minimum amounts of loan are usually specified and some do not require commission fees or make redemption charges.

14.4.2 Business loans

The banks provide a variety of loans for business purposes, e.g. for the purchase of a business, for property purchase or improvement or for product development.

The loans may be on an overdraft, on fixed rate of interest term loans or with variable rates on a term basis.

Venture capital may be available from a bank. It will be offered on a term basis, perhaps with a fixed rate, and on condition in many cases that the bank may have an option to take up shares in the company. Some banks require representation on the board of the borrower. In venture type loan arrangements it is common for business consulting services to be offered by the bank.

Some developers make arrangements with a bank to provide loans to buyers of property. Such arrangements are common in the multi-ownership markets for units in resorts, e.g. a time-share.

14.4.3 Banker's 'measurement' of borrowers

General criteria by which a bank may judge whether or not to make a facility available to a prospective seeker of funds for business purposes may include:

1. the nature of the industry or profession;

2. the objectives of the business in seeking the facility;

3. the standing and track record of the business;

4. the intrinsic merits of the product, property or service being considered;

5. the quality of the presentation made and supporting data supplied;

6. the business accounts and business data from external sources, e.g. credit ratings, references and the like;

7. the availability and quality of any participation or collateral offered or sought; and

8. the entrepreneur or manager as such.

14.5 Banking Ombudsman

Disputes which have arisen between banks and their customers since 1st January 1986 may have been referred to the Banking Ombudsman for an impartial determination. Numerous cases have been made (many of which were inappropriate), advice given and determinations made. Many of the cases have been important to the customer but were outside the field of investment and property.

14.6 Banking bodies

From the beginning of 1988, a newly formed association, the British Merchant Banking and Securities Houses Association, embraces the members of the Accepting Houses Committee and the Issuing Houses Association, together with others. Its work will cover asset management, corporate finance, market-making of securities and merchant banking.

The British Bankers Association represents the banks as a separate body.

15 BUILDING SOCIETIES

15.1 Role

15.1.1 Prime role

Although their role has changed, the prime role of the building societies is lending for house purchase. For a variety of reasons mergers of building societies are common so that the number of individual societies has declined markedly since the turn of the century when over 2,000 existed. There are now about a hundred building societies (with about 7,000 branches) in the United Kingdom but less than a dozen hold the bulk of the business. The number is likely to decline, perhaps more slowly, with further mergers and, perhaps for some, the transfer to public limited company status (like banks), e.g. Abbey National plc. Most building societies are members of the Building Societies Association.

The essence of their traditional role is to borrow short, with cash virtually on demand for the depositor but by no means invariably so, and to lend long, say up to 30 years on mortgage. Traditionally, the funds lent by the building societies come from depositors, the so-called 'retail' funds, but this source has been less buoyant in the last few years so the money market or 'wholesale funding' has become a more prominent source for them, e.g. the international bond market.

Persons may become either shareholder members of a building society with a share account, or investors with the rank of creditor; their accounts comprise the bulk of liabilities of the building societies. The bulk of building societies' assets are mortgages on dwellings but a proportion of assets must be held in liquid form.

15.1.2 Other services

Hitherto, their business has been almost exclusively for domestic house purchase although some lending has been in respect of business property. However, the Building Societies Act 1986 has considerably widened the powers which the building societies enjoy and this will inevitably widen the range of services they provide.

Already, several building societies have moved into the field of estate agency with an established network of branches. Conveyancing and insurance are an obvious areas for 'channel development' in the markets for house purchase.

Housing development, particularly in inner city locations, may be a continuing growth business for the larger building society.

Housing associations have established links with building societies and at least one building society is involved in the Business Expansion Scheme.

15.2 Mortgages

A variety of forms of mortgage have been developed to meet the needs of borrowers. Personal Equity Plan linked and pension linked mortgages together with the traditional repayment mortgages and endowment mortgages (a term mortgage linked to life insurance) are offered with various starter home devices to assist the first time buyers.

The buyer of a house from a developer may find that the developer has established an arrangement with a building society to lend to purchasers. Similarly, an estate agent may have such links with a building society.

15.2.1 Repayment mortgage

The repayments under this kind of mortgage provide for capital and interest payments at the same time. Over time the capital element becomes larger and the interest correspondingly smaller. Tax relief on the first £30,000 of the loan is enjoyed on the interest payments only. The loan period is long-term, say 20 to 30 years, but could be shorter. Rates are usually variable and the building society sometimes extends the period of the loan to maintain the level of monthly repayments.

An insurance policy to cover the demise of the borrower (and spouse sometimes) during the period of the loan is common, in which case in the event of death the loan is paid off.

15.2.2 Endowment mortgage

The endowment mortgage provides for purchase of the residence with the payment of interest only and an endowment policy to accumulate the capital over the term of the loan. If the borrower dies the loan is repaid. Such policies pay off the loan by the end of the loan period, usually with profits as a bonus for the borrower.

15.2.3 'Equity participation' mortgage

Innovative schemes of house purchase which allow particular persons to buy/ rent houses have been introduced by some building societies. In effect, the house-buyer purchases say 50% of the dwelling on mortgage and rents the other 50%. When the property is sold the equity is shared between the parties.

15.2.4 'Measurement' in the transaction

In effect the building society 'measures' both the borrower and the property offered as security when considering whether or not to make a loan. The borrower is measured on such matters as;

1. profession or occupation;
2. level of income, salary or wages, including, perhaps, spouse's income (for young professionals as much as four times annual income may be lent);
3. level of 'collateral', e.g. deposit;
4. standing as a householder, e.g. previous house ownership; and,
5. availability of references or confirmations, e.g. banker's reference and employer's confirmation of position held.

'Measurement' in relation to the property offered as security for a loan may include consideration of:

1. the value of the dwelling for mortgage purposes;
2. the proportion of loan sought to value;
3. the need for any improvements or immediate repairs;
4. the tenure, e.g. freehold or leasehold, and the duration of any term of lease remaining after the loan period has expired;
5. in the case of a lease, obligations under it; and
6. the need to prohibit any lettings and any use for business purposes.

15.3 Taxation

The principal aspects of taxation concern the society itself in relation to depositors or account holders and the taxation relief enjoyed by borrowers.

15.3.1 Composite rate

Building society interest is received by the depositors net of income tax unless other arrangements are authorised. Depositors cannot therefore reclaim tax but must account for higher tax rates if they are liable; this will be charged on the interest grossed up.

15.3.2 MIRAS

Borrowers who use the money for house purchase are allowed tax relief on interest they pay on any principal up to a maximum amount of the loan, which is currently £30,000. (The relief has been limited to standard rate income tax from 1991/92.)

It may be noted, however, that continuing debate in recent years has focused on the continuation of such tax relief and it is conceivable that a start will be made to dismantle it in future.

15.3.3 Corporation Tax

Building societies pay corporation tax on capital gains from the disposal of gilt-edged securities (prior to 24th February 1984 such holdings were exempt if held for more than 12 months).

15.3.4 Net or gross payments of interest

Building societies are permitted to pay certain investors on a gross of tax basis but otherwise deduct income tax at the basic rate. The investors included are charities, registered friendly societies, non-resident individuals and quoted Eurobond holders. In some instances a certificate of their exemption is required of the investor.

15.4 Ombudsman

The Building Societies' Ombudsman was appointed from 1st July 1987 with powers provided under the Building Societies Act 1986.

It is unlikely that the Ombudsman will take up a case until the complainant has used the customer complaints procedures available from the building society. He is empowered to make awards to aggrieved parties up to a sum of £100,000. However, any determination must depend on his goodwill or power of persuasion, since there is no provision for enforcement in law.

Matters of complaint which the Ombudsman will not investigate include:

(a) the reasons why an offer has not been made to an individual, i.e. the credit rating of that person; and,

(b) the enforcement of any legal right.

An award is binding on the building society but not on the complainant. In the event of dissatisfaction the latter may, for instance, take legal action against the building society.

Complaints have tended to be concerned with such matters as insurance, e.g. charges, automatic teller machines, and problems with valuation surveys.

15.5 Building Societies Investor Protection Board

Sections 24 to 30 of the Building Societies Act 1986 provides for the Building Societies Investor Protection Board. It has powers to levy contributions from building societies and to raise funds by other means. The principal purpose is to protect investors in the event of any building society becoming insolvent.

15.6 Building Societies Commission

Section 1 of the Building Societies Act provides for the Building Societies Commission with prime functions set out in section 1(4), e.g. 'to promote the financial stability of building societies generally' or 'to administer the system of regulation of building societies provided for by or under this Act'.

16 FINANCE HOUSES

16.1 Role

There are about one hundred and forty finance houses who are members or associate members of the Finance and Leasing Association. Ownership of many finance houses rests in other financial institutions; some finance houses are banks and others are licensed as deposit-takers.

Their main role is to provide short-term funds for the purchase of goods and equipment; hire purchase is the generally accepted means by which they operate but leasing is also significant. Other services they may offer include factoring and bank accounting (as a bank). Some lend on mortgage secured on the customer's house, mainly for home improvement.

The finance houses borrow funds from the banks, mainly on term loans, and take deposits from companies, generally on a short-term basis.

16.2 Terms and conditions of lending

The terms and conditions upon which a hire purchase agreement will be set up include the following:

1. a deposit of say 20% for the time being;
2. a pre determined duration of up to five years, but less than a year is common;
3. the rate of interest charged for the 'package' offered is relatively high since the lending is on credit and, in the event of default, the goods and equipment afford relatively poor security for the outstanding principal and interest;
4. possession and use of the goods and equipment lies in the hands of the borrower;
5. ownership of the assets vests in the finance house;
6. re possession of the goods and equipment in the event of default; and,
7. ownership is transferred to the borrower at the end of the agreed period a nominal charge maybe made for this purpose.

16.3 Assets covered

The assets normally covered by this type of transaction include plant and machinery, furniture, catering and other equipment used by commercial, industrial and professional clients of the company.

16.4 Representative groups

There are over 40 members of the Association. Itestablished a renewed code of conduct for its members in 1987. The code covers such matters as advertising standards, customers in financial difficulties, the treatment of young applicants for credit, and the creditworthiness of customers.

16.5 Chartered Institute of Arbitrators

The Chartered Institute of Arbitrators provides an arbitration service for the parties to a finance credit agreement covering both the consumer and industrial sectors.

17 PROPERTY UNITS

17.1 Role

Considerable discussion on the creation of a unitised property market took place some years ago and it seems possible that property units in one or more forms will appear in due course. The Barkshire Committee reported on the subject in 1985 and favoured the unitisation of property; PINCs (Property Income Certificates) are being progressed by Richard Ellis Financial Services and County Bank, whilst the Barkshire Committee proposed Single Property Ownership Trusts (SPOTs) and Single Asset Property Companies (SAPCOs).

The unitised property market would enable owners of a building to dispose of the whole or part of a property by way of units in it. The unit holder would own equity in a building directly or indirectly in a readily realisable form. This may to be of particular interest to small charities, pension funds and individuals wishing to invest in particular properties but who would otherwise not have the means to do so.

17.2 Form

When the Royal Institution of Chartered Surveyors reviewed property units they suggested that any forms promulgated should be 'tax transparent', neutral in the market, readily marketable, and as safe as other similar investments from the investor's perspective.

In the event, the property unit or 'single asset property vehicle' did not come to the market. In due course, the property units would be 'owned' by the unit holders and the building owned and managed by a property management company. The units could become available on the Stock Exchange.

17.3 Availability

It may be expected that the units in a particular fund would be traded after the issue of a prospectus inviting unit holding on the basis of the details supplied. No doubt the particulars would describe the property in some detail, with perhaps some indication of the locality. Whether considerable information about the latter may be expected is in doubt but it is conceivable that secondary sources would develop in the property press. Other data in the prospectus would set out the rights of the unit holders, and the duties of the managers and professional advisers. Independent valuations would be required and a valuer's Report and Certificate of Value would, no doubt, be published in the prospectus and subsequent annual reports of the unitised property.

17.4 Property Income Certificate (PINC)

17.4.1 Introduction

The Property Income Certificates (PINCs) would be units giving the owner a right to income from an investment in a single prime commercial property. No interest in land, would in fact, held by the unit holder.

17.4.2 PINCs Association

The PINCs Association was created by its fourteen founder members as a marketing, educational, developmental and advisory body for its members and others concerned with PINCs and other single asset property vehicles. Membership was opened to corporate property investors, banks, stockbrokers, chartered surveying firms and others involved in developing this area of investment.

17.5 Single Property Ownership Trust (SPOT)

The Single Property Ownership Trust (SPOT) was promoted by the Barkshire Committee. As yet the positioning of SPOTs, like PINCs, has to be established in the market place.

18 STOCKS, SHARES, BONDS AND OTHER ISSUES

18.1 Markets

18.1.1 Introduction

Raising funds for a company may be undertaken in several ways but the issue of shares, i.e. equities or ordinary shares, enables the shareholders to participate in any profits by way of dividends. It is outside the scope of this text to look at detail. Shares may be issued on a personal basis to relatives, for instance. More commonly they come to the open market by a public issue, an 'offering' or a 'placing'. The last two methods are cheaper but may be criticised in that ordinary investors are not 'in the market' as readily as others.

Hitherto the principal markets for equities fell into three categories, namely the full Stock Exchange quote, the Unlisted Securities Market (USM) and the Third Market. Entrants to the three markets were required to comply with the Stock Exchange regulations.

However, the Third Market has been folded and the Unlisted Securities Market is likely to fold in the near future.

18.1.2 Stock Exchange full quote

An issue of equity on the International Stock Exchange's full quotation now requires at least five years, accounts and at least 25% of the shares must be offered to the public. In general it is the safest area of equity investment when compared with the other markets, involving somewhat large companies. However, the controls imposed by the International Stock Exchange and the costs of an issue and underwriting fees are relatively costly for those seeking funds by this route.

Several thousand companies have a full listing although only a selection are listed in the newspapers and financial journals.

18.1.3 Unlisted Securities Market

Under the control of the International Stock Exchange, the Unlisted Securities Market has been running since November 1980 and peaked with nearly 450 quotes. However, for a variety of reasons the USM is likely to cease operating in the near future.

18.1.4 Rule

In certain circumstances the sale and purchase of shares is permitted under the International Stock Exchange's Rule.

18.2 Business Expansion Scheme

A Business Expansion Scheme sections 289 to 312 of the Income and Corporation Taxes Act 1988 (as amended) is an issue of equity to which special taxation advantages are available to the shareholder. Since the shareholders should hold the shares for five years in order to obtain the full tax benefits, the market is relatively dormant. However, some shares in companies which were issued as Business Expansion Schemes are traded, but they must not be traded on the Stock Exchange.

Property development as such and dealing in property are outside the Business Expansion Scheme. In fact any proposal for a company with more than 50% of its assets in property would not be eligible. It seems, however, that concurrent borrowing enables a proposed Business Expansion Scheme to be created with the concomitant taxation advantages for the subscribing shareholders; this may enable, for example, the development of a hotel.

The advantage to the prospective shareholder in a BES is the total tax write-off allowed. Between £500 and £40,000 is allowed provided the holding is kept for at least fiveyears. In the event of disposal after five years, any capital gain is free of capital gains tax.

However, there have been criticisms of some of these flotations, e.g. the prospectuses, seemingly generous terms to the sponsors and uncertainty about the future market for the shares and so on. The schemes are sponsored and the standing of the sponsor may be important for the prospective investors. Generally, the investor should examine any proposal with care; the tax advantages will be of no value in the absence of a commercially viable project!

The limitation of £750,000 for BES fund-raising severely restricts, in general, the viability of such projects. However, by virtue of section 50 and schedule 4 of the Finance Act 1988 up to £5 million may be raised for housing to rent on assured tenancies under the Housing Act 1988. Indeed, the growth of BES projects in rented housing has been spectacular with several hundred million pounds being secured for such operations. The scheme is due to end by 31 December 1993 but it may be continued in another form.

18.3 Securitisation

Another field of investment which may grow in the United Kingdom in the next few years is the securitisation of debt. It seems that an individual property or a portfolio of properties may be funded by means of securities, i.e. bonds. Similarly, existing mortgages may be clustered or aggregated and redistributed as securities, i.e. mortgage bonds.

The field has grown in the United Kingdom, and it is well established in the United States of America. However, there are indications that the regulatory authorities may make securitisation less attractive.

Of course, a mix of property units and property securities may well be used in project funding arrangements; if the field develops there is much scope for innovation and ingenuity.

19 PROTECTION OF INVESTORS AND OTHERS

19.1 Introduction

Following the publication of a report by Professor Gower and other events, the government introduced the Financial Services Act 1986 which provides a largely non-governmental system for the regulation of those offering investments or financial services of various kinds. Almost all aspects of the industry are covered by the legislation.

Apart from the considerable changes to investor protection introduced by the Financial Services Act 1986, other bodies provide ways of protecting investors and others. It is outside the scope of this section to give more than a flavour of the subject.

19.2 Financial services bodies

19.2.1 Securities and Investments Board

The Securities and Investments Board Ltd, a private company, is the principal organ for the regulation and control of the financial industry. The Board is responsible to the Secretary of State for Trade and Industry. The 1986 Act provides that the Board shall:

1. prepare regulations for the control of the financial industry;
2. authorise the Self-Regulatory Organisations (SROs);
3. authorise the Recognised Professional Bodies (RPBs); and
4. institute criminal proceedings or other measures in certain circumstances of a breach of regulations.

19.2.2 Self-Regulatory Organisations

The role of the SROs is to authorise members of its particular sector to act as an investment business, to provide regulations for the conduct of business and to monitor performance.

The five SROs are:

1. Association of Futures Brokers and Dealers (AFBD);
2. Financial Intermediaries, Managers and Brokers Regulatory Association (FIMBRA);
3. Investment Management Regulatory Organisation (IMRO);
4. Life Assurance and Unit Trust Regulatory Organisation (LAUTRO); and,
5. The Securities and Futures Association.

19.2.3 Recognised Professional Bodies

Professions are regulated under the Act by the setting up of the RPBs. They provide control and monitoring of participants in a way designed to protect investors. It seems that some professions, e.g. the Royal Institution of Chartered Surveyors, may establish links with an SRO for the few members who will need an authorisation under the 1986 Act. Where a professional person is not a member of an RPB authorisation may be made by an appropriate SRO or the SIB.

The RPB's include the Institute of Actuaries, the Insurance Brokers Registration Council and the Law Society.

19.3 Timetable for regulation

The main functions of the SIB came into full operation in 1988, with regulations which were submitted to and approved by the Department of Trade and Industry, having been laid before Parliament for legislative approval.

There is general acceptance of the need for a comprehensive regulatory framework but some aspects of the SIB's regulations resulted in controversy. For instance, the polarisation principle which is firmly held by the SIB has been opposed, inter alia, by the banks and building societies. Some aspects of the regulatory system may be changed in the future.

19.4 Principal functions of the system

The main functions of the regulatory system include the authorisation of those in investment services. The SROs are responsible in the main for this role. Investment advisors and others have been required to obtain their authorisation and it is an offence to do business in the field. The criteria are based upon such matters as:

1. financial standing of the person;
2. the reputation in the business of an individual or a company's senior representatives; and
3. professional indemnity insurances carried by the party concerned.

A compensation fund has been set up under the scheme and it is administered by the regulatory bodies.

Four types of participants were identified by the SIB; in ascending order of relative risk, the groups are:

(a) unit trusts which are controlled;

(b) financial intermediaries who do not handle 'savers' cash, e.g. certain life assurance companies and investment consultants;

(c) financial intermediaries who do handle 'savers' cash, e.g. certain life assurance groups; and,

(d) the others who run investment schemes, deal in options, securities, commodities and similar investments.

The regulations for supervision are framed to this pattern.

19.5 Insider dealings

The progress of the prohibition of insider dealing, which started in the United Kingdom with the Companies Act 1980, gained momentum with the Company Securities (Insider Dealing) Act 1985.

It is an area which is under the control of the Department of Trade and Industry, with responsibility for enforcement of the 'insider dealing' legislation. Insider dealing is, for instance, the use by some agent, consultant or trustee of confidential information to obtain personal gain, e.g. the purchase of shares in advance of a takeover bid.

The Company Securities (Insider Dealing) Act 1985 gave the Secretary of State powers to appoint inspectors to investigate insider dealing. The 1986 Act's provisions extended the inspector's powers of investigation and an order bringing the powers into effect has been in force since November 1986. The inspectors are able to investigate cases with confidentiality.

The penalties for insider dealing have been increased markedly, e.g. the term of imprisonment was increased from up to two years to seven years.

Any contracts entered into by unauthorised persons will be invalid, and it will be a criminal offence to so act.

Insider dealing provisions cover real estate consultants and their staff and some firms have taken action to review their management and staffing policies to ensure compliance, e.g. by creating'Chinese Walls' and by appointing a Compliance Officer.

Harmonisation of practice on insider dealing in the European Community underlies work in this area by Member States. The European Commission's Recommendation of 25th July 1977 promulgated a code and more recently the Insider Dealing Directive 89/592 was adopted on 13th November 1989 to come into force before 1 June 1992.

19.6 Remedies

19.6.1 The framework

The SIB and SROs have powers to sanction those investment advisors and businesses who transgress the regulations and codes set down. Reprimands, perhaps in public, or withdrawal of authorisation are possible remedies.

19.6.2 The aggrieved investor

A number of remedies will be available to the aggrieved investor once the scheme is running. They include:

1. a complaint to the relevant SRO or RPB for an investigation into an alleged breach of the regulations;
2. a complaint to the SIB for an investigation;
3. a complaint to the relevant sector Ombudsman, e.g. banking or insurance or the appropriate SROs Ombudsman;
4. going to arbitration or an independent expert if the agreement between the parties provides for it;
5. recourse to the courts for an appropriate legal action; and,
6. seeking compensation from the SIB or the SRO. The compensation arrangements are limited to £48,000 with losses up to £30,000 being covered in full and an additional £20,000 loss being covered at 90%.

19.7 Appeals

The Financial Services Tribunal has been created to hear appeals against certain decisions of the SIB on authorisation, i.e. refusals, suspensions or withdrawals.

APPENDIX 1

GOVERNMENT AND REGULATORY ORGANISATIONS

CUSTOMS & EXCISE
New King's Beam House
22 Upper Ground
London SE1 9PJ
071-620 1313

DEPARTMENT OF TRADE AND INDUSTRY
Ashdown House
123 Victoria Street
London SW1E 6RB
071-215 5000

FINANCIAL INTERMEDIARIES, MANAGERS AND BROKERS REGULATORY ASSOCIATION (FIMBRA)
Hertsmere House
Hertsmere Road
London E14 4AB
071-538 8860

INVESTMENT MANAGEMENT REGULATORY ORGANISATION (IMRO)
Broadwalk House
5 Appold Street
London EC2A 2LL
071-628 6022

LIFE ASSURANCE AND UNIT TRUST REGULATORY ORGANISATION (LAUTRO)
Centre Point
103 New Oxford Street
London WC1A 1QH
071-379 0444

OFFICE OF FAIR TRADING
Field House
15-25 Breams Buildings
London EC4A 1PR
071-242 2858

THE PANEL ON TAKE-OVERS AND MERGERS
PO Box 226
Stock Exchange Building
Old Broad Street
London EC2P 2JX
071-382 9026

THE SECURITIES AND INVESTMENTS BOARD (SIB)
Gavrelle House
2-14 Bunhill Row
London EC1Y 8RA
071-638 1240

THE SECURITIES AND FUTURES AUTHORITY
Cotton Centre
Cottons Lane
London SE1 2QB
071-378 9000

APPENDIX 2

OTHER ORGANISATIONS

AGRICULTURAL MORTGAGE CORPORATION
AMC House
Chantry Street
Andover
Hampshire SP11 1DD
0264 334344

ASSOCIATION OF CORPORATE TREASURERS
12 Devereux Court
London WC2R 3JJ
071-936 2354

ASSOCIATION OF CORPORATE TRUSTEES
2 Withdean Rise
Brighton
East Sussex BN1 6YN
0273 504276

ASSOCIATION OF FACILITIES MANAGERS
67 High Street
Saffron Walden
Essex
CB10 1AA
0799 513150

ASSOCIATION OF INVESTMENT TRUST COMPANIES (AITC)
6th Floor, Park House
16 Finsbury Circus
London EC2M 7JJ
071-588 5347

ASSOCIATION OF PROJECT MANAGERS
85 Oxford Road
High Wycombe
Buckinghamshire HP11 2DX
0494 440090

ASSOCIATION OF PROPERTY UNIT TRUSTS
11 Devonshire Square
London EC2M 4YR
071-626 3434

BRITISH FRANCHISE ASSOCIATION
Thames View
New Town Road
Henley-on-Thames
Oxfordshire RG9 1HG
0491 578049

BRITISH INSURANCE AND INVESTMENT ASSOCIATION
14 Bevis Marks
London EC3A 7NT
071-623 9043

BRITISH MERCHANT BANKING AND SECURITIES HOUSES ASSOCIATION (BMBA)
6 Fredericks Place
London EC2R 8BT
071-796 3606

BRITISH PROPERTY FEDERATION
35 Catherine Place
London SW1E 6DY
071-828 0111

BRITISH VENTURE CAPITAL ASSOCIATION (BCVA)
3 Catherine Place
London SW19E 6DX
071-233 5212

BUILDING SOCIETIES ASSOCIATION
3 Savile Row
London W1X 1AF
071-437 0655

BUSINESS EXPANSION SCHEME ASSOCIATION
Holywell Centre
1 Phipp Street
London EC2A 4PS
071-613 0032

COMPANY PENSIONS INFORMATION CENTRE
7 Old Park Lane
London W1
071-409 1933

FINANCE AND LEASING ASSOCIATION
18 Upper Grosvenor Street
London W1X 9PB
071-491 2783

INCORPORATED SOCIETY OF VALUERS AND AUCTIONEERS
3 Cadogan Gate
London SW1X 0AS
071-235 2282

INSOLVENCY PRACTITIONERS' ASSOCIATION
18-19 Long Acre
London EC1A 9HE
071-600 3601

INSTITUTE OF ACTUARIES
Staple Inn Hall
High Holborn
London WC1V 7QJ
071-242 0106

INSTITUTE OF CHARTERED ACCOUNTANTS IN ENGLAND AND WALES
PO Box 333
Chartered Accountants' Hall
Moorgate Place
London EC2P 2BJ
071-628 7060

INSTITUTE OF MANAGEMENT
2 Savoy Court
The Strand
London WC2R 0EZ
071-497 0580

INSTITUTE OF REVENUES RATING AND VALUATION
41 Doughty Street
London WC1N 2LF
071-831 3505

INSURANCE BROKERS REGISTRATION COUNCIL
15 St Helens Place
London EC3A 6DS
071-588 4387

INTERNATIONAL STOCK EXCHANGE OF THE UNITED KINGDOM
The Stock Exchange
Old Broad Street
London EC2N 1HP
071-588 2355

THE LAW SOCIETY
113 Chancery Lane
London WC2A 1PL
071-242 1222

LLOYDS OF LONDON
One Lime Street
London EC3M 7DQ
071-623 7100

NATIONAL ASSOCIATION OF ESTATE AGENTS
Arbon House
21 Jury Street
Warwick CV34 4EH
0926 496800

NATIONAL ASSOCIATION OF PENSION FUNDS
12 Grosvenor Gardens
London SW1W 0EB
071-730 0585

NATIONAL FEDERATION OF INDEPENDENT FINANCIAL ADVISERS
Westward House
Lancaster Road
High Wycombe
Buckinghamshire HP12 3PY
0494 442904

NATIONAL SAVINGS
Charles House
375 Kensington High Street
London W14 8QH
071-605 9300

OCCUPATIONAL PENSIONS ADVISORY SERVICE (OPAS)
11 Belgrave Road
London SW1V 1RB
071-233 8080

PINCs ASSOCIATION
Richard Ellis Financial Services
55 Old Broad Street
London EC2M 1LP
071-256 6411

RATING SURVEYORS ASSOCIATION
Regal House
Mengham Road
Hayling Island
Hampshire PO11 0BL

ROYAL INSTITUTE OF BRITISH ARCHITECTS
66 Portland Place
London W1N 4AD
071-580 5533 Fax 071-255 1541

ROYAL INSTITUTION OF CHARTERED SURVEYORS
12 Great George Street
Parliament Square
London SW1P 3AD
071-222 7000

ROYAL TOWN PLANNING INSTITUTE
26 Portland Place
London W1N 4BE
071-636 9107

RURAL DEVELOPMENT COMMISSION
11 Cowley Street
London SW1P 3NA
071-276 6969

UNIT TRUST ASSOCIATION
65 Kingsway
London WC2B 6TD
071-831 0898

WELSH DEVELOPMENT AGENCY
Pearl House
Greyfriars Road
Cardiff CF1 3XX
0222 222666

APPENDIX 3

COMPLAINTS, COMPENSATION SCHEMES, OMBUDSMEN AND ARBITRATION

BUILDING SOCIETIES COMMISSION
15 Great Marlborough Street
London W1V 2AX
071-437 9992

BUILDING SOCIETIES OMBUDSMAN
Grosvenor Gardens House
35-37 Grosvenor Gardens
London SW1X 7AW
071-931 0044

THE COMPLAINTS BUREAU
The Stock Exchange Bureau
Old Broad Street
London EC2N 1EQ

THE INSURANCE OMBUDSMAN
Insurance Ombudsman Bureau
City Gate One
135 Park Street
London SE1 9EA
071-928 7600

THE INVESTMENT REFEREE
6 Frederick Place
London EC2R 8BT

THE OFFICE OF BANKING OMBUDSMEN
Citadel House
5-11 Fetter Lane
London EC4A 1BR
071-583 1395

SOLICITORS' COMPLAINTS BUREAU
Portland House
Stag Place
London SW1E 5BL
071-834 2288

Chapter 2

Property Development and Investment Companies

Index

Others

A

B

D

E

F

G

H

I

J

K

L

M

N

O

P

Q

R

T

U

V

W

X

Y

Z

A A K Enterprises Limited
Units B2 & 3
The Dresser Centre
Whitorth Street
Openshaw
Manchester M11

A D C Properties Limited
58b Wimpole Street
London W1M

A H Property Developers
47 New Briggate
Leeds

A M Investments
1 Russell Court
108 Hammersmith Grove
London W6

A R & V Investments Limited
44 Shepherds Bush Road
London W6

A S W Holdings plc
PO Box 207
Conway House
Fortran Road
St Mellons
Cardiff CF3 0YJ
0222 471333
DIRECTORS: P J Rich (Managing); B Ford (Marketing)

ABI Property Developments Limited
Colonial House
Swinemoor Lane
Beverley
South Yorkshire HU17 0LJ
0482 870452
DIRECTOR: D Hible (Managing)

AMEC Properties Limited
7 Baker Street
London W1M 1AB
DIRECTOR: N Franklin (Managing)

ARC Properties
20 Manvers Street
Bath, Avon BA1 1LX
Tel: 0225 444200 Fax: 0225 466553
DIRECTOR: A P Hall (Managing)

Abaca Group plc
10 Bloomsbury Street
London WC1B

Abacus Developments Limited
40 Bernard Street
London WC1N
Tel: 071-833 3322 Fax: 071-730 4466
NATURE OF BUSINESS: Commercial and Investment Developers
DIRECTORS: Adrian N R McAlpine; D E A Budden FCA; MIR Lemerle BSc. ARICS

Abal Establishments
2 Greycoat Place
London SW1P

Abard Developments
163 Russell Road
Moseley
Birmingham B13

Abbey Properties Limited
Star House
Mutton Lane
Potters Bar
Hertfordshire EN6 2QP
0707 51266
NATURE OF BUSINESS: Development & Investment
DIRECTORS: D Gallen (Managing); G Gowers (Marketing) (Wholly owned subsidiary of Abbey plc); Charles Gallagher (Chairman); Raymond J Davies (Chief Executive); Patrick Brosnan; Dennis A Jackson; Charles H Gallagher; Peter B Meyer
MAJOR SHAREHOLDERS: Gallagher Holdings Limited
SUBSIDIARY COMPANIES: Abbey Homesteads (Developments) Limited; Abbey Homesteads (Investments) Limited; Abbey Properties Limited; M&J Engineers Limited; Term Rentals Limited; Abbey Properties Limited (Ireland); P J Mathers & Company Limited (Ireland)

Abbeygate Developments
Abbeygate House
St Andrews Street South
Bury St Edmonds
Tel: 0284 752277 Fax: 0284 701773
DIRECTORS: P Serlow (Managing)
(Sept 1992)

Abbeyvend Limited
22 Holmes Road
Kentish Town
London NW5 3AB
071-267 9119/0169
NATURE OF BUSINESS: Development
DIRECTORS: B Ashcroft (Managing); C D Torns; B Ascroft
DEVELOPMENT ACTIVITIES: Residential 100%

Abeje M Limited
336 Essex Road
London N1

Able Property Developers plc The
169 Knightsbridge
London SW7

Ablecity Securities
57 Upper Montague Street
London W1
071-706 1022

Absoren Limited
Gateway House
Milverton Street
London SE11

Acan Developments Limited
Hazelwood House
Hazelwood Road
Northampton NN1 1LT
0604 30686
DIRECTOR: R D Darby(Marketing)

Acrofame Properties Limited
96-98 Green Lane
Ilford
Essex ITI 1YQ
Tel: 081-478 6648 Fax: 081-471 9519
NATURE OF BUSINESS: Development & Investment
DIRECTORS: S R Patel BSc (Managing)
REGIONAL PREFERENCES: Greater London; Essex
INVESTMENT POLICY: To increase portfolio of commercial and residential property; by renovation, conversion and development
DEVELOPMENT ACTIVITIES: Shops 50%; residential 50%
DEVELOPMENT POLICY: Renovation and conversion
(Sept 1992)

Adamson Developments
34 Leazes Park Road
Newcastle-Upon-Tyne NE1 4PZ
091-232 8922
DIRECTORS: J R Adamson (Managing); M Price (Marketing)

Addison Properties
41d Holland Road
London W14

Adeline Properties
6 Maiden Lane
Covent Garden
London WC2E 7NW
071-836 9013
DIRECTOR: Mr Greenbaum (Managing)

Admillion Holdings Limited
16 Bermondsey Trading Estate
Rotherhithe New Road
London SE16

Adnams & Company Limited
Sole Bay Brewery
Southwold
Suffolk IP18 6JW

Aim Group plc
16 Carlton Crescent
Southampton SO1 2ES
0703 335111
DIRECTOR: J C Smith (Chairman)

Akeler Developments plc
Queens House
34 Wellington Street
Leeds LS1 2DE
Tel: 0532 460060 Fax: 0532 448340
DIRECTOR: M Glatman (Chief Executive)

Alan Homes Limited
120 Davy Hulme Road
Urmston
Manchester M31

Alan Roberts Developments
Byrom House
Quay Street
Manchester M33

Albermarle House Properties
10 Welbeck Way
London W1M

Aldernam Properties plc
22 Grosvenor Gardens
London SW1W 0DH

Alford Brothers Limited
Glanville House
Frobisher Way
Taunton
Somerset TA2 6BB
Tel: 0823 259777 Fax: 0823 259907
NATURE OF BUSINESS: Property Development and House Building
DIRECTORS: David Edwards (Managing Director)
MAJOR SHAREHOLDERS: Prowting plc
ANNUAL INCOME/TURNOVER: Group £61.8m (1990)

Alfred Cox & Company
144 Camden High Street
London NW1

Allamanda Estates
Craven House
West Street
Farnham
Surrey GU9 7ES
0252 722333

Entry missing ? Call HELPLINE Page v

Allen PLC
Wigan Road
New Springs
Wigan
Lancs WN2 1DL
0942 46265
DEVELOPMENTS MANAGER: P J Anderton

Allhus
124 Alderney Street
London SW1V 4HA
071-630 9788
DIRECTOR: Mr Gardelius (Managing)

Allied Commercial Investment
46 Queen Anne Street
London W1M

Allied Dunbar Property Funds Limited
Allied Dunbar Centre
Swindon
Wiltshire SN1 1FL
0793 513091
DIRECTORS: A Leitch (Managing); K Carby (Marketing)

Allied Freeland Property Trust Limited
77 South Audley Street
London W1Y 6EE
071-486 4684
DIRECTOR: E N Goodman (Managing)

Allied London Properties plc
Allied House
26 Manchester Square
London W1A 2HU
Tel:071-486 6080 Fax: 071-486 5486
(Sept 1992)
DIRECTORS: Morris Leigh PhD (Hon) (Life President); G N Leigh (Chairman); D Smith FCIOB; C Austin FCA, FCCA; A A Davis FCA; Sir Denis Mountain Bt; J E Lowe FCIS (Secretary)
DIRECTOR: D Ballin (Marketing)
MAJOR SHAREHOLDERS: Geoffrey Leigh Settlement; Morris Leigh Settlement; BAT Industries plc
ANNUAL PROFIT: £10.7m (1988)
VALUE OF PROPERTY PORTFOLIO: £165.3m (1988)
SUBSIDIARY COMPANIES: Allied London Investments Limited; Allied London Property Investments Limited; Alstone Developments Limited; Bodshire Limited; Bonabond Limited; Braddon Towers Limited; Cannons Project Limited; Castville Limited; Cavildec Limited; Central & West End Property Company Limited; Cheltenham Trade Park Limited; Coronet Hotel Holdings Limited; Desirable Homes Limited; Easiwork Homes Limited; Edwards (Brokerage) Limited; Edwards (Export) Limited; E J Nye & Sons Limited; Ellrock Limited; Ensign Properties Limited; Federated & General Investments Limited; G C Power Tools Limited; Gimquick Limited; Gomholt Limited; Gough Cooper & Company Limited; Gough Cooper (Contracts) Limited; Gough Cooper Land Limited; Gough Cooper (Midland) Limited; Gough Cooper Properties Limited; Gough Cooper (Rainham) Limited; Gough Cooper Services Limited; Gough Cooper (South East) Limited; Gough Cooper (Wessex) Limited; Gunscar Limited; Hounslow Centre Investments Limited; Inland Developments (London) Limited; Invicta Power Tools Limited; Landra Properties Limited; Langstone Homes Limited; Lissock Limited; Maycrest Property Investment Limited; Memro Limited; Metropolitan Railway Country Estates Limited (The); Nineteen Sixty Properties Limited; Nurstar Limited; One Hill Street Limited; Palmcrest Property Investment Company Limited, S D B Properties Limited; Sittingbourne Industrial Park Limited; Sterling Homes Limited; Sterling Homes (Contractors) Limited; Sterling Homes (Holdings) Limited; Sterling Homes (Plant) Limited; Sterling Property Investments Limited; Sterling Quality Homes Limited; Surplus Values Limited; Temple Island Development Limited; Verdeer Limited; Verglen Limited; Westongate Developments Limited; Wide Range Purchases Limited; Wintdell Limited; Yanacre Limited (Jan 1991)

Allied Partnership Group plc
Piccadilly House
55 Piccadilly
York YO1 1PL

Allis Holdings plc
535 Kings Road
London SW10

Alpha Estates plc
Victoria House
150 Archer Road
Sheffield
SY8 OJY
0742 367070

Alton House Holdings
Alton House
Norstead Place
London SW15 3SA
Tel: 081-789 5111 Fax: 081-785 6116
DIRECTOR: J Gregory

Amalgamated Developers Limited
16 Pall Mall
London SW1Y

Amber Centres Limited
Stubben Edge Hall
Ashover
Derbyshire
S45 0EU
0246 590543
DIRECTOR: M A Pass (Chairman)

Ambergrange
Wesley House
24 Grosvenor Road
Aldershot
Hants GU11 1DP
0252 341113
DIRECTORS: N Kubale; Mr Barranowski (Managing)

Amec plc
Sandiway House
Hartford
Northwich
Cheshire CS8 2YA

Amey Homes Limited
Sutton Courtney
Abingdon
Oxon OL14 4PP

Amston Properties
1 Thames Walk
Battersea Bridge Road
London SW11 3BG
071-924 2583
DIRECTOR: A Shead (Managing)

Anglia Secure Homes plc
Connaught House
Stephenson Road
Severall Business Park
Colchester
Essex CO4 4QR
Tel: 0206 752200 Fax: 0206 752225
DIRECTORS: P B Edmondson; R S Clough FCA (Managing); J R S Bryant; R A Meadows; P N Rudder
(Sept 1992)
MAJOR SHAREHOLDERS: British & Commonwealth (14.9%) Commercial Union Life (12.2%) Schroder Investments (7.9%) CIN Venture 4.9% UNEX Mechanical (4.7%) Naaz Holdings (4.4%) Robert Fleming (4.2%) Abbey Life (3.9%)
BRANCH OFFICES: Norwich
ANNUAL TURNOVER: Group £23.1m (1991)
SUBSIDIARY COMPANIES: Haven Management Services Limited; Cound Page Architects Limited; Trowbridge Estate Agents Limited

Anglo Holt Construction Limited
290 High Street
West Bromwich
West Midlands B70 8EN
021-525 6717
DIRECTOR: W J H Garland (Managing)

Anglo Metropolitan Holdings plc
53 Upper Brook Street
Grosvenor Square
London WIY IPG
071-493 6163

Anglo United plc
Newgate House
Broombank Road
Chesterfield
Derbyshire S41 9QJ

Anglo-French Estates
The Passage
Lena Gardens
London W6

Anglo-Park Group plc
Anglo-Park House
Southgate Street
Winchester
Hampshire SO23 9EH
Tel: 0962 844888 Fax: 0962 841225
(Sept 1992)
NATURE OF BUSINESS: Property Development and Investment
DIRECTORS: J Green (Chairman); D Elias (Dep.Chairman);
A R Burden (Managing); S Hanson (Finance Director)
SHAREHOLDERS: D Elias and A R Burden (Group)
REGIONAL PREFERENCES FOR ACTIVITIES: nationwide
PORTFOLIO: £5m
(Jan 1991)

Anston Investments Limited
6/7 Hatton Garden
London EC1N

Antartica Interiors Limited
48 Fulham Road
London SW3

Anthony Lipton Holdings Limited
125 New Bond Street
London W1Y

Antler Developments plc
The Antler Complex
Leeds Business Park
3 Bruntcliffe Way
Morley
Leeds
West Yorkshire LS27 OJG
0532 528101
DIRECTOR: R Kilty (Managing)
(Sept 1992)

Antler Property Corporation plc
Action International House
Crabtree Office Village
Eversley Way
Egham SY TW20 8RY
Tel: 0784-439670 Fax: 0784 432616
BUSINESS: Property Developers
DIRECTOR: I Ramsay (Managing)
(Sept 1992)
VALUE OF PORTFOLIO: £100m
INVESTMENT POLICY: All types of properties let to substantial covenants

Antler Property Northern plc
The Antler Complex
Leeds Business Park
3 Bruntcliffe Way
Morley
Leeds
West Yorkshire LS27 OJG

Entry missing ? Call HELPLINE Page v

0532 528101
DIRECTOR: R Kilty (Managing)
SUBSIDIARY COMPANIES: Antler Properties Corporation

Anvil Estates Limited
The Green
Elstead
Surrey GU8 6DD
0252 702287
DIRECTOR: J Robertson

Apex Properties Limited
Apex House
High Street
New Malden
Surrey
081-949 6297
NATURE OF BUSINESS: Development & Investment
DIRECTORS: John de Vere Hunt (Chairman); James William Jones ACIS
MAJOR SHAREHOLDERS: J de Vere Hunt; J W Jones; P A de Vere Hunt; Dalgety Pension Fund; Channel Hotels Properties Limited
BUILDING MANAGER: J Bell
BRANCH OFFICES: 243/247 Pavilion Road, Sloane Street, London SW1
DEVELOPMENT POLICY: Offices
SUBSIDIARY COMPANIES: Alkanvil Investments Limited; Apex Commercial Properties Limited; Apex Retail Properties Limtied; Broadlands Roc Investments Limited; Commercial & Centre Investments Limited; Concord Properties Limited; Howitt Close Properties Limited; Queens Gate Holdings; Scainfort Investments Limited; West End & Greater London Properties Limited

Appleford Developments
2nd Floor
Vandale House
Post Office Road
Bournemouth
Dorset BH1 1BX
0202 842713
DIRECTOR: R V Thomas (Managing)

Appleyard Group
Windsor House
Cornwall Road
Harrogate
N. Yorkshire HG1 2PW
0423 531999
DIRECTOR: Mr M.G. Williamson(Chairman & Chief Executive)

Aquic Estates
17 Bruton Street
London W1X 7AH
071-493 9596
DIRECTOR: M Baker (Managing)

Arcadia
Hill House
1 Little New Street
London EC4A 3TR
071-321 0399
DIRECTORS: P Smith (Managing); P Smith, P Hind (Marketing)

Arcadia Limited
27 John Adam Street
London WC2N

Arcadian International plc
Apollo House
56 New Bond Street
London W1Y 9DG
071-491 3070
ANNUAL TURNOVER £11.33m (30/4/87)
VALUE OF PROPERTY PORTFOLIO:£6.53m (30/4/87)

Archduke Limited
17 Grosvenor Square
London SW1W

Arcona Properties Limited
20/22 Queens Street
Mayfair
London W1X 7PT
Tel: 071-491 2388 Fax: 071-408 2152
DIRECTOR: P Despard (Managing)

Ardwall Holdings Limited
Gilchristland
Closeburn, Thornhill
Dumfriesshire DG4 5HN
0848 30827
DIRECTORS: A J McCulloch; F M G Gourlay

Argent Estates Limited
5 Albany Courtyard
Piccadilly
London W1V

Arkwright Developments Limited
3 Cranmer Street
Nottingham NG3 4GH
0602 626313
DIRECTORS: T R Kemp (Managing); W W Scholter (Marketing)

Arkwright, John & Co
35 Bruton Street
London W1X

Arlington Property Developments
Burwood House
14/16 Caxton Street
London SW1H OQT
071 222 2755
Major shareholder - British Aerospace

Arlington Securities Limited

1 Brewers Green
Buckingham Gate
London SW1H ORH
Tel: 071-629 1822/-222 8883 Fax: 071-222 9753
(Sept 1992)
DIRECTORS: Lord Keith of Castleacre (Chairman); H R Mould (Deputy Chairman & Chief Executive); P L Vaughan (Managing); B Holmes (Marketing); G M MacEchern; H J M Price FCA; S Stevenson Jnr CA (Non-Executive); R H Norris FRICS; R C Cholmeley
MAJOR SHAREHOLDERS: Kuwait Investments Office
ANNUAL TURNOVER: £69.7m (1988)
VALUE OF PROPERTY PORTFOLIO: £52.1m (1988)
DEVELOPMENT POLICY: Mainly business parks and retail schemes
SUBSIDIARY COMPANIES: Arlington & Henley Developments Limited (50%); Arlington Business Parks Limited; Arlington Estates Limited; Arlington Industrial Estates Limited; Arlington Property Developments Limited; Arlington Property Investments Limited; Arlington Property Services Limited; Arlington Retail Developments Limited; Arlington Retail Developments (Ireland) Limited; Bellstar Properties Limited; Business Parks Services Limited; Globe Park Securities Limited (60%); Gloucester Business Park Limited; Helmvale Building Limited; Joshua Tayler & Company Limited; Langstone Yachting plc; Lazerconic Limited; Linknext Limited; Lookwise Limited; Lynfield Limited; Marlin Estates Limited (50%); Norwich Riverside Limited; Port Solent Limited; Port Solent Marina Limited; Portway Business Park Limited; Probebit Limited; Waterside Leisure Services Limited (50%); Winner Developments Limited;
(Jan 1991)

Arly Properties Limited

22 Woodstock Street
London W1R

Arrowcroft Group PLC

24 Hanover Square
London W1R 9DD
Tel: 071-499 5432 Fax: 071 493 0323
DIRECTOR: Mr N Hay (Managing)

Arthur Andersen & Company

Bank House
9 Charlotte Street
Manchester M1 4EV
061-228 2121
DIRECTORS: J Priestley (Managing); D Lawson (Marketing)

Arundell House plc

12 Lion & Lamb Yard
Farnham
Surrey GU9 7LL
Tel: 0252 727201 Fax: 0252 725862
DIRECTOR: A N Sturt (Managing) G Windsor-Lewis (Marketing)

Asda Property Holdings plc

58 Queen Annes Street
London W1M 9LA
Tel: 071-224 1030 Fax: 071-224 0574
NATURE OF BUSINESS: Property Investment, Development & Trading
DIRECTORS: E W Davidson (Chairman & Managing); A D Roscoe ARICS; P L Huberman; G A Davidson; Lord Finsberg.
MAJOR SHAREHOLDERS: Trustees of The Manny Davidson Discretionary Trust - 28%; Trustees of The Brigitta Davidson Discretionary Trust - 12.8%; Rockleigh Corporation plc - 3.7%; Barclays Bank plc - 3.1%
ANNUAL TURNOVER: £35.8m
REGIONAL PREFERENCE: London & Home Counties
VALUE OF PROPERTY PORTFOLIO: £129.7m (12/5/92)
INVESTMENT POLICY: Offices - 31%; Retail - 23%; Industrial - 17%; Residential - 29%
SUBSIDIARY COMPANIES: Asda Properties Limited; Arvoline Limited; Asda Estates Limited; Asda Securities Limited; D W Bevan Limited (80%); Holwell Securities Limited; Proman Limited; Salmax Properties Limited.
(Sept 1992)

Ashby & Horner (London) plc

58-62 Scrutton Street
London EC2A 4PH
071-377 0266
DIRECTORS: I Soffe (Managing) J Thornton
NATURE OF BUSINESS: Refurbishment
(Sept 1992)

Ashby Homes Limited

Pensfold Shopping Centre
Gains Park
Shrewsbury
Shropshire
0743 231556
DIRECTOR: G Ashley (Managing)

Ashford Developments Limited

4 Greenbanks Drive
Horsforth
Leeds

Ashford, M J and Company Limited

Alcester Road
Wythall
Birmingham B47 6JN
0564 824313
DIRECTORS: M Ashford (Managing); J Knott (Marketing)

Ashtenne Limited

13 Craven Street
London WC2N

Ashville Group
Ashville House
The Broadway
Wimbledon
London SW19 1QJ
081-543 5111
DIRECTORS: N McNair (Managing); A Poole (Marketing)

Ashworth Properties Limited
36 St James Street
London W1M

Aspen Properties Limited
17 Bourdon Place
London W1X 9HZ
071-409 0670
DIRECTOR: I Croysdill (Managing)

Aspen Property Investments
17 Bourdon Place
London W1X 9HZ
071-409 0670
DIRECTOR: I Croysdill (Managing)

Asset Corporated Limited
10 Sherlock Mews
London W1M 3RH

Asset Corporation Limited
10 Sherlock Mews
London W1M 3RH

Assetguard
Premier House
313 Kilburn Lane
London W9 3EG

Associated British Ports Holdings plc
150 Holborn
London EC1N 2LR
071-430 1177
DIRECTORS: S Bradley (Managing)
BUSINESS DEVELOPMENT OFFICER: G Rabbitts

Associated Property Owners Limited
83 Woodchurch Lane
Birkenhead
Merseyside L42 9PL
051-608 6887

Association of Italian Works
114 Kings Cross Road
London WC1X

Asterplot Limited
Suite 220
Linen Hall
162-168 Regent Street
London W1R 5TB
071-439 3054 Fax 071-439 4276
NATURE OF BUSINESS: Development & Investment
DIRECTORS: Margaret Parsons (Managing); K Faith (Chairman); P Baker; A David; B Obank; S Butcher; S Orgin (Secretary)
MAJOR SHAREHOLDERS: K Faith; B Obank
BRANCH OFFICES: Camden
ANNUAL TURNOVER: £75,000-£150,000 (1989/90)
REGIONAL PREFERENCES: N London and suburbs
PROPERTY PORTFOLIO: offices 10%; residential 90%
VALUE OF PROPERTY PORTFOLIO: £100,000
INVESTMENT POLICY: Buying portfolios to manage and contract
DEVELOPMENT ACTIVITIES: offices 15%; shops 5%; residential 80%
DEVELOPMENT POLICY: Managing agents and contracting
SUBSIDIARY COMPANIES: Splicefam Limited

Astra Group
c/o Astra Trust plc
96/98 Baker Street
London W1M 1LA
071-935 4470
DIRECTORS: J Schryer (Managing); R Lewczynski; M Watkins; T Paphitis
DIRECTORS OF ASTRA TRUST plc: T Paphitis; J W D Clark; M J E Fevers
MAJOR SHAREHOLDERS: AFS is not a limited company. AFS is a division of Astra Trust plc, a fully quoted public company
ANNUAL GROSS TURNOVER: £4.7m (Astra Trust plc 1987)

Atlantic Estates plc
1st Floor
Chenil House
181/183 Kings Road
London SW3 5EB
Tel: 071-351 5353 Fax: 071-351 5350
DIRECTOR: Mrs L D Gordon (Managing)

Atmore Property Group
Minster House
Paradise Street
Liverpool L1 3EU
051-709 7187
DIRECTOR: M Grodner (Managing); Miss J Hannah

Aulay Estates
Mayfair Chambers
7 Broadbent Street
London W1X

Autumn Lake Investments
25 Ennismore Mews
London SW7 1AP
071-225 0971

Avening Properties
36 Bruton Street
London W1X
071-629 6404
DIRECTORS: P Codling

Avenue Property Holdings
4 Durweston Mews
Crawford Street
London W1H 1PB
Tel: 071-487 5772 Fax: 071-487 5385
DIRECTOR: B R Norman (Managing)

Avon Rose plc
37-39 Great Marlborough Street
London W1V 1HA
Tel: 071-439 1691 Fax: 071-734 9710
DIRECTOR: J Chestertan (Managing)

BBL Estates Limited
Water Lane House
Water Lane
Richmond-upon-Thames
Surrey TW9 1TG
081-332 1313
DIRECTORS: R Bailey (Managing)

BBS Property Co Limited
Onward Building
207 Deansgate
Manchester M3

BDA Holdings plc
James Yard
480 Larkshall Road
London E4 9UA
081-531 8211
DIRECTORS: B Duker (Managing); I Shenker (Marketing)

BEBC Limited
Bourne End Business Centre
Estate Office
Cores End Road
Bourne End
Bucks

BHH Group
Newstead House
Trentham
Stoke-on-Trent
Staffordshire ST4 8XB
0782 644222
DIRECTORS: D Fitzgerard (Managing); M Jones (Marketing)

BICC plc
Devonshire House
Mayfair Place
London W1X 6ET
071-629 6622
DIRECTOR: R Biggan (Chief Executive)

BJ Group
Beaufort House
Beaufort Road
Plasmarl Industrial Estate
Swansea SA6 8JG
0792 701414
DIRECTORS: M James (Managing); A Hill (Marketing)

BS Group plc
Eastgate Centre
Stapleton Road
Eastville
Bristol
Avon BS5 6NW

BSA International Limited
16 Davies Street
Berkeley Square
Mayfair
London W1Y

Bachard Developments
Europe House
15 St Dionis Road
London SW6 4UQ

Bagnalia Properties Limited
33 Newington Green Road
London N1

Bailey Investments Plc
Conway House
St Mellons Business Park
Fortran Road
St. Mellons
Cardiff CF3 OLT
Tel: 0222 777778 Fax: 0222 797105
(Sept 1992)
NATURE OF BUSINESS: Property Investment
DIRECTORS: P E Bailey; P M Guy ACA (Managing)
MAJOR SHAREHOLDERS: P E Bailey; P M Guy
REGIONAL OFFICES: Cardiff
ANNUAL INCOME/TURNOVER: £3m
VALUE OF PROPERTY PORTFOLIO: £13m (1990)
DISTRIBUTION OF PORTFOLIO (by value): Office 75%; industrial 15%; retail 10%
INVESTMENT POLICY: Via development programme
(Jan 1991)

Bailly, J C Construction
Bailey House
Bailey Industrial Park
Mariner Tamworth
Staffordshire B79 7XE
0827 52271
DIRECTOR: M Wilson (Managing)

Baird Investments
114 Brompton Road
Knightsbridge
London SW3 1JJ
071-581 5351
DIRECTOR: P Lucas (Managing)

Balfour Beatty Developments Limited
5 Princes Gate
London SW7 1QJ
071-581 9994

Ballan Investments
5 Avallon Close
Tottington
Manchester

Ballance, J J & Co Limited
61 Catherine Place
London SW1E

Baltic Developments plc
25/26 Albemarle Street
London W1X 4AD
071-493 9899
NATURE OF BUSINESS: Development & Investment: Trading company specialising in developing and financing commercial, industrial, and residential property, specialising in enterprise zones.
(Sept) 1992)

Bamberworth Limited
Michelle House
16 Richmond Street
Manchester M1

Bamfords Overseas Limited
Victoria House
114-116 Colmore Row
Birmingham B3

Bampton Property Group Limited, The
Freshwater House
158-162 Shaftesbury Avenue
London WC2H 8HR
071-836 1555 Fax: 071-379 6365
NATURE OF BUSINESS: Property Investment & Trading
DIRECTORS: B S E Freshwater (Managing Director); D Davis
MAJOR SHAREHOLDERS: A subsidiary through Bampton Holdings Limited and City & County Properties Limited of Daejan Holdings plc
ANNUAL TURNOVER: Company £3.9m
VALUE OF PORTFOLIO: £34m (31/3/91)
(Sept 1992)
SUBSIDIARY COMPANIES: Astral Estates (London) Limited; Bampton Homes Limited; Bampton (Redbridge) Limited; Pegasus Investment Company Limited; Seaglen Investments Limited

Banner Homes Group plc
Wycombe 3
Bourndary Road
Loudwater
High Wycombe
Bucks HP10 9PN

Barberry House Properties plc
13 Church Street
Stourbridge
West Midlands
DY8 1LT
Tel: 0384 377311 Fax: 0384 393077
DIRECTOR: G J Hickton (Managing)

Barlows plc
Canada House
3 Chepstow Street
Manchester
M15 5FN
Tel: 061-228 3525 Fax: 0244 311522
NATURE OF BUSINESS: Property Investment
DIRECTORS: R Weston (Managing)

Barnack Group
Barnack Business Centre
24-27 Blakey Road
Salisbury
Wiltshire SP1 2LP
Tel: 0722 336363 Fax: 0722 336457
DIRECTOR: R Croft (Managing)

Barnet, G Group
1 Churchill Court
58 Station Road
North Harrow
Middlesex HA2 7SA
081-863 0711
DIRECTOR: G Barnet (Managing)

Barnett, Curtis & King
70 Gloucester Place
London W1H

Barnsfold Limited
66 Waterpark Road
Salford
Manchester M7 OJ2
061-740 0116/740 3670
DIRECTOR: A Weis (Managing)

Barnwell Limited
Anchor Brewhouse
Shad Thames
London SE1

Barratt Developments plc
Wingrove House
Ponteland Road
Newscastle on Tyne NE5 3PD
Tel: 091-286 6811 Fax: 091-271 2242
(Sept 1992)
NATURE OF BUSINESS: Development & Investment
DIRECTORS: J S R Swanson (Chairman); W H Bruce (Deputy Chairman); A F Rawson; R W R James FCA ATII; J S R Swanson; T Van Ree FCIOB FBIM; M Norton; T P Hartley MDN CEng MICE MIHT FBIM
BRANCH OFFICES: Newcastle-upon-Tyne; London; Aberdeen; Falkirk; Glasgow; Ellon; Manchester; Chester; Bradford; York; Salford; Halesowen; Bristol; Nottingham; Cardiff; Luton; Colchester; Guildford; Eastleigh; USA - Irvine, San Diego
ANNUAL TURNOVER/INCOME/PROFIT: £529.5m (1988)
INVESTMENT POLICY: Residential, leisure
DEVELOPMENT POLICY: Residential, leisure
SUBSIDIARY COMPANIES: Barratt Commercial Limited; Barratt Multi-Ownership & Hotels Limited
(Jan 1991)

Barry Properties
Joclar Court
65 Upper Berkeley Street
London W1H

Bartlett Land plc
Essex House
141 Ringsroad
Brentwood
Essex CM14 4DR
0277 262802
DIRECTORS: R Bartlett (Managing); B Ford (Marketing)

Barvolder Johnson Developments Limited
3 Victoria Road
Leeds

Basi Properties
10 Holyhead Road
Birmingham B21

Bayford Developments
Bowcliffe Hall
Bramham, Wetherby
West Yorkshire LS23 6LP
0937 541111
DIRECTOR: D Fryer (Managing)

Baywood Securities Limited
195 Bury Old Road
Prestwich
Manchester M25

Beasleigh Property Group
'Drumsell'
Pains Hill
Limpsfield
Oxted
Surrey RH8 ORB
Tel: 0883 723409 Fax: 0883 723338

Beaverhomes West Limited
Cossington
Bridgewater
Somerset TA7 8LJ
0278 722456
DIRECTORS: P Hill (Managing); P Fernandez (Sales & Marketing)

Beazer Developments
Beazer House
Lower Bristol Road
Bath
Avon BA2 3EY
0225 428401
DIRECTORS: C Munday (Managing); Sandra Niven (Marketing)

Beazer Holdings plc
2 Midland Bridge Road
Bath,
Avon BA2 3EY
0225 428401
TAKEN OVER BY HANSON PLC
1 Grosvenor Place
London SW1X 7HJ
Tel: 071-245 1245 Fax: 071-245 1270

Beckman plc
111/113 Great Portland Street
London W1N 5FA

Bedford Estates
Bedford Office
29a Montague Street
London WC1
071-636 2713
STEWARD: C G Chester

Bedford Properties
113 Stephendale Road
London SW6

Belgrave Estates
20 Upper Grsovenor Street
London W1X

Belgrave Holdings plc
26-33 Queens Gardens
London W2 3BD
Tel: 071-723 4737 Fax: 071-724 5820
(Sept 1992)
NATURE OF BUSINESS: Investment

Entry missing ? Call HELPLINE Page v

DIRECTORS: A R Rabheru BA Hons (Managing); R C Rabheru; A Y Young ARICS; Sir Montague Prichard CBE MC
MAJOR SHAREHOLDERS: Larksila SA; International Securities AG
BRANCH OFFICES: Birmingham
PROPERTY PORTFOLIO: Factories 20%; leisure 80%
INVESTMENT POLICY: Seeking opportunities
SUBSIDIARY COMPANIES: Yes
(Jan 1991)

Belgrave Properties (Edinburgh) Limited

45 Frederick Street
Edinburgh EH2

Belgravia Property Company Limited

Chesham House
30-31 Chesham Place
London SW1
071-235 1961
DIRECTOR: F King (Managing)

Belgravia Property Trust plc

22 Headfort Place
London SW1X 7DH
Tel: 071-245 6566 Fax: 071-724 5820
(Sept 1992)
DIRECTOR: R Whybra (Managing)
ANNUAL TURNOVER: £11.83m (1988)
(Jan 1991)

Bellhouse & Joseph Investments

5 Princes Gate
London SW7 1QN
071-225 2757
JOINT CHAIRMEN: T E H Bellhouse; J L Joseph

Bellway plc

Horsley House
Regent Centre
Gosforth
Newcastle upon Tyne NE3 3LU
Tel: 091-285 0121 Fax: 091-284 6325
DIRECTORS: R Bell; A K Bell; H C Dawe (Managing); A G Robson
MAJOR SHAREHOLDERS: Prudential; D F W Golding
SUBSIDIARY COMPANIES: Nixon Fitted Furnishings Limited; Heron Electrical Contractors Limited; Blackett Limited

---

Bellway Builders Limited

Horsley House
Regent Centre
Gosforth
Newcastle upon Tyne NE3 3LU
091-285 0121
NATURE OF BUSINESS: Development & Investment
DIRECTORS: K Bell (Chairman); H C Dawe MCIOB (Managing); A G Robson FCA (Financial); A K Bell (Housebuilding - Northern); J Corscadden (Non-Executive); C F J Thompson MA (Oxon) 0FTII (Non-Executive)
MAJOR SHAREHOLDERS: K Bell; C F J Thompson
BRANCH OFFICES: Newcastle-upon-Tyne
ANNUAL TURNOVER: £102,485 (1988)
PROPERTY PORTFOLIO: Residential 100%
INVESTMENT POLICY: Residential
DEVELOPMENT POLICY: Residential
SUBSIDIARY COMPANIES: Bellway Homes Limited; Bellway Homes (Anglia) Limited; Bellway Homes (Herts) Limited; Bellway Homes (West Midlands) Limited; Bellway Urban Renewal Limited; Bellway Urban Renewals (Contracts) Limited; Bellway Urban Renewals (New Homes) Limited; Bellway (Services) Limited (motoring services); Blackett (UK) Limited; Heron Electrical Devices Limited; J T B (Chapel Farm) Limited; Nixons Fitted Furnishing Limited; Cramlington Developments Limited
OVERSEAS SUBSIDIARY COMPANY: Bellway Pty Limited (incorporated in Australia)

Bellwinch plc

Malcolm House
Empire Way
Wembley
Middlesex HA9 0LW

Belstead Properties Limited

14 Pratt Mews
London NW1

Ben/Bailey Construction plc

Elizabeth House
Cliff Street
Mexborough
South Yorkshire S64 9HU
0709 586261
DIRECTOR: B Wainwright (Managing)

Bencon Investments Limited

64 Cardigan Square
London SW1X

Bendigo Properties Limited

11-13 Goldsmith Street
Nottingham
Nottinghamshire NG1 5JS
0602 470185
DIRECTOR: K Grundy (Managing)

Benn Martin, JMA

13 Masons Yard
Lonson SW1X

Bennett, J F Limited

Hallmark Building
Lakenheath
Suffolk IP27 9ER
0842 860765
DIRECTOR: L C Noble (Managing); T Bugg (Marketing)

Benson Kayley Limited
25 Elystan Place
London SW3 3JY
071-581 8493
DIRECTOR: S R Clackett (Managing)

Bentray Investment Limited
22 Dorset Street
London W1H 3FD
071-486 2911
NATURE OF BUSINESS: Development & Investment
DIRECTORS: N F Langford BSc ARICS
MAJOR SHAREHOLDERS: R Holmes A'Court
INVESTMENT POLICY: Up to £6m - offices; industrial; retail
DEVELOPMENT POLICY: Schemes up to £10m - offices; industrial; retail
SUBSIDIARY COMPANIES: Inter Centre Developments Limited

Berisford Property Limited
1 Baker Street
London W1M 1AA
071-224 6063

Berkeley Group plc, The
The Old House
4 Heath Road
Weybridge
Surrey KT13 8TB
Tel: 0932 847222 Fax: 0932 858596
NATURE OF BUSINESS: Property Developers - Housebuilders
DIRECTORS: R Lewin; P Francis; P Read; G Roper; T Ridgley; D Jackson; J Jacobs; B Davies
MAJOR SHAREHOLDERS: SAAD Inv Ltd (10.16%); Grantham Mayo Van Otterloo & Co (5.03%); Eagle Star (4.34%); Commercial Union (3.75%); Robert Fleming (3.54%) Royal Insurance (3.13%)
REGIONAL OFFICES: Weybridge; Westerham; Brighton; Basingstoke; Bristol; Bedford.
ANNUAL TURNOVER: Group £126.6m (1992)
REGIONAL PREFERENCE FOR ACTIVITIES: Midlands & South East
INVESTMENT POLICY: Current trader, investing in land to fulfill short term trading needs.
DISTRIBUTION OF DEVELOPMENT ACTIVITIES: Residential building £97m, Commercial £1m.
UK DEVELOPMENT SUBSIDIARIES: James Crosby Group plc; St George plc; Berkeley Homes (Surrey & Thames Valley) Ltd; Berkeley Homes (Hampshire) Limited; Berkeley Homes (North London) Ltd; Berkely Homes (Kent) Limited; Berkeley Homes (Sussex) Limited; Berkeley Homes (Essex) Limited; Berkeley Homes (Midlands) Limited; Berkeley Homes (Western) Ltd
(Sept 1992)

Berkeley Hambro Property Co
41 Tower Hill
London EC3N 4HA
071-480 5000
(Formerly SIDA Holdings Limited) a subsidiary of Hambros plc
DIRECTORS: D D Bailey (Managing)
SUBSIDIARY COMPANIES: Glamborough Investments Limited; SIDA Properties Limited

Berkeley Homes Limited
Berkeley House
66-70 Baker Street
Weybridge
Surrey KT13 8AL
0932 853455
DIRECTOR: P Owen (Managing)
0234 272472

Berkley House Developments Limited
111 Regents Park Road
London NW1

Berrick Properties Limited
24 Grosvenor Hill Court
Bourdon Street
London W1X 9HT
Tel: 071-493 1759 Fax: 071-491 4929
NATURE OF BUSINESS: Property Development
MAJOR SHARE HOLDER: L Berrick
REGIONAL PREFERENCES: London & South East England
DISTRIBUTION BY PORTFOLIO: 100% Shops
DEVELOPMENT & INVESTMENT POLICY: To retain developments and build portfolio; buy vacant High Street shops/prime or good secondary
(Sept 1992)

Bestin Properties
4 Bank Mill
Manchester Road
Mossley
Manchester

Bestwood plc
Wellington House
Trust Road
Waltham Cross
Hertfordshire EN8 7HF

Bett Developments
9 Cox Street
Downfield
Dundee DD3 9HA
0382 84191
DIRECTOR: I C R Bett (Chairman)

Beverley Manor Limited
53 Sussex Street
London SW1V

Entry missing ? Call HELPLINE Page v

Bexbuild (Developments) plc
Third Floor
Fountain House
83 Fountain Street
Manchester
M2 2EE
061-236 7799
DIRECTOR: P M Shapiro (Managing)

Bigwood Properties Limited
The Old Rectory
Bargate
Grimsby
South Humberside BN 32 4SY
Tel: 0472 250005 Fax: 0472 240617
NATURE OF BUSINESS: Property Development
DIRECTORS: D W Smith
REGIONAL OFFICE: Grimsby
REGIONAL PREFERENCES: Anywhere in U.K.
DEVELOPMENT POLICY: Food + Non food retail; petrol filling stations; leisure, including golf.
(Sept 1992)

Birch Developments plc
Cedar House
25 Ashbourne Road
Derby DE3 3FQ
0323 291806
DIRECTOR: Mr Gadsby

Birchin Developments Limited
20 Church Street
Manchester M4

Birchwood Properties
The Coach House, Heawood Hall
Nether Alderley
Manchester
0625 585738
DIRECTOR: Nick Hall

Birmingham International Airport plc
New Terminal Building, B.I.A
Birmingham B26 3QJ
021-767 5511
DIRECTOR: E Taylor (Marketing)

Birse Group plc
Humber Road
Barton-on-Humber
South Humberside DN18 5BN

Birse Properties Limited
43 Dover Stret
London W1X
071-499 2402
DIRECTOR: D Downing (Managing)

Bishara Estates
20 Sherwood Court
Shouldham Street
London W1H

Black Country Development Corporation
Black Country House
Rounds Green Road
Oldbury
West Midlands B69 2DG
Tel: 021-511 2000 Fax: 021-544 5710

Black, W E Limited
Hall Farm
Shepherds Lane
Chorleywood
Hertfordshire WD3 5EX
09278 4266
DIRECTOR: Mr Gadsden (Managing)

Bleakrose Properties Limited
2 Woodcote View
Dean Row Road
Wilmslow
Cheshire SK9 2BY
0625 528258
DIRECTORS: A N Williamson; S J Clownes
MAJOR SHAREHOLDERS: A N Williamson
DEVELOPMENT ACTIVITIES: Offices; shops; factories; warehouses; industrial

Blegberry
55 South Audley Street
London W1Y 5FA
071-491 4821
JOINT DIRECTORS: R Draycott; C Bennett

Blenheim Management Limited
10 Sedley Place
London W1R

Bloomsbury Properties Limited
Le Hant
Clifton
St Peter Port
Guernsey
Channel Islands
Tel: 0481 721448 Fax: 0481 713956
DIRECTOR: R Coubrough (Chairman)

Bloor, J S & Company Limited
Ashby Road
Mesham
Nr Burton on Trent
Staffordshire DE12 7JP
0530 72737
DIRECTORS: L W Evans; J Bloor (Managing)

Blue Circle Industries plc
Ecclestone Square
London SW1V 1PX

Blue Circle Properties
Portland House
Aldermaston Park
Church Road
Aldermaston
Berks RG7 4HP

Blue Lamp Properties Limited
Ames House
6-7 Duke of York Street
St James
London SW1Y 6LA
071-976 1699
DIRECTORS: A J Collins (Managing Director); Foina Thompson (Director)
Subsidiary of Tarmac Properties

Bluechip Properties Limited
One Great Cumberland Place
London W1H 7AI
071-724 4344
DIRECTOR: J Curtis (Managing)

Bolton Estates plc
Bolton House
194 Old Brompton Road
London SW5

Bolton Group plc
334A Goswell Road
London EC1V 7LQ

Bom Holdings plc
Kingsnorth Industrial Estate
Kingsnorth-on-the-Medway
Hoo, Rochester
Kent ME3 9ND

Bonchester Limited
71 South Audley Street
London W1Y

Bond Co, The
180/182 Fazeley Street
Birmingham B5

Bond Street Properties
10 Three Kings Yard
London W1Y

Bonnington Bond Consortium Limited
2 Forbes Road
Edinburgh EH10 4EE

Boot, Henry & Sons plc
Banner Cross Hall
Sheffield S11 9PD
0742 555444 Fax: 0742 585548
NATURE OF BUSINESS: Property Development & Construction
DIRECTORS: D H Boot (Chairman); E J Boot (Managing Director); A M Bamford DMS FIPM; A P Cooper FCA; D Greaves ARICS MCIOB; J Redgrave; J S Reis MA
MAJOR SHAREHOLDERS: BAC Pension Funds (3.37%); Aberforth Partners (3.23%); A C Boot (3.86%); J H Boot (3.77%) GRE (5.1%); Employees (5.6%); Postal Investment (6.32%); Mrs G M Reis (6.41%)
ANNUAL TURNOVER: £129.9m (1988)
SUBSIDIARY COMPANIES: Henry Boot Northern Limited; Henry Boot Southern Limited; Henry Boot Scotland Limited; Henry Boot Management Limited; Henry Boot Homes Limited; Banner Plant Limited; Henry Boot Developments Limited; First National Housing Trust Limited; Henry Boot Estates Limited; Henry Boot Projects Limited; Henry Boot Training Limited; Henry Boot Inner City Limited
(Sept 1992)

Booth Estates Limited
Hilton House
104 St Georges' Road
Bolton M3

Boothbourne Properties
3 Castlefield Court
Church Street
Surrey RH2 0SN
07372 21111
DIRECTOR: P Pozzoni (Managing)

Boots Properties plc
1 Thame Road
Nottingham NG2 3AA
Tel: 0602 506255 Fax: 0602 492421
NATURE OF BUSINESS: Investment & Development
MAJOR SHAREHOLDERS: The Boots Company plc
ANNUAL INCOME/PROFIT BEFORE TAX: Group £374m, Trading Profit Company £70m
REGIONAL PREFERENCES: U.K.
VALUE OF PROPERTY PORTFOLIO: £810m (1992)
PROPERTY PORTFOLIO: Retail 90%; Offices 5%; Industrial 5%
INVESTMENT POLICY: To ensure that property assets provide a return to Boots' shareholders
DEVELOPMENT POLICY: Concentrated on a small high quality portfolio of retail properties
SUBSIDIARY COMPANIES: Boots Development Properties Limited
(Sept 1992)

Border Engineering Contractors (Estate Developers) Limited
PO Box 23
Coach Road, Whitehaven
Cumbria CA28 9DF
0946 693773
DIRECTORS: K Irving (Managing Director); S Shephard

(Marketing Director); Barker; N J Walker; J L W Bartholomew; J C Johnston; G A G Millner
BRANCH OFFICES: Carlisle; Earlston

Boscombe Property plc
50 The Terrace
Torquay
Devon TQ1 1DD
Tel: 0803 291100 Fax: 0803 293092
(Sept 1992)
DIRECTORS: T S Adams MA LLB BSc FRICS (Chairman & Managing); R D White FRICS; Mrs R A Adams MA (Secretary)
REGIONAL PREFERENCES: South West
(Sept 1992)

Boulding Group
302 Ringinglow Road
Bents Green
Sheffield
S Yorks S11 7PX
0742 309033
DIRECTORS: Mr & Mrs Boulding

Boultbeeland plc
435 The Highway
London E1

Boultee Land plc
100 Broad Street
Birmingham B15

Boultee Land plc
49 Kensington High Street
London W8

Bovis Limited
Bovis House
Northolt Road
Harrow
Middlesex HA2 OEE
Tel: 081-422 3488 Fax: 081-422 7827
(Sept 1992)
NATURE OF BUSINESS: development & investment
DIRECTORS: Sir Jeffrey Sterling CBE (Chairman); C J Spackman (Managing); A K Black; P G Cazalet; P J Ford; T C Harris; A G Hatchett; G G Hoyer Millar; F W Lampl; O Marriott; A M Robb; C D Stewart-Smith; P L Warner; B A Winham
MAJOR SHAREHOLDERS: Prudential Corporation plc; Commercial Union Assurance Company plc; Phoenix Assurance plc; Norwich Union Insurance Group; Guardian Royal Exchange plc; Iron Trades Insurance Group
PROPERTY PORTFOLIO: Central London: offices 92.5%, other 7.5%; Outer London: shops 24.5%, offices 17%, other 58.5%; Other UK: shops 69.1%, offices 12%, other 18.9%
INVESTMENT POLICY: Refurbishment and letting
DEVELOPMENT POLICY: Major projects in all sectors throughout UK
PRINCIPAL SUBSIDIARIES IN CONSTRUCTION & PROPERTY: Bovis Homes Limited; Bovis Construction Limited; Wyseplant Limited; Yeomans & Partners Limited; Bovis International Limited; Town & City Properties Limited; The Arndale Property Trust Limited; Charlwood Alliance Holdings Limited; Arndale Shopping Centres Limited; Arndale Communications Limited
OTHER SUBSIDIARIES IN: Service industry; transport; shipping; Australia
(Jan 1991)

Bowra, G E Group Limited
18 Leigh Road
Haine Industrial Park
Ramsgate
Kent CT12 5EU
Tel: 0843 597555 Fax: 0843 597770
NATURE OF BUSINESS: Development & Investment
DIRECTORS: C E Bowra; A A Bowra
MAJOR SHAREHOLDERS: C E Bowra; A A Bowra
ANNUAL TURNOVER: £5m
REGIONAL PREFERENCES FOR ACTIVITIES: South East
VALUE OF PROPERTY PORTFOLIO: £7m (1990)
DISTRIBUTION OF PROPERTY PORTFOLIO: offices 5%; shops 10%; factories 55%; leisure 10%; residential 20%
DISTRIBUTION OF DEVELOPMENT ACTIVITIES: Shops 50%; residential 50%
SUBSIDIARIES: Bowra Ltd (contracting); Acryneon Ltd (sign manufacturing)

Brace Bidwell Estates
7 The Crescent
Woldingham
Surrey CR3 7DB
0883 653040
DIRECTOR: P Brace (Managing)

Braemore Estates
Rutland Square House
12 Rutland Square
Edinburgh EH1 2BB
Tel: 031-228 2866 Fax: 031-228 3637
(Sept 1992)

Bradenham Developments
15 Bradenham Place
Penarth
South Glamorgan CF6 2AG
0222 707202
JOINT MANAGING DIRECTORS: A Hurst; A Watts

Bradford Property Trust Limited
69 Market Street
Bradford
West Yorkshire BD1 1NE
0274 723181
DIRECTORS: Sir Edward Courtenay Henry Warner Bt (Chairman, Non-Executive); H R J Burgess (Managing); E A C Denham (Non-Executive); J A Fooks MA FCA (Non-Executive); P D Gresswell FRICS (Non-Executive); P H Reddihough (Non-Executive); N A E Robinson FRICS ACIArb (Non-Executive); B Tetley FCA; P C T Warner (Non-Executive)

ANNUAL TURNOVER: £35.1m (1989)
VALUE OF PROPERTY PORTFOLIO: £64m (1989)
SUBSIDIARY COMPANIES: Ealing Tenants Limited; Eastbourne Artisans Dwellings Company Limited; Grelden Investment Company Limited; Margrave Estates Limited; Stoke-on-Trent Tenants Limited; Gracefield Properties Limited; B G Utting & Company Limited
RELATED COMPANIES: Bradbridge Property Company Limited; Donlo Investment-Developments Limited; Bradwa Limited

---

Bray Developments Moray Limited
Robinhill
Sheriff Brae
Forres, Moray
Scotland
IV36 ODP
0309 72854
DIRECTOR: R B M Braid (Managing)

Bream Valley Estates Limited
2 Junction Road
Harrow
Middlesex HA1 1NL
081-427 1235
DIRECTOR: N Frais (Managing)

Bredero Properties plc
The Clock House
4 Dorking Road
Epsom
Surrey KT18 7LX
Tel: 03727 26433 Fax: 03727 41598
NATURE OF BUSINESS: development & investment
DIRECTORS: A D Chisholm MA(Hons) (Managing); P C Badcock FCCA; A K Cook BSc(Hons) CEng MICE DipTP; G A Sutton MSc DIC CEng MICE MCIBSE; B W Burman MCIOB
MAJOR SHAREHOLDERS: Slough Estates plc; Scottish Amicable; Midland Montagu
REGIONAL OFFICES: Aberdeen; Paisley; Hammersmith
ANNUAL TURNOVER: £61m (1990)
VALUE OF PROPERTY PORTFOLIO: £100m (1989)
DISTRIBUTION OF DEVELOPMENT ACTIVITIES: retail 50%; offices 50%
INVESTMENT POLICY: Major shopping centres
DEVELOPMENT POLICY: major town centre schemes
SUBSIDIARY COMPANIES: Chequer Street Developments Limited; Ashley Avenue Developments Limited; Ashley Properties Limited; Bredero Dorking Limited; Bredero Developments Limited; Bredero Aberdeen Centre Limited; Bredero Fleet Limited; Bredero Centre West Limited; Bredero Grampian Limited; Bredero Homes Limited; Bredero Investments Limited; Bredero Property Management Limited; Bredero Construction Company Limited; Bredero Projects Limited; Bredero Buchanon Centre plc; Bredero Lewisham Limited; Bredero Regent Street Limited; Bredero (Southampton) Limited; Langley Estates Limited; Lenbell Limited; Paisley Developments Limited (Sept 1992)

Bremner plc
13A Alva Street
Edinburgh EH2 4PH

Brent Walker plc
19 Rupert Street
London W1V 7FS
071-465 0111
DIRECTOR: J Blackenbury (Managing)

Brickhill Developments
Brickhill House
701 South Fifth Street
Witan Gate East
Central Milton Keynes
Bucks MK9 2PR
0908 664551
DIRECTOR: Mr Prestidge (Managing)

Bride Hall plc
19 Queen Street
London W1X 7PJ
Tel: 071-493 3996 Fax: 071-499 4388
NATURE OF BUSINESS: Property Development & Investment
DIRECTORS: D Desmond (Chairman); A W B Fforde MA ACA; D J Stewart FRICS; The Hon T Noel ARICS (Associate)
MAJOR SHAREHOLDERS: D F Desmond and Family Trustees
LOCATION OF REGIONAL OFFICES: London only
ANNUAL INCOME/TURNOVER: £32m
REGIONAL PREFERENCES FOR ACTIVITIES: Anywhere in UK
VALUE OF PORTFOLIO: £13m (1991)
DISTRIBUTION OF PORTFOLIO: offices 60%; warehouses 25%; retail 15%
INVESTMENT POLICY: To expand portfolio of commercial investments mainly by development but with strategic acquisitions where appropriate.
DISTRIBUTION OF DEVELOPMENT ACTIVITIES: offices 10%
factories 5% retail 35% warehouses 15% hitech 25% (Sept 1992)
SUBSIDIARIES: Bride Hall Developments plc, Bride Hall Holdings Limited

---

Bridge Securities Limited
47 Dorset Street
London W1H

Bridgehampton plc
117 George Street
London W1H 5TB
Tel: 071-724 3481 Fax: 071-724 5621
DIRECTOR: P V Oldsberg (Managing)

Bridgers Commercial
55 High Street
Epsom
Surrey KT18 8DH
03727 41777
PARTNER: I Fasham

Brighouse Group plc
20 Conduit Street
London W1R

Briscard Developments
Stratton House
Cater Road
Bishopsworth
Bristol BS13 7UH
0272 358248
DIRECTOR: R Stokes (Managing); E S A Taylor (Marketing)

Bristol and England Properties
The Down House
Foxholes Lane
Tockington
Bristol
Avon BS12 4PF
0454 201321

Bristol Evening Post plc
Temple Way
Bristol
Avon BS99 7HD

Britannia Group plc
83 The Promenade
Cheltenham
Gloucestershire GL50 1PJ
0242 221322
DIRECTORS: J Rickards (Managing); M Mann (Marketing)

Britannic Securities & Investments Limited
375 Regents Park Road
London
N3
081-346 8834

British Coal Estates
Coal House
Doncaster
South Yorkshire
DN1 3HD
0302 321587
HEAD OF ESTATES: T C Rees

British Commercial Property Investment Trust Limited
Carlton House
33 Robert Adam Street
London W1M 5AH,
Tel: 071-935 3555 Fax: 071-935 3737
NATURE OF BUSINESS: Development & Investment
DIRECTORS: The Lord Rayne; M Millsom FRICS; (alternate to Mr Driver) R F Spier BCom FCA; E G Miller FCIOB; M Newman FRICS; N G E Driver (Director of Property)
MAJOR SHAREHOLDERS: Wholly owned subsidiary of London Merchant Securities plc
(Sept 1992)

British Ensign Estates Limited
23 Cavaye Place
London SW10

British Land Company plc
10 Cornwall Terrace
Regents Park
London NWI 4QP
Tel: 071-486 4466 Fax: 071-935 5552
(Sept 1992)
NATURE OF BUSINESS: Property Development & Investment
DIRECTORS: J Ritblat FSVA (Chairman & Managing Director); C Metliss FCA; J H Weston-Smith MA FCIS; D C Berry FCA; P Simon BSc PhD ACII; S L Kalman FRICS, J D Spink, Nicholas Ritblat
ANNUAL TURNOVER/INCOME: £70.3m (1990)
REGIONAL PREFERENCES FOR ACTIVITIES: 91% of portfolio is in UK (Central London 60%); 7% in Europe and 2% in USA
DISTRIBUTION OF PORTFOLIO: Offices 34%; retail 42%; industrial 8%; residential 1%
INVESTMENT POLICY: Even when money is expensive, our business is to buy for the long term when we think property is cheap.
SUBSIDIARY COMPANIES: Adamant Investment Corp Limited; B L Holdings Limited; British Land of America Inc; City Wall (Holdings) Limited; Clarendon Property Company Limited; Euston Centre Investments Limited; Firmount Limited; Industrial Real Estate Limited; Plantation House Limited; British Land Investments NV; Real Property and Finance Corp Limited; British Land Securities Limited; W Crowther & Sons Limited; Jarvis Brothers & Brewster (Construction) Limited; Actiontrain Limited; B L Atrium BV; Selected Land & Property Company Limited; Union Property Corp Limited; West London Leaseholds Limited; FCS Currency Management Limited; The Hale (Holdings) plc; Kingsmere Productions Limited
(Sept 1992)

British Petroleum Properties
Britannic Tower
Moor Lane
London EC2Y 9BU

British Rail Property Board
Great Northern House
79-81 Euston Road
London NW1 2RT
071-837 5800
DIRECTOR: D Leslie (Managing)

British Telecom Property
81 Newgate Street
London EC1A 7AJ
071-356 5000
DIRECTOR: K A D Brown (Managing)

British Waterways
Greycaine Road
Watford
Herts
WD2 4JR
0923 226422

Brixton Estate PLC
22-24 Ely Place
London EC1N 6TQ
071-242 6898/071-831 9908 Fax: 071-831 9908
(Sept 1992)
NATURE OF BUSINESS: Development & Investment
DIRECTORS: H S Axton FCA (Chairman); Sir D Morpeth TD FCA FRCM (Deputy Chairman); D F Gardner FRICS (Managing) L J Lane FRICS (Deputy Managing); Sir R B Wilbraham Bt; Sir M Beetham GCB CBE DFC AFC; P H D Crichton; Sir J Cuckney; T J Nagle FRICS
MAJOR SHAREHOLDERS: Clerical Medical & General Life Assurance Society; Royal Insurance plc; Cross Forth Limited; Mrs L M Baker; The Investment Company plc; Bassett-Patrick Securities Limited
ANNUAL TURNOVER/INCOME/PROFIT: £31.69m (1988)
REGIONAL PREFERENCES: South East
DEVELOPMENT/INVESTMENT POLICY: Offices; industrial; warehouses; hi-tech
VALUE OF PROPERTY PORTFOLIO: £589m (1989)
DISTRIBUTION OF PORTFOLIO: Offices 40%; modern industrial/ warehouses 60%
(Jan 1991)

Broadwell Land plc
Calico House
Plantation Wharf
London SW11 3UB
Tel: 071-924 3900 Fax: 071-924 3901
NATURE OF BUSINESS: Development & Investment
DIRECTORS: I L Shearer (Chairman & Chief Executive); M R Breen; R C Breen; D J T MacDonald; D Aarons (Non-Executive); A M Davies (Non-Executive); C A Fry (Non-Executive); P H Swan DSO DFC (Non-Executive)
ANNUAL TURNOVER: £33.7m (1989)
VALUE OF PROPERTY PORTFOLIO: £3.3m (1989)
SUBSIDIARY COMPANIES: Broadwell Land Management Limited; Beampay Limited; Bestmatch Properties Limited; Revolver Properties Limited

Brobal Developments Limited
Number One Lowther Close
Elstree
Hertfordshire WD6 3PY
081-458 8541

Brockett Investment Company Limited
436 Hook Road
Chessington, Surrey
081-397 4525
DIRECTOR: R L Ransom (Managing)

Brookclose Limited
220 High Street North
London E6 2JA
081-471 1678
DIRECTOR: J J Ward (Managing)

Brookfield Estates
Brookfield House
Elstead
Godalming
Surrey GU8 6LG
0252 703549
DIRECTOR: G C Stead (Managing)

Brookglade Properties Limited
113 New London Road
Chelmsford
Essex CM2 OQT
Tel: 0245 252595 Fax: 0245 252682
(Sept 1992)
NATURE OF BUSINESS: Development
DIRECTORS: C J Collins BSc FRICS; T Magee; C Z Collins
MAJOR SHAREHOLDERS: C J Collins; C Z Collins; Family Trust
REGIONAL PREFERENCES: South East
INVESTMENT POLICY: Hold what we can
DEVELOPMENT POLICY: Commercial & residential develoment
(Jan 1991)

Brookgreen Developments Limited
5 Court Lodge
48 Sloane Square
London SW1W

Brookley plc
Guardian House
Borough Road
Godalming
Surrey GU7 2AE
Tel: 0483 426212 Fax: 0483 426850
NATURE OF BUSINESS: Property Development
DIRECTORS: L C Allen-Vercoe FInstDir; R A Donald; M J Durak; D J Corney
MAJOR SHAREHOLDERS: L C Allen-Vercoe; R A Donald
ANNUAL TURNOVER: £5m
VALUE OF PORTFOLIO: £2m (1992)
REGIONAL PREFERENCES: South East preferred but also active in South West and Wales
INVESTMENT POLICY: High yielding industrial
DEVELOPMENT ACTIVITIES: offices 10%; factories 20%; residential 60%; leisure 10%
DEVELOPMENT POLICY: Development now centred on Europe

Entry missing ? Call HELPLINE Page v

SUBSIDIARY COMPANIES: Brookley Estates Limited; Brookley Commercial Limited
(Sept 1992)

Brookmount plc
Melrose House
4-6 Savile Row
London W1X 1AF
071-287 1616
NATURE OF BUSINESS: Development & Investment
DIRECTORS: J F Wilton (Chairman); B A Craig BSc FRICS (Chief Executive); T Leyland (Managing); C J Auden BSc ARICS; P H Dunn LLB FCA FCIS (Non-Executive); D A H Baer (Non-Executive); P A Lovegrove LLM (Non-Executive); D M Calverley FCA (Non-Executive)
MAJOR SHAREHOLDERS: Trafalgar House plc; British and Commonwealth Holdings plc
ANNUAL TURNOVER: £63.3m (1989)
VALUE OF PROPERTY PORTFOLIO: £77.6m (1989)
SUBSIDIARY COMPANIES: Brookmount Properties Limited; Brookmount Estates Limited; Atholl Developments (Scotland) Limited; Brookmount Trading Limited; Towermill Properties; Atholl Building Contractors (Scotland) Limited; Brasshold Limited; Brookmount Murray Limited; Atholl Land Limited; Atholl Holdings (Scotland) Limited; Centre Management Services Limited; Atholl Property Consultants (Scotland) Limited; Brookmount Investments Limited; CFF Partnership Associates Limited; Wright Oliphant Limited; Brookmount Developments Limited; Brookmount Development Management Limited; Brookmount (Science Park) Limited; Brookmount City Investments Limited

Brougham Developments Limited
111 Windsor Road
Oldham OL8

Brown, A & Sons
6 Queen Street
London W1X 7PH

Brown, N Group plc
53 Duke Street
Manchester
M60 6ES

Brown & Jackson plc
Battle Bridge House
300 Gray's Inn Road
London WC1X 8DX

Brown Property & Investment Co
16 Davies Street
London
W1Y 1LJ

Bruntwood Estates Limited
Abney Hall
Manchester Road
Cheadle
Cheshire
SK8 2TD
061-491 3911
DIRECTOR: M J Oglesvy (Managing)

Bruton Estate plc
22-24 Ely Place
London
EC1N 6TQ
Tel: 071 242 6898 Fax: 071 405 1630
NATURE OF BUSINESS: Property Investment/ Development
DIRECTORS: H S Axton (Chairman); Sir Douglas Mordeth (Deputy Chairman); D F Gardner (Managing Director); L J Lane (Deputy Managing) Sir Richard Baker Wilbraham BT; Sir Michael Beetham; Sir John Cuckney; T J Nagle.,
MAJOR SHAREHOLDERS: Clerical Medical Investment Group, Royal Insurance plc
ANNUAL INCOME/TURNOVER: Company £47.6m.
REGIONAL PREFERENCES: S.E.
VALUE OF PROPERTY PORTFOLIO: £711m (1989)
DISTRIBUTION OF PORTFOLIO: Offices 40%, modern industrial/warehousing 60%
DEVELOPMENT POLICY: Offices, industrial, warehouses, hightec.

Bryant Barlett Limited
30 Camden Road
Bexleyheath
Kent
DA5 3NR
081-303 5486
DIRECTOR: Mr Barlett (Managing)

Bryant Group plc
Cranmore House
Cranmore Boulevard
Shirley, Solihull
West Midlands B90 4SD
Tel: 021-711 1212 Fax: 021-711 2610
NATURE OF BUSINESS: Development & Investment
DIRECTORS: A C Bryant BSc FCIOB (Chairman); A Mackenzie BSc FCIOB (Managing Director); M C Chapman FCA (Secretary); H W Laughland CA ATH; W N Mason-Jones BSC ARICS; G F Potton FCIOB; S J Roberts
ANNUAL TURNOVER: £322.9m (1992)
LOCATION OF REGIONAL OFFICES: Bracknell, Hertford, Crawley, Wetherby, Bristol, Loughborough, London.
INVESTMENT POLICY: All assets are held on a trading basis within a five year period.
DEVELOPMENT POLICY: All residential, commercial property and construction opportunities.
SUBSIDIARY COMPANIES: Bryant Homes plc, Bryant Properties plc, Bryant Construction Group plc, Bryant Group Services Limited, Bryant Retirement Homes Limited.
SISTER COMPANIES: Cactusmere Limited, Padyear Limited, Shire Business Park Limited, Vallbury Limited, Vechter Limited, Waterlinks plc, Birmingham Heartlands plc.
(Sept 1992)

Bryant Properties plc
Cranmore House
Cranmore Boulevard
Solihull
West Midlands B90 4SD
Tel: 021-711 1212 Fax: 021-711 1693
DIRECTORS: A C Bryant; A MacKenzie; M C Chapman; W N Mason-Jones; N J Harris; B P Sullivan

Buckingham Properties Investments Limited
19 Brunswick Place
Southampton
SO1 2AQ
0703 637717
DIRECTOR: R B Jordan (Managing)

Bucks & Herts Property Company Limited
Hardrick
Shootersway
Berkhampstead
Hertfordshire HP4 3NJ
0442 863861

Budge, A F (Development) Limited
West Carr Road
Retford
Nottinghamshire DN22 7SW
Tel: 0777 706789 Fax: 0777 705-66
DIRECTORS: A F Budge (Managing); R J Budge; R J Budge; J R Bower; G W Jarrett; G Muir; M A Jates
SUBSIDIARY COMPANIES: A F Budge (Contractors) Limited; A F Budge (Plant) Limited; J & J Fee Limited; Fee Design & Build Limited
ANNUAL GROSS TURNOVER/INCOME: £285m
REGIONAL PREFERENCES: UK

Burford Group plc
1 Bentinck Mews
London
W1M 6DD
Tel: 071-872 0044 Fax: 071-872 0012
NATURE OF COMPANY: Property Investment
DIRECTORS: Nigel Wray (Chairman); Nicholas Leslau BSc ARICS (Chief Executive); Julian Gleek (Financial Director); John Gommes (Non Exec)
MAJOR SHAREHOLDERS: Nigel Wray, Singer & Friedlander, Gartmore, Standard Life Assurance Company, TSB Group, Scottish Widows Fund.
LOCATION OF OFFICES: None
ANNUAL INCOME: GROUP £10m
VALUE OF PROPERTY PORTFOLIO: £80m (1991)
REGIONAL PREFERENCE FOR ACTIVITIES: Throughout the UK
DISTRIBUTION OF PORTFOLIO: Offices 52%; shops 22%; industrial 12%; ground rents 10%; retail warehousing 5%; residential 5%; other 4%.
INVESTMENT POLICY: To acquire high yielding properties let at low base rents where majority of income is derived from very good covenants and management opportunities to add value
(Sept 1992)

Burhill Estates Co
Club House
Burhill
Walton-On-Thames
Surrey KT12 4BL

Burleigh Investments Limited
Haven House
Lakes Road
Keston
Bromley
Kent BR2 6BN
Tel: 0689 860320 Fax: 0689 858601
DIRECTORS: A R Cherry (Chairman); C D Parsons; M P Grover; S R Grover; D A Bird
NATURE OF BUSINESS: Investment

Burrel Contracts plc
174 High Street
The Royal Mile
Edinburgh EH1 1QS
031 220 3040
DIRECTOR: A Burrell (Managing); L Barras (Marketing)

Burrell Company, The
174 High Street
The Royal Mile
Edinburgh EH1 1QS
031-220 3040
DIRECTOR: A Burrell (Managing)

Bursha Holdings Limited
37 Upper Grosvenor Street
London W1X

Burton Property Trust Limited
1 Dean Street
London W1V
071-734 1040
DIRECTORS: J Bywater (Managing); C Miniham; S Rutherford

Burwood House Group
3rd Floor
65 Buckingham Gate
London SW1E

Bury & District Property Co Limited
39 Bury New Road
Prestwich
Manchester M25

Butlers Wharf Limited
The Butlers Wharf Building
36 Shad Thames
London SE1

CIN Properties Limited
66 Hanover Street
Edinburgh EH2

CIN Properties Limited
Hobart House
Grosvenor Place
London SW1X 7AE

CINIO Limited
105 Park Street
London W1Y 3FB

CIS Property Developments Limited
50 Berners Street
London W1P 3AD
071-323 9316 FAX: 071-436 5270

CP Holdings Limited
CP House
Otterspool Way
Watford Bypass
Watford WD2 8HG
0932 50500
DIRECTOR: B Schreier (Managing)

CP Trafalgar Securities (UK) Limited
62/65 Trafalgar Square
London WC2N

C & P Projects Limited
14 Grosvenor Crescent
London SW1X 7EE
071-245 6711
DIRECTOR: D Owen

CNC Properties Ltd
CNC House
33 High Street
Sunninghill, Ascot
Berkshire SL5 9NR
Tel: 0990 28721 Fax: 0990 28711

CTL Estates
Lissadel House
Lissadel Street, Salford
Greater Manchester M6 6QQ
Tel: 061-737 6056 Fax: 061-737 8118
NATURE OF BUSINESS: Property Development/ Investment
REGIONAL PREFERENCES: North/North E Midlands/ Scotland
INVESTMENT POLICY: Secondary offices/warehousing/ factories

Cabra Estates plc
4 Hill Street
Mayfair
London W1X 7FU
Tel: 071-408 1661 Fax: 071 629 9368
NATURE OF BUSINESS: Property Traders and Developers
DIRECTORS: J F Duggan; E J Cotter; A J Mackay; J A G Young
MAJOR SHAREHOLDERS: Mountleigh Securities Limited, Universities Superannuation Scheme Limited, Barclays Bank plc, The Merchant Navy Officers, J F Duggan, The Norwich Union Life Insurance Society, The Royal Bank of Scotland Group plc
ANNUAL TURNOVER/INCOME: £91.9m (1990) (Group)
VALUE OF PROPERTY PORTFOLIO: £133.7 million 31.3.90
DISTRIBUTION OF PORTFOLIO: UK £116.074 million, Ireland £17.626 million.
SUBSIDIARY COMPANIES: Marler Estates plc and subsidiaries Rohan Group plc and subsidiaries.

Caddick, Paul Limited
Calder Grange
Knottingley
W. Yorkshire WF11 8DA
0977 678181
SECRETARY: G Beaumont

Cadogan Estates Limited
The Cadogan Office
18 Cadogan Gardens
London SW3 2RP
071-730 4567
DIRECTOR: S Corbyn (Managing)

Cadogan Securities plc
11 Grosvenor Crescent
London SW1X 7EE
071-629 0242
MANAGING DIRECTORS: J D Billig; J B Barrymore; C P Colombott

CAEC Howard Group
Howard House
40/64 St John's Street
Bedford MK42 ODL
0234 63171
DIRECTOR: B Howard (Managing)

CALA City of Aberdeen Land Association
1 Golden Square
Aberdeen AB9 8BH
0224 647344
ANNUAL TURNOVER: £42.49m (1987)
CONTACT: Mrs Morrison

Cala plc
42 Colinton Road
Edinburgh
EH10 5BT
Tel: 031-346 0194 Fax: 031-346 4190
NATURE OF BUSINESS: Housebuilding and Property Development
DIRECTORS: R J W Dick, A J Kelley, M J Whittles, E T Razzall, A Ledingham, A W Downie

LOCATION OF REGIONAL OFFICES: Falkirk, Edinburgh, Birmingham, Basingstoke
ANNUAL TURNOVER: GROUP: 88m (1990)
DISTRIBUTION OF DEVELOPMENT ACTIVITIES: All UK
(Sept 1992)

Caldaire Holdings
24 Barnsley Road
Wakefield
W Yorkshire WF1 5JX
0924 383483
DIRECTOR: Mr M J Hunter (Managing)

Calder House Estates
Calder House
1 Dover Street
London W1X 3PJ
071-493 6120
DIRECTORS: G Bell FRICS (Managing); D Thompson

Caledon Park plc
2 Belford Road
Edinburgh EH4

Callander Land Securities Limited
24 Melville Street
Edinburgh EH3

Calthorpe Estate Office
16 Norfolk Road
Edgbaston
Birmingham
B15 3SN
021-456 1409
DIRECTOR: J P Neering (Managing)

Caltrust Development Limited
132 West Regent Street
Glasgow
G2 2RG
041 221 3965

Cambridge Land Securities Limited
36 Green Street
London W1Y

Cameron Hall Developments Limited
Wynyard Hall
Billingham
Cleveland
TS22 5NP
0740 644811

Campaniers Quinta S.A.
10a Drayton Gardens
London SW10

Canadian Business Parks plc
Juniper Court
Boxwell Road
Berkhamsted
Herts HP4 3ET
0442-870737

Canning Properties Limited
64 West Smithfield
London EC1A

Canynge Securities Limited
84 Pembridge Road
Bristol
Avon BS8 3EG
0272 743791
DIRECTOR: A Whicheloe

Caparo Properties plc
103 Baker Street
London W1M 1FD
071-486 1417

Capital & City Holdings Limited
Brookfield House
44 Davies Street
London W1Y 1LD
Tel: 071-499 0583 Fax: 071-499 6866
DIRECTOR: A R Hay (Managing)

Capital & City Management Limited
33 Davies Street
London W1Y

Capital & City plc
33 Davies Street
London W1Y 1FN

Capital & Counties plc
40 Broadway
London SW1H OBU
Tel: 071-222 7878 Fax: 071-222 2989
NATURE OF BUSINESS: Shopping Centre and Commercial Development and Portfolio Management
DIRECTORS: D Gordon CA (SA) (Chairman); M Rapp CA (SA) (Deputy Chairman); B A Jolly FRICS (Managing); J G Abel FRICS; R A M Baillie FCIBS (SCOT); W E Cesman CA (SA); H P de Villiers CA (SA); D A Fischel ACA; J I Saggers FRICS; P H Spriddell; K H Wallis
PARENT COMPANY: Transatlantic Insurance Holdings plc
ANNUAL TURNOVER: £97.9m (1991)
SUBSIDIARY COMPANIES: Greenhaven Securities Limited
INVESTMENT POLICY: Active
DEVELOPMENT POLICY: Principally large retail schemes. Campus style office parks.
(Sept 1992)

Entry missing ? Call HELPLINE Page v

Capital Estates Limited
1234/127 New Road
London E1

Capital Investments
Suite 627
Sunlight House
Quay Street
Manchester M3

Capital Investment Agency
Kings House
Widmore Road
Bromley
Kent BR1 1RY
081-464 4442
DIRECTOR: D E Dawkins (Managing)
(Sept 1992)

Capital & Regional Properties plc
22 Grosvenor Gardens
London SW1W 0DH
Tel: 071-730 5565 Fax: 071-730 0151
NATURE OF BUSINESS: Property Investment & Management
DIRECTORS: M Barber (Chairman); X Pullen (Managing); R M Boyland FCA; Lynda S Coral ACA; M H Gruselle FCA (Non-Executive); D D Martin-Jenkins (Non-Executive)
MAJOR SHAREHOLDERS: Scottish Amicable Pensions Investments (12.48%); British Gas Pension Fund (8.08%); Sun Life (6.84%); Invesco Mim (5.99%); Scottish Mutual Assurance (4.83%); Philips & Drew (4.73%); Clerical Medical & General Life Assurance (4.14%); Charterhouse Tilney (3.19%)
ANNUAL TURNOVER: £5.24m (1991)
VALUE OF PROPERTY PORTFOLIO: £47.05m (1991)
SUBSIDIARY COMPANIES: Branchlook Limited; Capital & Regional Estates Limited; Capital & Regional Investments Limited; Capital & Regional Property Management Limited; Cosmorole Limited; Dawncross Limited; Favourshaw Limited; Grovebury Properties (Holdings) Limited; Manchester Corn Exchange Estates Limited; Owlamber Limited; Capital & Regional Property Holdings Limited; Churchwick Investments Limited; Dawson Investments Limited; Denton Investments Limited; Jearon Properties Limited; Capital & Regional (Victoria) Limited (50%)
(Sept 1992)

Capital & Rural Properties
Lansdowne House
Berkeley Square
London W1X 6BP
071-495 7575
NATURE OF BUSINESS: Property Developer
DIRECTORS: Lord Sharp of Grimsdyke, Chairman; S Lipton (Managing); J Botts; D Dantzic; S Honeyman; R John; P Kershaw; P Reichmann; P Rogers; V Wang
(Sept 1992)

Capital Pride Properties Limited
281 Kentish Town Road
London NW5

Capital Property Developments Limited
288/292 Regent Street
London W1R 5HE
071-323 44300

Capital Real Estates Limited
49 Mount Street
London W1Y

Caran Investments Limited
9 Hanover Street
Hanover Square
London W1R 9HF
071-629 3841

Cardiff Property plc
56 Station Road
Egham
Surrey TW20 9LX
Tel: 0784 437444 Fax: 0784 439157
NATURE OF BUSINESS: Property Development & Investment
DIRECTORS: N D Jamieson; J R Wollenberg; A Zaph (Managing); W R Beck ACIS (Secretary)
ANNUAL TURNOVER: £790,669
VALUE OF PORTFOLIO: £11.6m (1991)
SUBSIDIARY COMPANIES: Wadharma Equities Limited; Wadharma Holdings Limited; Wadharma Investment Limited; Wadharma Securities Limited; Cardiff Property (Dev) Ltd; Cardiffi Property (Construction) Ltd; Village Residential plc
(Sept 1992)

Cardinal Developments Limited
15 Park Street
Windsor
Berkshire SL4 1LU
0753 830038
NATURE OF BUSINESS: Development
DIRECTORS: R C Greed FRICS; C L Greed CSD
MAJOR SHAREHOLDERS: Directors
REGIONAL PREFERENCES: Home Counties & West
DEVELOPMENT ACTIVITIES: offices 20%; residential 50%; science parks/hi-tech 20%; leisure 10%
DEVELOPMENT POLICY: Commercial development and refurbishment. Some residential and leisure

Caribbean Development (Holdings) Limited
9 Radnow Walk
London SW3

Carlton Gate Development Co
Carlton Gate
Harrow Road
London W9

Carlton House Group Limited
Carlton House
Albert Square
Manchester M2

Caroline Developments Limited
46 Priestgate
Peterborough
Cambridgeshire PE1 1LF
0733 64814
DIRECTOR: B Cheetham (Managing)

Carrington Properties Limited
Carrington House
130 Regent Street
London W1R

Carroll Group of Companies
2-6 Catherine Place
London SW1E 6HP
071-828 6842
(Sept 1992)
NATURE OF BUSINESS: Development & Investment
DIRECTOR: A Clarke (Managing)
MAJOR SHAREHOLDERS: Private Company, Family Trusts
INVESTMENT POLICY: Seeking further major inner city development & investment opportunities in partnership with Local Authorities, Statutory Bodies or Government Agencies
DEVELOPMENT POLICY: £60m Inner city programme to develop derelict sites. Throughout UK develop high quality business accommodation in partnership with Public Authorities
(Jan 1991)

Carroll Property Corporation
255 Cranbrook Road
Ilford
Essex IG1 4TG
0277 210661
DIRECTOR: P A Willis (Managing)

Carter Commercial Developments Limited
3 Vicarage Road
Edgbaston
Birmingham B15

Carter Holdings plc
Pilgrim House
High Street
Billericay
Essex CM12 9XY
Tel: 0277 659321 Fax: 0277 630020
DIRECTOR: M J Clarke (Managing)

Castle Keep Developments Limited
22 Grosvenor Gardens
London SW1W ODH
071-730 9960
NATURE OF BUSINESS: Development & Investment
DIRECTORS: R F Willmot FRICS; J F Willmott MCIOB MBIM; ANNUAL TURNOVER: £5.5m (30/6/88)
INVESTMENT POLICY: Intend to move into investment more when asset base is stronger
DEVELOPMENT ACTIVITIES: Offices 20%; shops 60%; warehouses 10%; residential 10%
DEVELOPMENT POLICY: Tendency for developments which can be traded on to institutions
SUBSIDIARY COMPANIES: John Willmot Developments; John Willmott Homes; John Willmott Investments

Castle Square Development Limited
6 & 7 Castle Hill
Lincoln
Lincolnshire LN1 3AA
0522 522243
DIRECTOR: C F Markham (Managing)

Castlemere Property Group Limited
12 Oxford Road
Altrincham
Cheshire WA14 2EB
Tel: 061-941 3499 Fax: 061-928 9515
NATURE OF BUSINESS: Fund Management, Investment and Development
DIRECTORS: S G Lindemann (CEO); C A Lindemann; J B Sherriff (Chairman); R Vezina (Canadian)
MAJOR SHAREHOLDERS: Laurential Life plc (100%)
BRANCH OFFICES: Gloucester (reg. office); London
ANNUAL TURNOVER: £2.9m (1992)
REGIONAL PREFERENCES: North West; Gloucester; Greater London
VALUE OF PROPERTY PORTFOLIO: £30m
PROPERTY PORTFOLIO: Offices 40%; shops 16%; factories 44%
DEVELOPMENT/INVESTMENT POLICIES: To add value to existing portfolio; Opportunistic
DEVELOPMENT ACTIVITIES: Offices 50%; Industrial 50%
SUBSIDIARY COMPANIES: Castlemere Developments Limited; Castlemere Properties Limited
(Sept 1992)

Castlemount Developments Limited
12th Floor
Silkhouse Court
Tithebarn Street
Liverpool L2 2LE

Castletone Investments Limited
6 Durweston Mews
Crawford Street
London W1H 1PB
071-935 0937

Caterham Development Company Limited
Croudace House
97 Godstone Road
Caterham
Surrey CR3 6XQ
0883 341458
DIRECTOR: R Edmunston (Managing)

Cavendish Estates
9 Cavendish Road
London W1M OBL

Cavendish and Gloucester Properties Limited
Gloucester House
Woodside Lane
London N12 8TP
Tel: 081-446 4216 Fax: 081-446 0519
DIRECTOR: P Murphy (Managing)

Cavendish Offices & Houses Inventments Limited
23 Welbeck Street
London W1M

Cedarlands Limited
20 Great Western Road
London W9 3NW
Tel: 071-289 6263 Fax: 071-289 6386
NATURE OF BUSINESS: Property Investment & Development
DIRECTORS: David Tarling; V A Keech BSc
MAJOR SHAREHOLDERS: Various
ANNUAL TURNOVER/INCOME: Company 3m; Group 3m
REGIONAL PREFERENCES: London and South East England
VALUE OF PROPERTY PORTFOLIO: £3.5m 1989
DISTRIBUTION OF PORTFOLIO: Shops 50%; residential 50%
INVESTMENT POLICY: Purchase of freehold shop investments and residential investments.
DEVELOPMENT ACTIVITIES: £1.5m shops
DEVELOPMENT POLICY: Acquisition of any potential development land in South East England.

Celus Properties Limited
1 Berners Mansions
34-36 Berners Street
London W1P 3DA
071-636 6041

Centerfield Investments Limited
14 Walker Street
Denton
Manchester M34

Central & City Investment Holdings
55 St James's Street
London SW1A 1LA
Tel: 071-491 2948 Fax; 071-629 0414
(Sept 1992)
NATURE OF BUSINESS: Commercial Property Development and Investment
DIRECTORS: David A King; Sir John A Mactaggart (Joint Managing)
REGIONAL PREFERENCE: Central London
DISTRIBUTION OF PORTFOLIO: Offices 90%; shops 10%
(Jan 1991)

Central & District Properties Limited
79 Pall Mall
London SW1Y 5ES
DIRECTORS: J M Sterling CBE (Chairman); B D MacPhail FCA; R D Mann FRICS; P H Grimson FCA; J G Lyon FRICS; E Wyatt (Secretary)
MAJOR SHAREHOLDERS: A subsidiary of Town & City Properties plc

Central & Provincial Estates Limited
The Fitzpatrick Building
188/194 York Way
London N7 9AX
Tel: 071 607 6867 Fax: 071 607 2088
NATURE OF BUSINESS: Property Investment Company & Developers
DIRECTORS: N L Bobroff (Managing)
MAJOR SHAREHOLDERS: N L Bobroff; A H Bobroff
REGIONAL PREFERENCES: England
INVESTMENT POLICY: Commercial, Retail & Residential Properties
(Sept 1992)

Central & Provincial Properties Limited
Mitre House
177 Regent Street
Lonon W1R 7FB

Central & Sheerwood plc
Caldwell Road
Nuneaton
Coventry CV11 4NE
Tel: 0203 341211 Fax: 071-408 1814
NATURE OF BUSINESS: development
DIRECTORS: J R K Bowdidge BSc ARICS; C J Emson
MAJOR SHAREHOLDERS: Pergamon Holdings Limited; Robert Fraser Group Limited
ANNUAL TURNOVER: £10m (1989)
REGIONAL PREFERENCES: London, Midlands, East Anglia
DEVELOPMENT ACTIVITIES: Offices 65%; shops 25%; factories 10%
DEVELOPMENT POLICY: Active in commercial property

Central Estates (Belgravia) Limited
Institution House
169 Knightsbridge
London SW7
071-581 4059

Central London Securities Limited
Chancel House
Neasden Lane
London NW10
081-451 0675

Central Manchester Development Corporation
Churchgate House
56 Oxford Street
Manchester M1 8DJ
061-236 1166

Central Parkes South Limited
Hale Court
Lincoln's Inn
London WC2A 3UL
0623 410100

Central Properties
24 Quarmby Road
Manchester M18

Central Properties Securities Limited
41 Beauchamp Place
London SW3 1NX
071-581 0516
NATURE OF BUSINESS: Development & Investment
DIRECTORS: P Mason; R Mellor FSVA
REGIONAL PREFERENCES: London & Home Counties
PROPERTY PORTFOLIO: Shops 85%; warehouses 15%
DEVELOPMENT ACTIVITIES: residential 50%; studio/workshop 50%
DEVELOPMENT POLICY: Residential and studio workshop developments

Central Union Property Group Limited
31 Imperial Square
Cheltenham
Gloucestershire GL50 1QZ
0242 222414
NATURE OF BUSINESS: Development & Investment
DIRECTORS: R A Martin FRICS; P W Thorneycroft FRICS

Centreland Group
36-38 Berkeley Square
London W1X 5DA
Tel: 071-355 4595 Fax: 071 355 4003
DIRECTOR: R Freeman (Managing)
(Sept 1992)

Centric Securities Limited
47 South Moulton Street
London W1Y 1HE
071-499 7171
DIRECTOR: R J Midda (Managing)

Centros Properties Limited
Stratton House
Stratton Street
London W1X 6NJ
Tel: 071-499 3917/-491 7452 Fax; 071-499 3741
(Sept 1992)

Centrovincial Estates Limited
4-6 Savile Row
London W1X 1AF
071-734 7551
Subsidiary of Singer & Friedlander
NATURE OF BUSINESS: Development & Investment
DIRECTORS: J Gold FRICS (Chairman & Joint Managing); P A Coster ARICS (Joint Managing); H A S Djanoghy CBE; B Gold FRBA Dip Arch (UCL); B C Marshall CA
MAJOR SHAREHOLDERS: Barclays Nominees (George Yard) Limited: 1m shares; General Accident Group: 2.8m shares; Count Bank Group: 0.9m shares
BRANCH OFFICES: London
INVESTMENT POLICY: Offices, shops
DEVELOPMENT POLICY: Offices, hi-tech, retail, warehouses
SUBSIDIARY COMPANIES: Golby-Hale Property & Investment Company Limited; Queensland Properties Limited; Burnham Estates Limited; Inmobo SA (incorporated in Spain)

Ceres Estates Limited
Buchanan House
24-30 Holborn
London EC1N 2HS
DIRECTOR: W J Parker

Chadlington House Limited
11 Lesley Court
Strutton Ground
London SW1P

Chadstock Properties
49-53 Kensington High Street
London W8 7RD

Chainbow Holdings plc
Hope House
Great Peter Street
London SW1P 3LT
Tel: 071-222 2837 Fax: 071-976 7252
DIRECTOR: R J Southam (Managing)
(Sept 1992)

Chalkhurst Limited
Flat 4
18 Hans Crescent
London SW1X

Challenge Developments (Northern) Limited
251 Parr Lane
Bury BL9

Chancel Construction Limited
Chancel Court
2 Wellington Road
Bilston
West Midlands WV14 6AA
0902 353432
DIRECTORS: P A Hardee (Marketing)

Chancery Lane Property Management Services Limited
22 South Audley Street
London W1Y
Fax: 071-935 3338

Chandos Investments Limited
44 Stamford Street
Stalybridge
Manchester SK15

Chanery Property Finance
100 Avenue Road
Swiss Cottage
London NW3 3HF
Tel: 071-722 0099 Fax: 071-722 5797/5226
NATURE OF BUSINESS: property finance
DIRECTORS: Brian Rubins; Hanan Baradon; Ian Rosenthal
MAJOR SHAREHOLDERS: Chancery plc
INVESTMENT POLICY: finance for residential and commercial development investment finance, bridging and term loans.

Chanic Group Limited, The
17/18 Clere Street
London EC2A

Chantry Developments Limited
'Birkrigg'
1B Dorchester Road
Hazel Grove
Stockport SK7 5HE
061-483 7028
NATURE OF BUSINESS: Development and Investment
DIRECTORS: C H Perrin BSc FRICS (Managing Director);A J Perrin
ANNUAL INCOME/TURNOVER: Company £2m (1989)
REGIONAL PREFERENCES: North West England
DISTRIBUTION OF PORTFOLIO: offices 25%, B1 40%, industrial 35%
VALUE OF PROPERTY PORTFOLIO: £3m (1990)
INVESTMENT POLICY: to continue Commercial Development Programme for disposal, with selective investment acquisitions
DEVELOPMENMT ACTIVITIES: Offices 20%, B1 50%, industrial 30%
DEVELOPMENT POLICY: To expand commercial development programme
(Sept 1992)

Charities Official Investment Fund
St Alphage House
2 Fore Street
London EC2Y 5AQ
Tel: 071-588 1815 Fax: 071-588 6291
DIRECTOR: Viscount Churchill (Managing)
(Sept 1992)

Charlecote Property Developments Limited
5A Charlecote Mews
Staple Gardens, Winchester
Hampshire SO23 8SR
Tel: 0962 842244 Fax: 0962 867037
NATURE OF BUSINESS: Property Development
DIRECTORS: R J Cleaver FRICS; B S Keys FRICS;
REGIONAL PREFERENCE: Southern half of country up to Birmingham including South Wales
DEVELOPMENT POLICY: Keen to acquire land and buildings for all types of commercial development

Charles Miller Properties Limited
58 High Street
Oxted
Surrey RH8 9LP
Tel: 0883 714285 Fax: 0883 730120
DIRECTOR: P Charles
REGIONAL PREFERENCES: South-East UK
DISTRIBUTION PORTFOLIO: Shops 70%; Offices 10%; Residential 20%
INVESTMENT POLICY: To expand portfolio by the acquisition of good/secondary shops and shopping parades.
(Sept 1992)

Charmar Developments
162 High Street
Stoke Newington
London N16

Charter Developments plc
10 The Pavillion
Exchange Quay
Salford
Manchester M5

Charter Group plc
Exchange Tower
1 Harbour Exchange Square
London E14 9GB
Tel: 071-355 1000 Fax: 071-355 3527
(Sept 1992)
NATURE OF BUSINESS: Development
DIRECTORS: S P Miller (Chairman); J B White (Managing Director); A T Davison; A P Hadley; K P Reynolds
ANNUAL TURNOVER: £37.8m (1988)
VALUE OF PROPERTY PORTFOLIO: £30.5m (1988)
SUBSIDIARY COMPANIES: Charter Group Developments plc; Interdec Design Group plc; Charter Group Finance Limited; Charter Group Marketing Limited; Harbour Exchange Management Company Limited; Charter Group Project Management Limited; Charter Group Estates Limited; Harbour Exchange Limited; Charter Group Investments Limited
ASSOCIATED COMPANIES: Charter Group Design Limited; Hill Charter Developments Limited
(Jan 1991)

Charter Group Developments plc
1 Harbour Exchange Square
Limeharbour
London E14
Tel: 071-538 3155 Fax: 071-355 3525
(Sept 1992)

Charter Investments Limited
155 Regents Park Road
London NW1

Chartered Developments Limited
451 London Road
Westcliff-on-Sea
Essex SSO 9LG
0702 345111
DIRECTOR: J Anderson (Managing)

Charterfield Properties Limited
9-10 Old Stone Link
Ship Street
East Grinstead
West Sussex RH19 4EF
Tel: 0342 410242 Fax: 0342 313493
NATURE OF BUSINESS: Development
DIRECTORS: T H Merchant MBA BSc MICE; D N Cowan RIBA; P S M Rogers
MAJOR SHAREHOLDERS: Directors
ANNUAL TURNOVER/INCOME/PROFIT: £0.25m
REGIONAL PREFERENCES: London, South East
VALUE OF PROPERTY PORTFOLIO: £1.1m 1992
DISTRIBUTION OF PORTFOLIO: Offices 100%
DEVELOPMENT ACTIVITIES: Offices 1000%
DEVELOPMENT POLICY: Quality housing and retirement schemes, offices
(Sept 1992)

Charterhall Properties
9 Chesterfield Street
London W1X
071-493 2627
DIRECTORS: J Smith; D Stacey FRICS (Managing)

Charterhouse Estates
5 Royalty Studios
105 Lancaster Road
London W11 1QF
071-792 2900
DIRECTOR: R Zogolovitch (Managing)

Charterhouse Estates Limited
61 Grange Road
London SE1
071-231 3723
DIRECTOR: R Zogolovitch (Managing)

Charterhouse Land Limited
10 Whitchurch Road
Pangbourne
Berkshire RG8 7BP
0734 844651

Charting Developments (Holdings) Limtied
32 Fleming House
Craig Park
Newcraighall
Edinburgh EH15

Chartwell Land plc
66 Chiltern Street
London W1M 2AL
Tel: 071-224 5522 Fax: 071-224 2964
(Sept 1992)
DIRECTORS: A Jones (Managing); N Light (Commercial); T Ayre (Investment); D Gregory (Retail Development); M Heald (Finance); R Hood (Business Development & Marketing); J Petit (Business Space Development)
MAJOR SHAREHOLDERS: 100% Kingfisher plc
PROPERTY ASSETS: £842m (Feb 1990)
PROFITS: £64.8m plus a further £84.9m of sales and leasebacks (Feb 1990)
REGIONAL PREFERENCES: Throughout the UK
INVESTMENT POLICY: Retail 85%; Office 7%; Industrial 8%
DEVELOPMENT POLICY: Retail; High Street, Retail Parks, Shopping Centres and Malls. Business Space; Industrial, Offices, Business Parks, Distributions Centres
(Jan 1991)

Charville Estates Limited
Broadbent House
64-65 Grosvenor Street
London W1X 9DB
071-493 5129
NATURE OF BUSINESS: Development & Investment
DIRECTORS: D J Pulford FRICS; R C Pulford FRICS
MAJOR SHAREHOLDERS: Directors
VALUE INVESTMENT AND DEVELOPMENT: Shops 100%
INVESTMENT POLICY: Prime locations in market towns throughout UK
DEVELOPMENT POLICY: Town Centre retail, conservation areas

Chase Redevelopments Limited
18 Bennets Hill
Birmingham B2

Chatburn Properties Limited
45 Welbeck Street
London W1M 7HF
071-792 0371
DIRECTOR: B Hodges (Managing)

Chatham Estates
Lower Chatham Street
Manchester M1

Chaucer Estates Limited
Chaucer House
6 Boltro Road
Haywards Heath
West Sussex RH16 1BB
Tel: 0444 416631 Fax: 0444 440700
DIRECTORS: L I Granville-Grossman (Managing); L B McCormick; B C Davis FCA; C E Bush BSc ARICS; H A Vice
(Sept 1992)

Cheamplace Limited
The Mount
Selby Road
Garforth
Leeds
West Yorkshire

Chelsfield plc
67 Brook Street
London W1Y 1YE
071-493 3977
DIRECTOR: M Broke (Managing)

Chessingham Estates
The White House
Chantry Lane
Bishopthorpe
York YO2 1QF
0904 708944
DIRECTOR: Mr R. Wood (Managing)

Chesterfield Developments Limited
Albany House
10 Wood Street
Barnet
Hertfordshire EN5 4BW

Chesterfield Properties plc
38 Curzon Street
Mayfair
London W1Y 8EY
Tel: 071-499 7571 Fax: 071-499 2018
(Sept 1992)
NATURE OF BUSINESS: Development & Investment
DIRECTORS: E L Erdman FSVA (Chairman) (Non-Executive); R Wingate BSc (Est Man) FRICS (Chief Executive); R Boas BA FCA (Non-Executive); R Wain MA (Non-Executive); R Cossey FRICS; D Kiernan FCCA; J Gamble ARICS
MAJOR SHAREHOLDERS: Prudential Corporation plc; Harold Hyam Wingate Charitable Foundation; Nominees (Jersey) Limited
ANNUAL TURNOVER: £28.6m (1989)
REGIONAL PREFERENCES: South East
VALUE OF PROPERTY PORTFOLIO: £499m (1989)
INVESTMENT POLICY: Offices, shops
DEVELOPMENT POLICY: Shops, offices, industrial, residential
SUBSIDIARY COMPANIES: Busher (Property Management) Limited; Cadfield Properties Limited; Cadmount Properties Limited; Chesterfield Properties (Merthyr) Limited; Chestergreen Properties Limited; Chestergrove Limited; Chestermount Properties Limited; Comchester Properties Limited; Comet Properties Limited; Comgrove Properties Limited; Corfield Properties Limited; Cormount Properties Limited; Fenfield Properties (Mayfair) Limited; Instrument Motors Limited; Kenfield Properties Limited; Meadfield Properties Limited; Penwind Limited; Phoenix Theatre Limited; Provincial Shop Properties Limited; Tenstall Limited; Titlerule Limited; Viaduct Properties Limited; Kengrove Properties Limited; Curzon Film Distributors Limited; GCT (Management) Limited; Continental Investment Development SA; SAI Elysee Roosevelt; Maybox Group plc, Anfield Properties Limited.
(Jan 1991)

Chestergate Properties
62/63 Queen Street
London EC4R

Chestergate Property Holdings Limited
213 Ashley Road
Hale
Cheshire WA15 9TB
061-941 4948
DIRECTORS: J Jackson; P Conn
REGIONAL PREFERENCES: South East England, North West England
DEVELOPMENT ACTIVITIES: Offices; shops; factories; warehouses
SUBSIDIARY COMPANIES: Chestergate Properties Limited; Chestergate Developments Limited; Chestergate Investments Limited

Cheveley Park Properties (Radcliffe) Limited
95 Radcliffe Road
Bury
Manchester BL9

Christian & Nielson
21-24 Grosvenor Place
London SW1X 7JE
071-235 4321
DIRECTOR: Mr Anstead (Managing); Mr Purves (Marketing)

Christopher Lawrence Limited
100 Warwick Way
London SW1V 1SD

Christopher St James Properties plc
12 The Broadway
London SW19 1RF

Church Commissioners for England, The
1 Millbank
London SW1P 3J2
Tel: 071-222 7010 Fax: 071-222 0653
(Sept 1992)
NATURE OF BUSINESS: Development & Investment
DIRECTORS: Committees & Board of Governors
FIRST COMMISSIONER: Sir D Lovelock
ANNUAL NET INCOME: £53.8m (1988) (Total property income); £40.1m (1988) (Commercial property)
VALUE OF PROPERTY PORTFOLIO: £1,326.8m; £941m (commercial)
TOTAL PROPERTY PORTFOLIO: offices 32%; factories/warehouses 2%; residential 18%; shops 28%; other 20%
COMMERCIAL PORTFOLIO: offices 45%; factories/warehouses 3%; shops 41%; other 11%
INVESTMENT POLICY: Industrial outside the South East; Retail - prime position with low zone A; Office - provincial centres (Leeds, Bristol, Manchester)
DEVELOPMENT ACTIVITIES: (approx) offices 20%; shops 60%; warehouses 10%
DEVELOPMENT POLICY: Keen to undertake developments, especially office/park/industrial
(Jan 1991)

Churchbury Estates plc
Leconfield House
Curzon Street
London W1Y 8JR
DIRECTORS: O Marriott (Chairman & Managing); A MacDonald; D Lucie-Smith FCA (Secretary); J Evans; D E Gourlay CA FCIS; E G Libby
SUBSIDIARY COMPANIES: Banderway Limited; Churchbury Investment Company Limited; Law Land plc; Oastbridge plc

Churchill Securities
1 Dartmouth Grove
London SE10 8AR

Churchmanor Estates Company,The
24 Binney Street
London W1Y 1YN
071-499 5854
DIRECTOR: S Clark (Managing)

Churchmoor
Garland Hall
Crowley
Northwich
Cheshire CW9 6NS
0565 777430
JOINT MANAGING DIRECTORS: M W Pickard; S L Pickard

Cignet
Belmont Road, Belmont
Surrey SM2 6DW
081-642 4456 081-643 0147
(Sept 1992)
DIRECTORS: P Stait FRICS; J J Bishop; B A Yates; P I McFarlan
MAJOR SHAREHOLDERS: Directors
ANNUAL INCOME TURNOVER: Group £8m (1989)
REGIONAL PREFERENCES: South East England
DISTRIBUTION OF PORTFOLIO: Industrial 100%
DEVELOPMENT ACTIVITIES: Offices 25%; Industrial 75%
SUBSIDIARY COMPANIES: Cignet Group Contractors Limited; Cignet Group Properties Limited; Erinhill Limited
(Jan 1991)

Circle Properties Limited
38 Cadogan Square
London SW1X

City Estates Limited
City House
5 Carlton Crescent
Southampton
Hampshire SO1 2EY
Tel: 0703 212060 Fax: 0703 212007
NATURE OF BUSINESS: Property Development and Investment
DIRECTORS: Mr Titheridge (Managing); D J Mallinson
MAJOR SHAREHOLDERS: Scottish Heritable Trust plc
REGIONAL OFFICES: Southampton/London
ANNUAL INCOME/TURNOVER: Company £10m; Group £90 million.
REGIONAL PREFERENCE: Southern England
VALUE OF PROPERTY PORTFOLIO: 60% offices; 20% shops, 20% industrial
DEVELOPMENT POLICY:To expand portfolio within Portsmouth/Southampton area
DEVELOPMENT ACTIVITIES:60% Offices, 20% Shops, 20% Industrial

City Land plc
12 Upper Berkley Street
London W1H 7PE
Tel: 071-723 0031 Fax: 071-724 7303
DIRECTOR: A Nissim (Managing)

City & London Group Limited
105 Boundary Road
St Johns Wood
London NW8 ORQ
071-372 1100

City of London Real Property Company Limited
Landsec House
5 Strand
London WC2N 5AF
Tel: 071-413 9000 Fax: 071-925 0202
DIRECTOR: P J Hunt (Managing)
MAJOR SHAREHOLDERS: Land Securities plc

City & Northern Limited
Shildon Grange
Corbridge
Northumberland NE45 5PT
Tel: 0434 633663 Fax: 0434 633042
NATURE OF BUSINESS: Property Development

City & Provincial Management Group Limited
14 Grosvenor Crescent
London SW1X 7EE
071-245 6711
DIRECTOR: P A Archer (Managing)

City & Provincial Properties Limited
43 Queen Anne Street
London W1M

City & Urban Securities Limited
2 Charterhouse Mews
London EC1M

City Conversions
Linton Court
Murleston Road
Edinburgh EH11

City Orbit Estates Limited
131 Baker Street
London W1M

Citygrove Leisure plc

1/18 Chelsea Garden Market
Chelsea Harbour
London SW10
Fax: 071-376 4918
(Sept 1992)

Citybridge plc

10 Kenyon Street
Birmingham B18

City Securities Group of Companies

19 Devonshire Street
London W1N 1FS
071-636 3021
DIRECTOR: D Mosselson (Managing)
(Sept 1992)

City Site Estates plc

116 Blythewood Street
Glasgow
Tel: 041-248 2534 Fax: 041-226 3321
(Sept 1992)
NATURE OF BUSINESS: Investment
DIRECTORS: L M Goodman; S M Silver LLB; A J Watt FRICS; W W Syson; B M Rose
MAJOR SHAREHOLDERS: F S Assurance Trustees Limited; Scottish Amicable; Royal Bank of Scotland Nominess Limited;
BRANCH OFFICES: London
VALUE OF THE PROPERTY PORTFOLIO: £160 million (1990)
PROPERTY PORTFOLIO: Offices 70%; shops 28%, industrials 2%
INVESTMENT POLICY: Acquisition and active management of mixed commercial properties with growth potential throughout the UK
SUBSIDIARY COMPANIES: City Site Properties Limited; Queensbridge Estates Limited; Mercantile Limited; Fargrange Properties Limited; Viking Property Group
(Jan 1991)

City Square Securities Limited

PO Box 132
Yorkshire House
East Parade, Leeds 1
0532 892548
DIRECTOR: Mr Black

Citygrove plc

77 South Audley Street
London W1Y 5TA
Tel: 071-493 4007 Fax: 071-409 3515
DIRECTORS: D Woolf FCA (Chairman & Chief Executive); T Ellis; N Hewson MA ACA; A Pratt BSc ARICS; P Whight Dip TP; N Roskill MA (Non-Executive); P Burks BSc ARICS; D White FCIT CBIM (Non-Executive)
MAJOR SHAREHOLDERS: Scottish Amicable, Norwich Union Pensions Management Limited
ANNUAL TURNOVER: £63.1m (1988)
VALUE OF THE PROPERTY PORTFOLIO: £1m (1988)
SUBSIDIARY COMPANIES: Citygrove Developments Limited; Citygrove Real Estates Limited; Citygrove Retail Developments Limited; Citygrove Properties (Swansea) Limited; Citygrove Petrol Stations Limited; Citygrove Leisure Developments Limited; Audley Trust Limited

Citywide Properties Limited

No 1 St John Street
London EC1M 4AA
071-253 6163
DIRECTOR: J Keller (Managing)

Civic Property Companies

77 George Street
London W1H

Civic Property Company Limited

Penarth Road
Cardiff CF1 7TW
0222 231425

Cladan Property Developments Limited

The Old Rectory
Bargate
Grimsby
South Humberside DN34 4SY
Tel: 0472 250005 Fax: 0472 240617
NATURE OF BUSINESS: Property Development
DIRECTORS: D W Smith BSc ARICS Dip (Proj Man)
REGIONAL PREFERENCES: Anywhere in U.K.
DEVELOPMENT POLICY: Food and Non food retail; petrol filling stations; leisure including golf
(Sept 1992)

Clarendon Trust

7 Catherine Place
London SW1

Clarke Nickolls & Coombs plc

CNC House, 33 High Street
Sunninghill, Ascot
Berkshire SL5 9NR
Tel: 0344 28721 Fax; 0344 28711
DIRECTORS: R A Mathieson MA MPhil ARICS; E Lyall CBE (Chairman); G Mathieson BSc FICE FCIArb; G Vincent ASVA; R Mais MCIOB (Managing Director); C Walker-Robson (Financial Director)
MAJOR SHAREHOLDERS: London Securities, Channel Hotels and Properties, M&G Investment Management Limited
ANNUAL TURNOVER/INCOME: £11.9m (1988)
VALUE OF PORPERTY PORTFOLIO: £25m (1989)
SUBSIDIARY COMPANIES: CNC Properties Limited; CNC (Ireland) Limited; Altbarn Properties Limited; CNC (Benfleet) Limited; CNC Delaware Incorporated; CNC London Properties Limited; Aldenbridge Limited; First Base Properties Limited
JOINT VENTURE COMPANIES: BCNC (Cheapside) Limited; Beacontree Estates Limited; Beacontree Plaza Limited; CNC Burlington Estates Limited; CNC (City) Limited; CNC (Epsom) Limited; CNC (Houndslow) Limited; CNC (Taplow) Limited; Philpot Management Limited.

Clayform Properties plc
24 Bruton Street
Mayfair
London W1X 7DA
Tel: 071-491 8400 Fax: 071-499 1053
NATURE OF BUSINESS: Development
CHAIRMAN: M D Wigley; MANAGING DIRECTOR: R T E Ware ACA; B S P Dowling FRICS; D Jones; P Gee
ANNUAL TURNOVER/INCOME/PROFIT: £49.4m (1988)
VALUE OF PROPERTY PORTFOLIO: £61.1m (1988)
SUBSIDIARY COMPANIES: Clayform Developments Limited; Russell Management (Properties) Limited; Clayform Holdings plc; Clayform Bathgate Limited; Clayform Properties (Wales) Limited; Elvington Properties Limited; Clayform Property Investments Limited; Saturn Hereditaments Limited; SCI San Diego; SCI Fleur de Lys
ASSOCIATED COMPANIES: Schofield Centre Limited; Tarmac Guildford Limited; Bryant-Clayform Properties Limited; Winggrade Limited; Landpack Limited; Cornerstatic Limited; Fireside Properties Limited
(Sept 1992)

Clayton Properties Limited
3 Wylam Hall
Wylam
Northumberland NE41 8AS
DIRECTOR: J Beach

Clemence Property Development Limited
268-272 North Street
Romford
Essex RM1 4QN
0708 722499

Clemo De Havilland Limited
9 Radnor Walk
London SW3

Cleveley Park Properties (Radcliffe) Limited
95 Radcliffe Road
Bury BL9

Clinton Scott Holdings
Islington House
313 Upper Street
Islington
London N1 2XQ
071-704 8040

Closegate Developments
Norfolk House
90 Grey Street
Newcastle-Upon-Tyne NE1 6AG
091-261 8311
DIRECTOR: N Cook (Managing)

Closs Nicholas
19 Devonshire Street
London W1N 7FS
071-323 2268

Coats Viyella plc
28 Savile Row
London W1X 2DD
071-734 4030
DIRECTOR: Sir David Alliance (Chairman)
(Sept 1992)

Cobden Commercial Properties Limited
3 The Lodge
80 Wimbledon Parkside
London SW19 5LL
Tel: 081-876 8666 Fax: 081-785 4162
NATURE OF BUSINESS: Development
DIRECTORS: J M P Newman FRICS; D J Tully
MAJOR SHAREHOLDERS: J M P Newman
ANNUAL GROSS INCOME/TURNOVER: £1.3m (1988)
DEVELOPMENT ACTIVITIES: Offices 100%
DEVELOPMENT POLICY: Development of small office schemes (new build or refurbish) in SE England
SUBSIDIARY COMPANIES: Cobden Developments
(Sept 1992)

Cobden Securities Limited
29 Barnes High Street
London SW13 9LW

Cockcroft Property Limited
8 Duke Street
Luddenden
Halifax
West Yorkshire HH2 6RD
0422 884025
DIRECTOR: P Cockcroft (Managing)

Coin Street Community Builders
99 Upper Ground
London SE1

College Estates
4 Garrick Street
London WC2E

Colmore Properties Limited
32 Oldbury Place
London W1M

Color Properties Limited
Moat House
Dorsington
Stratford-Upon-Avon
Warwickshire CV37 8AX
Tel: 0789 720270 Fax: (0789) 720988
(Sept 1992)
NATURE OF BUSINESS: Development & Investment
DIRECTORS: I Kolodotschko BSocSc BSc AADip RIBA; J Kolodotschko DipIng (Germany); M Kolodotschko BA(Hons)
MAJOR SHAREHOLDERS: I Kolodotschko; J Kolodotschko

Entry missing ? Call HELPLINE Page v

REGIONAL PREFERENCES: Midlands, Southern Germany
PROPERTY PORTFOLIO: Shops 10%; factories 30%; warehouses 40%; leisure 10%; other 10%
INVESTMENT POLICY: Hold and manage own industrial and commercial schemes in West Midlands
DEVELOPMENT ACTIVITIES: Offices 10%; shops 10% factories 10% warehouses 10%; other 60%
DEVELOPMENT POLICY: Part funded and let shopping projects throughout UK and retain leisure elements within portfolio or managed
SUBSIDIARY COMPANIES: Color Construction Limited; Color Development Limited
(Jan 1991)

Colour Court Properties plc

43 Pall Mall
London SW1Y 5JG
071-839 8700
DIRECTOR: J Juul-Hansen (Managing)

Colroy Homes

212 Bellingdon Road
Chesham
Bucks HP5 2NN
0494 775301
DIRECTORS: W H Hoggett (Managing); A F Taylor (Marketing)

Coltre Holdings Limited

31 Park Road
Moseley
Birmingham B13

Commandfield Properties Limited

Melbury Cottage
2 Melbury Road
London W14

Commercial Consolidated Limited

194 Queen's Gate
London SW7

Commercial Land

22/26 Albert Embankment
London SE1

Commercial & Industrial Properties Limited

3rd Floor
19 Mercer Street
Covent Garden
London WC2H 9QP
071-379 4142
DIRECTOR: D Flack (Managing)

Commercial Properties Limited

14 West Smithfield
London EC1
071-248 1212

Commercial & Residential plc

535 King's Road
London SW10

Commercial Union Properties Limited

Schomberg House
80-82 Pall Mall
London SW1Y 5HF
Tel: 071-283 7500 Fax: 071-930 3844
Managing Director: I D Mathieson
(Sept 1992)

Commission for the New Towns

Glen House
Stag Place
London SW1E

Compco Holdings plc

7 Albyn Place
Edinborough EH2 4NN
031-226 4771
DIRECTORS: J M Button; R A Nadler ARICS (Managing Director); J E Nadler BSc (Est Man) ARICS ASVA; D M Pickford FRICS (Chairman);
MAJOR SHAREHOLDERS: Rutero Corp; R C Bailey & A J Adler; Courtaulds Pensions Common Investment Fund; J A Franks & A J Adler; MacTuggart Third Fund
ANNUAL TURNOVER/INCOME: £1.5m (1992)
VALUE OF PROPERTY PORTFOLIO: £21.5m (1992)
SUBSIDIARY COMPANIES: Compco Colorado Limited; Compco Holdings Corporation; Esjohn Properties Limited; Leowell Limited; Ortonwood Limited; Seymour Development Limited; Terrington Properties Limited
(Sept 1992)

Compton Securities Limited

19 Bloomsbury Square
London WC1A

Compton Street Securities plc

10A Old Compton Street
London W1V 5PG
071-439 3970
DIRECTOR: T M H Payne (Managing)

Comstock Developments Limited

2 Mount Street
Manchester M2

Conder Developments Limited

Egginton Junction
Derbyshire DE65 6GU
Tel: 0283 732422 Fax: 0283 734325
NATURE OF BUSINESS: Development
DIRECTORS: P Shanley MBA MCIOB ARICS; I S Turner FCIS FCMA; J Bell
MAJOR SHAREHOLDERS: Conder Group plc
ANNUAL TURNOVER/INCOME: £150m (Group), £5m (Company)
BRANCH OFFICES: Winchester
DEVELOPMENT ACTIVITIES: Offices 30%; Industrial/ Warehouses 50%; Retail 15%; Residential 5%

DEVELOPMENT POLICY: Provide good guality developments to meet market requirements
ASSOCIATED SISTER COMPANIES: Conder UK Limited
(Sept 1992)

Condux Corporation Limited
14 Old Park Lane
London W1Y

Conifercourt Property Group
Fitznells Manor
Chessington Road
Ewell Village
Surrey KT17 1TF
081-393 8899
DIRECTOR: J Rogers (Managing)

Connor Clark Consultants Limited
17/18 Henrietta Street
Birmingham B19

Conrad Phoenix Properties
24 Fitzroy Square
London
W1P 5HJ
071 387 0244
DIRECTOR: M. Thorpe (Managing)

Consolidated Credits and Discounts Limited
West Worlds
West Gate
London W5 1DT
Tel: 081-991 2551 Fax: 081 991 5263
NATURE OF BUSINESS: Investment
DIRECTORS: C Lewis; J Lewis; John Moore
MAJOR SHAREHOLDERS: Lewis Trust Group
(Sept 1992)

Consolidated Property Developments Limited
89a Onslow Gardens
London SW7

Consortium Developments Limited
24 Haymarket
London SW1Y 4TP
081-930 8665
DIRECTORS: Lord Northfield (Chairman); Andrew Bennett (Managing Executive)
COMPRISES: Barratt Developments plc; Beazer Homes & Property Limited; Bovis Homes Limited; Ideal Homes Holdings plc; Laing Homes Limited; McCarthy & Stone; Y J Lovell (Holdings) plc; Tarmac plc; Wilson Homes Limited; Wimpey Homes Holdings Limited

Conspectus Project Management Consultants
25 Garrick Street
London WC2E

Construction Control Associates Limited
2 Bloomfield Court
London W9

Constructora Palma 30 (UK) Limited
10 Golden Square
London W1R

Control Securities Limited
Unit 3A
Southwark Bridge Office Village
60 Turale Street
London SE1 9HW
Tel: 071-815 0805 Fax: 071-815 0806
(Sept 1992)
NATURE OF BUSINESS: Development & Investment
DIRECTORS: N G Virani (Chairman & Chief Executive); A G Virani Dip Est Man; E J Hewitt FCA; R Parmar BA; B Solanki BA; R M Wilson CBE BSc FRICS; Z G Virani
MAJOR SHAREHOLDERS: Virani Group (UK) Limited; Mountleigh Group plc; Heron Securities Limited
ANNUAL TURNOVER: £108.8m (1989)
VALUE OF PROPERTY PORTFOLIO: £227.4m (1989)
PROPERTY PORTFOLIO: Offices 39%; residential 6%; industrial 16%; leisure 34%; retail 5%
SUBSIDIARY COMPANIES: Ascot Holdings plc; Ascot Estates Limited; Ascot Properties Limited; Balmcrest Estates Limited; Belhaven Brewery Company Limited; Bellhaven SA; Blezard Limited; H C Pubs Limited; Ledbury Estates Limited; Cardiff Commercial Properties Limited; Ellesmere Port Properties Limited; Harrowby Street Estates Limited; Harrowby Street Porperties Limited; Namebeam Limited; Purfleet Properties Limited; Warwick Court (Coventry) Limited; Yensen Limited
(Jan 1991)

Conversation Limited
9 Brynaston House
Dorset Street
London W1H

Co-operative Wholesale Society Limited
Property Group
New Century House
Manchester M60 4ES
061 834 1212 ext 6579

Co-ordinated Land & Estates plc
34 Grosvenor Gardens
London SW1W 0DH
Tel: 071-823 6766 Fax: 071-629 0005
DIRECTOR: T King (Managing)

Co-Partnership Property Group Limited
53-57 Queen Anne Street
London W1M OLJ
071-487 5821

Copley Square Group of Companies
Kestrel Court
Pacific Quays
Broadway
Manchester M5

Copley Square Limited
St James House
Pendleton Way
Salford
Manchester M6

Coralcorp Limited
5th Floor
Liberty House
222 Regent Street
London W1R 5DE

Cordwell Property Limited
23 Mount Street
London W1Y 5RB
071-491 1438
DIRECTOR: W Warrack (Managing)

Core Property plc
Suite A
30 Brighton Road
Sutton
Surrey SM2 5BN
Tel: 081-643 3332 Fax: 081-643 7768
NATURE OF BUSINESS: Development & Investment
DIRECTORS: R P Harwood FRICS FSVA; D E Walker
MAJOR SHAREHOLDERS: R P Harwood
ANNUAL TURNOVER: New company, still within first trading year (1989)
REGIONAL PREFERENCES: UK General
INVESTMENT POLICY: Limited to Surrey and Home Counties
DISTRIBUTION OF DEVELOPMENT ACTIVITIES: 100% Commercial
(Sept 1992)

Corman Group of Companies
58 Acacia Road
St Johns Wood
London NW8

Cornex Limited
23 Colmore Row
Birmingham B3

Corob Holdings
62 Grosvenor Street
London W1X 9DA
Tel: 071-499 4301 Fax: 071-491 0105
DIRECTORS: E Corob; J V Hajnal; L Wiseman; F Cook; S Wiseman; P A Corob; L E Corob; A L Corob
REGIONAL PREFERENCES: Throughout UK
CURRENT INVESTMENT POLICY: To expand the retail investment element of the portfolio by acquisition of prime retail investments let to first class covenants and shopping centres.
(Sept 1992)

Corporate Estates Properties plc
12 Blandford Street
London W1H 3HA
071-323 1574
MAJOR SHAREHOLDERS: Ensign Trust
ANNUAL TURNOVER: £5.42m (1987)
VALUE OF PROPERTY PORTFOLIO: £4.83m (1987)

Corrie Properties Limited
Rodwell House
Middlesex Street
London E1 7HJ
071-377 9366

Costain Property Development Limited
46 Green Street
London W1Y 3FJ
071-409 3040
NATURE OF BUSINESS: Development
DIRECTORS: C T Wyatt (Chairman); P J Costain (Group Chief Executive); T W Slee (Finance); B D Stillwell (Personnel); G R Haworth (Executive Director); J E Langford (Executive); J F Reeve OBE (Executive); W E Bell CBE (Non-Executive); L W Melville (Non-Executive); Sir G Messervy (Non-Executive); P B Sawdy (Non-Executive); Sir M Wilcox CBE (Non-Executive)
MANAGER: P Shaw
BRANCH OFFICES: Woking, Manchester, Calgary (Canada), Chicago (USA), Middlesborough, Jeddah (South Arabia), Maidenhead, Kingston-upon-Thames, London, Nottingham, Livingston (Scotland), Erith, Bramborough, Bahrain, Cairo (Egypt), Hong Kong, Oman (Jordan), Kuala Lumpar (Malaysia), Ruisi (Oman), Abu Dhabi, Dubai, Lagos (Nigeria), Southerton (Zimbabwe), Bloemendaal (Netherlands), Birmingham, Marlow, Melbourne (Australia)
ANNUAL TURNOVER/INCOME/PROFIT: £1.16bn (1988)
VALUE OF PROPERTY PORTFOLIO: £312.5m (1986)
PROPERTY PORTFOLIO: Engineering & construction 60.5%; mining 24.6%; housing (UK & Australia) 4.7%; property 5.2%
DEVELOPMENT POLICY: Engineering & construction, mining, housing & property
SUBSIDIARY COMPANIES: Byard Kenwest Engineering Limited (reg in Scotland); Consolidated X-Ray Service Corporation and subsidiary companies; Controlec Limited; Costain (Africa) Limited; Costain Australia Limited and subsidiary companies; Costain-Blankvoort International Dredging Company Limited; Costain-Blankvoort Limited; Costain-Blankvoort (UK) Dredging Company Limited; Costain Civil Engineering Limited; Costain Concrete Company Limited; Costain Construction Limited; Costain Holdings Inc; Costain Homes Limited; Costain International Limited; Costain Investments (Australia) Proprietary Limited; Costain Management Design Limited; Costain Mining Limited; Costain Overseas Services Limited; Costain Petrocarbon Limited; Costain Process Construction Limited; Costain Process Inc; Costain Process Limited and subsidiary

companies; Costain Property Developments Limited; Costain Property Investments Limited; Costain Renovations Limited; Costain UK Limited; County & District Properties Limited and subsidiary companies; E J Cook & Company (Engineers) Limited; Foundation Engineering (Nigeria) Limited; Haigh & Ringrose Limited; Industrial Fuels Corporation; John Shelbourne & Company Limited; Land & Marine Engineering Limited; Lysander Insurance Brokers Limited; Lysander Travel Service Limited; Pearson Bridge Holdings Limited and subsidiary companies; Richard Costain (Holdings) Limited; Richard Costain Limited; Richard Costain Properties Limited; Streeters of Godalming Limited and subsidiary companies; Stressed Concrete Design Limited; Tees Dredging Limited; Toplis Painters Limited; Westminster Plant Company Limited; Yahya Costain LLC; Yarmside Holdings Limited
RELATED COMPANIES: Britannia House Property SA; Coal Systems Companies (joint venture); Costain (West Africa) Limited; Foundation Construction Limited; Genstar Costain Tie Company Limited; Gulh-Cobla (Private) Limited; GKN Kwikform Holdings Limited; Hopewell Costain Limited; Jalal-Costain WLL; Pyro Mining Company (joint venture); R Costain & Sons Limited

---

Costain & Sons (Liverpool) Limited
Barlows Lane
Fazakerley
Liverpool
Merseyside L9 9EL
051-525 4141
DIRECTORS: L A Robinson; R C Bazley; D A Hughes; F Jenkins; H J Mullineaux; N P Williams
AREA MANAGER: Mr Dennis
BRANCH OFFICES: Chester, Liverpool

Couchmore Property Company Limited
Kingston House
15 Coombe Road
Kingston upon Thames
Surrey KT2 7AD
081-546 2177
DIRECTORS: John Hickman (Managing)
MANAGER PROPERTY: R Robinson

Country Estates (UK) Ltd
114 Sinclair Road
London W14
071-603 6065

Countryside Properties plc
Countryside House
The Warley Hill Business Park
The Drive, Brentwood
Essex CM13 3AT
0277 260000
NATURE OF BUSINESS: Development & Investment
DIRECTORS: A H Cherry MBE FRICS; M F Pearce FCA; Trisha Gupta BArch (Hons) RIBA; G S Cherry BSc (Hons) MCIOB; R S Cherry BSc (Hons) ARICS; C P Crook BSc (Hons) ARICS; D J Doig
MAJOR SHAREHOLDERS: A H Cherry; Nutraco; Sun Life Pensions; Devon County Council; M&G; Robert Fleming; Scottish Amicable
ANNUAL TURNOVER/INCOME/PROFIT: £95.58m (1988)
REGIONAL PREFERENCES: South East England
DEVELOPMENT POLICY: Expanding commercial and industrial development
PROPERTY PORTFOLIO: Investment: shops 100%
SUBSIDIARY COMPANIES: Country Investments Limited; Countryside Commercial & Industrial Properties Limited

---

County & District Properties
46 Green Street
London W1Y
071-409 3040

County Hall Properties (Manchester) Limited
Westminster House
11 Portland Street
Manchester M60

County Park Properties Limited
191 Bowes Road
London N11
081-368 6345

County Properties Group
Pavillion House
Pavillion Square
Scarborough
North Yorkshire YO11 2JR
DIRECTORS: J Guthrie MA FRICS (Chairman & Managing); G H Dodsworth FCA JP; C G Montgomery CA; M Guthrie FRICS; T Bisset CA; R Urquhart
MAJOR SHAREHOLDERS: Lady Legard, Trustees of S M Guthrie's 1965 settlement
SUBSIDIARY COMPANIES: County Properties Limited; County Properties (England) Limited; County Properties (Scotland) Limited; County Properties (Northern) Limited; The Learmoth Property Investment Company Limited; Carment Limited; Ganvogue Limited;
County Properties (Holdings) Limited; County Properties (Wokingham) Limited; County Properties (Southern) Limited; County Properties (Kirkcaldy) Limited; Rose Brothers & Company (Nairn) Limited; County Homes (Scotland) Limited; County Homes (England) Limited; County Homes (Southern) Limited; County Homes (Northern) Limited; Hutchinson Construction (Northern) Limited; Hutchinson Construction (Southern) Limited; Hutchinson Construction (Scotland) Limited

---

County Properties (Scotland) Limited
63/65 Shandwick Place
Edinburgh EH2

Court Group of Companies
The Grange
Market Square,
Westerham
Kent TN16 1AR

0959 564746
NATURE OF BUSINESS: Investment
DIRECTORS: M R Court BA Arch ARIBA AA dip TP; V R Stringer; O Court
MAJOR SHAREHOLDERS: M R Court; O Court; V R Stringer; H W R Court; A R Court; D R Court
PROPERTY PORTFOLIO: Offices 7%; residential 91%; other 2%
INVESTMENT POLICY: To expand portfolio of residential investments in the U.K.
SUBSIDIARY COMPANIES: J Court & Sons (Norwood) Limited; The Russell Court Properties Limited; NRC Properties Limited; Court Joint Properties Limited; Mariners Farms Limited; Stringer Court Company Limited; Russell Stedman Limited
(Sept 1992)

Courtfield Developments Limited
23 Motcomb Street
London SW1X

Courtney Investment Limited
1A Kensington Gore
London SW7 2AT
071-589 4466

Covent Garden Group Limited
34 Floral Street
London WC2E 9DJ
Tel: 071-836 0227 Fax: 071-240 3943
NATURE OF BUSINESS: Investment
DIRECTORS: D Shamash; D R Shamash
MAJOR SHAREHOLDERS: Directors
REGIONAL PREFERENCES: England
PROPERTY PORTFOLIO: Offices 40%; Residential 60%
DEVELOPMENT/INVESTMENT POLICY: Freehold Ground Rents
(Sept 1992)

Cozens-Smith Limited
Cranleigh Works
Cranleigh
Surrey GU6 8SB
0483 273131
DIRECTORS: J J Cozens-Smith (Managing); Mr Sparks

Cradleport Limited
362 Kingsland Road
London E8

Craig European Holdings plc
56 Grosvenor Street
London W1

Craigton Combined Securities Limited
Freshwater House
158-162 Shaftesbury Avenue
London WC2H 8HR
Tel: 071-836 1555 Fax: 071 379 6365
NATURE OF BUSINESS: Property Trading (Holding Co)
DIRECTORS: B S E Freshwater; D R Hodges; L Stempel; D G Weaver
MAJOR SHAREHOLDERS: Highdorn Co Limited - Owned by Freshwater Family
ANNUAL TURNOVER: £445,600
VALUE OF PORTFOLIO: £719,300 (31.3.91)
SUBSIDIARY COMPANIES: Craigton Properties Limited; London & Oxford Properties Limited
(Sept 1992)

Cramphorn plc
Cuton Mill
Springfield
Chelmsford CM2 6PD
0245 466221
DIRECTORS: Mr Cramphorn; Mr Barker (Joint Managing)

Cranford Estates plc
Olympic House
63 Woodside Road
Amersham
Bucks HP6 6AA
0494 728092
DIRECTOR: G Holden

Crawford Estates Limited
81 Crawford Street
London W1H 4AT
071-723 8534

Creegan Properties Limited
60 Durham Road
Raynes Park
London SW20
081-947 7384

Crescent Estates
18 Park Place Villas
London W2 1SP
071-262 7277
DIRECTOR: J Johnston (Managing)

Crest Estates
St Martins Court
37 Queens Road
Weybridge
Surrey KT13 9UQ
0932 840999
DIRECTORS: N Walker (Managing); J Bowyer (Marketing)

Crest Estates Limited
Crest House
39-41 Thames Street
Weybridge, Surrey
KT13 8JL
0932 847272
DIRECTOR: M Freshney (Managing)

Crest International Securities plc
36 Dover Street
London W1X 3RB

DIRECTORS: W A Stenson (Chairman); J Brown; T Farmer; E Landau; B Simmons BSc (Secretary)
MAJOR SHAREHOLDERS: A Subsidiary of Kwik-Fit (Tyres & Exhausts) plc
SUBSIDIARY COMPANIES: Arrowspeed Investments Limited; City & Cranbrook Securities Limited; Crest International Group Limited; Crest International Developments Limited; Crest International Properties Limited; London & Foreign Investment Trust Limited; Mirivale (TC Investments) Limited

---

Crest Nicholson plc

Crest House
Station Road
Egham
Surrey TW20 9NP
0784 438771
DIRECTOR: R Lewis (Managing)

Cresta Properties Limited

Peregrine House
Peel Road
Douglas
Isle of Man
0624 73800
DIRECTOR: I England (Managing)

Crewbridge Estates (Wessex) Limited

Estate House
122/124 Widmore Road
Bromley
Kent BR1 3BA
081-464 7777
DIRECTOR: Mr I Andrews (Managing)

Cringle Investments Limited

Alexandra House
Pilot Industrial Estate
Manchester Road
Bolton
Lancashire

Crisp, Thomas Developments

17A-17B Market Place
Loughborough
Leicester LE11 3EA
0509 233221
DIRECTOR: J W Crisp (Managing)

Crocker Group, The

12/14 Wigmore Street
London W1N

Cromwell Developments

1 Town Quay Wharf
Barking
Essex IG11 7BZ
081-591 3080
DIRECTOR: L Aldis (Managing)

Crossglade Limited

1 Silvester Square
The Maltings
Silvester Street
Hull HU1 3HA
Tel: 0482 586444 Fax: 0482 229654
DIRECTOR: R E Hatfield (Managing)
NATURE OF BUSINESS: Property Developers
MAJOR SHAREHOLDERS: R E Hatfield
REGIONAL PREFERENCE: Humberside
ANNUAL INCOME/TURNOVER: Company £700,000
VALUE OF PORTFOLIO: £9,000,000 (1992)
% DISTRIBUTION OF PORTFOLIO: The Maltings Complex Hull 90% Offices; 10% Leisure; Waterside Park Hull 100% Offices
INVESTMENT POLICY: Renovation & New Developments
DISTRIBUTION OF DEVELOPMENT: 90% Offices; 10% Leisure
(Sept 1992)

Cross Lane Business Parks Limited

2a Colbeck Row
Birstall
Leeds

Croudace Land Holdings Limited

Croudace House
Godstone Road
Caterham
Surrey CRE 6RE
0883 346464
DIRECTOR: Mr Wall (Managing)

Crowngap Developments Limited

Newark Lane
Ripley
Surrey GU23 6DF
0483 211111
DIRECTORS: J W Newman (Development Director); R Wright (Chairman); D Lacey; A Prescott

---

Crown Street Properties

Queensway House
57 Livery Street
Birmingham
West Midlands B3 1HA

Crowndell Investments Limited

14 Northwick Terrace
London NW8

Crowngate Developments Limited

60/64 Great Hampton Street
Birmingham B18

Cruden Investments Limited

Baberton House
Juniper Green
Edinburgh EH14 3HN
Tel: 031-442 3862 Fax: 031-442 4556

Entry missing ? Call HELPLINE Page v

DIRECTORS: E A Brian; A Matthews; J S G Kirkland; W R Douglas; M J Rowley
MAJOR SHAREHOLDERS: Cruden Foundation Limited
SUBSIDIARY COMPANIES: Hart Builders (Edinburgh) Limited; Cruden Building Limited; Cruden Homes (Scotland) Limited; Cruden Property Developments Limited
(Sept 1992)

Crystalmoor Properties Limited

Hattingley House
Medstead
Near Alton
Hampshire GU34 5NQ
0420 62294
DIRECTORS: J Assersohn FSVA (Managing)

Cue Property Holdings (Rotherhithe) Limited

128 Lower Road
London SE16

Cuffins Homes Limited

The Great North Road
Gosforth
Newcastle upon Tyne NE3 2DA
091-285 0567
DIRECTOR: W I Waites (Managing)

Culverpalm Limited

Bentley House
15-21 Headstone Drive
Wealdstone
Middlesex HA3 5QX
081-427 0303
DIRECTOR: H L Jaffer(Managing)

Cumber Developments (Devon) Limited

Beacon Boathouse
Southtown
Dartmouth
Devon TQ6 9BT
0803 832663
NATURE OF BUSINESS: Development
DIRECTORS: T P Freeman BSc MBA
DEVELOPMENT ACTIVITIES: Residential 100%

Cumberland Park Developments Limited

6th Floor
Cumberland House
26-100 Scrubs Lane
London NW10 6AH
081-968 9683
DIRECTOR: H A Lloyd (Managing)

Cussins Green Properties plc

44 Springfield Road
Horsham
East Sussex RH12 2PD
04032 41500
(Sept 1992)
DIRECTOR: B Burgess (Managing)
VALUE OF PROPERTY PORTFOLIO: £65m (1988)
(Jan 1991)

Cussins Property Group plc

155 Bishopsgate
London EC2M 3XJ
Tel: 071-374 4100 Fax: 071-256 8842
NATURE OF BUSINESS: Development & Investment
DIRECTORS: P I Cussins BSc (Chairman); J A Mackenzie FRICS; W I Waites; J F Gregory (Non-Executive); B M Wyllie FCIB (Non-Executive)
MAJOR SHAREHOLDERS: The Throgmorton Trust plc, Prudential Corporation Group
ANNUAL TURNOVER: £22.5m (1989)
REGIONAL PREFERENCES: Newcastle Upon Tyne
VALUE OF PROPERTY PORTFOLIO: £17.4m (1989)
DEVELOPMENT POLICY: The business of the Cussins Property Group and its subsidiaries is the development of commercial, industrial and residential property and the creation of a commercial investment portfolio.
SUBSIDIARY COMPANIES: Cussins Homes Limited; Cussins Commercial Developments Limited; Cussins Investment Properties Limited; Lemmington Estates Limited; Cussins South Limited
JOINT COMPANY: Cussins Green Properties plc, with the Throgmorton Trust

D & E Developments

171 New Street
Blackrod
Howrich
Manchester

D W Investments

Kinders Mill
Kinders Green
Greenfield
Saddleworth
Manchester

Daddy & Daughters plc

3 The Vale
London SW3

Daejan Holdings plc

Freshwater House
158-162 Shaftesbury Avenue
London WC2H 8HR
Tel: 071-836 1555 Fax: 071-379 6365
NATURE OF BUSINESS: Property Investment & Trading
DIRECTORS: B S E Freshwater (Chairman & Managing Director); D Davis; S I Freshwater
MAJOR SHAREHOLDERS: Freshwater Family & Trusts
ANNUAL GROSS PROFIT: £45.18m (1989)
VALUE OF PROPERTY PORTFOLIO: £220m (1992)
DISTRIBUTION OF PORTFOLIO: USA 6.46%; Central London 47.8%; South 14.83%; Midlands/Wales 8.38%; North 4.67%
DISTRIBUTION OF DEVELOPMENT ACTIVITIES: Office 22.21%; Shops 32.98%; Industrial/Leisure 6.09%; Miscellaneous 4.49%; Residential 34.23%

SUBSIDIARY COMPANIES: Astral Estates (London) Limited; Bampton Holdings Limited; Bampton (Redbridge) Limited (75%); Brickfield Properties Limited; Chilon Investment Company Limited; City & Country Properties Limited; City & Country Properties (Birmingham) Limited; City & Country Properties (Camberley) Limited; City & Country Properties (Midlands) Limited; Daejan Developments Limited; Daejan Enterprises Inc; Daejan Investments (Grove Hall) Limited; Daejan Investments (Harrow) Limited; Daejan Investments (Park) Limited; Daejan (Massachusetts) Inc; Daejan Holdings (US) Inc; Daejan (NY) Ltd; Daejan Enterprises Inc; Daejan Properties Limited; Daejan Securities Limited; Daejan (NY) Limited; Daejan Holdings (US) Inc; Hampstead Way Investments Limited; Limebridge Company Limited; Pegasus Investment Company Limited; Rosebel Holdings Limited; Seaglen Investments Limited; St Leonards Properties Limited; The Bampton Property Group Limited; The Cromlech Property Company Limited; The Halliard Property Company Limited; Daejan (Dartford) Ltd; Daejan (Durham) Ltd; Daejan Estates Ltd; Daejan (High Wycombe) Ltd; Daejan Invetments Ltd; Daejan (Kingston) Ltd; Daejan (Reading) Ltd; Daejan (Taunton) Ltd; Daejan (Warwick) Ltd; Daejan (Worcester) Ltd; Rapid 7533 Ltd
(Sept 92)

Daleside Limited
9 Cavendish Square
London W1M

Dalwood Properties Limited
PO Box 570
London N3 7TZ
081-346 7131

Damo Investments Limited
57 Whitechapel Road
London E1

Danbuild Construction (UK) Limited
77-85 Fulham Palace Road
London W6
081-748 4224

Danby Limited
Wellington House
Wellington Road
London NW10
081-969 7799

Danmerc International Property & Investment Consultants Limited
Danmerc House
18 Exeter Street
London WC2E

Dares Estates plc
1 Albermarle Street
London W1X

Darwin Estates
16 Berkeley Street
London W1X

David Izett & Company
131c Kensington Church Street
London W8

David Lewis Property Corporation Limited
76 Gloucester Place
London W1H 4DQ
071-487 3401

David Munns & Co
81 Walton Street
London SW3

Davies, Philip (Holdings)
Upper Kirby Street
Manchester M4 6SA
061-205 1393

Davis, William & Company Limited
Forest Field
Forest Road, Loughborough
Leicestershire LE11 3NS
0509 231181

Davro Homes Limited
Greenhill House
396 Cheetham Hill Road
Manchester M8

Davy Property Holdings
PO Box 43
Green Lane
Padgate
Warrington
Cheshire WA1 4JB
0925 820100
DIRECTOR: Mr Balmforth (Managing)

Dawnchurch Properties Limited
12 Craven Terrace
London W2

Day, C F Limited
705 High Road
North Finchley
London N12
081-445 3611
DIRECTOR: M J W Piercy (Managing)

Dayfield Properties Limited
70 Charlotte Street
London W1P

DB Securities
25 Bracken Park
Starcroft, Leeds
West Yorkshire LS14 3HZ
Tel: 0532 892548 Fax: 0532 893158
DIRECTORS: D I Black (Managing)

Deal Projects Limited
Carlton House
Wakefield House
Stourton
Leeds

Dean & Dyball Construction Limited
Ocean House
New Quay Road
Poole
Dorset BH15 4AB
0202 665665
DIRECTOR: M Hurst (Managing)

Deanson Properties Limited
4 Rabbit Row
London W8

Deauville Securities
100 Chalk Farm Road
London NW1 8EW
071-431 2500
DIRECTOR: Mr Bentley(Managing)

Declan Kelly Group plc
2/4 Cayton Street
London EC1V 9EH
NATURE OF BUSINESS: Development
DIRECTORS: D P Kelly MSc; D J Myddleton FRICS; R H Carter CA; L P Coyne MBA; D J Smith; M Marshall; B H Firmin FCA; D A Beety FRICS; L J Holliday FCIOB; E A Lowrie FIB
REGIONAL PREFERENCES: London; the South East; the South West
DEVELOPMENT ACTIVITIES: Residential 100%
SUBSIDIARY COMPANIES: Declan Kelly Associates Limited; Declan Kelly Commercial Developments Limited; KDC Construction Limited; Guildway Limited; Retirement Community Homes; Guildway Construction Limited; Declan Kelly Management Services
DEVELOPMENT POLICY: Declan Kelly Group develops a range of housing for first time purchasers and the retired in addition to upmarket schemes for middle income purchasers

Deeley, G W Limited
Hewgate Construction Division
Hewgate House
Rabans Lane
Aylesbury
Bucks HP19 3RT
Tel: 0296 81021 Fax: 0296 25226
NATURE OF BUSINESS: Design, Management & Construction of Commercial & Industrial Buildings.
DIVISIONAL DIRECTORS: G V Free (Divisional Director & General Manager); R J Newell BSc MCIDB MCIM (Divisional Director)
MAJOR SHAREHOLDERS: A division of G W Deeley Limited, a wholly owned subsidiary of Deeley Group Limited.
ANNUAL INCOME/TURNOVER: Group £13m; Company £7m
REGIONAL PREFERENCE FOR ACTIVITIES: Southern England & Midlands
SISTER COMPANIES: Deeley Northampton Limited, Deeley Homes Limited; Deeley (Properties) Limited; Deeley Investments Limited.
(Sept 1992)

Deeley Properties Limited
William House
Torrington Avenue
Coventry
Warwickshire CV4 9GY
Tel: 0203 462521 Fax: 0203 469533
(Sept 1992)
NATURE OF BUSINESS: Industrial/Commercial Developers
DIRECTORS: D A W Deeley; P R Goodgame; B N Crawford
MAJOR SHAREHOLDERS: Wholly owned subsidiary of Deeley Group Limited.
ANNUAL INCOME/TURNOVER: Company £2m; Group 15m
LOCATION OF REGIONAL OFFICES: Pond Wood Close, Moulton Park, Northampton
DISTRIBUTION OF PORTFOLIO: All investment property owned by Deeley Investments Limited.
INVESTMENT POLICY: Industrial Commercial Investments to continue
DEVELOPMENT ACTIVITIES: Industrial Offices 50%, Warehouses 50%
DEVELOPMENT POLICY: To continue in current market place
DEVELOPMENT SUBSIDIARIES: G W Deeley Ltd (Construction); Deeley Homes Limited (Residential development)
(Jan 1991)

Deepsure
Gun Hill, Dedham
Colchester, Essex
0206 323094
DIRECTOR: K E Dodd (Managing)

Deltavale Construction Limited
2 Willis Street
Birmingham B19

Dencora plc
Dencora House
Blyburgate
Beccles
Suffolk NR34 9TQ
Tel: 0502 712729 Fax: 0502 716821
(Sept 1992)
NATURE OF BUSINESS: Development & Investment
DIRECTORS: J K Laurence TD BL CA (Chairman); C R Holmes FCIOB FFB FGS; R C Youngs; R M Morritt FCA;

C H Armon Jones FRICS; T A Catchpole CEng MIStructE; A P Scott; A F Twist MA
MAJOR SHAREHOLDERS: Millsreeve Jersey Trustees Limited
ANNUAL TURNOVER: £32.2m (1988)
VALUE OF THE PROPERTY PORTFOLIO: £70m (1988)
PROPERTY PORTFOLIO: Industrial 59%, offices 36%, retail 5%
SUBSIDIARY COMPANIES: Dencora Securities Limited; Dencora Properties Limited; Harvey & Leech Limited; Spaulding & Holmes Limited; Rogers Bros Limited; Dencora Homes Limited; Dencora (Essex) Limited; Dencora Retirement Homes Limited; Masters & Skevens Limited; Masters & Skevens (Wreningham) Limited; Christchurch Management Services Limited
(Jan 1991)

Derwent Valley Holdings

87 Wimpole Street
London W1M 7DB
Tel: 071-486 4848 Fax: 071-465 8198
NATURE OF BUSINESS: Property Development & Investment
DIRECTORS: J C Ivey (Non-Executive Chairman); J D Burns (Managing); R E Cook; J E Dixon; S P Silver; C J Odum
MAJOR SHAREHOLDERS: Scottish Amicable, Topcastle Holdings; Scottish Americal Inv Co plc; T&N Pension Trustee Ltd; CNIM Smeker Companies Exempt Fund; TR Property Investment Trust plc; Chatsworth Management.
ANNUAL PROFIT: £6.17m (1991)
SUBSIDIARY COMPANIES: Itkin Properties (London) Limited; Derwent Valley Railway Co; Colebrook Estates Limited; Wilmar Estates Limited; Derwent Valley Properties Ltd; Derwent Valley Property Developments Ltd
(Sept 1992)

Desert Storm Trading Co Limited

12 Bolton Street
London W1Y

Development Realisation Trust

Development Realisation Trust Ltd
6 Hobart Place
London SW1W 0HU
071-235 0505
(Sept 1992)

Development Venture Associates

2 Heron Mews House
1A Balfour Road
Ilford
Essex IG1 4HP
081-478 4442
DIRECTOR: G Chalkley (Managing)

Developments Commercial & Industrial (Holdings) Limited

1 Northgate
Cowcaddens
Glasgow G4 0BB
Tel: 041-332 6668 Fax: 041-332 3696
NATURE OF BUSINESS: Development Investment & Allied Activities, Property Consultancy & Project Management
DIRECTORS: A Campbell Fraser (Chairman); J H Higgins (Technical); A W Coutts (Project & Developments); J McClements (Contracting)
MAJOR SHAREHOLDERS: A Campbell Fraser (Chairman); Witan Investment Company plc; J M Kerr Exectuers
REGIONAL OFFICE: Dee Street, Aberdeen
ANNUAL GROSS INCOME/TURNOVER: Group £40 m (1991/92)
REGIONAL PREFERENCES: Scotland - But U.K. and EC in general
VALUE OF PROPERTY PORTFOLIO: Nominal 92-93
DEVELOPMENT POLICY: To maintain DCI's lead in the field of intelligent office developments, to make more generally available to the industry DCI's skilled Project Management and Property Consultancy services and increase its subsidiary's (Permac, Real Security and PermaClean) contributions to Group turnover
DISTRIBUTION OF PROPERTY PORTFOLIO: The major part of DCI's portfolio was sold off last year in anticipation of the property slump. DCI thereafter cleared off all property borrowing and bank overdrafts.
INVESTMENT POLICY: The above action has allowed DCI to be efficiently geared to take advantage of the upswing in property development when the economy improves.
(Sept 1992)
DISTRIBUTION OF DEVELOPMENT: Activities: Commercial 50%; Industrial 10%; Retail 10%; Project Management & Property Consultancy 15% & Allied Activities (Permac) 5%
DEVELOPMENT ACTIVITIES: Offices 65%; residential 25%; shops 5%; science parks hi-tec 5%
U.K.DEVELOPMENT: DCI (Group) Limited - Property Services and Investment; DCI - PCS - Property Consultancy Services; DCI - PMC - Property Management Services; Permac Systems - contracting allied services; Real Security - Security Services; Permaclean -Clean Services
SISTER COMPANIES: Permac Limited
SUBSIDIARY COMPANIES: DCI (Northern) Limited; DCI (Scotland) Limited

---

Devonshire Estates plc

100 Crawford Street
London W1H 1AN
071-724 3759

Diamond Estates

10 Bridge Street
Northampton NN1 1NW
0604 233574

Dima Investments Limited

107 King Henry's Road
London NW3

Dimsdale Developments Limited
Rawdon House, High Street
Hoddesdon
Hertfordshire EN11 8BD
0992 441301
DIRECTOR: D H Beadle (Managing)
SALES MANAGER: M Davey

District Reversionary Estates Limited
115 Flood Street
London SW3 5TD

District & Urban Group plc
28 Hereford Road
London W2 5AJ
071-221 0005
DIRECTOR: Mr Graham (Managing)

Dixons Commercial Properties (UK) Limited
29 Farm Street
London W1X 7RD
Tel: 071-409 2322 Fax: 071-499 6696
NATURE OF BUSINESS: Development
DIRECTORS: M W Heaton BA BSc (Chairman); T Haines BSc FCA; T M Peake; T Holden.
MAJOR SHAREHOLDERS: Dixons Group plc
BRANCH OFFICES: Brussels, Dusseldorf, Stuttgart, Lisbon, Lille, Strasbourg, Hamburg
SUBSIDIARY COMPANIES: Dixons Investments Limited; Martin Brent Developments Limited; Codic SA (Belgium) Codic SA France; Codic GmbH, DCPP (Portugal)
(Sept 1992)

DJT Properties
171 Moston Lane
Blackley
Manchester M9

Docklands & East London Properties plc
1 Heron Mews House
1A Balfour Road
Ilford
Essex IG1 4HP
081-478 6070
DIRECTOR: S Cohen (Managing)

Dominion Estates Limited
Sackville House
40 Piccadilly
London W1V 9PA
071-439 8777

Dominion Property Holdings Limited
5 Vigo Street
London W1X

Domino Properties Limited
14a Cazenove Road
London N16

Domus Developments
County House
Cornwall Avenue
London N3
081-349 2711
DIRECTOR: C Woolf (Managing)

Don Little Property Developments
94 Kirkgate
Leeds
Yorkshire

Donegal Investments
Argyle House
Park Road
Middleton
Manchester M24

Dorodon Holdings Limited
PO Box 71
Meadens Church Lane
Warfield
Bracknell
Berks RG12 6DF
0344 882286
DIRECTOR: P Gray (Managing)

Dorrington Properties plc
14 Hans Road
London SW3
Tel: 071-581 1477 Fax: 071-589 3542
(Sept 1992)
NATURE OF BUSINESS: Development & Investment
DIRECTORS: M S Gorvy BCom FCA; A J Leibowitz BSc MSc; T Moross BA BSc(Est Man) FRICS; A M Silver BSc(Est Man) ARICS
REGIONAL PREFERENCES: London & South East
PROPERTY PORTFOLIO: Offices 60%; shops 35%; warehouses 5%
INVESTMENT POLICY: Buying investments with an opportunity to 'add value'
DEVELOPMENT POLICY: Buying opportunities on a cautious basis
(Jan 1991)

Double Properties
77 Disraeli Road
London SW15 2DR

Douglas, R M Property Development
George Road
Erdington
Birmingham B23 7RZ
Tel: 021-344 4888 Fax: 021-344 4801
NATURE OF BUSINESS: Property Development
DIRECTORS: J R T Douglas; R A Paine; R B Morgan (Managing); H E Green (Finance)
MAJOR SHAREHOLDERS: Robert M Douglas Holdings PLC

LOCATION OF REGIONAL OFFICES: Chiswick, London
ANNUAL INCOME/TURNOVER: Company £6m, Group £330m
VALUE OF PORTFOLIO: £40m (1990)
DISTRIBUTION OF DEVELOPMENT ACTIVITIES: Offices; industrial; warehousing; retail
UK/EUROPEAN DEVELOPMENT OR CONSTRUCTION SUBSIDIARIES: Douglas Hill Developments; Waterlinks plc; Star-Site plc
UK/EUROPEAN DEVELOPMENT OR CONSTRUCITON SISTER COMPANIES: Heartlands Industrial plc; R M Douglas Construction Limited; Douglas Homes Limited

---

Douglas Hill Developments Limited

395 George Road
Erdington
Birmingham B23 7RZ
Tel: 021-344 4888 Fax: 021-344 4801
BRANCH OFFICES: Wolverhampton
DIRECTOR: Mr Johnstone (Managing)

Douglas Homes Limited

395 George Road
Erdington
Birmingham B23 7RZ
Tel: 021-344 4888 Fax: 021-344 4801

Douglas, R M Property Developments

395 George Road
Erdington
Birmingham B23 7RZ
Tel: 021-344 4888 Fax: 021-344 4801
DIRECTORS: J R T Douglas; R A Paine; M V Manzoni; Mr Johnstone
SUBSIDIARY COMPANIES: R M Douglas Construction Limited; R M Douglas Asphalt & Paving Limited; Town & Country Tarpave Limtied; Douglas Technical Services; Rapid Metal Developments; Douglas Homes Limited; Douglas Hill Developments Limited; The Lakeland Village Limited; Lakeland Management; Douglas Contrete &1 Aggregates; Douglas Specialist Contractors; Douglas Plant Hire

---

Downland Homes Securities Limited

Lee House
Highfield Road
Edgbaston
Birmingham B15

DP Development Company Limited

21 Woodstock Street
London W1R 1HF
Tel: 071-495 6636 Fax: 071 499 0905
NATURE OF BUSINESS: Property Development & Investment
DIRECTOR: V de Peyrecave (Managing); R L de Peyrecave
ANNUAL INCOME/TURNOVER: £0.5m
REGIONAL PREFERENCES: England
VALUE OF PORTFOLIO: £3m (1992)
DISTRIBUTION OF PORTFOLIO: Offices 57%; Factories 33%; Residential 10%
INVESTMENT POLICY: To achieve a completely freehold portfolio
DISTRIBUTION OF DEVELOPMENT: Offices 90%; Residential 10%
DEVELOPMENT POLICY: To provide best quality in prime locations
(Sept 1992)

Drake & Scull Holdings

Hamlyn House
Highgate Hill
London N19 5PS
071-272 0233
DIRECTORS: G Britton (Managing); B McGregor (Marketing)

Drakeheights Limited

457 Smithdown Road
Liverpool L15 3JL
051-733 4259

Drew, Peter

The Dockmasters House
St Katherine's Way
London E1

Dropzend Limited

133 Bethnal Green Road
London E2

Drum Developments (Northwest) Limited

36 Young Street
Manchester M3

Duchess Estates Limited

Hill House
6 Albermarle Street
London W1X 3HF
071-491 1708

Duchy of Lancaster Office

Lancaster Place
London WC2E 7ED
071-836 8277
M K Ridley (Clerk of the Council)
(Sept 1992)

Dudrich (Holdings) Limited

HEAD OFFICE ADDRESS: Lonsto (International) Limited
Lonsto House
276 Chase Road
Southgate
London N14 6HA
Tel: 081-882 8575 Fax: 081 886 6676
NATURE OF BUSINESS: Property Investment - NHBC Developers
DIRECTOR: R Dudding (Managing)
MAJOR SHAREHOLDER: R I Dudding
ANNUAL INCOME/TURNOVER: Company £2m - Mainly rental income
REGIONAL PREFERENCES: England/Wales
VALUE OF PORTFOLIO: £20 m (1992)

Entry missing ? Call HELPLINE Page v

DISTRIBUTION OF PORTFOLIO: Lock-up Garages 85%; Offices/Shops/Flats 15%
INVESTMENT POLICY: Aquisition of lock-up garage sites
(Sept 1992)

Dufton Developments Limited
Kingsley House
5 High Street
Chislehurst
Kent BR7 5AB
081-295 1975
DIRECTOR: M Dufton (Managing)

Dukeminster plc
Newton House
118 Piccadilly
London W1V 9FJ
Tel: 071-495 0909 Fax: 071-491 4605
DIRECTOR: E Shohet (Managing)

Dunstone Management Limited
130 George Street
London W1H

Dwelling Development 1988 Limited
218 Blythe Road
London W14

Dwyer plc
10 Mount Row
Mayfair
London W1Y 5DA
Tel: 071-629 6666 Fax: 071-493 4701
NATURE OF BUSINESS: Property Development & Investment
DIRECTORS: D L Bloom (Chairman); M B Silverman; M J M Philips; M R Dwyer (Non-Executive); A M D Kirwan (Non-Executive)
MAJOR SHAREHOLDERS: Winglaw Develpment Ltd; La Gerta Properties SA; IBI Nominees Ltd; Sun Life Trust Management Ltd; Alibane Ltd; Norwich Union; Bankuwait Ltd; Bank of Ireland; Al Shang Ltd.
ANNUAL TURNOVER: £16.6 m (1991)
VALUE OF PROPERTY PORTFOLIO: £60.4m (1991)
DISTRIBUTION OF PORTFOLIO: Northern Ireland 25.18%; Scotland 8.47%; North east 19.2%; Midlands 11.43%; London & South East 18.64%
SUBSIDIARY COMPANIES: Dwyer (UK) Holdings Limited; Dwyer Property Limited; Dwyer Investments Limited; Hulburds (Sittingbourne) Limited; Annstar Properties Limited
(Sept 1992)

E & F Securities
63 Curzon Street
Mayfair
London W1Y 7PE
071-493 7071
DIRECTOR: T Clegg (Managing)

E I E International (UK) Limited
10 Yeoman's Row
London SW3

Eagle Management Co Limited
Broadbent House
65 Grosvenor Street
London W1X

Eagle Star Properties Limited
60 St Mary Axe
London EC3
Tel: 071-493 8411 Fax: 071-499 1867
(Sept 1992)
DIRECTORS: M Butt (Chief Executive); N B E Mountain; R E Brimblecombe FIA PMI; C N Jones FRICA; J F C Mills BSc FRICS; B Williams FCA; M Heath (Marketing)
MAJOR SHAREHOLDERS: Eagle Star Holdings plc
(Jan 1991)

Earlsdene Limited
65 Wigmore Street
London WIH 9LG
Tel: 071-935 0192 Fax: 071-935 3074
NATURE OF BUSINESS: Property Development & Trading
DIRECTORS: S M Brecker FRICS FCIArb; S Grossmith FRICS
MAJOR SHAREHOLDERS: S M Brecker; S Grossmith
REGIONAL PREFERENCES FOR ACTIVITIES: London & Home Counties
PROPERTY PORTFOLIO: Offices 35%; shops 35%; factories/warehouses 30%
INVESTMENT POLICY: Purchase freehold shops, offices, factories, warehouses portfolios, vacant/let for investment. Single units or parades any size
DEVELOPMENT POLICY: Development freehold properties and sites, vacant/let, with/without planning permission, for shops, offices, factories, warehouses
ASSOCIATED COMPANY: Wigmore Managements Limited
(Sept 1992)

East Cannon Estate Limited
Monks Hall
Monkmead Lane
West Chiltington
West Sussex RH20 2NH
0798 815155
DIRECTORS: G R H Howard FAAI; I N MacLachlan BSc (Eng)
MAJOR SHAREHOLDERS: G R H Howard; I N MacLachlan
BRANCH OFFICES: Horsham
SUBSIDIARY COMPANIES: Cannon Developments Limited; Cannon (UK) Limited

Easter Management Group Limited
22 Grosvenor Gardens
London SW1W

Eastheath Properties
Edward Court
Wellington Road
Wokingham
Berks RG11 2AN
0734 781558
MANAGING DIRECTOR: C W Hartman

East Mercia Developments Limited
Manor Stables
Langham
Nr Oakham
Leicestershire LE15 7JL
0753 37171
DIRECTORS: R Buce (Managing); M Watson (Marketing)

East Ridge Properties Limited
East Ridge
137 Totteridge Lane
London N20 8NS
081-445 2909
DIRECTOR: P Nelkin (Managing)

EBC Group Property Development Limited
2 Queens Terrace
Exeter
Devon EX4 4HR
0392 410612 / 52272
DIRECTORS: L Wint; P Evans (Managing); P Warner (Marketing)

Ebury Developments Limited
22 Headfort Place
London SW1X 7DH
Tel: 071-245 6566 Fax: 071 235 8408

Ebury Property Holdings
41 Praed Street
London W2
071-224 8138
DIRECTORS: J H P Harcourt (Managing); D J B Moss (Marketing);

Edger Investments Limited
142 Holborn Bars
London EC1N 2NW
Fax: 071-499 1614
DIRECTORS: The Hon D McAlpine; J R A Bishop FCA; I R Gordon FRICS; W A Lovell FRICS; D A Reid
MAJOR SHAREHOLDERS: The Prudential Assurance Company Limited
REGIONAL PREFERENCES: South Eastern Region & Southern Region
VALUE OF PROPERTY PORTFOLIO: £36.9m (1985)
DEVELOPMENT ACTIVITIES: Offices, shops, warehouses
SUBSIDIARY COMPANIES: Daysbridge Investments Limited; Kings Reach Development Company; Macsaga Investments Limited; Lenworth Investments Limited; Park Ave Investment Limited; Setcrest Limited; Proplands Limited; EMA Investments Limited

Edge Development Limited
25 Sackville Street
London W1X 1DA

Edge Properties Limited
Academy House
26/28 Sackville Street
London W1X 1DA

Edinburgh & Glasgow Investment Co Limited
2 India Street
Edinburgh EH2

Edinburgh & London Metropolitan Limited
3a Jordan Lane
Edinburgh EH10

Edinburgh Development & Investment Limited
1 Broughton Market
Edinburgh EH3

Edinburgh Maritime Limited
Tower Place
Leith Dock
Edinburgh EH6

Edinburgh Restoration Development Co Limited
Kinellan House
33 Murrayfield Road
London EH12

Egan Building Developments
Egan House
Barlow Street
Radcliffe
Manchester M26

Egg Builders Limited
24 Highbury Grove
London N5

Egerton Trust plc
9 Chesterfield Street
London W1X 7HF
Tel: 071-491 3817 Fax: 071-493 4082
NATURE OF BUSINESS: Development & Investment
DIRECTORS: M F Sanderson (Chairman & Chief Executive); M N Sanderson; W Esplen (Managing Director); D G Coombs; R W Beale; S T Wright; J A Leek FCA ATII (Non-Executive)
MAJOR SHAREHOLDERS: Sanderson Family Settlement; Caparo Group Limited; Darmont Securities Limited; 3i plc; Talbot Nominees
ANNUAL TURNOVER: £110.57m (1988)
VALUE OF PROPERTY PORTFOLIO: £1.96m (1988)

Entry missing ? Call HELPLINE Page v

SUBSIDIARY COMPANIES: Barnsdale Properties Limited; Barnsdale Developments Limited; Trentham Developments Limited; Maybourne Partnerships Limited; PPP Beaumont plc (50%); Beaumont Education Limited; Denehurst Homes Limited; Denehurst Properties Limited; Denehurst Homes West Limited; Ruskin Homes Limited (75.1%); Gayton Homes Limited; G Percy Trentham Limited; Egerton Financial Services plc; Brooklink plc; Culverline plc; Egerton Incorporated (94.55%); Egerton Development Corp (94.55%); Foxwood Homes Inc (94.55%); Emaral Corp (94.55%); Mass Sand & Gravel Colne (94.55%)

Elf Oil (GB) Limited

Elf House
PO Box 80
Woodlands Road
Altrincham
Cheshire WA14 1HD
061 953 1000

Elgar Estates

2 Bridge Street
Hereford HR4 9DF
0432 277773
NATURE OF BUSINESS: Development & Investment
DIRECTORS: P W Morris FRICS; A J Carlton FRICS; M J C King CA
MAJOR SHAREHOLDERS: Directors
REGIONAL PREFERENCES: West Midlands, Devon
DEVELOPMENT ACTIVITIES: shops 20%; residential 80%
DEVELOPMENT POLICY: Infill residential schemes, secondary shopping

Elite Homes

1 Berry Street
Peel Green
Manchester M30

Elliot, J A (Developments) Limited

54-56 Fairfax Road
Teddington
Middlesex TW11 9BZ
Tel: 081-943 5543 Fax: 081-943 5536

Ellis Campbell Group

Craven House
West Street
Farnham
Surrey GU9 7ES
Tel: 0252 722333 Fax: 0252 714189
NATURE OF BUSINESS: Property Investment and Development
DIRECTORS: M D C C Campbell; G G Donald; G C Exeter; A J Taylor
REGIONAL PREFERENCES: Anywhere in the UK

Ellison Harte Developments plc

6a Randolph Crescent
Edinburgh EH3

Eltham Properties Limited

Wesley Chambers
Union Street
Dewsbury
Leeds
West Yorkshire

EMAP Properties Limited

1 Lincoln Court
Lincoln Road
Peterborough PE1 2RF
0733 68900
CHIEF EXECUTIVE: R Miller
DIRECTOR: R Balam (Managing)

Embassy Property Group

Greswolde House
197A StationRoad
Knowle
Solihull
W Midlands B93 OPU
Tel: 0564 776271 Fax: 0564 770114
(Sept 1992)
DIRECTORS: M R Stone (Chairman); R M Holbeche FRICS (Chief Executive); M R Cleveley (Deputy Chief Executive) T Y Wong (non-exec); T L Wong (non-exec)
TURNOVER: £13.4m (1992)
MAJOR SHAREHOLDERS: The Embassy Property Group plc
SUBSIDIARY COMPANY: Embassy Developments Ltd
(Jan 1991)

Emco Estates Limited

5/7 New York Road
Leeds

Emerson Group

The Red House
Kings Ride Court
Kings Ride, Ascot
Berkshire SL5 7JR
0344 20115
DIRECTOR: D Robinson (Managing)

English Estates

St George's House
Kingsway
Team Valley
Gateshead
Tyne & Wear NE11 0NA
Tel: 091-487 8941 Fax: 091-487 5690
CHIEF EXECUTIVE: Mr Pender
MARKETING ASSISTANT: Miss J Miller
BRANCH OFFICES: English Estates North
(Sept 1992)

English Heritage

Fortress House
23 Savile Row
London W1X 2HE
071-973 3000

English & Overseas Properties plc
29 Buckingham Gate
London SW1E 6NF
Tel: 071-828 9929 Fax: 071-828 5767
NATURE OF BUSINESS: Property Development, Investment & Consultantcy
DIRECTORS: J R Clark FRICS; J N Lazarus ARICS; Mr Dear
MAJOR SHAREHOLDERS: Pentos plc; Benaa Limited; Standard Life; M&G Management; British Linen Securities; Save & Prosper
REGIONAL OFFICES: Manchester
ANNUAL INCOME/TURNOVER: Group: £1m; Company £500,000
REGIONAL PREFERENCES: London & South East
VALUE OF PORTFOLIO: £50 m (1993)
% DISTRIBUTION OF PORTFOLIO: London 70%; Milton Keynes 20%; Other 10%
DEVELOPMENT ACTIVITIES: Offices 40%; Shops 10%; Warehouses 5%
SUBSIDIARY COMPANIES: English & Overseas Project Management; English & Overseas Properties North Limited; de Sion
(Sept 1992)

English Property Corporation Limited
Brook House
113 Park Lane
London W1Y 4AY
071-499 0444
DIRECTORS: S H Honeyman FRICS; G Rothman; D J Hughes BSc FCA; I M Laing MA MSc; A Reichman; P Reichman; R Reichman; F B Mellett FCCA; D C Pratt FCIS
MAJOR SHAREHOLDERS: Subsidiary of Olympia and York Developments Limited
ANNUAL TURNOVER/INCOME: £23.5m (1985)
SUBSIDIARY COMPANIES: E P C Developments Limited; E P C Project Managements Limited; Lansdown Industrial Estates Limited; S C I de la Boursidiere; Second Covent Garden Property Company Limited; Star European Managements SA; Star European Properties SA; Star (Great Britain) Holdings Limited; Star Management France SA; Woolf Project Management Limited

English, Richard Properties
29 Buckingham Gate
London SW1 6NF
071-828 9929

Ensign Group plc
Westminster House
38/40 Palace Avenue
Paignton
Devon TQ3 3HB

Enterprise Edinburgh Limited
375 High Street
Edinburgh EH1

Enterprise Zone Developments
International House
World Trade Centre
St Katherine's Way
London E1 9UN
071-480 7513
DIRECTORS: B Williams (Managing); C Hobson (Marketing)
DEVELOPMENT ACTIVITIES: Industrial and Commercial

Equitable Land
78 Wimpole Street
London W1M 7DD

Equity Developments Limited
Unit 6
Penn Street Works, Penn Street
Amersham
Buckinghamshire HP7 OPU
0494 715546
DIRECTORS: R L Hastings (Managing)

Eric Newman Developments Limited
56 Ufton Road
London N1

Eros Property Investment Limited
22 Arlington Street
London SW1A 1RW
071-929 1111 Extn 53529
CHAIRMAN: I M Macinnes

Esse Developments Limited
Broadland House
53A South Park Road
Wimbledon
London SW19 8RT
081-543 6360
NATURE OF BUSINESS: Development
DIRECTORS: S M Etheridge BSc
MAJOR SHAREHOLDERS: S M Etheridge
ANNUAL TURNOVER/INCOME/PROFIT: £430,000 (1991-92)
REGIONAL PREFERENCES: SW London
DEVELOPMENT ACTIVITIES: Residential 100%
DEVELOPMENT POLICY: Residential house building
(Sept 1992)

Essex & Metropolitan Estates plc
Essex House
Astra Centre
Edinburgh Way
Harlow
Essex CM20 2BE
0279 451277
DIRECTOR: A Fordham (Managing)

Estates & Agency Holdings plc
Rosedimond House
11 Hatton Garden
London EC1N 8AH
Tel: 071-405 1411/2185 Fax: 071-831 5626

NATURE OF BUSINESS: Investment
DIRECTORS: J S I Rosefield BA MBA (Chairman); J G Bizley FCA; H M Paisner BA
MAJOR SHAREHOLDERS: Ventureset Holdings Limited; Capite Holdings Limited; D M King; J I S King; Jove Investment Trust plc; J C Glencross; G Rosenfield & J S I Rosenfield; M D Paisner; S A Rosefield; B W Frost; R J S Whiteside & A I M Murphy; The Catherine Lewis Foundation.
ANNUAL TURNOVER: £7.14m (1988)
VALUE OF PROPERTY PORTFOLIO: £62.3m (1988)
SUBSIDIARY COMPANIES: Edgbaston Investment Trust Limited; Estates & Agency (Warwick Street) Limited; Estates & Agency (Piccadilly) Limited; Estates & Agency (Charing Cross) Limited; Estates & Agency (Rainham) Limited; Estates & Agency (Plymouth) Limited; Estates & Agency (Barking) Limited; Estates & Agency (Blakes Market) Limited; Shop Developments (Exeter) Limited; Shop Developments (Suburban) Limited
(Sept 1992)

Estates & General Investments plc

51 Green Street
Mayfair
London W1Y 3RH
Tel: 071-409 1787 Fax: 071-408 1037
(Sept 1992)
NATURE OF BUSINESS: Development & Investment
DIRECTORS: P B Prowting (Chairman); D W Bloomfields ACIS (Managing Director); B S Clegg; P N Clayton; D G M Cull FCCA IPFA ACIB; R J Dossett MSC ARICS MCIOB; T F Wilson FRICS
MAJOR SHAREHOLDERS: D G Randall; Guardian Assurance plc; R A Oury
ANNUAL TURNOVER/INCOME/PROFIT: £11.6m (1988)
VALUE OF PROPERTY PORTFOLIO: £97m (1988)
PROPERTY PORTFOLIO: Offices 47%; shops 34%; industrial 19%
SUBSIDIARY COMPANIES: County & Suburban Holdings Limited; Copse Wood (Northwood) Investments Limited; County & Suburban Developments Limited; County & Suburban Securities Limited; County & Suburban Investments Limited; Flagon Securities Limited; Pacemaker Investments Limited; Worth (London) Limited; Paquin Investments Limited; Estates & General Developments Limited; Dixolines Developments Limited; Midfair Properties Limited; Wellfull Developments Limited; Castle Mall Securities Limited; Forecourt Properties Limited; County & Suburban Properties Limited; Crosstyre plc; Site Improvements Limited; Site Developments Limited; Estates & General Project Management Limited
DEVELOPMENT/INVESTMENT POLICY: To maximise asset base by investment and development whilst maintaining a progressive dividend policy for shareholders
(Jan 1991)

Estates, SMC

145-157 St John Street
London EC1V 4QJ
071-253 6106
DIRECTOR: C Sullivan (Managing)

Eton House Developments Limited

5 New Quebec Street
London W1H

European & Pacific Limited

75 Park Lane
London W1

European Land Limited

Borroughbridge Hall
Burroughbridge
North Yorkshire Y05 9AN
0423 322555

Eurotunnel Developments

Victoria Plaza
111 Buckingham Palace Road
London SW1W 0ST
071-224 4282
DIRECTORS: A Morton (Managing); Mr Hemmingway (Marketing)

Eurotunnel Developments Limited

11 North Street
Ashford
Kent TN24 8LF
Tel: 0233 646555 Fax: 0233 646446
NATURE OF BUSINESS: Development & Investment
MAJOR SHAREHOLDERS: Eurotunnel plc 100%
ANNUAL INCOME/TURNOVER: Company £250,000
REGIONAL PREFERENCES: S E England
VALUE OF PORTFOLIO: £3.2m (1991)
DISTRIBUTION OF PORTFOLIO: 50% Commercial; 50% Industrial
DISTRIBUTION OF DEVELOPMENT ACTIVITIES: 50% Commercial; 50% Industrial
(Sept 1992)

Evans of Leeds plc

Millshaw
Ring Road, Beeston
Leeds LS11 8EG
0532 711888
NATURE OF BUSINESS: Property development & investment
DIRECTORS: J A C Humphries OBE (Chairman); F R Evans OBE (Life President); M W Evans; J D Leavesley; G L Best; E L Curtis ASCA; I J Montgomery FCA; Mrs P E Horsbrough; D Helliwell BSc FRICS(Marketing); W M Gibson LIB FCA; R M Evans; P A Turner FRICS; A F Evans
MAJOR SHAREHOLDERS: Scottish Amicable Life Assurance Society & Subsidiary; N C Lombard Street Nominees Limited, The Equitable Life Assurance Society
ANNUAL INCOME/TURNOVER:£8.523m; £18.275m
VALUE OF PORTFOLIO: £211.5m (1992)
SUBSIDIARY COMPANIES: Astra House Limited; Boden Investments Limited; Dumfries Trading Estate Limited; Evans (Montague) Investments Limited; F R Evans (Administration) Limited; F R Evans (Leeds) Limited; Furnival Estates Limited; Garpool Limited; Hadcrest Limited; Jangay Investments Limited; Lichfield Securities Limited; Lonsdale Properties Limited; Marchington

Properties Limited; Millshaw Property Company Limited; Mulgate Investments Limited; Redvers Investments Limited; R H D Investments (Sheffield) Limited; Sealand Properties Limited; Spabourne Investments Limited; Speylands Limited; Studfair Limited; Tern Hill Securites Limited
(Sept 1992)

Evered plc
Radcliffe House
Blenheim Court
Lode Lane
Solihull
West Midlands B91 2AA
021-711 1717
DIRECTORS: R Kettle (Executive);
C Blasdale(Marketing)

Ewart plc
17 Bedford Street
Belfast BT2 7ES
Tel: 0232 321088 Fax: 0232 238983
NATURE OF BUSINESS: Property Development & Investment
DIRECTORS: B Gilligan; E Robinson; F Tughan; Capt. O Henderson; Sir W Ewart; D Deeney; P Monahan
MAJOR SHAREHOLDERS: P P Monahan; F Tughan; P Whymann; Prudential Corporation Group; Gamma Leasing; Barclays Bank; R S Ferguson
(Sept 1992)
ANNUAL INCOME: £217,997 (1992)
VALUE OF PROPERTY PORTFOLIO: £5.99m (1988)
SUBSIDIARY COMPANIES: William Ewart Properties Ltd; Fenset Properties Ltd; Eward (Southern) Ltd; West Kent Cold Storage Ltd; Eward Developments plc; Victoria Mall Ltd; Langanbank Dev Co Ltd

F E B C Limited
5 Netherwood Road
London W14

F S M Properties
Melrose House
4-6 Savile Row
London W1X 1AF
071-287 1616
DIRECTOR: A E Leyland

Fairbairn Estates (Harrogate) Limited
8 North Park Road
Harrogate
W. Yorkshire HG1 5PG
Tel: 0423 523771 Fax: 0423 520269
NATURE OF BUSINESS: Development & Construction
DIRECTORS: I Conroy; S Bowden
MAJOR SHAREHOLDERS: Conroy & Booth Limited
REGIONAL OFFICES: Huddersfield, Harrogate
ANNUAL INCOME/TURNOVER: Group £8m; Company £2m
REGIONAL PREFERENCES: South, West & North Yorkshire
VALUE OF PORTFOLIO: £4m (1992)
DISTRIBUTION OF PORTFOLIO: Office Investments 50%; Development Land 50%
DISTRIBUTION OF DEVELOPMENT ACTIVITIES: Office 50%; Residential 30%; Industrial 20%
DEVELOPMENT POLICY: Design & Build contracts - residential, industrial, office
(Sept 1992)

Fairclough Homes Limited
King & Queen Wharf
Rotherhithe Street
London SE16

Fairhome Estates Limited
7 The Square
Wimbourne
Dorset BH21 1JA
Tel: 0202 842717 Fax: 0202 842720
NATURE OF BUSINESS: Investors and Developers
DIRECTORS: C J Short; J L Berthet
MAJOR SHAREHOLDERS; C J Short
REGIONAL OFFICES: Wimborne Only
ANNUAL INCOME/TURNOVER: Company £500,000; Group £1m
REGIONAL PREFERENCE: South Hampshire, Dorset, S Wilts
PROPERTY PORTFOLIO: £2.5m (1989-90)
DISTRIBUTION PORTFOLIO: Industrial £2m, Shops £250,000, Residential £250,000, Land £750,000, Others £100,000
INVESTMENT POLICY: Strategic Land Buying on options, quick turnover of developments/refurbishments. Investments - Reversionary and high yielding
DISTRIBUTION ACTIVITIES: £750,000 allocated to quick turnover of developments, refurbishments. Split between industrial and shops.
DISTRIBUTION POLICY: To reduce bank borrowings and increase income
DEVELOPMENT SUBSIDIARIES: Fairhome Estates Limited (Investment only)
(Sept 1992)

Fairview Estates Investments Limited
50 Lancaster Road
Enfield
Middlesex EN2 0BY
Tel: 081-366 1271 Fax: 081-366 0189
DIRECTORS: J Bickel (Managing); S Lambe (Marketing)
ASSOCIATED COMPANY: Fairview New Homes plc

Fairview New Homes plc
Admiral Walk
Trundleys Road
London SE8

Fairview Securities Limited
Fairview House
277 Cranbrook Road
Ilford
Essex IG1 4TP
081-518 2323
DIRECTOR: M Stolkin (Managing)

Faithfold Properties & Investment (Splicefam Limited)

Suite 220
The Linen Hall
162-168 Regent Street
London W1R 5TB
Tel: 071-434 1757 Fax: 071-439 4276
NATURE OF BUSINESS: Development & Investment
DIRECTORS: K Faith (Chairman & Managing Director); P A Baker; S Orgin (Secretary); Mrs M Parsons (Marketing)
MAJOR SHAREHOLDERS: K Faith
ANNUAL GROSS TURNOVER: £0.5m (1987/8)
REGIONAL PREFERENCES: London & suburbs
VALUE OF PROPERTY PORTFOLIO: £250,000
PROPERTY PORTFOLIO: Offices 15%; shops 10%; residential 75%
DEVELOPMENT & INVESTMENT POLICY: Buying properties for refurbishment: buying freehold ground rent
DEVELOPMENT ACTIVITIES: Offices 5%; residential 95%
SUBSIDIARY COMPANIES: Asterplot Limited

Farlane Management UK Limited

21/22 Grosvenor Street
London W1X

Farnsworth Co Limited

Eldon House
2/3 Eldon Street
London EC2M

Farquhar Limited

Deveronside Works
Huntly
Aberdeenshire AB5 4PS
Tel: 0466 3231 Fax: 0466 3098
DIRECTOR: R F Shand (Managing); I Knox (Marketing)

Farr Properties Limited

No 2 Mill
Eagley Industrial Estate
Hough Lane
Bromley Cross
Bolton

Fearnley Developments

Constance House
5 Missouri Avenue
Salford M5 2NP
061-736 4576

Federated Housing plc

Swan House
Swan Court
Leatherhead
Surrey KT22 8AH

Fenwell Properties Limited

8 Silver Street
Bury BL9

Finlan Group plc

37 Ixworth Place
London SW3 3QH
071-584 4231
DIRECTOR: K Taylor-Smith (Managing)

Finland Skybridge plc

37 Ixworth Place
London SW3 3QH
071-584 4231
DIRECTOR: D Rippon (Managing)

Finsgate Properties Limited

48-50 Mortimer Street
London W1N 7DG
071-636 2313

First Argyle

10 Upper Berkeley Street
London W1H 7PE

First Foundations Property Company Limited

15 Albemarle Street
London W1X 3HA
071-491 1143
DIRECTORS; B Dehaan; P Okrent

First London Investments plc

239 Regents Park Road
London N3 3LF
Tel: 081-343 2266 Fax: 081-343 3857
DIRECTORS: A Goldberg; J Gold
(Sept 1992)

First Metropolitan Securities Limited

25 Castlereagh Street
London W1H 5YR
071-706 1989
DIRECTOR: G Jackson (Managing)

First National Housing Trust Limited

Banner Cross Hall
Sheffield
South Yorkshire S11 9PD
0742 555444

First National Developments plc

St Alphage House
Fore Street
London EC2
071-638 2855

First Regional Properties Limited

25 Castlereagh Street
London W1H 5YR
071-706 1989
MANAGING DIRECTOR: G Jackson

Entry missing ? Call HELPLINE Page v

First State Holdings Limited
Somerton Court
Somerton
Somerset TA11 7AH
Tel: 0458 74200 Fax: 0458 74201
DIRECTOR: R Byron-Collins (Managing)

Firstland Property & Finance Limited
104 Wigmore Street
London W1H

Firth Norman Developments Limited
2a Lobstock Road
Urmston
Manchester M31

Fiscal Properties Limited
94 Mount Street
London W1Y

Five Bridges Properties Limited
The Cottage
Archers Green
Nr Hertford
Hertfordshire
SG14 2NG
0438 717459
DIRECTOR: K Bridges (Managing)

Five Oaks Investments plc
130 Jermyn Street
St James's
London SW1Y 4UJ
Tel: 071-925 2393 Fax: 071-925 2448
NATURE OF BUSINESS: Property Investment & Development
DIRECTORS: John H Watkins (Managing Director); T P Walter (Finance); W Trevor Robinson (Chairman); D H Baker (Non-Executive).
MAJOR SHAREHOLDERS: The British Land Co plc; Phillips & Drew Fund Manangement Limited; NatWest Investment Bank; Equitable Life; Schroder Unit Trusts; Colonial Mutual Group
ANNUAL INCOME/TURNOVER: Group £4.9m
REGIONAL PREFERENCES: UK Provincial
VALUE OF PROPERTY PORTFOLIO: Industrial £35.2m; Development £8.1m (1991)
VALUE OF DISTRIBUTION OF INCOME PRODUCING PORTFOLIO: Midlands 48%; North 19% SE 22%; SW 7%; E.Anglia 3%; London 1%
INVESTMENT BY SECTOR: Office 32%; Industrial 28% Office/Retail 22%; Retail 18%
INVESTMENT POLICY: Active management of provincial reversionary property to produce above average capital appreciation and an inherently increasing income stream. Resources are targeted on sectors of the market and in locations considered to offer the most profitable opportunites
(Sept 1992)
SUBSIDIARY COMPANIES: Crescent Development Limited; Five Oaks City Limited; Five Oaks London Limited; Five Oaks Northern Limited; Five Oaks Southern Limited; Five Oaks Projects Limited; Five Oaks Properties Limited

Flagstone Holdings plc
Mill Ridge Estate
Mill Ridge
North Ascot
Berks SL5 8LT

Flair Estates
37/39 Great Marlborough Street
London W1V

Flaxman Properties Limited
53 Egerton Gardens
London SW3

Flaxyard Environmental Development Co Limited
The Granary
Hazelbury Manor
Near Box, Corsham
Wiltshire SN14 9HX
Tel: 0225 810715 Fax: 0225 810716
NATURE OF BUSINESS: Development and Design
DIRECTORS: I D Pollard ARICS; D Pollard
MAJOR SHAREHOLDERS: I D Pollard; D Pollard
ANNUAL TURNOVER: Group (Forecast 92/93) £500,000
REGIONAL PREFERENCES: London & South East
DEVELOPMENT ACTIVITIES: Offices 33%; Retail 33%; Leisure 33%
DEVELOPMENT POLICY: To create individual prestigious 'landmark' buildings - adopting design concepts and ideas which ensure buildings are environmentally and socially stimulating
SUBSIDIARY COMPANIES: Flaxyard Tec Centre Limited; Flaxyard Peckham Limited; Flaxyard Business Centres Limited
(Sept 1992)

Fleetway Properties plc
65 Knightsbridge
London SW1X 7RA
071-235 8424
DIRECTOR: I Markovitz (Managing)

Fletcher King
Stratton House
Stratton Street
London W1X 5FE
071 493 8400
DIRECTOR: A White (Managing)

Fletcher Estates Limited
95 Mount Pleasant Road
Shrewsbury
Shropshire SY1 3EL
0743 67278

Entry missing ? Call HELPLINE Page v

Flohouse Limited
1 Market House
Market Place
Chalfont St Peter
Buckinghamshire SL9 9HA
0753 886684
DIRECTOR: E C Bowen (Managing)

Floridan Properties Limited
Arden Wych
Vicarage Hill
Tanworth-In-Arden
Solihull
West Midlands B94 5EA
05644 2303
DIRECTOR: C L Marlow (Managing)

Folkes Properties Limited
Forge House
Old Forge Trading Estate
Dudley Road
Lye, Stourbridge
West Midlands DY9 8EL
Tel: 0384 424242 Fax: 0384 424455
NATURE OF BUSINESS: Development
DIRECTORS: C J Folkes; J E Folkes; H J Folkes; S Norley
MAJOR SHAREHOLDERS: Subsidiary of Folkes Group plc
ANNUAL GROSS TURNOVER/INCOME: £3.5m (1991)
REGIONAL PREFERENCES: West Midlands
VALUE OF PORTFOLIO: £30m (1991)
(Sept 1992)
PROPERTY PORTFOLIO: Factories 80%; warehouses 20%
DEVELOPMENT ACTIVITIES: Factories 70%; warehouses 30%
DEVELOPMENT POLICY: To construct high quality serviced trading estates: no units below 10,000 sq ft.
(Jan 1991)

Folkestone (UK) Limited
38 Park Street
London W1Y

Follet Property Holdings
18 Berkeley Street
London W1
Tel: 071-499 4645 Fax: 071-491 8883
(Sept 1992)

Ford Sellar Morris Developments
Melrose House
4-6 Savile Row
London W1X 1AF
071- 287 1616
DIRECTORS: A E Leyland (Managing); M Ellis (Marketing)

Ford Sellar Morris Properties plc
Melrose House
4,5,6 Savile Row
London W1X 1AF
071-287 1616
NATURE OF BUSINESS: Development & Investment
DIRECTORS: R W Aitken FCA; I G Sellar; A E Leyland BA AMSIA; M D Morris; N J Wallis BA; W B Johnston MA(Oxon); J J Wallis; Mrs M McAfee
ANNUAL TURNOVER: £16.9m (1988) (15months)
VALUE OF PROPERTY PORTFOLIO: £45.82m (1988)
PROPERTY PORTFOLIO: Offices/shops 27%; shops 27%; offices 16%; industrial 30%
SUBSIDIARY COMPANIES: Ford Sellar Morris Developments Limited; Centrovincial Estates Limited; City & Provincial Holdings Limited; City & Provincial Company (Properties) Limited; Barrie Menswear (London) Limited; Queensland Properties Limited; Centrovincial Estates (Derby) Limited; Centrovincial Estates (Mayfair) Limited; Burnham Estates Limited; Law 6 Limited; Brent & Collins (Unlimited)
RELATED COMPANY: Kitatom Limited

Forextra Limited
79 Grosvenor Street
London W1X

Fort Knight Group plc
Victoria House
Victoria Industrial Estate
Kent DA1 5AJ

Forth Properties Limited
Tower Place
Leith Docks
Edinburgh EH6

Fourth Avenue Estates Limited
18 Cardiff Road
Luton
Bedfordshire LU1 1PP
Tel: 0582 29851 Fax: 0582 481236
NATURE OF BUSINESS: Development
DIRECTORS: D M Traherne BSc (Hons) MICE ACGI; L K J Traherne; C C Bridge BSc MICE
MAJOR SHAREHOLDERS: D M Traherne; L A Traherne; L K J Traherne
ANNUAL GROUP TURNOVER: £1.29m (1991)
REGIONAL PREFERENCES: Herts, Beds, Cambs, Bucks, Norfolk, Suffolk
INVESTMENT POLICY: Very little involved at present.
DEVELOPMENT ACTIVITIES: offices 4%; residential 92%; factories 4%
DEVELOPMENT POLICY: Mainly new house development with some conversion and refurbishment. Includes sheltered housing for the elderly (but not ongoing managment of these schemes)
SUBSIDIARY COMPANIES: David Traherne Developments Limited; Cross Oak (Berkhamsted) Developments Limited
(Sept 1992)

Fox Properties Limited
17 Boulton Road
Reading
Berkshire RG2 ONH
Tel: 0734 313855 Fax: 0734 314557
NATURE OF BUSINESS: Property Investors/Developers

MAJOR SHAREHOLDERS: H A Fox; G S Fox (Joint M/D's)
REGIONAL OFFICE: London
ANNUAL INCOME/TURNOVER: Group £70,000
REGIONAL PREFERENCES: South East
VALUE OF PORTFOLIO: £900,000 (1991/2)
DISTRIBUTION OF PORTFOLIO: Development Sites £300,000; Investments £600,000
INVESTMENT POLICY: Tenanted investments with mid-term development potential - To £½m lot size
DISTRIBUTION OF DEVELOPMENT ACTIVITIES: Offices 100% (Seeking to diversify into leisure)
DEVELOPMENT POLICY: Fringe town centre sites suitable to derive mid-term income. Lot size to £½m
(Sept 1992)

Frankton House Developments Limited
St Johns House
East Street
Leicester LE1 6NB
Tel: 0533 553277 Fax: 0533 540965

Franthom Property Limited
Barker Chambers
Barker Road, Maidstone
Kent ME16 8FF
0622 685101
DIRECTORS: R F Rushton (Managing); J S Brown (Marketing)

Frayland Limited
Unit 4
111 Power Road
London W4 5PY
081-995 4753
DIRECTOR: J Flannery (Managing)

Freedom (Estates) Limited
18 Bramley Shopping Centre
Leeds
West Yorkshire

Freeway Investments plc
73 St James' Street
London SW1A

Fremantle Properties Limited
76 Palace Court
London W2 4JE
071-792 0451
NATURE OF BUSINESS: Development
DIRECTOR: Mr Collins (Managing)

Frenbury Properties Limited
The Old Manor
Fox Road
Framingham Pigot
Norwich NR14 7PZ
Tel: 05086 2082 Fax: 05086 4500
DIRECTOR: W French (Managing)
(Sept 1992)

Friday Street
59 High Street
Odiham
Hampshire RG25 1LF
Tel: 0256 704500 Fax: 0256 704717
NATURE OF BUSINESS: development, investment and the restoration of architectural interesting properties.
DIRECTORS: C A Hogben (Managing); R E Hogben
MAJOR SHAREHOLDER: C A Hogebn
REGIONAL OFFICES: Odiham, Hampshire
ANNUAL TURNOVER: Company £1.0m
REGIONAL PREFERENCES: Major County Towns and rural locations
INVESTMENT POLICY: To retain investments, expand services and office suite operation and build a well balanced portfolio of commercial property
DEVELOPMENT ACTIVITIES: Offices 50%; Industrial 20%; Retail 10%; Residential 20%
DEVELOPMENT POLICY: To acquire buildings/sites with planning and consveration problems in sensitive locations
(Sept 1992)

Friedman, Dr L
160a Earls Court Road
London SW5

Frincon Holdings
Estate House
Connaught Avenue
Frinton-On-Sea
Essex CO13 9AB
0255 674343
MANAGING DIRECTOR: A R W Tomkins

Frogmore Estates plc
Frogmore House
8 Manchester Square
London W1A 2JZ
Tel: 071-244 4343 Fax: 071-935 6476
(Sept 1992)
NATURE OF BUSINESS: Development & Investment
DIRECTORS: P G Davis (Managing); D K Wilmot FCA; G A McCullock; D J King FRICS; P C Shepherd; G H Birch (Non-Executive); D J Cope (Non-Executive Chairman)
MAJOR SHAREHOLDERS: Equitable Life Assurance Society; Markheath Securities plc
ANNUAL TURNOVER/INCOME/PROFIT: £75.6m (1988)
VALUE OF PROPERTY PORTFOLIO: £186.4m (1988)
PROPERTY PORTFOLIO: Commercial 58%; retail 18%; industrial 24%
SUBSIDIARY COMPANIES: Frogmore Estates (Investments) Limited; Portland Place Developments Limited; Frogmore Developments Limited; Highnooners Limited
(Jan 1991)

Frogmore Investments Ltd
Frogmore House
8 Manchester Square
London W1M 6BD
071-224 4343
DIRECTORS: P G Davies (Managing); P C Shepherd (Marketing)

Frost & Fenwick Partnership
4 Highmore Road
Blackheath
London SE3 7UA

Froy, C W & Sons Limited
34 East Dulwich
London SE22

Fujita Co (UK) Limited
31 Lancster Gate
London W2

Full House Property Company
167 Earl's Court Road
London SW5

Fussell Group
Horsefair Tower
The Horsefair
Romsey
Hampshire SO51 8EZ
Tel: 0794 524343 Fax: 0794 513425
NATURE OF BUSINESS: Development & Investment
DIRECTORS: D J Venables; S G Wall ACA
MAJOR SHAREHOLDERS: Directors
REGIONAL PREFERENCES: South of England
PROPERTY PORTFOLIO: Offices 10%; shops 15%; factories/warehouses 70%; residential 5%
INVESTMENT POLICY: Industrial, shops, both high yielding
DEVELOPMENT ACTIVITIES: Offices 15%; shops 5%; factories/warehouses 60%; residential 20%
DEVELOPMENT POLICY: Industrial break up to smaller units. Residential conversion from redundant buildings. New house building
SUBSIDIARY COMPANIES: Fussell Builders Limited; Fussell Estates Limited; Fussell Development Limited; Nobletown
(Sept 1992)

G & G Estates
37 Sloane Street
London SW1X

G S & P Limited
40 Crawford Street
London W1H

Gablecross Properties Limited
10 Bentinck Street
London W1M 6AT
071-935 1639
DIRECTOR: I Plummer (Managing)

Gabriel Securities Limited
Claridge House
32 Davies Street
London W1Y 1LG
071-629 3433
NATURE OF BUSINESS: Development & Investment
DIRECTORS: C Lawrence Chartered Surveyor; J English (Marketing)
MAJOR SHAREHOLDERS: C Lawrence and Family Trust
REGIONAL PREFERENCES: SE England only
DEVELOPMENT ACTIVITIES: offices 50%; science parks/hi-tech 50%
INVESTMENT POLICY: Seeking portfolios of high yielding investments
DEVELOPMENT POLICY: Seeking further commercial sites for development
SUBSIDIARY COMPANIES: Gabriel Properties Limited; Gabriel Developments Limited; Everdean Investment Company Limited

Gallagher, J J Limited
Gallagher House
51 Bordesley Green
Birmingham
West Midlands B9 4QS
Tel: 021-766 6789 Fax: 021-766 6767
(Sept 1992)
BUSINESS: Residential and retail estate developers, building and civil engineering contractors
DIRECTORS: J J Gallagher (Chairman & Managing); J P Gallagher, BSC; J G Gallagher FCA (Finance); A C Gallagher (Property); T J Gallagher
MAJOR SHAREHOLDERS: T J Gallagher; J P Gallagher; J G Gallagher; A C Gallagher
REGIONAL OFFICES: Malmesbury, Wiltshire
ANNUAL INCOME/TURNOVER: Group £54m (31.12.89)
REGIONAL ACTIVITIES: Anywhere in the UK
VALUE OF PROPERTY PORTFOLIO: £50m 1989 @ cost development and values £150m+
DISTRIBUTION OF PORTFOLIO: Residential 60%; retail 35%; factories 5%.
INVESTMENT POLICY: To purchase large sites, obtain planning permission, install infrastructure and develop on own account in consortium or onward sales of sites or complete package.
DEVELOPMENT ACTIVITIES: Residential 60%, Retail 35%, Factories 5%.
DEVELOPMENT POLICY: To consolidate existing land bank and promote its further development - utilise existing large liquid resources to maximise situations in the current depressed market.
SUBSIDIARY COMPANIES: Gallagher Estates Limited, J J Gallagher Construction, Thornborough Investments (2), Gallagher Developments, Astradon Property Co Limited, Longfield Garage.
(Jan 1991)

Galliford Brindley Properties Limited
Wolvey Grange
Wolvey
Hinckley
Leicestershire LE10 3JD
0455 220533
(Sept 1992)

Galliford plc
Wolvey Grange
Wolvey
Hinckley
Leicestershire LE10 3JD
Tel: 0455 220533 Fax: 0455 220779
NATURE OF BUSINESS: Construction
DIRECTORS: P Galliford (Chairman); G R Marsh (Managing); J Livingston (Financial); E G Flower; R M Miles; G A Taylor; J M Wardle; J A Bower (Secretary)
REGIONAL OFFICES: Throughout UK
ANNUAL GROSS TURNOVER/INCOME: £225m
REGIONAL PREFERENCES FOR ACTIVITIES: Throughout UK
(Sept 1992)

Galliford Sears
Castle House
Park Road
Banstead
Surrey SM7 3BU
0737 353411
MANAGING DIRECTOR: Mr D E Brill

Gardington Estates Limited
48 Seymour Street
York House
London W1H 6BB
Tel: 071-706 1111 Fax: 071-872 6799
MAJOR SHAREHOLDERS: Rank Organisation

Garrick Holdings Limited
81 Elizabeth Street
London SW1W 9PQ
071-730 1417
NATURE OF BUSINESS: Development & Investment
DIRECTORS: A G Saxby FRICS; C L Manton FRICS
MAJOR SHAREHOLDER: Directors
BRANCH OFFICES: Aspley Guise, Milton Keynes
REGIONAL PREFERENCES: South East. Housing mainly between Oxford and Cambridge, Watford and Northampton
PROPERTY PORTFOLIO: Offices 50%; Industrial 50%
INVESTMENT POLICY: Interested in high yielding industrial
DEVELOPMENT ACTIVITIES: Offices 30%; residential 70%
DEVELOPMENT POLICY: Actively looking for opportunities
SUBSIDIARY COMPANIES: Garrick Securities Limited; Andrew Garrick Homes Limited
(Sept 1992)

Garson Limited
14 Granville Street
Aylesbury
Buckinghamshire HP2 2JR
0296 87145
DIRECTORS: J Bryce (Managing); T Dell (Commercial)

Garthwood Developments
Hillidge Road
Leeds LS10 1DE
0532 703170
DIRECTOR: Mr Rostron; Mr Elliot (Managing)

Gatechurch Property Management Limited
99 Bishopsgate
London EC2N

Gauld Properties
10 Claremont Terrace
Glasgow G3 6AA
041-332 8509
DIRECTOR: D Mclean (Managing)

Gazeley Properties Limited
248 Marylebone Road
London
NW1
071-706 2162

General Continental Investments
72 New Bond Street
London W1Y 9DD

General Investment Portfolio Limited
108 New Bond Street
London W1Y

Geometry Properties
Unit A
83 Lynch Lane
Weymouth
Dorset
DT4 9DN
0305 777988
DIRECTOR: J Hanna (Managing)

George Harris & Associates (UK) Limited
19 Bow Street
London WC2E

Gibbs Mew plc
Anchor Brewery
Milford Street
Salisbury SP1 2AR

Giffard Securities Limited
Fisher House
6-6A Castilian Terrace
Northampton NN1 1LD
Tel: 0604 24627 Fax: 0604 230706
DIRECTOR: G Underwood (Managing)
(Sept 1992)

Gisborne Life Assurance
NLA Tower
12-16 Addiscombe Road
Croydon
Surrey
081-686 4355
DIRECTOR: S McCrumlish (Managing)

Glanmoor Investments Limited
115 Park Street
London W1Y

Glassedin Securities Limited
Fleming House
5 Kinnaird Road
Craig Park
Edinburgh EH15

Glaston Properties Limited
9 Wimpole Street
London W1M 7AB
Tel: 071-323 6666 Fax: 071-436 8409
DIRECTORS: S Carter; G Glover
(Sept 1992)

Glaxo Holdings
6-12 Clarges Street
London W1Y 8DH
071-493 4060
CHIEF EXECUTIVE: Dr E Mario

Gleeson, M J Group plc
Haredon House
London Road
North Cheam, Sutton
Surrey SM3 9BS
Tel: 081-644 4321 Fax: 081-641 6110
NATURE OF BUSINESS: Building, Civil Engineering Contractors & Residential & Commercial Property Developers
DIRECTORS: J P Gleeson (Chairman); D J Gleeson (Chief Executive); P J Gleeson; W S Bruce; J C Assender FRICS; R W J Radford; C W McLellan CA (Secretary); J D Kay FCIOB
MAJOR SHAREHOLDERS: B S Pension Fund Trustee Limited; Dr Mary M Cleary; Mrs J C Cooper; Prudential Corporation Group; Sun Alliance Investment Management Limited; Sun Life Corporation plc; Mrs P M West; Mr C M White; J P Gleeson; D J Gleeson
ANNUAL TURNOVER: £199m (1991)
REGIONAL OFFICES: Sheffield; Manchester; Newcastle-upon-Tyne; Stirling; Northampton
PROPERTY PORTFOLIO: £50m (1991)
DISTRIBUTION PORTFOLIO: Offices 60%, offices/retail 15%, industrial 25%
INVESTMENT POLICY: Expansion of portfolio by further developments and strategic acquisitions.
DEVELOPMENT ACTIVITIES: Offices 80%, retail 10%, industrial 10%
DEVELOPMENT POLICY: Increased Group turnover in conjunction with expansion of portfolio
PRINCIPAL SUBSIDIARIES: M J Gleeson (International) Limited; Gleeson Homes Limited; Gleeson Housing Development Limited; G L Plant Limited; Northern Woodworkers Limited; Joinery Manufacturers Limited; Powerminster Limited; Concrete Repairs Limited, Sealers Limited
OTHER SUBSIDIARIES: Central Parade Investment Limited, Gleeson (Amesbury) Limited, Haredon Developments Limited, HHNC Investments Limited, Lowbrook Investments Limited, MJG (Management) Limited, Peak Plastering Company Limited.
(Sept 1992)

Glengate Holdings plc
68 Berners Street
London W1P 4EP
Tel: 071-323 6699 Fax: 071 323 4576
(Sept 1992)
NATURE OF BUSINESS: Development & Investment
DIRECTORS: S B Beaumont ARICS; S J Markham; Sir G Johnson-Smith MP; S W Turner FRICS; J E Markham FSVA
VALUE OF PROPERTY PORTFOLIO: £220m approx
PROPERTY PORTFOLIO: Offices 20%; shops 80%
DEVELOPMENT ACTIVITIES: Offices 40%; shops 60%
(Jan1991)

Global Group plc
Cranbrook House
Redlands
Coulesdon
Surrey CR5 2HT

Global Securities Limited
Metropole Chambers
Salubrious Passage
Wind Street
Swansea SA1 3RT
0792 652799
NATURE OF BUSINESS: Development
DIRECTOR: R Waters (Managing)

Glovers Wood Developments Limited
9 Milstead Close
Tadworth
Surrey
0737 814870
DIRECTOR: M J Rose
(Sept 1992)

Goldcrest Land
Goldcrest House
20 Hurlingham Business Park
Sulivan Road
London SW6 3DU
Tel: 071-731 7111 Fax: 071 731 7782
DIRECTOR: M Collins (Managing)
(Sept 1992)

Goldman Investments Limited
81 Stonegate Road
Leeds
West Yorkshire

Goldquill Properties Limited
19 Berkeley Street
London W1
081-491 9101
DIRECTOR: I Besley (Managing)

Goldsborough
Chartwell House
12 Ladbroke Terrace
London W11

Goldside Limited
42 Hillmarton Road
London N7

Goldstone Investments Limited
Beaver House
Neachells Lane
Willenhall
West Midlands WV13 3SJ
0902 307181
DIRECTOR: D Unwin (Managing)

Golfrate Properties
59 Kingston Road
London SW19 1JN

Golf & Leisure Developments Limited
Chiswick Station House
Burlington Lane
London W4
081-994 4545
NATURE OF BUSINESS: Leisure Development

Goode Durrant Bank plc
22 Buckingham Street
London WC2N 6PU
Tel: 071-782 0010 Fax: 071-782 0995
NATURE OF BUSINESS: Development & Investment
DIRECTORS: L K Carter; F M Waring (Chairman); D S Thompson FCA
SHAREHOLDERS: 100% owned by Goode Durrant plc
ANNUAL GROSS INCOME/TURNOVER: £1.6m (1988)
REGIONAL PREFERENCES: SE England but would consider elsewhere in England
TYPES OF DEVELOPMENT: Offices 20%; residential 80%
DEVELOPMENT POLICY: Lend 70% of site cost and 70% development conversion costs

Grafton Estates plc
48 Mount Street
London W1Y 8JW
071-408 0888
DIRECTOR: G L Drake (Managing)

Grafton Securities Limited
2/3 Golden Square
London W1R

Grainger Trust plc
Chaucer Buildings
57 Grainger Street
Newcastle upon Tyne NE1 5LE
091 261 1819
NATURE OF BUSINESS: Property Investment
DIRECTORS: I J Dickinson (Chairman); S Dickinson FCA (Managing); R H Dickinson; T M Balch FRICS; M Creasey FRICS; The Earl of Portsmouth; P M Milburn; Sir R T Pease Bart; R J Rimington FCA
ANNUAL TURNOVER/INCOME: £17.29m (1988)
VALUE OF PROPERTY PORTFOLIO: £48.4m (1988)
SUBSIDIARY COMPANIES: Grainger BVI Limited; Mayaba Ridge Syndicate Limited; Northumberland & Durham Property Trust Limited; Atlantic Metropolitan (UK) plc Group; Channel Hotels & Properties (UK) Limited Group; Derment Developments Limited; Hatch Warren Limited

Grainhurst (Properties) Limited
55 North Wharf Road
London W2 1LA
071-706 1818
DIRECTOR: B Ring (Executive)

Grand Metropolitan Estates
River Court
50 Oxford Road
Denham
Uxbridge
Middlesex UP9 4DL
0895 74621
DIRECTOR: R Williams (Managing)

Grantham Developments
51 High Street
Whetherby
West Yorkshire SL22 4LR
0937 580686
DIRECTORS: T R Cansick (Managing); J D Granthem (Marketing)

Grant & Boyd Limited
56/60 St John Street
London EC1M

Graphic Developments Limited
91 Newberries Avenue
Radlett
Herts WD7 7EN
0923 855219
DIRECTOR: Mr Katz (Managing)

Grayling Developments
Grayling House
97 Tulketh Street
Southport PR8 1AW
0704 500960
DIRECTOR: M Howard (Managing)

Entry missing ? Call HELPLINE Page v

Graysim (Holdings) Limited
Saltley Market Hall
42 Alum Rock Road

GRE Properties Limited
17 Bruton Street
London W1X 7AH

Great Eastern Properties Limited
87 St Johns Street
Bury St Edmunds
Suffolk IP33 1SQ
0284 63685

Great Gable plc
15 Gosditch Street
Cirencester
Gloucestershire GL7 2AG
Tel: 0285 641146 Fax: 0285 641239
NATURE OF BUSINESS: Property Developer & Invester
DIRECTOR: R Ladenburg; N D Arthbuthnott; A W Grant (Chairman)
ANNUAL INCOME/TURNOVER: £4,500,000 (30/3/92)
REGIONAL PREFERENCES FOR ACTIVITIES: Birmingham/Taunton/London Triangle
DISTRIBUTION OF PORTFOLIO: Offices 50%; Residential 50%
INVESTMENT POLICY: Purchase of reversionary investments
DISTRIBUTION OF DEVELOPMENT: Offices 50%; Residential 50%
DEVELOPMENT POLICY: To joint venture properties where forward sales have been achieved.
(Sept 1992)

Great Portland Estates plc
Knighton House
56 Mortimer Street
London W1N 8BD
071-580 3040
NATURE OF BUSINESS: Development & Investment
DIRECTORS: Richard Peskin MA LLM FRSA (Chairman & Managing Director); M Edmondson FRICS; D F Desmond; D Witty CBE MA; T C Harvey CVO DSO; R Paynton LLB FRSA
MAJOR SHAREHOLDERS: Water Authorities Superannuation Fund; British Rail Trustee Company Limited; Mrs Basil Samuel
ANNUAL PRETAX INCOME: £29.36m (1989)
VALUE OF PROPERTY PORTFOLIO: £942m (1989)
PROPERTY PORTFOLIO: Offices 75.6%; retail & showrooms 13.3%; commercial & light industrial 11.1%
SUBSIDIARY COMPANIES: City & Corporate Holdings Limited; Collin Estates Limited; Courtana Investments Limited; J L P Investment Company Limited; Knighton Estates Limited; Limco Group plc; Petra Investments Limited; Pontsarn Investments Limited; Kenneth Orrin Limited
RELATED COMPANY: Bride Hall plc

Greater London Estates
39 Bruton Place
Berkley Square
London W1X 7AB
071-491 4566
DIRECTOR: S Goldenberg (Managing)
(Sept 1992)

Gredley Group Holdings Limited
Rosebury Court
14/15 Charles Street
London W1X

Greenbell Properties Limited
2 Bedford Gardens
London W8

Gregor Properties Limited
22a Rutland Street
Edinburgh EH1

Greenwich House Properties Limited
Weaver House
19 Chapel Road
London SE27 OTP
Tel: 081-766 6844 Fax: 081 766 6845
(Sept 1992)

Gregory Properties Limited
5 East Parade
Harrogate
North Yorkshire HG1 5LF
Tel: 0423 569961 Fax: 0423 500094
MANAGING DIRECTOR: D C A Bramall, (Chairman); G B Gregory (Managing Director); P J B Wilkinson

Greig Property Developments Limited
Eskhill House
Roslin
Edinburgh EH25

Gresham Estates Limited
9 Wimpole Street
London W1M

Gresham Trust Limited
Barrington House
Gresham Street
London EC2V 7HE
071-606 6474
DIRECTORS: N Baldock (Managing); M Thornton (Marketing)

Greyayne Properties
Rutland House
148 Edmund Street
Birmingham B3 2JQ

Greycoat plc
Leconfield House
Curzon Street
London W1Y 8AS
Tel: 071-491 8688 Fax: 071-491 0213
NATURE OF BUSINESS: Development & Investment

DIRECTORS: G Wilson FRICS (Chairman); R Spinney FRICS (Deputy Chairman & Joint Managing); P Thornton BSc FRICS MICE FCIOB (Joint Managing); B Cockerell FRICS FRVA (Asst Managing); G X Constantinidi MA; A Fergusson; N Fetterman FCA; R Guignard FCA MBIM (Finance); G S Pitt FCA; Sir J L E Smith CBE; C Strickland B Tech (Hons) C Eng MICE; J Weir FRICS (Executive, resident in the USA);
W Kumar MA FRICS
MAJOR SHAREHOLDERS: Legal & General Assurance Company Limited
BRANCH OFFICES: City of London, New York
ANNUAL TURNOVER/INCOME/PROFIT: £17.4m (1989)
VALUE OF PROPERTY PORTFOLIO: £554m (1989)
SUBSIDIARY COMPANIES: Churchbury Estates; Law Land plc; Dolphin Property Developments Limited; Wessex & City Investments Limited; The City Offices plc; Cumulus Investment Company Limited; Greycoat Central Limited; Greycoat City Developments Limited; Greycoat City Investments Limited; Greycoat Construction Limited; Greycoat Embankment Place Limited; Greycoat Estates Investments Limited; Greycoat Estates Management Limited; Greycoat Lutyens House Limited; Greycoat Shopping Centres plc (95%); Greycoat Overseas Investments Limited; Greycoat (USA) Corporation (Delaware USA); Greybridge Real Estates Corporation (New Jersey USA)

Griffin Development Limited
8 Drake Street
Rochdale

Griffon Lane and Estates Limited
1 Towers Place
Eton Street
Richmond upon Thames
Surrey TW9 1EG
Tel: 081-332 1777 Fax: 081-332 1334
DIRECTOR: M J Denholm (Managing)

Gross Hill Properties Limited
155 Regents Park Road
London NW1 8BB
Tel: 071-722 5960 Fax: 071-722 4808
DIRECTOR: M Gross (Managing)

Grosvenor Developments Limited
22 Alva Street
Edinburgh EH2

Grosvenor Developments Limited
Management Office
3rd Floor
The Market Place
Bolton
Lancashire

Grosvenor Developments Limited
26-28 Mount Row
London W17 5DA
Tel: 071-491 2672 Fax: 071-491 2356
(Sept 1992)
DIRECTORS: G H B Carter MA FRICS (Chairman); J N C James FRICS (Deputy Chairman); D R J de Broekert MICE (Managing Director); M Aldred FCA; Sir Charles Fraser KCVO WS DL; G Hammond FRICS; J H M Newsum FRICS; I M P Staines FCA
MAJOR SHAREHOLDERS: Grosvenor Estate Holdings
ANNUAL TURNOVER: £48m (1988)
BRANCH OFFICES: Northampton, Edinburgh
DEVELOPMENT ACTIVITIES: Offices/B1 40%; shops & some leisure 40%; factories/warehouses 20%
DEVELOPMENT POLICY: Prime locations, quality development, good spread
SUBSIDIARY COMPANIES: GECD (Gillingham) Limited; Grosvenor Investment Management Limited; Grosvenor (Perth) Limited
(Jan 1991)

Grosvenor Estates Holdings
53 Davies Street
London W1Y 1FH
Tel: 071-408 0988 Fax: 071-629 9115
NATURE OF BUSINESS: Property & Investment
DIRECTORS include: J N C James FRICS; J H M Newsum FRICS; D R J de Broekert MICE; G H B Carter, FRICS
MAJOR SHAREHOLDERS: Private company
LOCATION OF REGIONAL OFFICES: Chester, Northampton, Edinburgh
SUBSIDIARY COMPANIES include: Grosvenor Developments; Grosvenor Estate Restoration Limited; Grosvenor (Mayfair) Estate; Grosvenor Estate Belgravia

---

Grosvenor House Investments plc
Southon House
Station Approach
Edenbridge
Kent TN8 5LP

Grosvenor Park Developments Limited
Old Coach House
The Heath
Dunstarn Lane
Leeds
West Yorkshire

Grosvenor Place Investments Limited
14 Grosvenor Place
London SW1X

Grosvenor Securities Limited
Tilney House
5 Tilney Street
London W1Y 6JL
Tel: 071-629 9933 Fax: 071-493 5561
DIRECTORS: L D Moss CBE FSVA DL (Chairman); R S Moss BSc ARICS ASVA (Managing); S D Moss LLB MSc; A R L Moss
REGIONAL PREFERENCES: Greater London & the South
PROPERTY PORTFOLIO: Offices 90%; shops 5%; residential 5%
DEVELOPMENT ACTIVITIES: Offices 60%; shops 15%; residential 5%; industrial 15%; other 5%

Grosvenor Square Properties Group plc
59 New Cavendish Street
London W1M 8AX
Tel: 071-637 5353 Fax: 071-631 5210
(Sept 1992)
NATURE OF BUSINESS: Development & Investment
DIRECTORS: P B Marber BSc FRICS; J A D Holt FRICS; T J G Bowen FCA; M R Creasey FRICS; A J Tomsett OBE FCA; P G Elster ARICS; D J Griffiths FRICS; Miss G Stewart (Marketing)
MAJOR SHAREHOLDERS: Associated British Ports Holdings plc 100%
DEVELOPMENT ACTIVITIES: Offices 34%; retail 53%; business space 13%
DEVELOPMENT POLICY: Current developments programme - estimated end value in excess of £620m in addition to schemes being developed on land at ABP ports
(Jan 1991)

Grosvenor Terrace Developments plc
9th Floor
Hanover House
11/12 Paul's Square
Birmingham

Group One Investments
10 Loveridge Mews
London NW6 2DP
071-624 0555
JOINT MANAGING DIRECTORS: J Adelman; D Espinoza

Grove & Wright
Sealock Building
Bart Street
Cardiff CG1 6HZ
0222 462426

Guaranteed Property Co Limited
44 Harley Street
London W1N 1AD

Guildhall Properties Limited
40 Charles Street
London W1X 7PB
071-493 7447
(Formerly Slough Developments Limited)
Subsidiary of Slough Estates
DIRECTORS: C Handford FRICS (Managing)

Guinea Properties
24 Ainslie Place
Edinburgh EH3 6AJ
Scotland
031-220 6535
DIRECTOR: J S Drummond (Managing)

Guinea Properties Management Limited
18 Bruton Place
London W1
071-491 8730

Guiness Mahon Properties
32 St Mary Hill
London EC3P 3AJ
071-023 9333

Guiness Peat Properties Limited
32 St Mary at Hill
London EC3P 3AJ
071-623 6222/9333
DIRECTORS: M R Langdau; M Lindsay

GUS Property Management
Temple House
Seacroft Ring Road
Leeds LS14 1NH
0532 734022
DIRECTOR: J Mabbatts (Managing)

H & H Holman Properties Limited
Queensway House
57 Livery Street
Birmingham
West Midlands B3 1HA

H P H Limited
5 Kingsmead Square
Bath BA1
0225 447155

Halbury Estates Limited
27 Berkeley Square
London W1X

Hales Properties Group Limited
Rudgeway House
283-285 Chester Road
Castle Bromwich
Birmingham B36 OET
Tel: 021-747 2833/021-749 6161 Fax: 021-749 2529
NATURE OF BUSINESS: Property Investment/ Development
DIRECTORS: A Rabheru; R Rabheru; Mrs L D Thompson

Halford Developments Limited
Unlt 6
Cornwall Street Industrial Street
Openshaw
Manchester M11

Hall & Tawse City Limited
Lawrence House
River Front
Enfield
Middlesex EN1 3SY
Tel: 081-367 2999 Fax: 081-367 3739
DIRECTOR: A B Paxford (Marketing)
NATURE OF BUSINESS: Building Contractors
REGIONAL OFFICE: Raine Industries plc, Raine House,

Ashbourne Road, Mackworth.
ANNUAL INCOME/TURNOVER: Group £600m; Company £30m
REGIONAL PREFERENCES FOR ACTIVITIES: Within the M25, Bucks, Herts, Beds & Essex areas.
(Sept 1992)

Halla International Limited

3 Dunraven Street
London W1Y

Hallborough Properties Limited

Leathley Hall
Leathley
Leeds
West Yorkshire

Hambleberry Limited

Westfield Farm
Coopers Hill
Eversley
Hampshire RG27 OQA
Tel: 0252 876001 Fax: 0252 879327
NATURE OF BUSINESS: Development & Investment
DIRECTORS: J P Faulkner BSc (Hons); P G Faulkner
MAJOR SHAREHOLDERS: J P Faulkner
ANNUAL TURNOVER/INCOME/PROFIT: £5m (1988)
SUBSIDIARY COMPANIES: Hambleberry Homes Limited; Hambleberry Developments Limited;
PROPERTY PORTFOLIO: Offices 50%; residential 50%
DEVELOPMENT ACTIVITIES: Offices 10%; residential 90%

Hambros plc

41 Tower Hill
London EC3N 4HA

Hammerson Group of Companies

100 Park Lane
London W1Y 4AR
Tel: 071-629 9494 Fax: 071-629 0498
NATURE OF BUSINESS: Property Developers & Investors
DIRECTORS: S Mason (Chairman); J R Parry (Managing); H R Vogt; R A C Mordanti
MAJOR SHAREHOLDERS: Standard Life Assurance Co (23.59%); AMP Asset Management (9.2%); ABP Royal London Asset Management; ICI Pension Fund
ANNUAL TURNOVER: £166.5m
SUBSIDIARY COMPANIES: Principal subsidiary companies incorporated and operating in the UK: Hammerson Amethyst Properties Limited; DOB Estate Limited; Hammerson Group Management Limited; Hammerson UK Properties Limited; Hammerson (Newchat) Properties Limited; Hammerson International Holdings Limited
BRANCH OFFICES: Divisions in Canada, Australia, USA East, USA West, France, Germany, Holland
VALUE OF THE PROPERTY PORTFOLIO: £1,907.5m (1992)
DISTRIBUTION OF PORTFOLIO: U.K. (41%); Canada (26%); Australasia (14%); Continental Europe (16%); USA (3%)
(Sept 1992)

Hampton Trust plc

Larches House
188 Wllifield Way
London NW11
071-935 5737
DIRECTOR: P Morris
NATURE OF BUSINESS: Investment
DIRECTORS: T C Robey (Chairman); D J Lewis BSc FRICS; S L J Raynaud FCCA; J N Davis; S H Shohet; E Shohet; R H Watson; P Morris
MAJOR SHAREHOLDERS: A subsidiary of Southend Property Holdings
SUBSIDIARY COMPANIES: Dallad Properties Limited; Drancourt Properties Limited; Brinelynn Limited; Tarravale Eastern Limited; Oldbrook Estates Limited; Masonplan Limited; Envalynn Limited; Masonplan Securities Limited; Pilonlynn Limited; Toftplan Properties Limited
BRANCH OFFICE: London
INVESTMENT POLICY: Commercial properties in UK; 50% interest in trading, 50% interest in oil and gas in USA and Australia
REGIONAL PREFERENCES: South East
PROPERTY PORTFOLIO: Shops 60%; offices 35%; industrial/commercial 5%

Hanover Druce plc

21 Manchester Square
London W1A 2DD
071-486 1252

Hanover Lane Securities

52 Park Road
London NW1

Hanover Property Developments Limited

16 Hans Road
London SW3 1RS
071-581 1477
MARKETING DIRECTOR: T Morros

Harcooke Estates and Land Limited

183 Kingston Road
Wimbledon
SW19 1LH
081-543 9139

Hardaker Estates Limited

4th Floor
Hyde Park House
60 Knightsbridge
London SW1X 7JX
Tel: 071-235 6552 Fax: 071-245 0990
DIRECTORS: D A Hardaker; J Hardaker
MAJOR SHAREHOLDERS: D A Hardaker
REGIONAL PREFERENCES: London, S.E. and Manchester
VALUE OF PROPERTY PORTFOLIO: £8m 1990

Hardanger Properties plc
Minster House
8 Church Street
Kidderminster
Worcester DY10 2AD
Tel: 0562 820123 Fax: 0562 823324
NATURE OF BUSINESS: Development & Investment
DIRECTORS: D Coombs (Chairman); N Siviter ARICS (Managing); K Maslen LIB ACIB (Secretary); J Westwood
MAJOR SHAREHOLDERS: Prudential; Target Life
ANNUAL TURNOVER/INCOME/PROFIT: £27.57m (1988)
SUBSIDIARY COMPANIES: Keyshire Builders Limited; Hardanger Investments Limited; Aprax Properties Limited; Bressel Investments Limited; Hardanger Investments (Southern) Limited; Hardanger (Southern) Limited
VALUE OF PROPERTY PORTFOLIO: £44.9m (1988)

Harlinspear Limited
Accurist House
44 Baker Street
London W1M

Harrods Estates
87-135 Brompton Road
London SW1X 7XL
Tel: 071-584 6600 Fax: 071-581 1287
DIRECTOR: J Mayer (Managing)
(Sept 1992)

Hartland Estates (Croydon) Limited
12a Eccleston Street
London SW1W

Hartley Properties
143 Grove Hall Court
Hall Road
London NW8
(Sept 1992)

Hartley Property Trust Limited
39 Charles Street
London W1X 7PB
Tel: 071-409 0220 Fax: 071-409 3424
NATURE OF BUSINESS: Property Investment
DIRECTORS: R G Dwyer
(Sept 1992)

Hartola Properties Limited
188 Chorley New Road
Bolton

Hasington Management
Hastingwood Trading Estate
Harbert Road
Edmonton
London N18 3HR
081-884 1318
DIRECTORS: M Roat (Managing); Mr Irwin (Marketing)

Haslemere Estates plc
4 Carlos Place
Mayfair
London W1Y 5AE
071-629 1105
(Sept 1992)
DIRECTORS: D M Pickford FRICS; G L Powell; K A Phillips FRICS; M R Thody; P D Webster BA FCA; T C O'Rorke FRICS; C I Benham BSc(Econ); R V Wood BA FFA
SUBSIDIARY COMPANIES: Aidengate Limited; Bellwood Properties Limited; Bishopswood Properties Limited; Carlos Estates Limited; The Faircliffe Finance Company Limited; Hamastead Limited; Haslemere Estates (Developments) Limited; Haslemere Management Services Limited; Haslemere Management Services (Guernsey) Limited
REGIONAL PREFERENCES: London & South East
PROPERTY PORTFOLIO: Offices 75%; shops 4%; factories, warehouses, residential, science parks/mixed & industrial 21%
DEVELOPMENT ACTIVITIES: Offices, shops, factories, warehouses, industrial
(Jan 1991)

Hassall Homes Limited
Allerdale House
Brigham
Cockermouth
Cumbria
CA13 OXH
0900 825351
DIRECTOR: J W Smith (Managing)

Hatfield Estates
1 Forum Place
Hatfield
Herts AL10 ORN
0707 273333
DIRECTOR: K G Wilkins (Managing)

Hatfield Holdings
1 Silvester Square
The Maltings
Silvester Street
Hull HU1 3HA
Tel: 0482 586444 Fax: 0482 229654
NATURE OF BUSINESS: Property Investors
MAJOR SHAREHOLDERS: R E Hatfield; S M Hatfield
ANNUAL INCOME/TURNOVER: Company £250,000
VALUE OF PORTFOLIO: £4m (1992)
DISTRIBUTION OF PORTFOLIO: Commercial 40%; Residential 60%
REGIONAL PREFERENCES: Humberside
(Sept 1992)

Hawk Development Management plc
37 Queen Anne Street
London W1M

Hawkesworth Securities plc
115 Edbury Street
London SW1W

Hay, W G & Co
21 Causewayside
Edinburgh EH9

Haymills Holdings Limited
Empire House
Hanger Green
Ealing
London W5 3BD
081-997 5602
DIRECTORS: R E Butler (Managing); D Thornton (Marketing)

Headcrown Limited
12 Well Court
London EC4M

Headland Properties South
31 Main Street
Ratho
Edinburgh EH28

Headland Weald Limited
3 Chesham Street
London SW1X

Heathfield Group of Companies
11 Deer Park Walk
Lye Green
Buckinghamshire
0494 784 824

Heduco Property & Investments Company Limited
St Georges House
195-203 Waterloo Road
London SE1 8XJ
071-633 0238
DIRECTORS: J M Cooling BSc(Eng) CEng (Chairman); J H Duckworth CEng; N E Herring ATD
MAJOR SHAREHOLDERS: J M Cooling & family; J H Duckworth; N E Herring
SUBSIDIARY COMPANIES: Heduco Inc
PROPERTY PORTFOLIO: Offices 88%; residential 3%; overseas residential 9%

Helical Bar plc
11-15 Farm Street
London W1X 7RD
Tel: 071-629 0113 Fax: 071-408 1666
NATURE OF BUSINESS: Development & Investment
DIRECTORS: J P Southwell (Chairman & Non-Executive); L C K Kelly MA (Vice-Chairman & Non-Executive); M E Slade FRICS FSVA (Managing); N G M Scott MA FCA; C D Scott FSVA
MAJOR SHAREHOLDERS: TR Property Investment Trust plc; Pramton Company
ANNUAL TURNOVER: £123.5m (1989)
SUBSIDIARY COMPANIES: Aycliffe & Peterlee Investment Company Limited; Aycliffe & Peterlee Development Company Limited; Coltil Limited; Helical Investment Holdings Limited; Helical Properties Limited; Helical Properties (HSM) Limited; Helical Properties Investment Limited; Helical Properties (MF) Limited; Helical Properties (RS) Limited; Helical Properties (Western) Limited; Intercontinental Land & Development Company Limited; Intercontinental Land & Development (Cardiff) Limited; Intercontinental Land (City Road) Limited; Intercontinental Land Tritec Limited
VALUE OF PROPERTY PORTFOLIO: £62.3m (1989)

Helix Properties Limited
2 Henrietta Street
London WC2E

Hemdell Limited
98 New Bond Street
London W1Y

Hemingway Estates
11 Wellbeck Street
London W1
071-486 7063
DIRECTOR: L Phillips (Chairman)

Hemingway Properties Limited
62 Queen Anne Street
London W1M

Hemphurst Limited
Suite 1
Barry House
20/22 Worple Road
London SW19 4DH

Henderson Homes Limited
Woodend, Netherley Road
Tarbock
Liverpool L35 IQE
051-487 0666
NATURE OF BUSINESS: Development & Investment
DIRECTORS: M S Henderson
MAJOR SHAREHOLDERS: Private Trust
DEVELOPMENT/INVESTMENT POLICY: Expansion, The company has no borrowings and is cash rich.
PROPERTY PORTFOLIO: Offices 5%; shops 5%; factories 5%; warehouses 5%; residential 75%; leisure 5%
DEVELOPMENT ACTIVITIES: Residential 90%

Heneghan Developments Limited
26 Norford Way
Rochdale
Yorkshire

Henry Boot Developments
Eccleshall Road
Banner Cross Hall
Sheffield S11 9PD
0246 410111
DIRECTOR: K Gledhill (Managing)

Entry missing ? Call HELPLINE Page v

Henry Properties
Second Floor
45 Walm Lane
Willesden Green
London NW2 4QU
Tel: 081-451 1907 Fax: 081-451 5212
DIRECTOR: N Henry
(Sept 1992)

Heritable Trust
97 Old Brompton Road
London SW7 3LD
071-581 8422
DIRECTOR: J B Richmond-Dodd (Managing)

Heritage Land plc
39 Bruton Place
Berkeley Square
London W1X 7AB
Tel: 071-491 4566 Fax: 071-491 0809
NATURE OF BUSINESS: Property Investors and Developers
DIRECTORS: H M Goldenberg (Chairman); S A Goldenberg FSVA, IRRV, FRSH (Managing Director); B M Goldenberg
REGIONAL PREFERENCE: Throughout the UK.
Requirements include freehold ground rents
(Sept 1992)

Hermes Properties
Higher House
Stockland Road
Dalwood
Devon EX13 7HQ

Heron Hi-Tech Limited
Alexander Barn
1 Waverley Lane
Farnham
Surrey GU9 8BB

Heron Homesteads Limited
Heron House
PO Box 1701
Church Road
Yate, Bristol
Avon BS17 5YG
0454 312933
DIRECTORS: G M Ronson; P G H Lewis (Chief Executive); I D G Buck; H Dobin; D J Tucher; M Price (Marketing)
SUBSIDIARY COMPANIES: Heron International plc

Heron Property Corporation Limited
Heron House
19 Marylebone Road
London NW1 5JL
Tel: 071-486 4477 Fax: 071-487 3190
NATURE OF BUSINESS: Development & Investment
DIRECTORS: A W Royle FSVA (Chairman); G M Ronson (Managing); A Burnie; E M Walker; J Mackevoy
MAJOR SHAREHOLDERS: Privately owned
SUBSIDIARY COMPANIES: Heron Hi-tech; Heron Retail Parks
DEVELOPMENT POLICY: Commercial particularly retail town-centre schemes
INVESTMENT POLICY: Existing portfolio being enhanced by selective acquisitions and disposals
PROPERTY PORTFOLIO: Offices 20%; shops 80%
DEVELOPMENT ACTIVITIES: Offices 10%; shops 80%; science parks 10%

Heronhurst Homes
Pembroke House
Llantarnan Park
Cwmbran
Gwent
South Wales
Tel: 0633 838485 Fax: 0633 360063
DIRECTOR: N D Oswell (Finance)

Hertford Manor Estates Limited
20 Wayside Mews
Gants Hill
Ilford
Essex IG12 6XJ

Hesley Estates
79 Netherhall Road
Doncaster
0302 867222

Hestair Developments Limited
1st Floor
60 Charles Street
Leicester
Leicestershire LE1 1GP
0533 623881
DIRECTORS: D Gallagher (Managing); Lynn Phillips (Marketing)

Hetton Properties Limited
2 Wellington Road
London NW8

Hey & Croft Group plc
White Horse Lane
Chipping Hill
Witham
Essex CM8 2BX

Heywood Williams
Waverley
Edgerton Road
Huddersfield HD3 3AR
0484 435477
DIRECTOR: Mr Hinchlisse (Managing)

Higgins, D J Developments Limited
Hawke House
Old Station Road
Loughton
Essex IG10 4PE

Higgins Group of Companies
Hawke House
Old Station Road
Loughton
Essex IG10 4PE
081-508 5555
DIRECTORS: G Bent (Managing); B Sabin (Marketing)

Higgs & Hill Homes Limited
Crown House
Kingston Road
New Malden
Surrey KT3 3SJ
081-942 8921
DIRECTORS: D L Ridout LLB BSc(Econ) FCIS; S I Padmore FRICS; B J Hill MA FRICS; N Dancer (Managing)
MAJOR SHAREHOLDERS: Higgs & Hill plc
SUBSIDIARY COMPANIES: Higgs & Hill Properties Limited; Clement Avenue Properties Limited; Higgs & Hill Properties (Scotland) Limited
BRANCH OFFICES: Falkirk, Stirlingshire
VALUE OF PROPERTY PORTFOLIO: £14m (1986)
PROPERTY PORTFOLIO: Offices 30%; shops 11%; industrial 59%
DEVELOPMENT ACTIVITIES: All, but in varying amounts

Highcroft Investment Trust plc
Lamarsh Road
Botley Road
Oxford OX2 OHZ

Highcross Commercial Developments Limited
Toomers Wharf
Canal Walk
Newbury
Berkshire RG13 1DY
Tel: 0635 521088 Fax: 0635 35432
DIRECTOR: J Walters (Managing)

Highgold Properties Limited
8 Northbridge Street
Shefford
Bedfordshire SG17 5DH

Highland Developments Limited
11 Balfour Mews
London W1Y 5RJ
071-408 0501
DIRECTOR: R I Duckworth; C Collett

Highpoint Estates Limited
Royal Liver House
Westgate
Leeds

Hilfiger Limited
10 Chester Place
London NW1

Hillgate Developments
St George House
103 Tonbridge Road
Maidstone
Kent ME16 8JW
0622 692394
DIRECTOR: D Kay (Managing)

Hill Welsh
25 Queen Anne's Gate
London SW1H

Hillreed Homes
Hillreed House
54 Queen Street
Horsham
Sussex
0403 64210
BUILDING DIRECTOR: M Bruce
(Sept 1992)

Hills & Hills
12 Bear Street
London WC2H

Hilson Twigden Limited
The Shrubbery
Church Street
St Neots, Huntingdon
Cambridgeshire PE19 2BU
0480 72728
DIRECTORS: H Hemmings (Managing); C Smith (Sales)

Hilstone Developments Limited
1A Yeoman's Row
London SW3 2AL
071-225 1666

Hilton International Properties (UK) Limited
Norvic House
1 Hilton Street
Manchester M4

Hinchland Limited
36 Buckingham Palace Road
London SW1W

Hind Trading Co Limited
1 Harriet Walk
London SW1X

Hintsword Limited
25 Bracken Park
Scarcroft
Leeds
West Yorkshire LS14 3HZ
0532 892767

HJA Developments Limited
No 1 The Broadway
Winchester
Hampshire SO23 9BE
0962 61194
DIRECTORS: M J Ashby; F Ashby; R R C Guion BArch (Hons)
MAJOR SHAREHOLDERS: M J Ashby; F Ashby
SUBSIDIARY COMPANIES: Ashby Renovations Limited
REGIONAL PREFERENCES: Hampshire

Hofton Commercial
24 St Pauls Square
Birmingham B3

Hojgaard & Schultz UK Limited
19 Berkeley Street
London W1X

Holborn Property Company Limited
27 Maddox Street
London W1R 9LE
Tel: 071-629 3025 Fax: 071-629 6040
DIRECTOR: P Wayne (Managing)

Hollins Murray Group Limited
Hollins House
Cottesmore Gardens
Hale Barnes, Altrincham
Cheshire WA15 8TS
061-904 9412
DIRECTOR: A J Murray (Managing)

Holman, H & H Properties Limited
Queensway House
57 Livery Street
Birmingham B3 1HA
021-233 2202
DIRECTOR: P Holme (Managing)

Holyoake Estate Co Limited, The
28 Wimpole Street
London W1M

Holyoake Estate Co Limited, The
5 Berners Street
London W1P 3AG

Homedale Developments
Suite 2
19A Broadlands Road
Highgate
London N6 4AE
081-348 6363
DIRECTORS: Mrs L Mendoza; Mrs S Freeman (Joint Managing)

Homewise
77 Werneth Hall Road
Oldham OL8

Hortons Estate Limited
3IA Colmore Row
Birmingham
West Midlands B3 2BU
Tel: 021-236 6481 Fax: 021 236 6548
NATURE OF BUSINESS: Property Investment & Development
DIRECTORS: Mr R N Rowlatt (Managing); R E Blyth (Property); M S Horton (Chairman); M T Horton; G B Horton; R T Horton; P D Taylor
(Sept 1992)

Horton House Developments
133 Barton Road
Stretford
Manchester M32

Hotspur Investments
180 New Bridge Street East
Newcastle-Upon-Tyne
NE1 2TE
091-232 9232
DIRECTOR: I H Percy (Managing);
PROJECT MANAGER: P J Brown

Housebuilder Properties Limited
Unit C, Victoria Mill
Buckley Street
Droysden
Manchester M35

House of Orange Developments Limited
Ashbourne House
2 South Park Road
Harrogate
North Yorkshire HG1 5QX
0423 501137
DIRECTORS: T Orange (Managing); A Ballingall (Marketing)

Housing Projects Limited
Lancaster House
80 Princess Street
Manchester M1

Howard Holdings plc
7 Lyon Road
Merton
London SW19 2RZ

Howard-De-Walden Estates Limited
23 Queen Anne Street
London W1
071-580 3163

Hudson Conway Properties Limited
Waldron House
57-63 Old Church Street
Chelsea
London SW3 5BS
Tel: 071-352 4535 Fax: 071 376 8884

DIRECTOR: B S Sandhu BSc(Econ) ACA MBA ABIM MInstD; A D Cummins BSc(CE) MBA; R E Luke; B Hamilton B Comm FCA
(Sept 1992)

Hufvudstaden (UK) Limited

Cunard House
15 Lower Regent Street
London SW1Y

Hughes Investments Limited (Holdings) Limited

1 Dwynant Estates
Pontyates
Llanelli
Dyfed SA15 5RY
Tel: 0269 860455 Fax: 0269 860455
(Sept 1992)
DIRECTORS: R C Hughes; R M Hughes
MAJOR SHAREHOLDERS: Directors
PROPERTY PORTFOLIO: Warehouses 90%; industrial 10%
DEVELOPMENT ACTIVITIES: Warehouses 80%; science parks/mixed 10%; industrial 10%
(Jan 1991)

Hull Hampshire Estates plc

62 High Street
West End
Southampton
Hampshire SO3 3DT
Tel: 0703 477377 Fax: 0703 474252
DIRECTORS: P A H Grover FRICS (Managing); M A Chiswell ASVA
SUBSIDIARY COMPANIES: West End Land Company Limited;
Hull Hampshire Estates Services Limited
ANNUAL TURNOVER/INCOME: Less than £5m (1988)
REGIONAL PREFERENCES: Southern England
INVESTMENT ACTIVITIES: Offices/factories/shops

Humberside Properties Limited

The Bar House
Northbar-within
Beverley
North Humberside HU17 8DG
0482 862280
DIRECTOR: A D Osborne (Chairman)

Hunt & Nash Chartered Surveyors

15 Crendon Street
High Wycombe
Buckinghamshire
HP13 6LQ
0494 24884
NATURE OF BUSINESS: Chartered Surveyors

Huntingate Developments Limited

PO Box 4444
4 Hunting Gate
Hitchin
Hertfordshire SG4 OTB
Tel: 0462 434444 Fax: 0462 45592
NATURE OF BUSINESS: Property Developers
DIRECTORS: J P Walters (Managing); K Grundy; A Clayton; N J Needs; J Carslile; S W Holloway; M Freeman
MAJOR SHAREHOLDERS: Hunting Gate Group Limited
ANNUAL TURNOVER: £104m (1989)
REGIONAL PREFERENCES: UK
PROPERTY PORTFOLIO: £83M (1989)

Huntingdon Group Limited

Churchgate House
Churchgate
Bolton

Hunts Cross Limited

53 Frewin Road
Wandsworth Common
London SW18 3LR
Tel: 081-874 4555 Fax: 081-877 3747
NATURE OF BUSINESS: Distribution Development
DISTRIBUTION OF DEVELOPMENT: Warehousing 70%; Transport 20%; Offices 10%
DEVELOPMENT POLICY: UK + European Road/Rail Infrastructure & Development
(Sept 1992)

Hurlingham Management Limited

Grosvenor Garden House
Grosvenor Gardens
London SW1W

Hurstbourne Management Limited

6 Randolph Crescent
Edinburgh EH3

Hyde Park Investments Limited

199 Piccadilly
London W1
071-734 0363
DIRECTOR: J Mautner (Managing)

Hyperion Properties plc

The Merton Centre
45 St Peters Street
Bedford MK40 2UB
Tel: 0234 272222 Fax: 0234 217207
NATURE OF BUSINESS: Development
DIRECTORS: R P Gapper (Chairman); H Lafferty (Managing); R H Watson (Non-Exec); R Lucas (Non-Exec); R W Hinde (Non-Exec); A R Williams; J D Stokes; E J Davies; R M E Mann; J M T Howell, D L Kay.
MAJOR SHAREHOLDERS: NFC plc
SUBSIDIARY COMPANIES: We are a wholly owned subsidiary company.
ANNUAL INCOME/TURNOVER: Company £39m

Hystar Developments

Forum House
Brighton Road
Redhill
Surrey RH1 6YS
0737 767161
DIRECTOR: S A Hyde (Managing)

I M F C Limited
Century House
2 Eyre Street Mill
Clerkenwell Road
London EC1R

I P D Consultants Limited
8 Palace Gate
London W8

Ian Smith Associates
26a Davies Street
London W1Y

Ibstock Johnson plc
Lutterworth House
Lutterworth
Leicestershire LE17 4PS
0455 553071
DIRECTORS: R Boxhall (Managing); I MaCellen(Marketing)

ICI Estates Limited
ICI Group HQ
9 Millbank
London SW1P 3JF
071-834 4444
CHAIRMAN: Sir D Henderson

IDC Property Investments Limited
23 St James's Square
London SW1Y 4JH
071-839 6241
DIRECTOR: Neil Barnes

Ideal Homes Holdings plc
Goldsworth House
The Goldsworth
Park Centre
Woking
Surrey GU21 3LF
Tel: 0483 747474 Fax: 0483 772285
NATURE OF BUSINESS: Housebuilders & Residential Developers
DIRECTORS: D M Calverby; J D Low; J E Coker; D C Henderson; R P Lowes; J E King
MAJOR SHAREHOLDERS: Trafalgar House Property Limited
LOCATION OF REGIONAL OFFICES: Weybridge; Rickmansworth; Leicester; Exeter; Thornaby-on-Tees; Llantrisant; Leigh
DEVELOPMENT POLICY: Major mixed developments (Sept 1992)

IGP Investments Limited
Vicarage House
58-60 Kensington Church Street
London W8 4DB
Tel: 071-937 4600 Fax 071-937 3400
DIRECTOR: J Dwek (Managing)

IMC Holdings
Warren House
Argent Court
Sylvan Way
Basildon
Essex SS15 6TH
0268 541960
DIRECTOR: I Gibson (Managing)

Imperial Investment
Ball Wharf
Redcliff Street
Bristol BS1 6QR
0272 298444
DIRECTORS: P W Dunscombe; W G Mather (Joint Managing)

Imperial Land Limited
11/13 Young Street
London W8 5EH
071-938 1915
DIRECTOR: C Wong (Managing)

Imry Merchant Developers plc
19 St James's Square
London SW1Y 4JT
Tel: 071-321 0266 Fax: 071-321 0094
NATURE OF BUSINESS: Development & Investment
DIRECTORS: D J Davies MA (Chairman, Non-Executive); M R Landau FCA (Deputy Chairman); M T Myers BSc FRICS (Managing Director & Chief Executive); B F Martin FRICS (Deputy Managing Director); M J Chande ACA; L Freedman CBE FSVA Non-Executive); M M Kavanagh (Non-Executive); Lord McAlphe of West Green (Non-Executive); B J Webb (Non-Executive); Diana Midgen (Marketing)
MAJOR SHAREHOLDERS: Govett Stategic Investment Trust plc; Boots Pensions Limited; The Equitable Life Assurance Society
ANNUAL GROSS PROFIT: £22.8m (1989)
VALUE OF PROPERTY PORTFOLIO: £282.2m (1989)
SUBSIDIARY COMPANIES: IMD Investments plc; Macdet Investments Limited; CLE (Southern) Limited; Guildhall Yard Properties Limited; Harleigh Limited; IMD Developments plc; Imry Properties Developments Limited; Imry Properties Inc; CMD Property Developments Limited; IMD Trading Limited; Banestar Limited; Imry Property Holdings plc; IMD Securities Limited; IMD International Limited; Surpart BV; IMD Development Co-ordination Limited
RELATED COMPANIES: Ashford Great Park (Phase I) Limited; Ashford Great Park (Phase II) Limited; Golden Oak Developments (Maidenhead) Limited; Jumpcloud Limited; McGuinness Limited; PHD Limited; Precis (338) Limited; Rootbourne Limited; Townregal Limited; Trophy Properties Limited; Welkinsable Limited; West Regent Street Development Limited

In Shops Centres plc
Warwick House
35 Spring Road
Hall Green
Birmingham B11 3EA
021-778 2233
CHIEF EXECUTIVE: J Hoesli

Indescon Limited
Indescon House
117 Stanhope Road
Darlington
County Durham DL3 7SF
0325 351811
DIRECTORS: D H L Waiter (Managing); M Rogers(Marketing)

Indestates Developments Limited
Indescon House
117 Stanhope Road
Darlington
County Durham DL3 7SF
0325 351811
DIRECTOR: R J Fielder (Managing)

Industrial & General Properties Limited
16 St James Gardens
London W11

Industrial Ownership plc
105 Park Street
Mayfair
London W1Y 3FB
Tel: 071-499 8842 Fax: 071 491 4319
DIRECTORS: T Pain; J R Sims
MAJOR SHAREHOLDERS: Sunley Holdings plc; J R Sims
ANNUAL INCOME/TURNOVER: Company £5m
REGIONAL PREFERENCES: Anywhere in U.K.
VALUE OF PORTFOLIO: £5m (1992)
DISTRIBUTION OF PORTFOLIO: 100% Industrial
INVESTMENT POLICY: To continue to purchase multi-let estates
(Sept 1992)

Inner City Enterprises plc
52-53 Poland Street
London W1V 3DF
071-287 5858
DIRECTORS: C Brocklehurst (Managing); I D Harrabin (Development)

Inoco plc
St Clements House
2/16 Colegate
Norwich NR3 1BQ
0603 632350
DIRECTOR: Mr Robefon (Managing)

Insight Securities Limited
Binfield Place
Forest Road
Binfield, Bracknell
Berkshire RG12 5EA
0344 481123
DIRECTOR: G Thomas (Managing)

Institutional Property Consultants Limited
29 Buckingham Gate
London SW1E

Intercity Property Group Limited
Lawrence House
City Road
Manchester M15

Intercounty Property Limited
48 Portland Place
London
W1N 4AJ
071-930 0739

International Caledonian Assets Limited
3 Wyndham Place
London W1H

Intertrade & Developers Limited
Thrist House
12/14 Wigmore Street
London W1H

Interurban Limited
The Meridian Centre
King Street
Oldham OL8

Invesco Mim plc
11 Devonshire Square
London EC2M 4YR

D W Investments
Kinders Mill
Kinders Green
Greenfield
Saddleworth
Manchester

Ironcliffe Estates plc
27 St James Street
London SW1A 1HA
Tel: 071-925 2111 Fax: 071-930 0785
(Sept 1992)
NATURE OF BUSINESS: Property Developer
DIRECTORS: G A C Wood FRICS (Managing); N A Wood
MAJOR SHAREHOLDERS: Directors
REGIONAL OFFICE: Crawley
ANNUAL INCOME/TURNOVER: £500,000 p.a.
REGIONAL PREFERENCE: South East England
PORTFOLIO VALUE: £10m Trading
PORTFOLIO DISTRIBUTION: Offices 50%, residential 50%
INVESTMENT POLICY: Reversionary
DEVELOPMENT ACTIVITIES: Offices 50%; industrial 50%
DEVELOPMENT POLICY: Develop for the Investment Market
(Jan 1991)

Ironstone Freeholds Limited
118a Highgate Road
London NW5
071-267 6789
DIRECTOR: Mrs G Nagel (Managing)

Irwin Group Limited, The
Low Hall Road
Horsforth
West Yorkshire LS18 4EW

Islef Building & Construction Limited
303 Rotherhithe Street
London SE16

Ivygrove Developments
Racecourse Industrial Park
Mansfield Road
Derby DE2 4SX
0332 43247
DIRECTOR: J Blount (Managing)

J A P Holdings Limited
Aireside Alma Street
Woodlesford
Leeds

J D P Services (U.K.) Limited
Unit 517
Butler's Wharf Business Centre
45 Curlew Street
London SE1

J I P C
213 Kennington Lane
London SE11

Jackson Properties Limited
Dobbs Lane
Kesgrave
Ipswich
Suffolk IPS 7QQ

Jackson's Bourne End plc
8 St James's Square
London SW1Y

Jacobs Island Company Limited
The Harpy Mill Street
London SE1 2BA
081-232 1100
MANAGING DIRECTOR: R A Hand
DIRECTORS: Basil Dunning; Andrew Wadsworth
DEVELOPMENT POLICY: London Docklands Developers

Jaisons Holdings Limited
18 Berkeley Street
London W1X

James Developments
123 Victoria Road
Romford
Essex RM1 2NL
0708 743796
DIRECTOR: E J B Cooper (Managing)

James Property Development
8 Westminster Street
Cornbrook
Manchester M15

Jarvale Properties
Norton Church Road
Sheffield
South Yorkshire S8 8JQ
0742 748880
DIRECTORS: A Lee; D Lee; A Lee; L Lee
MAJOR SHAREHOLDERS: Directors
REGIONAL PREFERENCES: East Midlands, South Yorkshire, North Derbyshire

Jaymarke Developments
The Coach House
1 Queens Lane North
Aberdeen AB2 4DF
0224 645889

Jean Hennighan Properties
60 High Road
Broxbourne
Herts EN10 7NF
0992 445055
DIRECTOR: J A Hennighan (Managing)

Jeradean Property Limited
5 Inverness Mews
London W2

Jermyn Investment Company plc
3 Beeston Place
London SW1W OJJ
071-834 1014 Fax: 071 828 9363
NATURE OF BUSINESS: Investment
DIRECTORS: G M Newton (Chairman); G A Adkin FCA; J A M English FRICS; C H B Mills; A H Noel (Company Secretary)
(Sept 1992)

JMB Real Estate Group Inc
50 Curzon Street
London W1Y

Joint Properties Limited, The
81 Great King Street
Edinburgh EH3

Johnsey Estates
Newport Industrial Estate
Newport
Gwent NP1 OQU
0633 277638

Johnson Fry Corporate Finance Limited
20 Regent Street
London SW1Y 4PZ
Tel: 071 321 0220 Fax: 071 437 4844
DIRECTOR: A Altham
NATURE OF BUSINESS: BES and other investment syndication
MAJOR SHAREHOLDERS: LIT Group plc
VALUE OF PORTFOLIO: £460m
DISTRIBUTION OF PORTFOLIO: Residential property BES £200m; Enterprise Zone Trusts £50m; Client Investments Other £150
INVESTMENT POLICY: Sydication of property and other investments to private investors
(Sept 1992)

Johnston House Developments
Johnston House
Hatchland's Road
Redhill
Surrey RH1 1BG
0737 242466
DIRECTOR: Mr D G Matthews (Managing)

Joneve Limited
17 Milner Street
London SW3

Josujama Developments Limited
3 Stedham Place
London WC1A 1HU
071-631 0521

K & T Investments
29 Rectory Road
London N16

K V F Property Co
17a Bark Street
Bolton
Lancashire

Kajima UK Development Limited
Grove House
248A Marylebone Road
London NW1 6JZ

Kalon plc
Huddersfield Road
Birstall
Batley
West Yorkshire WF17 9XA
0924 477201

Kay-Le Property Investment Co Limited
Saville Mill
River Street
Bolton
Lancashire

Keeval
Betteridge Farm
Nether Whitacre
Nr Coleshill
Birmingham B46 2EG
0675 462937
DIRECTOR: J Brown (Managing)

Keith Donnelly Homes Limited
304A Haydons Road
Wimbledon
London SW19 8JZ
081 543 2619
NATURE OF BUSINESS: Development
DIRECTORS: K Donnelly; M J Nolley
MAJOR SHAREHOLDERS: K Donnelly; M J Nolley
REGIONAL OFFICES: Dorking Surrey
REGIONAL PREFERENCE: London and Southern Home Counties.
DEVELOPMENT ACTIVITIES: Residential 80%; commercial 20%
DEVELOPMENT POLICY: All types of residential except sheltered housing, any size of site. Office/warehouses/ industrial-commercial any size.
SUBSIDIARY COMPANIES: Dovemanor Limited

Kelburn Holdings Group
Earl Grey House
75-85 Grey Street
Newcastle-Upon-Tyne
NE99 1HE
091-261 5135
DIRECTOR: B Burnie (Managing)

Kelgrove Group Limited
15 Albermarle Street
London W1X 3HA
Tel: 071-491 1143 Fax: 071-355 4863
NATURE OF BUSINESS: Development/Hotels
DIRECTORS: D E Dell F INST D (Chairman); I D Scharfer FRICS (Managing); S G Saideman FCA (Finance Director)
MAJOR SHAREHOLDERS: D E Dell F INST D (Chairman)
REGIONAL OFFICES: 37 Rue Des Mathurins, 75015 Paris, France.
REGIONAL ACTIVITIES: UK, France and Germany
DEVELOPMENT ACTIVITIES: Factories/Warehousing 20%; Hotels 80%
DEVELOPMENT POLICY: To increase turnover particularly in hotels
(Sept 1992)

Kelsall Desiato Projects
33 Johns Mews
London WC1N

Entry missing ? Call HELPLINE Page v

Kelvinmoss Limited
59 St James's Street
London SW1A

Kenmore Investments Limited
23 Logie Mill
Beaverbank Office Park
Logie Green Road
Edinburgh EH7 4HG
Tel: 031 557 3233 Fax: 031 557 1122
NATURE OF BUSINESS: Property Development & Investment
MAJOR SHAREHOLDERS: John A B Kennedy - Managing Director
REGIONAL PREFERENCES FOR ACTIVITIES: Mainly Scotland; N England
VALUE OF PORTFOLIO: £11m
DISTRIBUTION OF PORTFOLIO: Commercial Property 100%
INVESTMENT POLICY: To expand portfolio of commercial investments mainly by development but with strategic acquistions
DISTRIBUTION OF DEVELOPMENT ACTIVITIES: Offices 60%; Shops 10%; Warehouses 30%
DEVELOPMENT POLICY: To increase turnover on commercial development over the next year to suit investment policy
(Sept 1992)

Kennedy, John
47 Restairig Road
Edinburgh EH6

Kensington Green Estate Office
53 Marloes Road
London W8

Kent & City Holdings Ltd
40 Curzon Street
London W1Y

Kenwood House
Oldfield Road
Birmingham B12

Kenwood Property Developments
43 Rotherfield Street
London N1

Kerandale Properties Limited
15 Abercorn Road
Edinburgh EH8

Kewal Investments Limited
20/30 Whitechapel Road
London E1

Keys, H H Estates Limited
27 St Albans Crescent
Woodford Green
Essex
081-504 1813
DIRECTOR: J R Keys (Managing)

Kimbell Properties
Humfrey Lane
Boughton
Northampton NN2 8RH
081-950 9556
CHAIRMAN: Mr Ruddle

Kindale
11 Bedford Road
Barton-Le-Clay
Bedfordshire MK45 4JU
0582 882635
DIRECTOR: C Hughes(Managing)

Kingfast Limited
22 Dorset Street
London W1H

Kingfisher Project Co-Ordination Limited
Flat 7
101 Mount Street
London W1Y

Kingstar Estates Limited
Colonial Buildings
59-61 Hatton Garden
London EC2N

Kingswell Properties Limited
Grafton House
2/3 Golden Square
London W1R

Kingsworthy Property Limited
25 Chehsam Street
London SW1X

Kirkton Investments Limited
39 Cumberland Street
Edinburgh EH3

Knightsbridge Management Services Limited
37 Upper Brook Street
London W1Y

Knill, Padgham & Grande
58 St James's Street
London SW1A 1LD
071-491 4723
DIRECTORS: J E Grande (Managing); C Pepler (Marketing)

Kumagai Gumi UK Limited
18 King William Street
London EC4N 7BP
Tel: 071-815 0600 Fax: 071 815 0804
NATURE OF BUSINESS: Property Development and Investment
DIRECTORS: Y Matsumoto; M Shibata; L J D Arnold; E A Goodbody
(Sept 1992)
MAJOR SHAREHOLDERS: Kumagai Gumi Company Limited, Japan
SUBSIDIARIES: Arnold Project Services Limited; The Ranelagh Group Limited
(Jan 1991)

Kyle Stewart Properties
Merit House
Edgware Road
Colindale
London NW9 5AF
Tel: 081-200 7070 Fax: 081 205 8100
NATURE OF BUSINESS: Development
DIRECTORS: J Trussler FCIOB (Chairman); E R Petrie BSc FRICS (General Manager); R O Hickson FCCA
MAJOR SHAREHOLDERS: Hollandsche Beton Group NV
ANNUAL INCOME/TURNOVER Company £40m; Group £1300m
REGIONAL ACTIVITIES: Anywhere in the UK
INVESTMENT POLICY: Properties will not be acquired for investment purposes
DEVELOPMENT POLICY: Office, Industrial and retail development. Parent company normally to be contractor.
DEVELOPMENT OR CONSTRUCTION SISTER COMPANIES: Kyle Stewart Limited (Contractors UK); Edmond Nuttall Limited (Civil Engineering); Mabon b.v.(Development Europe); Hollandsche Beton Group NV (Construction, Civil Engineering, Dredging Property worldwide-based in the Netherlands)

La Salle Partners International
James House
1 Babmaes Street
London SW1Y

Ladbroke City & County Land Company Limited
10 Cavendish Place
London
W1M 9DJ
Tel: 071-323 5000 Fax: 071-323 0907

Ladnor Developments
Woodgate House
2-8 Games Road
Cockfosters
Herts EN4 9HN
081-449 3232
DIRECTOR: R G Doe (Managing)

Laing Homes Limited
Caldew House
Garamonde Drive
Wymbush
Milton Keynes MK8 8DF
Tel: 0908 261500 Fax: 0908 264311

Laing, John Developments Limited
52 Portland Place
London W1N 3DG
Tel: 071-383 5152 Fax: 071-383 0683
NATURE OF BUSINESS: Development Company
DIRECTORS: J R Walshe (Chairman) E Airey (Managing Director) J Armstrong; D I Smith; Miss H Gordon; B J P Fitzgerald; A J H Ewer
MAJOR SHAREHOLDERS: Wholly owned subsidiary of John Laing plc
REGIONAL OFFICES: Barnfield, Rambledon Road, Godalming GU7 1QX; Sussex House, 83/85 Mosley Street, Manchester M2 3LG
(Sept 1992)

Laira Properties
11 The Crescent
Plymouth PL1 3AH

Lakefield Estate
1 Belsize Square
London NW3
071-794 8586
DIRECTOR: K Isfahani (Managing)

Lakeland Village Limited, The
Newby Bridge
Near Ulverston
Cumbria LA12 8PX
Tel: 0448 31133 Fax: 05395 31881
DIRECTOR: D T Forbes (Managing)

Lamont Holdings plc
Lamont House
Purdy's Lane
Belfast
Northern Ireland BT8 4AX

Lamrest Property Co Limited
21 Bentinck Street
London W1M

Lancaster Holdings
3 Vere Street
London W1M 9HQ
071-493 6480
CHIEF EXECUTIVE: Sir Henry Warner
MARKETING DIRECTOR: A Batty

Land & Equity Group
1230 High Road
Whetstone
London N20 0LH
Tel: 081-446 2391 Fax: 081-446 9017

Entry missing ? Call HELPLINE Page v

DIRECTORS: J Burns (Managing); B Berman (Marketing)
(Sept 1992)

Land & Property Trust Company plc

Enserch House
8 St James's Square
London SW1Y 4JU
Tel: 071-976 1666 Fax: 071-930 1300
DIRECTORS: S Reinhold; L Bloom; S Prenser; M Gurney; B Berger
VALUE OF PORTFOLIO: £500m
PROPERTY PORTFOLIO: Offices 90%; shops 2%; warehouses 5%; residential 3%
DEVELOPMENT ACTIVITY: Offices 100%
SUBSIDIARY COMPANIES: Adonis Properties Limited; Andromache Properties Limited; Antigone Properties Limited; Aquarius Properties Limited; Argent House Property Investments Company Limited; Baik Properties Limited; Betjohn Properties Limited; Braykle Limited; Cabinet Properties Limited; Central Real Investors Limited; Chair Properties Limited; Cronus Properties Limited; Data Properties Limited; Desk Properties Limited; Door Properties Limited; EC Construction Limited; Eleven Norwich Street Limited; Felt Properties Limited; Finance & Properties Securities Limited; Glancroft Investment Developments Limited; Hall Road Investments Limited; Harding Street Property Investment Limited; Hovemoor Investments Limited; Inguard Securities Limited; Kerusi Properties Limited; Klecube Limited; Land Company of Westminster Limited; Lyra Properties Limited; Mallorc Securities Limited; Manseway Property Investments Limited; Mensa Properties Limited; Muka Properties Limited; Pencil Properties Limited; Pisces Properties Limited; Quill Properties Limited; Quince Properties Limited; Radiator Properties Limited; Railkey Securities Limited; Rowlstone Company Limited; Rumah Properties Limited; Satin Properties Limited; Saurien Investments Limited; St Lawrence Properties Limited; Sparmoor Investments Limited; Stroudbrook Investments Limited; Swiftgale Investments Limited; Tail Properties Limited; Tulang Properties Limited; Uranus Properties Limited

Land & Urban plc

4 The Exchange
Brent Cross Gardens
London NW4 3RT
Tel: 081-203 9829 Fax: 081-203 0426
NATURE OF BUSINESS: Property Developers

Land Assets plc

4 The Exchange
Brent Cross Gardens
London NW4 3RY

Land Capital Limited

Kingsway Business Park
Oldfield Road
Hampton
Middlesex TW12 2HD

Land Securities plc

5 Strand
London WC2N 5AF
Tel: 071-413 9000 Fax: 071-925 0202
NATURE OF BUSINESS: Property Development & Investment
DIRECTORS: P J Hunt BSc (Est Man) FRICS (Chairman & Managing); W Mathieson FRICS; I J Henderson BSc (Est Man) FRICS; M R Griffiths FRICS; K Redshaw BSc(Est Man)FRICS; J K Murray MA, FCA;
MAJOR SHAREHOLDERS: Prudential Corporation plc; Schroder Investment Management Ltd; Scottish Widows Investment Management Ltd
REGIONAL OFFICES: Birmingham; Liverpool; Glasgow; Kingston.
BRANCH OFFICES: Kingston-upon-Thames; Birmingham; Glasgow; Liverpool
ANNUAL TURNOVER: £406.7m (31.3.90)
VALUE OF PROPERTY PORTFOLIO: £4300.6m (31.3.92)
PROPERTY PORTFOLIO: Offices (50.65%); Retail Shops (37.97%); Industrial (3.89%); Retail (out of town) (7.49%)
DEVELOPMENT/INVESTMENT POLICY: Offices, shops, retail warehouses, food superstores and industrial premises throughout the UK together with the management of its properties
SUBSIDIARY COMPANIES: Land Securities Properties Limited; Ravenseft Properties Limited; The City of London Real Property Company Limited; Ravenside Investments Limited; Revenseft Industrial Estates Limited
(Sept 1992)

Land Use Developments Limited

Mayfair Chambers
7 Broadbent Street
London W1X

Landbase

Tooke House
Ball Plain
Hertford
Hertfordshire OG14 1DT
0992 500565
DIRECTOR: J P Anderson (Managing)

Landbond Developments Limited

344 Kensington High Street
London W14

Landlink Two Limited

Mistress Page's House
13 High Street
Windsor
Berkshire SL4 1LD
0753 869771
MANAGING DIRECTOR: A Butcher
DEVELOPMENT MANAGER: S Keeler

Landmark Projects Limited

7/9 Queen Victoria Street
Reading
Berks RG1 1SY

Landmark Properties (UK) Limited

120 Crawford Street
London W1H

Landmark Securities Limited
1 Bentinck Street
London W1M 5RN
071-487 3234
(Sept 1992)
DIRECTOR: M Hersch (Managing)
(Jan 1991)

Lands Improvement Group Limited, The
1 Buckingham Palace
London SW1E

Landsowne Real Estates
111 Bishopsgate Street
Edgbaston
Birmingham B15 1ET
021-634 8277
DIRECTOR: G Roberts (Managing)

Lane Developments Limited
Everest House
48 Church Street
Maidstone
Kent ME14 1DU
0622 755111
DIRECTOR: M G I Betts (Chairman & Managing)

Langro Limited
47/50 Hockley Hill
Hockley
Birmingham B18

Lansbury Developments Limited
112-114 High Street
Billericay
Essex CM12 7BY

Lansbury Holdings Limited
112-114 High Street
Billericay
Essex CM12 7BY

Lanyon Fleming
24 Brook Mews
London W1Y

Lapid Developments Limited
6 Broad St Place
London EC2M

Larkcroft Properties Limited
Fl 14, Westfield Hall
Hagley Road
Birmingham B16

Larkmont Investments Limited
1 Dover Street
London W1X 3PJ
Tel: 071-491 8933 Fax: 071 409 0463
NATURE OF BUSINESS: Property Investment
JOINT DIRECTORS: A Welsh; H Davis; A Oliver
MAJOR SHAREHOLDERS: Thompson Holdings Limited
ANNUAL INCOME/TURNOVER: Group £4m; Company £1m
REGIONAL PREFERENCES FOR ACTIVITIES: United Kingdom
VALUE OF PORTFOLIO: £10m (1992)
DISTRIBUTION OF PORTFOLIO: Offices 54%; Retail 46%
INVESTMENT POLICY: To expand portfolio of commercial investments
(Sept 1992)

Laser Richmount Limited
Berkeley Square House
Berkeley Square
London W1X 6AN
Tel: 071-495 7788 Fax: 071-499 4407
DIRECTOR: A Altham
NATURE OF BUSINESS: Investment
MAJOR SHAREHOLDERS: Richmount Enterprise Zone Managers; Johnson Fry Corporate Finance
REGIONAL PREFERENCE FOR ACTIVITIES: All enterprise zones
VALUE OF PORTFOLIO: £250m
DISTRIBUTION OF PORTFOLIO: Enterprise Zone Property Trusts 100%
INVESTMENT POLICY: Syndication of Enterprise Zone Properties - Range £2m-£30m

Latchmere Properties Limited
Latchmere House
134/136 South Street
Dorking
Surrey RH4 2EU
Tel: 0306 876006 Fax: 0306 881287
NATURE OF BUSINESS: Development & Investment
DIRECTORS: R E Eshelby FRICS FSVA (Managing)
MAJOR SHAREHOLDERS: R E Eshelby (100%)
BRANCH OFFICES: London W1
ANNUAL TURNOVER/INCOME: £5m
REGIONAL PREFERENCES: Surrey
VALUE OF PROPERTY PORTFOLIO: £7m
PROPERTY PORTFOLIO: Offices 10%; shops 5%; residential 80%; other 5%
INVESTMENT POLICY: To purchase rent controlled houses
DEVELOPMENT ACTIVITIES: Offices 10%; shops 10%; residential 80%
DEVELOPMENT POLICY: Develop and refurbish houses, flats, shops and offices
SUBSIDIARY COMPANIES: Dialworth Limited; Unicastle Limited
(Sept 1992)

Lathan Developments
Bridgend Business Centre
Bridgend
0656 662100
(Sept 1992)
DIRECTOR: S P Lathan (Managing)
(Jan 1991)

Lathurst Limited
30 Lyme Street
London NW1

Laurence, Christopher Limited
100 Warwick Way
Westminster
London SW1V 1SD
071-834 2425
DIRECTOR: L Brazier (Managing)

Law Estates
2 Carlos Place
Mount Street
London W1Y 5AE
071-407 2963

Lawfield Estates Limited
Scottish Legal Building
95 Bothwell Street
Glasgow G2 7HY
Tel: 041-221 2375 Fax: 041 221 8325
(Sept 1992)
NATURE OF BUSINESS: Development
MANAGING DIRECTOR: A J Buick, FRICS; E M Buick
REGIONAL PREFERENCES: Scotland and North of England
DEVELOPMENT ACTIVITIES: Offices 20%; shops 80%
(Sept 1992)

Lawley Estates Limited
Lawley House
Sloane Court East
London SW3

Lawlor Land Co Limited
2 Prince Albert Road
London NW1

Lawrence, Walter plc
Lawrence House
Pishiobury
Sawbridgeworth
Hertfordshire CM12 0AF
0279 725001
CHIEF EXECUTIVE: T J C Mawby

Laybrook Properties Limited
20 Calthorpe Road
Edgbaston
Birmingham B15

Lazaris Property Investments Limited
189-219 Isledon Road
London N7

LCH Properties
58-60 Berners Street
London W1P 3AE
071-255 1843

LCP Properties Limited
Build 36
The Pensnett Estate
Kingswinford
West Midlands DY6 7NA

Leanse Family Investment Trust Limited, The
8/55 Portland Place
London W1N

Leasehold & Reversionary Estates Limited
19 Rodmarton Street
Baker Street
London W1H 3PW
071-935 8302
DIRECTOR: R Hofbauer (Managing)

Lee Savell Developments Limited
43 Stanley Road
Carshalton
Surrey SM5 4LE
081-773 2727
DIRECTORS: E B Rogers; A R Clark (Joint Managing)

Leeds City Developments Company
2nd Floor
Permanent House
72 The Headrow
Leeds LS1 8DL
0532 424293
CHIEF EXECUTIVE: M J E Burrell

Leepark Properties Limited
69 Corporation Street
Manchester M4

Leeside Properties Limited
34 Argyll Arcade
Glasgow G1
Tel: 041-420 1144 Fax: 041-429 1293
NATURE OF BUSINESS: Property Development & Investment
DIRECTORS: P Darroch; G Mair (Managing)
MAJOR SHAREHOLDERS: P Darroch; G Mair; P McKenna
VALUE OF PROPERTY PORTFOLIO: £2m
PROPERTY PORTFOLIO: shops 10%; residential 90%
DEVELOPMENT ACTIVITIES: residential 100%
SUBSIDIARY COMPANIES: None

Lelliot, John Group
265 Burlington Road
PO Box 92D
New Malden KT3 4LZ
081-947 7621
DIRECTOR: R Marshall (Managing)

Lemonpark Developments Limited
Green Lane
Heywood
Manchester

Lend Lease International plc
1 Northumberland Avenue
London WC2N

Lenspace Limited
105a Queensway
London W2

Leon, J & Co Limited
12 Warren Court
Euston Road
London NW1

Lescren Holdings Limited
Lescren House
68 High Street
Newport Pagnell
Buckinghamshire
MK16 8AQ
0908 613219
DIRECTOR: B G Tyrrell (Managing)

Lewis & Barrow Developments Limited
151 Malden Road
London NW5

Lewis Shop Holdings
Chelsea House
West Gate
Hanger Lane
Ealing
London W5 1DR
081 998 8822 (Ext 6000)
DIRECTOR: B Lewis (Managing)

Lexington Securities
49 Charles Street
London
W1X 7PA
071-408 0725
DIRECTOR: J Baker (Managing)

Liberty Properties
Godstall House
Godstall Lane
Chester CH1 1LN
0244 351306
DIRECTORS: P Morris (Managing); J Spaven

Liberty Standard
1 Northumberland Avenue
London WC2N

Lief Securities Limited
32 Warrender Park Road
Edinburgh EH9

Lightoaks Investments Limited
48 Princess Street
Leigh
Manchester

Lilley Developments
428 Carlton Hill
Carlton
Nottingham
0602 873121
DIRECTOR: D Walker (Managing)

Lilley plc
331 Charles Street
Glasgow G21 2QX
041-552 5222
DIRECTOR: D R H Walker (Managing)

Lilley Properties Limited
21 St James's Place
London SW1
071-493 2240

Limewood Developments Limited
St Andrews Chambers
20-21 Albert Square
Manchester M2 5PE
Tel: 061-832 4434 Fax: 061-832 1924
(Sept 1992)
DIRECTOR: B Wagzell (Managing)
(Jan 1991)

Lincoln Properties International plc
26 Lower Belgrave Street
London SW1W

Lindley (Holdings) Limited
Peel Mills
Commercial Street
Morley
Leeds

Ling Group plc
156-168 West Street
Erith
Kent DA8 1BL

Lingfield Securities plc
3 Temple Row West
Birmingham
West Midlands B2 5NY
021 236 9511
DIRECTOR: R G Hart (Managing)

Link Parks Group
32 Lancaster Gate
London W2

Linkmel Developments Limited
Wheatcroft Nursery
Landmear Lane
Nottingham NG12 4DE
Tel: 0602 406505 Fax: 0602 405303
(Sept 1992)
NATURE OF BUSINESS: Development & Investment
DIRECTORS: D G Chambers FCIS AIB (Managing); B A Newing FISE; B G Cannell
MAJOR SHAREHOLDERS: Directors
REGIONAL PREFERENCES: Midlands and South West
INVESTMENT POLICY: Small shops only
DEVELOPMENT ACTIVITIES: Offices 40%; shops 10%; factories 50%; warehouses 50%
DEVELOPMENT POLICY: Mainly interested in industrial and commercial developments on the basis of purchasing industrial land and developing new buildings and also refurbishment of prime commercial shops in town centres
SUBSIDIARY COMPANIES: Linkmel Estate Limited; Linkmel Construction Limited
(Jan 1991)

Linkwood Developments Limited
Monomark House
27 Old Gloucester Street
London WC1N

Linkwood Developments (Southern) Limited
14 Cromwell Crescent
London SW5

Lister Developments Limited
Devlin House
36 St George Street
London W1R 9FA
Tel: 071-495 7787 Fax: 071-495 6122
DIRECTOR: D R Lister (Managing)
(Sept 1992)

Littlecroft Properties Limited
Gable House
1 Balfour Road
Ilford
Essex 1G1 4HP
081-478 5947
081-478 5434
NATURE OF BUSINESS: Property Investment
DIRECTOR: H R Winston
PROPERTY PORTFOLIO: Residential and Commercial

Lloyds Chemists Group
Manor Road
Mancetter
Atherstone
Warwickshire CV9 1Q7
0827 718001
DIRECTORS: A Lloyd (Managing); R Warner (Marketing)

Lloyds Developments Limited
Monomark House
27 Old Gloucester Street
London WC1N

Lloyds Investment Managers
48 Chiswell Street
London EC1Y 4SB
071-600 4500
(Sept 1992)
DIRECTOR: Mr D'Adhema (Managing)
(Jan 1991)

LMS Services Limited
33 Robert Adam Street
London W1M

Local London Group plc
53 Mount Street
London W1Y 5RE
071-629 3345
DIRECTORS: A Bergbaum (Chaiman); R A Bourne FCA (Joint Managing); G A Bourne (Joint Managing); J S V McAvilley FCCA FCIS; C J Smith CA; M D Harford
MAJOR SHAREHOLDERS: Provident Mutual Life Assurance Association; The Property Investment Trust plc
ANNUAL TURNOVER/PROFIT: £9.02m (1987)
VALUE OF PROPERTY PORTFOLIO: £70.97m (1987)
DEVELOPMENT/INVESTMENT POLICY: Acquisition of commercial properties, their conversion into business centres containing small units with the benefit of shared office services and the subsequent licensing and management of these centres
SUBSIDIARY COMPANIES: Local London Group (Investments) Limited; Local London Group Holdings Limited; Local London Properties Limited; Local London (Promotions) Limited; Local London (Office Centres) Limited; London House Investments Limited; Noblehead Limited; Local London Limited; Kalfield Limited; Wentog Properties Limited; Standard Securities plc; Nationwide Storage

Lockton Developments
31 Old Burlington Street
London W1X 1LB
Tel: 071-439 3303 Fax: 071-439 3383
NATURE OF BUSINESS: Development
DIRECTOR: B Urfell (Chairman)
CONTACT: S Hanton (Development Executive)
General Manager: C S Forbes ARICS
REGIONAL PREFERENCES: South East England
ANNUAL GROSS TURNOVER/INCOME: £10m (1989)
DEVELOPMENT ACTIVITIES: Offices 75%; factories 15%; residential 10%
DEVELOPMENT POLICY: Industrial & office sites in the South East and major provincial centres

Logan Land Development Co Limited
Capital House
20/22 Craven Road
London W2

Londimium & Co Limited
36 Berkeley Square
London W1X

London & Auckland Estates Limited
41-51 Blandford Square
Newcastle ME1 4HP
091-281 4425
(Sept 1992)
MANAGER: G P Williamson
(Jan 1991)

London & Berkshire Estates plc
3 Astwood Mews
London SW7

London & Cambridge Properties Limited
LCP House
The Pensnett Estate
Kingswinford
West Midlands DY6 7NA
Tel: 0384 400123 Fax: 0384 400862
NATURE OF BUSINESS: Development & Investment
DIRECTORS: C MacDonald-Hall (Chairman); H I Taylor LLB (Chief Executive); J D Chandris; M D Chandris
MAJOR SHAREHOLDERS: Leathbond Limited; C MacDonald-Hall; H I Taylor
ANNUAL INCOME TURNOVER: £20.063m (31.3.92)
BRANCH OFFICES: London, Runcorn, Cannock
REGIONAL PREFERENCES: Any area considered
VALUE OF PROPERTY PORTFOLIO: £168.5m
DISTRIBUTION OF PROPERTY PORTFOLIO: Offices 10%; factories 80%; warehouses 10%
DEVELOPMENT POLICY: Industrial & offices, some rental
DEVELOPMENT ACTIVITIES: Offices 45%; shops 10%; factories 45%
SUBSIDIARY COMPANIES: LCP Properties Limited; LCP Developments Limited; LCP Investments Limited; LCP Securities Limited; Rookman Properties Limited
ASSOCIATED COMPANY: Deeley LCP Limited
(Sept 1992)

London & Chester Holdings Limited
Snow Hall
Gainford
County Durham DL2 3BE
0325 730217

London & City Estates
2-3 Cornwall Terrace
Regent's Park
London NW1 4QP
Tel: 071-935 2382 Fax: 071-486 7083
DIRECTORS: D Faber; N Bradman (Joint Managing)

London & City Holdings Limited
50 Carver Street
Birmingham B1

London & Cleveland Property Investment Companies
22 Ives Street
Draycott Avenue
London SW3 2ND
071-584 8292
DIRECTOR: P Cope (Managing)

London & Clydeside Holdings
1 Park Quadrant
Glasgow G3 6BS
041-333 9339
DIRECTOR: J McIntyre (Managing)
ANNUAL PRE-TAX PROFIT: £664,000 (6 mths to 31/3/89)

London & Commercial Property Limited
98 High Road
East Finchley
London N2 9PL
081-853 4661/-444 5683

London & Eastern Investments plc
2 Conduit Street
London W1R

London & Edinburgh Trust plc
243 Knightsbridge
London SW7 1DH
Tel: 071-581 1322 Fax: 071-584 2297
NATURE OF BUSINESS: Development & Investment
DIRECTORS: J L Beckwith FCA ATII (Chairman); P M Beckwith BA Hons (Cantab) (Deputy Chairman); P S McDonald MA Hons (Cantab) FCA (Joint Managing Director); N J P Sheehan FRICS (Joint Managing Director); C J Hoddell BSc(Est Man) FRICS (Non-Executive); J Newman BSc(Est Man) FRICS; R A L Phipps FRICS; M R F Langdon MA Hons (Cantab) FCA (Non-Executive); G H Millar (Non-Executive); R Rankin (Non-Executive)
MAJOR SHAREHOLDERS: J L Beckwith; P M Beckwith; Regent House Properties Limited
ANNUAL TURNOVER: £161.7m (1988)
VALUE OF PROPERTY PORTFOLIO: £366.6 (1988)
PROPERTY PORTFOLIO: Offices 59%; business parks/light industrial 15%; retail 14%; residential 8%; leisure 4%
DEVELOPMENT ACTIVITIES: Offices 41%; business parks/light industrial 26%; retail 22%; residential 7%; leisure 4%
SUBSIDIARY COMPANIES: Ciresty Limited; Jibspray Limited; Letinvest; Lyndean Investments Limited; 245 Hammersmith Road Investment Limited; Carlton Offices Limited; Charter Court Developments Limited; Cometship Limited; LET Birmingham Investments Limited; LET Birmingham Properties Limited; LET Industrial Limited; LET Inns Limited; LET Leisure plc; LET Offices Limited; LET Peacocks Limited; LET Retail Limited; LET Retail Warehouse Limited; Lightgrove Limited; London & Carlton International plc; Owen Owen plc; Richmond Ice Rink Limited; Richmond Properties Limited; Rysbridge Estates Limited; Trust Estates Limited; Vegaplan Limited; Washington Lands Limited;

Entry missing ? Call HELPLINE Page v

London & Edinburgh Investment Inc; London & Edinburgh Investment of Massachusetts One Inc; LET Pacific Limited; LET Europe NV; London & Edinburgh Properties BV; London & Edinburgh Investments BV; Lethill BV; Harpchange BV; Jibspray BV; Modores Limited; Teakvale Limited; LET Financial Holdings Limited; LET Financial Services Limited

London & Erskine Estates Limited

21 Manor Place
Edinburgh EH3

London & General Property Limited

17 Dover Street
London W1X

London & Guildford Investments plc

12 The Broadway
London SW19 1RF
081-944 1598
DIRECTOR: P Masters (Managing)

London & Lancashire Securities

9 Mulberry Close
Hampstead
London NW3 5UP
Tel: 071-794 1551 Fax: 071-435 1266
NATURE OF BUSINESS: Development & Investment
DIRECTORS: D A Kohler BSc(Hons) ARICS; N Kohler; R Kohler
MAJOR SHAREHOLDERS: Directors
BRANCH OFFICES: London, Blackpool
PROPERTY PORTFOLIO: Residential 40%; shops 60%
DEVELOPMENT ACTIVITIES: Offices 20%; shops 30%; residential 30%; leisure 10%; warehouses 10%

London & Manchester Group plc

Winslade Park
Exeter EX5 1DS
0392 52155
NATURE OF BUSINESS: Investment
DIRECTORS: J M Thomson MA (Chairman); The Rt Hon Lord Wakehurst MA LLB (Deputy Chairman); D C Bourdon FIA; D A L Jubb FIA (Chief Executive); J Leigh Pemberton MA MBA; Sir Ronald McIntosh KCB; The Rt Hon Lord Peyton of Yeovil PC; T A Pyne FIA ASA
MAJOR SHAREHOLDERS: Sun Alliance & London Insurance plc; Britannic Assurance plc; British Railways Board
BRANCH OFFICES: London
ANNUAL PROFIT AFTER TAX: £9.3m (1986)
SUBSIDIARY COMPANIES: London & Manchester Assurance Company Limited; London & Manchester (Managed Funds) Limited; London & Manchester (Pension) Ltd; London & Manchester (Asset Management) Limited; London & Manchester (Trust Management) Limited; London & Manchester (Mortgages) Limited; Leslie Lintott & Associates Limited; Seymour Adelaide & Company Limited

London & Metropolitan plc

3 Buchanan House
St James's Square
London SW1Y 4JU
071-925 2383
(Sept 1992)
NATURE OF BUSINESS: Development & Investment
DIRECTORS: N C Ireland CA FCMA (Chairman & Non-Executive); D Lewis FCIOB FRICS (Deputy Chairman & Chief Executive); C I K Harris (Managing Director); P H Gibbon; J A Theophilus FCA FCT; R G G Walton BSc(CEng) MICE; S J Davies FRICS; J Aiton CA (Non-Executive); P J Henwood FRICS (Non-Executive); P Braithwaite (Marketing);
MAJOR SHAREHOLDERS: Balfour Beatty Investments Limited; Merchant Navy Officers Pension Fund; Scottish Amicable Investment Managers Limited; Edinburgh Investment Trust plc; Provident Mutual Life Assurance Association
ANNUAL TURNOVER: £54.7m (1988)
VALUE OF PROPERTY PORTFOLIO: £13.5m (1988)
SUBSIDIARY COMPANIES: Challengerhold Limited; Edenhold Limited; Heathcove Limited; L&M Chestergate Limited; London & Metropolitan Estates Limited; L&M Europe BV; London & Metropolitan Investments Limited; London & Metropolitan Scotland Limited; London & Caltrust Properties Limited; L&M Project Management Limited; L&M Windsor Limited; Osterhold Limited; Rowanspon Limited; Deerspon Limited; Sealspon Limited
RELATED COMPANIES: Caphold Limited; Howsmoor Development Limited; Jumpcloud Limited; Olympichold Limited; Switchold Limited; Welcomebond Limited; Trophy Properties Limited; Welkinsable Limited;
(Jan 1991)

London & Midland Development plc

46 Maddox Street
London W1R 9PB
Tel: 071-629 9712 Fax: 071-629 5287

London & New York Estates

9 Harley Street
London W1
071-580 7413
DIRECTOR: L Kuston (Managing)

London & Northern Development Limited

11A Anyards Road
Cobham
Surrey KT11 2LW
Tel: 0932 66600/63963 Fax: 0932 68848
PROJECT MANAGER: Diana Warren

London & Northern Estate Company Limited

Manor Farm
Podington
Near Wellingborough
Northamptonshire NN9 7HP

London & Palatine Estates
5 Queens Street
Knutsford
Cheshire WA16 6HZ
0565 55685
DIRECTOR: R Wordsworth (Managing)

London & Paris Property Group plc
No 7 27 St James Street
London W1M
Tel: 071-493 6848 Fax: 071-930 3158
(Sept 1992)
NATURE OF BUSINESS: Development
DIRECTORS: P E Davidson FRICS; R S Berger MA FRICS; C F Dymond BSc ARICS; K P Despard MA ARICS; J R Hindle BArch DipArch RIBA; E N G Wills; G A Elliot MA FCA; R W Carey (Alternate) FRICS
MAJOR SHAREHOLDERS: P E Davidson; R S Berger; Slough Estates plc
ANNUAL PRE-TAX PROFIT: £5m (1988)
REGIONAL PREFERENCES: All major provincial centres and all South England
DEVELOPMENT ACTIVITIES: Offices 80%; warehouses 12%; science parks/hi-tech 8%
DEVELOPMENT POLICY: Office & industrial development in major centres
(Jan 1991)

London & Reading Developments
20 Piccadilly
London W1V 9PE
Tel: 071-439 7550 Fax: 071-494 4614

London & Regional Estates Limited
58 Broadwick Street
London W1V

London & Stockholme Properties
59A New Kings Road
London SW6
Tel: 071-736 5825 Fax: 071-736 5824

London & Stockholme Properties
11 Curzon Street
London W1Y
071-409 7050

London & Stratford Securities Limited
15 Penrhyn Road
Kingston upon Thames
Surrey KT1 2BZ
081-546 9441
DIRECTOR: W Barker (Managing)

London & Westminster Property Company Limited, The
Estates Department
Grayleigh, St Huberts Lane
Gerrards Cross
Buckinghamshire SL9 7BW
Tel: 0753 884702 Fax: 0753 888302
DIRECTORS: B H Fitch; S M Fitch; A H Fitch; J S Fitch
MAJOR SHAREHOLDER: S M Fitch
BRANCH OFFICES: London EC2
REGIONAL PREFERENCES: Within 100 miles of Gerrards Cross
PROPERTY PORTFOLIO: Offices 12%; warehouses 50%; residential 25%; industrial 13%; other
SUBSIDIARY COMPANIES: London Financial Agency Limited

London & Wiltshire Estates Limited
140 Brompton Road
Knightsbridge
London SW3 1HY
Tel: 071-584 1430 Fax: 071-584 1430
NATURE OF BUSINESS: Property Developers
DIRECTORS: R F Bradley (Chairman); B J Murphy BSc ARICS; J A Johnson BSc ARICS (Managing)
REGIONAL PREFERENCES: Good provincial towns, the motorway network
DEVELOPMENT POLICY: Joint Venture forward funding; debt finance
DEVELOPMENT ACTIVITIES: Offices 40%; warehouses 20%; residential 20%; science parks/hi-tech 10%; retail warehouses 20%

London & Winchester Estates Southern Limited
The Old Post Office
Easton
Winchester SO21 1EF
Tel: 0962 78683 Fax: 0962 78653
NATURE OF BUSINESS: Property Development and Investment
DIRECTORS: A Sterling; A Foster (Joint Managing)
MAJOR SHAREHOLDERS: The Directors
REGIONAL PREFERENCE: Within 75 miles of Winchester
INVESTMENT POLICY: Freehold, postwar industrial, warehouse and office preferably with reversionary potential. Lot size £1m-£5m
DEVELOPMENT POLICY: Industrial/warehouse 5-20 acres, offices 20,000 square feet

London and Hong Kong Investments plc
84 Kensington High Street
London W8

London Anglia Developments plc
10 Palace Gate
London W8

London City & Westcliffe Properties Limited
P O Box 55
11/13 Holborn Viaduct
London EC1P 1EL

London Commercial Properties
66 Gloucester Place
London W1
071-224 6010

London Docklands Development Corporation

Thames Quay
191 Marsh Wall
London E14 9TJ
Tel: 071-512 3000 Fax: 071-512 0777
NATURE OF BUSINESS: Urban Development Corporation
(Sept 1992)

London Gate Securities

1A Duke Street
Richmond-Upon-Thames
Surrey
TW9 1HP

London Generation Consortium plc

Regeneration House
York Way
Kings Cross
London N1 OBB
071-837 5533
DIRECTORS: Lord Sharp of Grimsdyke, Chairman; S Lipton; J Botts; D Dantzic; D Dickinson; S Honeyman; R John; P Kershaw; P Reichmann; P Rogers; V Wang; N Wilson; A Gay (Managing)

London Industrial plc

75 Whitechapel Road
London E1 1DU
071-247 7614
DIRECTOR: M Calder (Managing)

London Investment & Mortgage Company Limited

Talbot House
92 Park Lane
Croydon
Surrey CR9 1YH
081-686 6531

London Mayfair Properties plc

46 Queen Anne Street
London W1M OLA

London Merchant Securities plc

Carlton House
33 Robert Adam Street
London W1M 5AH
Tel: 071-935 3555 Fax: 071-935 3737
NATURE OF BUSINESS: Development & Investment
DIRECTORS: The Lord Rayne (Chairman); J N Butterwick; N G E Driver; P J Grant; R S Jayson; W Millsom; The Hon R A Rayne; R F J Spier (Finance and Administration); The Marquess Townsend of Raynham
MAJOR SHAREHOLDERS: General Accident Life Assurance Limited; Norwich Union Life Insurance Society; Barclays Bank plc.
ANNUAL GROSS RENTAL INCOME & TRADING TURNOVER: £23m (31/3/90)
BRANCH OFFICES: Bishopbriggs, Glasgow & New York
REGIONAL PREFERENCES: Central London; SE England; Will consider Glasgow & Edinburgh
VALUE OF PROPERTY PORTFOLIO: £464.5m (1990)
PROPERTY PORTFOLIO: Offices 90%; shops 5%; residential 5%
INVESTMENT POLICY: Still prepared to purchase suitable, primarily retail investments
DEVELOPMENT ACTIVITIES: Offices 90%; shops 5%; residential 5%
DEVELOPMENT POLICY: Actively interested in and prepared to proceed with suitable commercial development
PRINCIPAL SUBSIDIARY COMPANIES: British Commercial Property Investment Trust Limited; Caledonian Properties Ltd; Central London Commercial Estates Limited; City Commercial Real Estate Investments Limited; Carlton Construction & Development Company Limited; Kensington Commercial Property Investments Limited; Palaville Limited; Portman Investments (Baker Street) Limited; The New River Company Limited; Trendworthy Two Limited; West London & Suburban Property Investments Limited; Caledonian Properties Limited; LMS Industrial Finance Limited; LMS Properties Limited; LMS Shops Limited; LMS Services Limited; London Merchant Securities Services Inc; St James' Real Estate Company Limited; Corinium Estates Limited.

London Orbital Developments

7 St Peter's Street
Winchester
Hampshire SO23 8BW
Tel: 0962 877778 Fax: 0962 878777
(Sept 1992)
DIRECTOR: C Mitchell (Managing)
(Jan 1991)

London Regeneration Consortium

3 Generation House
York Way
Kings Cross
London N1 0BB
Tel: 071-837 5533 Fax: 071-278 6958
NATURE OF BUSINESS: Property Development
DIRECTORS: Andrew Gay (Managing); Kevin McGovern (Marketing)
MAJOR SHAREHOLDERS: Stanhope Properties plc

London Securities

Mill Ride Estate
Mill Ride
North Ascot
Berkshire
SL5 8LT
0344 885444
NATURE OF BUSINESS: Development & Investment
DIRECTORS: D B Pearl FCA (Chairman); C R Freemantle; R O Prickett FCA (Managing)
MAJOR SHAREHOLDERS: Phoenix Assurance plc
ANNUAL GROSS INCOME/TURNOVER: £703,000
VALUE OF PROPERTY PORTFOLIO: £357,000
SUBSIDIARY COMPANIES: Amalgamated Estates Trading & Developments Limited; Hanruff Associates Limited; Mill Ride Investments Limited; Cosmos House (East) Bromley Limited; 136 High Street Sevenoaks Limited; Copthall House Coventry Limited; Candyfleet

Limited; London Securities Management Services Limited; London Securities (Gloucester) Limited; Phasetop Limited; London Securities Middlesex House Limited; Ankermycke Estate Limited; London Securities France SA

London Transport Property
Townsend House
Greycoat Place
London SW1P 1BL
071-222 5600
DIRECTOR: G A Sullivan (Managing)

Longcroft Properties Limited
1 Kingswood Road
Hillesley
Near Wotton-under-Edge
Gloucestershire GL12 7RB
0453 521054
DIRECTOR: A Phillips (Managing)

Longford Investments Limited
6 Charles Street
London W1X

Longley, James & Company Limited
East Park
Crawley
West Sussex RH10 6AP
0293 561212
DIRECTORS: O Longley (Managing); G Todd (Marketing)

Longmile Group
53 Upper Brook Street
London W1Y

Longtrack Development Limited
51 Woodsford Square
London W14

Lordship Properties Limited
247/249 Vauxhall Bridge Road
London SW1V

Lovell Limited
Elm Tree Court
Long Street
Devizes
Wiltshire SN10 1NH
0380 722151
(Sept 1992)
DIRECTORS: D J Hinton; J B Heffer; A Turner (Managing); E G Wakenham; R M Woodward; J G Yard; C J J Gingell; J C Watts; J G Laing (Secretary)
SUBSIDIARY COMPANIES: Part of Lovell Group (Jan 1991)

Lovell Developments Limited (1)
10 Brickett Road
St Albans
Hertfordshire AL1 3JX
0727 46411 Fax: 0727 46667
NATURE OF BUSINESS: Commercial Property Development
DIRECTOR: P Butcher (Managing)
ANNUAL TURNOVER: £394.6m (1990)

Lovell Homes (London) Limited
Prospect House
Crendon Street
High Wycombe
Bucks HP13 6LT
Tel: 0494 443751 Fax: 0494 440262
NATURE OF BUSINESS: Residential Development
DIRECTOR: P D Wiltshire (Managing)
MAJOR SHAREHOLDERS: Y J Lovell Holdings
ANNUAL TURNOVER: £394.6m (1990)

Low, W M & Company Limited
PO Box 73
Baird Avenue
Dryburgh Industrial Estate
Dundee
Scotland DD1 9NF
0382 814022
DIRECTORS: C Blake (Chairman); J L Millar (Managing); H L Findlay (Secretary); R Johnson (Property); C R Mitchell; P D Stevenson; I W Stewart; A Turnbull (Marketing)

Lowndes Street Properties Limited
40 Lowndes Street
London SW1X

LSP Securities Limited
Mostyn Broadway
Llandudno
Gwynedd
North Wales LL30 1YR
0492 78217
DIRECTOR: P Lovell-Smith (Managing)

LTH Properties Limited
1364b High Road
Whetstone
London N20 9HJ
081-446 6501
DIRECTOR: M J Rubens(Managing)

Lundberg Developments Limited
Buckingham Court
78 Buckingham Gate
London SW1E

Lydnell Properties Limited
1 Ravens Close
Prestwich
Manchester M2

Entry missing ? Call HELPLINE Page v

Lyndale Developments Company
36 Preston Park Avenue
Brighton
Sussex BN1 6HG
0273 555555
DIRECTOR: J Cama (Managing)

Lynton plc
15/17 St Cross Street
London EC1N
071-405 8108

Lysander Securities
Birkett House
27 Albermarle Street
London W1X

M & D Development
36 High Street
Bishops Stortford
Herts CM23 2LS
0279 755609
DIRECTORS: D Harris (Managing)

M B W Group Limited
6 Coldbath Square
London EC1R

M E P C plc
35 Chesham Place
London SW1X

M P C Industries Limited
9-21 Shand Street
London SE1

M S Property Developments Limited
49 Park Lane
London W1Y

M S R Developments Limited
210 Harehills Lane
Leeds

MAB (UK) Limited
Cavendish House
92 Albion Street
Leeds LS1 6AG
Tel: 0532 421113 Fax: 0532 465763
DIRECTORS: R Holmes; A Homer (Finance Manager)
PARENT CO/GROUP NAME: MAB Groep BV Den HAAG
(Sept 1992)

Mabey Developments Limited
Elta House
Birmingham Road
Stratford Upon Avon
Warwickshire CV37 0AQ
0789 297933
DIRECTOR: Mr Grove (Managing)

Macalpine, Alfred Properties Limited
8 Suffolk Street
London SW1Y 4HG
Tel: 071-930 6255 Fax: 071-839 6902
DIRECTORS: R P Harwood FRICS FSVA; J T Smith; R J McAlpine FCIOB; C J Edwards MA FCA; G Odgers (Managing); T Pellman (Marketing)
MAJOR SHAREHOLDERS: Alfred McAlpine plc
ANNUAL GROSS INCOME/TURNOVER: £581.9m (1988)
BRANCH OFFICES: Chester
INVESTMENT POLICY: To retain existing portfolio
PROPERTY PORTFOLIO: Offices 40%; factories 40%; science parks/hi-tech 20%
DEVELOPMENT ACTIVITIES: Offices 20%; shops 50%; science parks/hi-tech 30%
DEVELOPMENT POLICY: Total development programme with variety of office/industrial/retail
SUBSIDIARY COMPANIES: Whyatt Properties Limited; Whyatt Securities Limited; Whyatt Properties Streatham Limited; Whyatt Developments Limited; Hopton Securities Limited

Macalpine, Sir Robert & Sons Limited
40 Bernard Street
London WC1N 1LG
071-837 3377

MacBryde Homes
7 Wynnstay Road
Colwyn Bay
Clwyd LL29 8NB
0492 534456
DIRECTORS: S MacBryde (Managing)

Maclan Developments Limited
8 Bourdon Street
London W1X

Maidsfield Properties
5 Malvern Drive
Llaneshen
Cardiff
S Glamorgan
0222 747077
NATURE OF BUSINESS: Property Developers

Malcolm, Roger Limited
Malcolm House
Empire Way
Wembley, Middlesex
081-902 1101

Malminster Limited
13/14 Hanover Street
London W1R

Maltbys
6 Sydney Street
London SW3

Maltings Structures Limited
The Maltings
High Street
Tingrith, Milton Keynes
Buckinghamshire MK17 9EN
052587 2617
NATURE OF BUSINESS: Development
DIRECTORS: A J Woodfield LCIOB (Managing); C A Woodfield
MAJOR SHAREHOLDERS: A J Woodfield; C A Woodfield
REGIONAL PREFERENCES: South Bedfordshire; Buckinghamshire; Hertfordshire; North London
DEVELOPMENT ACTIVITIES: residential 100%
DEVELOPMENT POLICY: Interested in residential/ commercial, new/refurbishment propositions in small lots
(Sept 1992)

Malvern Properties (London) Limited
7 Strathray Gardens
London NW3 4PA
071-431 2505
DIRECTOR: B Anderson (Managing)

Mamot Booth Heylin (Southern) Limited
12 Primrose Hill
Fitzroy Road
London NW1

Manchester & District Properties Limited
St Annes House
St Annes Place
Manchester M2

Manchester Ship Canal Company, The
Dock Office
Quay West
Trafford Wharf Road
Salford M17 1HH
Tel: 061-872 2411 Fax: 061-872 0344
NATURE OF BUSINESS: Development, Investment & Trading
MAJOR SHAREHOLDERS: Peel Holdings plc
DIRECTORS: R E Hough (Chairman & M D); M S Butterworth (Property); J Whittaker;
REGIONAL OFFICES: Runcorn
ANNUAL INCOME/TURNOVER: £20m
REGIONAL PREFERENCES: North West
VALUE OF PORTFOLIO: £130m (1991)
DISTRIBUTION OF PORTFOLIO: Investment Land 41%; Operations Land & Properties 21%; Offices 26%; Industrial 10%; Residential 2%
DISTRIBUTION OF DEVELOPMENT: Offices & Commercial 90%; Leisure 10%
SUBSIDIARIES: Ship Canal Land Ltd; MSC Services Ltd; MSC (Waste) Ltd; Ship Canal Enterprises Ltd; Ship Canal Investment Ltd; Manchester Ship Canal Development Ltd
(Sept 1992)

Manchester Square Property Company Limited
1A Duke Street
Manchester Square
London W1M 6HQ
071-935 1671
DIRECTOR: M Winkler (Managing)

Manders (Holdings) plc
PO Box 76
Old Heath Road
Wolverhampton WV1 2UP
0902 453122
PROPERTY MANAGER: Mr Evans

Manhattan Leisure Limited
25 Harrington Street
Liverpool l2 9QA
051-236 1877
NATURE OF BUSINESS: Leisure Department
DIRECTORS: M J Finnegan (Chairman)

Manlet Group Holdings Limited
Friars Court, Friars Passage
Aylesbury
Buckinghamshire HP20 2SJ
0296 88484
DIRECTOR: T Tompkins (Managing)

Mannai Properties
7 Old Park Lane
London W1Y 3LJ
071-493 0105
DIRECTOR: P Jackson (Managing)

Manor County Limited
91 Belgrave Road
London SW1V

Manor Estates
Lanivet Manor
Rectory Road
Lanivet
Bodmin
Cornwall PL30 5HG
0726 890555
NATURE OF BUSINESS: Property Developers & Consultants

Mansell Homes
Roman House
Grant Road
Croydon
Surrey CR9 6BU

Mansfield Properties Limited
31 Eastcastle Street
London W1N 7PD
071-580 0401
DIRECTOR: S R Cohen

Manton Estates Limited
Development House
191-195 Bradford Road
Castle Bromwich
Birmingham B36 9AQ
Tel: 021-776 7333 Fax: 021-776 7449
NATURE OF BUSINESS: Property Development
DIRECTORS: R J Manton; J B Manton

Manywell Heights Limited
15 Hall Road
London NW8

Maple Oak plc
Lion Court
Swan Street
Old Isleworth
Middlesex
Tel: 081-569 8382 Fax: 081-569 8374
NATURE OF BUSINESS: Development & Investment
DIRECTORS: R Clark (Managing); M J Foundly
DEVELOPMENT MANAGER: S M Lambert; G Allen
MAJOR SHAREHOLDERS: John Mowlem & Company plc
BRANCH OFFICES: Reigate; Bristol
REGIONAL PREFERENCES: Most areas of the country, but particularly the southern half
INVESTMENT POLICY: Not currently increasing our portfolio
DEVELOPMENT POLICY: Continually taking on new schemes, depending on viability
(Sept 1992)

Maple Properties (Yorkshire) Limited
45 St Michaels Lane
Leeds

Mara Group Holding International Limited
95A Chiltern Court
Baker Street
London W1

March Estates plc
11 Pall Mall
London SW1
071-839 7111
NATURE OF BUSINESS: Property Developers

Marchant Lane Property Company Limited
The Old Bakery
Golden Square
Petworth
West Sussex GU28 0AP
0789 42872
DIRECTOR: C E Marchant-Lane (Managing)

Marchday Group, The
43 Portland Place
London W1N

Margram Holdings plc
Suite 15E
CHallenge House
Sherwood Rrive
Letchlet
Milton Keynes MK3 6DP
Tel: 0908 370666 Fax: 0908 370555
NATURE OF BUSINESS: Development
DIRECTORS: J Bryant (Managing); D B A Davis (Chairman); S E W Snaith
ANNUAL INCOME/TURNOVER: Group £20m
PROPERTY PORTFOLIO: £20m
DEVELOPMENT ACTIVITIES: Service areas and petrol filling stations 100%.

Marinup plc
1 Sweden Gate
Baltic Quay
Plough Street
London SE16

Markheath Securities plc
Markheath House
31 St George Street
Hannover Square
London W1R 9FA
Tel: 071-355 2345 Fax: 071-491 2378
NATURE OF BUSINESS: Property Development & Investment
DIRECTORS: I B Creber; G A Springer
MAJOR SHAREHOLDERS: Adelaide Steamship (UK) Limited (49.9%); Eilloc PTY Ltd (10.3%); Howard Smith Ltd (8.5%)
REGIONAL PREFERENCES: North London/West London & Hertfordshire
ANNUAL TURNOVER: £4.3m (1989)
VALUE OF PROPERTY PORTFOLIO: £117m (1992)
DISTRIBUTION OF PORTFOLIO: Investment £73m including completed offices; £34m; Development £44m, including land and completed offices £28m
DEVELOPMENT/INVESTMENT POLICY: Commercial Property Development & Investment Properties.
SUBSIDIARY COMPANIES: Markheath Construction Limited; Markheath Developments Limited; Markheath Estates Limited; Markheath Homes Limited; Markheath Investments Limited; Markheath Properties Limited; Markheath Properties London Limited; Markheath Property Developments Limited; Oakleigh Building Supplies Limited
(Sept 1992)

Markvale Group Limited
248 Old Birmingham Road
Bromsgrove
Worcestershire B60 1NU
Tel: 021-445 1004 Fax: 021-447 7418
NATURE OF BUSINESS: Property Development and Investment
DIRECTORS: G G Vale; M J Vale; E R Vale
MAJOR SHAREHOLDERS: G G Vale; M J Vale; E R Vale
(Sept 1992)

Marler Estates plc
4 Hill Street
London
W1X 7FU
071-408 1661
DIRECTORS: A J Mackay; R L Crabtree; J F Duggers; E J Cotter; K McKeogh
MAJOR SHAREHOLDERS: Cabra Estates plc.
SUBSIDIARY COMPANIES: Apus Properties Limited; Broadweir and Southern Properties Limited; Alderite Limited; Bloomsbury Square Estate (Holdings) Limited; Chiefhaunt Limited; Lucaslodge Limited;
Marler Debwell Developments Limited; Marler Estates Developments (Chichester) Limited; Mayfair Executive Business Centre plc; Rivermore Properties Limited.
Marler Project Services Limited; SB Property Limited; Wembley Plaza Investments Limited; Woburn Walk Investments Limited. London Enterprise Property Company Limited.

Marley Properties Limited
24 South Park
Sevenoaks
Kent TN13 1DX
0732 455255
DIRECTOR: P R Baker (Managing)

Marncrest Homes
20 Q20 Queens Road
Weybridge
Surrey KT13 9UX
0932 856669

Marples Developments Limited
Marples Wharf
210 Lower Bristol Road
Bath BA1 1TY
0225 337700
DIRECTOR: A Thomson (Managing)

Marque Securities plc
Kingswood Hall
Kingswood
Surrey KT20 7BA
0737 221233
DIRECTORS: M C Heighes; J Reddin
MAJOR SHAREHOLDERS: M C Heighes
ANNUAL TURNOVER/INCOME: £2m
DEVELOPMENT ACTIVITIES: All types

Marrant Securities plc
291 Ballards Lane
Finchley
London N12 8NP

Marshamheath Limited
19 Green Street
London W1Y

Marwin Securities Limited
1a Duke Street
London W1M

Marwood Homes
Walnut House
63 St Davids Hill
Exeter
Devon EX4 4DW
0392 52272
DIRECTOR: Eric Speight (Managing)

Maryland Securities Limited
Sunlight House
Quay Street
Manchester M3

Marylebone Estates Co
12 Blandford Street
London W1H 3HA
071-486 7063
DIRECTORS: L Phillips (Chairman); L Salama (Marketing)

Mason Drage
68a Wigmore Street
London W1H

Mason Hugo Properties
35 Moreton Terrace
London SW1V

Masonbrook Limited
17-18 Dryden Court
Parkleys, Ham Common
Richmond
Surrey TW10 5LH
081-549 5201
DIRECTORS: M A Smith (Managing); P G Hook
DEVELOPMENT ACTIVITIES: Office, shops, factories, warehouses, residential, industrial
SUBSIDIARY COMPANIES: Masonbrook Construction Limited

Masterhouse Building Limited
'Badgers Sett'
Gateside Farm
Cartmel
Cumbria LA11 7NR
Tel: 05395 36675 Fax: 05395 36053
NATURE OF BUSINESS: Property Development

Matthew Homes Limited
Matthew House
45-47 High Street
Potters Bar
Herts EN6 5AW
0707 55550

Matzen Investments Limited
145 Kensington Church Street
London W8
DIRECTORS: Bruce Hodges; P Maxwell-Brown FRICS

Entry missing ? Call HELPLINE Page v

Maunders (John) Group plc
Development House
Crofts Bank Road
Urmston
Manchester M31 1UH
061-747 6656
DIRECTORS: J B Davies (Managing); D Wain (Sales)

Maunders Urban Renewal Limited
25 The Crescent
Salford
Manchester M5

Mavenham Properties
The Belgravia Hotel
431-441 Cheetham Hill Road
Manchester M8

Mavglen Limited
16 Davies Street
London W1Y 1LJ
071-493 6666
DIRECTOR: P S Hammerson (Managing)
MAJOR SHAREHOLDERS: P S Hammerson
REGIONAL PREFERENCES: Midlands & South East
PROPERTY PORTFOLIO: Offices 24%; factories 76%
INVESTMENT POLICY: Selective purchases made with a view to improvement and long term retention
DEVELOPMENT POLICY: No new major developments
SUBSIDIARY COMPANIES: Bellstan Properties Limited; Park Lane Films Limited; Stockwood Investments Limited; Taiberry Limited; Parkrose Properties Limited; Middlemore Industrial Management Limited

Maxply Securities Limited
Oak Grove
Brill Road
Horton-cum-Studley
Oxon OX9 1BU

May Gurney Group
Trowse
Norwich
Norfolk NR14 8SZ
0603 627281
DIRECTORS: D Neale (Managing); P Gainsford (Marketing)

Maybrook Properties plc
199 Piccadilly
London W1V 0JJ
Tel: 071-734 3438/1186 Fax: 071-434 4051
Subsidiary of Croudace Group
DIRECTORS: J B Ratcliffe DSO (Chairman); R C V Gardner BSc FRICS (Chief Executive); A R Carey BSc ACA; P N E Cole BSc ARICS (Company Secretary); C A Henley RCCA
(Sept 1992)

Mayfair & City Properties plc
7 Hill Street
Mayfair
London W1X 7FB
071-499 4301
DIRECTOR: S Corob (Managing)

McAlpine, Alfred plc
Hooton
South Wirral
Cheshire L66 7ND

McCarthy & Stone Developments Limited
Homerice House
Oxford Road
Bournemouth
Dorset
0202 292480
DIRECTOR: J McCarthy (Managing)
ANNUAL TURNOVER: £149.7m (1988)

McClean Homes
Langley House
West Mill
Oxted
Surrey RH8 9HU

McGregor, John G (Properties)
Seafield Road
Longman
Inverness IV1 1SG
0463 222791
DIRECTOR: D Troup (Managing)

McInerney Properties
McInerney House
Croxley Green, Rickmansworth
Hertfordshire WD3 3HZ
0923 776622
DIRECTORS: D McInerney (Chairman); B Bennett (Managing); G Milton; Mrs A Brodala (Marketing) R Allen (Secretary)
ANNUAL TURNOVER: £98.9m (1988)

McKay Securities plc
20 Greyfriars Road
Reading RG1 1NL
0734 502333
NATURE OF BUSINESS: Development & Investment
DIRECTORS: I A McKay (Chairman); E S G Lloyd FCA (Deputy Chairman & Managing); J R Chilton FRICS; D A L Bird FRICS; M J C Hawkes FRICS; I C Menzies CA
MAJOR SHAREHOLDERS: General Accident Assurance; Farringdon Property Trust Limited; Scottish Amicable Investment Managers Limited
ANNUAL TURNOVER/INCOME/PROFIT: £6.07m (31.3.88)
REGIONAL PREFERENCES: S and SE England
VALUE OF PROPERTY PORTFOLIO: £75.1m (31.3.88)
PROPERTY PORTFOLIO: Commercial 58.7%; industrial 27.2%; residential 14.1%
INVESTMENT POLICY: Will consider investments with

redevelopment/refurbishment potential
DEVELOPMENT POLICY: Active development programme in S&E England and in Glasgow. Actively seeking office, retail, warehousing, hi-tech in good locations in South of England
SUBSIDIARY COMPANIES: Baldwin House Limited; Camberley Central Properties Limited; Kirkland Properties Limited; McKay Securities Overseas Limited; Parkside Knightsbridge Limited; Princes Home Security Limited; St Georges Development Limited; S W Factories Limited; Western Properties (MAP) Limited

---

McKenzie International Developments Limited
14/16 Regent Street
St James
London SW1Y

McLaughlin & Harvey plc
15 Trench Road
Mallusk
Newtownabbey
County Antrim BT36 8FA

McLean Investments Limited
Crestwood House
Birches Rise, Willenhall
West Midlands WV13 2DD
0902 68511
DIRECTOR: S F Pickstock (Managing)

Meadow Projects Limited
1 Stable Courtyard
Broughton Hall
Skipton
N Yorks BD23 3AE
0756 700719
NATURE OF BUSINESS: Property Development

MEC UK Limited
Bow Bells House
Bread Street
London EC4M

Medran Developments Limited
78 Duke Street
London W1M

Melbourne Court Estates
45 Fernshaw Road
London SW10
071-352 4002

Melhome Developments Limited
The Manor
Main Street
Saxton
Nr Tadcaster
Leeds LS24 9PY
Tel: 0937 557193 Fax: 0937 557480
DIRECTORS: M B Spencer; M T Spencer
NATURE OF BUSINESS: Builders & Developers
MAJOR SHAREHOLDERS: M B Spencer; M T Spencer
ANNUAL INCOME/TURNOVER: Company £1m
DISTRIBUTION OF PORTFOLIO: 100% Residential
DEVELOPMENT POLICY: To increase turnover
(Sept 1992)

Mellawood Properties Limited
31 London End
Beaconsfield
Buckinghamshire HP9 2HW
0494 672513 Fax 0494 672976
DIRECTOR: B Galan (Managing)

Melville Place Investments plc
25a Blacket Place
Edinburgh EH9

Melville Properties
Winchester House
55 South Street
Epsom
Surrey KM8 7PX
0372 740550
(Sept 1992)
DIRECTOR: A Kliner (Managing)
(Jan 1991)

MEPC Developments Limited
Brook House
113 Park Lane
London W1Y 4AY
071-491 5300
DIRECTOR: C J Barwick (Managing)

MEPC Plc
12 St James Square
London SW1Y 4LB
Tel: 071-911 5300 Fax: 071-839 2340
(Sept 1992)
NATURE OF BUSINESS: Development & Investment
DIRECTORS: Sir C J Benson FRICS (Chairman); J A Beveridge MA FCA; The Lord Boardman MC TD DL (Non-Executive); Sir Patrick Meaney (Non-Executive); The Hon Angus Ogilvy (Non-Executive); R M Squire MA FRICS; J L Tuckey FRICS (Managing Director); I Watters FRICS
MAJOR SHAREHOLDERS: Co-operative Insurance; H J Hymans
BRANCH OFFICES: Birmingham, Manchester, Leeds
ANNUAL TURNOVER/INCOME/PROFIT: £217m (1988)
VALUE OF PROPERTY PORTFOLIO: £3079m
PROPERTY PORTFOLIO: Offices 59.7%; shops 20.9%; industrial 8.2%; residential 0.8%
INVESTMENT POLICY: To have a balanced international portfolio
DEVELOPMENT POLICY: To pursue a diversified programme
SUBSIDIARY COMPANIES: In UK: Eastern Central Properties Limited; English Property Corp plc; Fairfield Properties Limited; Farquhar Investments Limited; Fiveways Properties Limited; Kingsley Investment Trust Limited; Lansdown Estates Group Limited; The London

County Freehold & Leasehold Properties Limited; London County Properties (Developments) Limited; London Land & Property Company Limited; Manchester Commercial Buildings Company Limited; Marcus Estates Limited; Metestates Limited; The Metropolitan Railway Surplus Lands Company Limited; Monument Investment Trust Limited; Nonpareil Securities Limited; Oldham Estate Company plc; Ortem Estates Limited; Ortem Developments Limited; Southern Central Properties Limited; Star Great Britain Overseas Developments Limited; Star London Realty Limited; Threadneedle Property Company Limited; Town Investments Limited
OVERSEAS: in Sweden; Netherlands; Australia; France; Luxembourg; Germany; USA
(Jan 1991)

Merchant Manufactory Estate Company

84 Brook Street
London W1
071-408 1346
DIRECTOR: P Southall (Managing)

Merchant Property Group Ltd

6 Torriano Mews
London NW5

Merebrook Properties plc

Wren House
Portsmouth Road
Esher
Surrey KT10 9AA
0372 68033
NATURE OF BUSINESS: Development & Investment
DIRECTORS: G Maber; P J Clayton ARICS (Managing)
REGIONAL PREFERENCES: South East England; in particular Surrey, Sussex, Kent, Hampshire and Middlesex
DEVELOPMENT ACTIVITIES: Offices 15%; shops 20%; factories/warehouses 50%; science parks/hi-tech 15%
SUBSIDIARY COMPANIES: Merebrook Managment Limited; Merebrook Securities Limited; Tigaland Limited

Merivale Investments Limited

Park House
158/160 Artur Road
Wimbledon Park
London SW19 8AQ

Merivale Moore

3 - 4 Bentinck Street
London W1M 5RN
Tel: 071-581 5791 Fax: 071-581 8664
NATURE OF BUSINESS: Development & Investment
DIRECTORS: J G Dean MA (Chairman); E E Chapman BA; J S Neill (Managing Director); R A Brocksom (Chief Executive); D C MacDonald; L J Olivier BA FCIS;
MAJOR SHAREHOLDERS: Hill Samuel & Company Limited
ANNUAL TURNOVER/INCOME/PROFIT: £78.8m (1991) (Sept 1992)
VALUE OF PROPERTY PORTFOLIO: £107.8m (1988)
PROPERTY PORTFOLIO: Commercial investment 30%; commercial development 30%; residential investment 26%; residential development 14%
SUBSIDIARY COMPANIES: Britannia Elmsdale Properties Limited; Allen & Norris Holdings Limited; Easthome Limited; Wonham Properties Limited; Bartbell Limited; J Hornal Limited; Central & Southern Properties Limited; Liskin Investments Limited; Merival Moore Commercial Limited; De Vere Mews Limited; Four Square Properties Limited; Merival Moore Construction Limited; Merival Moore Residential Limited; Rathbone Estates Limited;
R Salisbury & Company Limited; Municipal Properties Limited; Tabrove Limited; The Housing & Land Development Corp Limited; Traverco Limited
(Jan 1991)

Merlin Great Northern

277 Deansgate
Manchester M3

Merlin International Properties (UK) Limited

47 Upper Grosvenor Street
London W1X 9PG
Tel: 071-408 2018 Fax: 071-493 7013
NATURE OF BUSINESS: Development & Investment
DIRECTORS: R T D Stott (Chairman); T C Hayson (Deputy Chairman); W L B Stott (Joint Managing Director); I C Hayson (Joint Managing Director); P T Jevans (Chief Executive); J W Rouse; M L Milspaugh; R N Kohler; R D Laurie; G Jury; A Thomas (Marketing)
BRANCH OFFICES: Australia, USA
ANNUAL GROSS PROFIT: £8.14m (1988)
VALUE OF PROPERTY PORTFOLIO: £87.67m (1988)
DEVELOPMENT POLICY: Development and management in the international marketplace of quality speciality retail shopping centres, festival marketplaces, mixed use developments and inner city urban renewal projects
SUBSIDIARY COMPANIES: Merlin International Properties (Australia) Pty Limited; Festival Market Place Unit Trust; Pitt Street Development Unit Trust; Manly Cove Unit Trust; Sensor Unit Trust; The Darling Walk Unit Trust; Hakgo Trust; Merlin International Properties (Europe) Limited; Merlin International Properties (UK) Limited; Merlin International Properties (Trowbridge) Limited; Merlin International Properties (USA) Inc; Northern Investments Limited; Lloyd Limited; Minim Enterprises Limited

Merseyside Development Corporation

Dept 6
Royal Liver Building
Pier Head
Liverpool L3 1JH
051-236 6090
DIRECTOR: Dr J Ritchie (Managing)

Meteor Properties Limited

6 Mount Row
London W1V

Metestates Limited

Centre Point
103 New Oxford Street
London WC1A

Metier Developments
Suite 611
Sunlight House
Quay Street
Manchester M3 3LE
061-832 0846
DIRECTOR: G Richardson (Managing)
(Sept 1992)

Metier Property Holdings Limited
St Peters Court
8 Trumpet Street
Manchester M1 5LW
Tel: 061-832 0846 Fax: 061-832 0847
NATURE OF BUSINESS: Property development & Investment
DIRECTORS: Graham Richardson FSVA (Chairman & Managing Director); Gilian M Richardson (Director); David R Brooks BA (Comm) FCA (Finance Director)
MAJOR SHAREHOLDERS: Graham Richardson FSVA
ANNUAL INCOME/TURNOVER: Company £2m; Group £5m
REGIONAL PREFERENCES: North West
PROPERTY PORTFOLIO: £1m 1990
DISTRIBUTION PORTFOLIO: All Commercial
INVESTMENT POLICY: Reversionary commercial/ industrial in improving locations.
DEVELOPMENT ACTIVITIES: Office £10m. Industrial £2m. Roadside £1m.
DEVELOPMENT POLICY: Prime areas only
UK DEVELOPMENT SUBSIDIARIES: Metier Developments Limited
(Sept 1992)

Metrolands Investments Limited
Cranberry Buildings
Cranberry Lane
Darwin
Lancashire BB3 2HU
0254 704262
DIRECTOR: R Horrochs (Managing)

Metropolitan & City Properties Limited
74 Wigmore Street
London W1
071-486 4445

Metropolitan & County Holdings plc
20 Bickenhall
Bickenhall Street
London W1H 3LF
Tel: 071-486 6714 Fax: 071-935 0354
NATURE OF BUSINESS: Property & Investment
DIRECTORS:S J Thoday BA(Hons); F A Kbar ACA; R Shutler FRICS; M C Hay BSc FCA (Managing); T Pugsley ARICS
MAJOR SHAREHOLDERS: Giltford Properties Ltd
ANNUAL TURNOVER/INCOME/PROFIT: £4m
REGIONAL PREFERENCES: SE England & Wales
VALUE OF PROPERTY PORTFOLIO: £11m (1992) (Sept 1992)
PROPERTY PORTFOLIO: Offices 60%; shops 20%; residential 10%; warehouses 10%
DISTRIBUTION OF PORTFOLIO: London £9m; Bristol £2m
INVESTMENT POLICY: High yielding, good quality
DEVELOPMENT ACTIVITIES: Offices 10%; residential 30%; shops 5%; science parks/hi-tech 55%
SUBSIDIARY COMPANIES: Metropolitan & County Trading Limited; Metropolitan & County Managements Limited; Shepherds Market Props Limited; Perthland Limited; M&C Properties Limited; Metropolitan & County Developments Limited
(Jan 1991)

Metropolitan Cattlemens Property Company Limited
114 Brompton Road
Knightsbridge
London SW3 1JJ
071-581 5351
DIRECTOR: P Lucas (Managing)

Mevenham Properties plc
430/441 Cheetham Hill Road
Manchester M8

Meyer International plc
Villiers House
41-47 Strand
London WC2N 5JG
071-839 7766
DIRECTOR: R W Jewson (Chairman); Sir Allen Sheppard (Deputy Chairman); J M Dobby (Managing Director); D W Ford CBE; H Langhorn; R T Reynolds; B Wright
TURNOVER: 1,125.8m (1992)
(Sept 1992)

Michael Shanley Group
Sorton
Aylesbury End
Beaconsfield
Bucks HP9 1LW
0494 671331
CHAIRMAN: M Shanley

Micklegate Group plc
Moorfield Business Park
Yeodon
Leeds

Mid Century Trust Limited
2nd Floor
Palladium House
1-4 Argyll Street
London W1V 1AD
071-734 4944
DIRECTOR: B Owen (Managing)

Mid UK Limited
65 Curzon Street
London W1Y

Midas International Properties Limited
Accurist House
44 Baker Street
London W1M 2HH
071-486 7686
DIRECTORS: C Morton-Firth; D Fenwick; P I Munday

Midgehall Properties
King Street Buildings
1 Ridgefield
Manchester M2 6EG
061 832 4183
JOINT MANAGING DIRECTORS: H J Tattersall;
M H Laycock

Midland Commercial Properties Limited
Queensway House
57 Livery Street
Birmingham
West Midlands B3 1HA

Midland Development Group of Companies
269 Castle Street
Dudley
West Midlands
0384 241747

Midland Oak Estates
19-20 Grosvenor Street
London W1X 9FD
Tel: 071-491 9864 Fax: 071-409 7251

Midland Real Estates
100 Hagley Road
Edgbaston
Birmingham B16

Milburn Estates (Bolton) Limited
Milburn House
Boundary Industrial Estate
Millfield Road
Newcastle-Upon-Tyne
NE1 1LE
091-232 0881
CHAIRMAN: G B Reed

Miller Developments Limited
White Hart House
Park Street
Colnbrook
Derkshire SL3 0HS
Tel: 0753 680700 Fax: 0753 684693
(Sept 1992)
DIRECTORS: N M Irvine (Managing); J Paske (Development); K M Miller BSc; J Miller CBE MA FCIOB FCIArb; R O S Miller BSc FCIOB; M G Ballard MCIOB; R Taylor; G R C Scott MA CA;
MAJOR SHAREHOLDERS: The Miller Group
BRANCH OFFICES: Edinburgh; Godalming
SUBSIDIARY COMPANIES: Miller Developments; Miller Construction; Miller Homes
(Jan 1991)

Million Dollar Properties
10 Aldford House
Park Street
London W1Y 7AE
071-491 0909
DIRECTOR: Miss R Green (Managing)

Milroy Developments
Milroy House
Sayers Lane
Tenterden
Kent TN30 6BW
05806 5766
DIRECTORS: I Corke (Managing); J Hawkins (Marketing)

Minerva Corporation
10 Gloucester Place
London W1H 3AX
071-935 2888

Minton Homes
Blayds Mews
Blayds Yard
Leeds
West Yorkshire

Mintz, Louis J Son & Partners
100a Chalk Farm Road
London NW1

Mip (Sophia Antipolis) Limited
44 Baker Street
London W1M

Miskin Group plc
Alban House
Brownfields
Welwyn Garden City
Hertfordshire AL7 1BE

Mitchell C.D. Limited
64 South Street
Epsom
Surrey KT18 7PH
0372 741995
NATURE OF BUSINESS: Builders
DIRECTORS: C D Mitchell; D M Mitchell; C M Mitchell

Mitre Estates
Boston House
Ridings Road, Ilkley
West Yorshire
0943 602555
DIRECTOR: M Whitaker (Managing)

Mitre Homes
Threaf House
54 Wallingford Road
Uxbridge
Middlesex UB8 2RW
0895 811927
DIRECTOR: Mr J Gitshan (Manging)

Mogul Securities Limited
41 Lowndes Street
London SW1
071 235 4439
DIRECTOR: A Cace (Managing)

Molineaux Properties Limited
3 Temple Row West
Birmingham B2

Molyneux Estates Limited
76 Gloucester Place
London W1H 4DQ
071-487 3401
NATURE OF BUSINESS: Investment
DIRECTORS: D J Lewis BSc FRICS (Managing); J N Davis; J Caplan FCA
MAJOR SHAREHOLDERS: Lewis & Davis family interests
REGIONAL PREFERENCES: Greater London; Home Counties and South Coast
INVESTMENT POLICY: Acquire high yielding (10% plus) shopping centres, office buildings, shopping parades, industrial/warehouse investment
SUBSIDIARY COMPANIES: Molyneux Securities (Estates) Limited; Molyneux Securities (Metropolitan) Limited; Nerston Limited

Monarch Investments Limited
Ventoulet
Rue de Fontaine
Trinity, Jersey
Channel Islands
0534 73321

Monk, A & Company Limited
Green Land
Padgate
Warrington
Cheshire WA1 4JB
0925 812000
DIRECTORS: A Lucas (Managing); C Daniels (Marketing)

Monument Trust, The
9 Red Lion Court
London EC4
071-936 2023

Moorfield Estates
Shern House
1st Floor
16 Melbourne Road
Bushey
Herts WD2 3LN
0923 227118
JOINT DIRECTORS: G Hoffmann; D L Edelman; A Phillips; K Jackson; S Jackson; Mrs G Parkin

Moran Holdings plc
Miniver House
19/20 Garlick Hill
London EC4V 2AL

Morcroft Property Development
Croft House
21 Station Road
Knowle, Solihull
West Midlands B93 0HL
Tel: 0564 775176 Fax: 0564 778031

Morrison Developments Limited
Atholl House
51 Melbille Street
Edinburgh EH3 7HL
Tel: 031-226 4666 Fax: 031-226 4166
(Sept 1992)
NATURE OF BUSINESS: Development
DIRECTORS: W D MacDonald (Managing)
MAJOR SHAREHOLDERS: Alexander Morrison (Builders) Limited
REGIONAL PREFERENCES: UK
INVESTMENT POLICY: Small holding
DEVELOPMENT POLICY: Acquisition of commercial opportunities in Scotland and England. Subsequent trade investments
(Jan 1991)

Moss Group of Companies
13 Park Square Mews
Upper Hartley Street
London NW1 4PP
071-935 3588
DIRECTOR: S Moss (Managing)

Mount Provincial Development Limited
11-13 Knightsbridge
London SW1X 7LY
Tel: 071-235 6070 Fax: 071-235 2646
DIRECTOR: D Houghton (Managing)

Mountain Development & Management Limited
Highland House
Main Road
Old Brampton
Chesterfield S42 7SG

Mountleigh Northern Developments Limited
Leigh House
Stanningley
Pudsey
West Yorkshire LS28 7XG

Mountleigh Group plc
49 Grosvenor Street
London W1X 9FH
071-493 5555
CHAIRMAN AND MANAGING DIRECTOR: N Peltz
CHIEF EXECUTIVE: C Strowger
REGIONAL OFFICES; Leigh Mills, Stanningley, Pudsey, Yorks LS28 7XG
DIRECTOR: G Goodwill (Managing)

Mountview Estates plc
16-20 High Road
Wood Green
London N22 6DB

Mountway Trading Limited
18 Doughty Street
London WC1N

Mowat Group
2 The Chase
John Tate Road
Hertfordshire SG13 7NN
0992 554333
DIRECTOR: M Nathanson (Managing)

Mowlem (John) & Co plc
Lion Court
Swan Street
Isleworth
Middlesex TW8 OQZ

Mowlem, John Homes
Unit House
33 London Road
Reigage
Surrey RH2 9HZ

MPH
28 Stamford Road
Bowden
Altrincham
Cheshire WA14 2JU
061-928 0886

MPH Limited
5 Kingsmead Square
Bath
Avon BA1 2AB

MSL International (UK) Limited
32 Aybrook Street
London W1M 3JL
071-487 5000
DIRECTOR: J Hodgeson (Managing)

Mucklow, A & J & Company Limited
Haden Cross
Hallsowen Road
Cradeley Heath
Warley
West Midlands B64 7JB
Tel: 021-550 1841 Fax: 021-550 7532
NATURE OF BUSINESS: Development & Investment
DIRECTORS: A J Mucklow ACIS (Chairman); T Mucklow; Alan J Mucklow; B H Wood; G C Evans
BRANCH OFFICES: Warley, Birmingham
ANNUAL TURNOVER: £4.9m (1988
REGIONAL PREFERENCES: West Midlands
VALUE OF PROPERTY PORTFOLIO: £114.9m (1988)
INVESTMENT POLICY: Residential, industrial, office
DEVELOPMENT POLICY: Residential, office, industrial
SUBSIDIARY COMPANIES: Barrs Industrial Limited; A&J Mucklow (Birmingham) Limited; A&J Mucklow (Investments) Limited; Belfont Homes (Birmingham) Limited; Kumclow Investments Limited; A&J Mucklow & Company Limited; A&J Mucklow (Joint Developments) Limited; A&J Mucklow (Lancashire) Limited; A&J Mucklow (Estates) Limited; A&J Mucklow Finance Limited

Municipal Properties plc
2A Pond Place
London SW3 6QJ
071-584 7060
NATURE OF BUSINESS: Investment
DIRECTORS: A W Allen FCA (Chairman); J B Davidson FSVA; R T Paice MA FIB
MANAGER: J Niell
MAJOR SHAREHOLDERS: Allen & Norris Limited; Western Heritable Investment Company Limited; Lloyds Bank SF Nominees Limited
REGIONAL PREFERENCES: Mainly SW London
PROPERTY PORTFOLIO: non-residential 17%; residential 83%
INVESTMENT POLICY: Residential property sold as becomes vacant to reduce maintenance costs, this cash invested in commercial property in good locations
SUBSIDIARY COMPANIES: Housing and Land Developments Corp Limited; Merival Moore Limited

Multi Developments Limited
Bird Hall Lane
Cheadle Heath,
Stockport
Cheshire SK3 0XP
Tel: 061-428 0766 Fax: 061-428 3157
NATURE OF BUSINESS: Development
DIRECTORS: R L Mower (Chief Executive); G M Hallworth (Development Manager); P C Clutton; T G White (Company Secretary)
MAJOR SHAREHOLDERS: Ellerby Investments Limited
BRANCH OFFICES: Langley (Buckinghamshire), Berkeley Street, Mayfair, London
REGIONAL PREFERENCES: North West, Hampshire, Home Counties, Scotland
INVESTMENT POLICY: Sell on completed developments
DEVELOPMENT ACTIVITIES: Offices 50%; factories 25%; warehouses 25%
DEVELOPMENT POLICY: Expand development activity by redevelopment or refurbishment opportunities
SUBSIDIARY COMPANIES: Oakhurst Developments (Stockport) Limited, Birdhall Developments Limited, Sumardale Developments Limited, Multi Developments (York) Limited.
SISTER COMPANIES: Multi Construction Limited, Peerage Homes Limited

Municipal Mutual Insurance
22 Old Queen Street
Westminster
London SW1H 9HW
071-222 7933
DIRECTORS: A Maclean (Managing); D Forster (Marketing)

Murrayfield Investments
8 Murrayfield Place
Edinburgh EH12

Mutley Properties (Holdings) Limited
Mutley House
1 Ambassador Place
Altrincham
Cheshire WA15 8DB
Tel: 061-941 3183 Fax: 061-927 7437
DIRECTORS: I B Black; H Marks; S Marks; D L Marks FSVA ARVA; H S Black BA BSc ARICS; M C A Ford BSc ACA (Secretary)
(Sept 1992)

Mytre Property Trust plc
104 Wigmore Street
London W1H 9DR
Tel: 071-486 1884 Fax: 071-487 4171
MANAGER: M Brilling

Nairn Construction plc
1 Battersea Bridge Road
London SW11 3BZ
071-924 2744
DIRECTOR: R Faber (Managing)

National Car Parks Limited
21 Bryanston Street
Marble Arch
London W1A 4NH
Tel: 071-499 7050 Fax: 071-491 3577
NATURE OF BUSINESS: Car Parking
JOINT CHAIRMEN: R F Hobson; Sir Donald Gosling

National-Nederlanden Vastgoed Inc
72 New Bond Street
London W1Y

Nationwide Properties Limited
Faulkner House
Faulkner Street
Manchester M1 4DY
061-228 6636
DIRECTORS: S Kay; M S Kay; M A Kay; T Evans
MAJOR SHAREHOLDERS: S Kay
PROPERTY PORTFOLIO: Offices 3%; shops 97%
SUBSIDIARY COMPANIES: Newmart Investments Limited

NCC Property Limited
26 King Street
Covent Garden
London WC2E 8JD
Tel: 071-753 4333 Fax: 071-753 4330
(Sept 1992)
NATURE OF BUSINESS: Property Development
MAJOR SHAREHOLDERS: Part of Nordstjernan Group (Sweden)
(Jan 1991)

Neale House Investments Limited
21 Coates Street
Edinburgh EH3

Neale House Management Limited
Neale House
62 St James's Street
London SW1A 1LY
071-491 4375

NEC Homes Limited
22 Highfield Road
Edgbaston
Birmingham B15

Neilcott Developments Limited
International House
Cray Avenue
Orpington
Kent BR5 3QA
0689 832199
GROUP MANAGING DIRECTOR: D Glynn

New Capital & Scottish Properties Co Limited
17 Hawthornbank Lane
Edinburgh EH10

New Cavendish Estates plc
43-44 Albemarle Street
London W1X 3FE
Tel: 071-355 1575 Fax: 071-355 1574
NATURE OF BUSINESS: Investment & Development
DIRECTORS: H E W Schep (Chairman); R P Farr BSc ARICS (Chief Executive); M D Ewing CA (Finance Director); A W Scott-Harden FRICS; P Driessen
MAJOR SHAREHOLDERS: Noro-Buckfield NV; T R Property Investment Trust
DISTRIBUTION OF PORTFOLIO: Mostly shops and offices in the South East.
INVESTMENT POLICY: With the exception of five small integral residential units, our portfolio is entirely commercial and located in the South East.
DEVELOPMENT POLICY: In the current market, we only envisage undertaking new development projects where they have been prelet or where completion is in the medium to long term.

New Craft
Park Lane
Aston
Birmingham B6

New England Properties plc
30 St James's Street
London SW1A 1HB
Tel: 071-925 0160 Fax: 071-930 8127
DIRECTORS: R E Treacher FCA (Chairman, Non-Executive); D Jackson FSVA (Joint Managing Director); J W Hackman MA ACIB FCIS (Joint Managing Director); A Peters ACIS (Non-Executive)
MAJOR SHAREHOLDERS: Hunting Gibson plc; T R Property Investment Trust plc; The Hon Jacob Rothschild and Five Arrows Limited
ANNUAL TURNOVER: £3m (1988)
VALUE OF PROPERTY PORTFOLIO: £25m (1988)
SUBSIDIARY COMPANIES: New England Developments Limited; New England (Northern) Limited; New England (Southern) Limited; Treehurst Limited; FGH (Newcastle) Limited; Sapco One Limited; Management & Investment Advisory Services (Northern) Limited

New Europe Limited
33 Belsize Park Gardens
London NW3

New Land Assets
9 Lynedoch Crescent
Glasgow G5 6EQ

New London Properties Limited
155 Queens Court
Queensway
London W2 4QU
Tel: 071-229 7611 Fax: 071-229 1818
NATURE OF BUSINESS: Development & Investment
DIRECTORS: R E Holland BSc FIA; P J Newbury FRICS; A E Orchard-Lisle CBE FRICS; J Case FRICS; D M Webber MA FIA
MAJOR SHAREHOLDERS: Pearl Insurance Group plc
ANNUAL TURNOVER: £6.7m (1988)
VALUE OF PORTFOLIO: £91m
SUBSIDIARY COMPANIES: Queens Ice Skating Limited

New Look Holdings
Unit A
Littlesea Industrial Park
83 Lynch Lane
Weymouth
Dorset DT4 9DN
0305 771477
DIRECTOR: J Hanna (Managing)

New Walk Properties Limited
The Cottage
Branston
Oakham
Leicestershire
021-456 2118
NATURE OF BUSINESS: Development
DIRECTOR: R Froggatt (Managing)
MAJOR SHAREHOLDERS: R L Froggatt
ANNUAL TURNOVER/INCOME/PROFIT: £1m in-house, £5m development programme
INVESTMENT POLICY: Separate company will hold a proportion of future developments. Properties held will be self created or with scope for active management,
DEVELOPMENT ACTIVITIES: Offices 20%; shops 70%; factories/warehouses 10%
DEVELOPMENT POLICY: Speculative retail developers in-house financed. Larger schemes jointly with others. Advisers and project managers to major third party companies.
ASSOCIATE COMPANY: Kestrel Clarke Limited

Newarthill plc
40 Bernard Street
London WC1N 1LG
071-837 3377
CHAIRMAN: Sir John Hedley-Greenborough

Newcombe Estates Limited
17 Northumberland Avenue
London WC2N 5AP
071-925 0616
DIRECTORS: J L Newcombe; E M Newcombe (Joint Managing)

Newman Tonks Group plc
Hospital Street
Birmingham B19 2YG
021-359 3221
CHIEF EXECUTIVE: G D Gahan

Newporte Developments
Newporte House
Low Moor Road
Lincoln LN6 3JY

Newton Corporation Limited
Newton Cross
118 Piccadilly
London W1V

Next plc
Desford Road
Enderby
Leicester LE9 5AT

NFC plc
The Merton Centre
45 St Peters Street
Bedford MK40 2UB

Nichelhome Limited
Pyramid House
856 High Road
Finchley
London N12 9RX
081-446 6911
MANAGING DIRECTOR: M Morris

Nilestar Properties
9 Bedford Park
Croydon
Surrey CRO 2AQ
081-948 5821
DIRECTOR: M Morris (Managing)

Nisses Millbank
100 Fetter Lane
London EC4A 1DD
071-589 9303
DIRECTOR: C G Peterson (Managing)

Nobility Properties
Empire House
175 Piccadilly
London W1V 9DB

Nomura Properties plc
19 Ludgate Hill
London EC4
071-248 4133

Norcros Estates Limited
Norcros House
Bagshot Road
Bracknell
Berks RG12 3SW
Tel: 0344 861878 Fax: 0344 867473
NATURE OF BUSINESS: Property Investment & Development
DIRECTORS: M Doherty (Managing); T P Rix; P Levinsohn (Marketing)
MAJOR SHAREHOLDERS: Norcros plc
BRANCH OFFICES: Reading
(Sept 1992)

Norcross Investments Limited
Gatehouse
Halfords Lane Industrial Estate
Smethwick
Birmingham B66

Nordrach
Nordrach House
Blagdon
Bristol
BS18 6XW
0761 62991
DIRECTOR: Mr Stokes (Managing)

Nordstrom, Rolf L
89 Piccadilly
London W1V

Normanby Estate Company Limited
Estate Office, Normanby
Scunthorpe
South Humberside DN15 9HS
Tel: 0724 720618 Fax: 0724 280129
NATURE OF BUSINESS: Development & Investment
DIRECTORS: R A B Sheffield; V P Sheffield; P Hill FBAA
MAJOR SHAREHOLDERS: Normanby Holding Company Limited
ANNUAL TURNOVER: £75,678 (1988)
REGIONAL PREFERENCES: South Humberside
VALUE OF PROPERTY PORTFOLIO: £2m (1988)
PROPERTY PORTFOLIO: Residential 30%; other 70%
DEVELOPMENT/INVESTMENT POLICY: Maximise income and capital
DEVELOPMENT ACTIVITIES: Warehouses 100%

Norseman Holdings Limited
Broadbent House
64/65 Grosvenor Street
London W1X

North Square Properties
2 Nottingham Street
London W1M

North West Central Developments Limited
29 Burnley Road East
Waterfoot, Rossendale
Lancashire BB4 9AG
0204 34224
NATURE OF BUSINESS: Development & Investment
JOINT MANAGING DIRECTORS: J R Niman; M J Willan
REGIONAL PREFERENCES: None, although most work in North England
DEVELOPMENT POLICY: Commercial and industrial

North Yorkshire Securities plc
2 Killingbeck Drive
Leeds LS14 6UF
0532 496611

Northern Property Investment Limited
2 Nottingham Street
London W1

Northern Rock Trust Limited, The
Northern Rock House
Gosforth
Newcastle upon Tyne NE3 9PL

Northside Developments Limited
39 Camden Lock
London NW1

Northwest Properties Limited
1 Moreton Drive
Bury BL8

Norwest Holst Limited
Toft Hall
Knutsford
Cheshire WA16 9PD
0565 55366
DIRECTORS: P J Mason (Managing); J Pilkington (Marketing)

Entry missing ? Call HELPLINE Page v

Nterprise
235 Stoke Newington Church Street
London N16

Nuttal, Edmund
St James House
Knoll Road
Camberley
Surrey GU15 3XW
0276 63484
DIRECTORS: J R Grice (Managing); P Morgan (Marketing)

NWW Properties
Chadwick House
Warrington Road
Risley
Warrington
Cheshire WA3 6AE

O & H Construction Limited
50f Brook Green
London W8

Oakland House Developments
56 Oxford Street
Manchester M1

Oakley Land Limited
(Formerley Broadoak Property Limited)
City Gates
2-4 Southgate
Chichester
West Sussex
Tel: 0243 786548 Fax: 0243 531417
NATURE OF BUSINESS: Development and Dealing
DIRECTORS: M A Swindall ARICS; D J Hutchings FRICS;
R M Orr FCA; C P Wilkins RIBA
MAJOR SHAREHOLDERS: Oakley Investments Limited
ANNUAL TURNOVER: Company £850,000
VALUE OF PROPERTY PORTFOLIO: £7.7m 1989
DISTRIBUTION OF PORTFOLIO: Shops 55%, residential 20%, offices 20%, factories 5%
DEVELOPMENT ACTIVITIES: Residential 40% offices 40% factories 10%
DEVELOPMENT POLICIES: Retail; residential; offices & industrial
UK DEVELOPMENT SUBSIDIARIES: Broadoak Homes Limited

Oakmount Properties Limited
70 Raeburn Avenue
Surbiton
Surrey KT5 9DR

Obayashi Europe BV
2nd Floor, 25-28 Old Burlington Street
London
W1X 1LB
Tel: 071-434 9595 Fax: 071-494 3249

Octagon Developments Limited
Weir House
Hurst Road
East Molesey
Surrey
081-941 4131
DIRECTOR: R Wyatt (Managing)

Ogden Group of Companies
Boston Hall
218 High Street
Boston Spa
Yorkshire
0937 541234
CHAIRMAN: R Ogden CBE; T J Garnet FRICS; F N Colvin C.A.

Old Chelsea Group
63A Kings Road
London SW3 4NT
071-730 2162
JOINT MANAGING DIRECTORS: M Fenwick; S Alder

Old Park Lane Securities Limited
7 Old Park Lane
London W1Y 3LJ
071-499 8136
DIRECTOR: J Bradley (Managing)

Oldway Property Group
Castle House, Castle Street
Merthyr Tydfil, Mid Glamorgan
Wales CF47 8YX
Tel: 0685 722386 Fax: 0685 721011
NATURE OF BUSINESS: Property Developers & Managing Agents
DIRECTORS: Peter Morgan; G H Davies FCA; Mrs J M Morgan BSC
MAJOR SHAREHOLDERS: P Morgan
REGIONAL OFFICES: Castle House, Castle Street, Merthyr Tydfil CF47 8H
ANNUAL TURNOVER/INCOME: Group £5m plus (1990)
REGIONAL PREFERENCES: England & Wales, South of Leicestershire, Swindon.
VALUE OF PROPERTY PORTFOLIO: £30m (1992)
DISTRIBUTION OF PORTFOLIO: Vast majority in office sector, B1 Business Parks and residential.
PROPERTY PORTFOLIO: Offices 90%; Residential 10%;
INVESTMENT POLICY: Part portfolio retention & part trading upon completion of scheme.
DEVELOPMENT ACTIVITIES: Offices and B1 40%; warehouses 20%; residential 40%
DEVELOPMENT POLICY: Stated preference for 'Green Field' site development.
(Sept 1992)
SUBSIDIARY COMPANIES: Oldway Developments Limited; Oldway Limited; Oldway House Development (Swansea) Limited; Oldway House Development (Pontypridd) Limited; Hillesdon Court Time Ownership Limited; Oldway Properties Limited; Grafton Court Torquay Limited; Oldway Management Services Limited (Jan 1991)

Olim Limited
Pollen House
10-12 Cork Street
London
W1X 1PD
Tel: 071-439 4400 Fax: 071-734 1445

Olivera, A
1 Greenland Place
London NW1

Olives Holdings plc
Dodington House
Chipping Sodbury
Avon BS17 6SF

Ollerton Developments Limited
Ollerton Grange
Chelford Road
Knutsford
Cheshire WA16 8RD
0565 3440
DIRECTOR: G A Bishop (Managing)

Ollerton Developments Limited
Victoria Tip
Liverpool Road
Eccles
Manchester M30

Olympia & York
1 Canada Square
London E14 5AB
Tel: 071-418 2000 Fax: 071-233 1110
DIRECTORS: M Dennis (Managing) R John (Marketing)

Omega Properties Estates
Broom Hall
Broom Hall Road
Sheffield S10 2DR

Onyx Property Managements Limited
17 Monson Road
Tunbridge Wells
Kent TN1 1LS
Tel: 0892 513111 Fax: 0892 516179
DIRECTOR: C E Kidby (Managing); L M Kidby
(Sept 1992)

Oppidan Etates
5 Princes Gate
Knightsbridge
London SW7 1QJ
071-225 1200
DIRECTOR: P Coates (Managing)

Orbit Development Limited
Kings Ride Court
Kings Ride, Ascot
Berkshire SL5 7JR
Tel: 0344 20115 Fax: 0344 23496
NATURE OF BUSINESS: Development & Investment
DIRECTORS: P E Jones (Chairman); S Annison (Managing); H Richards; A Jones
REGIONAL PREFERENCES: Primarily West London and Thames Valley
ASSOCIATED COMPANY: Emerson Developments (Holdings) Limited

Oriel Land & Estates Limited
15 Penrhyn Road
Kingston-upon-Thames
Surrey KT1 2BZ
081-546 9441
DIRECTOR: W Barker (Managing)

Orient & Overseas Co P.D.
46 Maple Street
London W1P

Orion Developments Limited
3 Northwest Business Park
Servia Hill
Leeds
Yorkshire

Orlik Property
29 Redhill Street
London NW1

Ortem Developments Limited
21 Upper Brook Street
London W1Y 1PD
071-493 6770
DIRECTOR: A Pearson (Managing)
MAJOR SHAREHOLDERS: MEPC

Ossory Estates plc
Heathcoat House
20 Savile Row
London W1X 1AE
Tel: 071-287 6677 Fax: 071-734 6663
NATURE OF BUSINESS: Development & Investment
DIRECTORS: M J M Walker MA Cantab; F R Gulmohamed FCA ATII; P L Everest; L J Spence (Non Exec)
(Sept 1992)
MAJOR SHAREHOLDERS: Directors; Simon Engineering plc; Scottish Amicable
BRANCH OFFICES: Manchester, Edinburgh, Birmingham, Ottowa, Philiadelphia
VALUE OF PROPERTY PORTFOLIO: £100m (1988)
PROPERTY PORTFOLIO: Offices 30%; shops 38%; factories 20%; residential 9%; other 3%
(Jan 1991)

Ossory Road Estates Limited
58 Albion Street
Leeds 1
West Yorkshire
0782 825210
Subsidiary of Ossory Estates plc

Outerwish Properties Limited
Assets House
17 Elverton Street
London SW1P

Overcourt Limited
23 Highbury Crescent
London N5

Overdale Securities Limited
Beck Field Main Street
East Keswick
Leeds
West Yorkshire

Owen Investments Limited
2nd Floor
Palladium House
1-4 Argyll Street
London W1V 1AD
071-734 4944
DIRECTOR: B Owen (Managing)

P & I Properties
The Gatehouse
24 Southend Road
Beckenham
Kent BR3 2AA
081-663 3088
DIRECTOR: P Knight (Managing)

P & O Developments Limited
4 Carlton Gardens
Pall Mall
London
SW1Y 5AB
Tel: 071-839 5611 Fax: 071-930 0992/2098
(Sept 1992)
DIRECTORS: B D MacPhail FCA (Chairman); J G Lyons FRICS; P H Grimson FCA; E Wyatt ACIS (Secretary)
ANNUAL TURNOVER/INCOME: £745,000 (1985)
SUBSIDIARY COMPANIES: Grosvenor Place Estates Limited
(Jan 1991)

P & O plc
79 Pall Mall
London SW1Y 3EJ

P & O Properties
220-222 Tottenham Court Road
London W1P 0HH
071-287 8531
DIRECTOR: R Ferguson (Managing)

P & O Shopping Centres Limited
3rd Floor
Arndale House
Arndale Centre
Manchester M4 3AA
061-832 6773
DIRECTORS: Mr Christmas (Managing) J Prosser (Marketing)

P F D Limited
19/20 Hyde Park Place
London W2

P K P Properties Limited
9 Islington High Street
London N1

P M Consultancy Limited
8 Bury Avenue
Ruislip

Pace Property Developments Limited
North Lane Studios
North Lane
Round Hay
Leeds
West Yorkshire

Palace Gate Estates
6 Palace Gate
London W8

Palmer & Hingston Estates Limited
16 Phillimore Place
London W8 7BU
Tel: 071-937 8359 Fax: 071-938 4231
NATURE OF BUSINESS: Development & Investment
DIRECTORS: C E Stevenson; M J Stevenson FCA; J M Hinton
MAJOR SHAREHOLDERS: MICA Holdings
(Sept 1992)
ANNUAL INCOME/TURNOVER: Company £0.38m; Group £4.8m
REGIONAL PREFERENCES: UK
VALUE OF PROPERTY PORTFOLIO: £6m (1990)
PROPERTY PORTFOLIO: Offices 40%; Shops 35%; Industrial 25%
INVESTMENT POLICY: Keep balanced portfolio of commercial properties.
DEVELOPMENT ACTIVITIES: £1.5m West London Industrial
DEVELOPMENT POLICY: Actively seeking developments below £0.5m.
SISTER COMPANIES: Gresley Estates Limited
(Jan 1991)

Palmerston Holdings
42 Welbeck Street
London W1M 8AY
071-487 5700
(Sept 1992)
DIRECTOR: C Gershinson (Managing)
ANNUAL TURNOVER: £11.6m (ye 31/3/89)
VALUE OF PROPERTY PORTFOLIO: £94.5m (ye 31/3/89)
(Jan 1991)

Palmerstone Properties Limited
Colton House
Princes Avenue
London N3 2DB

Palmerstone Property Developments plc
Colton House
Princes Avenue
London N3 2DB

Panar Properties Limited
4 The Slype
Gustard Wood
Wheathampstead
Hertfordshire AL4 8RY
Tel: 058-283 3278 Fax: 058-283 4632
NATURE OF BUSINESS: Development & Investment
DIRECTORS: R D Locks FSVA (Managing); S M Locks
REGIONAL PREFERENCES; East Anglia, S & SE Midlands, Lincolnshire, Home Counties and West Country
DEVELOPMENT/INVESTMENT POLICY: To acquire prime and good secondary freehold shops, offices and industrial/warehouse investments, rack rented or reversionary. Also similar properties required with vacant possession suitable for improvement and development sites

Panorama Homes
Suite 6
44 Baker Street
London KT12 4BL

Panther Securities plc
38 Mount Pleasant
London WC1X 0AP

Pan Gulf Group
Claremont House
Horton Road
W Drayton
0895 441000

Para Estates
378 East Park Road
Leicester
Leicestershire

Paragon Properties
Bath Brewery
Toll Bridge Road
Bath
Avon BA1 7DE
0225 852554
DIRECTOR: N Heggie (Managing)

Parc Securities Limited
16 Grosvenor Street
London W1
Tel: 071-495 6555 Fax: 071-499 0710
DIRECTOR: D Heyette (Managing)

Parchment Street Developments
12 The Hundred
Romsey
Hampshire SO51 8BU

Park Estates (Liverpool) Limited
1 Stanley Street
Liverpool L1 6AD

Park Home Estates Limited
Surrey Hills Park
Boxhill Road
Boxhill
Nr Tadworth
Surrey KT20 7LY
Tel: 0737 842011 Fax: 0737 844043
(Sept 1992)

Park House Properties
Delta House
181-183 Romford Road
London E15

Park Investments Limited
283 Brockley Road
London SE4
081-691 2959

Park Lane Estates
142a Park Lane
Whitefield
Manchester M25

Park Royal Estates
80 Clapham High Street
Clapham Park
London SW4 7UL

Park Square Development
41 Bedford Square
London WC1B

Park Tower International Limited
103 Mount Street
London
W1Y 5YE
Tel: 071-499 2660 Fax: 071-499 5228

Parkdale Property Development Company
Princes House
36-40 Jermyn Street
London SW1Y 6DT
081-531 4419

Parkes Incorporated Limited
7th Floor North
Brettenham House
Lancaster Place
London WC2E

Parkland Properties
1 Lincoln Grove
Bolton

Parkwood (Northern) Estates Limited
The Manor House
Cad Beaston
Leeds

Parkwood Estate
58B Wimpole Street
London W1
071-487 4488
DIRECTOR: P Gutkin (Managing)

Pass Group Limited
Stubben Edge Hall
Ashover
Derbyshire S45 OEU
Tel: 0246 590543 Fax: 0246 590449
BUSINESS: Property Developers and Investors
DIRECTORS: M A Pass; A Pass; R Brown; H A Brewer; D Neath
REGIONAL PREFERENCE: M25 North to Leeds
PORTFOLIO DISTRIBUTION: Group - Retail 27%; industrial 61%; offices 12%.
INVESTMENT POLICY: To expand the property portfolio on a long term basis by means of development projects and investment acquisitions.
SUBSIDIARY COMPANIES: Sissons Contractors Limited
SISTER COMPANIES: Amber Pass Limited; Amber Centre Estates Limited; Grangeheath Limited; Derbyshire Estates Limited; Sissons Contractors Limited; Amber Agriculture Limited.
(Sept 1992)

Patterson Developments
5 Eastgate Square
Pickering
North Yorkshire
0751 74909
DIRECTOR: G D Patterson (Managing)

Peachey Property Corporation Limited
19 Sloane Street
London SW1X 9NE
Tel: 071-235 2080/-262 0161 Fax: 071-245 9962
NATURE OF BUSINESS: Development & Investment
DIRECTORS: O Husken (Chairman); A Adams MA FCA (Finance); D Chance BSc FRICS; R Vigars; L Williams CBE DFC FCA; Sir S Eburne MC; M Jukes; G Verweij (Managing); K Grover
MAJOR SHAREHOLDERS: Imperial Chemical Staff Pension Fund; Wereldhave
BRANCH OFFICES: London
REGIONAL PREFERENCES: South East, especially London
PROPERTY PORTFOLIO: Retail 53%; offices 37%; industrial 9%; residential 1%
INVESTMENT POLICY: Offices, residential
DEVELOPMENT POLICY: Offices, retail, warehouse, shops, residential
SUBSIDIARY COMPANIES: A Peachey plc; Peachey Property Management Company Limited

Peal Southwest Limited
St Ann Way
Gloucester
Gloucestershire GL1 5SF
0452 418000
DIRECTORS: R Williams

Pearce, Alexander & Sons Limited
21 Brown Street
Salisbury
Wiltshire SP1 2AT
Tel: 0722 27631 Fax: 0722 411463
DIRECTOR: D J Pearce (Managing)

Pearce Developments
Parklands
Stoke Gifford
Bristol
Avon BS12 6QU
Tel: 0272 236262 Fax: 0272 236508
NATURE OF BUSINESS: Commercial Property Development
MAJOR SHAREHOLDERS: Wholly owned subsidiary of Crest Nicholson plc
DIRECTORS: P R Murray; J Callcutt; A T Yates (Managing); J R Allen; W L Clark; M Stanley-Smith
ANNUAL INCOME/TURNOVER: Group £300m; Company £15m
REGIONAL PREFERENCE: South West England & South Wales
VALUE OF PORTFOLIO: £25m (1992)
DISTRIBUTION OF DEVELOPMENT ACTIVITIES: Offices £10m; Retail £10m; Land £5m
DEVELOPMENT POLICY: Only looking at quick turn round schemes. Only building with pre-lets.
SISTER COMPANIES: Crest Estates; Pearce Construction.
(Sept 1992)

Pearl & Coutts
116 Clarence Road
London E5 8JA
081-985 5359
NATURE OF BUSINESS: Investment
DIRECTOR: D A Pearlman
Residential, shopping parades, refurbishments anywhere in UK

Pears, William Group
100A Avenue Road
Swiss Cottage
London NW3 3HF
071-722 7707
DIRECTOR: M Pears (Managing)

Peaston & Company
17 Lansdowne Crescent
Edinburgh EH12 5EH
031-337 8592
MANAGING DIRECTOR: C MacGregor
MARKETING MANAGER: M Cambell

Pecan Group

Pecan House
2 Shadwell Lane
Leeds
West Yorkshire LS17 6DR
0532 694226
DIRECTORS: M Levi (Managing); J Levi LLB; P Schiffeldrin
MAJOR SHAREHOLDERS: M Levi
PROPERTY PORTFOLIO: Offices 25%; shops 20%; warehouses 15%; residential 30%; other 10%
SUBSIDIARY COMPANIES: Pecan Estates; Pecan Properties (Leeds) Limited; Pecan Insurance

Peel Holdings plc

Quay West
Trafford Park Road
Manchester M17 1HH
Tel: 061-877 4714 Fax: 061-877 4720
NATURE OF BUSINESS: Property Investment & Management and Development
DIRECTORS: J Whittaker (Chairman); R E Hough LLB (Deputy Chairman); P A Scott FCCA (Managing Director); P P Wainscott (F.D.)
MAJOR SHAREHOLDERS: J P M Nominees Limited; Provident Mutual; Porenhowe Investments Ltd.
ANNUAL TURNOVER: £76,171,000 (1989)
REGIONAL OFFICES: Sutton; Hartlebury
VALUE OF PROPERTY PORTFOLIO: £623m (1992) (Sept 1992)
DISTRIBUTION OF PORTFOLIO: Out-of-town retail 23.7%; town centre retail 22.5%; offices 17.9%; industrial 17.1%; land 14.7%; overseas 4.1%.
SUBSIDIARY COMPANIES: Peel Homes Limited; Peel Investments (South) Ltd; Peel Investments (North) Ltd; Peel Developments (NW) Limited; Peel Overseas Limited; Peel Investments (NW) Limited; Peel Properties (SW) Limited; Bars Court Building Limited; Peel Properties (NW) Limited; Peel Commercial (NW) Limited; Colver Limited; Peel South East Limited; The Beaumont Property Trust Limited; Peel Developments (SE) Limited; Peel Securities (NW) Limited; Peel Investments (NE) Limited; Knight & Company (Services) Limited; Peel Developments (NE) Limited; London Shop Development Services Limited; Peel Securities (SE) Limited; Beaumont (Bahamas) Limited; Londrock (Bahamas) Limited; New Windsor Hotel Company Limited; Pittsdown Developments Limited; Washington Properties (Bermuda) Limited; Peel Developments Espana SA; Elljay Limited; Bathgate (Cayman) Limited
(Jan 1991)

Peel Investments (North) Lilmited

Quay Wharf
Rafford Wharf Road
Manchester M17 1HM
Tel: 061-877 4714 Fax: 061-877 4716
(Sept 1992)
DIRECTORS: B B Pugh MC MA LLB (Chairman); D K Redford CBE; J Holt (Managing Director); W A Bromley-Davenport FCA; R I Weston BSc FRICS; I W M Guthrie FCA (Secretary)
MAJOR SHAREHOLDERS: Largs Limited
REGIONAL PREFERENCES: Manchester Area
DEVELOPMENT ACTIVITIES: Residential 99%
SUBSIDIARY COMPANIES: Bridgewater Homes Limited (Jan 1991)

Pegasus Commercial Property Development UK

Ryebrook Studios
Woodcote Side
Epsom
Surrey KT18 7HD

Pegasus Retirement Homes Limited

43 Rodney Road
Cheltenham
Gloucestershire
GL50 1HX
0242 576610

Pelham Estate Limited

6 Sloane Street
London SW1X 9LF
Tel: 071-823 1623 Fax: 071-823 1582
DIRECTOR: J Hall (Managing)

Pelham Homes Limited

Tubs Hill
House South
Sevenoaks, Kent

Pembroke Developments Limited

2 Wake Green Road
Birmingham B13

Pendle Property

Brockett House
1 Montgomery Road
Nelheredge
Sheffield S7 1LN
0742 555888
DIRECTOR: R Walker (Managing)

Pengap Estates

214 Oxford Street
London W1N 9DF
071-493 6402
NATURE OF BUSINESS: Development
MAJOR SHAREHOLDERS: Burton Group
BRANCH OFFICES: St Albans
DEVELOPMENT POLICY: Developers of retail and industrial property for onward industrial sale
SUBSIDIARY COMPANIES: Pengap Mercantile Securities Limited; Pengap Industrial Developments Limited

Pennant Properties

Walter House
418-422 Strand
London WC2R 0PT

Penrith Developments
147 London Road South
Poynton
Cheshire
0625 871184
DIRECTOR: N Penrith (Managing)

Pentref Development Company Limited
c/o Bernard Williams Associates
Kings House
32-40 Widmore Road
Bromley, Kent BR1 1RY
Tel: 081-460 1111 Fax: 081-464 1167
NATURE OF BUSINESS: Development
DIRECTORS: James Grove FRTPI RIBA; Dr Nicholas Falk BA MBA PhD; Sydney Isaacs BComm; Bernard Williams FRICS AMBIM
ANNUAL GROSS INCOME/TURNOVER: £3m (est. 1991)
BRANCH OFFICES: Swansea
DEVELOPMENT ACTIVITIES: Shops 5%; residential 90%; leisure 5%
DEVELOPMENT POLICY: Social development of new village communities with a wide social range. Development profits to be gifted to the sponsoring trust, Pentref Private Development Trust, for redistribution to improve communities locally and nationally
(Sept 1992)

Penstone plc
8 Staple Inn
London WC1V

Penway Limited
54/56 Euston Street
London NW1

Percy Bilton plc
Bilton House
Wabridge Road
London W5 2TL

Permanent Land Limited
921 Fulham Road
London SW6 5HU
071-731 4330
NATURE OF BUSINESS: Development & Investment
DIRECTOR: B Fleming (Managing)
REGIONAL PREFERENCES: South England

Perseus Property Company Limited
Pearl Assurance House
128-130 Old Christchurch Road
Bournemouth
Dorset
0202 296931
DIRECTOR: R E Wright (Managing)

Persimmon plc
Persimmon House
Fulford
York YO1 4RE
Tel: 0904 642199 Fax: 0904 610014
NATURE OF BUSINESS: Residential Development
DIRECTORS: D H Davidson (Chairman), M J Allen, G Grewer, B D Taylor, J White, M P Farley, D G Bryant, J C L Keswick, H G Littlefair, Mrs S K Davidson.
ANNUAL GROSS INCOME/TURNOVER: £143.8 m (Dec 1991)
(Sept 1992)

Peterman Group of Companies
75 Herne Hill
London SE24 9NE
071-733 5454
JOINT MANAGING DIRECTORS: S H Peterman; M W Peterman

Petrel Developments Limited
8 Bourdon Street
London W1X

Petros Development Company Limited
Kingfisher House
Bridge Place
Altrincham
Cheshire WA14 1RL
061-941 4536
DIRECTOR: P Collins (Managing)

PHD Properties
98 Beulah Road
Thornton Heath
Surrey CR7 8JF
081653 0110
DIRECTOR: P H D D Jackson (Managing)

Philip George Properties Limited
12 Long Acre
London WC2E

Phoenix Securities (Properties) Limited
28 Dorset Street
London W1H

PI Consortium Managers Limited
138 Gloucester Place
London NW1

Pilcher Properties
Bishopthorpe Garth
Bishopthorpe
York YO2 1UE
0904 701771
DIRECTORS: R D S Pilcher (Managing) A Rutter (Marketing)

Pillar Property Investments plc
65 Buckingham Gate
London SW1E

Pilot Properties Limited
1 Kingsland Passage
London E8 2BB
Tel: 071-275 7676 Fax: 071-275 9348
NATURE OF BUSINESS: Development
(Sept 1992)
DIRECTOR: H Geddes (Managing)
(Jan 1991)

Pine Developments (Cambridge) Limited
8 Bridle Avenue
Maidenhead
Berkshire SL6 IRR
0628 71043
NATURE OF BUSINESS: Development
DIRECTORS: D A McGlinchey; M C Pascall (Managing)
MAJOR SHAREHOLDERS: Directors
REGIONAL PREFERENCES: London & SE
DEVELOPMENT ACTIVITIES: offices 20%; factories 20% science parks/hi-tech 60%
INVESTMENT POLICY: All our developments are pre-funded with institutions who retain the investment. We act entirely as developers
DEVELOPMENT POLICY: Industrial estates South East. Offices Thames Valley area
SUBSIDIARY COMPANIES: Pine Finance Limited

Pinstone Securities Limited
46 Bell Street
Henley on Thames
Oxfordshire RG9 2BG
0491 576593
DIRECTORS: R B Sturdy (Managing)

Pinto, D & Co
15 Dover Street
London W1X

Piper Trust
Eardley House
182-184 Campden Hill Road
London
W8 7AS
071-221 5488
DIRECTOR: Adrian Burford (Managing Director)

Pique Holdings plc
291A Brompton Road
London SW3 2DY
071-225 3877
DIRECTOR: C Pool (Managing)

PJJS Limited
Warmlake Estate
Maidstone Road
Sutton Valence
Kent ME17 3LR

Placedeal Corporation
16 Connaught Street
London W2

Planning Design Development
667 Silbury Boulevard
Central Milton Keynes
Milton Keynes
Bucks MK9 3LD
0908 690630
DIRECTORS: K Revill (Managing); A Lewis (Marketing)

Plaza Estates
29-31 Edgeware Road
London W2 2JE
071-724 3100
DIRECTOR: S Salama (Managing)

Plimley Holdings
7 Melville Terrace
Stirling FK8 2ND
0786 62161
DIRECTOR: P K Plimley (Managing)

Plimpto Properties
65 Commercial Street
London E1 6BD
071 321 0266
DIRECTOR: Mr C. Shamas (Managing)

Ploughland Estates Limited
Ploughland Court
George Street
Wakefield

Plynlimon Estates and Properties
17 John's Mews
London WC1N 2PU
071-405 1561
DIRECTOR: T J Davies (Managing)

Pochins plc
Brooks Lane
Middlewich
Cheshire CW10 OJQ
0606 843333
NATURE OF BUSINESS: Development
DIRECTORS: M A Pochin; N J Pochin MA (Managing); W R Verity; J H Woodcock; Mrs S Nicholson
MAJOR SHAREHOLDERS: A C Pochin; N J Pochin; S E Nicholson; W R Verity; M A Pochin
BRANCH OFFICES: Middlewich; Slough; Bathgate; Colesmill; Thirsk; Newport
REGIONAL PREFERENCES: North West
SUBSIDIARY COMPANIES: Pochin (Contractors) Limited; Contractors Plan (North West) Limited; Pochin (Development) Limited; William Griffith & Sons Limited; Pochin (Wales) Limited

Entry missing ? Call HELPLINE Page v

Poco Homes Limited
Britannia Road
Sale
Greater Manchester M33 2AB
061-969 2031
DIRECTOR: D W Broadbent (Managing)

Point West Developments Limited
West London Terminal
Cromwell Road
London SW7

Polar Construction and Development (UK) Ltd
6 Sackville Street
London W1X 1OD

Polton Investments Limited
Souther House
Station Approach
Woking
Surrey GU22 7UZ

Polypipe plc
Broomhouse Lane
Edlington
Doncaster
South Yorkshire DN12 1ES
0709 770000
MANAGING DIRECTOR: K McDonald
ADVERTISING MANAGER: V Roberts

Port of London Properties
5 Tilbury Gardens
Tilbury
Essex RM18 7NH
0375 852355

Portland Estates & Investments
20 Hanson Street
London W1P

Portland House Securities Limited
11 Kensington Court
London W8

Portman Family Settled Estates
The Portman Office
38 Seymour Street
London W1
071-262 1464
DIRECTOR: C A G Hatherell (Managing)

Portman New Homes Limited
Ramsbury House
20 High Street
Hungerford RG17 OUZ
Tel: 0488 681555 Fax: 0488 686200
NATURE OF BUSINESS: Housebuilder
DIRECTORS: N Howe (Managing Director); G H B Carter (Chairman); K Culley; D Gibson; H Westropp
MAJOR SHAREHOLDERS: Portman Building Society
ANNUAL INCOME/TURNOVER: Company: £10m
VALUE OF PROPERTY PORTFOLIO: £27m (1991)
DISTRIBUTION OF PORTFOLIO: Residential Land and Property £27m
INVESTMENT POLICY: To expand residential property portfolio.
DISTRIBUTION OF DEVELOPMENT: 100% Housebuilding
(Sept 1992)

Portmand Square Holdings plc
133 Ebury Street
LondonSW1W 9QU
Tel: 071-730 1363 Fax 071-730 1677
(Sept 1992)
DIRECTOR: G Randall (Managing)
(Jan 1991)

Portswood Developments Limited
Portswood House
1 Hampshire Corporate Park
Chandlers Ford
Eastleigh
Hampshire SO5 3YX
0703 256256
DIRECTORS: Terry Hartwell; Jim Adams
Subsidiary of Chartwell Land plc

Positive Location Properties
The Corner House
1 George Street
Alderley Edge
Cheshire SK9 7EJ
0625 582378
DIRECTOR: Mr A B Clowes (Managing)

Postal Properties
Strandon House
21 Mansell Street
London E1 8AA
071 702 0888
CHIEF EXECUTIVE: A Threadgold

Powell & Partner Investments
39/41 Station Road
East Oxted
Surrey RH8 OBD
0883 712315

Power Corporation (UK)
4 Walton Place
London SW3 1RH
071-823 9199

Power Securities (Manchester) Limited
Royal Exchange Shopping Centre
Cross Street
Manchester M2 7DB
061-834 3731
DIRECTOR: N Rome (Managing)

Entry missing ? Call HELPLINE Page v

Powergen plc (Property Services)
Haslucks Green Road
Shirley
Solihull
West Midlands B90 4PD

Princeton Investments plc
7/8 Conduit Street
London W1R OJY
071-493 2594
NATURE OF BUSINESS: Investment
DIRECTORS: Arnold Lee (Solicitor); Alan Lee ARICS; Edward Lee BSc (Econ); G Coughlan (Managing)
BRANCH OFFICES: New York USA
REGIONAL PREFERENCES: Central London and London suburbs, North Eastern USA, European capitals
PROPERTY PORTFOLIO: Offices 100%
INVESTMENT POLICY: Well located secondary office buildings actively sought. Active management situations particularly of interest
DEVELOPMENT POLICY: Office schemes considered for development or refurbishment
SUBSIDIARY COMPANIES: Princeton International Inc (USA)

Prince Estates Limited
65 Abbotsbury Road
London W14

Principal Hotels Group plc
8th Floor
Cophall House Tower
Station Parade
Harrogate
North Yorkshire HG1 1TS

Prior plc
3/4 Perry Street
London W1P 0ET
Tel: 071-409 2424 Fax: 071-409 1862
(Sept 1992)
NATURE OF BUSINESS: Investment
DIRECTORS: K H Clapp FRICS ACIArb; N C Gray BSc Solicitor; R Larkey FCA; J Prior (Chairman)
MAJOR SHAREHOLDERS: Directors; Scottish Amicable Life Assurance Group
ANNUAL TURNOVER: £22m (1989)
BRANCH OFFICES: None
REGIONAL PREFERENCES: None
VALUE OF PROPERTY PORTFOLIO: £35m
PROPERTY PORTFOLIO: 80% Industrial; 20% Offices & Shops
(Sept 1992)
INVESTMENT POLICY: Develop an asset base from successful trading of commercial properties
SUBSIDIARY COMPANIES: Prior Securities (Gloucester) Limited; Ringell Limited; Central & General Property Company Limited
(Jan 1991)

Priory Estates
6 Sackville Street
London W1X

Privilege Properties Limited
Shorefield House
Dunscar Fold
Egerton
Bolton

Property & Design Corporation
229 Kensington High Street
London W8

Property & Leisure Services
27 Hartington Place
Edinburgh EH10

Property Action & Marketing Limited
36 Langham Street
London W1N

Property Holdings Incorporated plc
RWF House
5 Renfield Street
Glasgow G2 5EZ
NATURE OF BUSINESS: Development & Investment
DIRECTORS: E I Commander FRICS; A Craddock; A Meirs FCIS
MAJOR SHAREHOLDERS: Directors
BRANCH OFFICES: London, Leamington Spa
REGIONAL PREFERENCES: Excluding: SE England & North of Manchester
PROPERTY PORTFOLIO: offices 60%; factories 20%; warehouses 20%
INVESTMENT POLICY: High yield investments either developed or puchased for retention
DEVELOPMENT ACTIVITIES: factories 40%; warehouses 40%; residential 20%
DEVELOPMENT POLICY: Acquisition of only prime sites for developments where pre-letting available or virtually guaranteed any form of development

Property International Limited
Britannia House
45-53 Prince of Wales Road
Norwich
Norfolk NR1 1BL
Tel: 0603 628112 Fax: 0603 620631
(Sept 1992)
NATURE OF BUSINESS: Development & Investment
DIRECTORS: W H Blatch (Managing); G M Villiers de Casanove FCIS;
MAJOR SHAREHOLDERS: W H Blatch Investments Limited; A R Gilbertson;
ANNUAL TURNOVER/INCOME/PROFIT: £2.8m (1989)
REGIONAL PREFERENCES: East of England from Lincolnshire downwards to Northern Home Counties and Greater London
DEVELOPMENT ACTIVITIES: Offices 20%; shops 7%; other 10%

DEVELOPMENT POLICY: Development/refurbishment of retail and retail warehouse schemes. Development/ refurbishment of offices and industrial property
SUBSIDIARY COMPANIES: Property Investments Phoenix BV
(Jan 1991)

Property Partnerships plc
Noverre House
Theatre Street
Norwich
Norfolk NR2 1RH
Tel: 0603 761260 Fax: 0603 633696
(Sept 1992)
NATURE OF BUSINESS: Development & Investment
DIRECTORS: P R King JP BSc FRICS (Chairman & Managing); W J Hayden DL FCA; M R King (Solicitor); N W Roskill MA; C Binns FHCIMA FBIM MI
JOINT MANAGING DIRECTORS: P Rudd; P Mackness
MAJOR SHAREHOLDERS: BBC New Pension Schemes; H E King
ANNUAL TURNOVER/INCOME: £5.41m (1988)
REGIONAL PREFERENCES: East Anglia
VALUE OF PROPERTY PORTFOLIO: £31.47m (1988)
SUBSIDIARY COMPANIES: Property Partnerships (Hotels) Limited
(Jan 1991)

Property Security Investment Trust plc
Fetcham Park House
Lower Road
Fetcham
Surrey KT22 9HD
Tel: 0372 376155 Fax: 0372 312338
NATURE OF BUSINESS: Investment
DIRECTORS: A R Perry (Chairman); L N Tucker; Sir H Cabitt CBE DL FRICS; P H Dunn LLB FCA FCIS; H L S Dilbey MA FRICS; G H Caines FCA MCT (Financial)
MAJOR SHAREHOLDERS: Harper Investment Limited; Royal Insurance plc
ANNUAL TURNOVER/INCOME/PROFIT: £9.26m (1988)
BRANCH OFFICES: Richmond
REGIONAL PREFERENCES: South East
VALUE OF PROPERTY PORTFOLIO: £170.12m (1988)
INVESTMENT POLICY: Hi-tech and industrial, office, retail
SUBSIDIARY COMPANIES: Albion Close Investments Limited; Dallow Road Investments Limited; Louisville Investment Limited; Property Security Belgium SA; Property Security Holland BV; Property Security Ireland Limited; Property Securities Overseas Limited; Triad (Bootle) Limited; Property Security Investment Trust (CI) Limited

---

Property Trust plc
35 Dover Street
London W1X 3RA
Tel: 071-629 7284 Fax: 071-493 5165
NATURE OF BUSINESS: Property Investment; Trading and Development
DIRECTORS: Anthony Kai Chiu Cheng BSc ACA; Frederik Louis Tsun Meng Hsu BA; Kevin James Newman; David Kai Ho Cheng LLM; Charles Yeh Kwong Lee LLM; Timothy Tufnell MC ERD FSVA.
ANNUAL GROSS INCOME/TURNOVER: £9,520,000 (31/3/92)
(Sept 1992)

Prospect International
143 Wardour Street
London W12 3TB
071-439 1919
DIRECTOR: J Plummer (Managing)

Protec Investments Limited
Bridge Mills
Holland Street
Pendleton
Manchester M6

Provincial House Group plc
1 Glynd Mews
Walton Street
London SW3 1SB
071-584 6391
(Sept 1992)
DIRECTOR: R Kenwood (Managing)
BRANCHES: Mayfair, London
(Jan 1991)

Provincial House Group plc
53 Mount Street
London W1Y

Provincial Trust Limited
Ashley House
30 Ashley Road
Altrincham
Cheshire WA14 2DW
Tel: 061-928 9011 Fax: 061-926 8194
(Sept 1992)
DIRECTOR: R E Basher (Managing)
NATURE OF BUSINESS: Investment
BRANCH OFFICES: Knightsbridge, London
INVESTMENT POLICY: Range of banking and deposit taking services to private and corporate customers
A wholly owned subsidiary of ABA Company Investments plc
(Jan 1991)

Prowting plc
Breakspear House
Bury Street
Ruislip
Middlesex HA4 7SY
Tel: 0895 633344 Fax: 0895 677190
(Sept 1992)
NATURE OF BUSINESS: Housing Development
DIRECTORS: P Prowting (Chairman); T R Roydon BCS, MBA (Managing); R Templeman LLB, FCA; T G Whitting; R A Oury, FCA; J B Willett, FCIB.
ANNUAL GROSS INCOME/TURNOVER: £60.8 (1990)
SUBSIDIARY COMPANIES: 18 in Housing Development
(Jan 1991)

Prowting Holdings Limited
Breakspear House
Bury Street
Ruislip
Middlesex HA4 7SY
0895 633344
DIRECTORS: P B Prowting; (Chairman) T R Roydon, MBA (Managing Director), T G Whitting; B Templeman LLB FCA; R A Oury, FCA; J B Willett, FCIB.
LARGE SHAREHOLDERS: B P Pension Fund; Target Financial Fund; Allied Dunbar Growths & Income Trust; Allied Dunbar Accumulator Trust; Robert Flemming Asset Management Limited
REGIONAL OFFICES: Chichester, Sussex, Taunton, Somerset, Malvern, Worcestershire.
ANNUAL INCOME/TURNOVER: Company £61.8m
REGIONAL PREFERENCES: Southern half of England
DEVELOPMENT ACTIVITIES: Residential 100%
SUBSIDIARY COMPANIES: Bilsby Limited; Cherry Hill Homes Limited; Corn Mill Developments Limited; Friary Homes Limited; Lazy Acre Investments Limited; Leisurama Homes Limited; Montague Developments Limited; Mount Row Securities Limited; Pacemaker Developments Limited; Pennant Developments Limited; AEA Prowting Limited; Prowting Estates Limited; Prowting Investments Limited; Prowting Southern Limited; Prowting Western Limited; Reprise Developments Limited; Sequoia Developments Limited; Servernbrook Investments Limited; Tela Properties Limited; Trydall Developments Limited; Wendron Securities Limited; Whippendell Developments Limited

Ptarmigan Properties & Securities Limited
3 West Parade
Wakefield
Yorkshire

Puffin Properties Limited
Lower Hone Lane
Bosham
West Sussex PO18 8QN
Tel: 0243 575018 Fax: 0243 575018
NATURE OF BUSINESS: Development, Commercial and Residential
DIRECTORS: J Bing; A J Gunton ACIOB (Managing)
REGIONAL PREFERENCES: South East & South West; South M4
DISTRIBUTION OF DEVELOPMENT ACTIVITIES: Residential 75%; Commercial 25%
DEVELOPMENT POLICY: Design Build

Pullhigh Properties Limited
15 Chapletown
Pudsey
Leeds

Purbeck Estates Limited
Flint House
London Road
St. Ippollitts
Hitchin
Herts SG4 7NF
0462 433816
DIRECTOR: M Goss (Managing)

Purton Property Company Limited
6 Porter Street
London W1
071-935 8430

Purvis Industries Limited
Guildhall Buildings
Navigation Street
Birmingham B2

Queens Moat Houses plc
Queens Court
9-17 Eastern Road
Romford
Essex RM1 1BR
Tel: 0708 730522 Fax: 0708 762691
(Sept 1992)
ANNUAL TURNOVER: £234.4m (1988)
(Jan 1991)

Queensgate Development
Tectonic Place
Holyport Road
Maidenhead
SL6 2EZ
0628 25266
DIRECTORS: Mr Peterson; Mr Smith

Quoin Homes Limited
Plot 3
Chimneys Court
Arterberry Road
London SW20
081-879 7898

Quorum Estates
Abnay Hall
Manchester Road
Cheadle
Cheshire SK8 2PD
061-491 3222
DIRECTORS: John Slater (Managing)

R V B Investments Limited
Smithfield House
Digbeth
Birmingham B5

Radco Holdings plc
11 Waterloo Place
London SW1Y

Radco Properties Limited
62 Pall Mall
London SW1Y 58Z
071-930 7951
JOINT MANAGING DIRECTORS: C Rayden; P Rayden

Entry missing ? Call HELPLINE Page v

Radmark Properties Limited
66/68 Brewer Street
London W1R

Raglan Industrial Enterprises
Skinner Lane
Pontefract
Leeds

Raglan Property Trust plc
Orion House
Grays Place
Slough
Bucks SL2 5AF
Tel: 0753 553388 Fax: 0753 551969
NATURE OF BUSINESS: Property Company
DIRECTORS: Hon C E Cecil (Chairman); R J Pearson (Managing Director); D A Smith; M J Ingall, B R Green (Non Executive)
MAJOR SHAREHOLDERS: Glynwed International plc;
ANNUAL TURNOVER: £12.5m (1990) (Group)
PROPERTY PORTFOLIO: £11.8M (1990)
DEVELOPMENT/INVESTMENT POLICY: Market Town Shopping Developments.
SUBSIDIARY COMPANIES: Raglan (Property Management) Limited; Raglan (Evesham) Limited; Raglan (Horsham) Limited; Raglan Estates Limited; Raglan (New Malden) Limited
(Sept 1992)

Ralwood Securities Limited
9/85 New Cavendish Street
London W1M

RAM Developments
The Coach House
South Hill Cottage
Bleadon
Weston-super-Mare
Somerset BS24 ONJ

Rams Investments Limited
187 Cranbrook Road
Ilford
Essex

Ramsdell Estates Limited
378 Shelton New Road
Basford
Stoke-On-Trent
Staffordshire ST4 6EW
0782 623882
DIRECTOR: K Humphreys (Managing)

Randsworth Trust plc
Landseer House
19 Charing Cross Road
London WC2H
071-930 1354
NATURE OF BUSINESS: Development & Investment
DIRECTORS: D H B Holland (Chairman); J A Nichols FCA (Chief Executive); A P Brayford FRICS; N J Kempner; B S Hodge CA; S H R Musgrave ARICS
MAJOR SHAREHOLDERS: Markheath Securities plc; Royal Insurance Group; John Govatt & Company Limited; Legal & General Assurance Society Limited; Baillie Gifford & Co
ANNUAL TURNOVER: £24.57m (1988)
VALUE OF PROPERTY PORTFOLIO: £373.46m (1988)
SUBSIDIARY COMPANIES: London & Provincial Shop Centres (Holdings) plc; LPSC (Goswell Road) Limited; London & Provincial Shop Centres Limited; Randsworth Limited; Clemhart Limited; Holtvale Limited; Portal Homes plc; Lorne Exploration plc; Apex Properties plc; Commercial & Centre Investments Limited; Hemkip Limited; Nextdeal Limited; Jetsolid Limited; Staplegrow Limited; Microcope Limited; Alderney Nursing Care Limited
RELATED COMPANIES: Branchempire Limited; Circuitport Limited

Ranelagh Developments Limited
18 King William Street
London EC4N 7BP
Tel: 071-815 0606 Fax: 071-815 0947
DIRECTOR: T C O'Rorke
NATURE OF BUSINESS: Commercial Development & Project Management
MAJOR SHAREHOLDERS: Kumagai-Gumi (UK) Limited
(Sept 1992)

Rank Organisation plc
6 Connaught Place
London W2 2EX
071-706 1111
DIRECTORS: M Gifford (Managing); R Rycroft (Marketing)

Ratcliffe General Industrial Holdings Limited
Hill House
6 Albermarle Street
London W1X 3HF

Ravenseft Properties & Industrial Estates Limited
5 Strand
London WC2N 5AF
Tel: 071-413 9000 Fax: 071-925 0202
(Sept 1992)
DIRECTORS: C J Hunt (Chairman); Mr Henderson (Managing)
Subsidiary of Land Securities
(Jan 1991)

Ravenside Investments Limited
5 The Strand
London WC2N 5AF

Ray Day Investments Limited
12 Connaught Place
London W2

Raycastle Developments
97 Old Brompton Road
London SW7 3LD
071-225 0211
DIRECTOR: Y Fattal (Managing)

Rayfield Estates
56 Grosvenor Street
London W1X

Rayford Properties
Rayford House
School Road
Hove
Sussex BN3 5HX
0273 206201
DIRECTOR: R Horney (Managing)

Raynsway Properties Limited
690 Melton Road
Thurmaston
Leicester
0533 694002
DIRECTOR: C A Raynes (Managing)

Reality Estates Limited
25 Rochdale Road
Manchester M4 4HT
Tel: 061-832 9447 Fax: 061-832 0065
NATURE OF BUSINESS: Property Investment & Development
MAJOR SHAREHOLDERS: Y Tishbi
ANNUAL INCOME/TURNOVER: £1m
REGIONAL PREFERENCES FOR ACTIVITIES: North West
(Sept 1992)

REDAB UK Limited
4 Millbank
London SW1P

Redbourn Group plc
Watling House
Dunstable Road
Redbourn
St Albans
Herts AL3 7RG
0582 794412
DIRECTOR: M Shaw (Managing)

Redcastle Properties
65 Westgate Road
Newcastle NE1 1S6
091-230 0088
DIRECTOR: G Gibson (Managing)

Redhead Properties Limited
52 Eardley Crescent
London SW5

Redrow Commercial Developments Limited
Redrow House
St David's Park
Clwyd CH5 3PW
0244 520044
DIRECTOR: J Williams (Managing)

Redwing Estates
10 Queen Street
London W1X 7PD
Tel: 071-491 1418 Fax: 071-629 3225
NATURE OF BUSINESS: Development and Investment
DIRECTORS: C J Towlson; Mr D Moore
ANNUAL TURNOVER: Company £2m
REGIONAL PREFERENCES: South East and Major UK Towns
VALUE OF PORTFOLIO: £7m 1990
DISTRIBUTIONOF PORTFOLIO: Offices 33%, Industrial 64%, Retail 3%
INVESTMENT POLICY: High yielding industrial required with a view to expanding portfolio nationally. The portfolio is to be enlarged by development and strategic purchases. Investment propositions with short/medium term redevelopment potential of particular interest.
DEVELOPMENT ACTIVITIES: 100% Industrial B1

Reed Developments Limited
Reed House
London Road, Great Shelford
Cambridge CB2 5DB
0223 843930

Reed International plc
Reed House
6 Chesterfield Gardens
London W1
071-499 4020
DIRECTOR: Jan Shawe (Marketing)

Regal Land Company, The
89 Addison Road
London W14 8ED
Tel: 071-371 3199 Fax: 071-602 7886
NATURE OF BUSINESS: Residential Developemnt Investment
DIRECTOR: R Hildebrand
REGIONAL PREFERENCES FOR ACTIVITIES: Greater London
INVESTMENT POLICY: Greater London Residential
DEVELOPMENT POLICY: Greater London Residential
(Sept 1992)

Regalian Properties plc
44 Grosvenor Hill
London W1X 9JE
Tel: 071-493 9613 Fax: 071-491 0692
(Sept 1992)
NATURE OF BUSINESS: Development
DIRECTORS: L J Walton FIB (Chairman, Non-Executive); D J Goldstone LLB(Lond) (Managing); J A Darby FRICS (Non-Executive); J L Goldstone; S A Hill FCA; R Perdeaux MA FCA (Secretary); R King

Entry missing ? Call HELPLINE Page v

MAJOR SHAREHOLDERS: Davstone (Holdings) Limited; Provident Mutual Managed Pension Funds Limited; Legal & General Investment Management Limited
ANNUAL TURNOVER/INCOME/PROFIT: £107.8m (1989)
DEVELOPMENT POLICY: Development and refurbishment of residential property for resale
SUBSIDIARY COMPANIES: Regalian Developments Limited; Regalian (Urban Renewal) Limited; Regalian (Estates) Limited; Regalian Properties (Commercial); Regalian Homes Limited; Regalian Properties (Northern) Limited; Spencer & Monk Construction 1985 Limited
(Jan 1991)

Regency Developments (North West) Limited
22 Regency House
Longworth Road
Horwich
Manchester

Regency Place Investments Limited
12 Regency Place
London
SW1P 2DZ
071-834 5400
DIRECTORS: T Habani (Managing); Mr Contractor (Marketing)

Regent Capital Holdings Limited
77 South Audley Street
London W1M

Regent Estates
237 Regents Park Road
London N3 3LF

Regents Developments
Regent House
Ascot Drive
Derby DE2 8ST
0628 25266
DIRECTORS: M Harris (Managing); J Ridgby (Marketing)

Regional Properties Limited
Pixham End
Dorking
Surrey RH4 1QA
Tel: 0306 740123 Fax: 0306 886463
(Sept 1992)
DIRECTORS: N S Conrad FRICS (Chairman TCE); V Lucas FSVA FCIArb; G J L Hill FRICS; P A Hipps FCA; P M King MA; M S Hardie CA; F G Cotton FIA; A M S Wolffsohn FCCA FCMA (Secretary)
MAJOR SHAREHOLDERS: Friends Provident Life Office; Scottish Amicable Life Assurance Society
SUBSIDIARY COMPANIES: Atlas Properties Limited; Gracechurch Securities Limited; Ibex Commercial & Industrial Properties Limited; Ibex Developments (Vauxhall) Limited; Ibex Properties (Ealing) Limited; Ibex Properties (City) Limited; Ibex Properties (St James) Limited; London Midland Associated Properties Limited; Regional Properties Management Limited; Regional Securities Limited; Regional (Shops & Offices) Limited
(Jan 1991)

Regis Property Holdings plc
10 Cornwall Terrace
Regents Park
London NW1 4QP
071-486 4466
DIRECTORS: J H Ritblat FSVA (Chairman); S J Berwin; D M Cohen FCA FCCA; C Metliss FCA; J H Weston-Smith MA FCIS; D Wilson (Secretary)
MAJOR SHAREHOLDERS: A member of the British Land Group

Renton-Euro-Properties
3 Hollylodge
Lindsey Road
Poole
Dorset BH13 6BQ
0202 763107

Research Property Co Limited
42 Portman Square
London W1H

Retail Property Investments Limited
Peter House
Oxford Street
Manchester M1

Reversionary & Secondary Property Investments plc
13 Park Square Mews
Upper Harley Street
London NW1 4PP
071-935 3588
DIRECTOR: S Moss (Managing)

Revival Properties Limited
39 Chorley New Road
Bolton

Revival Properties Limited
33 Park Square West
Leeds
West Yorkshire LS1 2PF
Tel: 0532 423545 Fax: 0532 423786

Revival Properties Limited
21 Melville Street
Edinburgh EH3

RH Property (Developments) Ltd
92b Snakes Lane East
Woodford Green
Essex IG8 7HX
081-559 1040
DIRECTOR: R Hopkins(Managing)

Rialto Group plc
26 Bloomsbury Place
London SW18
081-877 1359

Richardson Brothers Limited
Murdock Road
East Middlesbrough Ind. Est.
Middlesbrough TS3 8TB
0642 240242
DIRECTOR: J Coverdale (Managing)

Richardson Development Limited
100 Dudley Road East
Oldbury
Warley
West Midlands B69 3DY
021-544 7111
DIRECTOR: D Richardson (Managing); A Fulton (Marketing)

Richcliff Group Limited
13 Motcombe Street
London SW1X

Richmond Developments Limited
Richmond House
Hagley Road
Birmingham B16

Rightacres Property Co
255A Cathedral Road
Cardiff CF1 9PD
0222 236216

RIJAC Properties Ltd
9 Clonard Way
Hatch End
Middlesex HA5 4BT
081-428 5050
DIRECTOR: M Shields (Managing)

Rika UK Limited
11 Belgravia House
Halkin Place
London SW1X

Rington Properties Limited
Brownlow Rooms
Brownlow Road
Berkhamsted
Hertfordshire HP4 2AR
0442 866433

Ringway Developments Plc
Building 205
Manchester Airport
Manchester M22 5PG
061-436 2239
CHIEF EXECUTIVE: A Perkins

Risebrook Properties Limited
Stevens Building
62 Market Street
Manchester M1

RMC Properties Limited
53-55 High Street
Feltham
Middlesex TW13 4HA
0932 5678833
MANAGER: A Y Bateman

Robert Fraser Estates
Fraser House
29 Albemarle Street
London W1X 3FA
Tel: 071-493 3211 Fax: 071 408 1814
(Sept 1992)
DIRECTOR: C J Emerson (Managing)
(Jan 1991)

Robertsdale Property Investment Limited
63 Whitworth Street
Manchester M1

Rockeagle Holdings Limited
(Parent of Rockeagle Ltd)
Mamhead House
Mamhead
Exeter
Devon EX6 8HD
0626 890999 Fax: 0626 891491
DIRECTOR: M Kay (Managing)
MAJOR SHAREHOLDERS: M R Kay; Dr H Kay
REGIONAL PREFERENCES FOR ACTIVITIES: South West England
VALUE OF PORTFOLIO: £15.3 m (1992)
DISTRIBUTION OF PORTFOLIO: Offices 30%; Industrial/Warehouses 30%; Out of Town Shopping 20%; Residential 20%
DEVELOPMENT POLICY: To take advantage of market conditions
(Sept 1992)

Rockwell Properties Limited
Unit E
5 Fairchild Place
London EC2A

Rodwise Limited
Berkeley Square House
Berkeley Square
London W1Y

Rohan Group plc
1 Hill Street
London W1X 7FU
071-408 1661
NATURE OF BUSINESS: Development & Investment
DIRECTORS: J F Duggan; E J Cotter; P J Harrington; T G Cryan (Secretary)

Entry missing ? Call HELPLINE Page v

MAJOR SHAREHOLDERS: Cabra Estates
INVESTMENT POLICY: Business Park
DEVELOPMENT POLICY: Industrial & commercial; business park
SUBSIDIARY COMPANIES: Construction Division; Rohan Construction Limited; Rohan Construction Management Limited; Industrial Estates & Property Division; Rohan Industrial Estates Limited; Rohan Construction (UK) Limited; Rohan Commercial Properties Limited; Rohan Investments Limited; Field Commercial Investments Limited; DAD Properties Limited; Langley Business Park Limited; Rohan Colorado Inc; Rohdel Inc; Hanro NV; Merydale NV
ASSOCIATED COMPANIES: Garrison Park Incorporated
BRANCH OFFICES: Dublin, Midleton (County Cork), London, Denver.

Roland Industrial Limited

2a Duke Street
London W1M

Roland Park Estates

108-110 Brent Street
London NW4 2HH
081-882 8575

Romulus Construction

Burlington House
184 New Kings Road
London SW6 4SW
071-736 1214
DIRECTOR: D Woolf (Managing)

Ropemaker Properties Limited

56A Brompton Road
London SW3
071-581 5336

Ropner plc

140 Coniscliffe Road
Darlington
Co. Durham DL3 7RP
0325 462811
DIRECTOR: J V Ropner (Managing)

Rosebury Developments Limited

328 Upper Street
London N1 2XQ

Rosehaugh plc

9 Marylebone Lane
London W1M 5FB
Tel: 071-486 7100 Fax: 071-486 7600
(Sept 1992)
NATURE OF BUSINESS: Development & Investment
DIRECTORS: G M Bradman FCA (Chairman); S Adams FCA; R A Green AIB; T J Nardecchia OBE BSc FRICS (Non-Executive); K Tracey (Marketing); I M Rowberry BSc FRICS; R Howson LLB; T P Amos BSc MCIOB; A Ashendon BSc FRICS; C M J Forshaw FCA; A J Cray; G C Johnson MA; P D Rivlin BA ACMA
ANNUAL TURNOVER: £78.7m (1988)
VALUE OF PROPERTY PORTFOLIO: £253m (1988)
SUBSIDIARY COMPANIES: Baxtergate Investments Company Limited; Applied Property Research Limited; Cardwool Limited; Church Street Reality Inc; General Funds Investment Trust plc; Home for Life plc; Pelham Homes Limited; Pelham Homes (Whitely Park) Limited; Rosehaugh Co-Partnership Investments Limited; Rosehaugh Co-Partnership Developments Limited; Rosehaugh Estates plc; Rosehaugh Heritage plc; Rosehaugh Management Services Limited; Shearwater Property Holdings plc; London Mercantile Holdings Limited; Rosehaugh Project Services plc
RELATED COMPANIES: Rosehaugh Greycoat Estates Holdings Limited; London Regeneration Consortium plc; Rosehaugh Stanhope Developments (Holdings) plc; Shearwater Estates plc; Kerrykey Limited; Hartstreet Properties Limited; Rosehaugh Associated Ports Developments plc; RAPD Horsham Limited; Blue Water Park plc; Newcastle Quayside Developments plc; Chafford Hundred plc
(Jan 1991)

Rosethay Securities (UK) Limited

23 Conduit Street
LONDON W1R

Ross, James Homes

Orbital House
85-87 Croydon Road
Caterham
Surrey CR3 6PD
0883 340711/4
DIRECTOR: R McMillan (Managing)

Rotch Properties Group

7th Floor
Leconfield House
Curzon Street
London W1Y 7FB
071-409 1055
DIRECTOR: R Tchenquiz (Managing)

Rothal-Court Limited

17 Station Road
Hinckley
Leicestershire LE10 1AW

Rothesay Securities UK Limited

23 Conduit Street
Mayfair
London W1R 9TB
071-233 5122

Rothschild Asset Management Limited

Five Arrows House
PO Box 528
St Swithins Lane
London EC4N 8NR
Tel: 071-280 5000 Fax: 071-929 1643
NATURE OF BUSINESS: Development & Investment
DIRECTORS: T F H King FRICS (property only); W Ramsay (Marketing)
DEVELOPMENT/INVESTMENT POLICY: Offices, shops, warehouses

REGIONAL PREFERENCES: Southern half UK
VALUE OF CLIENTS PROPERTY PORTFOLIO: £140m
PROPERTY PORTFOLIO: Offices 60%; shops 25%; warehouses 15%
DEVELOPMENT ACTIVITIES: Offices 100%

Rover Estates

Rover House
11 Maddox Street
London W1R 9LE
Tel: 071-491 0003 Fax: 071-493 6641
DIRECTOR: R Cox (Managing)

Rowan Limited

Altay House
86 High Road
London N12 8QA
081-524 0923

Rowlinson Development Limited

17 Bourdon Place
London W1X

Rowlinson Securities plc

London House
London Road, Poynton
South Cheshire SK12 1YP
Tel: 0625 877177 Fax: 0625 879995
NATURE OF BUSINESS: Development, Investment & Construction
DIRECTORS: P J Rowlinson (Chairman & Managing); N K Rawlings; P M Rowlinson;
MAJOR SHAREHOLDERS: P M Rowlinson; P J Rowlinson; W J Rowlinson; Midland Bank Trust Company Limited; Sun Life Assurance Society plc; Omega Trust & Finance Limited
ANNUAL PROFIT: £2.1m (1989)
VALUE OF PROPERTY PORTFOLIO: £35m (1989)
DEVELOPMENT/INVESTMENT POLICY: Acquiring further property investments. Disposing of surplus land. Strengthening London property development. Expanding building contracting
SUBSIDIARY COMPANIES: Rowlinson Constructions Limited; Rowlinson Investments Limited; Rowlinson Developments Limited; Willowmead Estates (Prestbury); Sanctioned Securities Limited; North West Plant Hire Limited; Rowlinson Securities (Group Services) Limited (Sept 1992)

Roy Properties

17 Roy Square
Narrow Street
London E14
071-538 4440

Royal Developments Limited

8 Wimpole Street
London W1M 7AB
071-493 3149
DIRECTOR: C Warren (Managing)

Royal Victoria Dock Development Partnership

35 Dover Street
London W1X

Royco Group Limited

Royco House
Liston Road, Marlow
Buckinghamshire SL7 1BX
0628 486922
DIRECTOR: R Clark (Managing); L Ashcroft (Marketing)

RTZ Estates

Admiral Office
Historic Dockyard
Chatham
Kent ME4 4JQ

Rugby Estates plc

103/105 Jermyn Street
St James's
London SW1Y 6NA
Tel: 071-839 1255 Fax: 071-839 6166
DIRECTOR: D Tye (Managing)

Rugby Estates & Country Estates

St Allum Lane
Elstree
Hertfordshire WD6 3NG

Rushcliffe Development

Tudor House
13-15 Rectory Road
West Bridgeford
Notts NG2 6BE
0602 455300
DIRECTOR: N A Dunn (Managing)

Rutland Group Limited, The

11 Upper Brook Street
London W1Y 1PB
Tel: 071-499 1124/6616 Fax: 071-408 1459
NATURE OF BUSINESS: Property Investors and Developers
DIRECTORS: J A McAllister; R T H Helby; The Earl of Liverpool; W A Oliver; A R Wardle
MAJOR SHAREHOLDERS: Directors
REGIONAL PREFERENCES: Throughout UK
PORTFOLIO VALUE: £65m (1992)
REGIONAL OFFICES: Glasgow, Hounslow
PORTFOLIO DISTRIBUTION: London/SE 60%; Scotland 40%
INVESTMENT POLICY: High yielding Commercial/ Industrial Investments
DISTRIBUTION ACTIVITIES: London/SE 95% Scotland 5%
DEVELOPMENT POLICY: Longer term strategic opportunities. Industrial/Office trading opportunities
SUBSIDIARY COMPANIES: Rutland Group Developments Limited; Rutland Group Services Limited; Rutland Holdings Limited; Rutland Management Limited; Rutland Hall Limited; Rutland (Investments) Limited; Rutland (Developments) Ltd. (Sept 1992)

Rutland Trust Plc
Rutland House
Rutland Gardens
London SW7 1BX
MANAGING DIRECTOR: M Langdon
MARKETING MANAGERESS: S Holgate

Rycote Holdings Limited
The Coach House
Green End House
Rickfords Hill
Aylesbury
Buckinghamshire HP20 2RX
Tel: 0296 87264 Fax: 0296 392134
Commercial Property Developers and Investors
DIRECTORS: T J Bedford MBE BA(Hons) (Chairman) M R Lawrence BSc FRICS FRVA (Managing Director) I P Mcleish (Finance), M K Sandberg
MAJOR SHAREHOLDERS: M R Lawrence
REGIONAL PREFERENCES: Central Southern England
ANNUAL INCOME TURNOVER: £10m (1990) (Group)
VALUE OF PROPERTY PORTFOLIO: £8m (1990)
PROPERTY PORTFOLIO: Offices 85%; shops 15%
INVESTMENT POLICY: Expansion of portfolio primarily through own developments.
DEVELOPMENT ACTIVITIES: Offices 85%; shops 15%
DEVELOPMENT POLICY: Well located town centre sites preferred.
SUBSIDIARY COMPANIES: Rycote Property Company Limited; Rycote Developments Limited; Rycote Developments (Oxford) Ltd;

Ryde International plc
Metro House
58 St James's Street
London SW1A 1LD
071-493 6356
NATURE OF BUSINESS: Development
DIRECTORS: B W Rainbow; H Hine FCA; J O Strudwick
SUBSIDIARY COMPANIES: Ryde Finance Corporation Limited (equity finance company through joint venture)

S & D Properties Group
7 Dalmeny Street
Edinburgh EH6

S & S Homes Limited
Kingsbridge House
702 South Seventh Street
Central Milton Keynes
Buckinghamshire MK9 2PJ
Tel: 0908 692323 Fax: 0908 691094
DIRECTORS: J T Williams (Chairman); C C Newham (Joint Managing); G J Stewart (Joint Managing); M P O'Shea; C J Gammons P S Staden BA ACA; M G Noble ACMA & Company Secretary

S C Properties
110 St Martin's Lane
London WC2N 4PJ
Tel: 071-930 1873 Fax: 071-839 7245
MAJOR SHAREHOLDER: Shimuzu Corporation

Safeland plc
42 Hendon Lane
Finchley
London N3 1TT
Tel: 081-349 9090 Fax: 081-444 9919
(Sept 1992)
NATURE OF BUSINESS: Development & Investment
DIRECTORS: E L S R Lipman
MAJOR SHAREHOLDERS: Safeguard Holdings Corp
ANNUAL GROSS INCOME/TURNOVER: £18.2m (1989)
REGIONAL PREFERENCES: Greater London; Hertfordshire; Surrey; Gloucester
INVESTMENT POLICY: Secondary retail and all residential countrywide
VALUE OF PROPERTY PORTFOLIO: £3.37m (1989)
SUBSIDIARY COMPANIES: Safeland Investments Limited
BRANCH OFFICES: London
(Jan 1991)

Safeway Properties
PO Box 8
6 Millington Road
Hayes
Middlesex UB3 4AZ
081-848 8744
DIRECTOR: K R Wyatt (Managing)

Salamander Property Group Limited
29 Catherine Place
London SW1E 6DY
071-821 1775
NATURE OF BUSINESS: Development & Investment
DIRECTORS: A R Lewis FCA ATII; N H Dearsly BSc FRICS; M J Flanders BSC FRICS; N J Gerrett FRICS; R A Brooks FCIB (Non-Executive)
MAJOR SHAREHOLDERS: Executive Directors; Kleinwort Benson Investment Management Limited; Trycourt Financial Holdings
ANNUAL TURNOVER: £3m (1987)
REGIONAL PREFERNCES: S E England
VALUE OF PROPERTY PORTFOLIO: £10m (1988)
INVESTMENT POLICY: Acquisitive
DEVELOPMENT POLICY: Acquisitive
SUBSIDIARY COMPANIES: Numerous

Salmon Developments Limited
82 Mount Street
London W1
071-499 4378
DIRECTOR: D Baird (Managing Director)

Samar Developments Ltd
Bath Lane
Leicester LE3 5BA
0533 625000

Samara Properties
9/11 Hyde Park Road
Leeds

Sampson Properties plc
60 Pembroke Road
London W8

Sanar Developments
Bath Lane
Leicester
Leicestershire LE3 5BA
0533 625000

Sand Aire Developments
5/10 Bury Street
London EC3A 5AT
Tel: 071-929 5566 Fax: 071-929 5533
NATURE OF BUSINESS: Property Investment & Development
MAJOR SHAREHOLDERS: Provincial Group plc
ANNUAL INCOME/TURNOVER: Group £500m Company £1.0m
REGIONAL PREFERENCES: U.K.
VALUE OF PORTFOLIO: £7.0 m (1991)
DISTRUBUTION OF PORTFOLIO: Industrial 40%; Offices 40%; Retail 20%
INVESTMENT POLICY: Conservative
DISTRIBUTION OF DEVELOPMENT ACTIVITIES: Offices 80%; Retail 20%
DEVELOPMENT POLICY: To be consistant with investment policy - opportunist within policy parameters

Sandover Properties Limited
58a St Lane
Leeds

Sapcote Group plc
87 Camden Street
Birmingham
West Midlands B1 3DE
Tel: 021-233 1200 Fax: 021-236 8682
(Sept 1992)
NATURE OF BUSINESS: Development
DIRECTORS: S W Sapcote (Chairman); J R Blake BSc FCIOB FASI (Chief Executive); R C Blake BSc MCIOB MASI; R C K Holloway MCIOB (Property); P E Judge MCIOB FASI
MAJOR SHAREHOLDERS: S W Sapcote; J R Blake
ANNUAL TURNOVER/INCOME/PROFIT: £40m (1989)
REGIONAL PREFERENCES: London, Home Counties, South East and Midlands
INVESTMENT POLICY: We are seeking part let properties which can be sub-divided and part sold off
DEVELOPMENT ACTIVITIES: offices 10%; factories 40%; warehouses 40%
DEVELOPMENT POLICY: We are seeking refurbishment projects in the industrial, commercial and office fields
SUBSIDIARY COMPANIES: William Sapcote & Sons Limited; William Sapcote Development Limited; Harricks (Birmingham) Limited; Cramb & Dean (London) Limited
(Jan 1991)

Sasson Developments Limited
65 Newman Street
London W1P

Sato Kogyo Co Limited
Suite 106
Princes House
36 Jermyn Street
London SW1Y

Saturnbridge Limited
3 Maida Avenue
London W2

Saunderson Holdings
Saunderson House
8 Hayne Street
London EC1A 9HH
Tel: 071-315 6500 Fax: 071-315 6550
DIRECTOR: D Saunderson

Saville, J Group Estates plc
Saville Gordon House
4 Wharfedale Road
Tyseley
Birmingham B11 2SB

Scammell Securities plc
Scammell House
High Street
Ascot
Berkshire SL5 7JF
Tel: 0344 28555 Fax: 0344 26141
DIRECTORS: P J Scammell. A H Scammell
MAJOR SHAREHOLDERS: P J Scammell
ANNUAL INCOME/TURNOVER: Group £10m
REGIONAL PREFERENCE: South East England
PORTFOLIO VALUE: £4m (1990)
INVESTMENT POLICY: Offices

Scandinavian Developments Limited
196A Cromwell Road
London SW5
071-259 2519

Scanscot Properties Limited
43 Ellen's Glen Road
Edinburgh EH17

Schroder Properties Limited
Regina House
5 Queen Street
London EC4N 1SP
Tel: 071-382 6000 Fax: 071-382 3960
(Sept 1992)
NATURE OF BUSINESS: Development & Investment
DIRECTOR: A D Strang BSc FRICS
MAJOR SHAREHOLDERS: Schroders plc
DEVELOPMENT POLICY: Direct development, joint ventures or prelet traditional funding
INVESTMENT POLICY: Particularly industrial and retail sectors; the properties must perform well either through market movement or active management

Entry missing ? Call HELPLINE Page v

VALUE OF PROPERTY PORTFOLIO: £180m (1990)
PROPERTY PORTFOLIO: Offices 38%; Industrial 35%; Shops 27%
(Jan 1991)

Scott Enterprise
233 Westbourne Grove
London W11

Scottish Homes
Thistle House
91 Haymarket Terrace
Edinburgh EH12 5HE
Tel: 031-313 0044 Fax: 031-313 2680

Scottish Metropolitan Property PLC
Royal Exchange House
100 Queen Street
Glasgow G1 3DL
Tel: 041-248 7333 Fax: 041-221 1196
NATURE OF BUSINESS: Property Investment
DIRECTORS: D Walton CStJ JP LLD Hon FRCPS (Glasg) (Chairman); A H Thomson CA (Financial); Prof R B Jack CSt MA LLB; J H Forbes Macpherson CBE OStJ CA; D Malcom MA FCII; N E Shepherd MA; J S Cairns BA FRICS
ANNUAL TURNOVER/INCOME/PROFIT: £19.5m (1991)
REGIONAL PREFERENCES: Scotland & North England
VALUE OF PROPERTY PORTFOLIO: £337m (1991)
PROPERTY PORTFOLIO: Shops 35%; Offices 55%; Industrial 10%
INVESTMENT POLICY: Commercial and industrial in UK
SUBSIDIARY COMPANIES: Aberdeen Heritable Securities & Investment Company Limited; Achnacree Investment Company Limited; Arthur Square Properties Limited (Reg in Northern Ireland); Cilix Investment Company Limited (Reg in England); G J McDowall & Company Limited; Scottish Metropolitan Lands & Investments Company Limited; Northrents Limited; The Scottish Lands & Buildings Company Limited; The Scottish Metropolitan Property Company (Edinburgh) Limited; The Scottish Metropolitan Property Company (Guarantees) Limited; The Scottish Metropolitan Property Company (Securities) Limited; Span Estates Limited; Union Investment Company Limited; Waltons Heritable Assets Limited; Waltons Property Holdings (Glasgow) Limited; The Whytehouse Estate Company Limited
(Sept 1992)

Sears Property Developments Ltd
Wembley Road
Leicester LE3 1UT
0533 31466
DIRECTOR: R Groom (Managing)

Sears Retail Properties Ltd
Wembley Road
Leicester LE3 1UT
0533 314666
DIRECTOR: R Groom (Managing)

Sears Property Developments Ltd
51 High Street
Wetherby
W Yorks LS22 4LR
Tel: 0937 580686 Fax: 0937 580659

Seaward plc
Drayton House
Chichester
West Sussex PO20 6EW
Tel: 0243 778800 Fax: 0243 776963
(Sept 1992)
NATURE OF BUSINESS: Development & Investment
DIRECTORS: B H D Sampson FCA; N T Fee BSc; H G Bridgewater ACA; J A Coombes ARICS DipTP
MAJOR SHAREHOLDERS: B H D Sampson
BRANCH OFFICES: Canterbury
ANNUAL TURNOVER/INCOME/PROFIT: £22m (1989)
REGIONAL PREFERENCES: South and South East
INVESTMENT POLICY: Long term site assembly and small portfolio acquisition
DEVELOPMENT ACTIVITIES: offices 10%; shops 10%; factories & warehouses 10%; residential 70%
DEVELOPMENT POLICY: Expansion throughout South East of commercial and residential
SUBSIDIARY COMPANIES: Seaward Properties Limited; Townscape Homes Limited; Seaward Homes Limited
(Jan 1991)

Secure Retirement plc
25 Whatley Road
Clifton
Bristol
Avon BS18 2PS

Seddon Estates
Park House
Parkway
Holmes Chapel, Nr Crewe
Cheshire WC4 8NU
0477 34422
DIRECTOR: A Brown (Managing)

Sedgebrook plc
Elizabeth House
13-19 London Road
Newbury
Berkshire RG13 1JL
Tel: 0635 524074 Fax: 0635 529105
BUSINESS: Commercial Developers
DIRECTOR: A L G Hedges (Managing)

Sedgwick Group Properties Limited
The Sedgwick Centre
10 Whitechapel High Street
London E1 8DX
071-377 3456
MARKETING DIRECTOR: T Kendrick

Sedley Properties Limited
121 Gloucester Place
London W1H 3PJ
071-486 2486
DIRECTOR: P J Allan (Managing)

Selective Construction Projects Plc
107 Jermyn Street
London SW1Y 6EE
071-930 2415
DIRECTOR: M Jerrow (Managing)

Sellwell Properties Limited
67 Grove Hall
Court Mall
London NW8

Shaftesbury plc
11 Waterloo Place
London SW1Y 4AU
071-839 4024
DIRECTORS: Peter Levy; Jonathon Lane (Managing)
ANNUAL TURNOVER: £2.43m (1988)
VALUE OF PROPERTY PORTFOLIO: £46.95m (1988)

Shanks & McEwan
22 Woodside Place
Glasgow G3 7QY
041-331 2614
DIRECTOR: M A Hewitt (Managing)

Sheafbank Properties Trust Plc
St Anns House
St Anns Place
Manchester M2 7LP
061-832 2663
DIRECTOR: D Gradel (Managing)

Shearwater Property Holdings plc
9 Marylebone Lane
London W1M 5FB
071-491 0906
DIRECTOR: D Shaw

Shellbridge Holdings Limited
Well Croft, Market Square
Shipley
West Yorkshire BD18 3QH
Tel: 0274 595039 Fax: 0274 531593
DIRECTORS: T M Duggan FGS FCPS MRSH CGLI (Chairman); P Duggan MRSH CGLI
MAJOR SHAREHOLDERS: Directors
REGIONAL PREFERENCES: West Yorkshire
PROPERTY PORTFOLIO: Shops/Offices 50%; Industrial/Business Parks 50%
DEVELOPMENT ACTIVITIES: Offices 50%; shops 15%; factories 35%
SUBSIDIARY COMPANIES: Shellbridge Limited; Thomas Duggan Limited; Vendatrust Limited; Shellbridge Pension Fund, Knotford Nook Country Club Limited; Duggan Bros Peroperties Ltd; Shipley Squash Club
(Sept 1992)

Shenewood Properties Limited
220 High Street North
East Ham
London E6 2JA
081-471 1678

Shepherd Development Company Limited
Prudential House
Blossom Street, York
North Yorkshire YO2 2AQ
Tel: 0904 659361 Fax: 0904 610817
DIRECTORS: Sir Peter Shepherd CBE DL DSc DUniv FCIOB CBIM; D W Shepherd FCIOB CBIM; C S Shepherd FCIOB FBIM; C M Branchette
MAJOR SHAREHOLDERS: Shepherd Building Group Limited
DEVELOPMENT ACTIVITIES: Offices 20%; shops 70%; factories/warehouses 10%
(Sept 1992)

Shepherd Homes Limited
89 The Mount
York
North Yorkshire YO2 2AX
0904 653040

Shepperton Properties Limited
6B High Street
Shepperton
Middlesex TW17 9AW
09322 25340

Sheraton Securities International plc
Leconfield House
Curzon Street
London W1Y 7FB
Tel: 071-629 4049 Fax 071-491 2735
NATURE OF BUSINESS: Development & Investment
DIRECTORS: P Taylor FRICS (Managing Director); J F Trapp FCA; R M Cox-Johnson (Chairman, Non-Executive); N B M Kittoe; J L Greenwood BSc (Est Man)
ANNUAL TURNOVER/INCOME/PROFIT: £2.43m (1989)
VALUE OF PROPERTY PORTFOLIO: £22.07m (1988)
SUBSIDIARY COMPANIES: Sheraton UK Limited; Sheraton USA Inc; Sheraton Investment Porperties Limited; Ballint Properties Limited; Dickerage Properties Limited; International Hotel Developments Limited; Old Temple Developments Limited; Weald Investments Limited; Gordon Property Investment Co; Caversham Bridge Group Limited; Caversham Build Limited; Rickworth Securities Limited; IHD Amsterdam Limited; IHD Flanders NV; IHD Netherland BV
RELATED COMPANIES: Sheraton JT Limited; Sheraton Caltrust plc; Caltrust Limited; Malvern Property Company plc; Edinburgh Development Group plc; Kinfield Limited

Sheraton St James Limited
81 Walton Street
London SW3

Sheridan Estates Limited
16 Sheridan Road
London SW19 3HP
081-542 6489
CHAIRMAN: D P Hearsum

Shield Group plc
PO Box 2117
London NW3 7RQ
071-433 3233
NATURE OF BUSINESS: Property Development
DIRECTORS: N R Mazure (Chairman); B.J. Markeson (Finance); A Rubin (Chief Executive); B J Emden (Non Exec)
MAJOR SHAREHOLDERS: R J Herd; Mars Security Limited; Prudential Assurance; N R Mazure; A R Rubin
ANNUAL TURNOVER: £7.5m (Group 1990)
REGIONAL PREFERENCES: Greater London and Home Counties
VALUE OF PROPERTY PORTFOLIO: £15m (1990)
DISTRIBUTION OF DEVELOPMENT ACTIVITIES: Residential 90%
DEVELOPMENT POLICY: Quality residential development
SUBSIDIARY COMPANIES: Shield Industrial Properties Limited

Shimizu Corporation
110 St Martin's Lane
London WC2N 4PJ
071-930 1873
DIRECTOR: H Uchida (Managing)

Shop & Store Developments Limited
Burley House, Bradford Road
Burley in Wharfdale
Ilkley
West Yorkshire LS29 7DZ
0943 864333
NATURE OF BUSINESS: Development
DIRECTORS: R B Kilty BSc (Hons) Est Man FRICS; G B Greenwood; S W Urry LLB FCA; D B Greenwood; M J Jenkins FFS; D J Parker BA ACA
REGIONAL PREFERENCES: Throughout England and Wales
DEVELOPMENT ACTIVITIES: Shops 100%
DEVELOPMENT POLICY: Shops ranging from single unit refurbishments to town centre schemes
SUBSIDIARY COMPANIES: Shop & Store Properties Limited

Shops & Properties Investments Limited
48 East Street
London SE17

Silver Estates Limited
11 Crescent Parade
Uxbridge Road
Hillingdon
Middlesex UB10 0LG
0895 234877
NATURE OF BUSINESS: Property & Investment
(Sept 1992)

DIRECTORS: A M Smith (Managing); N A Chalmers CA; R B Twinch
REGIONAL PREFERENCES: South
VALUE OF PROPERTY PORTFOLIO: £4m (1990)
(Jan 1991)

Silverman Group of Companies
91 Regent Street
London W1R

Silvermist Properties (Chelmsford) Limited
Fairacres
Stock Lane
Ingatestone
Essex CM4 9QL
0277 353171
DIRECTOR: G R Keen (Managing)

Simand Investments Limited
36 Ivor Place
Baker Street
London NW1 6EA
Tel: 071-724 3336 Fax: 071-723 6769
DIRECTOR: Adrew Ellinas LLB
NATURE OF BUSINESS: Property Investment
ANNUAL INCOME/TURNOVER: Company £5m
REGIONAL PREFERENCES FOR ACTIVITIES: Anywhere in U.K.
VALUE OF PORTFOLIO: £15m
DISTRIBUTION OF PORTFOLIO: Retail £11m (80%); Offices £1m (5%); Industrial £3m (15%)
INVESTMENT POLICY: Primary investment requirement, secondary parades of shops.
(Sept 1992)

Simon Hawthorn Property (Europe) Limited
3 Queen's Gate Mews
London SW7

Simons Property Limited
Beech House
Witham Park
Waterside South
Lincoln LN5 7JP
0522 510000
NATURE OF BUSINESS: Development & Investment
DIRECTORS: P D Hodgkinson (Managing); A L Pickering FRICS; H M Brooks; G M Walter ARICS
MAJOR SHAREHOLDERS: Simon Group Limited 100%.
REGIONAL PREFERENCES: Cathedral/market towns, Midlands, East Anglia and North of England
DEVELOPMENT/INVESTMENT POLICY: Active
PROPERTY PORTFOLIO: Shops 40%; factories/ warehouses 20%; residential 20%; offices 20%
DEVELOPMENT ACTIVITIES: Shops 100%
SUBSIDIARY COMPANIES: Simon Lincoln Securities

Simons Property Limited
Beech House
Witham Park
Waterside South
Lincoln LN5 9JP
Tel: 0522 514513 Fax: 0522 521164

Singer & Friedlander Limited

21 New Street
Bishopsgate
London EC2M 4HR
071-623 3000
NATURE OF BUSINESS: Investment
DIRECTORS: A N Solomons (Chairman & Chief Executive); B H Buckley (Deputy Chairman); A G O Walker (Deputy Chairman); R C Callinan; Sir Timothy Harford Bt; L A Coppel; R P Corbett; M S Pougatch; A R J Dyas; M E L Melluish; T S Rowan; V M Segal; P G Cordrey; B N Gorst; D C Courtman; J Hodson; M P Sutton; B D F Mansfield; R R Clough
DIRECTORS (NON-EXECUTIVE): P C Baker; P F Benton; P Brackfield; A D Chesterfield CBE; H J Clark; N C England; A Hanbury; Rt Hon Lord Lever; P Moores; K P Ney; J Renyi; Rt Hon G Rippon QC MP; M W Schubert
BRANCH OFFICES: Leeds, Birmingham, Nottingham, Glasgow, Bristol, Cambridge, Switzerland, Isle of Man
SUBSIDIARY COMPANIES: The First British American Corp Limited; Singer & Friedlander Trust & Assurance Corp Limited; Sinjul Investments Limited; Singer & Friedlander (Jersey) Limited; Singer & Friedlander (Isle of Man) Limited; Singer & Friedlander AG; Singer & Friedlander Managers Limited; Singer & Friedlander Leasing Limited; West City Securities Limited; Sinjul SA; Singer & Friedlander Investment Fund SA; Appledale Limited; Bread Street Investments Limited; Weniver Investments Limited; Hillgrove Estates Limited; Hillgrove Homes Limited; Quinarins Investments Limited; Melbreck Securities Limited; Nedcloe Investments Limited; Straker Bros Limited; Dupmead Limited; Gilbert House Investments Limited; Clarke London Limited (45%)

Sinoia Estates Limited

Phoenix House
Church Street
Bathford, Bath
Avon BA1 7RS
0225 852456
NATURE OF BUSINESS: Development & Investment
DIRECTORS: R G A Sankey HSc FSVA ARICS; K M Sankey
MAJOR SHAREHOLDERS: Directors
INVESTMENT POLICY: County towns, cathedral and market towns. Retail in secondary locations. Policy for 1988 commencement
DEVELOPMENT ACTIVITIES: Offices 2.5%; shops 97.5%
DEVELOPMENT POLICY: Retail development town centres and out of town in England and Wales

Sitac Enterprises Limited

57 Princes Gate
Exhibition Road
London SW7

Skanksa

23 Thomas More Street
London E1

Skillion plc

Swedish Gate
Baltic Quay
London SE16
071-232 1234

Sky Group of Companies plc

Crawford Mews
York Street
London W1H 1PT
Tel: 071-258 3998 Fax: 071 724 2044
NATURE OF BUSINESS: Property Development & Investment
DIRECTORS: M Rose BSc ARICS ASVA; J Rose; A Eves; E Robson BA
ANNUAL INCOME/TURNOVER: Group £8m
REGIONAL PREFERENCES: U.K.
PROPERTY PORTFOLIO: Offices 50%; shops 20%; residential 25%; other 5%
INVESTMENT POLICY: Offices and retail properties maximum investment value £10m. To show minimum of 8.5%
DEVELOPMENT ACTIVITIES: Offices 60%; residential 30%; other 10%
DEVELOPMENT POLICY: Office and studio developments generating total sale value of up to £20m. Residential development - total sale value of up to £10m (Sept 1992)

Slough Estates plc

234 Bath Road
Slough
Berkshire SL1 4EE
Tel: 0753 537171 Fax: 0753 820585
NATURE OF BUSINESS: Industrial and Commercial Property Development, Construction and Investment, The Supply of Utility Services
DIRECTORS: Executive: Sir Nigel Mobbs DL; R W Carey; D R Wilson; D E F Simons; H L Thomson.
MAJOR SHAREHOLDERS: R W Diggens (5.44%); Schreder Investments (3.85%); Morgan Stanley (3.05%); Philips & Drew (3.06%); C Heather, W Mackenzie, S Turner & M D Wilcox (7.74%).
ANNUAL TURNOVER: £128.5m
(Sept 1992)
SISTER COMPANIES: Bredero Properties plc; (49.5%) London & Paris Property Group; Property Equity Fund Ltd.
Services: Slough Estates Administration Limited; Slough Estates Finance plc; Slough Estates Luxembourg SA (Incorporated and operating in Luxembourg) Joint Venture Partnership: SDK Industrial Parks (USA) (80%) Associates: 33 West Monroe Associates (USA) (25%); Charterhouse Group International plc (USA) (20%); London & Paris Property Group plc (20%); Pentagon developments (Chatham) Limited (50%)
BRANCH OFFICES: London; Australia - Melbourne; Belgium - Woluwe; Canada - Mississauga; USA - Chicago, France - Paris; Germany - Dusseldorf.
VALUE OF PROPERTY PORTFOLIO: £1.656m (1991)
PROPERTY PORTFOLIO: UK: offices 7.8%; shops 2.7%; warehouses 21.8%; industrial 67.7% Overseas: offices 18.27%; retail 3.84%; industrial 77.88%
INVESTMENT POLICY: Industrial, warehousing, offices, retail

Entry missing ? Call HELPLINE Page v

DEVELOPMENT POLICY: Planning, design, development, ownership and management of industrial estates, offices and shopping centres in major commercial centres
(Jan 1991)

Smart, J & Co (Contractors) plc
28 Crammond Road South
Edinburgh EH4 6AB

Smithdown Group Limited
Spring Court
Spring Road
Hale
Altrincham
Cheshire WA14 2UQ
061-941 1262
MANAGING DIRECTOR: J O'Toole

Smithmann European Homes
3 Warstone Lane
Hockley
Birmingham B18 8JE

SOL Construction
Vale Road
Colwick
Notts NG4 2EG
0602 613100
DIRECTORS: A Whiteside (Managing); P Hughes (Marketing)

Solar Enterprises
21 Gate Hill Court
Notting Hill Gate
London W11

Somerset Properties
24 Sandyford Place
Glasgow G3 7NG

Sotra Property Co Limited
10 Sedley Place
London W1R

South Bank Estates Limited
Camelford House
87 Albert Embankment
London SE1

South Bank Homes (Construction)
Regency House
1 Albion Street
Lewes
East Sussex BN7 2ND
0273 478061
DIRECTOR: N Lock (Sales)

South Eastern Recovery Ass'd Homes plc
31 Sackville Street
London W1X

Southbrook Limited
33/37 Bell Street
London NW1

Southdale Properties Limited
2 Neville Avenue
New Malden
Surrey
081-949 6026

Southend Property Holdings plc
1 Dancastle Court
Arcadia Avenue
London N3 2JU
Tel: 081-458 8833 Fax: 081-458 1138
NATURE OF BUSINESS: Development & Investment
DIRECTORS: M Dagul (Chairman & Managing Director); L S Lebor FRICS; J J W R Main; A Nathan (Non Executive)
MAJOR SHAREHOLDERS: Shop Constructions
ANNUAL TURNOVER: £68.7m (1989)
DEVELOPMENT POLICY: The principal activities of the company are that of property investment and acting as an investing holding company.
SUBSIDIARY COMPANIES: Brimelyn Ltd; Curtin Mining NL; Drancourt Properties Ltd; Envalymn Ltd; H T A Pty Ltd; Hampton Health Care plc; H T Oil & Gas Ltd; Masonplan Ltd; Masonplan Securities Ltd; Mt Martin Gold Mines NL; Oil Ventures Pty Ltd; Oldbrook Estates Ltd; Pilonlymn Ltd; Tarravle Eastern Ltd; Toftplan Properties Ltd; Southend Property Management Ltd
NON-TRADING Hampton Retirement Homes PLC.
(Sept 1992)

Southern & City Developments Limited
17 Grosvenor Street
London W1X 9FD
Tel: 071-629 1593 Fax: 071-491 4849
NATURE OF BUSINESS: Development
DIRECTORS: A M Watts FRICS; R Jowett FSCA
(Sept 1992)
MAJOR SHAREHOLDERS: Directors
BRANCH OFFICES: Bruton, Somerset
REGIONAL PREFERENCES: Offices - South and West England; shops - throughout UK
DEVELOPMENT ACTIVITIES: offices 40%; shops 60%
DEVELOPMENT POLICY: We are at present undertaking shop and office developments throughout the South of England and South Wales. Schemes range in size from £0.6m to £8.5m
SUBSIDIARY COMPANIES: Southern & City Group Limited; Southern & City (Project Management) Limited
(Jan 1991)

Southwestern Shop & Office Investments Limited
No 6, 27 St James's Street
London SW1 1HA
071-930 2244
DIRECTOR: C A Cyzer (Managing)

Sovereign Land
81 Grosvenor Street
London W1X 9DE
071-491 3682
DIRECTORS: T Binnington; G Newman

Space Interspace Limited
20 Dock Street
London E1

Speciality Shops plc
11-13 Knightsbridge
London SW1X 7LY
Tel: 071-235 6070 Fax: 071-235 2646
NATURE OF BUSINESS: Development & Investment
DIRECTORS: P L Goldie; D J Houghton; S R Jaffe; M H Feeney; J Garlick; S McLean; S McDonald; R Richards
MAJOR SHAREHOLDERS: Canada Life Assurance Co; London & Edinburgh Trust plc; London & Manchester Group plc
ANNUAL TURNOVER: £5.8m (1988)
VALUE OF PROPERTY PORTFOLIO: £30m (1988)
INVESTMENT POLICY: Main activity is the identification, development and management of speciality shopping centres in all parts of the country
DEVELOPMENT POLICY: Property development activity undertaken anywhere in the UK in all sectors of the market

Spellhoe Estates Limited
Fisher House
6 Castillian Terrace
Northampton NN11 1JX

Spen Hill Properties
ANA House
6-8 Old Bond Street
London W1X 3TA
Tel: 071-495 0865 Fax: 071-499 1495
(Sept 1992)
DIRECTOR: P Mercer (Managing)
(Jan 1991)

Speyhawk Land & Estates Limited
Osprey House
Lower Square
Old Isleworth
Middlesex TW7 6BN
Tel: 081-560 2161 Fax: 081-568 8097
(Sept 1992)
NATURE OF BUSINESS: Development
DIRECTORS: T Osborne FRICS (Chairman); B Shrubsall FCIOB FFB (Vice-Chairman); R Burgess FCA; A Whitehorn BSc (Managing) FRICS; C Kennedy FRICS; S Short CEng MICE; R Maxted BA(Hons) FRICS; B Ashby; J Carter
MAJOR SHAREHOLDERS: British Airways Pension Trustees Limited
ANNUAL TURNOVER/INCOME/PROFIT: £77.8m (1988)
VALUE OF PROPERTY PORTFOLIO: £24.5m (1988)
SUBSIDIARY COMPANIES: Speyhawk Land & Estates Limited; Speyhawk (Maidenhead) Limited; Speyhawk Retirement Homes Limited; Speyhawk New York Corporation; Good Luck Limited; Guidefront Limited; Speyhawk NV; Allstate Realty Inc; Speyhawk Mount Row Limited; Carter Holdings Limited; Carter Commercial Developments Limited; Speyhawk Estates Limited; Speyhawk Hotels Limited; McMurdo Webb Limited Insurance Brokers; The Osprey Management Company Limited Property Management; Speyhawk Investments Limited; Speyhawk Securities Limited; Speyhawk Development Management Limited; Tellings Limited
(Jan 1991)

Spiralmoor Limited
69 Upper Berkeley Street
London W1H

Spitalfields Development Group
Bishops Court
Artillery Lane
London E1
071-377 1496

Spitaman Limited
80 Northend House
Fitzjames Avenue
London W14

Sports & Leisure Development
The Ice Bowl
Ambly Road
Gillingham Business Park
Gillingham
Kent ME8 0PP
0634 376800
MANAGING DIRECTOR: Dr D Price

Springvale Property Holdings
2 South Audley Street
London W1Y

St Andrews Land
111 Park Road
London NW8
071-262 3223

St Andrew's Trust plc
29 Charlotte Square
Edinburgh EH2 4HA
031-225 3811
DIRECTORS: J Scott-Plummer; M Kennedy
INVESTMENT MANAGER: M Curry

Entry missing ? Call HELPLINE Page v

St George Estates Limited
1st Floor
Arkwright House
Parsonage Gardens
Manchester M3

St George plc
St George House
The Green
Twickenham
Middlesex TW2 5AG

St George's Securities
6 Bedford Square
London
WC1B 3RA
071-631 3329
NATURE OF BUSINESS: Development & Investment
DIRECTORS: P A Waddington ARICS (Managing); D Whiting

St Giles Estates
Arkwright House
Parsonage Gardens
Manchester M3 2LE
061-8320219
DIRECTOR: A Gradel (Managing)

St James's Street Group
No 4, 27 St James's Street
London SW1A 1HA
071-839 6726
DIRECTOR: A Gordon-James (Managing); P Croysdill

St James Securities
6 Lisbon Square
Leeds LS1 4LY
0532 430231
DIRECTOR: R Stroff(Managing)

St John's Wood Estate Limited
39 Bruton Place
Berkeley Square
London W1X 7AB
071-491 4566
DIRECTOR: S Goldberg (Managing)

St Katharine by the Tower Limited
Ivory House
St Katharine by the Tower
London E1 9AT
071-488 2400
NATURE OF BUSINESS: Development & Investment
DIRECTORS: P R L Drew OBE (Chairman & Managing); J Topping FRICS (Deputy Chairman); D J Frudd ARICS (Marketing); Lady Taylor; A L Strachan CBE BSc (Est Man) FRICS; J Wolkind CBE LLM (Managing); S D Goodenough RICS Dip Proj Man; The Lord Taylor of Hatfield; C J Leamy FSCA (Secretary); K D Taylor; The Rt Hon Lord Bellwin JP LLB
MAJOR SHAREHOLDERS: Taylor Woodrow plc
VALUE OF PROPERTY PORTFOLIO: £225m (1989)
PROPERTY PORTFOLIO: Offices 80%; shops 5%; residential 10%; leisure 5%
INVESTMENT POLICY: Consolidation
DEVELOPMENT POLICY: Expansion
TYPES OF DEVELOMENT UNDERTAKEN: Offices 85%; residential 15%
SUBSIDIARY COMPANIES: More Street Management Limited; St Katharine Yacht Haven Limited; World Trade Centre in London Limited

St Lawrence Properties Limited
26a Davies Street
London W1Y

St Martins Property Corporation Limited
Adelaide House
London Bridge
London EC4 9DT
071-626 3411/7211
DIRECTORS: F M Al-Sabah (Chairman); F K Jaffar BA (Vice-Chairman); B A Dawson MA; D F Buchanan CA ACMA; L W Neal; D R Betts FCA; B L Cann FRICS (Managing); K N Al-Sabah; M E H Al-Sabah; M G Savage FRICS (Deputy Managing); A R Al-Mulla BA
EXECUTIVE DIRECTORS: C E Bellhouse FRICS; E Rippier FRICS; G Lambert FRICS; J M Durrant FRICS; A R O'Hagan TD FCA; R N Pearson BA Barrister

St Marylebone Property Company Limited
33 Warren Street
London W1P 5DI
071-383 4559

St Modwen Properties plc
Lyndon House
Hagley Road, Edgbaston
Birmingham B16 8PE
Tel: 021-456 2800 Fax: 021-456 1829
NATURE OF BUSINESS: Development & Investment
DIRECTORS: S W Clarke (Chairman & Chief Executive); C C Anthony Glossop MA (Managing Director); P E Doona BA(Hons) FCA; J D Leavesley (Non-Executive); C H Lewis FRICS FSVA (Non-Executive); C E Rosliner MA FCA (Non-Executive); Sir David Tripples RD JP MSI
ANNUAL TURNOVER: £45.11m (1991)
VALUE OF PROPERTY PORTFOLIO: £37.7m (1988)
SUBSIDIARY COMPANIES: Barton Property Investments Limited; Barton Property Investments (Northern) Limited; Blackpole Trading Estate (1978) Limited; Redman Heenan Properties Limited; St Modwen Developments Limited; Leisure Living Limited;
RELATED COMPANIES: Allied Investment & Property Holdings Limited; Clarke London Limited
(Sept 1992)

St Paul's Properties Limited
36 St Paul's Square
Birmingham B3

Stadium Developments Limited
Welton Grange
Welton, Brough
North Humberside HU15 1NB
0482 667149
DIRECTOR: Mr Healey (Managing)

Stafford Estates
26 Gillespie Road
Edinburgh EH13 ONN
031-225 9299
DIRECTOR: J Perry (Managing)

Standen Homes Limited
428 Carlton Hill
Carlton, Nottingham
0602 873121
DIRECTORS: M Dean (Managing); J Williams (Marketing)

Stangrange Limited
54/56 Euston Street
London NW1

Stanhope County Limited
135 Bishopsgate
London EC2M 3UR
Tel: 071-375 5000 Fax: 071-375 8012
DIRECTOR: John Fender
MAJOR SHAREHOLDERS: Stanhope Properties plc, County Nat West

Stanhope Properties plc
Lansdowne House
Berkeley Square
London W1X 6BP
Tel: 071-495 7575 Fax 071-495 3330/1
NATURE OF BUSINESS: Development & Investment
DIRECTORS: Lord Sharp of Grimsdyke (Chairman, Non-Executive); S Lipton (Chief Executive); J Botts (Non-Executive); S Honeyman FRICS (Non-Executive); R Jonn MA(Cantab) (Non-Executive); P Kershaw BSc ARICS; P Reichmann (Non-Executive); P Rogers BSc CEng MICE; V Wang BSc RIBA; R Dantzic (Finance Director); D Camp (Development Director)
ANNUAL TURNOVER: £4.5m (1988)
VALUE OF PROPERTY PORTFOLIO: £110.16m (1988)
SUBSIDIARY COMPANIES: Capital & Rural Properties Limited; Stanhope Construction Limited; Stanhope City Developments Limited; Rosehaugh Stanhope Developments (Holdings) plc (50%); London Regeneration Consortium plc (33.3%); Stanhope Kajima Developments Limited (50%)

Stanhope Trafalgar Chiswick Limited
Devonshire House
Mayfair Place
London W1A 3AG
MAJOR SHAREHOLDERS: Stanhope Properties plc

Stanley Properties Investment Limited
20 Stamford Street
Stalybridge
Manchester

Star Group plc
Star House
Linford Road
Chadwell St Mary
Grays
Essex RM16 4LR
0375 858844
DIRECTORS: I Drury (Chairman); C D Hartley MCIOB (Managing)
MAJOR SHAREHOLDER: Star Group plc
ANNUAL INCOME/TURNOVER: Company £8m Group 22m
REGIONAL PREFERENCE: National
VALUE OF PORTFOLIO: £10m (1990)
DISTRIBUTION OF PORTFOLIO: Hotel 50%, Industrial 50%
INVESTMENT POLICY: Established Portfolio by development and acquisition when possible.
DEVELOPMENT ACTIVITIES: Industrial 100%
DEVELOPMENT POLICY: Design and Build speculative and specific buildings, mostly warehouse and industrial
SUBSIDIARY COMPANIES: Star Groundworks, Star Plant, R W Hill Civil Engineers, R W Hill, Star Geotechnical Engineering Services, Star Waste, PPW Transport.

Steetley Industrial Associates
Bean Road
Birmingham New Road
Cosley
West Midlands DE14 9EE
0902 887644
Taken over by:
Redland Properties Limited
The Barons
Church Street
Reigate RH2 OJN
MAJOR SHAREHOLDERS: Redland plc
VALUE OF PORTFOLIO: £10m
(Sept 1992)

Stellenbosch Investment Corporation
84a Kensington High Street
London W8

Stemford Limited
70 Guildhall Buildings
Navigation Street
Birmingham B2

Stephen I Graham Partnership, The
144/146 New Bond Street
London W1Y

Sterland Leisure
5 Milner Street
Chelsea
London SW3

Entry missing ? Call HELPLINE Page v

Sterling Homes Limited
Allied House
26 Manchester Square
London W14 2HU
071-486 6080

Sterling Securities plc
6 Arlington Street
London SW1A

Stevens Properties Limited
45 Holland Park Mews
London W11

Stewart & Wright plc
24 Weymouth Mews
London W1N 3FN

Stier Homes Limited
45 St Michaels Lane
Headingley
Leeds

Stirling Construction & Development Limited
Stirling House
24 Manchester Road
Wilmslow
Cheshire
SK9 1BG
0625 531602
NATURE OF BUSINESS: Development & Investment
MAJOR SHAREHOLDERS: Stirling Management Group Ltd.
REGIONAL PREFERENCES FOR ACTIVITIES: North West England
(Sept 1992)

Stockbourne PLC
119/120 High Street Eton
Windsor
Berks SL4 6AN
0753 830155
DIRECTOR: M J Richards (Managing)

Stock Harvard Developments Limited
South Grange
Sibton
Saxmundham
Suffolk IP17 2ND
Tel: 0728 79562 Fax: 0728 79462
NATURE OF BUSINESS: Development and Development Co-ordination
DIRECTORS: R Catchpole; S Catchpole
MAJOR SHAREHOLDERS: Directors
REGIONAL OFFICES: Colchester; London
REGIONAL PREFERENCES FOR ACTIVITIES: Anywhere in U.K.
DISTRIBUTION OF DEVELOPMENT: Leisure 50%; Retail 25%; Business 25%
DEVELOPMENT POLICY: No scheme too large, local authority partnerships, town centre redevelopments, mixed leisure schemes
SUBSIDIARIES: Stock Harvard Leisure; Stock Harvard Cambridge Limited
(Sept 1992)

Stockton Estates Limited
42 Montagu Square
London W1H

Stone & Co New Homes
140 Redland Road
Redland
Bristol BS6 6YB
0272 739221
DIRECTOR: C Setter (Managing)

Stone Lime Investments Limited
3 Barclay Place
Edinburgh EH10

Stonepeter Developments Limited
228 Fulham Road
London SW10

Stonewood Securities plc
5 Commercial Street
Birmingham B1

Store Property Investments Limited
4 Churchill Court
The Street
Rustington
West Sussex BN16 2TB
Tel: 0903 783292 Fax: 0903 783294
NATURE OF BUSINESS: Development & Investment
DIRECTORS: R F Wickens FCA; J J Wickens; J V F Hobden; V L F Collyer; M R Standing MBIAT; D J S Hughes BSc ARICS; J H Smithers BSc FRICS
SISTER COMPANIES: Store Property Construction Limited.
REGIONAL PREFERENCES: Southern Counties
PROPERTY PORTFOLIO: Factories/Warehouses 50%; Retail 30%; Hi-Tec/Offices 17%; Residential 3%
INVESTMENT POLICY: Expansion of current commercial portfolio by development and direct acquisition
DEVELOPMENT ACTIVITIES: Factories/Warehouses 60%; Retail 30%; Hi-Tec/Offices 10%
DEVELOPMENT POLICY: Expansion of current programme in the B1/B8 and out of town retail sectors.

Storehouse plc
The Heal's Building
196 Tottenham Court Road
London W1P OES
071-631 0101
DIRECTOR: M Julien (Managing)

Strathedin Properties Limited
2 St Margarets Road
Edinburgh EH9

Stratton Estates Limited
Albert Bridge House
127 Albert Bridge Road
London SW11 4PL
Tel: 071-924 4199 Fax: 071-924 5825
NATURE OF BUSINESS: Development & Project Management
MAJOR SHAREHOLDERS: J F Sheridan ARICS (Managing Director); H I P Haydon ARICS
DEVELOPMENT POLICY: Industrial primarily throughout UK, also supermarkets in London area.
(Sept 1992)

Straudley Investments Limited
First Floor
92 Cavendish Street
London W1M

Structadene Limited
116 Clarence Road
Clapton
London E5 8JA
Tel: 081-985 5359 Fax: 081-985 8458
DIRECTOR: D A Pearl (Managing)

Studio Properties
15 Sydney Mews
London SW3

Sturgis International
33 Sloane Street
London SW1X

Styles & Wood Developments Limited
Copley Square
The Empress Building
380 Chester Road
Manchester M16 9EA
Tel: 061-954 0311 Fax: 061-877 5580
(Sept 1992)
BUSINESS: Development and Investment
DIRECTORS: D Barker; E R Madden
REGIONAL OFFICES: London; Manchester; Liverpool
ANNUAL INCOME/TURNOVER: Company £500,000; Group £30m
REGIONAL PREFERENCES: Anywhere in the UK
VALUE OF PORTFOLIO: £4m (1990)
DISTRIBUTION OF PORTFOLIO: Shops 90%; Factories 10%
INVESTMENT POLICY: Expansion of Commercial Investments by Development
SUBSIDIARY COMPANIES: Meridian Investment Properties Limited (Property Investment); Copley Square Limited (Property Investment); Styles & Wood (Contracting) Limited (Construction)
(Jan 1991)

Sucal Developments Limited
Show House
Staley Road
Mossley
Manchester

Summerfield Developments
Tauntfield
South Road
Taunton
Somerset TA1 3ND
0823 257961
DIRECTOR: M Foden (Managing)

Sun Alliance Group Properties Ltd
25 Floral Street
Covent Garden
London WC2E 9BU
071-836 1211
DIRECTOR: M Dew (Managing)

Sun Life Properties Limited
107 Cheapside
London EC2V 6DT
071-589 3477
DIRECTOR: J M Nichollsk (Managing)

Sun Life Properties Limited
160 Brompton Road
London SW3

Sunley Estates Limited
92 Park Lane
Croydon
Surrey CR9 1TU
081-688 6881
DIRECTOR: L Brunwin (Managing)
SUBSIDIARY COMPANIES: Sunley Holdings

Sunley Holdings Limited
79A Park Street
London W1Y 3HP
071-499 8842
DIRECTOR: C Hoskisson (Managing)

Surrey Group plc
Surrey House
2 The Green
Hersham
Walton-on-Thames
Surrey KT12 3SQ

Sutton's, Sir Richard Settled Estates Limited
5 Bolton Street
Piccadilly
London W1Y 7PA
071-499 2008
DIRECTOR: Mr Wilkinson (Managing)

Swan Properties
52 Poland Street
London W1
071-2878 9209

Swissdeal Co Limited
2 Dudley House
North Wharf Road
London W2

Symphony Estates Limited
New Progress Works
Gelderd Lane
Leeds
West Yorkshire LS12 6AI
0532 792521

T K Developments Limited
535 King's Road
London NW10

Tan Victor
92 Loudoun Road
London NW8

Tarian Developments
32 Llandaff Road
Canton
Cardiff
CF1 9NJ
Tel: 0222 664555 Fax: 0222 668901
(Sept 1992)

Tarmac Burford Developments Limited
25 Hill Street
London W1X 7FB
071-491 3377
NATURE OF BUSINESS: Development
DIRECTORS: P G Burford FRICS
MAJOR SHAREHOLDERS: Tarmac Properties Limited
ANNUAL GROSS TURNOVER: £15m (1988)
REGIONAL PREFERENCES: Greater Midlands
DEVELOPMENT ACTIVITIES: Offices 70%; shops 10%; science parks/hi-tech 20%
DEVELOPMENT POLICY: Careful selective commercial schemes sought

Tarmac Properties Limited
1 Hay Hill
London W1X
071-495 2858
DIRECTOR: A Collins (Managing)
PROPERTY DIVISION: John McLean and Associates; Farmcote Developments Limited; Tarmac Properties Home Counties Limited; Tarmac Provincial Properties Limited; Tarmac Brookglade Properties Limited; Tarmac Burford Development Limited; Tarmac Brookglade Management Company Limited; Blue Lamp Properties Limited; Tarmac Swindon Limited; Tarmac Central Properties
PRINCIPLE RELATED COMPANIES: Schofield Centre Ltd; Tarmac Guildford Limited; Foxholes Business Park Limited; Waterside Park Limited
HOUSING DIVISION TURNOVER: £920m (1989)
HOUSING DIVISION OPERATING PROFIT: £183.5m

Tartan Developments
1st Floor Bridge House
Jordans Yard
Bridge Street
Cambridge
CB2 1UG
0223 315280
DIRECTOR: R Perrin (Managing)

Tay Homes plc
West Bar Chambers
38 Boar Lane
Leeds LS1 5OA
0532 426262
MANAGING DIRECTOR: M Griffiths

Taylor Woodrow Property Company Limited
10 Park Street
London W1Y 4DD
Tel: 071-499 8871 Fax: 071-702 2377
(Sept 1992)
Wholly owned subsidiary of Taylor Woodrow plc
DIRECTORS: J Topping FRICS (Chairman); P R L Drew OBE (Deputy Chairman); P Hedges (Managing); N C Baker; J H Brooks FCA; R J Dillion; J M Eastwood ARICS; B F Higgs BSc FICE; B A Judd FRICS FCIArb; C R Knott FCIS (Secretary); L C Parnell FRICS
MAJOR SHAREHOLDERS: Taylor Woodrow plc
SUBSIDIARY COMPANIES: Taylor Woodrow Developments Limited; Churchill Square Management Company Limited; Park Street Management Company Limited; Taylor Woodrow (Leisure Services) Limited; Taylor Woodrow Property Holdings SA; Taylor Woodrow Property Holdings Inc; Taylor Woodrow Property Company of America Inc; Taylor Woodrow Property Company (South Carolina) Inc; Taylor Woodrow Property Company (Georgia) Inc; Taylor Woodrow Property Company (California) Inc; Taylor Woodrow Property Company (Texas) Inc; Taylor Woodrow Property Company (Florida) Inc; Taylor Woodrow of California Inc; Taylor Woodrow of San Francisco Inc; Taylor Woodrow Property Holdings Pty Limited; Taylor Woodrow Property Company of Australia Pty Limited; Taylor Woodrow Developments of Australia Pty Limited; City Arcade Pty Limited; Birtley Engineering
PARTICULARS OF RELATED COMPANIES: Hanger Lane Holdings Limited, Great Britain; Taylor Woodrow Chippindale Properties Limited, Great Britain; Wrights Lane Developments Limited, Great Britain; Gamgee Pty Limited, Australia; Margaret Street Pty Limited, Australia; Thurat Pty Limited
BRANCH OFFICES: Glasgow, Leicester, Swindon, Southampton, Brighton, Tampa - Florida, Atlanta - Georgia, San Francisco - California, Sydney, Brussells

Taylor Woodrow Property Co Limited
4 Dunraven Street
London W1Y
Fax 071-702 2377

Neil G.Taylor
21/6 Hall Road
London NW8

Tea Trade Properties
Sir John Lyon House
5 High Timber
Upper Thames Street
London EC4V 3NS
071 248 2185

Teesland Development Company Limited
11th Floor, Corporation House
Albert Road
Middlesborough
Cleveland TS1 2RU
BRANCH OFFICES: Scarborough

TEL Developments
230 Grange Road
Hyde
Manchester SK14

Telfos Holding plc
Hunslet Engine Works
Leeds LS10 1BT

Teltscher Estates Limited
17 Carlyle Square
London SW3

Temple Bar Properties
32 St Mary-At-Hill
London EC3P 3AJ
071-623 9333
COMPANY SECRETARY: A Marsh

Terrace Hill Group
31 Sackville Street
London W1X

Thames House Estate Limited
Thames House
Millbank
London SW1 4QN
071-834 9107

Thames Investments & Buildings Limited
59 Woodsford Square
London W14 8DS

Thanmeris Properties Limited
18 Shackwell Lane
London E8

Tharsis Company plc
136 West George Street
Glasgow G2 2HF

Thermoglobe Limited
3 Warstone Lane
Birmingham B18

THI Developments
5 Heritage Court
Lower Bridge Street
Chester CH1 1RD
0244 320600
DIRECTOR: J D Henley (Managing)
(Sept 1992)

Thirlby, Richard & June & Co
The Garden House
8a Hays Mews
London W1X

Thistle Property Co Limited
3 Ponton Street
Edinburgh EH3

Thomas , P
17 St Asaph
London SE4

Thorbourne plc
Edinburgh House
82-90 London Road
St Albans
Hertfordshire AL1 1TR
0727 50505
NATURE OF BUSINESS: Development
DIRECTORS: C J Yuill (Managing); R J H Bretherton; M W Pollard BSc ARICS; J E Yuill; A Mills-Baker FCA
ASSOCIATED COMPANY: Myring Investments plc; Rancon Securities plc

Thorn EMI PLC
The Quadrangle
Westmount Centre
Uxbridge Road
Hayes
Middlesex UB4 0HB
081-848 0011
DIRECTOR: Mr G Cant (Managing)

Thorn High Street Properties
Church House
18-20 Church Street
Staines
Middlesex TW18 4EP
0784 66177

Thornfield Development Limited
12 Park Place
Leeds

Thornfield Holdings plc
12 Park Place
Leeds LS1 2RU

Thornhill Properties Limited
429 Bearwood Road
Bearwood
Birmingham B66

Entry missing ? Call HELPLINE Page v

Thoroughbred Property Group

2 Landon Court
Tanbank
Wellington
Telford
Shropshire TF11 1HE

Thornsett Properties Ltd

Building No 3
126 Colindale Avenue
London NW9 5HU
Tel: 081-905 9899 Fax: 081-905 9879
NATURE OF BUSINESS: Development, Investment, Construction
DIRECTOR: G Cunningham (Managing)
MAJOR SHAREHOLDERS: D Cunningham; G Cunningham
REGIONAL OFFICES: Harringay
ANNUAL INCOME/TURNOVER: Group £18m; Company £11m
REGIONAL PREFERENCES FOR ACTIVITIES: London & South East
DISTRIBUTION OF PORTFOLIO: Office 50%; Housing 50%
DEVELOPMENT POLICY: To increase public sector housing, local authority joint ventures
SISTER COMPANIES: London Building Co Limited
(Sept 1992)

Thornstone Developments Limited

Assets House
17 Elverton Street
London SW1P

Tilbury Developments Limited

395 George Road
Erdington
Birmingham
B23 7RX
Tel: 0342 410721 Fax: 021 344 3774
(Sept 1992)
DIRECTORS: T Slater (Chairman); S M Brown (Managing Director); A C Hill (Director); G Wheeler (Finance Director);
G Norris (Development Surveyor); S D Sadler (Development Surveyor) S P Parsk (Project Manager)
MAJOR SHAREHOLDERS: Tilbury Group plc
ANNUAL INCOME/TURNOVER: Property Division: £67m, Group: £231.2m (1989)
SISTER COMPANIES: Tilbury Construction Limited; Clough Smith Limited; Tilbury City Limited; Westpile Limited; United Kingdon Construction and Engineering Company Limited; Tilbury Investments Limited; Tilbury Estates Limited; Tilbury Homes Limited
(Jan 1991)

Timberlaine Limited

Amelia House
Crescent Road
Worthing
West Sussex BN11 1RP
0903 34348
DIRECTOR: Mr Tuley (Mangaging)

Tokenspire Properties

100 Spellowgate
Driffield
North Humberside YO25 7UP
0482 868356
DIRECTOR: P W Theaston (Managing)

Tompkins, R C Group of Companies

7A The Broadway
Highams Park
London E4 9LQ
081-523 1438
DIRECTOR: R C Tompkins (Managing)

Tops Estates plc

77 South Audley Street
London W1Y 6EE
071-486 4684
DIRECTORS: E N Goodman FCA (Chairman & Managing Director); A Peters ACIS; E V Desson FRICS; T H W Piper; A C M Rintool, FRICS; A E Laycock; Adam H Cohen (Secretary)
ANNUAL TURNOVER/INCOME: £10.7m (1992)
VALUE OF PROPERTY PORTFOLIO: £124m (1990)
DEVELOPMENT ACTIVITIES: Mainly retail
(Sept 1992)

Towerclyde plc

Charter House
177 Angel Road
London N18 3BW
081-803 9066
DIRECTOR: B Simmon (Managing)

Town & City Properties Limited

4 Carlton Gardens
London
SW1
071-839 5611

Town & Country Developments

Beatty House
Westview Close
London NW10 1RH
081-208 2244

Town Centre Securities plc

Town Centre House
The Merrion Centre
Leeds
West Yorkshire LS2 8LY
Tel: 0532 459172 Fax: 0532 421026
NATURE OF BUSINESS: Development & Investment
DIRECTORS: I A Ziff OBE (Chairman); D C Whitehead; E M Ziff; J K Leadbeater FRICS; K W Attrill FSVA (Non-Executive); G H Cox
MAJOR SHAREHOLDERS: Barclays Bank Pension Trust Fund; General Accident Fire & Life Assurance Corp Limited; Courtaulds CIF Nominees Limited; WGTC Nominees Limited; Junction Nominees; Port Employers & Registered Dock Workers Pension Fund Trustees Limited.

ANNUAL GROSS PROFIT: £6.5m (1991)
VALUE OF PROPERTY PORTFOLIO: £172.1m (1991)
SUBSIDIARY COMPANIES: Town Centre Securities (Scotland) Limited; Town Centre Enterprises Limited; Rochdale Canal Co; Blackpool Markets Limited; T Herbert Kaye's Estates Limited; Zulon Limited; Town Centre Securities (Manchester) Limited
BRANCH OFFICES: London/Manchester
(Sept 1992)

Trafalgar House Industrial Development Limited

9 Berkeley Street
London W1X 3AG
Tel: 071-499 9020 Fax: 071-629 7542
(Sept 1992)
DIRECTORS: Sir N Broakes (Chairman); Lord Matthews; E W Parker; Sir Francis Sandilands CBE; C H B Carter (Property); W B Slater CBE VRD; The Marquess of Tavistock; V A Grundy; P R Howell; H W A Francis CBE; D M Taylor; A W Clements; G E Knight CBE; I Fowler BA FCA (Secretary)
ANNUAL TURNOVER/INCOME/PROFIT: £2.5bn (1988)
VALUE OF PROPERTY PORTFOLIO: £44.8m (1987)
SUBSIDIARY COMPANIES: Trafalgar House Property Limited; Trafalgar House Developments Limited; Trafalgar House Group Estates; Trafalgar House Business Parks; Trafalgar House Management Limited; T H M Developments Limited; Trafalgar House Real Estate Inc (USA); Builders Amalgamated Company Limited; New Ideal Holdings Limited; Central Ideal Homes Limited; E F G H Limited; New Ideal Homes Limited; Northern Ideal Homes Limited; Southern Ideal Homes Limited; Trollope & Colls Limited; Chase Property Holdings; Goldquill Properties Limited
(Jan 1991)

Trafford Park Estates

Estate Office
Trafford Park Road
Manchester M17 1AU
Tel: 061-872 5426 Fax: 061-872 7644
(Sept1992)
DIRECTORS: N G Westbrook CBE MA FRICS (Chairman); R O Gerrard MA FIOB (Secretary); N D Toosey BA FCA; T Woolfenden MC FRICS; C J Hoddell BSc FRICS; I F Smith ARICS (Joint Managing); R Winsby FCIS ATII
ANNUAL TURNOVER/INCOME: £6.98m (1988)
VALUE OF PROPERTY PORTFOLIO: £63.08m (1988)
SUBSIDIARY COMPANIES: Calder Vale Estates Limited; Faveway Limited; Port of Manchester Warehouses plc; Trafford Extensions Limited; Trafford Industrial Buildings Limited; Trafford Park Compnay (The); Williamson Corrosion Control Limited
(Jan 1991)

Trans Arrealty Limited

69/70 Mark Lane
London EC3R

TransAct Hotel & Tourism Property Limited

20 Conduit Street
London W1R

Translloyd Securities Limited

84 Baker Street
London W1M

Transomas Property Co

51 Gloucester Terrace
London W2

Transworld Investments Limited

24 Northways Parade
London NW3
071-722 1212

Tranville Developments Limited

The Hall
Moor Road
Bramhope
Leeds LS16 9HJ
0532 843553
DIRECTOR: P Holmes (Managing)
(Sept 1992)

Trebaer Limited

16 Needham Road
London W11

Trencherwood Estates

Trencherwood House
21-23 The Broadway
Newbury
Berkshire RG13 1AS
Tel: 0635 521200 Fax: 0635 521346
(Sept 1992)
NATURE OF BUSINESS: Development & Investment
DIRECTORS: J A Norgate FRICS (Chairman); M T Bull ASVA ARVA; B P Eighteen ACA (Managing); R A McDowell; C R Davis
MAJOR SHAREHOLDERS: Unilever Superannuation Fund
ANNUAL TURNOVER: £51.4m (1988)
VALUE OF PROPERTY PORTFOLIO: £2.6m (1988)
SUBSIDIARY COMPANIES: Trencherwood New Homes Limited; Trencherwood Construction Limited; Trencherwood Investments Limited; Trencherwood Commercial Limited; Grandmount Limited; Elmthorpe Construction Limited; Lindmere Construction Limited; Crossbourne Construction Limited; Redbourne Builders Limited; Trencherwood Group Services Limited; Trencherwood Retirement Homes Limited; Ledbury Markets & Fairs Company Limited; Trencherwood Estates Limited
RELATED COMPANIES: Rockhold Commercial Limited; Trencherwood Developments Limited; Sedgebrook plc; Winchcombe Developments Limited
(Jan 1991)

Trevian Holdings plc

341-349 Oxford Street
London W1R 1HB
Tel: 071-499 1213 Fax: 071-495 6234

BUSINESS: Property Development and Investment
DIRECTORS: Dennis Cope (Chairman); Lewis Davis (Managing), Brian Cotton; Philip Davies; Gerald Newton; David Wilmot
MAJOR SHAREHOLDERS: Frogmore Estates plc, Southend Property Holdings plc

---

Tri-Star International
Worldwide Investments Limited
Rugby Chambers
2 Rugby Street
London WC1N

Trident Group plc
Trident House
15 Bath Road
Slough
Berkshire SL1 3UJ
0753 33444
DIRECTORS: N Wicks (Managing); Mr Rowntree (Marketing)

Trinity Business Centre
305/309 Rotherhithe Street
London SE16

Trinity Estates plc
Buckingham House
62-63 Queen Street
London EC4R 1AD
Tel: 071-248 0881 Fax: 071-236 3346
DIRECTOR: K Price (Managing)

Trinity Tower Power Co Limited
26 Thomas More Street
London E1

Tristar Estates Limited
Queens Chambers
5 John Dalton Street
Manchester M2

Tritec Investments Limited
9 Queen Street
Mayfair
London W1X 7PH
071-408 0034
DIRECTOR: I Hilton (Managing)

Trollope & Colls Limited
Trafalgar House Group Services
Mitcham House
681 Mitcham Road
Croydon
Surrey CR9 3AP
081-689 2266
MAJOR SHAREHOLDERS: A subsidiary of Trafalgar House plc

Trust of Property Shares plc
77 South Audley Street
London W1Y 6EE
Tel: 071-486 4684 Fax: 071 499 9481
DIRECTOR: E Goodman (Chairman & Managing)
(Sept 1992)

Try Group
Cowley Business Park
High Street
Cowley
Uxbridge
Middlesex UB8 2AL
Tel: 0895 251222 Fax: 0895 259090
DIRECTORS: H W Try (Chairman);P Hull (Managing); R Bowen (Marketing)

Try Mistletoe Properties Limited
High Street
Cowley
Uxbridge
Middlesex UB8 2AL
0895 51222

Turner, A H Property Developments Limited
23 Grove Street
Retford
Notts. DN22 6NR
0777-860860

Turner, P S Construction
Skipton Road
Cross Hills
North Yorkshire
BD20 7BX
Tel: 0535 636116 Fax: 0535 632739
(Jan 1991)
DIRECTORS: M Wormald (Managing) M Smith (Marketing)
(Sept 1992)

Turnstone Estates
85 Springfield Road
Chelmsford
Essex CM2 6JL
Tel: 0245 490418 Fax: 0245 490308
BUSINESS: Property Development and Investment
DIRECTORS: C W Goldsmith (Managing Director); C R Holmes.
MAJOR SHAREHOLDERS; Dencora plc
REGIONAL PREFERENCES: Eastern part or south east
INVESTMENT POLICY: Purchase investments with angles, also portfolios and companies
DEVELOPMENT POLICY: Prelet of very high quality, speculative at present
VALUE OF PORTFOLIO: £5m (1992)
TURNOVER: £5m
(Sept 1992)

Turriff Properties Limited
Budbrook Road
Warwick
Warwickshire
CV34 5XJ
0926 410400
DIRECTORS: J Wyatt (Managing); T Godfrey (Marketing)

Tussac Estates Ltd
Lime Tree Business Park
22 Lime Tree Road
Matlock
Derbyshire DE4 3EJ
0629 580222
DIRECTORS: B Money (Managing) P Harkins (Marketing)

Tustin, P C & Co Limited
94 York Street
London W1H

Twyn Developments
7 West Market Street
Newport
Gwent
0633 257406

Tyburn Hill Limited
Linburn House
West Hampstead
London NW6 2QJ
Tel: 071-328 8688 Fax: 071-624 4100
(Sept 1992)
NATURE OF BUSINESS: Development & Investment
DIRECTORS: D A Sanders (Managing); J B Gertler
MAJOR SHAREHOLDERS: D A Sanders; J B Gertler
DEVELOPMENT POLICY: Residential propositions of all types. Also secondary vacant shops with vacant upper parts
INVESTMENT POLICY: Secondary and prime retail investments, tenanted or part tenanted residential properties
BRANCH OFFICES: London and Home Counties
(Jan 1991)

Tyne River Properties Plc
Pearson House
Wincomblee Road
Walker
Newcastle-Upon-Tyne NE99 1HE
091-262 7178
DIRECTOR: W J Peacock (Marketing)

Tyrone Investment Limited
35 Clarence Terrace
London NW1

UA Properties Limited
23 Glasgow Road
Perth
Scotland PH2 ONZ
Tel: 0738 31636 Fax: 0738 29390
(Sept 1992)
DIRECTOR: D E Carter (Managing)
BRANCH OFFICES: Sterling, Edinburgh, Inverness, Oban, Cupar
(Jan 1991)

UK Land plc
145 Kensington Church Street
London W8
071-221 1544

UK Property Company plc
10 Cornwall Terrace
Regents Park
London NW1 4QP
071-486 4466
DIRECTORS: J H Ritblat (Managing); D M Cohen; C Metliss; D Wilson (Secretary)
MAJOR SHAREHOLDERS: A subsidiary of British Land Company plc
ANNUAL TURNOVER/INCOME: £2.76m (1988)
VALUE OF PROPERTY PORTFOLIO: £22.28m (1988)
SUBSIDIARY COMPANIES: Codergrange Limited; Heywood Industrial Estates Limited; LDB Developments Limited; Landforge Limited; Rexmead Limited (84/85)

Unex Group
Unex House
Church Lane
Stetchworth
Newmarket CB8 9TN
Tel: 0638 768144 Fax: 0638 507449
(Sept 1992)
NATURE OF BUSINESS: Development & Investment
DIRECTORS: W J Gredley (Chairman); A J A Helme (Managing); V W McElroy (Property)
BRANCH OFFICES: Mayfair
REGIONAL PREFERENCES: East Anglia, London Docklands
VALUE OF PROPERTY PORTFOLIO: £115m
PROPERTY PORTFOLIO: Offices 34%; factories 14%; residential 8%; shops 7%; warehouses 17%; science parks/hi-tech 11%; bloodstock use 9%
DEVELOPMENT ACTIVITIES: Offices 50%; factories 10%; shops 5%; warehouses 10%; science parks/hi-tech 25%
(Jan 1991)

Unigate Properties Limited
40 Wayden Lane
Farnham
Surrey GU9 8UP
0252 733737
A subsidiary of Unigate plc

Entry missing ? Call HELPLINE Page v

Union Group plc
2 Queen Anne Mews
London
W1M 9DF

Union Square PLC
Calder House
Dover Street
London W1X 3PJ
Tel: 071-491 1802 Fax: 071-408 2162
(Sept 1992)
DIRECTOR: R Thompson (Managing)

United Dominions Property Trust Limited
116 Cockfosters Road
Barnet
Middlesex EN4 0DX
081-449 5533
DIRECTORS: J Davis (Managing); Mrs Foulkes (Marketing)

United Dutch UK Limited
22 Gilbert Street
London W1Y

United Kingdom Property Company plc
10 Cornwall Terrace
Regents Park
London
NW1 4QP
BUSINESS: Property Investment
DIRECTORS: J Ritblatt; C Metliss; J H Weston Smith;
MAJOR SHAREHOLDERS: The British Land Company plc

United Lane Plc
101 Elgin Crescent
London W1Y

United Realty Investment plc
No 5
21 Park Road
Regents Park
London NW1 6XN
071-262 2732
DIRECTOR: M Moss (Managing)

United Scientific Holdings Plc
United Scientific House
215 Vauxhall Bridge Road
London SW1V IEN
071-821 8080
DIRECTORS: N Prest (Managing); I Hilier (Marketing)

Universal Consolidated Group Plc
7 Stafford Street
London
W1X 3PG

Universal Land Developers
39 South Street
Mayfair
London W1Y 5PD
071-493 4048
MANAGING DIRECTOR: C White

Urban Space Management
39 Camden Lock Place
London NW1 8AF
071-485 4457
DIRECTORS: E Reynolds (Managing); R Priestman (Marketing)

Urban Waterside Limited
The Estate Office
Merchants Quay
Salford Quays
Manchester M5

Urquhart Securities
1 Queen Anne Mews
London W1
071-436 5195
DIRECTOR: R Hryncyszwn (Managing)

Usborne Developments
Dairy Hill
Busstwick
Hull HU12 9HF
0964 671144
DIRECTOR: Mr Frame (Managing)

V K M International Real Estate plc
47/50 Hockley Hill
Birmingham B18

Validhill Limited
48 Charles II Place
77 Kings Road
Chelsea
London SW3

Valla Group Plc
The Brewery
Sunderland SR1 3AN

Vanbrugh Land plc
96-98 Baker Street
London W1M 1LA
Tel: 071-224 4282 Fax: 071 224 4428
NATURE OF BUSINESS: Property Development
DIRECTOR: A M Slipper (Managing)
Subsidiary of Chartwell Land plc
MAJOR SHAREHOLDERS: Chartwell Land plc
ANNUAL INCOME/TURNOVER: Company £20m
REGIONAL PREFERENCES FOR ACTIVITIES: Anywhere in England
DISTRIBUTION OF PORTFOLIO: Warehousing for distribution 80%; retail warehousing 20%

DISTRIBUTION OF DEVELOPMENT ACTIVITIES: £16m Warehousing; £4m Retail warehousing
DEVELOPMENT POLICY: Development for trading

VAT Watkins
Watkins House
Pegamoid Road
Edmonton
London N18 2NG
081-803 6688
DIRECTOR: C Simmons (Managing)

Vaughan Land Securities
Aylestone Mill
Old Aylestone
Disraeli Street
Leicester LE2 8LX
0533 440723
DIRECTOR: J R P Vaughan (Managing)

VEJ Investments Limited
142 Merton Road
Wimbledon
London SW19
081-542 4675
DIRECTOR: Mrs J Hobbs (Managing)

Venaglass Limited
56/58 Whitcomb Street
London WC2H 7DN
Tel: 071-930 5724 Fax: 071-930 0666
DIRECTOR: P Vaughan
(Sept 1992)
NATURE OF BUSINESS: Investment/Development
REGIONAL PREFERENCES FOR ACTIVITIES: London Area
VALUE OF PORTFOLIO: £40m (1990)
(Jan 1991)

Vestey Estates
24 West Smithfield
London EC1A

Vic Hallam plc
Langley Mill
Nottingham NG16 4AN
Tel: 0773 531153 Fax: 0773 530128
(Sept 1992)
CHAIRMAN: Mr Burt
MAJOR SHAREHOLDERS: A member of May & Hassell Group
NATURE OF BUSINESS: System Builders
REGIONAL PREFERENCES FOR ACTIVITIES: Anywhere in U.K.
(Jan 1991)

Vickers Properties Limited
Vickers House
Millbank Tower
Millbank
London SW1P 4RA
071-828 7777
DIRECTOR: Sir Colin Chandler (Managing)

VICO Development Limited
Derriaghy Industrial Park
Dunmurry
Belfast BT17 9HU
Tel: 0232 628331 Fax: 0232 624200
NATURE OF BUSINESS: Development & Investment
DIRECTORS: C J Carvill (Chairman); M Carvill (Deputy Chairman); J M Bouche (Managing); T Carvill
MAJOR SHAREHOLDERS: C J Carvill; T Carvill

Victory Land Limited
46/47 Pall Mall
London SW1Y 5JG
071-408 1067
NATURE OF BUSINESS: Development & Investment
DIRECTORS: P M Jackson FRICS; R A F Lascelles ACIS
REGIONAL PREFERENCES: Central London and the South East
INVESTMENT POLICY: To acquire high yielding investments or special situations with 'hope value'
DEVELOPMENT POLICY: To seek out and acquire prime freehold or leasehold property suitable for development or refurbishment, particularly in London and the South East

Viewpoint Developments Limited
22 Greencoat Place
Westminster
London SW1P 1DX
071-828 5420
DIRECTOR: R T S T G Saunders

Viking Property Group
City Site Estates
15 Berkeley Street
Mayfair
London W1X 5AE
071-495 3818
MAJOR SHAREHOLDERS: City Site Estates

Vivat Holdings Plc
Denmark House
The Broadway NW9 7BU
081-203 7095
DIRECTOR: M Cooper (Managing); D Woodgate (Marketing)

Vogue Property Group Ltd
Bardsey Grange
Cornhill Close
Leeds

Vom (UK) Limited
35 Dover Street
London W1X

W M Low & Co Plc
P O Box 73
Baird Avenue
Dryburgh Industrial Estate
Dundee
DD1 9NF
Tel: 0382 814022 Fax: 0382 811420
BUSINESS: Grocery Retailing
DIRECTORS: J L Millar (Chairman, Chief Exec); C C R Mitchell (Managing); H L Findlay; A L Leslie; R K Johnson (Property); D K Rae; P D Stevenson
MAJOR SHAREHOLDERS: I E P Securities Limited; General Accident
REGIONAL OFFICE: West Road, Gateshead
ANNUAL INCOME/TURNOVER: 354.43 million
PROPERTY VALUE: £117m (1989/90)
DISTRIBUTION OF PORTFOLIO: Supermarkets 82%; Warehouses 10%; Shops 5%; Offices 2%; Houses 1%.
DEVELOPMENT ACTIVITIES: As for existing property portfolio.
SUBSIDIARY COMPANIES: Faraday Properties Limited (Supermarket and Investment Portfolio Development)

Walco Developments (Edinburgh) Ltd
7 Forres Street
Edinburgh EH3

Walden Properties
98/99 Jermyn Street
London SW1
071-839 5053
DIRECTOR: Mr C J Auden (Managing)

Waldon Construction Limited
Lakesmere House
Allington Lane
Fair Oak
Eastleigh
Hampshire SO5 7DB
0703 601818
DIRECTORS: J Start (Managing); P Tranter (Marketing)

Ward Dove Limited
25 Park Crescent
Emsworth
Hampshire PO10 7NT
0243 373520
NATURE OF BUSINESS: Development & Project Management

Ward Holdings plc
2 Ash Tree Lane
Chatham
Kent ME5 7BZ
Tel: 0634 855111 Fax: 0634 577172
(Sept 1992)
NATURE OF BUSINESS: Housing and Property Development
DIRECTORS: D J Ward (Managing); J V Walker D Pead
MAJOR SHAREHOLDERS: 59% Family Owned
REGIONAL OFFICE: Maidstone
ANNUAL TURNOVER/INCOME: £64m (1985)
REGIONAL PREFERENCES: South East of England
DEVELOPMENT ACTIVITIES: Housing £37m; Property £38m; Plant Hire 7m.
DEVELOPMENT POLICY: Housing, commercial and industrial also plant hire
SUBSIDIARY COMPANIES: Wards Construction (Medway) Limited; Wards Construction (Industrial) Ltd; Troy Developments Limited; P A Barden & Sons Limited
(Jan 1991)

Wardell Holdings
Barley Castle Lane
Appleton
Warrington
Cheshire WA4 4RW
Tel: 0925 261356 Fax: 0925 262210
DIRECTOR: R Lewis (Managing); A Strickland (Finance)
NATURE OF BUSINESS: Warehousing & Warehouse Development
ANNUAL INCOME/TURNOVER: Group £5m
REGIONAL PREFERENCES FOR ACTIVITIES: North West
VALUE OF PORTFOLIO: Group £20m (1992)
DISTRIBUTION OF PORTFOLIO: Warehouses 95% Offices 5%
INVESTMENT POLICY: Capital growth
DISTRIBUTION OF DEVELOPMENT ACTIVITIES: Warehouses 100%
DEVELOPMENT POLICY: Long term growth
(Sept 1992)

Wards Construction (Investments) Ltd
Weavering House
Grovewood Drive
Maidstone
Kent ME14 5PR
0622 39988
DIRECTOR: J Walker (Managing)

Warleggan Estates
154 Brompton Road
Knightsbridge
London SW3 1HX
071-823 9494
DIRECTOR: D Walsh (Managing)

Warner Estate Holdings Limited
3 Vere Street
London W1M 9HQ
071-493 6480
NATURE OF BUSINESS: Property Investment
DIRECTORS: Sir H Warner Bt (Chairman & Chief Executive); J G Day; A N Batty BSc FRICS; H R J Burgess; D J Veaser FCIS; P C T Warner; R W Ferrand FRICS
MAJOR SHAREHOLDERS: Provident Mutual Life Assurance Association
ANNUAL TURNOVER/INCOME: £13.74m (1988)

REGIONAL PREFERENCES: London
VALUE OF PROPERTY PORTFOLIO: £141.98m (1988)
BRANCH OFFICES: London, Walthamstow
INVESTMENT POLICY: Residential, industrial, offices, shops
SUBSIDIARY COMPANIES: Warner Estate Limited; Donlo Investment-Developments Limited; Lancaster Group Development Limited; Lotkeep Limited; A H Herbert & Company Limited; Marriott & Price Limited; Cardiff & Provincial Properties plc; Clapham Supermarket Limited; Bradbridge Property Company Limited; Bradwa Limited; Lancaster Holdings Limited

---

Warnford Investments plc

465 Salisbury House
London Wall
London EC2M 5RQ
071-588 6856
NATURE OF BUSINESS: Investment
DIRECTORS: G R Goobey FIA (Managing); L Sebba BA(Hons) DipTP FSVA; M Sebba BSc(Eng); E L Erdman FSVA; M Ross FCA; F Martyn FCA; T J Nardecchia OBE BSc FRICS
MAJOR SHAREHOLDERS: Sebba Holdings Limited; Co-op Insurance Society; Stanley Trust Holdings Limited
ANNUAL TURNOVER/INCOME: £10M (1989)
VALUE OF PROPERTY PORTFOLIO: £159.4m (1988)
SUBSIDIARY COMPANIES: Cumber Properties Limited; Dewarn Properties Limited; Evos Limited; Evos (Subsidiary) Limited; Portman Square Properties Limited; Salisbury House Offices Limited; Wardrobe Court Limited; Warnbridge Developments Limited; Warnbridge Properties Limited; Warnford Court (Canada) Limited; Parwick Investments Limited

---

Warrant Securities plc

Charles House
108-110 Finchley Road
Swiss Cottage
London NW3 5JJ
Tel: 071-431 4333 Fax: 071-794 0898
NATURE OF BUSINESS: Property Developers and Investors
DIRECTORS: Anthony I Fine; Jeremy L Stevens
REGIONAL PREFERENCES: London and the Home Counties
INVESTMENT POLICY: To acquire good secondary retail investments at yields of 8% plus and to enhance the value of our existing commercial portfolio through good estate management.
DEVELOPMENT ACTIVITIES: London and the Home Counties
DEVELOPMENT POLICY: To enhance the value of our existing portfolio through the maximisation of the development potential of selected properties.

Warrington Commercial Developments Limited

Stansfield House
Chester Business Park
Wrexham Road
Chester
Cheshire CH4 9QQ
0244 680041
DIRECTOR: G Jackson (Managing)

Warringtons plc

74 Grosvenor Street
London W1X 9DD
Tel: 071-491 2768 Fax: 071-499 0589
DIRECTOR: Mr Robins (Managing)

Warwick Homes Limited

8/9 Giltspur Street
London EC1A

Washington Developments

No.1 Cuthbert House
Glover Estate
District 11, Washington
Tyne and Wear NE37 2SH
091-415 3777
DIRECTOR: N R Bachelor (Marketing)

Waterglade International Holdings plc

Waterglade House
5-7 Ireland Yard
London EC4V 5DQ
Tel: 071-248 8301 Fax: 071-248 3278
NATURE OF BUSINESS: Development & Investment
DIRECTORS: R Nathan (Managing); P B Wilson FRICS; W H Adams FRICS FSVA; M S P Garvin LLB; R Archer BSc ARICS;
J M Edwards BSc (Econ) FCA; E R Smith FCIB
MAJOR SHAREHOLDERS: R Nathan; Hill Samuel Investments Limited; Scottish Amicable Investment Managers Limited; Prudential Assurance Company Limited; DRG Pensions Investment;
Target Investment Management Limited.
ANNUAL TURNOVER/INCOME: £28.2m (31/3/90)
VALUE OF PROPERTY PORTFOLIO: £85m (31/3/90)
PROPERTY PORTFOLIO: Offices 25%; shops 50%; warehouses 25%
DEVELOPMENT/INVESTMENT POLICY: Emphasis on all commercial schemes including industrial, retail and offices in major provincial centres throughout Europe.
DEVELOPMENT ACTIVITIES: Retail 70%;
Industrial 30%;
SUBSIDIARY COMPANIES: Waterglade Developments Limited; Waterglade Securities Limited; Waterglade Properties Limited; Waterglade Developments (Havant) Limited; Waterglade Developments (Clacton High Street) Limited; Waterglade Developments (Orpington) Limited; Waterglade Investments Limited; Waterglade (West Thurrock) Limited; Sidecard Limited; Fountains Development Limited; Polepact Limited; Waterglade Management Services Ltd;
Waterglade Ildway developments Llimited;
NETHERLANDS: Waterglade International BV, Larfefrade BV; Pemuco BV; Daran (Mainz) BV, SPAIN: Waterglade Espana SA; Gladeduke SA; PORTUGAL: Waterglade (Portugal) Propriedades Lda; WEST GERMANY; Waterglade Immobilien Management GmbH; Welott Grundstucksgesellschaft GmbH;
BRANCH OFFICES: Frankfurt, Amsterdam, Madrid

Waterlinks Plc

Aston Cross
Rocky Lane
Birmingham B6

Entry missing ? Call HELPLINE Page v

Wates City of London Properties plc

Level 21
City Tower
40 Basinghall Street
London EC2V 5DE
071-588 2888
NATURE OF BUSINESS: Development & Investment
DIRECTORS: J D Hamilton CBE (Non-Executive Chairman); P C R W Wates FSVA (Managing); J D Nettleton; R Clutton FRICS; C S Wates FCA (Non-Executive)
ANNUAL GROSS PROFIT: £30.2m (1988)
VALUE OF PROPERTY PORTFOLIO: £384m (1988)
SUBSIDIARY COMPANIES: 9-10 Philpot Lane Limited; 43-45 Eastcheap Limited; City Tower Limited; Number 80 Cheapside Limited; Philpot Lane Properties Limited; Retmoon Limited; Wates Philpot Lane Investments Limited; Wates Sixth Property Holdings Limited; W H (Cannon Street) Limited (75%); 100 Old Broad Street Limited; Wates City Property Management Limited; Vintners' Place Limited

Wates Properties Limited

1260 London Road
Norbury
London SW16 4EG
081-764 5000
NATURE OF BUSINESS: Development
DIRECTORS: C S Wates; P S Lord; G R Kinally
MAJOR SHAREHOLDERS: Private Company
REGIONAL PREFERENCES: South & South East England with the exception of retail developments
DEVELOPMENT ACTIVITIES: Offices 30%; shops 60%; warehouses 10%
DEVELOPMENT POLICY: Funds available to purchase sites on private treaty basis. Willing to finance joint venture developments

Waverly Properties Limited

89 Giles Street
Edinburgh EH6

Weatherall Green & Smith

22 Chancery Lane
London WC2A 1LT
071-405 6944

Webster Properties (Developments) Limited

Belcon House
Essex Road
Hoddesdon
Hertfordshire EN11 ODR
0992 467141
DIRECTORS: S Ellis (Managing); R Evans (Marketing)

Wedge Developments Limited

Wedge House
White Hart Lane
Tottenham
London N17 8HJ
081-801 4892
DIRECTOR: P Groom (Managing)
Subsidiary of Wedge Group plc

Wedgestone Properties Limited

62 Shaftesbury Avenue
London W1V

Weir Group Plc

149 Newlands Road
Cathcart
Glasgow G44 4EX
041-637 7111
DIRECTOR: R Garrick (Managing)

Welbeck Estates Company Limited

Portland Estate Office
Welbeck, Worksop
Nottinghamshire SH0 3LT
0909 500610

Welfare Dwellings Trust

20 Great Western Road
London W9

Welsh Development Agency

Property Division
Pearl House
Greyfriars Road
Cardiff CF1 3XX
Tel: 0222 222666 Fax: 0222 640030
(Property Services Unit)
NATURE OF BUSINESS: Property Development
DIRECTORS: G E Moore FRICS (Executive Director); K J Thomas ARICS (Property Development Director); C Munday (Property Management Director); D Swallow ARICS (Private Funding Director)
MAJOR SHAREHOLDERS: Development Agency supported by Grant Aid
REGIONAL PREFERENCES: Wales
PROPERTY PORTFOLIO: Mixed Industrial and Commercial with Science and Business Parks, Industrial Estates, Distribution Centres, and Hi-Tech Parks.
DEVELOPMENT ACTIVITIES: Factories 98%; science parks/hi-tech 2%
DEVELOPMENT PORTFOLIO: Acquisition and development of commercial and industrial premises and sites either directly or through joint venture partnerships
SUBSIDIARY COMPANIES: Welsh Venture Capital Limited; WDA (Holdings) Limited; A&E Circuits Limited
BRANCH OFFICES: Bangor, Carmarthen, Merthyr Tydfil, Newport, Swansea, Wrexham
(Sept 1992)

Wereldhave Property Corporation plc

19 Sloane Street
London
S1X 9NE
Tel: 071-235 2080 Fax: 071-823 1903
SECRETARY: John S L Watson, FCIA
ANNUAL INCOME/TURNOVER: 58.5m (1989)

Wesdon Investments Ltd

20 Hallam Street
London W1N

Westbrook Property Developments Limited

11 Market Square
Alton
Hampshire GU34 1HA
Tel: 0420 541542 Fax: 0420 541322
NATURE OF BUSINESS: Development
DIRECTORS: A N Lyndon-Skeggs MA FRICS; N E C Talbot-Ponsonby FRICS
MAJOR SHAREHOLDERS: Private Company
ANNUAL TURNOVER/INCOME: £3m 1988/89
REGIONAL PREFERENCES: SE England, Home Counties and Midlands
DEVELOPMENT ACTIVITIES: Offices 10%; shops 30%; Industrial & warehousing 50%; Residential 10%
DEVELOPMENT POLICY: Commercial/retail/industrial hi-tech developments on a speculative and forward sold let basis either as sole developer or in conjunction with others seeking further projects
SUBSIDIARY COMPANIES: Several
(Sept 1992)

Westbury Homes

Westbury House
Lansdown Road
Cheltenham
Gloucestershire
GL50 2JA
0242 236191
DIRECTOR: R L Fraser (Managing)

West End Estates

322 West End Lane
London NW6 1LN
071-794 1000
DIRECTOR: Mr Kay (Managing)

West End & Metropolitan Estates Limited

60 Queen Anne Street
London
W1M

Western Heritable Investments Company

55 St James's Street
London SW1A 1LA
071-491 2948

West London Property Agents & Developers Limited

28 Nottingham Place
London W1M

West Norfolk Tomatoes Ltd

55 Princes Gate
London SW7

Westminster Property Group plc

43 Gower Street
London WC1E 6ES
DIRECTORS: A P Ravenhill FCA (Chairman); P E Newall (Managing Director); S J Grafham; Sir Charles E M Hardie CBE FCA; T L F Royle FINSTM; G H Challis ACIS AIB MBIM; R Rowan FCII; J E Burden (Secretary)
MAJOR SHAREHOLDERS: Saint Piram Limited
SUBSIDIARY COMPANIES: Eaglemoor Limited; Westminster Property (Developments) Limited; Westminster Property Group (Management) Limited; Westminster Property Group (Estates) Limited; Westminster Property (Investment) Limited; Cerro Grande Lda

Westbridge Developments Ltd

23 Wood Street
Bolton

Wester Hailes Land & Property

17 Hailesland Place
Edinburgh EH14

Westminster Land Group Ltd

9 Golden Square
London W1R

Westmoreland Properties Limited

84 Grosvenor Street
London W1X 0HS
071-493 1295

Westpark Developments

8 Percy Road
Denton
Manchester M34

Wetting Properties Limited, Messrs

The Grove
Barnham
Norfolk NR16 2HE
09538 7345

Whitaker, S G Limited

Hope House
45 Great Peter Street
London SW1P 3LT
Tel: 071-222 2837 Fax: 071-976 7252
DIRECTORS: C A Coward MA FRICS; C E Coward; M F Coward; R J Southam BSc ARICS
NATURE OF BUSINESS: Property Investment & Development
REGIONAL PREFERENCES: Anywhere in U.K.
PROPERTY PORTFOLIO: Offices 65%; shops 20%; residential 5%; other 10%
DEVELOPMENT ACTIVITIES: Offices 75%; shops 25%
ASSOCIATED COMPANY: Chainbow Holdings plc
(Sept 1992)

Whitbread Developments Limited
Whitbread Property
Oakley Road
Leagrave
Luton
Bedfordshire LU4 9QH
Tel: 0582 499499 Fax: 0582 499244
DIRECTOR: H Siegle (Managing)
NATURE OF BUSINESS: Property Development
MAJOR SHAREHOLDERS: Whitbread plc
(Sept 1992)

White Group Leisure
40-42 Oxford Street
Manchester M1 5EJ
061-228 0808
DIRECTORS: D White; C White

Whitecroft plc
51 Water Lane
Wilmslow
Cheshire SK9 5BX
0625 524677
DIRECTORS: P Goold (Chief Executive); T Weatherby (Chairman)

Whitegates Construction (Swansea) Limited
52 Walter Road
Swansea SA1 5PW
0792 470037
DIRECTORS: J F Morse; K Church; G Bryant
MAJOR SHAREHOLDERS: Directors
PROPERTY PORTFOLIO: Offices 5%; shops 30%; warehouses 30%; residential 5%; other 30%
DEVELOPMENT ACTIVITIES: All types
SUBSIDIARY COMPANIES: Sabre Builders; Stag Estates Limited; Cotegate Limited

White Horse Property Holdings Limited
Stanley House
65 Victoria Road
Swindon SN1 3BB
Tel: 0793 618566 Fax: 0793 488428
NATURE OF BUSINESS: Property Investment
MAJOR SHAREHOLDERS: S R Lay; H P Lay; H Orr-Ewing
REGIONAL OFFICES: Newport, South Wales & Gravesend, Kent
ANNUAL INCOME/TURNOVER: Group £3m; Company £1m
REGIONAL PREFERENCES FOR ACTIVITIES: No preference
VALUE OF PORTFOLIO: £10m (1991)
DISTRIBUTION OF PORTFOLIO: Residential 20%; Industrial 30%; Commercial 35%; Retail 15%
INVESTMENT POLICY: No set policy in current market
DISTRIBUTION OF DEVELOPMENT ACTIVITIES: UK evenly
SUBSIDIARIES: White Horse Houses Ltd; Entertainment & Leisure Marketing Ltd; White Horse Land & Property Ltd; White Horse Investment Properties Ltd.
(Sept 1992)

Whitelands House Property Limited
188 Fulham Road
London SW10

Whitelane Securities Limited
29 Ropergate
Pontefract

Whiteleys Development Partnership
24 Redan Place
London W2
071-727 8841

Whittaker, C G Developments Limited
Wheatley Hill Road
Doncaster DN2 4PE
0302 369351

Whittingham Properties Southern Ltd
23 Mount Street
London W1Y

Whittome Properties Limited
Willowhayne House
Sutton, Wansford
Peterborough
Cambridgeshire PE5 7XA
0780 782771
NATURE OF BUSINESS: Development
DIRECTORS: R A Whittome; J C Whittome
MAJOR SHAREHOLDERS: R A Whittome; A A Whittome; H K P Whittome; T J E Whittome
REGIONAL PREFERENCES: East Anglia; SE England
INVESTMENT POLICY: Property investments are generally held for future development
DEVELOPMENT POLICY: Main activity - retail development/refurbishment in prominent provincial towns
DEVELOPMENT ACTIVITIES: offices 10%; shops 90%
(Sept 1992)

Wicks, B E
5 Princes Gate
London SW7

Wickes Properties
19/21 Mortimer Street
London W1N 7RJ
071-323 6667
DIRECTOR: P Jones (Managing)

Wickland Holdings
Lyon House
Lyon Road
Romford
Essex RM1 2BA
0708 755414
DIRECTOR: Mr Collins (Managing)

Wiggin Gee Group Limited

10/11 Argent Court
Sylvan Way
Basildon
Essex SS15 6TG
Tel: 0268 541654 Fax: 0268 414964
NATURE OF BUSINESS: Developer Building Contractor
DIRECTORS: E A Brian; J N Newby
MAJOR SHAREHOLDERS: Headcrown Limited
REGIONAL OFFICES: Basildon, London, Bridgend (Wales)
ANNUAL INCOME/TURNOVER: Company £25m; Group £100m
REGIONAL PREFERENCE: South East England and South Wales
VALUE OF PORTFOLIO: £2m (1992)
DISTRIBUTION OF PORTFOLIO: Offices £1m; Distribution £1m
DISTRIBUTION OF ACTIVITIES: Offices 50%, Residential 50%
DEVELOPMENT POLICY: To develop sites to clients' requirements.
(Sept 1992)

Wiggins Group plc

57 Hart Road
Thundersley
Byfleet
Essex SS7 3PD
DIRECTORS: J A C Edwards; S P Hayklan; E Pickard; P D Warren; J G Wiggins

Wigmore Management Limited

65 Wigmore Street
London W1H 9LG
Tel: 071-935 0192 Fax: 071-935 3074
DIRECTORS: S M Brecker FRICS FCIArb; S Grossmith FRICS
MAJOR SHAREHOLDERS: S M Brecker; S Grossmith

Wildoak Properties

Enterprise House
370-386 Farnham Road
Slough
Berkshire SL2 1JD
0753 34888
DIRECTOR: P Sim (Managing)

Wilky Group Limited

Pembroke House
Mary Road
Guildford
Surrey GU1 4QA
0483 37131
NATURE OF BUSINESS: Development & Investment
DIRECTORS: A Wilkinson; H C Wilkinson; S D Young; M R Young
MAJOR SHAREHOLDERS: Directors
BRANCH OFFICES: Farnborough, Hampshire
REGIONAL PREFERENCES: South East
PROPERTY PORTFOLIO: Factories/warehouses 100%
INVESTMENT POLICY: Retain some completed developments
DEVELOPMENT POLICY: Purchase industrial/ commercial land £0.5m - £3m
DEVELOPMENT ACTIVITIES: Factories/warehouses/ science parks/hi-tech 100%

William Pears Group of Co's Limited, The

100A Avenue Road
London
NW3 3HF

Willan, R Estates Limited

2 Brooklands Road
Sale
Cheshire M33 3SS
061-973 6262
DIRECTOR: P Willan (Managing)

Willis Dawson

Eagle & Child Court
1-5 Market Square
Leighton Buzzard
Bedfordshire LU7 7EU
05253 322557
DIRECTORS: W D Willis; A S Dawson; P R Willis; R C Willis; R V Willis
SUBSIDIARY COMPANIES: Rochpa Holdings Limited

Willmott Dixon

34 Upper Brook Street
London W1Y 1PE
071-272 0233
DIRECTOR: C Ticknap (Managing)

Wilson Bowden plc

Leicester Road
Ibstock
Leicester LE16 1HP
Tel: 0530 60777 Fax: 0530 62805
NATURE OF BUSINESS: Development & Investment
DIRECTORS: D W Wilson (Chairman); C E Bourke CEng MICE; A Greasley; T G Neiland (Non-Executive); Professor R Smith BA MSc PhD(Econ) (Non-Executive); G R G Berwick BA FCA FCT; G Crisp (Managing)
MAJOR SHAREHOLDERS: Wilson group
ANNUAL GROSS/TURNOVER: £149.5m (1988)
VALUE OF PROPERTY PORTFOLIO: £1.9m (1988)
SUBSIDIARY COMPANIES: David Wilson Homes Limited; David Wilson Homes (North Midlands) Limited; Wilson Bowden Properties Limited; David Wilson Homes (Central) Limited; David Wilson Homes (Anglia) Limited; David Wilson Developments Limited; David Wilson Homes (East Midlands) Limited; David Wilson Homes (Southern) Limited; David Wilson Homes (South Midlands) Limited; David Wilson Estates Limited; Wilson Bowden Business Parks Limited; Wilson Bowden Properties (Southern) Limited

Wilson (Connolly) Holdings plc

10 Grafton Street
London W1X 3LA
071-495 8844
DIRECTOR: A Michell (Managing)
ANNUAL TURNOVER: £161.6m (1988)

Entry missing ? Call HELPLINE Page v

Wilson Properties
16 Westwood Park Road
Peterborough PE3 6JL
0733 315423
DIRECTORS: W D Wilson; J H Wilson; J L Wilson; D Elliot; B Martelli
MAJOR SHAREHOLDERS: Directors, their families and family Trusts
REGIONAL PREFERENCES: Central London
PROPERTY PORTFOLIO: Residential 100%
DEVELOPMENT ACTIVITIES: Residential 100%
SUBSIDIARY COMPANIES: Wilson Holdings Limited; Wilson Contracts Limited; W D W Properties Limited; Wilson Holdings (Investments) Limited

Wilson UK Development Limited
Chantry House
High Street
Coleshill
West Midlands B46 3AX
0675 462444
DIRECTOR: A R Brown (Managing)

Wilton Group plc
9 West Halkin Street
London SW1X 8JL

Wimbledon-Preco
Wimbledon House
9/10 Hampshire Terrace
Portsmouth
Hants PO1 2QF
0705 824700
DIRECTOR: W A Whitenstall (Managing)

Wimpey, George Property Holdings Limited
26-28 Hammersmith Grove
London W6 7EN
Tel: 081-748 2000 Fax: 081-846 9670
DIRECTORS: C J Chetwood FCIOB (Chairman); T T Candish BSc FEng FICE; S S Jardine BSc ARCST FInstHE; R Cowan MA FCIS; R N Oliver FCIOB; The Viscount Hood; A M Coane BSc; L R Pincott CBE FCA MInstM; R B Ferris BEng; L C T Sallabank FICE FCIOB; D J T Graves MA MPhil; G A Wright ACMA; C B Smith; A D McDowall FICE FCIOB; Dr J Birks CBE; D Garrod (Property)
MAJOR SHAREHOLDERS: Grove Charity Management Limited
ANNUAL TURNOVER/INCOME: £1,694m (1988)
SUBSIDIARY COMPANIES: The Brightside Mechanical & Electrical Services Group Limited; George Wimpey Australia Pty Limited; George Wimpey Canada Limited; George Wimpey (Carribbean) Limited; George Wimpey Inc (USA); George Wimpey International Limited; Glenthorne Insurance Brokers Limited; Monteith Building Services Limited; OMIS Company Limited; Robert Hobbs Limited; Wimgrove Developments Limited; Wimgrove Investments Limited; Wimpey Alawi LLC; Wimpey Ashphalt Limited; Wimpey Construction UK Limited; Wimpey Engineering Limited; Wimpey Group Services Limited; Wimpey Homes Holdings Limited; Wimpey Laboratories Limited; Wimpey Major Projects Limited; Wimpey Marine Limited; Wimpey Offshore Engineers & Constructors Limited; Wimpey Plant & Transport Limited; Wimpey Property Holdings Limited; Wimpey Waste Managment Limited; Wimpol Limited; W W Hall Limited

Winchester Land plc
St Paul's Gate
Croft Street
Winchester SO23 HSZ
0962 55959

Winchester London Trust
16 Bedford Street
Covent Garden
London
WC2R 9HF

Winchester Property Holdings Limited
19 Minster Precinct
Peterborough
Cambridgeshire PE1 1XX
0733 558581
DIRECTOR: I Williams (Managing)

Windborne International Ltd
20 Suffolk Street
London SW1Y

Windex
Trinity House
33 Lynedoch Street
Glasgow G3 6AA
041-332 7640
DIRECTOR: J Oliver (Managing)

Windsor Plc
Lyon House
160/166 Borough High Street
London SE1 1JB
071-407 7144

Winglaw Group Limited
40 Park Street
London Wl 3PF
071-491 3590
NATURE OF BUSINESS: Development & Investment
DIRECTORS: Joey Esfandi (Managing)

Witting Liverpool Limited
Lynwood House
24-32 Kilburn High Road
London NW6 5UJ

Wood, F E Developments Limited
Charterhouse
169 Newhall Street
Birmingham B3

Woodborne Property Co (Birmingham) Ltd

617a Bearwood Road
Smethwick
Birmingham B66

Woodhead Investments & Development Services Ltd

22 St Johns North
Wakefield

Woodside Estates

2-3 Woodstock Street
London W1R 1HD

Woodstock Land plc

5 Albany Courtyard
Piccadilly
London W1V 9RB
071-734 3721
JOINT MANAGING DIRECTORS: Peter Freeman; Michael Freeman
Subsidiary of Chartwell Land plc

Woolwich Homes Limited

54 Shandwick Place
Edinburgh EH2

Woolwich Industrial Properties Limited

302 Broadway
Bexleyheath
Kent DA6 8AB
081-303 7755
(Sept 1992)
NATURE OF BUSINESS: Investment
DIRECTORS: T Boyd-Whyte LLB (Managing Director); L H Cowell; J M Cotgrove (Mrs); C A Pyle; E B Dennison BSc DA (Secretary)
REGIONAL PREFERENCES: SE London, Kent
ANNUAL TURNOVER: £120,000 (1988)
VALUE OF PROPERTY PORTFOLIO: Approximately £1.25m
PROPERTY PORTFOLIO: Shops 100%
INVESTMENT POLICY: Investment and some improvement of old properties
(Jan 1991)

World Class Homes Limited

1B Town Street
Farsley
Leeds

Wright Properties

Bridgewater Lodge
Bridge Road
Maidenhead
Berkshire SL6 8DG
0628 773133
DIRECTOR: A Cook (Managing)

Wrights Estates & Developments

65 Regent Street
Eccles
Manchester M30

WSJ Holdings Limited

71 Salop Road
Oswestry
Shropshire SY11 2RJ
0691 655201
NATURE OF BUSINESS: Development & Investment
DIRECTORS: W E Clarillon FCA; L Wood; R Bagnall
REGIONAL PREFERENCES: Midlands
BRANCH OFFICES: Stoke on Trent, Kidderminster, Shrewsbury
INVESTMENT POLICY: Progressive within the group
DEVELOPMENT ACTIVITIES: Offices 12%; residential 66%
DEVELOPMENT POLICY: Progressive
SUBSIDIARY COMPANIES: Watkin Starbuck & Jones Limited; WSJ Homes Limited; WSJ Training Limited

Wyncote Developments plc

125 Queens Road
Brighton
West Sussex BN1 3WB
Tel: 0273 205621 Fax: 0273 778524
DIRECTOR: C Gilbert (Managing)

Wynnstay Properties Plc

Union House
6 Martin Lane
London EC4R 0DP

Wyvern Homes Limited

Bond House
Link Way
Howsell Road
Malvern
Worcestershire WR14 1TF
Tel: 0684 561238 Fax: 0684 893428
DIRECTORS: M S Wilesmith (Chairman); C T W Hewitt; W A Gibbard; J N Chamberlain (Managing)
LOCATION OF REGIONAL OFFICES: Malvern, Worcestershire
ANNUAL INCOME/TURNOVER: £3m
REGIONAL PREFERENCES: 30 mile radius of Malvern
VALUE OF PROPERTY PORTFOLIO: £2m
DISTRIBUTION OF PORTFOLIO: Houses 66%; Land 34%
INVESTMENT POLICY: To acquire further land for development and increased sales and profit.
DEVELOPMENT ACTIVITIES: Private houses for sale
DEVELOPMENT POLICY: To increase turnover and profit to build 50 houses per annum to 1993 and then 75 houses in 1994.
(Part of Wilesmith Group)
(Sept 1992)

Entry missing ? Call HELPLINE Page v

Xygon Properties Limited
26 Newland Street
Crumpsall
Manchester
M8

Yarmouth Group (UK) L.P.
6/8 Old Bond Street
London
W1X

Yeates, W S Plc
249 Derby Road
Loughborough
Leicestershire
Le11 9HJ

Yeates, W S Plc
Brand Hill House
Brand Hill
Woodhouse Eaves
Loughborough,
Leicestershire
LE12 8S7

Yorkshire Commercial Properties Ltd
400 Shadwell Lane
Leeds
Yorkshire

Yorkshire Metropolitan Properties Limited
Wadworth Hall
Wadworth, Doncaster
South Yorkshire DN11 9BA
Tel: 0302 310606 Fax: 0302 310148
DIRECTOR: D Blunt (Managing)

Yorkshire Rider
1 Swinegate
Leeds LS1 4DQ
0532 451601
DIRECTORS: Bill Cuthan (Managing); N Bulinski (Marketing)

Yuill, C M Ltd
Cecil House
Loyalty Road
Hartlepool
Cleveland TS25 5BD
0429 266620
DIRECTORS: Mr P G Yuill (Managing); M Drabble (Marketing)

Zodeco Limited
Lenton Lodge
Woolaton Hall Drive
Nottingham
NG8 1AF

Zurich Group Plc
10 Bloomsbury Street
London
WC1B 3EX

3i Commercial Properties Limited
Warley Business Park
The Drive
Warley
Brentwood
Essex CM13 3BE
0277 263131
DIRECTOR: Mr Cartledge (Managing)

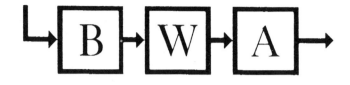

Chapter 3

Pension Funds

Index

Others

C

 Entry missing ? Call HELPLINE Page v

M

S

T

U

V

W

Y

Z

A A H Holdings plc Staff Pension Fund
76 South Pack
Lincoln LN5 8ES
0522-46577

A E plc Pension Fund
Caawston House
Rugby
Warwickshire CV22 7SB
0788-816677

Aarque Systems Limited Pension & Life Assurance Scheme
PO Box 70
Blackthorne Road
Colnbrook
Slough SL3 0AR
0753-680411

Abbey Life Assurance Company Limited Staff Pension Scheme
Abbey Life House
80 Holdenhurst Road
Bournemouth
Dorset BH8 8AL
0202-292373

Abbey National Building Society Pension Fund
Abbey House
207 Grafton Gate
Milton Keynes MK9 1AN
0908-691122

Abbott Laboratories Limited Pension Fund
Queensborough
Kent ME11 5EL
0795-663371

Adams Foods Limited Pension Scheme
Buxton Road
Leek
Staffordshire ST13 6EN
0538-385111

Addis Limited Pension Scheme
Ware Road
Hertford
Hertfordshire SG13 7HL
0992-54221

AEG Telefunken Limited Pension Fund
217 Bath Road
Slough
Berkshire SL1 4AW
0753-872350

Agricultural Mortgage Corporation plc Pension Fund
AMC House
27 Camperdown Street
London E1
071-480 7658

Air Canada Pension Scheme
140 Regent Street
London W1
071-439 7941

Air France Pension & Life Assurance Scheme
Georgian House
69 Boston Manor Road
Brentford
Middlesex TW8 8JQ
081-568 4411

Air Products Limited Pension Scheme
Hersham Place
Molesey Road
Walton on Thames
Surrey KT12 4RZ
0932-249200

Airflow 1973 Pension Scheme, The
Lancaster Road
High Wycombe
Buckinghamshire HP12 3QP
0494-525252
CAPITAL VALUE OF THE FUND: £8.1m
SIZE OF PROPERTY PORTFOLIO: 9.6%
PROPERTY INVESTMENT MANAGERS: Provident Mutual Managed Pensions Limited & Confederation Life Insurance Company
(Sept 1992)

Albright & Wilson Staff Superannuation Fund & Works Pension Fund
1 Knightsbridge Green
London SW1X 7QD
071-589 6393

Alcoa Europe Limited
Portman House
104 College Road
Harrow
Middlesex HA1 1BQ
081-427 4313

Alexander Towing Company Limited Pension Scheme
Castle Chambers
43 Castle Street
Liverpool L2 9TA
051-227 2151

Allen & Overy Pension Fund
9 Cheapside
London EC2V 6AD
071-248 9898

Alliance & Leicester Building Society Pension Fund
Alliance House
Hove Park
East Sussex BN3 7AZ
Tel: 0273-775454 Fax: 0273 224069

Allied Dunbar Assurance plc Pension Fund
Allied Dunbar Centre
Swindon
Wiltshire SN1 1EL
0793-28291

Allied Irish Bank plc
Bankcentre
Ballsbridge
Dublin 4

Allied Lyons Pension Fund
Wyndham Court
Pritchard Street
Bristol BS2 8RH
Tel: 0272-244244 Fax: 0272 244570
CAPITAL VALUE OF THE FUND: £950m (1991)
SIZE OF PROPERTY PORTFOLIO: £450m (1992)
INVESTMENT CATEGORIES: shops 40.7%; offices 31.4%; industrial 11.9%; hi-tech 9.7%; in the course of development 6.3% (1991)
PROPERTY INVESTMENT CONSULTANT(S): Debenham, Tewson & Chinnocks; Fletcher & King
SUBSIDIARY DEVELOPMENT COMPANIES: Let Peacocks Ltd; Ampwyn Developments Ltd; Wyn-Ro Properties Ltd.
(Sept 1992)

Allstate Insurance Company Limited
Marsland House
Marsland Road
Sale
Cheshire M33 3AQ
061-969 7311

Alsford J Pension Trustees Limited
Twickenham Road
Hanworth
Feltham
Middlesex TW13 6JJ
081-894 1011

Amalgamated Metal Corporation Pension Schemes
Adelaide House
London Bridge
London EC4R 9DT
071-626 4521

AMEC plc Staff Pension Scheme
14 South Audley Street
London W1Y 5DP
071-499 3656

American Express Pension Scheme
Prestamex House
171-173 Preston Road
Brighton
Sussex BN1I 6BX
0273-693555

AMI Hospitals Limited Pension Scheme
4-7 Cornwall Terrace,
Regents Park
London NW1 4QP
071-486 1266

AMP of Great Britain Limited Pension Plan
Terminal House
Merrion Avenue
Stanmore
Middlesex HA7 4RS
081-954 2356
CAPITAL VALUE OF FUND: £14m
SIZE OF PROPERTY PORTFOLIO: 5%
CURRENT POLICY FOR INVESTMENT IN PROPERTY: Phillips & Drew have discretion
PROPERTY INVESTMENT MANAGERS: Phillips & Drew
(Jan 1991)

Anderson Strathclyde plc Pension Fund
Anderson House
47 Broad Street
Glasgow
G40 2QW
041-554 1800

Andrews & Partners Limited
12 Badminton Road
Downend
Bristol
BS16 6BQ

ARC Limited
The Ridge
Chipping Sodbury
Bristol, Avon
BS17 6AY

Argyll Foods Pension Scheme
Argyll House
Millington Road
Hayes
Middlesex UB3 4AY
081-848 8744

Entry missing ? Call HELPLINE Page v

Armstrong Equipment plc Pension Scheme
Gibson Lane
Melton
North Ferriby
North Humberside HU14 3HY
0482-633311

Arnotts plc
PO Box 405
Henry Street
Dublin 1

Ash & Lacy plc
Alma Street
Smethwick
Warley
West Midlands
B66 2RP

Associated British Foods Pension Scheme
50-51 Russell Square
London WC1B 4LA
071-631 3535

Associated British Ports Pension Schemes
150 Holborn
London EC1N 2LR
071-430 1177

Associated Communications Corporation Group Pension Scheme
17 Great Cumberland Place
London W1A 1AG
071-262 8040

Associated Newspaper Holdings plc Pension Fund
Carmelite House
Carmelite Street
London EC4Y OJA
071-353 6000

Associated Octel Company Limited Pension Plan
PO Box 17
Oil Sites Road
Ellesmere Port
South Wirral
Cheshire L65 4HF
051-355 3611

Atkins, W S & Staff Retirement Benefits Plan
Woodcote Grove
Ashley Road
Epsom
Surrey KE18 5BW
03727-26140

Australia & New Zealand Banking
Minerva House
PO Box 7
Montague Close
London SE1 9DH

Automobile Association Staff Pension Scheme
Fanum House
Basingstoke
Hampshire RG21 2EA
Tel: 0256 20123 Fax: 0256 493637
(Sept 1992)
CAPITAL VALUE OF THE FUND: £10m
INVESTMENT CATEGORIES: offices 70%, shops 30%
CURRENT POLICY FOR INVESTMENT IN PROPERTY: Pension fund has presently withdrawn from the Property Investment Market
PROPERTY INVESTMENT MANAGER(S): J P Davies FRVA - Executive Estates Manager
(Jan 1991)

Automotive Products plc Pension Scheme
Tachbrook Road
Leamington Spa
Warwickshire CV3 3ER
0926-27000

Avon Cosmetics Pension Plan
Nunn Mills Road
Northampton NN1 5PA
0604-34722

Avon County Council Superannuation Fund
PO Box 22
Avon House
The Haymarket
Bristol BS99 7RT
0272-290777

Avon Rubber plc Retirement & Death Benefits Plan
PO Box 2
Melksham
Wiltshire SN12 8AA
0225-703101

BP Pension Services Limited
BP House
Third Avenue
Harlow
Essex CM19 5AG
0279 448132
INVESTMENT MANAGER: John Martin
PROPERTY INVESTMENT CONSULTANTS: Debenham, Tewson & Chinnocks
CAPITAL VALUE OF FUND: £3042.5m
SIZE OF PROPERTY PORTFOLIO: £841m (Dec 1990)
INVESTMENT CATEGORIES: offices 58.4%; shops 33.2%; industrial 5.8%; residential 1.9%; land 0.7%

CURRENT POLICY FOR INVESTMENT IN PROPERTY: All types of prime property considered on merits (Sept 1992)

BAA plc Pension Scheme

Saxley Court
121-129 Victoria Road
Horley
Surrey, RH6 7AS
Tel: 0293 821717 Fax: 0293 821777
PROPERTY INVESTMENT MANAGERS: Jones Lang Wootton

Babcock International Group Pension Scheme

The Lodge
Badminton Court
Church Street
Amersham
Bucks HP7 ODD
PROPERTY INVESTMENT MANAGERS: Hill Samuel Property Services Ltd.
SIZE OF PROPERTY PORTFOLIO: £25m (1992)
NORMAL INVESTMENT POLICY: Emphasis on retail, industrial with some offices. (Sept 1992)

Baker Perkins Holdings plc Group Pension & Life Assurance Scheme

Westfield Road
Peterborough
PE3 6TA
0733-261261

Bank of America Retirement & Benefit Plan

25 Cannon Street
London EC4P 4HN
071-313 2364

Bank of England Pension Fund

New Change
London EC4M 9AA
071-601 4444

Bank of Montreal

2nd Floor
11 Walbrook
London EC4N 8ED

Bank of Scotland 1976 Pension Fund

c/o Gillies Melville Associates
8 Fredericks Place
London EC2R 8AT
Tel: 071-600 2500 Fax: 071-796 4794
PROPERTY INVESTMENT MANAGER: D K A Madigan ARICS
PROPERTY INVESTMENT CONSULTANTS: Gillies Melville Associates
LOCATION OF REGIONAL OFFICES: Edinburgh & London
SIZE OF PROPERTY PORTFOLIO: £32m (1992)
DISTRIBUTION OF PORTFOLIO: Retail 35%; Offices 48%; Industrial 17%
NORMAL INVESTMENT POLICY: Freehold properties let to Triple A tenants on leases with a minimum of 15 years unexpired at yields in excess of 8% in lot sizes £0.5m to £3.0m
(Sept 1992)

Bankers Trust Company Pension Scheme

Dashwood House
69 Old Broad Street
London EC2P 2EE
071-726 4141

Baptist Union of Great Britain

Baptist House
129 Broadway
Didcot
Oxon OX11 8RT

Barclays Bank plc Pension Fund

Barclays House
1 Wimbourne Road
Poole
Dorset BH15 2BB
0202-671212

Barclays De Zoete Wedd

Ebbgate House
2 Swan Lane
London EC4R 3TS

Baring Brothers & Company Limited Pension Trust

8 Bishopsgate
London EC2N 4AE
071-283 8833

Barr & Wallace Arnold Trust plc

3 Killingbeck Drive
Killingbeck
Leeds LS1 6UF

Bass plc Employees Security Plan

Guardian House
PO Box 49
Cronehills
Linkway
West Bromwich B70 8SE
081-553 6141

BBA Group Pension Fund

PO Box 20
Whitechapel Road
Cleckheaton
West Yorkshire BD19 6HP
0274-874444

BDH Limited 1973 Pension Scheme

Broom Road
Poole
Dorset BH12 4NN
0202-745520

Entry missing ? Call HELPLINE Page v

BEC Pension Trustee Limited
82 New Cavendish Street
London W1M 8AD
071-580 5588

Bechtel GB Limited Pension Fund
Bechtel House
245 Hammersmith Road
London W6 8DP
071-846 4872

Bedfordshire County Council Superannuation Fund
County Hall
Bedford
Bedfordshire MK42 9AP
0234-63222

Beecham UK Pension Fund
Beecham House
Brentford
Middlesex TW8 9BD
081-560 5151

Berkshire County Council Superannuation Fund
PO Box 12 Shire Hall
Reading
Berkshire RG2 9XB
0734-8754444

Bestobell plc Pension Fund & Life Assurance Scheme
Farrs House
Cowgrove
Withborne
Dorset BH21 4EL
(Registered Office)

BET Public Limited Company
Stratton House
Piccadilly
London W1X 6AS

Bibby & Sons Pension Scheme
Richmond House
1 Rumford Place
Liverpool L3 9QQ
051-227 1291

BICC Group Pension Fund
PO Box 1
Prescot
Merseyside L34 5SZ
051-430 2000

Birmid Qualcast plc Pension Fund
Dartmouth Road
Smethwick
Warley
West Midlands B66 1BW
021-558 1431

Bison Holdings Limited
Thorney Lane
Iver
Bucks SL10 9HQ

Bissco Group Limited Pension Scheme
PO Box 1
Long Lane
Aintree
Liverpool L9 7BQ
051-525 3661

BL plc Pension Fund
6th Floor
Belgrave House
1 Greyfriars
Northampton NN1 2BL
0604-30632

Black & Decker Pension Plan
Westpoint
The Grove
Slough
Berkshire SL1 1QQ
0753-74277

Blue Circle Industries plc Pension Scheme
Portland House
Aldermaston
Berkshire RG7 4HP
07536-78000

Blue Star Line Limited Staff Pension Scheme
Albion House
20 Queen Elizabeth Street
London SE1 2LS
071-488 4567

BOC Group plc Pension Schemes
PO Box 39
Great West Road
Brentford
Middlesex TW8 9DQ
081-560 5166

Booker plc
Glynswood House
62-68 Oak End Way
Gerrards Cross
Bucks SL9 8BR

Boots Company plc Pension Scheme
1 Thane Road West
Nottingham
Nottinghamshire
NG2 3AA
0602-506111

Borg-Warner Limited Pension Plans
PO Box 38
Latchmore Court
10 Brand Street
Hitchin
Hertfordshire SG5 1HN
0462-36441

Bovis Pension Funds
Liscartan House
127 Sloane Street
London SW1X 9BA
071-730 0811

Bowring Group Pension Plan
The Bowring Building
Tower Place
London EC3P 3BE
071-283 3100

BPB Industries plc
Langley Park House
Uxbridge Road
Slough SL3 6DU

BPM Holdings plc Pension Scheme
Post & Mail House
28 Colmore Circus
Birmingham B4 6AX
021-236 3366

Bradbury Wilkinson plc Pension & Life Assurance Scheme
265 Burlington Road
New Malden
Surrey KT3 4NH
081-947 3271

Bradford & Bingley Building Society Staff Pension Scheme
PO Box 2
Bingley
West Yorkshire BO16 2LW
0274-568111

British Aerospace Pension Funds Trustees Limited
101 Cannon Street
London EC4N 5AD
Tel: 071-626 6111 Fax: 071-621 9204
PROPERTY INVESTMENT CONSULTANT(S): Jones Lang Wooton OLIM Limited
SIZE OF PROPERTY PORTFOLIO: Approx £166m (April '92)
DISTRIBUTION OF PORTFOLIO (BY VALUE): 49% retail; 17% offices; 24% industrial; £1m agricultural; warehouses 9%
(Sept 1992)

British Airports Authority Superannuation Scheme
Gatwick Airport
West Sussex RH6 OHZ
0293-517755

British Airways
Heathrow Airport
London
071-759 5511

British American Tobacco Company Limited Staff, Payroll & Overseas Pension Funds
Westminster House
Millbank
London SW1P 3JE
071-222 1222

British Broadcasting Corporation New Pension Scheme
Broadcasting House
London W1A 1AA
071-580 4468

British Caledonian Airways Limited Group & Life Assurance Scheme
Caledonian House
Crawley
West Sussex RH10
0293-27890

British Ceramic Research Limited
Queens Road
Penkhull
Stoke-on-Trent
Staffordshire ST4 7LQ

British Coal Corporation
Hobart House
Grosvenor Place
London SW1X 7AE
071-245 6911
British Coal Pension Funds UK Property Portfolio:
CAPITAL VALUE OF FUND: £10,000m
INVESTMENT CATEGORIES: shops & shopping centres 44%; factories/warehouses 13%; offices 42%
PROPERTY INVESTMENT MANAGER: Bob Juddery
CONSULTANTS: Healey & Baker
British Coal Pension Funds - British Coal Superannuation Scheme and Mine Workers Pension Scheme:
CIN PROPERTIES LIMITED: £1,500m
PROPERTY INVESTMENT MANAGER: Bob Juddery

Entry missing ? Call HELPLINE Page v

British Council Superannuation Scheme
65 Davies Street
London W1Y 2AA
071-499 8011

British Ever Ready Pension Fund
1255 High Street
Whetstone
London N20 0EJ
081-446 1313

British Fermentation Products Ltd
Dock Road
Felixstowe
Suffolk IP11 8QW

British Gas Corporation Pension Schemes
152 Grosvenor Road
London SW1V 3JL
Tel: 071-821 1444 Fax: 071-821 8522
(Sept 1992)
British Gas Corporation Staff Pension Scheme:
CAPITAL VALUE OF FUND: £4bn
SIZE OF PROPERTY PORTOFOLIO: £312.836m
INVESTMENT CATEGORIES: shops 30%; offices 32%; industrial/warehouse 24%; other 6%
PROPERTY INVESTMENT MANAGER: G Dent
CONSULTANTS: Weatherall Green & Smith; Humberts
British Gas Corporation Scheme:
CAPITAL VALUE OF FUND: £1bn
SIZE OF PROPERTY PROTFOLIO: £69.48m
INVESTMENT CATEGORIES: offices 39%; retail 48%; industrial 11%; other
PROPERTY MANAGER: G T Dent
CONSULTANTS: Stiles Harold Williams; Humberts
(Jan 1991)

British Olivetti Limited Retirement Benefits Plan
PO Box 89
88 Upper Richmond Road
London SW15
081-785 6666

British Railways Board Pension Fund
50 Liverpool Street
London EC2P 2BP
071-247 7600
CAPITAL VALUE OF FUND: £6bn
SIZE OF PROPERTY PORTFOLIO: £586m
INVESTMENT CATEGORIES: offices 50%; shops 35%; industrial 7%; agricultural 5%; retail warehouses 3%
PROPERTY INVESTMENT MANAGER: R English

British Shipbuilders Pension Trustee Limited
Hadrian House
61 Victoria Street
Farnborough
Hampshire GU14 7PA
0252-519255

British Standards Institution Retirement Benefits Plan
2 Park Street
London W1A 2BS
071-629 9000

British Steel Corporation Pension Scheme
9 Albert Embankment
London SE1 7SN
071-735 7654

British Sugar plc Staff Superannuation Scheme
PO Box 26
Oundle Road
Peterborough PE3 9QU
0733-63171

British Telecom Pension Fund
See Postel Property Services

British Waterways (1990) Pension Fund
Willow Grange
Church Road
Watford
Hertfordshire WD1 3QA
0923-26422
(Sept 1992)

Brooke Bond Group plc Pension Scheme
No 1 Watergate
London EC4Y 0EA
071-686 8899

Brown & Root Limited Retirement Benefits Plan
Brown & Root House
125 High Street
Colliers Wood
London SW19 2JR

BTR plc Pension Fund
Silverton House
Vincent Square
London SW1P 2PL
071-834 3848

Buckinghamshire County Council Superannuation Fund
County Hall
Aylesbury
Buckinghamshire HP20 1DU
0296-5000

Building Design Partnership Pension Fund
16 Grease Street
London W1
071-580 2621

Bull HN Information Systems Ltd
Computer House
Great West Road
Brentford
Hertfordshire EN6 5BA

Burmah Oil plc Group Pension Plans
Burmah House
Pipers Way
Swindon
Wiltshire SN3 1R
0793-30151

Burton Group plc Staff Superannuation Fund
Hudson Road Mills
Leeds
West Yorkshire LS9 7DN
0532-494949

Cable & Wireless Common Investment Fund
Mercury House
Theobalds Road
London WC1X 8RX
Tel: 071-315 4705 Fax: 071-315 5198
(Sept 1992)
CAPITAL VALUE FUND: £410m
SIZE OF PROPERTY PORTFOLIO: Nil
INVESTMENT CATEGORIES: PUTS 100%
CURRENT POLICY FOR INVESTMENT IN PROPERTY: Only PUTS
PROPERTY INVESTMENT MANAGER: Nil
(Jan 1991)

Cadbury Schweppes Pension Fund
PO Box 171
Franklin House
Bournville
Birmingham B30 2NA
Tel: 021-458 2000 Fax: 021-451 3199
CAPITAL VALUE OF FUND: £571m
SIZE OF PROPERTY PORTFOLIO: £66m
INVESTMENT CATEGORIES: industrial 13%; offices 50%; shops 23%; business space 13%
PROPERTY INVESTMENT MANAGER: S J Smith FRICS
CONSULTANT(S): Strutt & Parker
(Sept 1992)

Calor Group Limited Retirement Benefits Plan
Appleton Park
Riding Court Road
Datchet
Slough
Berkshire SL3 9JG
Tel: 0753 540000 Fax: 0753 48121
CAPITAL VALUE OF FUND: £145.5m (05/04/92)
SIZE OF PROPERTY PORTFOLIO: £9.35m (31/12/91)
INVESTMENT CATEGORIES: offices 3%; shops 39%; warehouses 58%
CURRENT POLICY FOR INVESTMENT IN PROPERTY: up to 10% of total fund value
PROPERTY INVESTMENT CONSULTANTS: Hillier Parker
(Sept 1992)

Cambridgeshire County Council Superannuation Fund
Shire Hall
Castle Hill
Cambridge CB3 0AP
0223-317233

Canadian Pacific Companies (Europe) Pension Funds
105 Victoria Street
London SW1E 6QT
071-839 5883

Cannon Lincoln
1 Olympic Way
Wembley
Middlesec HA9 0NB

Cape Industries plc Staff Pension & Life Insurance Scheme
114 Park Street
London W1Y 4AB
071-499 6022

Carborundum Company Limited Employees Pension Scheme & Management Plan
PO Box 55
Trafford Park
Manchester M17 1HP
061-872 2381

Carreras Rothmans Limited Pension Fund
Christopher Martin Road
Basildon
Essex SS14 3EP
0268-22840

Case Tractors Executive Staff & Works Benefit Plans
Meltham Mills
Meltham
Huddersfield
Yorkshire HD7 3AR
0484-850361

Caterpillar Tractor Company Limited Pension Plan
Old Edinburgh Road
Glasgow G2 1JP
0689-812921

Entry missing ? Call HELPLINE Page v

Central Independent Television
Central House
Compass Centre North
Chatham Maritime
Kent ME4 4UL

Charter Consolidated Services Limited Pension Scheme
PO Box 104
Charter House
Park Street
Ashford
Kent TB24 84Q
0233-25700

Charterhouse Systems Holdings Limited
34-35 Furnival Street
London EC4A 1JU
071-831 3031

Cheshire County Council Superannuation Fund
Richard House
80 Lower Bridge Street
Chester
Cheshire CH1 1SW
0244-602501

Chevron Petroleum (Formerly Gulf UK) Pension Fund
93 Wigmore Street
London W1H 9AA
071-487 8100

Chloride Group plc Pension Scheme
130 Wilton Road
London SW1V 1LQ
071-834 5500

Chubb & Son plc 1972 Pension Fund
Western Road
Bracknell
Berkshire RG12 1RG
(Registered Office)

CIBA Geigy plc Pension Fund
PO Box 47
Hurdsfield Industrial Estate
Macclesfield
Cheshire SK10 2NT
0625-21933

Civil Aviation Authority Superannuation Scheme
Aviation House
129 Kingsway
London WC2B 6NN
071-405 6922

Claas UK Limited
Saxham
Bury St Edmunds
Suffolk IP28 6QZ

Clark C & J Limited Pension Fund
40 High Street
Street
Somerset BA16 0YA
0458-43131

Clarke Nickolls & Coombs plc
CNC House
33 High Street
Sunninghill
Ascot
Berkshire SL5 9NR

Clayton Dewandre Holdings Limited Works Staff & Senior Staff Retirement Benefit Scheme
90 Newbold Road
Rugby
Warwickshire CV21 2N1
0788-74561

Clerical Medical & General Life Assurance Society Staff Superannuation Fund
Narrow Plain, Bristol
Avon BS2 0JH
0272-290566

Cleveland County Council Superannuation Fund
PO Box 100
Municipal Buildings
Middlesborough
Cleveland TS1 2QH
0642-248155

Clwyd County Council Superannuation Fund
Shire Hall
Mold
Clwyd CH7 6NA
0352-2121

Clydesdale Bank plc Pension Scheme
30 St Vincent Place
Glasgow
Strathclyde G1 2HL
041-248 7070

Co-operative Insurance Society Limited Employees Pension & Death Benefit Scheme
Miller Street
Manchester M60 0AL
061-832 8686

Co-operative Retail Services Limited Employees Superannuation Scheme
29 Dantzic Street
Manchester M4 4BA
061-832 8152

Co-operative Wholesale Society Employees Pension & Death Benefit Scheme
PO Box 53
New Century House
Manchester M60 4ES
061-834 1212

Coats Patons plc Superannuation Fund
155 St Vincent Street
Glasgow G2 5PA
041-221 8711

Colt International Limited Life Assurance & Retirement Scheme
New Lane
Havant
Hampshire PO9 2LY
0705-45111

Commercial Union Group Staff Retirement & Death Benefits Scheme
Commercial Unions House
69 Park Lane
Croydon
Surrey CR9 1BG
081-283 7500

Commonwealth Development Corporation Pension Scheme
33 High Street
London W1A 3AR
071-629 8484

Compair Limited Retirement Benefits Plan
PO Box 285
Appleton Park
Datchet
Berkshire SL3 9JF
0753-40000

Conder Group plc Pension Scheme
Kingsworth Court
Kingsworthy
Winchester
Hampshire S023 7QA
Tel: 0962-882222 Fax 0962-885016

Conoco Pension Plans
Park House
116 Park Street
London W1Y 4NN
071-493 1235

Cookson Group plc
1974 Works Staff & 1971 Senior Executive Pension Plans
14 Gresham Street
London EC2V 7AT
071-606 4400

Cope Allman International plc Group Pension Fund
40 Bernhard Street
London WC1N 1LE
071-833 0411

Cornhill Insurance plc Retirement & Death Benefits Fund
57 Ladymead
Guildford
Surrey GU1 1DB
0483-68161

Corning Limited Pension Plan
Wear Glass Works
Sunderland
Tyne & Wear
SR4 6EJ
0783-76222

Cornwall County Council Superannuation Fund
County Hall
Truro
Cornwall TR1 3AY
0872-74282

Corporation of Lloyds
Gun Wharf Dock Road
Chatham
Kent ME4 4TU
0634-407333

Corporation of London Superannuation Fund
PO Box 270
Guildhall
London EC2P 2EJ
071-606 3030

Costain Group plc Pension Scheme
111 Westminster Bridge Road
London SE1 7UE
071-928 4977

County of South Glamorgan
County Hall
Atlantic Wharf
Cardiff CF1 5UW

Entry missing ? Call HELPLINE Page v

Courtaulds Pensions Investment Trustees Limited
18 Hanover Square
London W1A 2BB
Tel: 071-629 9080 Fax: 071-629 2586
(Sept 1992)
PROPERTY INVESTMENT MANAGER: J B Evans
PROPERTY INVESTMENT CONSULTANTS: Hillier Parker
SIZE OF PROPERTY PORTFOLIO: £145m (1990)
DISTRIBUTION OF PORTFOLIO (BY VALUE): Offices 11%; shops 14%; retail warehouses 14%; hotels 5%; industrials 5%
NORMAL INVESTMENT POLICY: Accent on high-yielding, secondary properties
(Jan 1991)

Coutts & Company Staff Pension Scheme
440 Strand
London WC2R OQS
071-379 6262

CPC Limited & Death Benefits Scheme
Claygate House
Esher
Surrey KT10 9PN
0372-62181

Crane Limited Staff & 1978 Pension Schemes
11-12 Bouverie Street
London EC4Y 8AH
071-353 6511

Crown House plc Staff Pension Scheme
No 1 King Street
Manchester M2 6AW
(Registered Office)

Crusader Insurance plc
Reigate
Surrey RH2 8BL

CSO Valuations AG
17 Charterhouse Street
London EC1N 6RA

Cumbria County Council Superannuation Fund
The Courts
Carlisle CA3 8NA
0228-23456

Cummins Engine Company Limited Pension Fund & Life Assurance Scheme
Pensions Department
Cummins Engine Co Ltd
Yarm Road
Darlington
Co Durham DL1 4PW
Tel: 0325-460606 Fax: 0325-359380
LOCATION OF REGIONAL OFFICES: Shotts, Daventry, Huddersfield, Halifax, New Malden.
SIZE OF PROPERTY PORTFOLIO: £ Nil (1992)
DISTRIBUTION OF PORTFOLIO: None in property
NORMAL INVESTMENT POLICY: Equities, Fixed Interest etc.
(Sept 1992)

Currys Group plc Pension Plans
45-50 Uxbridge Road
Ealing
London W5 2SU
081-567 6611

Daily Telegraph Group Pension Fund
135 Fleet Street
London EC4P 4BL
071-353 4242

Dalgety UK Limited Pension Fund
19 Hanover Square
London W1R 9DA
071-629 9402

Danish Bacon Company
Howardsgate
Welwyn Garden City
Hertfordshire AL8 6NN

D'Arcy Macmanus & Masius Limited
2 St James's Square
London SW1Y 4JY
071-839 3422

Davy Corporation plc Staff & Works Pension Plans
15 Portland Place
London W1A 4DD
071-637 2821

De La Rue plc Pension Funds
De La Rue House
3-5 Burlington Gardens
London W1A 1DL
071-734 8020

Debenham Tewson & Chinnocks Limited
44 Brook Street
London W1A 4AG

Debenhams Pension Trust Limited
214 Oxford Street
London W1N 9DF
071-580 3000

Delta Group Pension Plans
Greets Green Road
West Bromwich
West Midlands B70 9ER
021-553 6188

Derbyshire County Council Superannuation Fund
County Offices
Matlock
Derbyshire DE4 3AH
0629-3411

Digital Equipment Company Limited Staff Pension Plan
Digital Park
Worton Grange
Imperial Way
Reading, Berkshire RG2 OTE
0734-868711

Distillers Company plc Companies Pension Scheme
Distillers House
33 Ellerfly Road
Edinburgh EH2 6JW
031-337 7373

Dixons Group plc Retirement & Employee Security Scheme
18-24 High Street
Edgware
Middlesex HA8 7EG
081-952 2345

Dorset County Council Superannuation Fund
County Hall
Dorchester
Dorset DT1 1XJ
0305-63131

Dow Chemical Company Limited Pension Plan
Meadowbank
Bath Road
Hounslow
Middlesex TW4 9QY
081-734 6329

Dowty Group plc Pension Fund
Arle Court
Cheltenham
Gloucester GL51 0TP
0242-521411

DRG Pension Trustee Limited
1 Redcliff Road
Bristol BS99 7QY
0272-294294

Du Pont UK Limited Pension Fund
Wedgwood Way
Stevenage
Hertfordshire SH1 4QN
0438-73400

Dumfries & Galloway Regional Council Superannuation Fund
Council Offices
Dumfries DG1 2DD
Tel: 0387 61234 Fax: 0387 60034
INVESTMENT MANAGERS: Morgan Grenfell Trust Corporation (CI) Ltd
(Sept 1992)

Dunham Mount Group Staff Pension Plan
Ruthven Road
Seaforth
Liverpool L21 2QB
051-920 8100

Dunlop Limited Pension Scheme
148-158 Westgate Road
Newcastle upon Tyne NE99 1TG
0632-322656

Dunn, G A & Co
1 Apsley Way
North Circular Road
London NW2 7HF

Duphar Limited
Duphar House
Gaters Hill
West End
Southampton SO3 3JD

Duport Group Staff & Works Pension & Life Assurance Plans
Sedgeley Road East
Tipton
West Midlands DY4 7YU
021-557 7591

Durham County Council Superannuation Fund
County Hall
Durham DH1 5UE
Tel: 091-386 4411 Fax: 091-383 0228
(Sept 1992)
SIZE OF PROPERTY PORTFOLIO: £20.08m (1989/90)
DISTRIBUTION OF PORTFOLIO (BY VALUE): Property unit trusts £20.08m
(Jan 1991)

Dyfed County Council Superannuation Fund
County Council
Camarthen
Dyfed SA31 1JP
0267-233333

Eagle Star Pension Funds
56 St Mary Avenue
London
EC3A 8SQ
071-929 1111
INVESTMENT MANAGER: R Brignell (Managing)

East Sussex County Council Superannuation Fund
County Hall
Lewes
East Sussex BN7 1SF
0273-475400

Ecclesiastical Insurance Group
Beauford House
Brunswick Road
Gloucester GL1 1JZ

Edmundson Electrical Limited
PO Box 1
Tatton Street
Knutsford
Cheshire WA16 6AY

Edward Erdman
6 Grosvenor Street
London W1X 0AD

Electricity Association
30 Millbank
London SW1P 4RD

Electricity Supply Pension Scheme
Electricity Council
30 Millbank
London SW1P 4RD
071-834 2333
(Sept 1992)
CAPITAL VALUE OF FUND: £6,000m
SIZE OF PROPERTY PORTFOLIO: £700m
INVESTMENT CATEGORIES: Offices 50%; shops 20%; factories 10%; warehouses 5%; other 5%
INVESTMENT MANAGER: G I M Cockburn
(Jan 1991)

Electrolux Limited Works Pension Scheme & Group Staff Pension Fund
Electrolux Works
Oakley Road
Luton
Bedfordshire LU4 9QQ
0582-573255

Electronic Rentals Group plc Pension Scheme
57-63 Ringway
Preston
Lancashire PR1 2SR
0772-51311

Eli Lilly Group Pension Trustees Limited
Dextra Court
Chappel Hill
Basingstoke
Hampshire RG21 2SY
0256 485096

Elliott B plc Pension Schemes
167 Imperial Drive
Harrow
Middlesex HA2 7JP
071-866 1244

Ellis, Richard
55 Old Broad Street
London EC2M 1LP

Emhart International Ltd
Lyn House
39 The Parade
Oadby
Leicester LE2 5BB

Englehard Industries Pension Scheme
Englehard House
8 Throgmorton Avenue
London EC2N 2DL
071-588 4080

English China Clays Group plc Staff Pension Schemes
John Keay House
St Austell
Cornwall PL25 4DJ
0726-623283

Equitable Life Property Pension Fund
Equitable Life Assruance Society
4 Coleman Street
London EC2R 5AP
071-606 6611

Equity & Law Life Assurance Society
Amersham Road
High Wycombe
Buckinghamshire HP13 5AL

Ernst & Whinney Staff Pension & Life Assurance Scheme
Becket House
1 Lambeth Palace Road
London SE1 7EU
071-928 2000

Essex County Council Superannuation Fund
County Hall
Chelmsford
Essex CM1 1JZ

Tel: 0245 492211 Fax: 0245 494650
CAPITAL VALUE OF FUND: £719m
SIZE OF PROPERTY PORTFOLIO: £50.5m
INVESTMENT CATEGORIES: offices 26%; retail 45%; warehouses 20%; other 9%
CURRENT POLICY FOR INVESTMENT IN PROPERTY: Rationalise portfolio and maintain current weighting
PROPERTY INVESTMENT MANAGER(S): Weatherall Green & Smith
CONSULTANTS: Weatherhall Green & Smith
(Sept 1992)

Esso Petroleum Company Limited Retirement & Death Benefit Plan
76-118 Victoria Street
London SW1E 5JW
071-834 6677

Extel Group plc Pension Fund
Extel House
East Harding Street
London EC4P 4HB
071-353 1080

Ferranti plc Pension Scheme
Bridge House
Park Road
Gatley, Cheadle
Cheshire SK8 4HZ
061-428 3644/ 01-588 4080

Fife Regional Council Superrannuation Fund
Fife House
North Street, Glenrothes
Fife KY7 5LT
0592-754411

Fina Pension Scheme
Fina House
Ashley Avenue
Epsom
Surrey KT18 5AD
0372-726226

Findus Pension Fund
Pelham Road
Cleethorpes
South Humberside DN35 7JU
0472-59141

Fisher Controls Limited Pension Plan
Fisher House
Chineham Court
Chineham, Basingstoke
Hampshire RG24 0UW
0256-55731

Fitch Lovell plc Pension Scheme
Glynswood House
62-68 Oak End Way
Gerrards Cross
Bucks SL9 8BR
Tel: 0753 888161 Fax: 0753 880091
PROPERTY INVESTMENT MANAGER: Connell Wilson
PROPERTY INVESTMENT CONSULTANT: Connell Wilson
SIZE OF PROPERTY PORTFOLIO: £6¼m (1991)
DISTRIBUTION OF PORTFOLIO: Offices 95%; Shops 5%
NORMAL INVESTMENT POLICY: Small office developments
(Sept 1992)

Ford Motor Company Limited Salaried & Hourly Paid Contributory Pension Fund
Eagle Way
Warley
Brentwood
Essex CM13 3BW
0277-253000

Forth Ports Authority Pension Scheme
Tower Place
Leith
Edinburgh EH6 7DB
031-554 4343

Foster Brothers plc Pension & Life Assurance Plan
Marshall Lake Road
Shirley, Solihull
West Midlands
021-774 8555

Freemans plc Retirement & Life Assurance Plan
139 Clapham Road
London SW9 0HR
071-735 7644

French Kier Holdings plc Pension & Assurance Scheme
Tempsford Hall
Sandy
Bedfordshire SG19 0HR
0767-40111

Furness Pension Scheme
Furness House
53 Brighton Road
Redhill
Surrey RH1 6YL
0737-771122
PROPERTY INVESTMENT MANAGER: MIM Limited
PROPERTY INVESTMENT CONSULTANTS: MIM Property Services

Fyffes Group Limited Pension Scheme
15 Station Street
Piccadilly
London W1A 2LI
071-499 3411

G Plan
Spring Gardens
PO Box 27
High Wycombe
Buckinghamshire HP13 7AD

Gallaher Pensions Limited
PO Box 14
Rowdell Road
Northolt
Middlesex UB5 5QU
Tel: 081-845 2366 Fax: 081-841 3744
PROPERTY INVESTMENT MANAGER: Chesterton
SIZE OF PROPERTY PORTFOLIO: Less than £50m (1992)
(Sept 1992)

Gateway Corporation Limited, The
Stockley House
130 Wilton Road
London SW1V 1LUH

GBE International Pension Fund
GBE House
Chantry House
Andover
Hampshire SP10 1DD
0264-58611

Geest Limited Pension Schemes
White House Chambers
Spalding
Lincolnshire PE11 2AI
0775-61111

General & Municipal Workers Pension Trustee Company Limited
Thorne House
Ruxley Ridge
Claygate
Esher
Surrey KT10 0TL
0372-62081

General Accident Assurance Companies Pension Scheme
Pitheavlis
Perth
Scotland PH2 0NH
0738-21202

General Electric Company plc Benefits Scheme
132 Long Acre
London WC2E 9AH
071-836 3444

General Foods Limited Pension Scheme
Banbury
Oxfordshire OX16 7QU
0295-4433

Gestetner Holdings plc Pension Scheme
PO Box 466
London B17 9LT
071-808 1050

Gillette UK Limited Pension Scheme
Great West Road
Isleworth
Middlesex TW7 5NP
081-560 1234

Glaxco Group Pension Scheme
Graham Street
London N1 8JZ
071-253 3060

Gloucester County Council Superannuation Fund
Quayside Wing
Shire Hall
Gloucester
Gloucestershire GL1 2TJ
0452-425878
(Sept 1992)

Glynwed International plc Group Pension Scheme
Headland House
New Coventry Road
Sheldon
Birmingham B26 3AZ
021-742 2366

Goodyear Tyre & Rubber Company Staff Pension Plan
Bushbury
Wolverhampton WV10 6DH
0902-22321

Grace, WR Limited Pension Plan
Northdale House
North Circular Road
London NW10 7UH
071-965 0611

Grampian Regional Council Superannuation Fund
Woodhill House
Ashgrove Road West
Aberdeen AB9 2LU
0224-682222

Grand Metropolitan Group & Senior Executives Pension Scheme
Cambridge House
Highbridge Industrial Estate
Oxford Road
Uxbridge
Middlesex UB8 1UN
0895-58111

CAPITAL VALUE OF FUND: £590m
SIZE OF PROPERTY PORTFOLIO: £81m
INVESTMENT CATEGORIES: offices 57%; shops 35%; factories/warehouses 16%
CURRENT POLICY FOR INVESTMENT IN PROPERTY: Acquire retail warehouse investment
PROPERTY INVESTMENT MANAGER(S): R A Lucas
CONSULTANT(S): Knight Frank & Rutley
(Sept 1992)

Greater London Council Superannuation Fund
County Hall
London SE1 7PB
071-633 6500

Greater Manchester Council Supperannuation Fund
County Hall
Piccadilly Gardens
Manchester M60 3HR
061-247 3610

Greater Manchester County Superannuation Fund
Tameside Metropolitan Borough Council
Finance Department
Council Offices
Wellington Road
Ashton-Under-Lyne
Tameside OL6 6DL
061-301 2418

Greater Nottingham Co-operative Society Limited Superannuation Fund
243 Derby Road
Lenton
Nottingham NG7 1QP
0602-474021

Greene King plc
Westgate Brewery
Westgate Street
Bury St Edmunds
Suffolk IP33 1QT

Grindlays Bank UK Group Pension Schemes
Minerva House
PO Box 7
Montague Close
London SE1 9DH
071-626 0545

Guardian & Manchester Evening News Pension Scheme
164 Deansgate
Manchester M60 2RR
061-832 7200

Guardian Royal Exchange Pension Fund
Royal Exchange
London EC3V 3LS
071-283 7101

Guinness United Distillers Pension Trust
33 Pinkhill Road
Edinburgh
EH12 7BA
Tel: 031-346 4373 Fax: 031-337 9872
(Sept 1992)
CAPITAL VALUE OF FUND: £700m (31/3/89)
SIZE OF PROPERTY PORTFOLIO: £60m
INVESTMENT CATEGORIES: offices 80%; warehouses 20%
CURRENT POLICY FOR INVESTMENT IN PROPERTY: Manager's discretion. Up to 15% of fund
PROPERTY INVESTMENT MANAGERS: Savills
(Jan 1991)

Gwent County Council Supperannuation Fund
County Hall
Cumbran
Gwent NP44 2XD
06333-67711

HP Foods Limited
45 Northampton Road
Market Harborough
Leicestershire LE16 9BQ

Hadrian Trustees Limited
Hadrian House
61-65 Victoria Road
Farnborough
Hampshire GU14 7PA

Halifax Building Society Staff Retirement Fund
PO Box 60
Trinity Road
Halifax HX1 2RG
Tel: 0422 330506 Fax: 0422 333006
PROPERTY INVESTMENT MANAGER(s): T S Postill - Group pension fund manager.
PROPERTY INVESTMENT CONSULTANTS: Michael Laurie
(Sept 1992)

Hall Engineering plc Pension Scheme
Harlescott Lane
Shrewsbury
Shropshire SY1 3AS
0743-59541

Halliburton Geodata Limited
Howe Moss Place
Kirkhill Industrial Estate
Dyce
Aberdeen AB2 0GL

Entry missing ? Call HELPLINE Page v

Hambros plc Staff Pension Scheme
41 Bishopsgate
London EC2P 2AA
01-588 2851

Hampshire County Council Superannuation Fund
The Castle
Winchester
Hampshire SO23 8UB
0962-54411

Harris Systems Limited
Eskdale Road
Winnersh
Wokingham
Berkshire RG11 5TR

Harrisons & Crossfield plc
14 Lower Street
Ipswich
Suffolk IP4 1AP

Hays Group Limited Pension Scheme
Hays Wharf
Millmead
Guildford
Surrey GU2 5HJ
0483-65000

Headington Holdings Limited
4-12 Dorrington Street
London EC1N 7TB

Healey & Baker
29 St George Street
London W1A 3BG

Heinz Company Limited Pension Plan
Hayes Park
Hayes
Middlesex UB4 8AL
081-573 7757

Hepworth Ceramic Holdings plc Pension Schemes
Genefax House
Tapton Park Road
Sheffield S10 3FJ
0742-306577

Hepworth J & Son plc Pension Scheme
Hepworth House
Claypit Lane
Leeds
West Yorkshire LS2 8AP
0532-440265

Hereford & Worcester County Coucil Superannuation Fund
County Hall
Spetchley Road
Worcester WR5 2NP
0905-35366

Hertfordshire County Council Superannuation Fund
County Hall
Hertford
Hertfordshire SG13 8DQ
0992-556650

Hickson UK Limited Group Pension Scheme
Castleford
West Yorkshire WF10 2JF
0977-556565

Hill Samuel Group plc Pension Scheme
100 Wood Street
London EC2P 2AJ
071-628 8011

Hoare Govett Limited Staff & Special Executives Pension Fund
4 Broadgate
London EC2M 7LE
Tel: 071-394 7005 Fax: 071-374 4670
(Sept 1992)

Hoechst UK Limited Pension & Life Assurance Scheme
Hoescht House
Salisbury Road
Hounslow
Middlesex TW4 6JH
081-570 7712

Honeywell Pension Funds
Charles Square
Bracknell
Berkshire RG12 1EB
0344-424555

Hong Kong Bank Group London Staff Pension Fund
PO Box 199
99 Bishopsgate
London EC2P 2LA
071-638 2300

Hoover plc Pension Scheme
Perivale
Greenford
Middlesex UB6 8DX
081-997 3311

House of Fraser plc Pension Plans
PO Box 142
69 Buckanan Street
Glasgow
Strathclyde G1 5LE
041-221 6401

HTV Wales Pension Fund
The Television Centre
Cardiff
South Glamorgan CF1 6XJ

Humberside County Council Superannuation Fund
PO Box 13
County Hall
Beverley
Humberside HU17 9AB
0482-867131

Hydroboard Superannuation Fund North of Scotland Hydro-Electric Board
16 Rothesay Terrace
Edinburgh EH3 7SE
031-225 1361

IBM Pension & Life Assurance Plan
PO Box 41
North Harbour
Portsmouth
Hampshire PO6 3AU
0705-321212

ICL Pension Fund
93-99 Uppper Richmond Road
Putney
London SW15 2TE
071-788 7272

Ilford Limited
Town Lane
Mobberley
Cheshire WA16 7HA

IMI plc Pension Fund
PO Box 216
Kynock Works
Witton
Birmingham B6 7BA
021-356 4848

Imperial Cancer Research Fund Pension Fund
PO Box 123
Lincoln`s Inn Fields
London WC2A 3PX
071-242 0200

Imperial Chemicals Industries plc Pension Funds
Bessemer Road
Welwyn Garden City
Hertfordshire AL7 1HD
07073-23400

Imperial Tobacco Limited
PO Box 244
Southville
Bristol
Avon BS99 7UJ

Inchcape plc Pension Fund
40 St Mary Avenue
London EC3A 8EU
071-283 4680

Inco Europe Limited Pension & Life Cover Plan
Thames House
Millbank
London SW1P 4QF
071-834 3888

Industrial Training Board Pension Funds, The
Star House
69-71 Clarendon Road
Watford
Hertfordshire WD1 1QL
0923-26264

International Harvester Company of GB Managerial & Non Managerial Pension Schemes
Wheatley Hall Road
Doncaster
South Yorkshire DN2 4PG
0302-66631

International Nickel Trustees Limited
Inco Alloys Limited
Holmer Road
Hereford HR4 9SL

International Thomson Organisation plc Pension Scheme
The Quadrangle
180 Wardour Street
London W1A 4YG
071-437 9987

Iron Trades Insurance Group Staff Trust
Iron Trades House
21-24 Grosvenor Place
London SW1X 7JA
071-235 6033

Entry missing ? Call HELPLINE Page v

Isle of Wight County Council Superannuation Fund
County Hall
Newport
Isle of Wight PO30 1UD
0983-524031

ITB Pensions Funds
Star House
69/71 Clarendon Road
Watford
Hertfordshire WD1 1QL

James Neill Holdings plc Pension Plan
Handsworth Road
Sheffield
South Yorkshire S13 9BR
0742-449911

John Holt Group Limited Pension Plan
380 India Buildings
Water Street
Liverpool
Merseyside L2 0QF
051-236 8881

John Lewis Partnership Pensions Trust
171 Victoria Street
London
SW1E 5NN
071-828 1000
DIRECTORS: R A Dennis (Managing)

Johnson & Firth Brown Trustees Limited
Western House
Manchester Road
Clifton
Manchester M27 2ND
061-7930275

Johnson & Johnson Limited Group Retirement Plan
Brunel Way
Slough
Berkshire SL1 1XR
0753-31234

Johnson Mathey Employees Pension Scheme
New Garden house
78 Hatton Garden
London EC1 8JP
Tel: 071-269 8124 Fax: 071-269 8129
(Sept 1992)
CAPITAL VALUE: £240m (1989)
PROPERTY PROTFOLIO: £12m
INVESTMENT CATEGORIES: Offices 31%; shops 34%; warehouses 35%
INVESTMENT POLICY: 5% of market value of fund
INVESTMENT MANAGERS: Mercury Asset Management, 33 King William Street, London EC4R 9AS

K Shoes Pension Schemes
Netherfield House
Kendal
Cumbria LA9 7BT
0539-24343

Kalamazoo plc 1973 Pension & Life Assurance Plan
Mill Lane
Northfield
Birmingham B31 2RW
021-475 2191

Kenning Motor Group plc Staff Pension Scheme
Manor Offices
Old Road
Chesterfield
Derbyshire S40 3QT
0246-77241

Kent County Council Superannuation Fund
County Hall
Maidstone
Kent ME14 1XE
0622-671411

Kimberly Clark Limited Pension Scheme
Larkfield
Aylesford
Kent ME20 7PS
0622-782486
(Sept 1992)

Kleeneze Holdings plc
Martins Road
Hanham
Bristol
Avon BS15 3DY

Kleinwort Benson Pension Scheme
20 Fenchurch Street
London EC3P 3DB
071-623 8000

Kodak Limited Pension Plan
Kodak House
Station Road
Hemel Hempstead
Hertfordshire HP1 1JU
0442-61122

Laing, John plc
Studio House
Elstree Way
Borehamwood
Herts WD6 1SD

Lancashire County Council
County Hall
Preston PR1 0LD

Lancashire County Council Superannuation Fund
County Hall
Preston
Lancs PR1 8XJ
0772-264742

Laporte Industries Holdings plc Pension Fund
Hanover House
14 Hanover Saqaure
London W1R 0BE
071-629 6603

Lawson Mardon Group (Europe) Limited
Boyce's Building
Regent Street
Clifton
Bristol BS8 4HU

Lazard Brothers & Co. Ltd
21 Moorfields
London EC2P 2HT

LCR International plc Pension Scheme
Glasshouse Yard
London EC1A 4JN
071-250 3078

Legal & General Assurance Society Pensions Management
Kingswood House
Tadworth
Surrey KT20 6EU
07373-53456

Leicestershire Co-operative Society Employees Superannuation Fund
4 Union Street
Leicester LE1 4HA
0533-20431

Leicestershire County Council Superannuation Fund
County Hall
Glenfield
Leicester LE3 8RB
0533-871313

LEX Service Pension Scheme
17 Great Cumberland Place
London W1H 8AD
071-723 1212

Liberty Life Assurance Co Ltd
Liberty House
Station Road
New Barnet
Herts EN5 1PA

Lilly Industries Ltd
Kingsclere Road
Basingstoke
Hampshire RG21 2XA

Lincolnshire County Council Superannuation Fund
County Offices
Newland
Lincoln
Lincolnshire LN1 1YG
0522-41651

Lindsey Oil Refinery Limited Pension Scheme
Killingholme
Grimsbury
Humberside DN40 3LW
0469-73211

Lindustries Limited Pension Scheme & CI Pension Scheme
Southgate House
Stevenage
Hertfordshire SG1 1HG
0483-65461

Littlewoods Staff Pension Scheme, The
JM Centre
Old Hall Street
Liverpool
Merseyside XL70 1AB
051-235 2764

Liverpool Victoria Friendly Society Staff Pension Scheme
Victoria House
Southampton Row
London WC1B 4DB
Tel: 071-405 4377 Fax: 071-430 0078
PROPERTY INVESTMENT DIRECTOR: T S Philpot F.S.A.
PROPERTY INVESTMENT CONSULTANTS: M McLafferty; R S Humphreys
SIZE OF PROPERTY PORTFOLIO: £500m (1991)
NORMAL INVESTMENT POLICY: All sectors except residential & agricultural & leisure
(Sept 1992)

Entry missing ? Call HELPLINE Page v

Lloyds Bank International Pension Fund
40-66 Queen Victoria Street
London EC4P 4EL
071-248 9822

Lloyds Bank plc Pension Scheme
78 Cannon Street
London EC4P 4LN
071-626 1500

Lloyds of London Superannuation Fund
Lloyds
Lime Street
London EC3M 7HA
071-623 7100

Lloyds Register of Shipping Superannuation Fund Association
71 Fenchurch Street
London EC3M 4BS
071-709 9166

London & Manchester Group Pension Scheme
Winslade Park
Clyst St Mary
Exeter
Devon EX5 1DS
0392-52155

London Borough of Barking & Dagenham
Civic Centre
Dagenham
Essex RM10 7BY
081-592 4500

London Borough of Barnet Superannuation Fund
Town Hall
Hendon
London NW4 4BG
081-202 8282

London Borough of Bexley Superannuation Fund
Town Hall
Erith
Kent DA8 1TL
081-303 7777

London Borough of Brent Superannuation Fund
Brent Town Hall
Forty Lane
Wembley
Middlesex HA9 9HR
081-903 1400

London Borough of Bromley Superannuation Fund
Bromley Civic Centre
Rochester Avenue
Bromley
Kent BR1 3UH
081-464 3333

London Borough of Camden Superannuation Fund
Town Hall
Euston Road
London NW1 2RX
071-278 4444

London Borough of Croydon Superannuation Fund
Municipal Offices
Fell Road
Croydon
Surrey CR9 1BQ
081-686 4433

London Borough of Ealing Superannuation Fund
Town Hall
New Broadway
Ealing
London W5 2BY
071-579 2424

London Borough of Enfield Superannuation Fund
Director of Finance
Civic Centre
Silver Street
Enfield
Middlesex EN1 3XF
Tel: 081-366 6565 Fax: 081-367 8701
(Sept 1992)
CAPITAL VALUE: £108m (1989)
PROPERTY PROTFOLIO: No Direct Property
(Jan 1991)

London Borough of Greenwich Superannuation Fund
Municipal Offices
45-53 Wellington STreet
London SE18 6RA
081-848 8888

London Borough of Hackney Superannuation Fund
Municipal Offices
Stoke Newington Church Street
London N16 0JR
081-800 1282

London Borough of Hammersmith & Fulham Superannuation Fund
Town Hall
King Street, Hammersmith
London W6 9JU
081-748 3020

London Borough of Harringay Superannuation Fund
Civic Centre
PO Box 264
High Road, Wood Green
London N22 4LE
081-881 3000

London Borough of Hillingdon Superannuation Fund
Civic Centre
Uxbridge
Middlesex UB8 1UW
Tel: 081-863 5611 Fax: 0895 273636

London Borough of Hounslow Superannuation Fund
Civic Centre
Lampton Road, Hounslow
Middlesex TW3 4DN
0895-50111
CAPITAL VALUE OF FUND: £69m
SIZE OF PROPERTY PORTFOLIO: 4.15%
INVESTMENT CATEGORIES: offices 33.68%; shops 66.32%
CURRENT POLICY FOR INVESTMENT IN PROPERTY: From time to time seek investment in the range £250,000 - £500,000
PROPERTY INVESTMENT MANAGER(S): Borough Treasurer - Borough Valuer

London Borough of Islington Superannuation Fund
New Municipal Offices
222 Upper Street
Islington
London N1 1XR
071-226 1234

London Borough of Lambeth Superannuation Fund
18 Brixton Hill
London SW2 1RL
071-274 7722

London Borough of Lewisham Superannuation Fund
Town Hall
Catford
London SE6 4RX
081-690 4343

London Borough of Merton Superannuation Fund
Crown House
London Road
Morden
Surrey SM4 5DX
081-543 2222

London Borough of Newham Superannuation Fund
New Municipal Offices
91 The Grove
Stratford
London E15 1EW
081-534 4545

London Borough of Redbridge Superannuation Fund
22-26 Clements Road
Ilford
Essex IG1 1BD
081-478 3020

London Borough of Richmond upon Thames Pension Scheme
Municipal Offices
Twickenham
Middlesex TW1 3AA
081-891 1411

London Borough of Southwark Superannuation Fund
Municipal Offices
Spa Road
Bermondsey
London SE16 3QN
071-237 6677

London Borough of Sutton Superannuation Fund
Civic Offices
St Nicholas Way
Sutton
Surrey SM1 1EA
081-661 5000

London Borough of the City of Westminster Superannuation Fund
Westminster City Hall
Victoria Street
London SW1E 6QP
071-828 8070

London Borough of Tower Hamlets Superannuation Fund
Town Hall
Patriot Square
London E2 9LN
071-980 4831

London Borough of Waltham Forest Superannuation Fund
Town Hall
Walthamstow
London E17 4JF
081-527 5544

London Borough of Wandsworth Superannuation Fund
Town Hall
Wandsworth High Street
London SW18 2PU
081-874 1545

London Brick Company plc
305 Ballards Lane
London N12
081-446 6711

London Life Association Limited Staff Superannuation Scheme
100 Temple Street
Bristol BS1 6EA
0272-27919

London Regional Transport Pension Fund
55 Broadway
London SW1H 0BD
Tel: 071-222 5600 Fax: 01-222 5102
CAPITAL VALUE OF FUND: £1.4bn
SIZE OF PROPERTY PORTFOLIO: £110m
PROPERTY ADVISERS: Jones Lang Wootton

London Royal Borough of Kensington & Chelsea Superannuation Fund
Town Hall
Horton Street
London W8 7NX
071-937 5464

London Weekend Television Superannuation Fund
Kent House
Upper Ground
London SE1 9LT
071-261 3434

Lothian Regional Council Superannuation Fund
George IV Bridge
Edinburgh
Lothian EH1 1UQ
Tel: 031-229 9292 Fax: 031-225 6356
PROPERTY INVESTMENT MANAGER: Donaldsons Property Management
PROPERTY INVESTMENT CONSULTANTS: Donaldsons Property Management
SIZE OF PROPERTY PORTFOLIO: £39.3m (1992)
DISTRIBUTION OF PORTFOLIO (BY VALUE): Offices 46%; shops 23%; warehouses 31% (Sept 1992)

Lovell, Y J Group plc Pension Scheme
Marsham House
Gerrards Cross
Buckinghamshire SL9 8ER
0753-882211

Lucas Industries plc Pension Fund
Great King Street
Birmingham B19 2XF
021-554 5252

MAA Pensions Limited The MAA National Motor Industry Pension Fund
10 Church Square
Leighton Buzzard
Bedfordshire LU7 7AE
Tel: 0525-348237 Fax: 0525-373899
CAPITAL VALUE OF FUND: £70m (88/89)

MacPherson Donald Group plc Retirement Benefits Plan
Rookwood Way
Haverhill
Suffolk CB9 5PB
(Registered Office)

Magnet & Southerns plc Group Pension Scheme
Sasco House
Mill Lane
Widnes
Cheshire WA8 0UJ
051-424 5500

Manchester Ship Canal Company Staff Superannuation Fund & General Pension Scheme
Dock Office
Trafford Road
Manchester M5 2XB
061-872 2411

Marathon Service (GB) Ltd
Marathon House
174 Marlyebone Road
London NW1 5AT

Marks & Spencer Pension Scheme
Michael House
47 Baker Street
London W1A 1DN
071-935 4422

Marley plc
London
Riverhed
Sevonoaks
Kent TN13 2DS

Marley plc Pension Fund
London Road
Riverhead
Sevenoaks
Kent TN13 2DS
0732-455255

Mars Security Pension Fund
Dundee Road
Slough
Berks Sl1 4JX
0753 693000

Mason, Joseph plc
Notingham Road
Derby DE2 6AR

Mather & Platt Staff & Works Retirement Benefits Scheme
Park Works
Manchester M10 6BA
061-205 2321

Matthew Hall plc Pension Scheme
Matthew Hall House
7 Baker Street
London W1M 1AB
071-935 9384

May & Baker Limited Pension Fund
Dagenham
Essex RM10 7XS
081-592 3060

McAlpine Pension Scheme
Hooton
Soouth Wirral
Cheshire L66 7ND
051-339 4141

McAlpine, Sir Robert & Sons Limited Staff Pension & Life Assurance Scheme
40 Barnard Street
London WC1N 1LG
071-837 3377

McCorquodale plc Pension Funds
PO Box 66
Telford Road
Basingstoke
Hampshire RG21 2YA
0256-65811

Medical Research Council MRC Pension Scheme
20 Park Crescent
London W1N 4AI
071-636 5422

Merchant Navy Pension Funds
Ashcombe House
The Crescent
Leatherhead
Surrey KT22 8LQ
Tel: 0372-386000 Fax: 0372 386666
(Sept 1992)
Merchant Navy Officers Pension Fund:
CAPITAL VALUE OF FUND: £1.845bn
SIZE OF PROPERTY PORTFOLIO: £266.8m
INVESTMENT CATEGORIES: offices 56.4%; retail 24.9%; industrial 18.7%
PROPERTY INVESTMENT MANAGER: Argosy Asset Management plc
CONSULTANT(S): Sir N Wakefield FCIOB CBIM of Lovell Holdings
Merchant Navy Ratings Funds:
CAPITAL VALUE OF FUND: £242m
SIZE OF PROPERTY PORTFOLIO: £36.6m
INVESTMENT CATEGORIES: offices 40.8%; retail 59.2%
PROPERTY INVESTMENT MANAGER: Argosy Asset Management plc

Mersey Docks & Harbour Company Staff Funds
Port of Liverpool Building
Pier Head
Liverpool
Merseyside L3 1BZ
051-200 2020

Merseyside County Council Superannuation Fund
Metropolitan House
Old Hall Street
Liverpool
Merseyside L69 3EL
051-227 5234

Metal Box plc Pension Scheme
Queens House
Forbury Road
Reading
Berkshire RG1 3JH
0734-581177

Metal Closures Group Staff Scheme & Works Fund
Bromford Lane
West Bromwich
West Midlands B70 7HY
021-5533 2900

Methodist Ministers Retirement Fund
1 Central Buildings
Westminster
SW1H 9NP
071-222 8010

Entry missing ? Call HELPLINE Page v

Metropolitan Borough of Wirral
Superannuation Fund
PO Box 120
Castle Chambers
4/6 Cook Street
Liverpool L69 2NW

Meyer International plc Pension Fund
PO Box 118
Carpenter Road
London E15 2DY
081-985 3300

Michelin Tyre plc Pension & Life Assurance Plans for Monthly & Weekly Staff
Campbell Road
Stoke on Trent
Staffordshire ST4 4EY
0782-48101

Mid Glamorgan County Council Superannuation Fund
County Hall, Cathays Park
Cardiff CF1 3NJ
0222-28033

Midland Bank Pension Trust Ltd
c/o James Capel Fund Managers Ltd
7 Devonshire Square
London EC2M 4HU
PROPERTY INVESTMENT MANAGER: A A Jones
PROPERTY INVESTMENT CONSULTANTS: Jones Lang Wootton
SIZE OF PROPERTY PORTFOLIO: £230m (1991)
(Sept 1992)

Milk Marketing Board Pension Fund
Giggs Hill Green
Thames Ditton
Surrey KT7 0EL
081-398 4101
CAPITAL VALUE OF FUND: £303m
SIZE OF PROPERTY PORTFOLIO: £33m
INVESTMENT CATEGORIES: shops 32%; warehouses 11%; offices 13%; factories 44%
CURRENT POLICY FOR INVESTMENT IN PROPERTY: No more investment at present
PROPERTY INVESTMENT MANAGER: M Wheldon - Richard Ellis
CONSULTANT(S): Richard Ellis
(Sept 1992)

Minster Trust Limited
Minster House, Arthur Street
London EC4R 9BH
071-623 1050

Mitchell Cotts Transports Limited Pension Schemes
23 Parkhouse Street
London SE5
071-703 0299

MK Electric Group plc Pension Fund
Shrubbery Road
Edmonton
London N9 0PB
081-803 3355

Mobil Oil Company Limited Pension Fund
Mobil House
54-60 Victoria Street
London SW1E 6QB
Tel: 071-828 9777 Fax: 071-828 1081
(Sept 1992)
PROPERTY INVESTMENT MANAGERS: Jones Lang Wootton
SIZE OF PROPERTY PORTFOLIO: £19m (1990)
DISTRIBUTION OF PORTFOLIO: Offices 27%; shops 70%; warehouses 3%.
(Jan 1991)

Molins plc Pension Fund
2 Evelyn Street
London SE8 5DH
071-237 4581

Montague, Samuel, Company Pension Scheme
Wilec House
City Road
London EC1
071-253 6755

Morgan Grenfell & Company Limited Staff Pension Scheme
23 Great Winchester Street
London EC2P 2AX
071-588 4545

Morgan Guaranty Trust Company of NY Pension Plan
PO Box 161, Morgan House
1 Angel Court
London EC2R 7AE
071-555 3111

Morris & Co (Shrewsbury) Limited
Welsh Bridge
Shrewsbury SY3 8LH

Moto Agents Association Pension Fund
201 Great Portland Street
London W1N 6AB
071-580 9122

Mouchel Association Limited
West Hall
Pavis Road
West Byfleet
Surrey KT14 6EZ

Mowlem, John & Company plc Staff Pension & Life Assurance Scheme
Westgate House
Ealing Road
Brentford
Middlesex TW8 0YZ
081-568 9111

Nabisco Limited Pension Fund
PO Box 1
Long Lane
Liverpool L9 7BQ
051-525 3661

National & Provincial Building Society Pension Fund
Provincial House
Bradford
West Yorkshire BD1 1NL
0274-733444
(Sept 1992)
PROPERTY INVESTMENT MANAGER: R W Watson FRICS
(Jan 1991)

National Bus Company Pension Fund & Employees Superannuation Trust
172 Buckingham Palace Road
London SW1W 9TN
071-730 3453

National Coal Board Pension Fund
Hobart House
Grosvenor Place
London SW1X 7AE
071-235 2020

National Deposit Friendly Society
4/5 Worcester Road
Clifton
Bristol
Avon BS8 3JL

National Freight Consortium plc Pension Funds
The Merton Centre
45 St Peter's Street
Bedford
Bedfordshire MK40 2UB
0234-67444

National Nuclear Corporation Limited Pension Scheme
Booths Hall
Chelford Road
Knutsford
Cheshire WA16 8QZ
0656 3800

National Provident Property Pension Funds
48 Gracechurch Street
London EC3P 3HH
071-623 4200

National Westminster Bank plc
Wettern House
56 Dingwall Road
Croydon
Surrey CR9 3HB

Nationwide Building Society Superannuation Fund
New Oxford House
High Holborn
London WC1V 6PW
071-242 8822

Navy Army Air Force Institutes Pension Fund
Imperial Court
Kennington Lane
London SE11 5QX
Tel: 071-735 1200 Fax: 071 793 0402
(Sept 1992)
NATURE OF BUSINESS: Employee Pension Fund
INVESTMENT MANAGERS: P W Sexton FRICS
SIZE OF PROPERTY PORTFOLIO: £26m (1990)
DISTRIBUTION OF PORTFOLIO: Offices 26%; Shops 49%; Industrial/Warehouse 25%
NORMAL IMVESTMENT POLICY: Shops; Offices; Industrial/Warehouse. Lot Sizes: £1-2m
(Jan 1991)

NCR Limited Pension Plan
206 Marleybond Road
London NW1 6LY
071-358 8103

Nestle Company Limited Pension Fund
St George's House
Park Lane
Croydon
Surrey CR9 1NR
081-686 3333

New Towns Pension Fund, The
158 Ramsons Avenue
Conniburrow
Milton Keynes
Buckinghamshire MK14 7NN
Tel: 0908-607728 Fax: 0908-607729

News Group Newspapers Limited Pension & Life Assurance Plan
30 Bouverie Street
London EC4Y 8EX
071-353 3030

Norcros plc Security Pension Plan
Norcros House
Bracknell
Berkshire RG12 3SW
Tel: 0344-861878 Fax: 0344 861642
PROPERTY INVESTMENT MANAGER: Rothschild Asset Management
SIZE OF PROPERTY PORTFOLIO: £14,050,000 (1992)
(Sept 1992)

Norfolk County Council Superannuation Fund
County Hall
Martineau Lane
Norwich NR1 2DW
0603-222222

North Yorkshire County Council Superannuation Fund
County Hall
Northallerton
North Yorkshire DL7 8AL
Tel: 0609-780780 Fax: 0609-780447
(Sept 1992)
CAPITAL VALUE OF FUND: £247.3m (31/3/89)
SIZE OF PROPERTY PORTFOLIO: £23.8m
INVESTMENT CATEGORIES: shops 100%
CURRENT POLICY FOR INVESTMENT IN PROPERTY: To invest about 10% of the value of the fund in property
PROPERTY INVESTMENT MANAGER(S): Cluttons
PROPERTY INVESTMENT CONSULTANT: G N Fearn, Langley Estates Limited
(Jan 1991)

Northamptonshire County Council Superannuation Fund
County Hall
Northampton NN1 1DN
0604 34833

Northern Bank Limited Pension Schemes
Donegall Square
West Belfast
Northern Ireland BT1 6JS
0232-245277

Northern Engineering Industries plc Group Pension Scheme
NEI House
Regent Centre
Gosforth
Newcastle on Tyne NE3 3SB
0632-843191

Northern Foods plc Superannuation Fund
Essex House
Manor Street
Hull HU1 1YQ
0482-27194

Northern Ireland Electricity Service Superannuation Fund
120 Malone Road
Belfast BY9 5HT
0232-661100

Northern Ireland Local Government Officers Superannuation Committee
Templeton House
411 Holywood Road
Belfast
Northern Ireland BT4 2LP
Tel: 0232-768025 Fax: 0232 768790
PROPERTY INVESTMENT CONSULTANTS: J W Burgess FRICS
SIZE OF PROPERTY PORTFOLIO: £62.3m (1992)
(Sept 1992)

Northern Telecom Europe Limited
Corporate Headquarters
Oakleigh Road South
New Southgate
London N11 1HB

Northumberland County Council Superannuation Fund
County Hall
Morpeth
Northumberland NE61 2EF
0670-514343

Norwich Union Pensions Management Limited
Norwich Union Investment Managers Ltd
Sentinel House
37 Surrey Street
Norwich NR1 3PW
Tel: 0603-622200 Fax: 0603-683950
PROPERTY INVESTMENT MANAGER: P M Sexton BSc ARICS
SIZE OF PROPERTY PORTFOLIO: £103m (1991)
DISTRIBUTION OF PORTFOLIO (BY VALUE): Offices 35%; retail 42%; industrial 19%; retail warehouse 4%
NORMAL INVESTMENT POLICY: Every investment proposition considered on its merits. Performance time horizon 12/24 months. At present very limited development exposure
(Sept 1992)

Nottinghamshire County Council Superannuation Fund
County Hall
West Bridgford
Nottingham BG2 7QP
0602-823823

Nurdin & Peacock plc Retirement Benefit Fund
Bushey Road
Raynes Park
London SW20 9JJ
081- 946 9111

Occidental International OIC Pension Fund
16 Palace Street
London SW1E 5BU
071-828 5600

Ocean Transport & Trading plc Ocean Nestor Pension Fund
India Buildings
Water Street
Liverpool
Merseyside L2 0RB
051-236 9292

Ogilvy & Mather Group Pension & Life Assurance Plan
10 Cabot Square
Canary Wharf
London E14 4QB
Tel: 071-712 3000 Fax: 071-712 9000

Otis Elevator plc
The Otis Building
43/59 Clapham Road
London SW9 OJZ

Overseas Containers Limited Pension Scheme
Beagle House
Braham Street
London E1 8EP
071-488 1313

Oxfordshire County Council Superannuation Fund
County Hall
New Road
Oxford OX1 1TH
0865-722422

P & O Group Pension Scheme
47 Middlesex Street
London E1 7AL
071-283 8000

Parker Pen UK Limited
Newhaven
East Sussex BN9 OAU

Pearl Assurance Company plc Staff Superannuation Fund
The Pearl Gates
Lynch Wood
Peterborough PE2 6FY
0733 470470
PROPERTY MANAGER: J Case FRICS.
SIZE OF PROPERTY PORTFOLIO: £75.5m end 1991
PORTFOLIO DISTRIBUTION: Office, 44%, Retail 51%. Industrial 5%
CURRENT POLICY FOR INVESTMENT IN PROPERTY: Selective freehold purchases of standing investments in lot sizes £1m to £5m.
(Sept 1992)

Peat Marwick Mitchell & Company Staff Pension Fund
1 Puddle Dock
Blackfriars
London EC4V 3PD
071-236 8000

Pegler Hattersley Staff & Works Pension Fund
St Catherine's Avenue
Doncaster
South Yorkshire DN4 8DF
0302-68581

Pensions Trust For Charities & Voluntary Organisations, The
13/15 Rathbone Street
London W1P 2AJ
PROPERTY INVESTMENT MANAGER: Richard Ellis
SIZE OF PROPERTY PORTFOLIO: £13.4m (1992)
DISTRIBUTION OF PORTFOLIO: Industrial - £6.9m; Retail - £3.46m; Offices - £1.49m; Retail Warehouse - £1.52m
NORMAL INVESTMENT POLICY: Freehold investments, target portfolio split of: Industrial 25%; Retail 30%; Offices 30%; Retail Warehouse 15%
(Sept 1992)

Pergammon/AGB Research plc Group Retirement Benefits Scheme
76 Shoe Lane
London EC4
071-822 2358

Phoenix Assurance plc Pension Fund
Phoenix House
Redcliffe Hill
Bristol BS1 6SU
0272-294941

Phillips & Drew Pension Fund
120 Moorgate
London EC2M 6XP
071-628 4444

Entry missing ? Call HELPLINE Page v

Phillips Pension Fund
64 Queen Street
London EC4R 1AD
Tel: 071-489 8514 Fax: 071-489 8530
PROPERTY INVESTMENT MANAGER: A T Keen FRICS
SIZE OF PROPERTY PORTFOLIO: £135m (1992)
DISTRIBUTION OF PORTFOLIO (BY VALUE): Offices 34%; shops 40%; industrial 240%; leisure 2%
SUBSIDIARY DEVELOPMENT COMPANIES: Joint Venture Company, UK Estates Limited
(Sept 1992)

Phillips Petroleum UK Retirement Plan
The Adelphi
John Adam Street
London WC2N 6BW
071-839 8833

Pilkington Brothers plc Pension Schemes
Prescot Road
St Helens
Merseyside WA10 3TT
0744-28882

Pitney Bowes Pension Fund
The Pinnacles
Harlow
Essex CM19 5BD
0279-26731

Plessey Pension Trust Limited
Vicarage Lane
Ilford
Essex IG1 4AQ
081-478 3040

Plumbing & Mechanical Services Pension Scheme
4 Walker Street
Edinburgh EH3 7EH
031-225 2255

Plysu plc
120 StationRoad
Woburn Sands
Milton Keynes
Bucks MK17 8SE

Port of London Authority Pension Fund
Tilbury Docks
Tilbury
Essex RM18 7EH
03572-3444

Post Office Insurance Society
County House
Conway Mews
London W1P 5HF

Post Office Staff Superannuation Scheme
See Postel Property Services

The Post Office Superannuation Headquarters
Standon House
21 Mansell Street
London E1 8AA

Postel Property Services
Postel Investment Management Limited
Standon House
21 Mansell Street
London E1 BAA
Tel: 071-702 0888 Fax: 071-702 9453
SIZE OF PROPERTY PORTFOLIO: £3,060m
VALUE INVESTMENT CATEGORIES: Offices £849m; shops £1031m; industrial £584m; agricultural £32m
(Sept 1992)

Powys County Council
County Hall
Llandrindod Wells
Powys LD1 5LE
Tel: 0597-3711 Fax: 0597 826230
(Sept 1992)
CAPITAL VALUE OF FUND: £50m
CURRENT POLICY FOR INVESTMENT IN PROPERTY: Property Unit Trusts
PROPERTY INVESTMENT MANAGER(S): Barclays de Zoete Wedd Securities Limited
(Jan 1991)

Press Association Pension Fund, The
Southwart Towers
32 London Bridge Street
London SE1 9SY
071-353 7440

Price & Pearce (Holding Co) Limited
Dukes Court
Dukes Street
Woking
Surrey GU21 5HB

Price Waterhouse Pension Fund
Southwark Towers
32 London Bridge Street
London SE1 9SY
071-407 8989

Proctor & Gamble Limited Staff Pension Fund & Manual Employees Pension Fund
Hedley House
St Nicholas Avenue
Gosforth
Newcastle on Tyne NE99 1EE
091-279 2000

Provident Mutual Life Assurance Association Staff Superannuation Fund
25-31 Moorgate
London EC2R 6BA
071-628 3232

Provincial Group Pension Fund
Sand Aire House
Stramongate
Kendal
Cumbria LA9 4BE
0539-723415
(Sept 1992)
CAPITAL VALUE OF FUND: £81.306m (as at 31.3.87)
SIZE OF PROPERTY PORTFOLIO: £6.383m (as at 31.3.87)
INVESTMENT CATEGORIES: offices 43.24%; shops 32.87%; factories 23.89%
CURRENT POLICY FOR INVESTMENT IN PROPERTY: Investment of up to 11% of the total market value of the fund, invested as: offices 40%; shops 40%; industrial units 20%. Reviewed from time to time
PROPERTY INVESTMENT MANAGER(S): R J Bruce FRICS
CONSULTANT(S): Profilic Asset Management plc
(Jan 1991)

Prudential Assurance Company Limited Staff Pension Fund
142 Holborn Bars
London EC1N 2NH
071-405 9222

Racal Electronic plc
Racal Group Services
309 Fleet Road
Fleet GU13 8BU

Rank Hovis McDougall plc Pension Funds
Pembroke House
44 Wellesley Road
Croydon CR9 3PA
081-686 5699

Rank Organisation plc Pension Plan, The
439 Godstone Road
Whyteleafe
Surrey CR3 0YG
0883-23355

Rank Xerox Pension Scheme
24-24 Temple End
High Wycombe
Bucks HP13 5DR
PROPERTY INVESTMENT MANAGER: Baring Houston & Saunders
SIZE OF PROPERTY PORTFOLIO: £46m (1992)
DISTRIBUTION OF PORTFOLIO: Offices 37%; Retail 40%; Industrial 23%
NORMAL INVESTMENT POLICY: UK Commercial
(Sept 1992)

Reckitt & Colman plc Pension Fund
Dansom Lane
Hull HU8 7DS
0582-26151

Redland plc Pension Scheme
Redland House
Reigate
Surrey RH2 0SJ
07372-42488

Reed International plc Pension Scheme
Cobdown House
London Road
Ditton
Maidstone
Kent ME20 6QD
0622-77777

Reed Stenhouse Pension Scheme
145 St Vincent Street
Glasgow G2 5NX
041-248 5070

Refuge Assurance plc Superannuation Fund
Oxford Street
Manchester M60 7HA
061-236 9432

Renold plc Group Pension Schemes
Renold House
Styal Road
Wythenshaw
Manchester M22 5WL
061-437 5221

Rentokil plc Staff Pension & Life Assurance Plan
Felcourt
East Grinstead
West Sussex RH19 2JY
0342-833022

Reuters Pension Fund
85 Fleet Street
London EC4P 4AJ
071-250 1122

Rigid Containers Holdings Limited
PO Box 7
Rushton Road
Desborough
Kettering
Northants NN14 2RY

Entry missing ? Call HELPLINE Page v

RMC Pension Trust
RMC House
Cold Harbour Lane
Thorpe
Egham
Surrey TW20 8TO
0932 568833
PROPERTY MANAGERS: P J Owen (Managing); G Tyler (Marketing)

Robert Bradford Holdings plc Group & Death Benefit Schemes
Minster House
Arthur Street
London EC4R 9BU
071-623 3050

Rockware Group plc Staff & Works Pension Schemes
Riverside House
Riverside Way
Northampton NN1 5DW
0604-26931

Rolls-Royce Pension Fund, The
PO Box 31
Derby DE2 8BJ
0332-243230

Rothmans International plc
Bakers Court
12 Widegate Street
London E1 7HP

Rover Group Holdings plc
c/o Nuffield Services Limited
6th Floor
Belgrave House
1 Greyfriars
Northampton NN1 2BL

Rover Group Pension Scheme
Belgrave House
1 Greyfriars
Northampton NN1 2BL
Tel: 0604 230632 Fax: 0604 239880
INVESTMENT COMPANY: Legal & General Property Limited, Bucklebury House, 3 Queen Street, Victoria Street, London EC4N 8EL
INVESTMENT CONSULTANT: J R Grimley
SIZE OF PROPERTY PORTFOLIO: £130m (5th April 1992)
PORTFOLIO DISTRIBUTION: offices 33%; shops 49%; industrial 17%; agricultural 1%
(Sept 1992)

Rowntree Mackintosh Pension Fund
York
Yorkshire YO1 1XY
0904-53071

Royal Automobile Club Pension Fund
PO Box 100
RAC House
Lansdown Road
Croydon CR9 2JA
081-688 2525

Royal Bank of Scotland plc Staff Pension Scheme
42 St Andrews Square
Edinburgh EH2 2YE
031-556 8555

Royal Doulton Tableware Limited Pension Plan
Leek New Road
Baddley Green
Stoke on Trent
Staffordshire ST2 7HS
0782-533121

Royal Insurance Group Pension Scheme
PO Box 144
New Hall Place
Liverpool L69 3EN
051-227 4422

Royal Liver Friendly Society Superannuation Fund
Royal Liver Buildings
Pier Head
Liverpool L3 1HT
051-236 1451

Royal London Mutual Insurance Society Limited, The
Royal London House
Middlesborough
Colchester
Essex CO1 1RA

Royal National Pension Fund for Nurses
Burdett House
15 Buckingham Street
Strand
London WC2N 6DU
Tel: 071-839 6785 Fax: 071 925 2287
PROPERTY INVESTMENT MANAGER: H S Clarke
PROPERTY INVESTMENT CONSULTANTS: Messrs: Gooch & Wagstaff
SIZE OF PROPERTY PORTFOLIO: £140m (1992)
(Sept 1992)

Royal Ordnance plc
Euxton Lane
Euxton
Chorley
Lancs PR7 6AD

RTZ Corporation plc, The
PO Box 133
6 St James's Square
London SW1Y 4LD

Rubery Owen Group Staff Pension Scheme
Darlaston
PO Box 10
Wednesdbury
West Midland WS10 8JD
021-526 3131

Safeway Foodstores Limited Retirement Benefits Plan
Stoneborough House
King Street
Maidstone
Kent ME15 6AW
0622-54922

Sainsbury Pension & Death Benefit Scheme
Stamford House
Stamford Street
London SE1 9LL
071-921 6000

Sara Lee H&PC Pension Scheme
225 Bath Road
Slough
Berkshire SL1 4AU
0753-508030
PROPERTY INVESTMENT MANAGER: Mercer Fraser
PROPERTY INVESTMENT CONSULTANT: Mercer Fraser
LOCATION OF REGIONAL OFFICE: London
SIZE OF PROPERTY PORTFOLIO: £0.5m (1992)
DISTRIBUTION OF PORTFOLIO: Industrial - 1.25% (Total)
NORMAL INVESTMENT POLICY: Emphasis on industrial investments
(Sept 1992)

Schering Holdings Limited
Mount Pleasant House
Huntingdon Road
Cambridge CR3 ODA

Schroder, J. Henry, Wagg & Co Limited
120 Cheapside
London ECV2V 6DS

Scottish & Newcastle Breweries plc Pension Schemes
Abbey Brewery
111 Holyrood Road
Edinburgh EH8 8YS
031-556 2591

Scottish Agricultural Industries Pension Fund
West Mains of Ingliston
Ingliston
Newbridge
Midlothian EH28 8ND
031-335 3100

Scottish Heritable Trust plc, The
Millbank House
18/20 Skeldergate
York YO1 1DH

Scottish Homes
Rosebury house
91 Haymarket Terrace
Edinburgh
EH12 5HE
031-337 0044
REGIONAL AND DISTRICT OFFICES ACROSS SCOTLAND:
Our aim is to improve the quality and choice of housing available to the people of Scotland by working in partnership with the public and private sector. Budget of around £285 million this year to support change and tackle housing problems.
We give grants to encourage private housebuilding in areas which developers might not normally choose. We support landlords willing to provide rented accommodation and we promote social and environmental initiatives so that communities get added benefit from new housing projects.

Scottish Legal Life Assurance & Society
95 Rothwell Street
Glasgow G2 8HY

Scottish Transport Group Staff Pension Funds
Carron House
114 George Street
Edinburgh EH2 4LX
031-226 7491

Scottish Widows Fund & Life Assurance Society Staff Retirement Benefits Scheme
15 Dalkeith Road
Edinburgh EH16 5BJ
031-655 6000

Scottishpower plc
Cathcart House
Spean Street
Glasgow G44 4BE

Searle UK Pension Fund
PO Box 53
Lane End Road
High Wycombe
Buckinghamshire HP12 4HL
0494 21124

Sears Holdings plc Pension Fund
40 Duke Street
London W1A 2HP
071-408 1180

Sedgwick Group plc Pension Scheme
Sedgwick Centre
10 Whitechapel Lane
London E1 8DX
071-377 3456

SGB Group Staff Pension & Family Security Scheme
23 Willow Lane
Mitcham
Surrey CR4 4TQ
081-640 3393

Sheerness Steel Company plc Group Pension Fund
Sheerness
Kent ME12 1TH
07956-663333

Shell Oil Pension Fund
Shell Centre
London SE1 7NA
071-934 1234

Shepherd Buildings Group Limited
Blue Bridge Lane
York YO1 4AS

Short Brothers plc Staff & Industrial Workers Pension Schemes
Arpert Road
Belfast BT3 9DZ
0232-58444

Shropshire County Council Superannuation Scheme
Shirehall Abbey
Foregate
Shrewsbury
Shropshire SY2 6ND
0743-222243

Simon Engineering plc Staff & Works Pension Fund
PO Box 31
Cheadle Heath
Stockport
Cheshire SK3 0RT
061-428 3600

Smith & Nephew Group of Companies Pension Fund
2 Temple Place
Victoria Embankment
London WC2R 2BP
071-836 7922

Smith Kline & French Laboratories Limited Pension Fund
Mundells
Welwyn Garden City
Hertfordshire AL7 1EY
0707-325111

Smith, W H & Sons Holding Pension Trust
Strand House
10 New Fetter Lane
London EC4A 1AD
071-353 0277

Smith, W H Pension Trust
Milton Hill House
Milton Hill
Abingdon
Oxon OX13 6AF

Smiths Industries Pension Scheme
765 Finchley Road
Childs Hill
London NW11 8DS
081-458 3232
(Sept 1992)

Social Workers Pension Fund
93 Borough High Street
London SE1 1NL
071-403 0301

Solicitors Staff Pension Fund, The
Bartya House
29 Victoria Avenue
Southend on Sea
Essex SS2 6AF
Tel: 0702-354024 Fax: 0702 354364
PROPERTY INVESTMENT MANAGERS: Mellersh & Harding
PROPERTY PORTFOLIO: £8,660,000
(Sept 1992)

Somerset County Council Superannuation Fund
County Hall, Taunton
Somerset TA1 4DY
0823-333451
(Sept 1992)

South Glamorgan County Council Superannuation Fund
County Hall
Atlantic Wharf
Cardiff CF1 5UW
Tel: 0222-872000 Fax: 0222-872106/872333
CAPITAL VALUE OF FUND: £232.5m(Market value @ 31.3.92)
SIZE OF PROPERTY PORTFOLIO: £11.2m (31.3.92)
CURRENT POLICY FOR INVESTMENT IN PROPERTY: Cautious & opportunistic
PROPERTY INVESTMENT MANAGER(S): Knight, Frank & Rutley
(Sept 1992)

South of Scotland Electricity Board Superannuation Scheme
Cathcart House
Spean Street
Glasgow G44 4BE
041-637 7177
CAPITAL VALUE OF FUND: £626.9m
SIZE OF PROPERTY PORTFOLIO: £34.9m
INVESTMENT CATEGORIES: offices 36.9%; shops 11%; factories/warehouse/science parks/hi-tech/leisure/ other 52.1%
CURRENT POLICY FOR INVESTMENT IN PROPERTY: No further investment for the moment
PROPERTY INVESTMENT MANAGER(S)/ CONSULTANT(S): Richard Ellis

South Staffordshire Water Works Company Superannuation Fund
50 Sheepcote Street
Birmingham B16 8AR
021-643 8731

South Yorkshire Pension Fund
PO Box 37
Regent Street
Barnsley
South Yorkshire S70 2PQ
Tel: 0226-770770 Fax: 0226 772999
CAPITAL VALUE OF FUND: £875m (approx)
SIZE OF PROPERTY PORTFOLIO: £90m (1992)
PROPERTY INVESTMENT MANAGER(S): Richard Ellis, Knight, Frank & Rutley
NORMAL INVESTMENT POLICY: Normal institutional pension fund portfolio including developments
(Sept 1992)

Sperry Pension Plan
Sperry House
78 Portsmouth Road
Cobham
Surrey KT11 1JZ
09326-7333

Squibb 1965 Pension & Life Assurance Scheme, The
Squibb House
141 Staines Road
Hounslow
Middlesex TW3 3JA
081-572 7422

Staffordshire County Council Superannuation Fund
County Buildings
Eastgate Street
Stafford
Staffordshire ST16 2NF
0785-3121

Standard Chartered Bank plc Group Pension Fund
10 Clements Lane
London EC4N 7AB
071-623 7500

Standard Life Assurance Company Staff Pension Fund
3 George Street
Edinburgh EH2 2XZ
031-225 2552

States of Jersey Pension Funds
State Treasury
PO Box 353
Cyril Le Marquand House
The Parade, St Helier
Jersey
0534-79111

Staveley Industries plc Retirement Benefits Scheme
Staveley House
11 Dingwall Road
Croydon CR9 3DB
081-688 4404

Steetley plc Staff & Works Pension Funds
PO Box 6
Gateford Hill
Worksop
Nottinghamshire S81 8AF
0909-474551

Sterling Winthrop Group Pension Funds
Sterling Winthrop House
Onslow Street
Guildford
Surrey GU1 4YS
0483-505515

Stewart Wrightson Holdings plc Pension Fund
1 Camomile Street
London EC3A 7HJ
071-623 7511

Stock Exchange Pension Fund, The
The Stock Exchange
London EC2N 1HP
071-588 2355

Storehouse plc
Central Pensions Office
The Heal's Building
196 Tottenham Court Road
London W1 5QD

Strathclyde Regional Council Superannuation Fund
2 India Street
Glasgow G2 4PF
Tel: 041-204 2900 Fax: 041-227 2870
PROPERTY INVESTMENT MANAGERS: Scottish Amicable Investment Managers
CAPITAL VALUE OF FUND: £2163m (31/11/90)
SIZE OF CURRENT PROPERTY PORTFOLIO: £200m (1992)
INVESTMENT CATEGORIES: offices 43%; industrial 20%; retail 33%; retail warehouses 4%
(Sept 1992)

Suffolk County Council Superannuation Fund
PO Box 38
St Giles House
County Hall
Ipswich
Suffolk IP4 2JP
Tel: 0473-230000 Fax: 0473 230240
(Sept 1992)
PROPERTY INVESTMENT MANAGERS: Hill Samuel Property Services Limited
SIZE OF PROPERTY PORTFOLIO: £13.9m (1990)
DISTRIBUTION OF PORTFOLIO (BY VALUE): Industrial 23%; offices 38.7%; retail 33%; mixed 6%
(Jan 1991)

Sun Alliance Insurance Group Pension Scheme
1 Bartholomew Lane
London EC2N 2AB
071-588 2345

Sun Life Assurance Society plc Staff Pension & Widows & Orphans Club
107 Cheapside
London EC2V 6DU
071-606 7788

Surrey County Council Superannuation Scheme
County Hall
Kingston upon Thames
Surrey KT1 2EA
081-541 8911
CAPITAL VALUE OF FUND: £385m (31-3-92)
SIZE OF PROPERTY PORTFOLIO: Direct property - Nil; Property Unit Trusts £5.9m
INVESTMENT CATEGORIES: All in Property Unit Trusts
(Sept 1992)

Swiss Bank Corporation
Swiss Bank House
1 High Timber Street
London EC4V 3SB

Swiss Life Insurance & Pension Co
P O Box 127
Swiss Life House
101 London Road
Sevenoaks TN13 1BQ

T & N plc
Bowdon House
Ashburton Road West
Trafford Park
Manchester M17 1RA

TAC Corporation Limited
12 Christchurch Road
Bournemouth
London BH1 2LW

Talbot Motor Company Limited Pension Fund
International House
Bickenhill Lane
Marston Green
Birmingham B37 7HZ
021-779 6565

Tarmac plc Staff Pension Scheme
(Main Office)
Tarmac plc
Hilton Hall
Essington
Wolverhampton WV11 2BQ
0902-307407
(Administration)
5th Floor
Norwich Union House
Waterloo Road
Wolverhampton WV1 4DZ
Tel: 0902-310455 Fax: 0902-640055
PROPERTY INVESTMENT MANAGERS: Strutt & Parker
PROPERTY INVESTMENT CONSULTANTS: Strutt & Parker
LOCATION OF REGIONAL OFFICES: London
SIZE OF PROPERTY PORTFOLIO: £20.538m (1991)
DISTRIBUTION OF PORTFOLIO: 100% in UK

NORMAL INVESTMENT POLICY: balanced portfolio in respect of both location and type of commercial property
(Sept 1992)

Tate & Lyle Group Pension Scheme
Enterprise House
45 Homesdale Road
Bromley
Kent BR2 9TE
Tel: 081-464 6556 Fax: 071-895 5719
PROPERTY INVESTMENT MANAGERS: Richard Ellis
PROPERTY INVESTMENT CONSULTANTS: Richard Ellis
CAPITAL VALUE OF FUND: £385m
SIZE OF PROPERTY PORTFOLIO: £30m
INVESTMENT CATEGORIES: offices 39%; shops 27%; warehouses 28%; retail warehouses 6%
(Sept 1992)

Tayside Regional Council Superannuation Fund
Tayside House
28 Crichton Street
Dundee DD1 3RF
0382-23281

Tees & Hartlepool Port Authority Pension Scheme
Queens Square
Middlesborough
Cleveland TS2 1AH
0642-241121

Texaco Limited Pension Plan
1 Knightsbridge Green
London SW1X 7QJ
071-584 241121

Texas Instruments Limited Pension Plan
Manton Lane
Bedford MK41 7PA
0234-67466

Thomas Borthwick & Sons plc Staff Superannuation Scheme
Prior House
St Johns Lane
London EC1M 4BX
071-253 8661

Thomas Cook Pension Fund
PO Box 36
Thorpe Wood
Petersborough PE3 6SB
0733-502290

Thomas W Ward Limited Pensions Schemes
Albion Works
Sheffield
South Yorkshire S4 7UL
0742-26311

Thompson, J. Walker, & Company Pension Scheme
40 Berkley Square
London W1X 6AD
071-629 9496

Thompson Organisation plc Pension Fund, The
4 Stratford Place
London W1
071-629 8111

Thorntons plc
Thornton Park
Somercotes
Derby DE55 4XJ

Thorton Limited Pension Fund
Derwent Street
Belper
Derbyshire DE5 1WP
077382-4181

TI Group plc Staff & General Pension Schemes
TI House
Fiveways
Birmingham B16 8SQ
021-454 4838

Tilbury Group Pension Fund
Tilbury House
Rusper Road
Horsham
West Sussex RH12 4BB
0403-69031

Times Newspapers Limited Pension Funds
Pennington Street
The Highway
Wapping
London E1
071-481 4100

Timex Corporation UK Retirement Benefits Plan
Harrison Road
Dundee DD2 3XL
0382-819211

Tioxide Europe Limited
Haventon Hill Road
Billingham
Cleveland
TS23 1PS
Fax: 0642 370290
(Sept 1992)

Entry missing ? Call HELPLINE Page v

Tootal Group plc Staff Pension Scheme
Tootal House
19-21 Spring Gardens
Manchester M60 2TL
061-831 7777

Total Oil GB Limited Pension Scheme
33 Cavendish Square
London W1M 0JE
071-499 6393

Touche Ross & Company Pension Scheme
Hill House
1 Little New Street
London EC4A 3TR
071-353 8011

Town & Country Building Society
Jackson Road
Clacton-on-Sea
Essex CO15 1JF

Tozer Kemsley & Millbourne Pension Scheme
1 Lygon Place
Ebury Street
London SW1W 0JR
071-730 0288

Trafalgar House Group Pension Fund
Mitcham House
681 Mitcham Road, Croydon
Surrey CR9 3AP
081-689 2266

Transport & General Workers Union Officials & Staff Superannuation Fund
Transport House
Smith Square
London SW1P 3JB
071-828 7788

Trebor Group Pension Scheme 1978
Trebor House
Woodford Green
Essex IG8 8EX
081-550 8800

Trident Television plc Pension Scheme
The Television Centre
Leeds LS3 1JS
0532-38283

Triplex Holdings Limited Pension Fund
Triplex House
Eckersall Road
Kings Norton
Birmingham B38 8SR
021-458 2031

Trustee Savings Bank Group Pension Scheme
25 Milk Street
London EC2 8LU
Tel: 071-606 7070 Fax: 071 726 8227
PROPERTY INVESTMENT MANAGER(S): Hill Samuel Property Services Limited
PROPERTY INVESTMENT CONSULTANTS: Hill Samuel Property Services Limited
SIZE OF PROPERTY PORTFOLIO: £160m (1991)
DISTRIBUTION OF PORTFOLIO (BY VALUE): Offices 31%; shops 34%; industrial 27%; retail warehouses 8%
NORMAL INVESTMENT POLICY: Investment and development fundings in all sectors
(Sept 1992)

Trusthouse Forte plc Group Pension Fund
12 Sherwood Street
London W1V 7RD
071-437 7788

Turner & Newhall plc Retirement Benefit Schemes
20 St Mary's Parsonage
Manchester M3 2N1
061-872 0155

Tyne & Wear County Council Superannuation Fund
Sandyford House
Archbold Terrace
Newcastle upon Tyne NE2 1ED
0632-816144

UBM Group Pension Fund
Avon Works
Winterstoke Road
Bristol BS99

UKF Fertilisers Limited Pension Fund
Ince
Chester CH2 4LB

Unigate plc
Unigate House
Wood Land
London W12 7RP
Tel: 081-749 8888 Fax: 081 576 6161
CAPITAL VALUE OF FUND: £394.6m (end Sept 1992)
INVESTMENT CATEGORIES: 5% cash remainder in equities (sold all property)
(Sept 1992)

Unilever Pensions Investments Limited
Unilever House
Blackfriars
London EC4 4BQ
Tel: 071-822 5252 Fax: 071-822 5865
(Sept 1992)
CAPITAL VALUE OF FUND: £2,138m

SIZE OF PROPERTY PORTFOLIO: £163m
INVESTMENT CATEGORIES: shops 30.4%; retail warehouses 5.5%; offices 43.1%; industrials 12%; developments 8.5%; woodlands 0.5%
PROPERTY INVESTMENT MANAGER: Keith Goulborn FRICS
(Jan 1991)

United Biscuits Limited Pension Fund
Grant House
Syon Lane
Isleworth
Middlesex TW7 5NN
081-560 3131

United Friendly Insurance plc Pension & Superannuation Fund
42 Southwark Bridge Road
London SE1 9HE
071-928 5644

United Glass Holdings plc Pension Schemes
Kingston Road, Staines
Middlesex TW18 1AD
0784-51321

United Kingdom Atomic & Energy Authority Superannuation Schemes
11 Charles II Street
London SW14 4QP
071-930 5454

United Newspapers Publications Limited
23 Tudor Street
London EC4Y OHR
071-583 9199

Union International plc Pension Fund
13 West Smithfield
London EC1A 9JN
071-248 1212

Universities Superannuation Scheme
Richmond House
Rumford Place
Liverpool L3 9FD
051-227 4711

University of Bristol Pension & Assurance Scheme
Senate House
Tyndall Avenue
Bristol BS8 1TH
0272-24161

University of Cambridge Contributory Pension Fund
The Old Schools
Cambridge CB2 1TS
0223-358933

University of Leeds Pension & Assurance Scheme
The University
Leeds LS2 9JT
0532-431751

University of Liverpool Pension Fund
PO Box 147
Liverpool L69 3BX
051-709 6022

University of London Superannuation Arrangements
4 Gower Street
London WC1E 6HA
071-636 8000

Varity Holdings Pension Trust Limited
Frank Perkins Way
Eastfield
Peterborough
PE1 5NA
Tel: 0733-552622 Fax: 0733-51629
(Sept 1992)
INVESTMENT CONSULTANTS: Hillier Parker May Rowden
SIZE OF PORTFOLIO: £23m (end Aug 1990)
PORTFOLIO DISTRIBUTION: Offices 38%; industrials 38%; retail warehouses 6%; retail 8%; cash 10%.
(Jan 1991)

Vauxhall Motors & Associated Companies Pension Fund
PO Box 3, Kimpton Road
Luton
Bedfordshire LE2 OSY
0582-21122

Vickers plc Group Pension Scheme
Vickers House
Millbank Tower
Millbank
London SW1P 4RA
071-828 7777

Warburg & Company Pension Scheme
33 King William Street
London EC4R 9AS
071-280 2222

Warner Lambert Limited Pension Scheme
Chestnut Avenue
Eastleigh
Hampshire SO5 3ZQ
0703-619777

Warwickshire County Council Superannuation Fund
PO Box 3,
Shire Hall
Warwick CV34 4RH
Tel: 0926-412227 Fax: 0926-410302
CAPITAL VALUE OF FUND: £250m (31/3/92)
SIZE OF PROPERTY PORTFOLIO: £1.25m
CONSULTANTS: Mr P H Ridley, Director Property Services Warwickshire County Council
(Sept 1992)

Water Authorities Superannuation Fund
St Peter's House
Hartsmead
Sheffield S1 1EU
0742-737331

Wedgewood plc Pension Schemes
Barlaston
Stoke on Trent
Staffordshire ST12 9ES
078139-4141

Weir Group plc Staff Pension Scheme, The
149 Newlands Road
Cathcart
Glasgow G44 4EX
041-637 7111

Wellbeck Pension Services Limited
Welbeck House
Bond Street
Bristol BS1 3LB
0272-428804

Wellcome Group Pension Fund
The Wellcome Building
183 Euston Road
London NW1 2BP
071-387 4477

Wesleyan & General Assurance Society Employees Benefit Scheme
Colmore Circus
Birmingham B4 6AR
Tel: 021-200 3003 Fax: 021-200 2971
(Sept 1992)
CAPITAL VALUE OF FUND: £800m (1988)
SIZE OF PROPERTY PORTFOLIO: £95m
INVESTMENT CATEGORIES: offices 50%; factories/ warehouses 20%; shops 28%; other 2%
PROPERTY INVESTMENT MANAGER: J P Shingler ARICS, ARVA
(Jan 1991)

West Glamorgan County Council Superannuation Fund
County Hall
Swansea SA1 3SN
0792-471111

West Midlands Metropolitan Authorities
Superannuation Fund
Wolverhampton Borough Council
Finance Department
Civic Centre
Wolverhampton WV1 1RL

West Sussex County Council Superannuation Fund
County Hall
Chichester
West Sussex PO19 1RG
0243-777100

West Yorkshire Metropolitan County Council Superannuation Fund
County Hall
Wakefield
West Yorkshire WF1 2QW
0294-367111

West Yorkshire Superannuation Fund
City of Bradford Metropolitan Council
Britannia House
Hall Ings
Bradford BD1 1HX
0274-752317
CAPITAL VALUE OF FUND: £1,800m
CURRENT POLICY FOR INVESTMENT IN PROPERTY: No direct investment in property; Investment confined to Shares in property companies and property unit trusts
(Sept 1992)

Western United Investment Co Limited
13/16 Smithfield
London EC1A 9JN

Westinghouse Electric SA
Regal House
London Road
Twickenham TW1 3QT

Westland plc Pension Schemes
Westland Works
Yeovil
Somerset BA20 2YB
0935-75222

Whitbread & Company plc Group Pension Fund
The Brewery
Chiswell Street
London EC1Y 4SD
071-606 4455

Wiggins Teape Pension Scheme
Gateway House
Basing View
Basingstoke
Hampshire RG21 2EE
0256-20262

Wilkinson Sword Group plc Pension Fund
Longley Hall
Slough
Berkshire SL3 8BZ
0753-44212

Willis Faber Pension Schemes
10 Trinity Square
London EC3P 3AX
071-481 8271

Wiltshire County Council Superannuation Fund
County Hall
Trowbridge
Wiltshire BA14 8JN
022214-3641

Wolverhampton Borough Council Superannuation Fund
Finance Department
Superannuation Division
Civic Centre
St Peter's Square
Wolverhampton WV1 1SL

Woolwich Equitable Building Society Pension Fund
Equitable House
Woolwich
London SE18 6AB
071-854 2400

Woolworth plc Pension Fund
Woolworth House
242 Marleybone Road
London NW1 6JL
071-262 1222

Yorkshire Bank plc Superannuation Funds
20 Merrion Way
Leeds LS2 8NZ
0532-441 244

Zurich Insurance Company UK Pension Fund
Zurich House
Stanhope Road
Portsmouth
Hampshire PO1 1DU
0705-822200

Entry missing ? Call HELPLINE Page v

Chapter 4

Building Societies

Index

Alliance & Leicester Building Society

49 Park Lane
London WIY 4EQ
Tel: 01-629 6661 Fax: 01-408 1399
DIRECTORS: F W Crawley JP FCIB, CBIM (Chairman); S Everard TD, DL, BA (Deputy Chairman); N Crowley FCA (Deputy Chairman); E J Baden MA, CA, ATII, CIT, FRSA, CBIM, FCIB; C J Baker LLB BSc (Econ), FIA, ACII; F A Cairncross MA; P Clifton BSc, CEng, FBICS; G N Corah DL, CBIM; R E M Elborne MA; L J Evans Dip Ed, FCIB; W J Hamilton FCA, ACBSI; Prof Sir M Thompson DSc. FInstP; P R White FCA, RCT (Managing Director)
TYPES OF COMMERCIAL PROPERTY ON WHICH LOANS GRANTED: Equity mortgages for 100% funding of commercial developments worth £5m-£20m
VALUE OF TOTAL ASSETS: £20.47m (1991)
(Sept 1992)

Barnsley Building Society

Permanent Building
Regent Street
Barnsley
South Yorkshire S70 2EH
Tel: 0226-733999 Fax: 0226-287374
DIRECTORS: D A Roebuck FCBSI; CHIEF EXECUTIVE: R H Gibson FCA (Chairman); N P Goodyear JP (Vice Chairman); K Goodal JP FRICS, MCIOB; B R Eldred; S Mitchell BA, ACA; A L Sherriff FCMA, AMBIM
BRANCH OFFICES: Rotherham; Chesterfield; Wakefield; Barnsley; Cudworth; Womberell; Mexborough; Doncaster
VALUE OF ASSETS: £155.2m (1991)
APPLY FOR LOANS TO: Any branch office
MORTGAGES GRANTED ON: Freehold/Leasehold; Residential Properties; Some Commercial.
MAXIMUM ADVANCE: £100k (Res), £500k (Comm)
VALUE ADVANCED: 95% (Res), 75% (Comm)
INTEREST CALCULATED: 1st January on balance due, to end of month on redemption.
(Sept 1992)

Bath Investment Building Society

20 Charles Street
Bath
Avon BA1 1HY
0225-423271
CHIEF EXECUTIVE: R S Hodgman FBIM
VALUE OF TOAL ASSETS: £26.5m (1988)

Bedford Building Society

65 Midland Road
Bedford MK40 1PR
0234-44123/4
DIRECTORS: G D Payne (Chief Executive)
VALUE OF TOTAL ASSETS: £40.3m (1988)

Bedford Crown Building Society

117 Midland Road
Bedford MK40 IDE
Tel: 0234-356112 Fax: 0234 354351
DIRECTORS: G H Gentle (Chairman); R E Harding FSCA (Director & Chief Executive); R Sharman; P C Chester; H F J Fowler
VALUE OF TOTAL ASSETS: £14m (1990)
APPLY FOR LOAN: J W Gurney
MORTAGES GRANTED ON: Residential properties within 50 mile radius of Bedford
MAXIMUM ADVANCE: £100,000
VALUE ADVANCED: 90%
MAXIMUM REPAYMENT PERIOD: 40 years
INTEREST CALCULATED: Current base rate 14.50%
GENERAL LENDING POLICY: Mortgage advances to owner occupied residential properties

Bexhill on Sea Building Society

2 Devonshire Square
Bexhill on Sea
East Sussex TN40 1AE
0424-210542
CHIEF EXECUTIVE: M A Varney FCIS FCBSI
VALUE OF TOTAL ASSETS: £10.8m (1988)

Birmingham Midshires Building Society

P O Box 81
35/49 Lichfield Street
Wolverhampton WV1 1EZ
Tel: 0902 710710 Fax: 0902-713412
CHIEF EXECUTIVE: M Jackson
VALUE OF TOTAL ASSETS: £3.74m (1991)
(Sept 1992)

Bolton Building Society

235-237 Baker Street
London NW1 6XE
071-935 0138
CHIEF EXECUTIVE: L F Tompsett FCBSI AFA
VALUE OF TOTAL ASSETS: £93.2m (1988)
(Sept 1992)

Bradford & Bingley Building Society

PO Box 88
Crossflatts
Bingley
West Yorkshire BD16 2UA
Tel: 0274-555555 Fax: 0274-554422
CHIEF EXECUTIVE: G R Lister FCA
VALUE OF TOTAL ASSETS: £4.9m (1988)

Bristol & West Building Society

P O Box 27
Broadquay
Bristol BS99 7AX
Tel: 0272-294271 Fax: 0272 211632
CHIEF EXECUTIVE: R W Linden AIB (Scot) FBIM
VALUE OF TOTAL ASSETS: £2.9m (1988)

Britannia Building Society

PO Box 20
Newton House
Leek
Staffordshire ST13 5RG
Tel: 0538-399399 Fax: 0538 399149
CHIEF EXECUTIVE: F M Shaw FCA
VALUE OF TOTAL ASSETS: £8.5bn (1991)
TYPES OF COMMERCIAL PROPERTY ON WHICH FINANCE IS ADVANCED: Offices (100% of Portfolio)
(Sept 1992)

Buckinghamshire Building Society
High Street
Chalfont St Giles
Buckinghamshire HP8 4QB
Tel: 0494 873064 Fax: 0494 876256
DIRECTORS: H Desmond Hall RIBA (Chairman); L F Magee FCA (Vice Chairman); A C Godwin; J C Parker; E J Payne RIBA; J A Stringer C.Eng; MI Struct E; Miss C L Wilson LLB; C: A C Godwin
VALUE OF TOTAL ASSETS: £40.3m (1991)
(Sept 1992)

Bury St Edmunds Building Society
8 Guildhall Street
Bury St Edmunds IP33 1PR
0284-61251
CHIEF EXECUTIVE: L M Marshall
Does not lend for development
VALUE OF TOTAL ASSETS: £20.7m (1988)

Cambridge Building Society
32 St Andrews Street
Cambridge CB2 3AR
Tel: 0223-315440 Fax: 0223 355175
(Sept 1992)
DIRECTORS: Chairman: E G Parker; Vice-Chairman: J S Cook; H A F Aston; R C Bailey; J R G Bradford; J M Dyke; N Hefler; G S Minto; R H Jackson
VALUE OF TOTAL ASSETS: £208m (1989)
TYPES OF COMMERCIAL PROPERTY ON WHICH FINANCE IS ADVANCED: Freehold/leasehold residential properties, some commercial properties in the region
MAXIMUM ADVANCE: Negotiable
VALUE ADVANCED: up to 95%
MAXIMUM REPAYMENT PERIOD: 25 years
INTEREST CALCULATED: Daily
LIKELY TO BECOME INVOLVED IN DIRECT DEVELOPMENT: Yes, but not immediately
(Jan 1991)

Catholic Building Society
7 Strutton Ground
Westminster
London SW1P 2HY
071-222 6736
CHIEF EXECUTIVE: F P Higgins
VALUE OF TOTAL ASSETS: £20m (1991)
(Sept 1992)

Chelsea Building Society
Thirlestaine Hall,
Thirlestaine Road
Cheltenham
Gloucestershire GL53 7AL
Tel: 0242-521391 Fax: 0242-222892
CHIEF EXECUTIVE: M Bage ACIS ASCA
GENERAL MANAGER FOR PROPERTY: R M Small LLB.
VALUE OF TOTAL ASSETS: £2.277m (1991)
(Sept 1992)

Cheltenham & Gloucester Building Society
Chief Office
Barnet Way
Gloucestershire GL4 7RL
Tel: 0452-372372 Fax: 0452 373955
DIRECTORS: J N Bays (Chairman); S Price (V Chairman); A H Longhurst BSc (Chief Executive); R F Burden (Operations Director); D Barnes (Finance Director)
REGIONAL OFFICES: More than 200 branch offices nationwide
VALUE OF TOTAL ASSETS: £14.500m (1991)
MORTGAGES GRANTED ON: Freehold/Leashold Residential Properties
SUBSIDIARY DEVELOPMENT COMPANIES: C & G Homes Limited - involved in development
OTHER MAJOR SUBSIDIARIES: C&G Channel Islands; C&G Guardian

Chesham Building Society
12 Market Square
Chesham HP5 1ER
Tel: 0494-782575 Fax: 0494-778399
CHIEF EXECUTIVE: K Starky
VALUE OF TOTAL ASSETS: £57m (1991)
TYPES OF COMMERCIAL PROPERTY ON WHICH FINANCE IS ADVANCED: offices and shops up to 60% of freehold value
(Sept 1992)

Cheshire Building Society
Castle Street
Macclesfield
Derbyshire SK11 6AH
Tel: 0625-613612 Fax: 0625 617246
CHIEF EXECUTIVE: J D P Hughes FCA
VALUE OF TOTAL ASSETS: £542.8m (1988)
(Sept 1992)

Cheshunt Building Society
100 Crossbrook Street
Waltham Cross
Hertfordshire EN8 8JJ
Tel: 0922-26261 Fax: 0992 35176
CHIEF EXECUTIVE: A Reece FCBSI FBIM
VALUE OF TOTAL ASSETS: £410m (1990)
14% of total lending is on commercial property
Does not provide bridging finance for residential/commercial development. Not involved in direct development

Chorley & District Building Society
49-51 St Thomas's Road
Chorley
Lancashire PR7 1JL
Tel: 0257-279373/4 Fax: 0257-241371
CHIEF EXECUTIVE: S Bullock FCBSI ACIS
VALUE OF TOTAL ASSETS: £48.3m (1992)
(Sept 1992)

City & Metropolitan Building Society
219 High Street
Bromley
Kent BR1 1PR
081-464 0814

DIRECTORS: J C Smethers JP, FCA (Chairman); D C G Brown (Vice Chairman); G J Gass FCIS, FCBSI; D O Simmons FCA, FCBSI; D M Sauders RD; N R Miller FRICS; T W Mingay FCBSI, ACII (Managing Director); R E Lane FCA
Does not lend for property development
VALUE OF TOTAL ASSETS: £84,740,173 (1991)
(Sept 1992)

City of London Building Society, The
54 Gresham Street
London EC2V 7LL
Tel: 071-920 9100 Fax: 071-606 2213
CHIEF EXECUTIVE: R P Harding BSc (Econ)
No property development finance at the moment
VALUE OF TOTAL ASSETS: £180m (1988)

Clay Cross Benefit Building Society
Eyre Street
Clay Cross
Chesterfield
Derbyshire S45 9JT
Tel: 0246-862120 Fax: 0246-250397
GENERAL MANAGER: J D Hawley
VALUE OF TOTAL ASSETS: £14.5m (1992)
MORTGAGES GRANTED ON: Residential Property
MAXIMUM ADVANCED: £100,000
VALUE ADVANCE: 90%
MAXIMUM REPAYMENT PERIOD: 25 Years
GENERAL LENDING POLICY: Residential Property In England & Wales
(Sept 1992)

Coventry Building Society
Economic House
PO Box 9
High Street
Coventry CV1 5QN
Tel: 0203-226469 Fax: 0203-227899
(Sept 1992)
CHIEF EXECUTIVE: P B Forde BCom FCA FCBSI
Will lend finance for the right type of development - preferably well designed housing estates by reputable local builders. Houses must be reasonably priced and the Society retains the mortgages on a proportion of them
VALUE OF TOTAL ASSETS: £1m (1988)
(Jan 1991)

Darlington Building Society
Tubwell Row
Darlington
Co Durham DL1 1NX
Tel: 0325-487171 Fax: 0325-380340
(Sept 1992)
CHIEF EXECUTIVE: A B Wood
Property development finance in selected local cases
VALUE OF TOTAL ASSETS: £143.5m (1988)
(Jan 1991)

Derbyshire Building Society
PO Box 1
Duffield Hall
Duffield
Derbyshire DE5 1AG
Tel: 0332-841791 Fax: 0332-840350
CHIEF EXECUTIVE: R E Hollick FCBSI MBIM
May lend for property development in future
VALUE OF TOTAL ASSTS: £804m (1988)

Dudley Building Society
Dudley House
Stone Street
Dudley
West Midlands DYI INP
0384-231414
CHIEF EXECUTIVE: A Johnson
Will only lend to individuals to build their own property
VALUE OF TOTAL ASSETS: £42.9m (1988)
(Sept 1992)

Dunfermline Building Society
12 East Port
Dunfermline KY12 7LD
Tel: 0383-721621 Fax: 0383-738845
DIRECTORS: J I Scott (Chairman); D B B Smith MA LLB NP (Chief Executive); J M Glover (Deputy Chief Executive)
LOCATION OF REGIONAL OFFICES: 45A George Street, Edinburgh; 39 Bath Street, Glasgow.
VALUE OF TOTAL ASSETS: £644m (1991)
BRIDGING FINANCE PROVIDED: Residential Purchases only
APPLY FOR LOAN TO: Any of Society's branches and agencies
MORTGAGES GRANTED ON: Freehold/Leasehold residential and commercial properties
MAXIMUM ADVANCE: No set maximum
VALUE ADVANCED: 95%
INTEREST CALCULATED: Annually on outstanding balance
GENERAL LENDING POLICY: All propositions considered on merit
(Sept 1992)

Earl Shilton Building Society
22 The Hollow
Earl Shilton
Leicester LE9 7NB
Tel: 0455-844422 Fax: 0455-845857
(Sept 1992)
CHIEF EXECUTIVE: J W Gilbert RD JP BSc (Eng)
Does not lend for property development
VALUE OF TOTAL ASSETS: £30.6m (1988)
(Jan 1991)

Frome Selwood Permanent Building Society
3 Market Place
Frome
Somerset BA11 1DQ
Tel: 0373-64367/8 Fax: 0373-51211
GENERAL MANAGER: J W Marshall FCBSI MBIM
Unlikely that will lend for property development
VALUE OF TOTAL ASSETS: £37.7m (1988)

Furness Building Society
51-55 Duke Street
Barrow in Furness LA14 1RT
Tel: 0229-824560 Fax: 0229-837043

CHIEF EXECUTIVE: K W Ackred FCBSI
VALUE OF TOTAL ASSETS: £304m (1991)
(Sept 1992)

Gainsborough Building Society

26 Lord Street
Gainsborough
Lincolnshire DN21 2DB
Tel: 0427-612956 Fax: 0427-617546
CHIEF EXECUTIVE: C R Bramham FCBSI
VALUE OF TOTAL ASSETS: £20m (1991)
BRIDGING FINANCE FOR RESIDENTIAL OR COMMERCIAL PROPERTY DEVELOPMENT: No
INVOLVED IN DIRECT DEVELOPMENT: No
(Sept 1992)

Gateway Building Society

223-227 Regent Street
London W1R 8AR
071-408 2424
(Merged with Woolwich)

Greenwich Building Society

279-283 Greenwich High Road
London SE10 8NL
Tel: 081-858 8212 Fax: 081-305 2187
DIRECTORS: Chairman: J C Butcher; Managing Director: R A Nichols; Operations Director: K J Borrett; K B Buchan; R E George; G C Grant; Finance Director: J Mundell; D W Poultney; Mrs L A Prentice
BRANCHES: Greenwich; Lewisham; Blackheath; West Wickham; Downham; Romford
VALUE OF TOTAL ASSETS: £139m (1992)
Does not provide bridging finance for residential/commercial development
Not involved in direct development
(Sept 1992)

Guardian Building Society

Guardian House
120 High Holborn
London WCIV 6RH
Tel: 071-242 0811/3142 Fax: 071-242 6364
(Merged with Cheltenham & Gloucester)

Halifax Building Society

PO Box 60
Trinity Road
Halifax
West Yorkshire HX1 2RG
0422-333333
(Sept 1992)
CHIEF EXECUTIVE: J D Birrell FCA
VALUE OF TOTAL ASSETS: £33,039m (1988)
TYPES OF COMMERCIAL PROPERTY ON WHICH FINANCE IS ADVANCED: offices, shops, leisure, other
BRIDGING FINANCE FOR RESIDENTIAL DEVELOPMENT: Yes
FINANCE FOR PROPERTY DEVELOPMENT: Housing development; private rented sector
Halifax Homes formed 1987, Managing Director: D Coutie
Equity partner in PROBE
(Jan 1991)

Hampshire Building Society

Anchor House
Kingston Crescent
Portsmouth
Hampshire PO2 8BX
Tel: 0705-668911 Fax: 0705-697633
CHIEF EXECUTIVE: B C Nichols
(Merged with Bradford & Bingley)

Hanley Economic Building Society

Granville House
42 Cheapside
Hanley
Stoke on Trent
Staffordshire STIIEX
Tel: 0782-208733 Fax: 0722-212977
CHIEF EXECUTIVE: B Thomas FCBSI
VALUE OF TOTAL ASSETS: £92.5m (1988)
(Sept 1992)

Harpenden Building Society

Aberdeen House
14/16 Station Road
Harpenden
Hertfordshire AL5 4SE
Tel: 0582-7654ll Fax: 0582-462673 DX 80470 HARP
(Sept 1992)
CHIEF EXECUTIVE: M P Read
VALUE OF TOTAL ASSETS: £36m
TYPES OF COMMERCIAL PROPERTY ON WHICH LOANS GRANTED: offices, shops
(Jan 1991)

Haywards Heath Building Society

33 Boltro Road
Haywards Heath
West Sussex RH16 1BQ
Tel: 0444-451844 Fax: 0444-414274
(Merged with Yorkshire)

Heart of England Building Society

Olympus Avenue
Tachbrook Park
Warwick CV34 6NQ
Tel: 0926-496111 Fax: 0926-490435
(Sept 1992)
CHIEF EXECUTIVE: M O Travis FCCA
VALUE OF TOTAL ASSETS: £428.5m (1988)
TYPES OF COMMERCIAL PROPERTY ON WHICH LOANS GRANTED: Shops 1%; other 1% (2% of total lending)
FINANCE FOR PROPERTY DEVELOPMENT: Mainly housing
(Jan 1991)

Hendon Building Society

9 Central Circus
Hendon
London NW4 3JS
081-202 6384
(Now Bradford & Bingley)

Skipton Building Society 303
Stafford Railway Building Society 303
Staffordshire Building Society 303

Herts & Essex Building Society
Saffron House
1A Market Street
Saffron Walden
Essex CB10 1MX
Fax: 0799-513622
CHIEF EXECUTIVE: K C Morgan ACBSI
VALUE OF TOTAL ASSETS: £16.7m (1988)

Hinkley & Rugby Building Society
81 Upper Bond Street
Hinkley
Leicestershire LE10 1DG
Tel: 0455-251234 Fax: 0455-618506
(Sept 1992)
CHIEF EXECUTIVE: A J Payne FCIS, ACBSI
TYPES OF COMMERCIAL PROPERTY ON WHICH LOANS GRANTED: Applications considered on merit
FINANCE FOR PROPERTY DEVELOPMENT: Applications considered on merit
VALUE OF TOTAL ASSETS £219.6m (1990)
(Jan 1991)

Holmesdale Benefit Building Society
43 Church Street
Reigate
Surrey RH2 0AE
07372-45716
CHIEF EXECUTIVE: I L Booth
VALUE OF TOTAL ASSETS: £54m (1991)
(Sept 1992)

Ilkeston Permanent Building Society
24-26 South Street
Ilkeston
Derbyshire DE7 5HQ
0602-325350
CHIEF EXECUTIVE: J R Macpherson ACBSI
VALUE OF TOTAL ASSETS: £10.3m (1988)

Ipswich Building Society
44 Upper Brook Street
Ipswich
Suffolk IP4 1DP
Tel: 0473-211021 Fax: 0473 231435
CHIEF EXECUTIVE: R W Coe
LOCATION OF BRANCH OFFICES: Alderburgh, Hadleigh, Halesworth, Ipswich, Saxmundham, Woodbridge.
VALUE OF TOTAL ASSETS: £153m (1991)
MORTGAGES GRANTED ON: Residential property in England & Wales
MAXIMUM ADVANCE: £250,000
VALUE ADVANCED: 95%
MAXIMUM REPAYMENT PERIOD: 40 Years
INTEREST CALCULATED: Annually
(Sept 1992)

Kent Reliance Building Society
Reliance House
Manor Road
Chatham
Kent ME4 6AF
Tel: 0634-848944 Fax: 0634-830912
CHIEF EXECUTIVE: I R Robinson
VALUE OF TOTAL ASSETS: £142m (1988)
TYPES OF COMMERCIAL PROPERTY ON WHICH LOANS GRANTED: Offices 20%; Shops 70%; factories 10% (4% of total lending)
FINANCE FOR PROPERTY DEVELOPMENT: Housing Associations
(Sept 1992)

Lambeth Building Society
118-120 Westminster Bridge Road
London SE1 7XE
Tel: 071-928 1331 Fax: 071-261 0193
CHIEF EXECUTIVE: D O Hayward FCCA FCBSI
VALUE OF TOTAL ASSETS: £409m (1989)
TOTAL LENDING ON COMMERCIAL PROPERTY: approx 1%
CATEGORIES: Offices (professional only) 0.5%; shops (usually with living accommodation) 0.5%
BRIDGING FINANCE FOR RESIDENTIAL PROPERTY DEVELOPMENT: Yes
BRIDGING FINANCE FOR COMMERCIAL PROPERTY DEVELOPMENT: No
INVOLVED IN DIRECT DEVELOPMENT: No

Leamington Spa Building Society
Leamington House, Milverton Hill
Leamington Spa
Warwickshire CV32 5FE
Tel: 0926-450045 Fax: 0926-311655
(Merged with Bradford & Bingley)

Leeds & Holbeck Building Society
105 Albion Street
Leeds LS1 5AS
Tel: 0532-459511 Fax: 0532-446003
CHIEF EXECUTIVE: A E Stone FCIS, FCBSI
Does not lend for property development
VALUE OF TOTAL ASSETS: £967.5m (1988)

Leeds Permanent Building Society
Permanent House
The Headrow
Leeds LS1 1NS
Tel: 0532-438181 Fax: 0532-437559
CHIEF EXECUTIVE: J M Blackburn FCIB, CBIM
Housing development envisaged
VALUE OF TOTAL ASSETS: £18bn (1991/92) approx
(Sept 1992)

Leek United Building Society
50 St Edward Street
Leek
Staffordshire ST13 5DH
Tel: 0538-384151 Fax: 0538-399179

(Sept 1992)
CHIEF EXECUTIVE: N McFadden
VALUE OF TOTAL ASSETS: £211m (1989)
(Jan 1991)

Londonderry Provident Building Society

7 Castle Street
Londonderry
Northern Ireland BT48 6HQ
Tel: 0504-370037 Fax: 0504-371508
(Sept 1992)
CHIEF EXECUTIVE: H Haslett
VALUE OF TOTAL ASSETS: £3.4m (1988)
(Jan 1991)

Loughborough Building Society

6 High Street
Loughborough
Leicestershire LE11 2PY
Tel: 0509-610707 Fax: 0509-231058
DIRECTORS: W Moss (Chairman); K R E Prince (Deputy Chairman); A C Pearson; A R Brooks; E L Messom; P R Blakemore
CHIEF EXECUTIVE: D F Smith FCBSI MBIM
VALUE OF TOTAL ASSETS: £78.5m (1990/1)
(Sept 1992)

Manchester Building Society

18-20 Bridge Street
Manchester M3 3BU
Tel: 061-834 9465 Fax: 061-833 2796
(Sept 1992)
CHIEF EXECUTIVE: P K Cross JP BA(Com) ACBSI
VALUE OF TOTAL ASSETS: £36.8m (1988)
(Jan 1991)

Mansfield Building Society

Regent House
Regent Street
Mansfield
Nottinghamshire NG18 1SS
Tel: 0623-649921 Fax: 0623-440162
(Sept 1992)
CHIEF EXECUTIVE: D J Fisher FCBSI/Chairman: M A Bull
VALUE OF TOTAL ASSETS: £61.4m (1988)
BRIDGING FINANCE FOR RESIDENTIAL DEVELOPMENT: Yes
BRANCH OFFICES: Sutton in Ashfield, Kirkby in Ashfield, Chesterfield, Mansfield
(Jan 1991)

Market Harborough Building Society

Wellands House
The Square
Market Harborough
Leicestershire LE16 7PD
0858-463244
CHIEF EXECUTIVE: R S Harris FCIS, ACBSI
Will lend for right type of development and if funds available
VALUE OF TOTAL ASSETS: £181.6m (1991)
(Sept 1992)

Marsden Building Society

6-20 Russell Street
Nelson
Lancashire BB9 7NJ
Tel: 0282-692821 Fax: 0282-698110
CHIEF EXECUTIVE: E Shapland FCBSI DMS MBIM
VALUE OF TOTAL ASSETS: £218.4m (31 Dec '91)
TYPES OF COMMERCIAL PROPERTY ON WHICH LOANS GRANTED: offices, shops, leisure (10% of total lending)
BRIDGING FINANCE FOR RESIDENTIAL DEVELOPMENT: Yes
FINANCE FOR PROPERTY DEVELOPMENT: Residential, owner occupation, sheltered housing
(Sept 1992)

Melton Mowbray Building Society

39 Nottingham Street
Melton Mowbray
Leicestershire LE13 1NR
Tel: 0664-63937 Fax: 0664-480205
DIRECTORS: C E I Thornton; R A Brownlow; R J Green; R W Ladbury; R F Leman; CHIEF EXECUTIVE: G F Wells FCBSI, MBIM
VALUE OF TOTAL ASSETS: £168.9m (1991)
(Sept 1992)

Mercantile Building Society

75 Howard Street
North Shields
Tyne and Wear NE30 1AQ
Tel: 091-296 0222 Fax: 091-258 5917
97% Residential; 3% Commercial
PROVIDE BRIDGING FINANCE FOR RESIDENTIAL PROPERTY DEVELOPMENT: Yes
(Sept 1992)

Mid-Sussex Building Society

Mid-Sussex House
66 Church Road
Burgess Hill
West Sussex RH15 9AU
0444-870700
(Merged with Cheltenham & Gloucester)

Monmouthshire Building Society

John Frost Square
Newport
Gwent NP9 1PX
Tel: 0633-840454 Fax: 0633 840325
GENERAL MANAGER: D A Powis
VALUE OF TOTAL ASSETS: £67.3m (1988)
Do not lend for property development
(Sept 1992)

Mornington Building Society

158 Kentish Town Road
London NW5 2BT
Tel: 071-485 5575 Fax: 071-485 4280
(Merged with Brittania)

National & Provincial Building Society

Provincial House
Bradford BD1 1NL
0274-733444
CHIEF EXECUTIVE: B Thompson-McCausland
LENDING BUSINESS MANAGER: D S Cox
VALUE OF TOTAL ASSETS: £7,856bn (1989)
LENDING ON COMMERCIAL PROPERTY: approx 2%
CATEGORIES: offices 0.4%; shops 1%; factories 0.1%; other 0.5%
BRIDGING FINANCE FOR RESIDENTIAL PROPERTY DEVELOPMENT: Yes
BRIDGING FINANCE FOR COMMERCIAL PROPERTY DEVELOPMENT: No
INVOLVED IN DIRECT DEVELOPMENT: No

National Counties Building Society

Church Street
Epsom
Surrey KT17 4NL
Tel: 0372-742211 Fax: 0372 745607
CHIEF EXECUTIVE: J Wayt
TOTAL LENDING ON COMMERCIAL PROPERTY - 0.3%
CATEGORIES: offices 100%
BRIDGING FINANCE FOR RESIDENTIAL PROPERTY DEVELOPMENT: No, but may consider
BRIDGING FINANCE FOR COMMERCIAL PROPERTY DEVELOPMENT: No, but may consider
INVOLVED IN DIRECT DEVELOPMENT: Not yet
(Sept 1992)

Nationwide Anglia Building Society

Chesterfield House
Bloomsbury Way
London WC1V 6PW
071-242 8822
CHIEF EXECUTIVE: T Melville-Ross FCIS FRSA CBIM
VALUE OF TOTAL ASSETS: £21,060m (1988)
FINANCE FOR PROPERTY DEVELOPMENT: Nationwide Housing Trust Ltd. Anglia Housing Association. Equity partner in PROBE. Quality Street; Manager P Mugnaioni, aims to invest £600m over next 5 years in provision of 40,000 private rented homes

Newbury Building Society

17-20 Bartholomew Street
Newbury
Berkshire RG14 5LY
Tel: 0635-43676 Fax: 0635-38790
(Sept 1992)
CHIEF EXECUTIVE: T H Butler FCBSI MBIM
VALUE OF TOTAL ASSETS: £136m (1988)
TOTAL LENDING ON COMMERCIAL PROPERTY: 10%
(Jan 1991)

Newcastle Building Society

Hood Street
Newcastle on Tyne NE1 6JP
Tel: 091-232 6676 Fax: 091 261 0015
GROUP MANAGING DIRECTOR: D W Midgley FCBSI MBIM
VALUE OF TOTAL ASSETS: £1bn (1992)
SUBSIDIARY COMPANY: Adamscastle
(Sept 1992)

North of England Building Society

50 Fawcett Street
Sunderland SR1 1SA
Tel: 091-565 6272 Fax: 091-5101231
DIRECTORS: R Shiel (Chairman); R W Linden AIB (Scot) FBIM (Chief Executive); J H Elsy FIIM; Sir David Chapman Bt. B Comm; T Collin ACIB; R A Edmonds FRICS ACIArb; S M Featherstone BA,FCA; A M Griffin ACIB,FCI,FBIM; K L Hayton LLB; R Hudson; D K Wilson FCA
VALUE OF TOTAL ASSETS: £1.2bn (1991)
MORTGAGES GRANTED ON: Freehold/leasehold residential & commercial investment & business premises
MAXIMUM ADVANCE: 95%
VALUE ADVANCED: Negotiable
MAXIMUM REPAYMENT PERIOD: Negotiable
INTEREST CALCULATED: Daily basis
GENERAL LENDING POLICY: Flexible approach to tailor facilities according to loan requirement
(Sept 1992)

North Wiltshire Rideway

18-19 Commercial Road
Swindon
Wiltshire SN1 5NP
Tel: 0793-481353 Fax: 0793-512383
(Merged with Portman BS)

Northern Rock Building Society

Northern Rock House
Gosforth
Newcastle upon Tyne NE3 4PL
Tel: 091-285 7191 Fax: 091-213 0820
CHIEF EXECUTIVE: J C Sharp
VALUE OF TOTAL ASSETS: £5,700m
TYPES OF COMMERCIAL PROPERTY ON WHICH LOANS GRANTED: Up to 75% LTV on residential & commercial investment
BRIDGING FINANCE FOR RESIDENTIAL DEVELOPMENTS: No
BRIDGING FINANCE FOR COMMERCIAL DEVELOPMENTS: No
CATEGORIES: offices, other
INVOLVED IN DIRECT DEVELOPMENT: Yes. Northern Rock Homes
(Sept 1992)

Norwich & Peterborough Building Society

Peterborough Business Park
Lynchwood
Peterborough PE2 0FZ
Tel: 0733-371371 Fax: 0733-371372
DIRECTORS: R M Mays-Smith MC, ECIB (Chairman); R W Bird MBE (Deputy Chairman); J E Sharman (Vice Chairman); M L Armstrong
REGIONAL OFFICES: 64 branches and mortgage shops throughout the Eastern Counties
VALUE OF TOTAL ASSETS: £1.27bn
BRIDGING FINANCE FOR RESIDENTIAL

DEVELOPMENT: No
APPLY FOR LOANS TO: Local branch or mortgage shop
MORTGAGES GRANTED ON: Residential and Semi-commercial properties
MAXIMUM ADVANCE: Negotiable
VALUE ADVANCED: Up to 95%
MAXIMUM REPAYMENT PERIOD: 30 Years (Pension Mortgages)
INTEREST CALCULATED: On a monthly basis on the opening balance in advance
GENERAL LENDING POLICY: For private residential owner; occupied property or semi-commercial purposes
MAJOR SUBSIDIARIES: Waters Lunniss & Co Ltd (Stockbrokers); Hockleys Ltd (Estate Agents); Catours Travel Ltd; Norwich & Peterborough Financial Planning Ltd.
(Sept 1992)

Nottingham Building Society

5-13 Upper Parliament Street
Nottingham NG1 2BX
Tel: 0602-481444 Fax: 0602-483948
MANAGING DIRECTOR: S E Brandreth FCBSI ACII FBIM
VALUE OF TOTAL ASSETS: £427.73m (1989)

Nottingham Imperial Building Society

Imperial Buildings
29 Bridgford Road
West Bridgford
Nottingham NG2 6AU
0602-817220
CHIEF EXECUTIVE: K A Hurst
VALUE OF TOTAL ASSETS: £32m (1991)
Not considering involvement in property development at the moment
(Sept 1992)

Peckham Building Society

1 Copers Cope Road
Beckenham BR3 1NB
Tel: 081-658 7221 Fax: 081-650 9259
CHIEF EXECUTIVE: N J Guest
VALUE OF TOTAL ASSETS: £70m (1989)
POLICY FOR LENDING ON COMMERCIAL PROPERTY: No new lending on commercial property. A small % of existing loans

---

Penrith Building Society

7 King Street
Penrith
Cumbria CA11 7AR
Tel: 0768-63675 Fax: 0768-891275
(Sept 1992)
GENERAL MANAGER: D Davey ACBSI
VALUE OF TOTAL ASSETS: £28.9m (1988)
May consider financing small project
(Jan 1991)

Portman Building Society

Principal Office
Portman House
Richmond Hill
Bournemouth
Dorset BH2 6EP
Tel: 0202-292444 Fax: 0202-292503
(Merged with Cheltenham & Gloucester)

Portsmouth Building Society

Churchill House
Winston Churchill Avenue
Portsmouth
Hampshire PO1 2EP
Tel: 0705-291291 Fax: 0705-291999
CHIEF EXECUTIVE: J R King
VALUE OF TOTAL ASSETS: £651.9m (1988)
TOTAL LENDING ON COMMERCIAL PROPERTY: approx 10%
CATEGORIES: offices 10%; shops 80%; factories 2%; warehouses 6%; leisure 2%
BRIDGING FINANCE FOR RESIDENTIAL PROPERTY DEVELOPMENT: No
BRIDGING FINANCE FOR COMMERCIAL PROPERTY DEVELOPMENT: No
INVOLVED IN DIRECT DEVELOPMENT: No

Principality Building Society

Principality Buildings
PO Box 89
Queen Street
Cardiff CF1 1UA
Tel: 0222-344188 Fax: 0222-644628
CHIEF EXECUTIVE: J D Mitchell FCBSI
VALUE OF TOTAL ASSETS: £910m (1988)
(Sept 1992)

Progressive Building Society

Progressive House
33-37 Wellington Place
Belfast BT1 6HH
Tel: 0232-244926 Fax: 0232 330431
(Sept 1992)
MANAGING DIRECTOR: W Ebb LLB MBIM
VALUE OF TOTAL ASSETS: £121.8m (1988)
(Jan 1991)

Rowley Regis Building Society

217-223 Halesowen Road
Cradley Heath
Warley
West Midlands B64 6QJ
Tel :0384-41000 Fax: 0384-410947
CHIEF EXECUTIVE: R G Frier FCBSI
VALUE OF TOTAL ASSETS: £82m (1988)
May consider finance for property development

Saffron Walden & Essex Building Society

Saffron House
1a Market Street
Saffron Walden
Essex CB10 IHX
0799-22211
CHIEF EXECUTIVE: R W Hockley FCA
VALUE OF TOTAL ASSETS: £101m (1988)
TYPES OF COMMERCIAL PROPERTY ON WHICH LOANS GRANTED: offices, shops, other (6.1% of total lending)
FINANCE FOR PROPERTY DEVELOPMENT: residential

Saint Pancras Building Society
200 Finchley Road
London NW3 6DA
Tel: 071-794 2000 Fax: 071-794 7088
DIRECTORS: CHIEF EXECUTIVE: J Heusen FAAI; (Chairman); H Disley (Vice Chairman); K L Wood MBIM; D A R May ACII; J L Clarke FCA
VALUE OF TOTAL ASSETS: £95m (1991)
Does not lend for property development
(Sept 1992)

Scarborough Building Society
Prospect House
PO Box 6
Scarborough
Yorkshire YO12 6EQ
Tel: 0723-368155 Fax: 0723-500322
DIRECTORS: G T V Pindar OBE; F Coopland JP; R L Grunwell; J B Mitchell; G F Winn B Comm FCA; J J Carrier FCBSI; The Rt Hon Lord Derwent LVO DL.
VALUE OF TOTAL ASSETS: £371m (April 1992)
MORTGAGES GRANTED ON: Residential and commercial securities
MAXIMUM ADVANCE: £1,000,000
VALUE ADVANCED: 90% residential
MAXIMUM REPAYMENT PERIOD: 25 years
INTEREST CALCULATED: Annually
GENERAL LENDING POLICY: Traditional residential properties
OTHER MAJOR SUBSIDIARIES: Scarborough Finance Ltd, Specialist Mortgages Services Ltd
(Sept 1992)

Scottish Building Society
23 Manor Place
Edinburgh EH3 7XE
Tel: 031-220 1111 Fax: 031-220 2888
VALUE OF TOTAL ASSETS: £91.8m (Jan 1992)
(Sept 1992)

Sheffield Building Society
66 Campo Lane
Sheffield S1 2EG
Tel: 0742-725588 Fax: 0742 722226
(Merged with Bradford & Bingley)

Shepshed Building Society
Bull Ring
Shepshed
Loughborough
Leicestershire LE12 9QD
0509-503302
CHIEF EXECUTIVE: G Aisbitt ACIS FCBSI FAAI
VALUE OF TOTAL ASSETS: £30m (1992)
Do not lend for property development
(Sept 1992)

Skipton Building Society
The Bailey
Skipton
North Yorkshire BD23 1DN
Tel: 0756-700500 Fax: 0756-700400
DIRECTOR/CHIEF EXECUTIVE: J G Goodfellow
VALUE OF TOTAL ASSETS: £2.8bn (1991)
MORTGAGES GRANTED ON: Most types of businesses
MAXIMUM ADVANCE: 65%
VALUE ADVANCED: Minimum loan £20,000; minimum valuation £75,000
MAXIMUM REPAYMENT PERIOD: 25 years
INTEREST CACLULATED: Normally between 1.5% to 3% above bank base rate
GENERAL LENDING POLICY: Most types of business considered
OTHER MAJOR SUBSIDIARIES: Homeloan Management Ltd; Skipton Financial Services Ltd
(Sept 1992)

Stafford Railway Building Society
4 Market Square
Stafford ST16 2JH
0785-223212
CHIEF EXECUTIVE: W R Dean BA FCA, M R Heenan BSc FCA
VALUE OF TOTAL ASSETS: £25m (1988)
Does not lend for property development
(Sept 1992)

Staffordshire Building Society
Jubilee House
PO Box 66
84 Salop Street
Wolverhampton WV3 0SA
Tel: 0902-772611 Fax: 0902-21546
(Sept 1992)
CHIEF EXECUTIVES: V E Pratt FCBS, DMS; P W Clarke IPFA, FRVA
VALUE OF TOTAL ASSETS: £464.4m (1988)
Would lend for local development
(Jan 1991)

Standard Building Society
64 Church Way
North Shields
Tyne & Wear NE29 0AF
Tel: 091-2574123 Fax: 091 258 0575
GENERAL MANAGER: M B Anderson LLB ACBSI
VALUE OF TOTAL ASSETS: £9.6m (1988)
Do not lend for property development

Stroud & Swindon Building Society
Rowcroft
Stroud
Gloucester GL5 3BG
Tel: 0453-757011 Fax: 0453-764044
DIRECTORS: Chief Executive: R L Payne FCBSI; P J Gadden (Chairman); J H Parker (Managing Director); + 8 Directors
VALUE OF TOTAL ASSETS: £520 (1992 - Est.)
(Sept 1992)

Surrey Building Society
10/12 Masseb Road
Horley
Surrey RH6 7DF
Tel: 0293-771525 Fax: 0293-820622
(Sept 1992)
GENERAL MANAGER: R A Dommett BA FCIS FCBSI MIPM

VALUE OF TOTAL ASSETS: £61m (1988)
FINANCE FOR PROPERTY DEVELOPMENT: Mainly occupied property
(Jan 1991)

Sussex County Building Society

40-42 Friars Walk
Lewes
East Sussex BN7 2LW
Tel: 0273-471671 Fax: 0273-478439
(Merged with Leeds BS)

Swansea Building Society

11 Craddock Street
Swansea SA1 3EW
Tel: 0792-641155 Fax: 0792-644785
(Sept 1992)
MANAGING DIRECTOR: P Protheroe BSc, FCBSI
VALUE OF TOTAL ASSETS: £14.5m (1988)
Does not lend for property development
(Jan 1991)

Teachers Building Society

Allenview House
Hanham Road
Wimbourne
Dorset BH21 IAG
Tel: 0202-887171 Fax: 0202-841694
CHIEF EXECUTIVE: D Smalley
VALUE OF TOTAL ASSETS: £80.4m (1988)
Would only provide finance after completion of development
(Sept 1992)

Tipton & Cosely Building Society

70 Owen Street
Tipton
West Midlands DY4 8HG
021-557 2551/2
CHIEF EXECUTIVE: C J Martin FCBSI MBIM
VALUE OF TOTAL ASSETS: £73m (1991)
TYPES OF COMMERCIAL PROPERTY ON WHICH LOANS GRANTED: Mainly shops, but offices, shops, factories, warehouses considered

Town & Country Building Society

215 Strand
London WC2R 1AY
Tel: 071-353 1476 Fax: 071-583 2933
(Now Woolwich)

Tynemouth Building Society

53-55 Howard Street
North Shields
Tyne & Wear NE30 IAF
091-257 5366
CHIEF EXECUTIVE: R H Mande
VALUE OF TOTAL ASSETS: £27.4m (1988)

Universal Building Society

41 Pilgrim Street
Newcastle on Tyne NE1 6BT
Tel: 091-232 0973 Fax: 091-222 0546
(Sept 1992)
CHIEF EXECUTIVE: A J Winder JP FABE FBIM
VALUE OF TOTAL ASSETS: £100.5m (1988)
Not involved in property development:
(Jan 1991)

Vernon Building Society

26 St Petersgate
Stockport
Cheshire SK1 1HF
Tel: 061-429 6262 Fax: 061-429 6996
(Sept 1992)
CHIEF EXECUTIVE: J Sutton FCA
VALUE OF TOTAL ASSETS: £54m (1988)
TYPES OF COMMERCIAL PROPERTY ON WHICH LOANS GRANTED: shops 2%; leisure 3%; offices 2% (7% of total lending)
(Jan 1991)

Walthamstow Building Society

869 Forest Road
Walthamstow
London E17 4BB
Tel: 081-531 3231/6 Fax: 081-523 2889
(Now Cheltenham & Glouster)

Wessex Building Society

115 Old Christchurch Road
Bournemouth BH1 1HB
Tel: 0202-767171 Fax: 0202-752164
(Now Portman BS)

West Bromwich Building Society

374 High Street
West Bromwich
West Midlands WV6 7XY
Tel: 021-525 7070 Fax: 021-500 5961
(Sept 1992)
MANAGING DIRECTOR: J T Allard FCBSI
VALUE OF TOTAL ASSETS: £586m (1988)
Active in lending for property development
(Jan 1991)

West Cumbria Building Society

Cumbria House
Murray Road
Workington CA14 2AD
Tel: 0900-605717 Fax: 0900-68767
DIRECTORS: P V Sanders FCBSI (Chief Executive)
VALUE OF TOTAL ASSETS: £31.5m (1991)
APPLY FOR LOANS TO: Mortgage Manager; Head Office
MORTGAGES GRANTED ON: Freehold/Leasehold

Residential Properties
MAXIMUM ADVANCE: £200,000
VALUE ADVANCED: Up to 95%
MAXIMUM REPAYMENT PERIOD: 25 years
INTEREST CALCULATED: Annual
GENERAL LENDING POLICY: Some semi-commercial properties
(Sept 1992)

Yorkshire Building Society
Yorkshire House
Westgate, Bradford
Yorkshire BDI 2AU
Tel: 0274-734822 Fax: 0274-735571
(Sept 1992)
CHIEF EXECUTIVE: D F Roberts FCII FCBSI
VALUE OF TOTAL ASSETS: £2,373m (1988)
TYPES OF COMMERCIAL PROPERTY ON WHICH LOANS GRANTED: offices, shops, other
FINANCE FOR PROPERTY DEVELOPMENT: Willing to consider all types of propositions
(Jan 1991)

Chapter 5

Banks

Index

Others

A

B

C

D

E

F

G

U

V

W

Y

Z

31 plc
91 Waterloo Road
London SE1

77 Bank Limited, The
Finsbury Circus House
12/15 Finsbury Circus
London EC2M

ANZ Grindleys Bank plc
Minerva House
Montague Close
London SE1

ABN Amro Bank
101 Moorgate
London EC2M

Adische Kommunale Landesbank-Girozentrale
Princes House
95 Gresham Street
London EC2V 7NA
071-606 0391

Afcan Continental Bank Limited
24-28 Moorgate
London EC2R 6DJ
071-628 7131/5680

Afghan National Credit & Finance Limited
New Roman House
10 East Road
London N1 6AD
071-251 4100

African Continental Bank
24 Moorgate
London EC2R

African Development Bank
58/60 Moorgate
London EC2M

Aitama Kyowa Bank, The
30 Cannon Street
London EC4M

Aitken Hume Limited
30 City Road
London EC1Y 2AY
071-638 6070

AK International Limited
10 Finsbury Square
London EC2A
071-628 3844

AlBaraka International Limited
73 Brook Street
London W1Y
071-499 9111

Allied Bank of Pakistan Limited
14 Trinity Square
London EC3N 4AA
071-481 0207

Allied Banking Corporation
114 Rochester Row
London SW1P
071-233 6311

Allied Irish Banks plc
32 Bruton Street
London W1X
071-629 8881

Allied Irish Investment Bank Limited
Pinners Hall
Austin Friars
London EC2N 2AE
071-920 9155

Allied Trust Bank Limited
97-101 Cannon Street
London EC4N 5AD
Tel: 071-283 9111 Fax: 071-626 1212
(Sept 1992)
TYPES OF PROPERTY FOR WHICH SHORT TERM FINANCE PROVIDED: Offices, shops, factories, warehouses, residential, science parks/hi-tech, leisure, other
POLICY FOR LENDING TO PROPERTY DEVELOPERS: Cautious but flexible
MORTGAGES ON COMMERCIAL PROPERTY: Yes
SIZE OF LOAN: £250,000 - £5m
VALUATION ADVANCED: 70%
REPAYMENT PERIOD: 25 Years
INTEREST CALCULATED: Daily
TYPES OF PROPERTY CONSIDERED: offices, shops, factories, warehouses, leisure, science parks, hi-tech, other
DIRECTORS: A R P Carden (Chairman); J A Champion (Deputy Chairman)
SENIOR EXECUTIVES: A C Wakelin (Chief Executive); J C Wray (General Manager); A M James (General Manager - Commercial Banking); J D R Margarson (Group Financial Controller); J D Sisson (Senior Manager - Resources); C G Stewart (Senior Manager - Retail Banking); R A Goodgame (Chief Dealer/Treasurer)
(Jan 1991)

American Express Bank Limited
60 Buckingham Palace Road
London SW1W
071-583 6666

Amsterdam-Rotterdam Bank NV
101 Moorgate
London EC2M 6SB
071-638 2700

Anglo-Romanian Bank
42 Moorgate
London EC2R 6EL
071-588 4150

Anglo-Yugoslav (Bank) Limited
11-15 St Mary-at-Hill,
London EC3R 8EE
071-283 2335

Arab African International Bank
19 Berkeley Street
London
W1X 5AE
Tel: 071-495 4881 Fax: 071-495 3702

Arbuthnot Latham Bank Limited
131 Finsbury Pavement
London EC2A 1AY
071-628 9876

Ashikaga Bank Limited
155 Bishopgate
London EC2M

Australia & New Zealand Banking Group Limited
Minerva House
Montague Close
London SE1 9DH
071-378 2121

Bahrain Middle East Bank
1 College Hill
London EC4R

Balfour Maclain International (UK) Limited
The Royal Exchange
London EC3V

Banca Commerciale Italiana SpA
42 Gresham Street
London EC2V 7LA
071-600 8651

Banca March
Peek House
Eastcheap
London EC3M

Banca Nazionale del Agricoltura SpA
4th Floor
85 Gracechurch Street
London EC3V 0AR
071-623 2773

Banca Nazionale del Lavoro
33-35 Cornhill
London EC3V 3QD
071-623 4222/-626 6211

Banca Popolare di Milano
51 Moorgate
London EC2R

Banca Serfin SNC
Stratton House
Stratton Street
London W1X
071-408 2151

Banco Ambrosiano Veneto
73 Cornhill
London EC3V

Banco Bilbao Vizcaya
100 Cannon Street
London EC4N

Banco Bradesco SA
45 Cornhill
London EC3V

Banco Central SA
Triton Court
Finsbury Square
London EC2A 1AB
071-588 0181

Banco De Gallego
55 St George Street
London SW1V

Banco de la Nacion Argentian
14 Chiswell street
London EC1Y

Banco de Napoli
1 Moorgate
London EC2R 6JH
071-726 4131

Banco de Sicilia
99 Bishopsgate
London EC2P 2LA
071-638 0201

Banco de Vizcaya
100 Cannon Street
London EC4N
071-623 6030

Banco do Brasil SA
15/17 King Street
London EC2P

Banco Economico SA
1 Gracechurch Street
London EC3V

Banco Espanol de Credito SA
33 King Street
London EC2V 8CH
071-606 4883

Banco Nacional de Mexico SNC
3 Creed Court
Ludgate Hill
London EC4M

Banco Popolare di Milano SCARL
51 Moorgate
London EC2R
071-628 6210

Banco Real SA
20 St Dunstans Hill
London EC3R

Bangkok Bank Limited
61 St Mary Axe
London EC3A 8BY
071-929 4422

Bank Bumiputra Malaysia Berhad
36-38 Leadenhall Street
London EC3A 1AP
071-488 2021

Bank Centrade
Bartlett House
9 Basinghall Street
London EC2V

Bank Central Asia
28 Austin Place
London EC2N

Bank Ekspor Impor Indonesia
Senator House
85 Queen Victoria Street
London EC4V

Bank Handlowy W Warzawie SA
4 Coleman Street
London EC2R

Bank Hapolim BM
8-12 Brook Street
London W1Y 1AA
071-872 9912

Bank Julius Baer & Co
Bevis Marks House
Bevis Marks
London EC3A 7NE
071-623 4211

Bank Leumi (UK) plc
PO Box 2AF
4-7 Woodstock Street
London W1A 2AF
071-629 1205

Bank Mees & Hope NV
Princes House
95 Gresham Street
London EC2V 7NA
071-606 4022

Bank Melli Iran
4 Moorgate
London EC2R 6AL
071-600 3636

Bank Negara Indonesia 1946
3 Finsbury Square
London EC2A

Bank Saderat Iran
(The Export Bank of Iran)
5 Lothbury
London EC2R 7HD
071-606 0951

Bank Sepah - Iran
5-7 Eastcheap
London EC3M 1JT
071-623 1371/5

Bank Tejarat
6 Clements Lane
London EC4N

Bank of America
National Trust & Savings Association
1 Alie Street
London E1

Bank of America International Limited
PO Box 262
1 Ave Street
London E1 8DG
071-634 4000

Entry missing ? Call HELPLINE Page v

Bank of Baroda
30b Commercial Road
London E1
071-488 4345

Bank of California NA
18 Finsbury Circus
London EC2M
071-628 1883

Bank of Ceylon
22 City Road
London EC2Y

Bank of China
8 Mansion House Place
London EC4N

Bank of Crete
8 Moorgate
London EC2R

Bank of Cyprus (London) Limited
27-31 Charlotte Street
London W1P 4BH
071-637 3961

Bank of East Asia Limited
75 Shaftesbury Avenue
London W1V

Bank of Fukuoka Limited
Royal Bank of Canada Centre
71 Queen Victoria Street
London EC4V

Bank of India
Park House
Finsbury Circus
London EC2M
071-628 3165

Bank of Indonesia
10 City Road
London EC1Y

Bank of Ireland
36 Queen Street
London EC4R
071-329 4500

Bank of Korea
Plantation House
Fenchurch Street
London EC3M

Bank of Kuwait & Middle East
66 Warnford Court
Throgmorton Street
London EC2N

Bank of Kyoto
62 Cornhill
London EC3V

Bank of Montreal
11 Walbrook
London EC4N 8ED
071-236 1010

Bank of New York
46 Berkeley Street
London W1X 8AA
071-499 1234

Bank of New Zealand
BNZ House
91 Gresham Street
London EC2V 7BL
071-726 4060

Bank of Nova Scotia
Scotia House
33 Finsbury Square
London EC2A 1BB
071-638 5644

Bank of Oman Limited
138 Park Lane
London W1Y
071-408 0349

Bank of Scotland
38 Threadneedle Street
London EC2P 2EH
071-601 6615

Bank of Scotland
The Mound
Edinburgh EH1 1YZ
031-442 7777
ASSISTANT GENERAL MANAGER PROPERTY: R H Hirst
(Sept 1992)

Bank of Seoul
3 Finsbury Square
London EC2A
071-588 6162

Bank of Tokyo International Limited
Northgate House
20-24 Moorgate
London EC2R 6DH
071-638 1271

Bank of Tokyo Limited
Finsbury Circus House
12/15 Finsbury Circus
London EC2M

Bank of Yokohama
40 Basinghall Street
London EC2V
071-628 9973

Bankorp Limited
90 Long Acre
London WC2E

Banque Bruxelles Lambert SA
1 Apollo Street
London EC2A
071-247 5566

Banque de L'Orient Arabe et D'Outre-Mer
195 Brompton Road
London SW3

Banque De La Meditterranean (UK) Limited
50/52 Curzon Street
London W1Y

Banque Francaise de L'Orient
31 Berkeley Street
London W1X

Banque Francaise du Commerce Exterieur
4-6 Throgmorton Avenue
London EC2N
071-638 0088

Banque Internationale a Luxembourg
Priory House
1 Mitre Square
London EC3A

Banque Internationale Pour L'Afrique
Occidentale
10 St James Street
London SW1A

Banque La Henin
48 Cambridge Street
London SW1V

Banque Nationale de Paris Limited
PO Box 416
8-13 King William Street
London EC4P 4AS
071-626 5678/5231

Banque Paribas
68 Lombard Street
London EC3V 9EH
071-929 4545

Banque Transatilantique
36 St James's
London SW1A

Banque Worms
15 St Swithins Lane
London
EC4N 8AN
071-626 6121

Barclays Bank plc
54 Lombard Street
London EC3P 3AH
071-626 1567
DIVISIONAL DIRECTOR PROPERTY: D J Turner

Baring Brothers & Company Limited
8 Bishopsgate
London EC2N 4AE
071-280 1000

Baronsmead plc
Clerkenwell House
Clerkenwell Road
London EC1R

Barry Edward & Associates
130-132 New Kings Road
Fulham
SW6 4LZ
071-371 0222

Bayerische Hyupotheken Und Weschel Bank
41 Moorgate
London EC2R

Bayerische Landesbank Girozentrale
13-14 Appold Street
London EC2A 2AA
071-247 0056

Bayerische Vereinsbank AG
1 Royal Exchange Buildings
London EC3V

BCH Property Limited
10 Lombard Street
London EC3V

BCI Limited
42 Gresham Street
London EC2V 7LA
071-606 4235

Entry missing ? Call HELPLINE Page v

Beirut Riyad Bank SAL
9 Basinghall Street
London EC2V

Berliner Bank
81 Gracechurch Street
London EC3V

BFG Bank AG
33 Lombard Street
London EC3V

BHF-Bank
61 Queen Street
London EC4R

Bikuben Bank UK
18 Cannon Street
London EC4M

Boston Safe Deposit & Trust Co (UK) Limited
Princes House
Bush Lane
London EC4R

Bred
76 Cannon Street
London EC4N

British Bank of the Middle East
18c Curzon Street
London W1Y
071-493 8331

British and Commonwealth Merchant Bank plc
62 Cannon Street
London EC4N 6AE
Tel: 071-249 0900 Fax: 071-248 0900
DIRECTORS: A J L Whimster, M J Chicken, B G Deeks
BRIDGING FINANCE PROVIDED FOR PROPERTY DEVELOPMENT: offices, shops, factories, warehouses, science parks, hi-tech, leisure
POLICY FOR LENDING TO PROPERTY DEVELOPERS: No fixed parameters. Flexibility dependent on individual project - provide senior debt, mezzanin and equity finance
MORTGAGES ON COMMERCIAL PROPERTY: Yes
SIZE OF LOAN: £1m - £5m with larger amounts being syndicated
VALUATION ADVANCED: Up to 100% (with an expected return from profits)
REPAYMENT PERIODS: Max 5 years
INTEREST CALCULATED: LIBOR + MARGIN + COLA
TYPES OF PROPERTY CONSIDERED: offices, shops, factories, warehouses, leisure, science parks, hi-tech
MORTGAGES GRANTED ON LEASEHOLD PROPERTY: Yes

British Linen Bank Limited
4 Melville Street
Edinburgh EH3 7NZ
Tel: 031-453 1919 Fax: 031-243 8393
(Sept 1992)
DIRECTORS: E F Sanderson (Chief Executive); A D Nicol (Depty Chief Executive); J S Hunter; A A Murray; M D McPhail; N M Suess; W D Marr
LOCATION OF REGIONAL HEAD OFFICES: London; Manchester; Glasgow
NON-EXECUTIVE: J E Boyd (Governor); I F Brown; P A Burt; P G Livesey; J Miller CBE; D J MacLeod CBE; D B Pattullo BA FIB (Depty Governor); Sir T N Risk; J M Young
(Jan 1991)

Brown Shipley & Company Limited
Founders Court
Lothbury
London EC2R 7HE
Tel: 071-606 9833 Fax: 071-726 0135
(Jan 1991)

BSI-Banca Della Svizzera Italiana
Windsor House
39 King Street
London EC2V 8DQ

Bulgarian Foreign Trade Bank
1 Gracehurch Street
London EC3V 0DD
071-626 1888

Caisse Centrale des Banques Populaires
4 London Wall Buildings
Blomfield Street
London EC2M 5NT
071-588 3281

Caja De Ahorros Municipal De Bilbao
100 Warnford Court
Throgmorton Street
London EC2N

Camara Bank
14 Chigwell Street
London EC1Y

Casse Nationale de Credit Agricole
Conder House
14 St Pauls Churchyard
London EC4M 8BD
Tel: 071-248 1400 Fax: 071-334 9376
(Sept 1992)
DIRECTORS: A De Trachis (General Manager); D Kingsmill, D Barros (Assts)
TYPES OF PROPERTY FOR WHICH SHORT TERM FINANCE PROVIDED: offices, shops, factories, warehouses, science parks/hi-tech, leisure, residential, other
POLICY FOR LENDING TO PROPERTY NEGOTIATORS: Terms are negotiated with individual Property Developers
(Jan 1991)

Canadian Imperial Bank of Commerce
Cottons Centre
Cottons Lane
London SE1 2QL
Tel: 071-234 6000 Fax: 071-407 4127
MORTGAGES GRANTED ON: Commercial not hotels/leisure
REPAYMENT PERIOD: 8 years
(Sept 1992)

Cassa di Risparmio delle Provincie Lombarde
Wax Chandler's Hall
Gresham Street
London EC2V
071-606 8225

Cassa di Risparmio delle Provincie Lombarde
1/6 Lombard Street
London EC3V

Chancery Bank plc
100 Avenue Road
London
NW3 3HF
071-722 0099

Chartered Westlandis Bank Limited
33/36 Gracechurch Street
London
EC3V OAX
071-623 8711
(JAN 1991)

Charterhouse Bank Limited
1 Paternoster Row
St Pauls
London EC4M 7DH
Tel: 071-248 4000 Fax: 071-248 4317
(Sept 1992)
A wholly owned subsidiary of The Royal Bank of Scotland Group plc
DIRECTORS: M V Blank (Chairman & Chief Executive); I M Beith; E G Cox; M R B Gatenby; R Kilsby; M H Mason; A W Muirhead; P H W Rix
(Jan 1991)

Chase Manhattan NA
Woolgate House
Coleman Street
London EC2P 2HD
Tel: 071-962 5203 Fax: 071-962 5361
Owned by Chase Manhattan Capital Markets International
DIRECTORS: Patrick Scott/Tim Hayne Vice Presidents
(Sept 1992)

Chemical Bank International Limited
Chemical Bank House
180 Strand
London WC2R 1ET
071-379 7674
A wholly owned subsidiary of Chemical NY Corp

Cho Hung Bank Limited
Plantation House
Fenchurch Street
London EC3M

Christians Bank
21 Lloyds Chambers
Portoken Street
London E1

Chugoku Bank Limited, The
Pennisular House
Monument Street
London EC3R

CIC Union Europeene International Et CIE
74 London Wall
London EC2M

Citibank NA
3 Finsbury Square
London EC2A
071-638 7878

Citibank Mortgage
St Martins House
1 Hammersmith Grove
Hammersmith
London W6 0NY
Tel: 081-741-8000 Fax: 081-846-8274
(Residential)
DIRECTORS: P A Cohan (MD); S W Balme (Marketing); J H Flynn (Sales); D C Moore (Business & Commercial Moartgages)
MORTGAGES GRANTED ON: Freehold, freehold or leasehold owner occupied residential properties with no part letting & commercial properties
MAXIMUM ADVANCE: £150,000
REPAYMENT PERIOD: 40 years
(Commercial)
MAXIMUM ADVANCE: £1m
REPAYMENT PERIOD: 25 years
(Sept 1992)

Citicorp Investment Bank Limited
PO Box 242
335 Strand
London WC2R 1LS
071-836 1230
A subsidiary of Citicorp New York through Citicorp International Group Inc

City Merchants Bank Limited
13 Austin Friars
London EC2N

Close Brothers Limited
36 Great St helen's
London EC3A 6AP
Tel: 071-283 2241 Fax: 01-632 9699
(Sept 1992)

DIRECTORS: M E A Keeling (Chairman); R D Kent (Managing Director); The Lord Denman CBE, MC; P J Gaynor; M H F Morley; P J Stone (Executive); A J Tennant; J G T Thornton (Executive); P L Winkworth (Executive)
(Jan 1991)

Clive Discount Company Limited
9 Devonshire Square
London EC3M 4HP
Tel: 071-283 1401 Fax: 071-548 5306
DIRECTORS: M Walker (Chief Executive)

Clydesdale Bank plc
30 St Vincent Place
Glasgow G1 2HL
Tel: 041-248 7070 Fax: 041-204 0828
(Sept 1992)
Owned by Midland Bank plc
OTHER MAJOR SUBSIDIARIES: Clydesdale Bank Insurance Brokers Ltd, Scottish Computer Services Ltd, Clydesdale Bank Equity Ltd, Clyde General Finance Ltd, Clydesdale Bank Finance Corporation Ltd
(Jan 1991)

Commercial Bank of Korea
27th Floor
Centre Point
103 New Oxford Street
London WC1A
071-379 7835

Commercial Bank of London plc
107/112 Leadenhall Street
London EC3A

Commercial Bank of London plc
69/71 Haymarket
Charles II Street
London SW1Y

Commerzbank AG
10/11 Austin Friars
London EC2N 2HE
071-638 5895

Commonwealth Bank of Australia
8 Old Jewry
London EC2R 8ED
071-600 0822

Consolidado (UK) Limited
Vestry House
Laurence Pountney Hill
London EC4R

Consolidated Credits Bank Limited
West World
West Gate
London W5 1DT
Tel: 081-991 2551 Fax: 01-991 5263
(Sept 1992)
TYPES OF PROPERTY FOR WHICH SHORT TERM FINANCE PROVIDED: offices, shops, residential, leisure, science parks/hi-tech
POLICY FOR LENDING TO PROPERTY DEVELOPERS: 70% advance against value of undeveloped property + 70% advance against architects certificates for work done. Joint venture/ Equity participation in some cases. Lending Range: £50,000 - £2m: 6-30 months. Finance open ended bridges including property portfolios. Bridge residential acquisitions for purchasers in broken or incomplete chains
MORTGAGES ON COMMERCIAL PROPERTY: Yes
(a) SIZE OF LOAN: £50,000 - £500,000
(b) % VALUATION ADVANCED: 60-70%
(c) REPAYMENT PERIOD: 1-5 years
(d) INTEREST CALCULATED: By negotiation
(e) TYPES OF PROPERTY CONSIDERED: offices, shops, leisure
MORTGAGES GRANTED ON LEASEHOLD PROPERTY: Yes
(Jan 1991)

Continental Bank NA
162 Queen Victoria Street
London EC4V

Co-operative Bank plc
PO Box 101
1 Balloon Street
Manchester M60 4EP
061-832 3456

Copleys Limited
14 King Street
London EC2V

County NatWest Limited
135 Bishopsgate
London EC2M

Coutts & Company
440 Strand
London WC2R 0QS
071-379 6262
A member of the National Westminster Group

Credit du Nord
10 Old Jewry
London EC2R 8DU
071-606 0621

Credit Commercial de France
Peninsula House
36 Monument Street
London EC2R 8LJ
071-623 1131

Credito Italiano SpA
17 Moorgate
London EC2R 6HX
071-606 9011

Credit Lyonnais SA
84/94 Queen Victoria Street
London EC4P 4LX
071-634 8000

Credit Lyonnais Bank Nederland NV
41/43 Maddox Street
London W1R

Credit Suisse
24 Bishopsgate
London EC2N 4BQ
071-623 3488

Creditanstait Bankverein
29 Gresham Street
London EC2V

Credito Italiano International Limited
Princes House
95 Gresham Street
London EC2V

Cyprus Credit Bank Limited
89/93 Newington Causeway
London SE1

Cyprus Popular Bank Limited
19 Fitzroy Street
London W1P 6BA
071-580 6091

Daiwa Bank Limited CAPITAL MANAGEMENT LTD
Level 19
City Tower
40 Basinghall Street
London
EC2V 5DE
Tel: 071-315 3900 Fax: 071-782 0875

4 BROADGATE
LONDON
EC2M 7LE

Danske Bank AF
Danske House
10 Broadgate
London EC2N 2RA
071-628 3090

Den Norske Bank plc
Nordic Bank House
20 St. Dunstan's Hill
London EC3R 8HY
Tel: 071-621 1111 Fax: 071-626 7400

Deutsche Aussenhandels Bank AG
150 Leadenhall Street
London EC3

Deutsche Bank AG
PO Box 441
6 Bishopsgate
London EC2P 2AT
071-971 7000

Discount Bank & Trust Company
34 Grosvenor Square
London W1X 9LL
071-629 0801

DKB International Limited
24 King William Street
London EC4R

Dai-Ichi Kangyo Bank Limited
DKB House
24 King William Street
London EC4R

Daiwa Investment Advisers (Europe) Limited
40 Basinghall Street
London EC3V

Deutsche Shiffbank AG
Grocers Hill
Princes Street
London EC2R

Development Bank of Singapore Limited
19/21 Moorgate
London EC2R

DG Bank
10 Aldersgate Street
London EC1A 4XX

DG Investment Bank Limited
10 Aldergate Street
London EC2R

Dillion Read Limited
Devonshire House
Mayfair Place
London W1X

Diners Club ENEA
364 Kensington High Street
London W14

Discount Copr. of New York (London) Limited
16 St Helens Place
London EC3A

Dresdner Bank AG
Dresdner House
125 Wood Street
London EV2V

Entry missing ? Call HELPLINE Page v

Dunbar Bank plc
9 Sackville Street
London W1X

Duncan Lawrie Limited
1 Hobart Place
London SW1W 0HU
071-245 1234
Wholly owned subsidiary of Walter Duncan & Goodnicke plc

EBC Amro Limited
10 Devonshire Square
London EC2M 4HS
071-621 0101
Wholly owned subsidiary of Amsterdam-Rotterdam Bank NV

Equator Bank Limited
Equator House
66 Warwick Square
London SW1V
071-821 8797

Equatorial Bank plc
10 Bucklersbury House
Walbrook
London EC4N 8EL
071-236 0666

Ermgassen & Co
24 Lombard Street
London EC3V

Etrufin Reserco Limited
3 St Helen`s Place
London EC3A

Exeter Bank
9 Berkeley Street
London W1X

Export Import Bank of Japan, The
7/11 Finsbury Circus
London EC2M

Export-Import Bank Korea
Moorgate Hall
155 Moorgate
London
EC2M 6XB
071-628 8384

Fennoscandia Bank Limited
The Old Deanery
Deans Court
London EC4V

FIBA Bank (UK) Limited
2 London Wall Buildings
London Wall
London EC2M

Fidelity Bank
1 Bishopsgate
London EC2N 3AB
071-621 1477

Fiduciary Trust International SA
30 Old Burlington Street
London W1X

Fieldstone Private Capital Group Limited
42 Queen Anne's Gate
London SW1H

Financial & General Bank plc
13 Lowndes Street
London SW1X

First Austrian International Limited
Eldon House
2 Eldon Street
London EC2M

First Bank of Nigeria Limited
29/30 King Street
London EC2
071-606 6411

First Commercial Bank
Ground Floor
2 South Place
London EC2M
071-628 2612

First Interstate Bank of California
First Interstate House
6 Agar Street
London WC2N 4HN
071-836 3560

First Mortgage Securities Limited
1 Lancaster Place
London WC2E

First National Bank plc
85 Uxbridge Road
London W13 8RA
081-840 7058

First National Bank of Boston
39 Victoria Street
London SW1H
071-799 3333
Wholly owned subsidiary of First National Boston Corporation

First National Bank of Chicago
90 Long Acre
London WC2E
071-240 7240

First National Bank of Maryland
12 Old Jewry
London EC2R 8DP
071-726 4082

First National Commercial Bank plc
2 South Place
London EC2M 2RB
071-628 2612

Fleet Bank of Massachusetts NA
40-41 St Andrew`s Hill
London EC4V 5DE
01-248 9531

Fleming (Robert) & Company Limited
25 Copthall Avenue
London EC2R 7DR
071-638 5858

Fokus Bank SA
99 Gresham Street
London EC2V

Fraser (Robert) & Partners
Fraser House
29 Albemarle Street
London W1X 3FA
Tel: 071-493 3211 Fax: 071-408 1814
DIRECTORS: J M Bottomley; C J Emson
POLICY FOR LENDING TO PROPERTY DEVELOPERS:
Prepared to finance on a selective basis - commercial property only
(Sept 1992)

French Bank of Southern Africa
64 Bishopsgate
London EC2N

Fuji Bank Limited
Riverplate House
7-11 Finsbury Circus
London EC2M
071-588 2211

Garanti Bankasi Turkiye
141 Fenchurch Street
London EC3M

Gartmore Money Management Limited
16/18 Gartmore House
Monument Street
London EC3R

Gefinor (UK) Limited
Gefinor House
18b Charles Street
London W1X

Generale Bank
Bavaria House
13/14 Appold Street
London EC2A

Gerrard & National plc
33 Lombard Street
London EC3V 9BE
071-623 9981

Ghana Commercial Bank
69 Cheapside
London EC2P 2BB
071-248 2384

Girobank plc
Operations Centre
Bridle Road
Bootle
Merseyside G1R 0AA
051-996 2234
REGIONAL OFFICES: Edinburgh/Ashford/Birmingham/Liverpool/Leeds.
(Part of Alliance and Leicester)
(Sept 1992)

Girobank plc
10 Milk Street
London EC2V 8JH
071-600 6020

Girozentrale Vienna
68 Cornhill
London EC3V

Goode Durrant Bank plc
22 Buckingham Street
London WC2N 6PU
071-782 0010

Gotabanken
Gota House
70/74 Cannon Street
London EC4N

Granville & Co Limited
Mint House
77 Mansell Street
London EC4N

Gresham Trust plc
Barrington House
Gresham Street
London EC2V

Greyhound Bank plc
11 Albermarle Street
London W1X

Grindlays Bank plc
13 St James`s Square
London SW1
071-930 4011

Gruppo Nordest
3 St Helen's Place
Bishopsgate
London EC3A

Guinness Mahon & Company Limited
32 St Mary at Hill
London EC3P 3AJ
Tel: 071-623 9333 Fax: 071-283 4811
(Sept 1992)
DIRECTORS: T D Walker-Arnott BSC, FRICS
TYPES OF PROPERTY FOR WHICH SHORT TERM FINANCE PROVIDED: offices, shops, factories, warehouses, residential, science parks, hi-tech, leisure, other
MORTGAGES GRANTED ON COMMERCIAL PROPERTY: No
(Jan 1991)

Gulf Bank KSC
1 College Hill
London EC4R

Gulf International Bank BSC
2/6 Cannon Street
London EC4M

HFC Bank plc
62 Trafalgar Square
London WC2N

Habib Bank AG Zurich
92 Moorgate
London EC2P

Habib Bank Limited
Granite House
97 Cannon Street
London EC4N

Habibsons Bank Limited
55-56 St James's Street
London SW1A 1LA
Tel: 071-895 1100 Fax: 071-895 1104
(Sept 1992)
DIRECTORS: H M D Habib; M H Hanafi; D W Kendrick; K Bradford; H D Habib; A R D Habib; A D Habib
(Jan 1991)

Hachijuni Bank Limited
37 Lombard Street
London EC3V

Hambros Bank Limited
41 Tower Hill
London EC3N 4HA
Tel: 071-480 5000 Fax: 071-702 4424
(Sept 1992)
TYPES OF PROPERTY/DEVELOPMENTS FOR WHICH SHORT TERM FINANCE PROVIDED: offices, shops, factories, warehouses, residential, science parks/hi-tech, leisure
POLICY FOR LENDING TO PROPERTY DEVELOPERS: will look at any properly documented presentation to established developers. The covenant of the borrower will be an important factor
MORTGAGES ON COMMERCIAL PROPERTY: Yes
SIZE OF LOAN: Appropriate to the investment - not less than £0.5m
% VALUATION ADVANCED: No fixed criteria say 50%-100%
REPAYMENT PERIOD: Generally up to 5 years, may be longer
TYPE OF PROPERTY CONSIDERED: offices, shops, factories, warehouses
MORTGAGES GRANTED ON LEASEHOLD PROPERTY: Yes
(Jan 1991)

Hamburgische Landesbank
5/7 St Helen`s Place
London EC3A

Hanil Bank Limited
Ropemaker Place
25 Ropemaker Street
London EC27
071-638 3981

Harris Trust Savings Bank
3 Queen Victoria Street
London EC4N 8EL
071-248 0364

Havana International Bank Limited
20 Ironmonger Lane
London EC2V 8EY
071-606 0781
Wholly owned subsidiary of Banco National de Cuba

Henry Ansbacher & Co Limited
Priory House
1 Mitre Square
London EC3A

Hessische Landesbank Girozentrale
8 Moorgate
London EC2R 6DD
071-726 4500

Hill Samuel Bank Limited
100 Wood Street
London EC2P 2AJ
Tel: 071-628 8011 Fax: 071-726 4671
DIRECTORS: E R Smith FIB; A W Clark FIB; D D S Crawley AIB
TYPES OF PROPERTY FOR WHICH SHORT TERM FINANCE PROVIDED: Offices, shops, factories, warehouses, science park/hi-tech, residential, leisure
POLICY FOR LENDING TO PROPERTY DEVELOPERS: Prepared to lend against most forms of property development. In the main only prepared to advance 2/3 of site purchase and construction costs. Occasional advances of 85-90% of costs in return for a percentage of profits on the overall development. Equities: will subscribe for a maximum of 20% of shares and will consider joint ventures on particular developments
MORTGAGES ON COMMERCIAL PROPERTY:
(a) SIZE OF LOAN: Minimum £250,000
(b) % VALUATION ADVANCED: 2/3
(c) REPAYMENT PERIODS: Negotiable
(d) INTEREST CALCULATED: On a floating basis or base rate or LIBOR
(Jan 1991)

Hill Samuel Property Finance Limited
5th Floor
E Section
Plantation House
10-15 Mincing Lane
London EC3M
071 929 1208

Hoare C & Company
37 Fleet Street
London EC4P 4DQ
071-353 4522

Hong Kong Bank Limited
PO Box 199
99 Bishopsate
London EC2P 2LA
071-638 2306
Wholly owned subsidiary of Hong Kong & Shanghai Banking Corp

Hokkaido Takushoku Bank Limited
33 Lombard Street
London EC3V
071-621 9295

Hau Nan Commercial Bank
19 Great Winchester Street
London EC2N

Hungarian International Bank Limited
Princes House
95 Gresham Street
London EC2V 7LU
071-606 5371
Owned by National Bank of Hungary (60%)

Hyakajushi Bank Limited
43 London Wall
London EC2M

Hyogo Bank Limited, The
5th Floor Peninsula House
30/36 Monument Street
London EC3R

IBCA Limited
Eldon House
2 Eldon Street
London EC2P

IB Finance (UK) plc
11 Golden Square
London W1R

IBJ
The Industrial Bank of Japan, Limited
London Branch
Bracken House
One Friday Street
London EC4M 9JA
Tel: 071-248 1111 Fax: 071-248 1114

IBJ International Limited
Bucklersbury House
3 Queen Victoria Street
London EC4N

Industrial Bank of Japan Limited
Bucklersbury House
14 Walbrook
London EC4N 8BR
071-236 8310

Internallianz Bank Zurich
21/23 St Swithins Lane
London EC4N

International Mexican Bank Limited
29 Gresham Street
London EC2V 7ES
071-600 0880

International Clearing Services Limited
LIFE Floor
Royal Exchange
London EC3V

International Currency Exchange plc
22 Old Bond Street
London W1X

International Investment Finance
Corporation Limited
6 Queen Street
London W1X

International Trade & Investment Bank
23 Gresham Street
London SW1X

Investcorp International Limited
Investcorp
65 Brook Street
London W1Y

Iran Overseas Investment Bank Limited
120 Moorgate
London EC3

Israel Discount Bank
120 Wigmore Street
London W1H

Isveimer
65 Queen Street
London EC4R

Italian International Bank Limited
122 Leadenhall Street
London EC3V 4PT
071-623 8700
A wholly owned subsidiary of Monte dei Paschi di Siena Banking Group

Iyo Bank Limited
40 Basinghall Street
London EC2V

Japan Development Bank
City Tower
40 Basinghall Street
London EC2V

Japan International Bank Limited
107 Cheapside
London EC2V 6BR
071-600 0931

JHI International Limited
20 Regent Street
London SW1Y

Jordan International Bank
103 Mount Street
London W1Y

Julian Hodge Bank Limited
10 Windsor Place
Cardiff CF1 3BX
Tel: 0222 220800 Fax: 0222 344061
DIRECTORS: J J Hodge; ; E M Hammonds FCIB, R E Cave FCIS; P F Coleman; D L Jones FCA; B S Morris FCIB; H M Gwyther FCA; D M Austin ACA
REGIONAL OFFICES: All enquiries to Head Office address
Part of Carlyle Trust Limited
UK DEPOSITS: £44m (1992)
BRIDGING FINANCE PROVIDED: Offices, Shops & Factories.
APPLY FOR LOAN TO: Manager, Commercial Lending, Head Office.
MORTGAGES GRANTED ON: Freehold/ Long Leasehold properties
MAXIMUM ADVANCE: £2m
VALUE ADVANCED: 65%
MAXIMUM REPAYMENT PERIOD: 15 Years
INTEREST CALCULATED: Monthly
GENERAL LENDING POLICY: Prepared to consider any viable proposition within 1/2 day's travelling distance from Cardiff.
OTHER MAJOR SUBSIDIARY: Carlyle Finance Limited
(Sept 1992)

Juroku Bank Limited
4th Floor
6 Broadgate
London EC2M

Jyske Bank
119 Chancery Lane
London WC2A

KCA Limited
Suite 525
Salisbury House
29 Finsbury Circus
London EC2M

Kansallis-Osake-Pankki
Kansallis House
19 Thomas Square
London E1

KDB Bank (UK) Limited
Plantation House
31/35 Fenchurch Street
London EC3M

Kenya Commercial Bank
24/25 New Bond Street
London W1Y

King & Shaxson plc
52 Cornhill
London ECV 3PD
071-623 5433

Kleinwort Benson Limited
20 Fenchurch Street
London EC3P 3DB
071-623 8000

Koram Bank
1 Alle Street
London E1

Korea Exchange Bank
1 Old Jewry
London EC3R

Korea First Bank
80 Cannon Street
London EC4N

Korea London Term Credit Bank
65/66 Queen Street
London EC4R

Kredietbank NV
40 Basinghall Street
London EC2V

Kyowa Bank Limited
Princes House
93-95 Gresham Street
London EC2V 7NA
071-606 9231

Aubrey G Lanston & Co Inc
Bucklesbury House
3 Queen Victoria Street
London EC4N

Lazard Brothers & Company Limited
21 Moorfields
London EC2P 2HT
Tel: 071-588 2721 Fax: 071-638 2165
Wholly owned by Lazard Partners Limited
(Sept 1992)

Leopold Joseph & Sons Limited
31/45 Gresham Street
London EC2V

Litex Bank SAL
1 Gracechurch Street
London EC3V

Lloyds Bank plc
71 Lombard Street
London EC3P 3BS
071-626 1500

Lloyds Merchant Bank Limited
40-66 Queen Victoria Street
London EC4P 4EL
071-248 2244/248 3738 (Treasurer)
Wholly owned subsidiary of Lloyds Merchant Bank Holdings Limited

Lordsvale Finance plc
111/113 Wandsworth High Street
London SW18 4HY
Tel: 081 874 7511 Fax: 081-877 1384
(Sept 1992)
PROVISION OF SHORT TERM FINANCE TO PROPERTY DEVELOPERS: Yes
CATEGORY: Leisure
PRESENT POLICIES FOR LENDING TO PROPERTY DEVELOPERS: Practically all business transacted is in the Amusement section of the leisure trade. Authorised under the 1987 Banking Act.
PROVISION OF MORTGAGES ON COMMERCIAL PROPERTY: Yes
(a) SIZE OF LOAN: Only in leisure trade £100,000 - £500,000
(b) % VALUATION ADVANCED: Each application considered on its merits
(c) REPAYMENT PERIOD: Normally 5 Years or less
(d) INTEREST CALCULATED: Normally as a flat rate
(e) TYPE OF PROPERTY ON WHICH MORTGAGES LIKELY TO BE GRANTED: Leisure
PROVISION OF MORTGAGES ON LEASEHOLD PROPERTY: Yes
(Jan 1991)

Ljubljanska Banka
7 Birchin Lane
London EC3V

Lombard Odier
Private Asset Management Limited
22 Southampton Place
London WC1A

London & City Management Limited
2/3 Cornwall Terrace
London NW1

London & International Mercantile Limited
17/19 Sun Street
London EC2M

London Italian Bank
20 Cannon Street
London EC4M

London Trust Bank plc
30 Upper Grosvenor Street
London W1X

London Ventures (Fund Managers)
14 St Christopher Place
London W1M

Entry missing ? Call HELPLINE Page v

McDonnell Douglas Bank Limited
4th Floor
Rothschild House
Whitgift Centre
Croydon CR0 0XB
Tel: 081-681 8120 Fax: 081-681 5814

Macquarie Securities Limited
69 Mark Lane
London EC3R

Madison Trust
6 Duke of York Street
London SW1Y

Malayan Banking Berhard
74 Coleman Street
London EC2R 5BN
0781-638 0561/4

Manchester Exchange & Investment Bank Limited
International House
1 St Katherine Way
London E1

Manufacturers Hanover Limited
1-11 John Adam Street
London WC2N 6HT
071-932 4000
Member of group of Manufacturers Hanover Trust Company

Marubeni International Finance plc
120 Moorgate
London EC2M

Mase Westpack Limited
Westpac House
75 King William Street
London EC4N

Matlock Bank Limited
Hesketh House
Portman Square
London W1H

Meghral Bank Limited
Meghral Court
18 Jockey`s Fields
London WC1R

Mellon Bank NA
6 Devonshire Square
London EC2M

Mercadian Securities International Limited
12 Masons Avenue
London EC2V

Merrill Lynch International Bank Limited
97 Park Street
London W1Y
071-499 7812

Middle East Bank Limited
Shakleton House
Battlebridge Lane
London SE1
071-357 6262

Midland Agriculture
70 Pall Mall
London SW1Y

Midland Bank plc
27-32 Poultry
London EC2P 2BX
071-260 8000

Midland Montagu
4/15 Lower Thames Street
London EC3R

Minories Finance Limited
123 Minories
London EC3N

Minister Trust Limited
Minister House
Arthur Street
London EC4R

Mitsui Taiyo Kobe Bank Limited
6 Broadgate
London EC2M

Mitsui Trust & Banking Co Limited
5th Floor
6 Broadgate
London EC2M

Mitsui Trust International Limited
41 Tower Hill
London EC3N

Mitsubishi Bank Limited
6 Broadgate
London EC2M
071-638 2222

Mitsubishi Trust & Banking Co
24 Lombard Street
London EC3V
071-929 2323

Monte Del Paschi Di Siena
122 Leadenhall Street
London EC3V

Montagu (Samuel) & Company Limited
114 Old Broad Street
London EC2P 2HY
071-588 6464
Wholly owned subsidiary of Midland Bank plc

Morgan Grenfell & Company Limited
23 Great Winchester Street
London EC2P 2AX
071-588 4545

Morgan Grenfell Asset Management Limited
20 Finsbury Circus
London EC2M

Morgan Guaranty Trust Co of New York
60 Victoria Embankment
London EC4Y

JP Morgan Investment Management Inc.
83 Pall Mall
London SW1Y 5ES

JP Morgan
60 Victoria Embankment
London EC4Y OJP

Moscow Narodny Bank Limited
81 King William Street
London EC4P 4JS
071-623 2500/2066

Mount Banking Corporation Limited
5 Mount Street
Mayfair
London W1Y 5AA
Tel: 071-409 1613 Fax: 071-493 1604
(Sept 1992)
DIRECTORS: S B R Shah (Chairman); N B Shah (Deputy Chairman); P E Tucker (Chief Executive); D C Shah (General Manager); I W McNab; P Hargreaves
PART OF GROUP: I & M Holdings Ltd
SIZE OF UK DEPOSITS/FUNDS: £150 million (1990); The Group: £170 million (1990)
BRIDGING FINANCE PROVIDED: All property
APPLY FOR LOAN TO: Bank address
MORTGAGES GRANTED ON: First legal charge
MAXIMUM ADVANCE: £2 million
VALUE ADVANCE: 70%
MAXIMUM REPAYMENT PERIOD: 10 years
INTEREST CALCULATED: Monthly in arrears
GENERAL LENDING POLICY: Ability to pay interest essential
SUBSIDIARY DEVELOPMENT COMPANY: Mount Bank (Cayman) Ltd
(Jan 1991)

Multibanco Comermex SNC
14 Austin Friars
London EC2N

NAFIN
17th Floor
99 Bishopgate
London EC2M

NMB Bank
2 Copthall Avenue
London EC2R

National Australia Bank Limited
6/8 Tokenhouse Yard
London EC2R 7AJ
071-606 8070

National Bank of Abu Dhabi
90 Bishopsgate
London EC2N 4AS
Tel: 071-626 8961 Fax: 071-626 1288
(Sept 1992)
DIRECTORS: K Haywood; M B Bowles; S L Petherick
TYPES OF PROPERTY FOR WHICH SHORT TERM FINANCE PROVIDED: offices, shops, factories, residential, leisure
MORTGAGES ON COMMERCIAL PROPERTY:
(a) SIZE OF LOAN: £0.5m - £5m
(b) % VALUATION ADVANCED: 70% maximum
(c) REPAYMENT PERIOD: 5 years maximum
(d) INTEREST CALCULATED: Bank Base Rate or LIBOR plus margin
(e) TYPES OF PROPERTY CONSIDERED: offices, factories
MORTGAGES GRANTED ON RESIDENTIAL PROPERTY: Yes - houses, flats
MORTGAGES GRANTED ON LEASEHOLD PROPERTY: Yes
(Jan 1991)

National Bank of Canada
Princes House
95 Gresham Street
London EC2V 7LU
071-726 6581

National Bank of Detroit
PO Box 51
Salisbury House
Finsbury Circus
London EC2M

National Bank of Dubai
207 Sloane Street
London SW1X

NBD Bank, NA
28 Finsbury Circus
London EC2M 7AU

071-920 0921

National Bank of Egypt
10 Finsbury Circus
London EC2M
071-374 6446

National Bank of Greece
7 Waterloo Place
London SW1 4BE
071-925 2775

National Bank of Kuwait SAK
13 George Street
London W1H

National Bank of Nigeria Limited
62 Pymers Mead
Croxted Road
London SE21 8NH
Tel: 081-761 5341 Fax: 081-766 7897

National Bank of Pakistan
18 Finsbury Circus
London EC2M 7BJ
071-588 1511

National Westminster Bank plc
Level 14, Nat West Tower
25 Old Broad Street
London EC2B 1HQ
071-920 5555

Natwest Estate Management & Development
41 Lothbury
London EC2P 2BP
071-726 1000

NCNB National Bank of North Carolina
14 Moorfields Highwalk
London EC2Y

Neoperm Bank Limited
20 Abchurch Lane
London EC4 7AD
071-623 1077

New Nigeria Bank Limited
53/53a Pall Mall
London SW1Y

Nikko Bank (UK) plc
Nikko House
17 Godiham Street
London EC4V

Nippon Credit Bank, The
City Tower
40 Basinghall Street
London EC2V 5DE
071-638 6411
DIRECTORS: Mr Tabei (Managing)

Nippon Trust & Banking Co Limited
22 Lovat Lane
London EC3R

Nomura Bank International plc
Nomura House
1 St Martin's-le-Grand
London EC1A

Noble Grossart Limited
64 Lincoln's Inn Fields
London WC2A
071-242 1414

Nordeutsche Landesbank Gironzentrale
20 Ironmonger Lane
London EC2V

Norinchukin Bank
1st Floor
Security Pacific House
4 Broadgate
London EC2M

Northern Bank Limited
PO Box 183
Donegal Square West
Belfast BT1 6JS
Wholly owned subsidiary of Midland Bank plc
Tel: 0232 245277 Fax: 0232 893214
DIRECTORS: Sir Desmond Lorimer (Chairman); D R Argus; The Duke of Abercorn; M J Bray; W Ervin CBE; Sir Dennis Faulkner CBE; T G McLaughlin; Hon H T O'Neill; S H Torbens (also Chief Executive)
SUBSIDIARIES: Northern Bank Development Corporation Limited; Northern Bank Executor and Trustee Company Limited; Northern Bank Factors Limited; Northern Bank Insurance Services Limited; Northern Bank (IOM) Limited; Northern Bank Leasing Limited
(Sept 1992)

Northern Trust Co, The
155 Bishopgate
London EC2M

Nykredit Mortgage Bank plc
27 Grosvenor Street
London W1X 9FE
Tel: 071-499 4191 Fax: 071-493 7926
(Sept 1992)
DIRECTORS: Thorlief Krarup (Chairman); A J Davison; R O Challis; P E Lockyear; B C B Clarke; T Hausen
PART OF GROUP: Nykredit
LOCATION OF REGIONAL HEAD OFFICE: Plymouth
APPLY FOR LOAN TO: P Lockyear - Head Office
MORTGAGES GRANTED ON: Freehold commercial properties

MAXIMUM ADVANCE: £40,000,000
VALUE OF ADVANCE: Up to 75% with indemnity
MAXIMUM REPAYMENT PERIOD: 20 years
INTEREST CALCULATED: Day to day, charged monthly/quarterly
(Jan 1991)

Omega Trust Co Limited
140 Brompton Road
London SW3

Orion Royal Bank Limited
71 Queen Victoria Street
London EC4V
071-489 1177
Wholly owned subsidiary of Royal Bank of Canada

Ottoman Bank
King William House
2a Eastcheap
London EC2M

Overseas Chinese Banking Corporation
111 Cannon Street
London EC4N
071-929 1394

Overseas Trust Bank Limited
6th Floor
36/38 Leadenhall Street
London EC3A

Overseas Union Bank Limited
61-62 Coleman Street
London EC2P 2EU
071-628 0361

Panmure Gordon Bankers Limited
14 Moorfields Highwalk
London EC2Y

Paribus Capital Markets Group
33 Wigmore Street
London W1H

Peoples Construction Bank of China, The
6th Floor
30 Cornhill
London EC3V

Philadelphia National Bank
3 Gracechurch Street
London EC3V 0AD
071-623 8144

Philippine National Bank
103 Cannon Street
London EC4N

PK Christiana Bank (UK) Limited
9 King Street
London EC2V 8EA
071-726 6213

Postipankki Limited
10-12 Little Trinity Lane
London EC4V
Tel: 071-489 0303 Fax: 071-489 1142
(Sept 1992)
APPLY FOR LOAN TO: P A Stone
MORTGAGES GRANTED ON: Freehold/leasehold commercial properties
MAXIMUM ADVANCE: £10 million
MINIMUM ADVANCE: £3 million
VALUE ADVANCED: Up to 70%
MAXIMUM REPAYMENT PERIOD: 7 years
GENERAL LENDING POLICY: Fully let income producing properties only
(Jan 1991)

Qatar National Bank SAQ
135-141 Cannon Street
London EC4N 5AH
071-283 3911

Quanta Group (Holdings) Limited
Empire House
8/14 St Martin`s-le-Grand
London EC1A

R & I Bank of Western Australia Limited
Park House
16 Finsbury Circus
London EC2M

RZB Austria
36/38 Botolph Lane
London EC3R

Rabobank Nederland
108 Cannon Street
London EC4N

Rafidain Bank
Rafidain Bank Building
7/10 Leadenhall Street
London EC3V 1NL
071-626 3244

Rea Brothers plc
Aldermans House
Aldermans Walk
London EC2M 3XR
071-623 1155
CHAIRMAN: Sir John Hill FRS
DEPUTY CHAIRMAN: Anthony Townsend
MANAGING DIRECTORS: Anthony Hall; Roger Parsons

 Entry missing ? Call HELPLINE Page v

(Sept 1992)

Republic National Bank of NY
30 Monument Street
London EC3R
071-409 2426

Reserve Bank of Australia
10 Old Jewry
London EC2R

Riggs National Bank of Washington DC
21 Great Winchester Street
London EC2N 2HH
071-588 7772

Riyad Bank
Temple Court
11 Queen Victoria Street
London EC4N

Rothschild & Sons Limited
PO Box 185
New Court
St Swithin's Lane
London EC4P 4DU
071-280 5000

Royal Bank of Canada Limited
71 Queen Victoria Street
London EC4V
071-489 1188

Royal Bank of Scotland, The plc
67 Lombard Street
London EC3V 9LJ
071-623 4356

Royal Bank of Scotland, The plc
PO Box 31
36 St Andrew's Square
Edinburgh EH2 2YB
Tel: 031-556 8555 Fax: 031-229 6643

Royal Trust Bank
48-50 Cannon Street
London EC4N 6LD
Tel: 071-236 6044 Fax: 071-415 1120
MAXIMUM ADVANCE: £10,000,000
REPAYMENT PERIOD: 10 years
(Sept 1992)

Roxburge Bank Limited
294 Regent Street
London W1R 5HE
Tel: 071-493 8888/636-4666 Fax: 071-631 0257
DIRECTORS: R H Landman; J H Shah; R J Shah; K D Thakar
UK FUNDS: £47m (1991)
(Sept 1992)

Saitama Bank
30 Cannon Street
London EC4M 6XH
071-248 9421

Sakura Global Capital
42 New Broad Street
London EC2M

Salomon Brothers International Limited
Victoria Plaza
111 Buckingham Palace Road
London SW1W OSB
071-721 2000

Samuel Montagu Private Bank
110 Old Broad Street
London EC2P

San Paolo Bank
9 St Paul's Churchyard
Bank
London EC4M

Sanwa Bank Limited
1 Undershaft
London EC3A

Sanwa International plc
1 Undershaft
London EC3A

Sarasin International Securities Limited
37/39 St Andrew's Hill
London EC4V

Saudi American Bank
Nightinghale House
65 Curzon Street
London W1Y

Saudi British Bank, The
4 Stanhope Gate
London W1Y

Saudi International Bank
99 Bishopsgate
London EC2M 3TB
071-638 2323

Scandinavian Bank Limited
Scandinavian Bank
2/6 Cannon Street
London EC4M 6XX
071-236 6090

Schroder Wagg (J Henry) & Company
120 Cheapside
London EC2V 6DS
071-382 6000
Wholly owned by Schroders Plc

Scimitar Development Capital Limited
Osprey House
78 Wigmore Street
London W1H

Seccombe Marshall & Campion plc
7 Birchin Lane
London EC3V 9DE
071-283 5031
Wholly owned subsidiary of Citicorp Investment Bank Ltd.

Security Pacific National Bank
4 Broadgate
London EC2M 7LE
071-588 0303

Shanghai Commercial Bank Limited
5 Bow Churchyard
London EC4M 9DH
071-248 8291

Shinan Bank
51 Gresham Street
London EC2V

Siam Commercial Bank Limited
1 Founders Court
Lothbury
London EC2R 7DB
071-606 7596

Singer & Friedlander Limited
21 New Street
Bishopsgate
London EC2M 4HR
071-623 3000
Britannia Arrow Holdings own 87.5% interest

Skandinaviska Enskilda Banken
ScandinavianHouse
2/6 Cannon Street
London EC4
071-588 3494

Societe Generale
7th Floor
60 Gracechurch Street
London EC3V OET
071-626 5400

Societe Generale Merchant Bank plc
Exchange House
Primrose Street
Broadgate
London EC2A 2DD
Tel: 071-496 0044 Fax: 071-374 0775

Sonali Bank
123 Commercial Street
London EC1
071-247 1658

Sovereign Trust
35 Maida Vale
London W9

Standard Bank Investment Corp Limited
28a Eaton Row
London SW1W

Standard Chartered Bank
38 Bishopgate
London EC2N 4DE
071-280 7500

Standard Chartered PLC
1 Aldermanbury Square
London EC2V 7SB
071-280 7500

State Bank of New South Wales
110 Fenchurch Street
London EC2M

State Bank of India
PO Box 801
State Bank House
1 Milk Street
London EC2P 2JP
071-600 6444

State of New York Banking Department
Sardinia House
52 Lincoln`s Inn Fields
London WC2A

State Street Bank & Trust Company
Bitchin Court
20 Bitchin Lane
London EC3V
071-283 4931

Stopanska Banka Skopje
103 Kingsway
London WC2B

Entry missing ? Call HELPLINE Page v

Sumitomo Bank Limited
Temple Court
11 Queen Victoria Street
London EC4N 4TA
071-236 7400

Sumitomo Finance International
107 Cheapside
London EC2V

Sumitomo Trust & Banking Company Limited
155 Bisopsgate
London EC2M 3XU
071-965 7000

Swedbank
Orient House
42/45 Old Broad Street
London EC2M

Swiss Bank Corporation
Swiss Bank House
1 High Timber Street
London EC4V 3SB
Tel: 071-329 0329 Fax: 071-329 8700

Swiss Cantobank (International)
Moor House
London Wall
London EC2Y

Swiss Volksbank
48/54 Moorgate
London EC2R

Syndicate Bank
2a Eastcheap
London EC3M

Taiyo Kobe Bank Limited
1 Undershaft
London EC3A 8TB
071-621 1430

Texas Commerce Bank NA
180 Strand
London WC2R
071-836 1677

Thai Farmers Bank Limited
80 Cannon Street
London EC4N 6HA
071-623 4975

Tijari Finance Limited
23 St James's Square
London SW1Y

Tokaibank Limited
99 Bishopsgate
London EC2M 3TA
Tel: 071-283 8500 Fax: 071-626 0020
SENIOR MANAGING DIRECTORS: Motohiko Watanabe; Kenji Mizutani; Satoru Nishigaki
(Sept 1992)

Toronto-Dominion Bank
Triton Court
14-18 Finsbury Square
London EC2A 1DB
071-920 0272

Toyo Trust & Banking Company Limited
5th Floor
Bucklersbury House
83 Cannon Street
London EC4N 8AJ
071-236 4020

Trust Bank of Africa Limited
20 Cannon Street
London EC4M 6XD
071-236 7424

TSB Bank
60 Lombard Street
London
EC3V 9EA
071-600 6000
DIRECTORS: Mr P Edwood (Chief Executive)

Turk Ticaret Bankasi
103 Mount Street
London W1Y

Turkish Bank Limited
84/86 Borough High Street
London SE1
Tel: 071-403 5656 Fax 071-407 7406
(Sept 1992)
HEAD OFFICE: 92 Girne Caddesi
Lefkosa
Mersin 10 Turkey
DIRECTORS: All resident in the Turkish Republic of Northern Cyprus, E Neng (Assistant General Manager and local Director)
APPLY FOR LOAN: Elephant and Castle/Harringay branches
MORTGAGES GRANTED ON: Freehold, residential and commercial properties
MAXIMUM ADVANCED: £0.5m freehold
VALUE ADVANCE: Up to 75%
MAXIMUM REPAYMENT PERIOD: 3, 5, 7 years
INTEREST CALCULATED: Day to day basis, quarterly
GENERAL LENDING POLICY: Short and medium term lending to commercial entrepreneurs
(Jan 1991)

Turkiye Is Bankasi AS
21 Aldermanbury
London EC2P

UBAF Bank Limited

30 Gresham Street
London EC2V 7LP
071-606 7777

UCB Bank plc

UCB House
Wallington
Surrey SM6 0DY
081-773 3111
PROVISION OF SHORT TERM FINANCE TO PROPERTY DEVELOPERS: Yes
CATEGORIES: offices, shops, factories, warehouses, science parks/hi-tech, residential
PRESENT POLICY FOR LENDING TO PROPERTY DEVELOPERS: Require to see proven track record of 3 years successful development or pre-let/sale situation. 75% on land cost plus 75% of build cost. Will consider 85% land cost and 85% build cost on new residential developments
PROVISION OF MORTGAGES ON COMMERCIAL PROPERTY: Yes
(a) SIZE OF LOAN: £15,001 - £1,250,000
(b) % VALUATION ADVANCED: 75%
(c) REPAYMENT PERIOD: 3-25 years
(d) INTEREST CALCULATED: Fixed or variable over FHBR
(e) TYPES OF PROPERTY ON WHICH MORTGAGES LIKELY TO BE GRANTED: offices, shops, factories, warehouses, science parks/hi-tech, nursing homes, licensed premises, investment properties
MORTGAGES GRANTED ON RESIDENTIAL PROPERTY: Yes, any with commercial use
MORTGAGES GRANTED ON LEASEHOLD PROPERTY: Yes long lease only (not rack rental)

Uco Bank

23 Finsbury Circus
London EC2M

Uganda Commercial Bank

(London Representative Office)
Uganda House
58/59 Trafalgar Square
London WC2N

ULC Trust Limited

1 Great Cumberland Place
London W1H 7AL
Tel: 071-258 0094 Fax: 071-262 4273
DIRECTORS: G D Stebbens ACIB; E Mani FCA; R Et Shepherd ACIB
MORTGAGES GRANTED ON: Freehold & long leasehold property
MAXIMUM DAVANCE: £150,000
REPAYMENT PERIOD: 12 months
INTEREST CALCULATED: Quarterly on day to day balance outstanding
LENDING POLICY: Short term bridging, refurbishment and development
SUBSIDIARY: Motor Care Finance by way of hire purchase
(Sept 1992)

Ulster Bank Limited

47 Donegal Place
Belfast BT1 5AU
0232-320222
Member of National Westminster Group

Ulster Investment Bank Limited

2 Linenhall Street
Belfast
Northern Ireland BT2 8BA
0232 326222

Unibanco-Unaio De Bancos Brasileiros SA

21 Lovat Lane
London EC3R

Unibank plc

107 Cheapside
London EC2V 6DA
071-726 6000
PART OF GROUP: Unibank Danmark

Union Bancaire Privee

39 Upper Brook Street
London W1Y

Union Bank of Finland

46 Cannon Street
London EC4N

Union Bank of Nigeria Limited

PO Box 148
14/18 Copthall Avenue
London EC2R

Union Bank of Switzerland

100 Liverpool Street
London EC2M

Union Discount Company of London plc

39 Cornhill
London EC3V 3NU
071-623 1020

United Bank Limited

2 Commercial Street
London E1
071-247 2577

United Bank for Africa Limited

Plantation House
Fenchurch Street
London EC3M

United Bank of Kuwait Limited

3 Lombard Street
London EC3V 9DT
071-626 3422

United Mizrahi Bank Limited
Finsbury House
23 Finsbury Circus
London EC2M

United Overseas Bank - Geneva
123 Pall Mall
London SW1Y

United Overseas Bank Limited
19 Great Winchester Street
London EC2N 2BH
071-628 3504

United Trust Bank plc
PO Box 909
9 Prescott Street
London E1

Visa International
99 Kensington High Street
London W8

Vojvodanska Banka-Udruzena Banka
308 Regent Street
London W1R

Wachovia Corporate Services Inc
7 Albermarle Street
London W1X

Warburg S G & Company Limited
1/2 Finsbury Avenue
London EC2M
071-606 1066

Westdeutsche Landesbank Girozentrale
51 Moorgate
London EC2R

Westpac Banking Corporation
75 King William Street
London EC4N 7AH

Wintrust Securities Limited
21 College Hill
London EC4R 2RP
071-236 2360

Wintschafts-Und Privatbank, Zurich
1 Devonshire Square
London EC2M

Wood Gundy Inc
Cottons Centre
Cottons Lane
London SE1

Yamaichi Bank (UK) Limited
Guildhall House
81/87 Gresham Street
London EC2V

Yapi Ve Kredi Bankasi AS
Stock Exchange Building
Eleventh Floor
Old Broad Street
London EC2N

Yasuda Trust & Banking Company Limited
1 Liverpool Street
London EC2M
071-628 5721

Yorkshire Bank plc
20 Merrion Way
Leeds LS2 8NZ
0532-472000
DIRECTORS: Lord Clitheroe Chairman; Rt Hon Viscount Downe; H North; A W Diplock; H R Sykes; F G Sunderland; D R Argus
TYPES OF PROPERTY FOR WHICH SHORT TERM FINANCE PROVIDED: offices, shops, factories, science parks/hi-tech, residential, leisure
POLICY FOR LENDING TO PROPERTY DEVELOPERS: The bank will consider any proposition for good business lending
MORTGAGES ON COMMERCIAL PROPERTY:
(a) SIZE OF LOAN: No limits
(b) % VALUATION ADVANCED: No fixed %
(c) REPAYMENT PERIODS: Normally over 10 years
(d) INTEREST CALCULATED: Daily and capitalised quarterly
(e) TYPES OF PROPERTY CONSIDERED: offices, shops, factories, warehouses, science parks/hi-tech, leisure, other
MORTGAGES GRANTED ON RESIDENTIAL PROPERTY: Yes - houses, flats, other
MORTGAGES GRANTED ON LEASEHOLD PROPERTY: Yes
(Sept 1992)

Zambia National & Commercial Bank Limited
19/23 Moorgate
London EC2R 6AR
071-588 4382

Z-Laenderbank Austria AG
32/36 City Road
London EC1Y

Ziraat Bankasi TC
48 Bishopgate
London EC2N

Chapter 6

Finance Houses

Index

A

B

C

D

E

Abbey National Treasury Services Limited
Genesis House
201 Midsummer Boulevard
Central Milton Keynes MK9 1AN
Tel: 0908-343776 Fax: 0908 343884

ACB Limited
27 Fleetwood Road
London NW10
081 452-7249

AFE Finance Limited
Bluegate Farm
Stanbridge
Leighton Buzzard
Bedfordshire
(Registered Office)

Agricultural Mortgage Corporation plc
AMC House
Chantry Street
Andover
Hants SP10 1DD
0264 334334

Ainsbury Financial Services Limited
Forthright House
238A Wellington Road
South Stockport
Cheshire SK2 6NW
061-477 2555

Albany Finance Company Limited
141 Wolverhampton Road
Codsall
North Wolverhampton
West Midlands WV8 1PD
09074-2316

Alert Finance Company Limited
Dorset House
West Derby Road
Liverpool 7
051-263 7527

Alliance & Leicester Personal Finance Limited
Heritage House
61 Southgates
Leicester
LE1 5RR
0533 515333 Fax: 0533 621993

Allied Irish Finance Company Limited
Commercial Mortgage Division
Bankcentre
Belmont Road
Uxbridge
Middlesex UB8 1SA
Tel: 0895-72222 Fax: 0895-56991
PRESENT POLICY FOR LENDING TO PROPERTY DEVELOPERS: Policy currently under review. Not a traditional market but may enter in the future.
MORTGAGES ON COMMERCIAL PROPERTY: Yes
(a) SIZE OF LOAN: £50,000 - £1m
(b) % OF VALUATION ADVANCED: For investment properties - residential or commercial standard terms are 30% of bricks and mortar but can go higher. For some businesses lending against goodwill fixtures & fittings but this can take lending to circa 130% of bricks & mortar value.
(c) REPAYMENT PERIOD: Capital & interest 20 years. Pension linked to retirement. Endowment linked - 25 years.
(d) INTEREST CALCULATION: Daily
(e) TYPES OF PROPERTY ON WHICH COMMERCIAL MORTGAGES LIKELY TO BE GRANTED: offices, shops, factories, warehouse, leisure, medical.
PROVISION OF COMMERCIAL MORTGAGES ON RESIDENTIAL PROPERTY: Yes
CATEGORIES: Houses, flats
PROVISION OF MORTGAGES ON LEASEHOLD PROPERTY: Yes

Alwyl Investments Limited
99 Wolverhampton Street
Dudley
West Midlands
DV1 1OA
0384-53288

Anglo Dominion Finance Company Limited
26 Park Square
Leeds 4
West Yorkshire
LS1 1RD
0532-29068

Anglo Leasing plc
2 Clerkenwell Green
London EC1R ODH
071-253 4300

Appleyard Finance Limited
North Street
Leeds LS7 1RD
0532-32731

Associated Credit Limited
Lancaster House
Blackburn Street
Radcliff
Manchester M26 9TS
061-723 3211

Associates Capital Corporation Limited
Associates House
PO Box 200
Windsor
Buckinghamshire SL4 1SW
Tel: 0753-857100 Fax: 0753-856569

Entry missing ? Call HELPLINE Page v

Atlasco (Hull) Limited
170 Anlaby Road
Hull
Yorkshire
HU3 2JN
0482-23631

Avco Trust Limited
Avco House
Castle Street
Reading
Berkshire RG1 7DW
0734-586123 Fax: 0734 594710

Babour Securities Limited
184 Beverley Road
Hull
North Humberside HU3 1US
0482-28573

Bank of Ireland Finance (NI) Limited
54 Donegal Place
Belfast
BT1 5BX
0232-234334
(Sept 1992)
PROVISION OF MORTGAGES ON COMMERCIAL PROPERTY:
(a) SIZE OF LOAN: £20,000 minimum
(b) % OF VALUATION ADVANCED: 65%
(c) REPAYMENT PERIODS: Maximum 10 years
(d) INTEREST CALCULATION: Varies
(e) TYPES OF PROPERTY ON WHICH COMMERCIAL MORTGAGES LIKELY TO BE GRANTED: factories, warehouses, offices, retail shop premises, non-retail shop premises, hotels, restaurants.
(Jan 1991)

Barclays Mercantile Highland Finance Limited
Highland Business Centre
Elstree House
Elstree Way
Borehamwood
Hertfordshire WD6 1DW
081-207 4488
SENIOR EXECUTIVES: Brian Hassell (Chairman); Brian Handley (Managing Director); David Smith (Director); John Callender (Director); Don Clackson (Director)
SECRETARY: Kate Coxhead
SUBSIDIARIES: Fiatagri Finance Limited; Barclays Mercantile Highland Finance Ireland Limited; Doe Leasing Limited; Barclays Mercantile Highland Business Systems Limited; Barclays Mercantile Espana SA; Barclays Mercantile Landbouw Financiering BV; Highland Contracts Limited

Barcon Finance Company Limited
391 Palatine Road
Northenden
Manchester 22
061-998 3427

Barlindwood Finance Company Limited
23 Commercial Street
Mansfield
Nottinghamshire
0623-23248

Bear Stearns International Corporation
9 Devonshire Square
London EC2
071-626 5656

Beaton Finance Company
170 Chester Road
Greenbank
Northwich
Cheshire
0606-76311

Bedfordia Industrial Credit Limited
4 Goldington Road
Bedford MK40 3NH
0234-54587

Belvoir Finance Company Limited
2 Eastfield Road
Western Park
Leicester LE3 6FD
0533-856131

Beneficial Bank plc
Prudential House
Wellesley Road
Croydon, Surrey
CR0 9XY

Benton Finance Limited
Benton Road
Newcastle upon Tyne
NE99 1DS
0632-666361

Berliner Handles
7 Birchin Lane
London EC3
071-628 9715

Bethnon Limited
279 Mitcham Road
London SW17
081-671 4022

Birks Finance Limited
23-25 Glebe Street
Stoke on Trent
Staffordshire ST4 1HL
Tel: 0782 747111 Fax: 0782 744676
DIRECTORS: D E Rawlins
BRIDGING FINANCE PROVIDED: None
APPLY FOR LOAN TO: Head Office
INTEREST CALCULATED: On a day to day basis
(Sept 1992)

Bisman Finance Company Limited
143 Ringwood Road
St Leonard's
Kingswood
Hampshire BH24 2NP
(Registered office)

Blemain Finance Company Limited
Sadaewick Mill
Amwats
Manchester
061-236 4904

Bluescarf Limited
Pebble Court
Danaway Maidstone Road
Sittingbournc
Kent ME9 7OB
0795-842429

BNP Leasing Limited
8-13 King William Street
London
EC4P 4HS

BNP Mortgages Limited
Trinity Court
21/27 Newport Road
Cardiff
South Glamorgan
CF2 1AA
0222 497977
(Sept 1992)

Borzo Investments Limited
104 Southampton Row
London WC1
071-278 3272

Boston Trust & Savings Limited
Boston House
Lower Dagnall Street
St Albans
Hertfordshire AL3 4PG
0727-32241
PROVISION OF MORTGAGES ON COMMERCIAL PROPERTY:
(a) SIZE OF LOAN: £5,000 TO £100,000
(b) % OF VALUATION ADVANCED: Up to 70%
(c) REPAYMENT PERIOD: Up to 10 years
(d) INTEREST CALCULATION: Linked to each individual mortgage; linked to base rate.
(e) TYPES OF PROPERTY ON WHICH MORTGAGES LIKELY TO BE GRANTED: Retail shop premises, non-retail shop premises, hotels, nursing homes, restaurants.
PROVISION OF MORTGAGES ON RESIDENTIAL PROPERTY: Yes
PROVISION OF MORTGAGES ON LEASEHOLD PROPERTY: Yes

Bowmaker (Commercial) Limited
Bowmaker House
Christchurch Road
Bournemouth
Dorset BH1 3LG
0202 22077

Brad Webb Finance Limited
42A South Audley Street
London W1Y 6ER
071-493 7705

Bradway Finance Company
Huttons Buildings
146 West Street
Sheffield
South Yorkshire S1 4ES
0742 28481/2

Bradwell Finance Company Limited
Bradwell House
16 Kings Street
Newcastle
Staffordshire
ST5 1ET
0782 617870

Brandcrest Finance Limited
1304-10 Pershore Road
Birmingham
West Midlands B30 2XU
021-459 1400

British Credit Trust Limited
British Credit House
High Street
Slough SL1 1ED
Tel: 0753 73211 Fax: 0753 821390
DIRECTORS: R Keenan; T G O'Neill; A Khan
LOCATION OF REGIONAL HEAD OFFICES: Bristol; Luton; Doncaster; Warrington
GENERAL LENDING POLICY: Asset based finance; H P leasing

Broadwood Finance Limited
Millfield
Sunderland
Tyne & Wear
078377611

Brompton Finance Limited
Brompton House
4 Athol Street
Douglas
Isle of Man
0624 75440

Brooks Associates
35 Lower Brook Street
Ipswich
Suffolk
0473-225031

Brownhill Finance Limited
Mayfield Ribchester Road
Clayton-Le-Dale
Blackburn
Lancashire
0254 40644

BSG Finance
Burgess House
1270 Coventry Road
Yardley
Birmingham B25 8BB
021-707 0490

Burton Group Financial Services plc
32 Haymarket
London SW1Y 4TP
Tel: 071-925 0777 Fax: 071-925 2787

Butterfield, N T & Son
24 Chiswell Street
London EC1Y 4TY
071-814 8800
DIRECTOR: I De Leschery

C & A Collins Limited
309 Stapleton Road
Bristol
BS6 0NN
0272 559913

C & A Finance (Croydon) Limited
280 Thornton Road
Croydon
Surrey
081-940 5424/5

Cann (Finance) Limited
III Bouverie Avenue South
Salisbury
Wiltshire
0722 335062

Carlyle Trust
31 Windsor Place
Cardiff CF1 3UR
Tel: 0222 371726 Fax: 0222 222597

Cattles Holdings Finance Limited
PO Box 17
Haltemprice Court
38 Springfield Way
Anlaby
Hull HU10 6RR
Tel: 0482 564422 Fax: 0482 505350

Cave Acceptances Limited
282 Park Avenue East
Hull
Yorkshire
0482 881408

Centenary Finance Limited
11 Laidlaw Street
Glasgow G5 8LP
041 429 2100

Central London Securities Limited
Glen House
Stag Place
Victoria
London SW1E 5AG
071 973 0600

Chalk Farm Acceptances Limited
314 High Road
Wood Green
London N22 6BH
081-881 5196

Chancery Securities PLC
20 John Street
London WC1N 2DL
071-242 0599
DIRECTORS: B L Rubens, I M Rosentital BSc, A Gilbey FCA, G D Nykerk
PROVISION OF SHORT TERM FINANCE TO PROPERTY DEVELOPERS: Yes
CATEGORIES: offices, shops, factories, warehouses, science parks/hi-tech, residential.
PRESENT POLICIES FOR LENDING TO PROPERTY DEVELOPERS: Lend to professionals in property on secured or participating basis. Flexible lending policy. Facilities from £100,000.
MORTGAGES ON COMMERCIAL PROPERTY: Yes
(a) SIZE OF LOAN: £100,000 - £5m
(b) % OF VALUATION ADVANCED: 70%
(c) REPAYMENT PERIOD: 5-20 years
(d) INTEREST CALCULATION: Balance outstanding variable rate over base or fixed.
CATEGORIES: offices, shops, factories, warehouses, science parks/hi-tech.
MORTGAGES ON LEASEHOLD PROPERTY: Yes

Chartered Trust PLC
24/26 Newport Road
Cardiff CF2 1SR
Tel: 0222 473000 Fax: 0222 495180
(Sept 1992)
SHORT TERM FINANCE TO PROPERTY DEVELOPERS: Yes
CATEGORIES: offices, shops, factories, warehouses, science parks/hi-tech, residential, leisure, other.
MORTGAGES ON COMMERCIAL PROPERTY: Yes
(a) SIZE OF LOAN: £250,000 - £2m
(b) % VALUATION ADVANCED: 66.66% up to 75%
(c) REPAYMENT PERIOD: Up to 15 years
(d) INTEREST CALCULATED: On a day to day basis at a % over base rate

(e) TYPE OF PROPERTY ON WHICH MORTGAGES ARE LIKELY TO BE GRANTED: offices, shops, factories, warehouses, science parks/hi-tech, leisure, other.
PROVISION OF MORTGAGES ON RESIDENTIAL PROPERTY: Yes
CATEGORIES: Houses, flats, other
MORTGAGES ON LEASEHOLD PROPERTY: Yes, long leasehold only.
(Jan 1991)

Charters Finance Company Limited
215 Lower Addiscombe Road
Croydon
Surrey CR9 6HH
081-656 2266

Chartwell Leasing
Victoria House
Kingsbury Road
Sutton Coldfield
West Midlands
0675-70135

Cheshire Commercial Finance Limited
Bank House
The Paddock
Handforth
Wilmslow
Cheshire SK9 3HQ

Cheshunt Trading & Finance Company Limited
Bank House
The Paddock
Handforth
Wilmslow
Cheshire SK9 3HQ
0992 25166

Chevron Finance Limited
23 Ella Combe Road
Longwell Green
Bristol
Avon BS15 6BG
0272 563668

Citibank Financial Trust Limited
St Martins House
1 Hammersmith Grove
Hammersmith
London W6 0NY
Tel: 081-846 8100 Fax: 081-846 8488

Close Asset Finance Limited
5th Floor
Tolworth Tower
Ewell Road
Tolworth, Surbiton
Surrey KT6 7EL
Tel: 081-390 8201 Fax: 081-390 6168

Club 24 Limited
Hepworth House
Claypit Lane
Leeds LS2 8DE
Tel: 0532-440265 Fax: 0532-430435

Coldunell Finance Limited
53A High Street
Esher
Surrey
(Registered Office)

Coleman Finance Limited
33 Herbert Road
Seven Kings, Essex
(Registered Office)

Colliers Credit Limited
Birch Lane
Garage Durkfield
Cheshire
061-330 2089

Colne Investment Corporation Limited
Colne House
5 George Street
Colchester
Essex CO1 1TR
0206 77631

Commercial Credit & Discount Limited
Crown House, High Road
Loughton, Essex
081-508 0041

Conister Trust Limited
PO Box 17
18 Finch Road
Douglas
Isle of Man
0624-74455

Consolidated Finance Holdings Limited
35 John Street
London
WC1N 2AT
071-404 5899

Consumer Loans Company Limited
Homer Road
Solihull, West Midlands
B91 3QJ

Continental Illinois Bank
Continental Bank House
162 Queen Victoria Street
London EC4V 4BS
071-236 5292
(Sept 1992)

DIRECTORS: WH Adams, MD Posen
PROVISION OF SHORT TERM FINANCE FOR PROPERTY DEVELOPERS: Yes
CATEGORIES: factories, warehouses, offices, retail shop premises, non-retail shop premises, hotels, nursing homes, science parks/mixed.
PRESENT POLICY FOR LENDING TO PROPERTY DEVELOPERS: Short and medium term construction finance for commercial developers. Re-financing available in Europe and USA.
PROVISION OF MORTGAGES ON COMMERCIAL PROPERTY: Yes
(a) SIZE OF LOAN: £500,000 upwards
(b) % VALUATION ADVANCED: 75%
(c) REPAYMENT PERIOD: Up to 7 years
(d) INTEREST CALCULATION: LIBOR Bank
(e) TYPES OF PROPERTY ON WHICH MORTGAGES LIKELY TO BE GRANTED: Factories, warehouses, offices, retail shop premises, non-retail shop premises, hotels, restaurants, nursing homes, other.
PROVISION OF MORTGAGES ON LEASEHOLD PROPERTY: Yes
(Jan 1991)

Copleys Limited
14 King Street
London
EC2V 8EA
Tel: 071-606 1101 Fax: 071-606 1104

Crane Frue Hauf Finance Limited
Toftwood
Dereham
Norfolk NR19 1JF
(Registered Office)

Crangate Castle Securities Limited
3 Parkgate Road
Wallington
Surrey
081-647 3378

Credit & Data Marketing Services Limited
JM Centre
Old Hall Street
Liverpool L70 1AB
Tel: 051-235 2475 Fax: 051-255 1604

Credit Extensions Limited
59 North Hills
Highgate
London N6 4BS
081-340 0929

Cromwell Finance Corporation Limited
54 Le Pollett Street
Peter Port
Guernsey
Channel Islands
0481-26754

Cross & Bevingtons (Finance) Limited
29 The Thyllings
Worcester
0905 21371

Currie Finance & Leasing Company Limited
161 Chertsey Road
Twickenham
Middlesex TW1 1ER
081-892 0041

Cyprus Finance Corporation (London) Limited
27-31 Charlotte Street
London W1P 2HJ
071-637 3961

Daiwa Europe Limited
5 King William Street
London
EC4N 7AX
Tel: 071-548 8080 Fax: 071-548 8303
(Sept 1992)
DIRECTORS: Minoru Mori (Managing Director)
BRANCH OFFICES: Amsterdam; Frankfurt; Zurich; Paris; Brussels; Bahrain; Milan; Stockholm; New York; New Jersey; Toronto; Hong Kong; Singapore; Melbourne; Sydney; Seoul; Beijing; Shanghai; Bangkok; Kuala Lumpur;
(Jan 1991)

Dalbeattie Finance Company Limited
15/33 Maxwell Street
Dalbeattie DG5 4AJ
0556-610243
(Sept 1992)
PRESENT POLICY FOR LENDING TO PROPERTY DEVELOPERS: Lending based entirely on strength of balance sheets. Bridging loans not normally granted for individual developments
PROVISION OF MORTGAGES ON COMMERCIAL PROPERTY: Yes
(a) SIZE OF LOAN: £100,000
(b) % VALUATION ADVANCED: 75%
(c) REPAYMENT PERIOD: Up to 7 years
(d) INTEREST CALCULATION: APR-flat rate for fixed period
(e) TYPE OF PROPERTY ON WHICH COMMERCIAL MORTGAGES LIKELY TO BE GRANTED: offices, shops, factories, warehouses, science parks/hi-tech, leisure, other
PROVISION OF MORTGAGES ON RESIDENTIAL PROPERTY: Yes
CATEGORIES: houses, flats, other
(Jan 1991)

Darlington Finance Limited
21 Skinnergate
Darlington
County Durham
0325-67445

Darlington Merchant Credits Limited
21 Skinnergate
Darlington
County Durham
0325-67445

Darvell Finance Limited
5 Station Parade
Dorchester Road
Northolt Park
Middlesex
081-864 9877

Davenport Securities Limited
London Road
High Wycombe
Buckinghamshire
0494 30021

Dealvic Finance Limited
20 Strawberry Bank
Blackburn
Lancashire BB2 6AA
0254 59516

Deva Finance Limited
18 Church Street
Frodsham
Cheshire WA6 6QN
0928-32358

Doncaster Transport & General Finance Company
5 Thorne Road
Doncaster
South Yorkshire DN1 2HJ
0302 66586

Douglas Finance
139 Lion Road
Bexleyheath
Kent DA6 8PB
081-303 4974

Douglas Valley Finance Company Limited
Albion House
Queen Street
Oldham
Lancashire OL9 6AF
061-633 1616

Durham Downs Finance Limited
3 Station Road
Yate
Bristol
0454-314974

Eagle Credit Limited
239 Green Lane
Palmers Green
London N13 4UH
081-882 4611

East Anglian Facilities (Romford) Limited
4-5 The Parade
Gallows Corner
Romford
Essex
0708-42057

Edward Manson & Company l.imited
Henrietta House
Henrietta Place
London W1M 9AG
071-637 1124
DIRECTORS: J M Mowat FIB Scotland; L C Kwek, Barrister at Law (Malaysia); R Williams AIB; L B Kwek LLB AICS (Singapore); J H B Muenter BScEcon (Denmark)
PROVISION OF SHORT TERM FINANCE FOR PROPERTY DEVELOPERS: Yes
CATEGORIES: factories, warehouses, offices, retail shop premises, non-retail shop premises, hotels, restaurants, nursing homes, other.
PRESENT POLICY FOR LENDING TO PROPERTY DEVELOPERS: Maximum loans £500,000 to £750,000 otherwise indicated.
PROVISION OF MORTGAGES ON COMMERCIAL PROPERTY: Yes
(a) SIZE OF LOAN: Min £20,000 normal max £500,000
(b) % OF VALUATION ADVANCED: 60-80%
(c) REPAYMENT PERIOD: 5-20 years
(d) INTEREST CALCULATION: Variable - Annuity System
(e) TYPES OF PROPERTY ON WHICH MORTGAGES ARE LIKELY TO BE GRANTED: All subject to merit
PROVISION OF MORTGAGES ON RESIDENTIAL PROPERTY: Yes
PROVISION OF MORTGAGES ON LEASEHOLD PROPERTY: Yes

Endeavour Finance Limited
90 Preston Road
Brighton
Sussex BN1 6AT
0273-506331

Export Engineering & General Finance Company Limited
49 Sloane Square
London SW1X 9LU
071-730 0436

F & T Holdings Limited
53 Savile Street
Hull
Yorkshire
0482-23669

Entry missing ? Call HELPLINE Page v

Fairholme Finance Limited
Warley Chambers
Warley Road
Hayes
Middlesex
081-903 3222

Ferriby Finance Limited
Temple Chambers
4 Abbey Road
Grimsby
South Humberside
DN32 OHF
0472-58251

Finance Acceptance Limited
Fitzroy House
69-79 Lake Street
Leighton Buzzard
Bedfordshire LU7 3RZ
0525-32041

Finance Facilities (London) Limited
Station Road
Cuxton
Rochester
Kent
0634-721941

Finova Finance Limited
Westminster Bank Chambers
Burystead Place
Wellingborough
Northamptonshire NN8 1AH
09333 2162

First Co-operative Finance Limited
1 Balloon Street
Manchester M4 4BE
061-832 3300

First National Bank Limited
First National House
College Road
Harrow
Middlesex HA1 1FB
081-861 1313

Ford Motor Credit Company Limited
Jubilee House
The Drive
Warley
CM13 3AR
Tel: 0277 692500 Fax: 0277 233722

Foreign Exchange
48 Berkeley Square
London W1
081-748 0778

Forthright Finance Limited
Bank of Wales Building
Kingsway
Cardiff
South Glamorgan CF1 4YF
Tel: 0222-396131 Fax: 0222-220708

Forward Trust Group Limited
Forward Asset Finance
PO Box 1811
Metropolitan House
1 Hagley Road
Edgbaston
Birmingham B16 8SS
Tel: 021-455 4500 Fax: 021-455 4650
MANAGER PROPERTY FINANCE: M C Jobbins FRICS
PROVISION OF SHORT TERM FINANCE TO PROPERTY DEVELOPERS: Yes
CATEGORIES: Offices, shops, factories, warehouses, private residential, sheltered housing for the elderly.
PROVISION OF MORTGAGES ON COMMERCIAL PROPERTY: Yes
(a) SIZE OF LOAN: freehold or long lease minimum £250,000.
(b) % VALUATION ADVANCED: up to 80% subject to rental income/company cashflow.
(c) REPAYMENT PERIOD: 3-15 years
(d) INTEREST CALCULATED: usually payable quarterly in arrears on day to day balance o/s. Fixed or fluctuating payments of capital & interest can be arranged.
CATEGORIES: Investment properties preferred, including offices, shops, factories, warehouses.

Frizzell Banking Services Limited
300 Poole Road
Bournemouth
Dorset BH1 3NQ
Tel: 0202-295544 Fax: 0202-588712

General Finance (Yeovil) Limited
33 The Avenue
Somerset
0935-22793/4

General Guarantee Corporation Limited
Ambassador House
Brigstock Road
Thornton Heath
Surrey CR7 7XD
Tel: 081-684 9831 Fax 081-689 2184
DIRECTORS: M Dobb; A Clark; G Rex; I Grant
LOCATION OF REGIONAL HEAD OFFICES: Newcastle upon Tyne; Stoke
PART OF GROUP: Great Universal Stores plc

General Merchandise Credit Limited
Associates House
PO Box 200
Windsor
Berkshire SL4 1SW
(Registered office)

Georgian Finance Limited
24 Sandyford Place
Glasgow G3 7NG
(Registered Office)

Glenavon Finance Company Limited
26 Glenavon Park
Old Sneyd Park
Bristol BS9 1RW
(Registered Office)

Gordon Finance Company Limited
45 Leicester Road
Salford
Manchester 7
061-792 2272

Gorner, H L (Finance) Limited
Nicol Road
Bryn, Wigan
Lancashire WN4 8RY
0942-78588

Graysell Securities Limited
Bury Gate
Pulborough RH20 1NW
079-881 304

Gregmar Credits Limited
5 Fitzhardinge Street
Portman Square
London SE27 9AF
071-934 1400

Gresham Trust PLC
Barrington House
Gresham Street
London EC2V 7HE
Tel: 071-606 6474 Fax: 071-606 3370
PROVISION OF SHORT TERM FINANCE TO PROPERTY DEVELOPERS: Yes
CATEGORIES: offices, shops, factories, warehouses, residential
PRESENT POLICY FOR LENDING TO PROPERTY DEVELOPERS: Between £100,000 - £500,000. Security - first charge.
No mortgages on commercial property.

Greyhound Financial Services Limited
11 Albemarle Street
London W1
071-493 5518

H & H Factors Limited
Randolph House
46-48 Wellesley Road
Croydon CR9 3PS
081-681 2641

H & J Finance Company (Midlands) Limited
Dudley Road
Halesowen
North Birmingham
021-550 2031

Hallgate Finance Limited
Renault Building
Helham Street
Belby Bridge
Doncaster
Yorkshire
0302-66912

Hambros Bank Limited
41 Tower Hill
London, EC3N 4HA

Hanneford Finance Company Limited
254 Ashley Road
Parkstone
Poole, Dorset
0202-742957

Hardware Federation Finance Company Limited
225 Bristol Road
Edgbaston
Birmingham B5 7UB
021-446 6688

Harton Securities Limited
6 Lombard Street
Abingdon
Oxfordshire OX14 5SD
(Registered Office)

Hemson Finance Limited
28 Salisbury Street
North Humberside HU13 0SE
0482-643147

Hendon Finance Company Limited
159 Brent Street
London NW4 4ET
081-203 5151/2/3

HFC Trust & Savings Limited
North Street
Winkfield
Windsor
Berkshire S2G 4TD
Tel: 0344-890000 Fax: 0344-890014
PROVISION OF MORTGAGES ON COMMERCIAL PROPERTY: Yes
(a) SIZE OF LOAN
(b) % OF VALUATION ADVANCED: 70%
(c) REPAYMENT PERIOD: 15 Years
(d) INTEREST CALCULATION: LIBOR or bank base rate + margin of 1.5 - 4.0 % p.a. Fixed rates for periods of up to 5 years may be available on application.

(e) TYPES OF PROPERTY ON WHICH MORTGAGES ARE LIKELY TO BE GRANTED: Factories, warehouses, offices, retail shop premises, non-retail shop premises, & other.
PROVISION OF COMMERCIAL MORTGAGES ON RESIDENTIAL PROPERTY: No
PROVISION OF MORTGAGES ON LEASEHOLD PROPERTY: Yes
(Registered Office)

Highway Finance Limited
231A Hartford Road
Enfield
Middlesex
081-804 5686

Hilvale Finance Limited
London House
82 Barnards Green Road
Malvern WR14 3LY
06845-63939

Hinchley Nominees Limited
2 Fitzhardinge Street
London W1H 9PN
(Registered Office)

Hitachi Credit (UK) Limited
Hitachi Credit House
Stable's Courtyard
Church Road
Hayes
Middlesex UB3 2UH
Tel: 081-561 8466 Fax: 081-561 1206

Home Supply Finance Limited
530 King Street
Lougton
Stoke on Trent
Staffordshire
0782-313626

House of Fraser plc
1 Howick Place
London SW1P 1BH
Tel: 071-834 1515 Fax: 071-828 8885

Humber Finance Limited
Prince Dock Chambers
Prince Dock Side
Hull
Yorkshire HU1 2LH
0482-225656

Hutchinson Discount Limited
330 Upper Richmond Road
London SW14 7JN
081-878 0984

HWS Finance Limited
1030 London Road
Leigh on Sea
Essex
0702-715271

IAF Group Plc
107 Cannon Street
London
EC4N 5AD
Impact Securities
355 Wellingborough Road
Northampton NN1 4ER
0604-34404

Imperial House Finance Limited
28A Crown Lane
Morden
Surrey SM4 5BL
081-542 7843/4/5

Industrial Finance Limited
591 London Road
North Cheam
Surrey SM3 9AG
(Registered Office)

Industrial Funding Trust Limited
Moor House
119 London Wall
London EC2Y 5ET
Tel: 071-628 4004 Fax: 071-628 4458

Industries & General Mortgage Company Limited
30/31 Windsor Place
Cardiff CF1 3UR
0222-371726

Ironguild Finance Company Limited
73 Sheffield Road
Rotherham
South Yorkshire S60 1DA
Tel: 0709 820303 Fax: 0709 372373

Itexton Finance Limited
18 Rothesay Road
Luton
Bedfordshire BL1 1QX
0582-21033

Ivory Securities Limited
36 Southampton Street
Strand
London WC2
071-836 0621

James Simpson's Trustees Limited
33 Rodney Street
Liverpool 1
051-709 9273

JCB Credit Limited
The Mill
Rocester
Staffordshire ST14 5JW
Tel: 0889-590800 Fax: 0889-590360

Jefferies, Alan
206 Saltaire Road
Shipley
Yorkshire
0274-587451

John Butters Limited
28 Friar Gate
Derby DE1 1BX
0332-46411

JTG Finance Company Limited
210-212 Caledonian Road
London N1
071-278 4566

Julian Hodge Bank Limited
30 Windsor Place
Cardiff, South Glamorgan
CR1 3UR

Kendall, A B Limited
4 Birch Lane
Manchester M13 0NN
061-969 9229

Kenmar Export
2267 Coventry Road
Sheldon
Birmingham B26 3PD
021-742 6073

Kent, M Finn Insurance Service
53 Coniseliffe Road
Darlington
Co Durham DL3 7EH
0325-55266

King, E M & Company
388 Two Mile Hill
Kingswood
Bristol
Avon BS15 2JP
0272 673982

Kings Lynn Finance Limited
24-26 King Street
King`s Lynn
Norfolk PE30 1HJ
(Registered Office)

Kredietfinance Corporation Ltd
14/15 Quarry Street
Guildford, Surrey
GU1 3UY

KS Facilities Limited
94 Roebuck House
Palace Street
London SW1
071-828 7138

L T Finance Limited
80-86 Lord Street
Liverpool 2
051 236 2659

Landhurst Leasing
6/7 Queen Street
London
EC4N 1SP

Langley House Finance Company Limited
2-6 Rushey Green
London SE6 4JF
(Registered Office)

Lease Management Services Limited
81 High Street
Esher, Surrey
0374-67711

Lease Plan (UK) Ltd
Thames Side
Windsor, Berkshire
SL4 1TY

Leeds Acceptances Limited
61 High Street
Yeadon, Leeds
South Yorkshire
0532-054084

Leigh Finance Limited
1080 London Road
Leigh-on-Sea
Essex
0702-715271

Lendalot Limited
115-116 Ickneild Street
Hockley
Birmingham 18
021-233 1058

Entry missing ? Call HELPLINE Page v

Lex Vehicle Leasing
2 Park Avenue
Sale
Cheshire M33 1HJ
061-865 2441

Link Securities Limited
191 High Street
Barnet
Hertfordshire
081-440 6773

Lloyds Bowmaker Limited
Finance House
Christchurch Road
Bournemouth BH1 3LG
Tel: 0202-299777 Fax: 0202-559177
MANAGER OF COMMERCIAL LENDING: J O Bricknell
PROVISION OF SHORT TERM FINANCE TO PROPERTY DEVELOPERS: Yes
CATEGORIES: commercial, industrial & residential
PRESENT POLICIES FOR LENDING TO PROPERTY DEVELOPERS: Developer must be experienced with proven record of satisfactory projects.
SIZE OF LOAN: min £50,000 no upper limit
REPAYMENT PERIOD: 2 years maximum term
LAND PURCHASE: 70% of forced sale value with planning consent, or up to 90% with mortgage indemnity cover.
BUILDING COSTS: 70% by monthly stage payments against Architect certificates verified by surveyor or up to 90% with mortgage indemnity cover.
INTEREST CALCULATED: Rolled up. Rates & Fees. By negotiation.
(a) SIZE OF LOAN: Min £50,000, no upper limit
(b) % VALUATION ADVANCED: 70% of forced land sale bricks and mortar value, or 90% with mortgage indemnity cover.
(c) REPAYMENT PERIOD: Min. 2 years - Max. 20 years.
(d) INTEREST CALCULATED: Variable linked to base rate
(e) TYPES OF PROPERTY ON WHICH MORTGAGES ARE LIKELY TO BE GRANTED: offices, shops, factories, warehouses, science parks/hi-tech, leisure, other.
PROVISION OF COMMERCIAL MORTGAGES ON RESIDENTIAL PROPERTY: Yes if owner occupied.
CATEGORIES: houses, flats, other.
PROVISION: Yes subject to unexpired term of 30 years.

Lombard North Central plc
Lombard House
3 Princess Way
Redhill
Surrey RH1 1NP
Tel: 0737-774111 Fax: 0737-76003

London & European Finance Limited
7th Floor
Regent House
89 Kingsway
London WC2B 6RH
(Registered office)

London & Scottish Finance Corporation Limited
Arndale House
Arndale Centre
Manchester M4 3AQ
Tel: 061-834 2861 Fax: 061-834 2536
PROVISION OF MORTGAGES ON LEASEHOLD PROPERTY: Yes

Lucran Finance Limited
67 Chorley Old Road
Bolton BL1 3AJ
0204 23263

M I Finance (Wakefield) Limited
Finance House
27 Cheapside
Wakefield
Yorkshire
0924-74116

Madoc Finance Limited
Fernwood House
47 London Road
Portsmouth
Hampshire PO8 8DQ
0705-14066

Mann & Overton Finance Limited
15 Carnwath Road
London SW6 3HR
071-731 1341

Marks & Spencer Financial Services Limited
Michael House
57 Baker Street
London W1A 1DN
Tel: 071-935 4422 Fax: 071-486 2679

Martin & Pehtard Limited
Church Green House
3 Church Green
East Redditch
Worcester
0527-62701

Medens Limited
Medens House
Station Way
Crawley
West Sussex RH10 1HH
0293-518877

Mercantile Credit Personal Finance
Windsor House
High Street
Esher
Surrey KT1O 9RY
Tel: 0372 469677 Fax: 0372 468344

Mexborough Investment Company Limited
Waveney House
Adwick Road
Mexborough
South Yorkshire
0709-88 2991

Midland Bank Finance Corporation Limited
Broad Street House
55 Old Broad Street
London EC2M 1RX
071-920 0141

Midland Finance Limited
25 Market Street
Swaffham
Norfolk
0760 21994

Midland Leasing Services Limited
Cleveland Road
Wolverhampton WV2 1BL
0902-25961

Milford Mutual Facilities Limited
Milford House
29 Ardwick Green
North Manchester M12 6HB
061-273 2531

Moorgate Mercantile Holdings plc
Woodchester House
Seldon Way
Docklands
London E14 9GL
Tel: 071-538 9500 Fax: 071-538 2210

Moorgate Services Limited
Boundary House
91-93 Charterhouse Street
London EC1
071-253 0101

Musters Finance Company Limited
562 Woodborough Road
Nottingham
0602-83493

Nationwide Trust Ltd
Nationwide House
Lower Dagnall Street
St Albans, Herts
AL3 4RR

Nationwide Anglia Trust Limited
The Old Meeting House
Lower Dagnall Street
St Albans
Hertfordshire AL3 4PG
Tel: 0727 32241 Fax: 0727 34508

New Guarantee Trust Finance Company Limited
27 Hill Street
St Helier
Jersey
0534 20548

Nidd Finance Company Limited
46 Bond End
Knaresborough
Yorkshire HG5 9AN
042-376 2191

NIIB Group Limited
32 Central Avenue
Bangor County Down BT20 3AF
Tel: 0247-469415 Fax: 0247-461434
(Sept 1992)
PROVISION OF SHORT TERM FINANCE FOR PROPERTY DEVELOPERS: Yes
CATEGORIES: Residential
PROVISION OF MORTGAGES ON COMMERCIAL PROPERTY: Yes
SIZE OF LOAN: £15,100 - £500,000
% VALUATION ADVANCED: 70-75% of cost
REPAYMENT PERIOD: On a daily basis with a margin over UK Finance House base rate.
TYPES OF PROPERTY ON WHICH MORTGAGES ARE LIKELY TO BE GRANTED: offices, shops, factories, warehouses
PROVISION OF COMMERCIAL MORTGAGES ON RESIDENTIAL PROPERTY: Yes
PROVISION OF MORTGAGES ON LEASEHOLD PROPERTY: No
(Jan. 1991)

Nikko Securities Co
17 Godliman Street
London, EC4
071-329 4154

Nomis Finance Limited
849 Sheffield Road
Chesterfield
Derbyshire
0246 51106

Nomura International Finance Limited
25 Monument Street
London EC3
071-929 2366

Norfolk & Suffolk Finance Limited
117 London Road
North Lowestoft
Suffolk NR32 1LZ
0502-63165

Norman Finance Company Limited
Stoke Prior
25 Poole Road
Bournemouth
Hampshire BH4 9DF
0202-64172

North Derbyshire Credit Company Limited
12 Terrace Road
Chapel-en-le-Frith
Stockport SK12 6EY
092-881 2403

North Manchester Finance Limited
8 Nursery Road
Prestwich
Manchester M25 7DN
061-773 8914

North Minster Finance Limited
30 De Montfort Street
Leicester LE1 7GD
0533-23996

North Star Securities Limited
249 Selhurst Road
London SE25
081-653 3901

North West Finance Limited
70 Chorley New Road
Bolton
Lancashire
0772-520592

North West Securities Limited
Northwest House
City Road
Chester CH1 3AN
0244-690000

North Western Finance Limited
Norwest House
377 Borough Road
Birkenhead
Cheshire L42 OHF
051-652 2223

Northern Counties Guarantee Corporation
715 Durham Road
Low Fell
Gateshead
Tyne & West NE9 5HB
0632-815348

Northern Finance Company
46 Priory Road
Liverpool L4
051-933 3466

Northern Trading Company (Manchester) Limited
13-17 Grecian Street
Lower Broughton
Salford 7
061-792 6331/2/3

Norwich Union Leasing Ltd
PO Box 21
Surrey Street
Norwich, Norfolk NR1 3NJ

Norwood Finance Limited
9A Beechwood Avenue
Hanham
Bristol
Avon BS15 3Q
0272-541459

Novic Finance Limited
297 Alysham Road
Mile Cross
Norwich NOR 1SN
0603-410861

Nutrade Limited
Lloyds Bank Chambers
128 Stamford Street
Ashton-under-Lyne
Lancashire
061-3302969

NWS Bank plc
North West House
City Road
Chester CH99 3AN
Tel: 0244 690000 Fax: 0244 312067

OKO Finance Ltd
Heron House
5 Heron Square
Richmond Upon Thames, Surrey
TW9 1EL

Orix Europe Limited
33 Lombard Street
London
EC3V 9BQ

Parc International Limited
Edinburgh House
Windsor Road
Slough, Berkshire
SL1 2DU

Phillips Finance Services Limited

The Westbrook Centre
Milton Road
Cambridge
CB4 1DS

Provincial Finance Co

13A Dalton Square
Lancaster LA1 1PL
Tel: 0524-68413 Fax: 0524-382235
PROVISION FOR SHORT TERM FINANCE FOR PROPERTY DEVELOPERS: Yes
CATEGORIES: residential
POLICY FOR LENDING TO PROPERTY DEVELOPERS: Any residential property considered.
PROVISION OF MORTGAGES ON COMMERCIAL PROPERTY:
(a) SIZE OF LOAN: Min £15,500, no max
(b) % OF VALUATION ADVANCED: 70%
(c) REPAYMENT PERIOD: 25 years
(d) INTEREST CALCULATED: FHBR + or Building Society rate
(e) TYPE OF PROPERTY ON WHICH MORTGAGES ARE LIKELY TO BE GRANTED: offices, shops, factories, warehouses, leisure, science parks/hi-tech, other.
PROVISION OF COMMERCIAL MORTGAGES ON RESIDENTIAL PROPERTY: Yes
CATEGORIES: Houses, flats, other
PROVISION OF MORTGAGES ON LEASEHOLD PROPERTY: Yes
(Sept 1992)

Royal Trust plc, The

Cromar House
Broad Street
Wokingham
Berkshire
Tel: 0734-790202 Fax: 0734-323712

Royscot Finance Group plc

Royscot House
The Promenade
Cheltenham
Gloucestershire GL50 1PL
Tel: 0242-224455 Fax: 0242-570524

Rydale Finance Commercial

Haltemprice Court
38 Springfield Way
Anlaby
Hull HU10 6RR
0482-564400

Schroder Leasing Limited

Townsend House
160 Northolt Road
Harrow
Middlesex HA2 0PG
081-422 7101

Sears Financial Services Limited

Radcliffe House
Blenheim Court
Solihull
W Midlands B91 2AA
Tel: 021-704 0077 Fax: 021-711 4097

Security Pacific Trust Limited

308/314 Kings Road
Reading
Berkshire RG1 4PA
Tel: 0734-61022 Fax: 0734-352802
BRANCH OFFICES: Birmingham, Bristol, Colchester, London, Luton, Manchester, Reading, Southampton, Tunbridge Wells.
PROVISION OF MORTGAGES ON COMMERCIAL PROPERTY: Yes
(a) SIZE OF LOAN: £15,000 upwards
(b) % OF VALUATION ADVANCED: up to 75%
(c) REPAYMENT PERIOD: 5-15 years
(d) INTEREST CALCULATED: Monthly payments of capital + interest equalises at a margin over FHBR using a notional base rate.
(e) TYPE OF PROPERTY ON WHICH MORTGAGES LIKELY TO BE GRANTED: offices, shops, factories, warehouses, science parks/hi-tech, leisure + majority of commercial property.
PROVISION OF MORTGAGES ON RESIDENTIAL PROPERTY: Yes
PROVISION OF MORTGAGES ON LEASEHOLD PROPERTY: Yes

Seymour Adelaide & Company Limited

Allington House
136-142 Victoria Street
London SW1E 5LD
Tel: 071-828 5282 Fax: 071-828 5549
NATURE OF BUSINESS: Property Financiers
DIRECTORS: K A Burgess; J A Sprawson; R J Berkley; A R Swinburn-Johnson; D Low
MAJOR SHAREHOLDERS: Wholly owned subsidiary of London & Manchester Group plc
INVESTMENT POLICY: Providers of mezzanine development finance - as principals (Project size £250,00 to £15m)

Shawlands Securities Liminted

8 Christchurch Road
Landsdowne
Bournemouth BH1 5NQ
0202-295544

Southern Finance Company Limited

Southern House
80 Shirley Road
Southampton
Hampshire SO1 3EY
Tel: 0703-226745 Fax: 0703-224745

Southern Funding Limited

62 Welbeck Street
London W1M 7HB
Tel: 071-935-9151 Fax: 071-935-9695
DIRECTOR: Brian Rubins

Entry missing ? Call HELPLINE Page v

Sports & General Finance Limited
29 Queens Drive
Thames Ditton
Surrey K17 0TJ
081-876 6600

St Margaret's Trust Limited
The Quadrangle
Imperial Square
Cheltenham
Gloucester GL50 1PZ
0242-36141
BRANCH OFFICES: Birmingham, Bristol, Bromley, Cheltenham, Harrogate, Luton, Reading.
PROVISION OF MORTGAGES ON COMMERCIAL PROPERTY: Yes
(a) SIZE OF LOAN: £15,000 - £250,000
(b) % OF VALUATION ADVANCED: 75%
(c) REPAYMENT PERIOD: 5-12 years
(d) INTEREST CALCULATED: Capital & Quarterly interest
(e) TYPES OF PROPERTY ON WHICH MORTGAGES ARE LIKELY TO BE GRANTED: factories, offices, warehouses, retail shop premises, non-retail shop premises, hotels, restaurants, nursing homes.
PROVISION OF MORTGAGES ON LEASEHOLD PROPERTY: Yes

St Michael Financial Services Limited
47-67 Baker Street
London W1A 1DN
071-935 4422

Steeple Finance Limited
Park Place House
Tunnel Street
St Helier
Jersey CI
0534-27829

Sterling Group Limited
1 South Terrace
Moorgate Street
Rotherham
South Yorkshire S60 2EU
(Registered Office)

Sun Finance Limited
902 Garratt Lane
London SW17 0NB
081-672 8111

TBF Thompson (Finance) Limited
Garvach Coleraine
County Londonderry
N Ireland
0265-353 74405

Teron Finance Limited
67-71 High Street
Wollaston
Wellingborough
Northamptonshire
0933 63340

Terwell Finance Company Limited
Mill Road
Ilford, Essex
081-478 4863

TGS Finance Limited
320 Wigan Lane
Wigan
Lancashire
0942-42156

Three Counties Finance Limited
Estate House
Union Road
Crediton, Devon
03632 3761/2

Town & Country Brokers (Derby) Limited
35-36 Irongate
Derby
Tel: 0332-48776 Fax: 0332-43976

Townsend Finance (Soton) Limited
Ivy Lane
West End
Southampton SP3 3AF
042-183413

Tramp Group
Crosby House
Elmfield Road
Bromley Kent
081-464 9931
MANAGER FINANCIAL SERVICES: R Farmer
Company will consider finance for right property development

Treloan Limited
20 Litchdon Street
Exeter
Devon EX32 8HS
0271-45391
(Sept 1992)
PROVISION OF SHORT TERM FINANCE FOR PROPERTY DEVELOPMENT: Yes
CATEGORIES: offices, shops, residential, leisure
POLICY FOR LENDING TO PROPERTY DEVELOPERS: up to a maximum of 10 years. Must be located south-west of Bristol
PROVISION OF MORTGAGES ON COMMERCIAL PROPERTY:
(a) SIZE OF LOAN: £15,001-£100,000
(b) % VALUATION ADVANCED: 70%
(c) REPAYMENT PERIOD: monthly/quarterly
(d) INTEREST CALCULATED: Monthly in arrears

(e) TYPES OF PROPERTY ON WHICH MORTGAGES ARE LIKELY TO BE GRANTED: offices, shops, leisure, other
PROVISION OF COMMERCIAL MORTGAGES ON RESIDENTIALPROPERTY: Yes
CATEGORIES: Houses
PROVISIONOFMORTGAGESONLEASEHOLD PROPERTY: Yes
(Jan 1991)

Tri-Riding Finance Company Limited
12 Calthorpe Road
Edgbaston
Birmingham 15
021-454 6141

Tricity Finance Limited
Lombard House
Southerby Road
Enfield, Middlesex
081-804 8161

Trinity House Finance plc
Trinity House
Liston Road
Marlow
Buckinghamshire SL7 1XW
Tel: 0628 898022 Fax: 0628 898008

Turfco Finance Limited
20 Brighton Road
Crawley
Sussex
0293-29673

Tyndale Investments
Orchard House
Priest Popple
Hexham
Northumberland
0434-603516

Tyne Tees Finance Limited
62-93 Westmorland Road
Newcastle upon Tyne
0632-28281

Tyneside Scottish Credits
c/o Harison Business Services
97 Front Street
Wickham
Newcastle upon Tyne
0329-3887558

Unifund Finance Limited
The Riding
Albury End
Ware
Hertfordshire
0920-74341

United Dominions Trust Limited
Holbrook House
116 Cockfosters Road
Barnet
Hertfordshire EN4 0DY
Tel: 081-449 5533 Fax: 081-447 0169

V & J Finance (Midlands) Limited
815B Bristol Road
South Northfield
Birmingham B31 2NQ
021-475 6317

Venture Finance Limited
Fairway House
13 Mont le Grand
Exeter, Devon
0392-71715

Verden Finance Limited
48 Division Lane
St Annes
Lancashire
0253-64938

Wagon Finance Limited
Argyle House
Joel Street
Northwood Hills
Middlesex HA6 1NW
Tel: 09274-26199 Fax: 0923-835349

Wakefield Securities Limited
4 & 6 Providence Street
Wakefield
Yorkshire
0924-73249

Waldorf Finance Limited
Wrendel House
2 Whitworth Street
West Manchester M1 5WX
061-236 6918/9

Warburg, S G Securities
1 Finsbury Avenue
London EC2M 2PA
Tel: 071-860 0311 Fax: 071-860 0860

Welbeck Finance PLC
Welbeck House
Bond Street
Bristol BS1 3LB
0272 277442

Entry missing ? Call HELPLINE Page v

Westpac General Finance

Babbage House
55 King Street
Maidenhead
Berkshire SL6 1DU
0628-771111
PROVISION OF SHORT TERM FINANCE FOR PROPERTY DEVELOPERS: Yes
CATEGORIES: Offices, shops, factories, warehouses, science parks/hi-tech, residential, leisure, other.
PRESENT POLICIES FOR LENDING TO PROPERTY DEVELOPERS: Up to 80% of value or purchase price of property or land. Planning consent must be in place. Up to 80% of actual costs of refurbishment/new build etc. Facility has to be serviced monthly and knowledge of where equity will come from.
PROVISION OF MORTGAGES ON COMMERCIAL PROPERTY:
(a) SIZE OF LOAN: min £100,000
(b) % OF VALUATION ADVANCED: up to 80%
(c) REPAYMENT PERIOD: max term 15 years
(d) INTEREST CALCULATED: day to day balance payable monthly.
(e) TYPE OF PROPERTY ON WHICH MORTGAGES ARE LIKELY TO BE GRANTED: offices, shops, factories, warehouses, science parks/hi-tech.
PROVISION OF MORTGAGES ON RESIDENTIAL PROPERTY: Yes
PROVISION OF MORTGAGES ON LEASEHOLD PROPERTY: Yes

Woodchester Investments (UK) Limited

Woodchester House
Docklands
London E14 9GL

Wrenwood Group Finance Limited

Lancaster House
Blackburn Street
Radcliffe
Manchester M26 9TS
Tel: 061-723 1628 Fax: 061-725 9160

WRM Finance Limited

314 St Mary's Lane
Upminster, Essex
0402 224511

Yorkshire Bank Finance Limited

Brunswick Point
Wade Lane
Leeds LS2 8NQ
Tel: 0532-315000 Fax: 0532-465875

Yorkshire Bank Retail Services Limited

PO Box 9
Gibson Lane
Melton, North Ferriby
North Humberside HU14 3JA
Tel: 0482-631006 Fax: 0482-633805

Chapter 7

Insurance Companies

Index

Abbey Life Assurance Company

(Abbey Life Property Fund)
PO Box 33
100 Holdenhurst Road
Bournemouth
Dorset BH8 8AL
Tel: 0202-292373 Fax: 0202-290536
PROPERTY INVESTMENT MANAGER: David Weston BSc, FRICS
PROPERTY INVESTMENT DIRECTOR: Ray Hilton FRICS
SIZE OF PROPERTY PORTFOLIO: £470m (1992)
PROPERTY PORTFOLIO: Offices 29%; Retail 29%; Industrial 23%; Agricultural 3%; Developments 7%; Liquidity 9%
INVESTMENT POLICY: The active investment management of the portfolio to produce enhanced returns to policyholders involving the acquisition, development, refurbishment and sale of property. Current emphasis is in the retail and industrial sector and lot sizes of £2-£5m.
(Sept 1992)

Aetna Life Assurance Company Limited

2-12 Pentonville Road
London N1 9XG
Tel: 071-837 6494 Fax: 071-837 3967

Albany Life Assurance Company Limited

Station House
3 Darkes Lane
Potters Bar
Hertfordshire EN6 1AJ
0707-42311
(Sept 1992)
INVESTMENT MANAGERS: Lambert Smith & Hampton
INVESTMENT CONSULTANTS: Wetherall, Green & Smith
PROPERTY FUND: Highly selective portfolio of quality commercial properties, occupied by first class tenants who include household names in banking, insurance and other fields
SIZE OF PROPERTY PORTFOLIO: £51.5m (1989)
PROPERTY PORTFOLIO: offices 34%; shops 26%; warehouses 23%; retail warehouses 17%
POLICY: Any property considered good value in market
(Jan 1991)

Albany Life Property Pension Fund

(Albany Life Assurance Company Limited)
3 Darkes Lane
Potters Bar
Hertfordshire EN6 1AJ
0707-42311
INVESTMENT MANAGER: Stephen Adolphus

Allied Dunbar Assurance plc

Allied Dunbar Centre
Swindon SN1 1EL
Tel: 0793-514514 Fax: 0793-524319
(Sept 1992)
PROPERTY MANAGING DIRECTOR: M Boggis
SIZE OF PROPERTY PORTFOLIO: £526m (1987)
THE PENSION PROPERTY FUND SIZE: £291m
DISTRIBUTION: retail 29%; office 34%; industrial 19%; cash 18%
THE PROPERTY FUND SIZE: £238m
DISTRIBUTION: retail 28%; office 34%; industrial 18%; cash 20%
THE AMERICAN PROPERTY FUND SIZE: £10m
DISTRIBUTION: retail 8%; office 70%; cash 22%
(Jan 1991)

Ambassador Life Assurance Company Limited

80 Holdenhurst Road
Bournemouth
Dorset BH8 8A1
0202-292373

American Life Insurance Company UK

American International Building
2-8 Altyre Road
Croydon CR9 2LG
081-680 6000

Assicurazioni Generali SpA

117 Fenchurch Street
London EC3M 5DY
071 488 0733

Australian Mutual Provident Society

(Trading as Pearl Assurance Co. Ltd)
Amp House
Dingwall Road
Croydon
Surrey CR9 2AP
Tel: 081-686 5611 Fax: 081-688 3046
(Sept 1992)
SIZE OF PROPERTY PORTFOLIO: £33m (1988)
PROPERTY PORTFOLIO (UK): offices 66%, shops 27%; industrial 7%
INVESTMENT POLICY: Prime retail and offices
INVESTMENT MANAGER: W Cairns DipAgr, FAIV, FSLE, FRVA
CONSULTANT(S): Howell Brooks & Partners
(Jan 1991)

Barclays Life Assurance Company Limited

252 Romford Road
London E7 9JB
081-534 5544
(Sept 1992)
VALUE OF PROPERTY INVESTMENT FUND: £65m (1988)
VALUE OF PROPERTY PENSION FUND: £18m (1988)
(Jan 1991)

Black Horse Life Assurance Company Limited

Mountbatten House
Chatham
Kent ME4 4JF
0634-834000

Britannic Assurance plc

Moor Green
Moseley
Birmingham
West Midlands B13 8QF
Tel: 021-449 4444 Fax: 021-449 0456

PROPERTYMANAGER: C J RaineFRICS
(Sept 1992)
SIZE OF PORTFOLIO: £91m (1988)
PROPERTY PORTFOLIO: offices 31%; industrial 17%; retail 51%; retail/warehouse 1%
(Jan 1991)

Canada Life Assurance Company

Pellipar House
Cloak Lane
London EC4R 2 RU
Tel: 071-955 0155 Fax: 071-955 0150
PROPERTY INVESTMENT MANAGERS: John S Garlick, Michael A White & Wendy Tyreman
NORMAL INVESTMENT POLICY: Active investment policy in all commercial and industrial sectors.
(Sept 1992)

Canada Life Property Pension Fund

(Canada Life Assurance Company)
18 High Street, Potters Bar
Hertfordshire EN6 5BA
Tel: 0707-51122 Fax: 0707-46088
INVESTMENT MANAGER: Jeff Richards (Based at Canada Life Assurance Company in London)
(Sept 1992)
SIZE OF PROPERTY PORTFOLIO: £47m (1987)
INVESTMENT POLICY: Active investment policy in all commercial and industrial sectors
(Jan 1991)

Cannon Lincoln Group

(Investment Management Division)
30 City Road
London EC1Y 2EE
Tel: 071-638 0044 Fax: 071-638 0424
PROPERTY INVESTMENT MANAGER: G J Regester ARICS
PROPERTY INVESTMENT CONSULTANTS: Conrad Ritblat & Company
LOCATION OF REGIONAL OFFICES: Nationwide
SIZE OF PROPERTY PORTFOLIO: £32m (Dec 1991)
DISTRIBUTION OF PORTFOLIO (BY VALUE): Retail 50%; offices 30%; industrial 20%
NORMAL INVESTMENT POLICY: Acquisitions across all sectors nationwide.
SUBSIDIARY DEVELOPMENT COMPANIES: Culverin Property Services Limited
OTHER MAJOR SUBSIDIARIES: Cannon Assurance Limited
(Sept 1992)

Canterbury Life Assurance Company Limited

St Paul's House
Broad Street
Canterbury
Kent CT1 2LY
0227-457375

Citibank Life

(Formerly British National Life Assurance Company Limited)
21-23 Perrymount Road
Hayward`s Heath
West Sussex RH16 3TP
Tel: 0444-414111 Fax: 0444-419337
INVESTMENT MANAGER: Richard Balmer
(Sept 1992)
SIZE OF PROPERTY PORTFOLIO: £1.2m (1986)
PROPERTY PORTFOLIO: Quoted Shares 100%
INVESTMENT POLICY: Quoted Shares only
(Jan 1991)

City of Westminster Assurance Company Limited

Sentry House
500 Avebury Boulevard
Saxon Gate West
Central Milton Keynes MK9 2NU
0908-690888

Clerical Medical Investment Group

15 St James's Square
London SW1Y 4LQ
Tel: 071-930 5474 Fax: 071-321 1846
INVESTMENT MANAGER: Mr R Walther
(Sept 1992)
SIZE OF PROPERTY PORTFOLIO: £279.9m (1986)
PROPERTY PORTFOLIO: offices 50%; shops 45%; factories/warehouses 40%; science/hi-tech 1%
INVESTMENT POLICY: Unit shops in market towns central west end/city offices. Retail warehouses in south. Industrial on western approaches M25
(Jan 1991)

Co-operative Insurance Society Limited

Miller Street
Manchester M60 0AL
061-832 8686

Colonial Mutual Group

Dominican House
Priory Court
Pilgrim Street
London EC4
Tel: 071-329 3838 Fax 071-489 9409
(Sept 1992)
PROPERTY INVESTMENT MANAGER(S): E H Borrill MCIT FRICS
SIZE OF PROPERTY PORTFOLIO: £190m (1990)
DISTRIBUTION OF PORTFOLIO (BY VALUE): Offices 46%; retail 28%; industrial 25%; other 1%
(Jan 1991)

Commercial Union Group

St Helens
1 Undershaft
London EC3P 3DQ
071-283 7500
(Commercial Union Properties Limited)
Schomberg House, 80-82 Pall Mall, London SWIY 5HF
Tel: 071-283 7500 Fax: 071-930 3844 Telex: 887626
OFFICE MANAGER: R P Locke
SIZE OF PROPERTY PORTFOLIO: £900m (1991)
INVESTMENT POLICY: Highly selective to maximise returns of holding funds
(Sept 1992)

Entry missing ? Call HELPLINE Page v

Confederation Life Assurance Company Limited
(UK Head Office)
Lytton Way
Stevenage
Hertfordshire SG1 2NN
Tel: 0438-741741 Fax: 0438-744999
Telex: 825037 CONFEDG
PROPERTY MANAGER: Mr Jonathan Tate
(Sept 1992)

Cornhill Insurance plc
32 Cornhill
London EC3V 3LJ
071-626 5410

Credit and Commerce Life Assurance Limited
74 Shepherd's Bush Green
London W12 8SD
01-740 7070

Criterion Insurance Company
Swan Court
Petersfield
Hampshire GU32 3AF
0730-63281

Crown Financial Management Limited
Duke Court
Duke Street
Woking
Surrey GU21 5XW
Tel: 0483-715033 Fax: 0483-720718
INVESTMENT MANAGER: Stuart Fraser
(Sept 1992)
SIZE OF PROPERTY PORTFOLIO: £20.63m (1988)
CROWN LIFE ASSURANCE COMPANY FUND: £10.445m
PROPERTY PORTFOLIO: offices 42%; shops 24%; industrial 12%; retail warehouse 22%
CROWN LIFE PENSIONS FUND: £10.185m
PROPERTY PORTFOLIO: offices 23%; retail 32%; industrial 4.5%; hi-tech 10%; business use 30.5%
(Jan 1991)

Crusader Insurance plc
Crusader House
Reigate
Surrey RH2 8BL
07372-42424

Devonshire Life
29 Glasshouse Street
London W1R 5RG
071-434 3511

Eagle Star Insurance Company
60 St Mary Avenue
London EC3A
071-929 1111

Ecclesiastical Insurance Office plc
Beaufort House
Brunswick Road
Gloucester GL1 1JZ
0452-28533

Equitable Life Assurance Society
4 Coleman Street
London EC2R 5AP
Tel: 071-606 6611 Fax: 071-796 4824
INVESTMENT MANAGERS: C L Winter - Chief Surveyor; G R Lauder - Deputy Chief Surveyor; P R Bates - Senior Management Surveyor.
SIZE OF PROPERTY PORTFOLIO: £750m (1991)
PROPERTY PORTFOLIO: Offices 48%; retail 34%; industrial/warehouses 17%
POLICY: Investment for long term rental and capital growth in all categories and sectors
(Sept 1992)

Equity and Law Life Assurance Society plc
20 Lincoln's Inn Fields
London WC2A 3ES
071-242 6844

Eurolife Assurance Group
Eurolife House
16 St John Street
London EC1M 4AY
Tel: 071-454 1151 Fax: 071-454 1277

Family Assurance Society
17 West Street
Brighton
East Sussex BN1 2RL
INVESTMENT DIRECTOR: Mr Christopher Edge
(Sept 1992)
CONSULTANT(S): Hartnell Taylor Cook, 35 Bruton St, London W1
SIZE OF PROPERTY PORTFOLIO: £6m (1987)
PROPERTY PORTFOLIO: offices 100%
INVESTMENT POLICY: Very flexible - up to 15% of total funds may be invested in property
(Jan 1991)

Federation Mutual Insurance Limited
1st Floor
Suffolk House
College Road
Croydon CR0 1PF
081-686 5685

Friends' Provident Life Office
Pixham End
Dorking
Surrey RH4 1QA
Tel: 0306-740123 Fax: 0306-886463 Telex 859262
INVESTMENT MANAGER: D J M Doubble
SIZE OF PROPERTY PORTFOLIO: Approx.£1,000m (1992)

PROPERTY PORTFOLIO: offices 57.6%; shops 23.4%; industrial 6.8%; residential 0.4%; shops/offices 11.9%; land 0.1%
INVESTMENT POLICY: On-going long term commitment to property
(Sept 1992)

FS Assurance Limited

190 West George Street
Strathclyde G2 2PA
041-332 6462

General Accident Fire & Life Assurance Corporation plc

Pitheavlis
Perth
Scotland PH2 0NH
Tel: 0738-21202 Fax: 0738-21843
(Sept 1992)
DEPUTY INVESTMENT MANAGER: D S Hay
SIZE OF PROPERTY PORTFOLIO: £586.7m (1988)
(Jan 1991)

General Portfolio Life Insurance plc

General Portfolio House
Harlow
Essex CM20 2EW
0279-626262
ASSOCIATED DIRECTOR: John Waller
(Sept 1992)

Growth and Security Life Assurance Society

23 Boltro Road
Hayward`s Heath
West Sussex RH16 1XJ
Tel: 0444-413307 Fax: 0444-450514

GT Management Limited

8th Floor
8 Devonshire Square
London EC2M 4YJ
071-283 2575

Guardian Royal Exchange Assurance plc

Royal Exchange
London EC3V 3LS
Tel: 071-283 7101 Fax: 071-629 1515
(Sept 1992)
PROPERTY INVESTMENT: £656.1m (1986)
(Jan 1991)
Subsidiary Co:
GUARDIAN ROYAL EXCHANGE PROPERTIES:
17 Bruton Street, London W1X 7AH
Tel: 071-493 9596 Fax: 071-629 1515
PROPERTY INVESTMENT MANAGER: Martyn Baker BSc FRICS
SIZE OF PROPERTY PORTFOLIO: £800m (1992)
PROPERTY PORTFOLIO: Mixed: Offices, Retail and Industrial
NORMAL INVESTMENT POLICY: Constantly being updated
SISTER COMPANY: Aquis Securities plc
(Sept 1992)

Hearts of Oak Insurance Group

84 Kingsway
London WC2B 6NF
071-404 0393

Henderson Administration Group plc

3 Finsbury Avenue
London EC2M 2PA
071-638 5757

Hill Samuel Investment Service Group Limited

NLA Tower
12-16 Addiscombe Road
Croydon
Surrey CR9 6BP
Tel: 081-686 4355 Fax: 081-681 1194
SENIOR PROPERTY MANAGER: Mr Gregory
PROPERTY INVESTMENT: £50m (1987)
(Jan 1991)

Irish Life Assurance Company plc

Irish Life Centre
Lower Abbey Street
Dublin 1
Ireland
0001-704 2000
(Sept 1992)
PROPERTY INVESTMENT MANAGER: Sean O'Brien BEARICS
Property Division
SIZE OF PROPERTY PORTFOLIO: £500m (1990)
DISTRIBUTION OF PORTFOLIO (BY VALUE): Offices 65%; retail 25%; industrial 10%
NORMAL INVESTMENT POLICY: Prime CBD commercial investments and developments
(Jan 1991)

Iron Trades Insurance Group

Iron Trades House
21/24 Grosvenor Place
London SW1X 7JA
Tel: 071-235 6033 Fax: 071-245 6308
INVESTMENT MANAGER: J M Hovey FCCA
INVESTMENT CONSULTANT: J D Wood
(Sept 1992)
SIZE OF PROPERTY PORTFOLIO: £54.5m (1989)
DISTRIBUTION OF PORTFOLIO: Shop 10.4%, retail warehouse 2%, offices 87.2%, residential 0.4%
INVESTMENT POLICY: Emphasis on Offices
(Jan 1991)

Kleinwort Benson Investment Management

20 Fenchurch Street
London EC3P 3DB
071-623 8000

Kleinwort Benson Property Pension Fund
20 Fenchurch Street
London EC3P 3DB
071-623 8000

Knight Williams & Company Limited
161 New Bond Street
London WIY OLA
071-408 1138

Langham Life Assurance Company Limited
Langham House
Holmbrook Drive
London NW4 2NX
071-203 5211

Laspen Property Fund
The LAS Group (Life Association of Scotland)
10 George Street
Edinburgh EH2 2YH
031-225 8494

Laurentian Life Property Fund
Laurentian Fund Management Ltd
Laurentian House
Barnwood
Gloucester GL4 7RZ
Tel: 061-941 3499 Fax: 061-928 9515
PROPERTY INVESTMENT MANAGERS: Castlemere Property Group Ltd (Fund Manager)
PROPERTY INVESTMENT CONSULTANTS: Castlemere Property Group Ltd
REGIONAL OFFICES: 12 Oxford Road, Altrincham, Cheshire WA14 2EB
SIZE OF PROPERTY PORTFOLIO: £53m (1992)
DISTRIBUTION OF PORTFOLIO: Offices 51.3%; retail 34.7%; Mixed 8.5%; Industrial 5.5%;
NORMAL INVESTMENT POLICY: Opportunistic industrial element likely to increase.
(Sept 1992)

Legal & General Group plc
Temple Court
11 Queen Victoria Street
London EC4N 4TP
Tel: 071-528 6200 Fax: 071-528 6222
LEGAL AND GENERAL LIFE ASSURANCE FUND
MANAGING DIRECTOR OF INVESTMENTS: Mr David Rough
(Sept 1992)
SIZE OF PROPERTY PORTFOLIO: £650m (1988)
(Jan 1991)

Liberty Life Assurance Company Limited
Liberty House
Station Road
New Barnet
Hertfordshire EN5 1PA
081-440 8210

Life Association of Scotland Limited
113 Dundee Street
Edinburgh EH3 5EB
Tel: 031-550 5000 Fax: 031-550 5123
INVESTMENT MANAGER: Robin Binnie BSc ARICS
INVESTMENT CONSULTANTS: Edward Erdman, Jones Lang Wooton
REGIONAL OFFICES: UK Network
(Sept 1992)

Liverpool Victoria Insurance
Southampton Row
London WC1B 4DB
Tel: 071-405 4377 Fax: 071-430 0078
INVESTMENT DIRECTOR: Mr T S B Philpot FSA
INVESTMENT CONSULTANTS: Mr P McLafferty, Mr R S Humphreys
SIZE OF PROPERTY PORTFOLIO: £500m (1991)

Lloyds Life Assurance Limited
20 Clifton Street
London EC2A 4HX
071-920 0202

London & Manchester Assurance Company Limited
Winslade Park
Exeter
Devon EX5 1DS
0392-52155

London & Manchester Property Funds
(London & Manchester Assurance Company Limited)
Winslade Park
Exeter
Devon EX5 1DS
0392-52155

London, Aberdeen & Northern Mutual Assurance
84 Kingsway
London WC2B 6NF
071-404 0393

London Indemnity & General Insurance Company Limited
18-20 The Forbury
Reading
Berkshire
0734-583511

London Life Assurance Limited
215 Bishopsgate
London EC2M 3XX
071-377 0660

M & G Assurance Group Limited
M & G House
Victoria Road
Chelmsford CM1 1FB
Tel: 0245-266266 Fax: 0245-267789
PROPERTY MANAGER: Mr Eills
(Sept 1992)
M & G PROPERTY BONDS
SIZE OF PROPERTY PORTFOLIO: £10.4m (1989)
INVESTMENT POLICY: To invest in first class industrial and commercial properties occupied by tenants of high reliability
(Jan 1991)

Manufacturers Life Insurance Company (UK) Limited
Manulife House
St George's Way
Stevenage, Hertfordshire SG1 1HP
0438-356101

Medical Sickness Annuity & Life Assurance Society Limited
7-10 Chandos Street
Cavendish Square
London W1M 9DE
Tel: 071-636 1686 Fax: 071-637 1048
INVESTMENT MANAGER: Christopher Dawson
(Sept 1992)
SIZE OF PROPERTY PORTFOLIO: £100m
(Jan. 1991)

Mercantile & General Reinsurance Company plc
Moorfields House
Moorfields
London EC2Y 9AL
Tel: 071-628 7070 Fax: 071-588 4629
(Sept 1992)
PROPERTY MANAGER: R O Lofts FRICS
PROPERTY PORTFOLIO: offices 50%; shops 25%; factories/warehouses 5%; agriculture 20%
(Jan 1991)

Merchant Investors Assurance Company Limited
83 Parkside
Wimbledon
London SW19 5LP
081-788 8000

MGM Assurance
MGM House
Heene Road
Worthing
West Sussex BN11 2DY
0903-204631

Municipal Life Assurance Limited
1 Sessions House Square
Maidstone
Kent ME14 1XX
0622-690555

National Employers' Life Assurance Company Limited
Milton Court
Dorking
Surrey RH4 3LZ
0306-887766

National Farmers Union Mutual & Avon Insurance Group
Tiddington Road
Stratford-upon-Avon
Warwickshire CV37 7BJ
Tel: 0789-204211 Fax 0789-298992
INVESTMENT MANAGER: R Martin ARICS
SIZE OF PROPERTY PORTFOLIO: £250m (1990)
PROPERTY PORTFOLIO: offices 50%; shops 40%; industrial 10%
NORMAL INVESTMENT POLICY: Prime shops, high quality distribution warehouses in Midlands and North, good modern well let offices
SUBSIDIARY DEVELOPMENT COMPANIES: Harvester Properties Limited
OTHER MAJOR SUBSIDIARIES: Knights Property Company Ltd.

National Mutual Life
The Priory
Priory Park
Hitchin
Hertfordshire SG5 2DW
Tel: 0462-422422 Fax: 0462-420010
INVESTMENT MANAGER: Mr Jeremy Bishop
(Sept 1992)
SIZE OF PROPERTY PORTFOLIO: £100m (1987)
PROPERTY & DISTRIBUTION: retail 9%; offices 83%; industrial/warehouse 8%
(Jan 1991)

National Mutual Schroder Life Assurance Limited
Enterprise House
Isambard Brunel Road
Portsmouth PO1 2AW
Tel: 0705-827733 Fax: 0705-830216
PROPERTY INVESTMENT MANAGER: Mr Parrett
(Sept 1992)
RESIDENTIAL PROPERTY FUND:
SIZE OF PROPERTY PORTFOLIO: £21m (1988)
NM SCHRODER PROPERTY FUND:
SIZE OF PROPERTY PORTFOLIO £15m (1988)
PROPERTY PORTFOLIO: shops 43%; offices 21%; industrial 30%; agriculture 2%
INVESTMENT POLICY: a fund for individuals via insurance and pension contracts
(Jan 1991)

National Provident Institution
PO Box 227
48 Gracechurch Street
London EC3P 3HH
Tel: 071-623 4200 Fax: 071-280 3380
PROPERTY INVESTMENT MANAGER: Miss P A L Craddock
SIZE OF PROPERTY PORTFOLIO: £450m (1991)
(Sept 1992)

New Zealand Insurance plc

110/114 Baster Avenue
Southend
Essex SS2 6FF
0702 344555

Norwich Union Group

Surrey Street
Norwich
Norfolk NR1 3NS
Tel: 0603-622200 Fax: 0603-683659
ESTATES MANAGER: Mr N Price
(Sept 1992)
NORWICH UNION INSURANCE GROUP (PENSIONS MANAGEMENT) LIMITED
NORWICH UNION INSURANCE GROUP (MANAGED FUNDS) LIMITED
NORWICH UNION FIRE INSURANCE SOCIETY
SIZE OF PROPERTY PORTFOLIO: £5 Billion
INVESTMENT CONSULTANT: In house, with agents selected as appropriate
PROPERTY PORTFOLIO: offices; shops; factories/warehouses
INVESTMENT POLICY: Continue to seek good development, funding and investment opportunities
(Jan 1991)

Pearl Assurance plc

55 Moorgate
London EC2R 6PA
Tel: 071-638 1717 Fax: 071-638 0405
PROPERTY INVESTMENT MANAGER: Mr J Whalley
(Sept 1992)
SIZE OF PROPERTY PORTFOLIO: £1475m (1989)
(Jan 1991)

Phoenix Assurance Company Limited

1 Bartholomew Lane
London EC2N 2AB
071-588 2345

Pinnacle Insurance Company Limited

Woodchester House
Seldson Way
London E14 9GL
081-801 3361

Pioneer Mutual Insurance Company Limited

16 Crosby Road
North Waterloo
Liverpool
Merseyside L22 0NY
051-928 6655

Premium Life Assurance Company Limited

37-39 Perrymount Road
Hayward`s Heath
West Sussex RH16 3BN
Tel: 0444-458721 Fax: 0444-452561
(Sept 1992)
SIZE OF PROPERTY PORTFOLIO: £3.3m (1.6.89)
PROPERTY PORTFOLIO: offices 41%; shops 28%; warehouses 7%; other 25%
INVESTMENT POLICY: seeking opportunities for redevelopment schemes, primarily non-residential
PROPERTY INVESTMENT MANAGER: A Iremonger
(Jan 1991)

Prolific Life & Pensions Limited

Stramongate
Kendal
Cumbria LA9 4UB
0539-733733

Property Equity & Life Assurance Company Limited

Baxter Avenue
Southend-on-Sea
Essex SS2 6HQ
0702-333433

Property Growth Assurance Company Limited

1 Bartholomew Lane
London EC2N 2AB
071-588 2345

Providence Capitol Life Property Pension Fund

Providence House
2 Bartley Way
Hook
Nr Basingstoke
Hampshire RG27 9XA
Tel: 0256-768888 Fax: 0256-768804
INVESTMENT CONTACT: John Gordon
(Sept 1992)

Provident Life Association (of London) Limited

Provident Way
Basingstoke R21 2FZ
0256-470707

Provident Mutual Life Assurance Association

25-31 Moorgate
London EC2R 6BA
Tel: 071-628 3232 Fax: 071-628 3238
SENIOR PROPERTY MANAGER: N A Hill ARICS
(Sept 1992)
SIZE OF PROPERTY PORTFOLIO: £850m (1989)
(Jan 1991)

Provincial Life Assurance Company Limited

5-10 Berry Street
London EC3A 5AT
Tel: 071-247 6533 Fax: 071-626 1631

Provincial Life Property Pension Accumulation Fund

Provincial Life Assurance Company Limited
222 Bishopsgate
London EC2N 4JS
071-247 6533

Prudential Assurance Company Limited

1 Stephen Street
London WIP 2AP
071-405 9222

Prudential Holborn Life & Pensions

Kings Reach
28-50 Kings Road
Reading RG1 3AA
Tel: 0734-391101 Fax: 0734-509117
(Sept 1992)
INVESTMENT MANAGER: Prudential Portfolio Managers
SIZE OF PROPERTY PORTFOLIO: £51.8m (Jan 1988)
PROPERTY PORTFOLIO: Offices 27.7%; shops 60.9%; factories 11.4%
(Jan 1991)

Refuge Assurance & Investments plc

Refuge House
Alderley Road
Wilmslow
Cheshire SK9 1PF
0625-535959
INVESTMENT MANAGER: Mr Gerrity

Regency Life Assurance Company Limited

Lanark Square
Cross Harbour
London
071-538 8800

Reliance Mutual Insurance Society Limited

Reliance House
76 Mount Ephraim
Tunbridge Wells
Kent TN4 8BL
0892-22271
INVESTMENT MANAGER: A Foulkes

Royal Heritage Life Assurance Limited

Bretton
Peterborough PE3
0733-262524

Royal Insurance (UK) Limited

New Hall Place
Liverpool L69 3EN
051 227 4422

Royal Insurance plc

1 Cornhill
London EC3V 3QR
Tel: 071-283 4300 Fax: 071-623 5282
(Sept 1992)
PROPERTY MANAGER: G F Linehan
INVESTMENT CONSULTANTS: St Quintin; Hillier Parker May & Rowden
SIZE OF PROPERTY PORTFOLIO: £950m (1987)
PROPERTY PORTFOLIO: offices 40%; shops 40%; factories/warehouses/science parks/hi-tech 20%
INVESTMENT POLICY: Upwards of £60m pa
(Jan 1991)

Royal London Mutual Insurance Society Limited

Royal London House
27 Middlesborough
Colchester
Essex CO1 1RA
Tel: 0206-761761 Fax: 0206-761693
PROPERTY INVESTMENT MANAGER: N C S Robson BSc (Hons), ARICS
PROPERTY INVESTMENT CONSULTANTS: Royal London Asset Management Ltd.
SIZE OF PROPERTY PORTFOLIO: £385m (1991)
DISTRIBUTION OF PROPERTY PORTFOLIO: Offices 50%; Industrial 20%; Retail 15%; Hi-tech 7%; Warehousing 6%; Land 2%
NORMAL INVESTMENT POLICY: Development, redevelopment and countercyclical aquisition of high quality commercial and industrial properties.
OTHER MAJOR SUBSIDIARIES: Royal London General Insurance; Lion Insurance.
(Sept 1992)

Save & Prosper Insurance Limited

(Save & Prosper Group Limited)
1 Finsbury Avenue
London EC2M 2QY
Tel: 071-588 1717 Fax 071-831 4040
(Sept 1992)
INVESTMENT MANAGER: John Stuart BSc ARICS
INVESTMENT CONSULTANT: Healey & Baker
(Jan 1991)

Save & Prosper Property Fund

(Save & Prosper Group Limited)
1 Finsbury Avenue
London EC2M 2QY
Tel: 071-588 1717 Fax: 071-831 4040
(Sept 1992)
SIZE OF PROPERTY PORTFOLIO: £59m (1989)
PROPERTY PORTFOLIO: Offices 7.9%; shops 60.8%; warehouses 7.9%; retail warehouses 9.4%; cash 14%
(Jan 1991)

Scottish Amicable Life Assurance Company

150 St. Vincent Place
Glasgow G2 5NQ
Tel: 041-248 2323 Fax: 041-221 4762
INVESTMENT MANAGER: Mr D I Hunter
(Sept 1992)
SIZE OF PROPERTY PORTFOLIO: £1,000m (1989)
PROPERTY PORTFOLIO: offices 43%; shops 24%; warehouses 20%; other 13%
INVESTMENT POLICY: Seeking investments which offer good rental/capital growth prospects or which offer attractive management opportunities
(Jan 1991)

Entry missing ? Call HELPLINE Page v

Scottish Equitable Life Assurance Society
28 St Andrew Square
Edinburgh EH2 1YF
031-556 9101
PROPERTY INVESTMENT MANAGER: M Jackson
SIZE OF PROPERTY PORTFOLIO: £200m (1/1/92)
PROPERTY PORTFOLIO: offices 51%; shops 32%; industrial 15%; other 2%
(Sept 1992)

Scottish Life Investments
19 St Andrew Square
Edinburgh EH2 1YE
Tel: 031-225 2211 Fax: 031-226 6155
PROPERTY MANAGER: R C Pugh
(Sept 1992)
SIZE OF PROPERTY PORTFOLIO: £200m (1988)
SCOTTISH LIFE MAIN FUND: £190m
FUND: offices 63%; shops 20%; industrial 9%; hi-tech 6%; farms 2%
SCOTTISH LIFE PENSIONS ANNUITY COMPANY LIMITED PROPERTY FUND
PROPERTY PORTFOLIO: £10.35m
PROPERTY PORTFOLIO: retail 46%; offices 31%; industrial 10%; other 13%
SCOTTISH LIFE INVESTMENT ASSURANCE COMPANY LIMITED PROPERTY FUND: £3.65m
FUND: retail 46%; offices 43%; industrial 11%
(Jan 1991)

Scottish Mutual Assurance Society
109 Vincent Street
Glasgow G2 5HN
Tel: 041-248 6321 Fax: 041-221 1230

Scottish Provident Institution
6 St Andrew Square
Edinburgh EH2 2YA
Tel: 031-556 9181 Fax: 081 558 2486
PROPERTY INVESTMENT MANAGER: E P Coupe FRICS
SIZE OF PROPERTY PORTFOLIO: £324m (1991)
DISTRIBUTION OF PORTFOLIO: Office 40%; Retail 43%; Industrial 25%; Others 27%
(Sept 1992)

Scottish Widows Fund & Life Assurance Society
15 Dalkeith Road
Edinburgh EH16 5BU
Tel: 031-655 6000 Fax: 031-662 4053
PROPERTY INVESTMENT MANAGER: Tom Laidlow
(Sept 1992)
MAIN LIFE FUND SIZE: £6.7bn (1990)
PROPERTY PORTFOLIO: £716m
DISTRIBUTION: shops 16%; offices 75%; industrial/warehouses 8%
PROPERTY PORTFOLIO: £45m
DISTRIBUTION: Retail 38%; offices 50%; industrial/warehouses 12%
SCOTTISH WIDOWS UNIT FUNDS: £900m
(Jan.1991)

Sentinel Life plc
2 Eyre Street Hill
London EC1R 5AE
071-278 4488

Skandia Life Assurance Company Limited
Frobisher House
Nelson Gate
Southampton
0703-334411

Stalwart Assurance Company Limited
Stalwart House
142 South Street
Dorking
Surrey RH4 2EU
Tel: 0306-876581 Fax: 0306-888717
SALES DIRECTOR: W M McLay
PROPERTY INVESTMENT MANAGER(S): Internal
PROPERTY INVESTMENT CONSULTANTS: Internal
SIZE OF PROPERTY PORTFOLIO: £70m (1991)
DISTRIBUTION OF PORTFOLIO (BY VALUE): 100% residential
NORMAL INVESTMENT POLICY: Purchase of reversionary interest
(Sept 1992)

Standard Life Assurance Company
3 George Street
Edinburgh EH2 2XZ
031-225 2552

Sun Alliance Insurance Group
1 Bartholomew Lane
London EC2N 2AB
Tel: 071-588 2345 Fax: 071-826 1159
INVESTMENT MANAGER: M Dew BSc FRICS
(Sept 1992)
SIZE OF PROPERTY PORTFOLIO: £1,342.1m (1988)
PROPERTY PORTFOLIO: Offices 66%; shops 18%; industrial 14%; agricultural 1%; other 1%
INVESTMENT POLICY ON BEHALF OF: Sun Alliance & London Assurance Company; Sun Alliance Pension Fund; Sun Alliance Pensions Limited; Sun Alliance Linked Life Assurance; Phoenix Life
(Jan 1991)
(Sun Alliance Property Group)
25 Floral Street
Covent Garden
London WC2E 9BU
Tel: 071-836 1211 Fax: 071-836 5124
PROPERTY MANAGER: M Dew BSc FRICS
(Sept 1992)

Sun Life Assurance Company of Canada
Burdett House
15 Buckingham Street
London WC2N 6DU
Tel: 071-925 0030 Fax: 071-930 5250
(Sept 1992)
INVESTMENT MANAGERS: Paul Neil Bellack FSVA Senior Officer; Warwick Kelvin Hoyle FRICS Assistant Vice President

SIZE OF PROPERTY PORTFOLIO: £350m (1990)
PROPERTY PORTFOLIO: shops 25%; offices 40%; warehouses/ factories 35%
INVESTMENT POLICY: Commercial Property from £1m - £15m giving above average returns
(Jan 1991)

Sun Life Unit Assurance Limited

Property Investment Department
107 Cheapside
London EC2V 6DU
071-606 7788
SIZE OF PROPERTY PORTFOLIO: £14.1m (1988)
PROPERTY PORTFOLIO: office 9.46%; retail 60.34%; industrial/warehouses 11.79%; other 18.41%

Swiss Life (UK) plc

PO Box 127
101 London Road
Sevenoaks
Kent TN13 1BG
Tel: 0732-450161 Fax: 0732-463801
(Sept 1992)
PROPERTY INVESTMENT MANAGER(S): T McIntosh
SIZE OF PROPERTY PORTFOLIO: £1,444,420 (Jan 1991)
DISTRIBUTION OF PORTFOLIO (BY VALUE): All property shares/cash
REGIONAL SALES OFFICES: London 071-734 8822
Manchester 061-834 6283
(Jan. 1991)

Terra Nova Insurance Company Limited

Terra Nova House
41-43 Mincing Lane
London EC3R 7SP
071-283 3000

Transinternational Life Insurance Company Limited

55-57 High Holborn
London WC1N 6DU
071-831 7481

TSB Insurance plc

Charlton Place
Andover
Hampshire SP10 1RE
Tel: 0264-345678 Fax: 0264-346844
(Sept 1992)
INVESTMENT MANAGER: R Dismorr
TSB GROUP PENSION FUND SIZE OF PROPERTY PORTFOLIO: £236m (1989)
PROPERTY PORTFOLIO: offices 33%; shops 30%; retail warehousing 9%; industrial 14%; hi-tech 3%; US offices 12%
(Jan 1991)

Tunbridge Wells Equitable

Abbey Court
Tunbridge Wells
Kent
0882-41466

United Friendly Insurance plc

42 Southwark Bridge Road
London SE1 9HE
071-928 5644

University Life Assurance Society

4 Coleman Street
London EC2R 5AP
Tel: 071-606 6611 Fax 071-796 4824

Victory Re-insurance Company Limited, NRG

Victory House
Castle Hill Avenue
Folkestone
Kent CT20 2TF
Tel: 0303-851234 Fax: 0303-850145 (General) Telex 965231

Western Australian Insurance Company Limited

Swan Court
Mansel Road
Wimbledon
London SW19 4AA
081-946 7777

Windsor Life Assurance Company Limited

Windsor House
Telford Centre
Telford TF3 4NB
0952 292929

Chapter 8

Property Unit Trusts

Index

A

B

C

D

F

G

H

I

K

L

M

N

P

S

T

U

W

Abbotstone Agricultural Property Unit Trust

155 Bishopsgate
London EC2M 3XY
Tel: 071-628 6000 Fax: 071-214 1630
SIZE OF PROPERTY PORTFOLIO: £13m (Jan 1992)
PROPERTY PORTFOLIO: Agricultural 73.7%; cash 26.3%
INVESTMENT POLICY: Active search for agricultural investment properties throughout England with substantial funds available
INVESTMENT COMMITTEE: Dr J R G Bradfield CBE (Chairman); T G Abell; C J Bartram FRICS; G N Mainwaring FRICS; O B Harris FCA; A J Sheppeck FCA ATII
PROPERTY INVESTMENT CONSULTANTS: Smiths Gore
(Sept 1992)

Aetna Financial & Property Unit Trust

Aetna Life Assurance Company Limited
85 London Wall
London EC2M 7AD
071-454 7900

Allied Dunbar Property Funds Limited

9-15 Sackville Street
London W1H 2JP
Tel: 071-434 3211 Fax: 071-494 2377

American Property Trust

43/44 Crutched Friars
London EC3N 2NX
071-374 3000

Arbuthnot Securities Limited

131 Finsbury Pavement
Moorgate
London EC2A 1AY
071-628 9876
ARBUTHNOT FINANCE & PROPERTY SHARE FUND:
FUND MANAGER: Christopher Bomford
INVESTMENT POLICY: Invests in carefully selected areas of property and financial sectors of UK equity market aimed at sustained capital growth
INVESTMENT MANAGER: P Ashley Miller

Barclays Unicorn Limited

Gredley House
11 Broadway
London E15 4BJ
081-534 5544
(Sept 1992)
BARCLAYS UNICORN FINANCIAL TRUST:
Financial and Property Shares:
Value: £86.9m (1986)
INVESTMENT POLICY: Long term capital and income growth
INVESTMENT MANAGER: Robin Evans
INVESTMENT CONSULTANTS: International Barclays Investment Management
(Jan 1991)

Brown Shipley Unit Trust Managers Limited

Founders Court
Lothbury
London EC2R 7HE
071-606 9833
(Sept 1992)
BROWN SHIPLEY FINANCIAL FUND
VALUE: £2m (Jan 1991)
MANAGER: Michael Beggs
(Jan 1991)

Charities Official Investment Fund

St Alphage House
2 Fore Street
London EC2Y 5AU
071-588 1815
PROPERTY INVESTMENT MANAGER: The Viscount Churchill
SIZE OF PROPERTY PORTFOLIO: £12m (1989)
CHIEF SURVEYOR: J McAuslan FRICS

Church Charity & Local Authority Fund Managers Limited

(Formerly Central Board of Finance of the Church of England)
St Alphage House
2 Fore Street
London EC2Y 5AQ
071-588 1815
SIZE OF PROPERTY PORTFOLIO: £130m (1991)
CHIEF SURVEYOR: J McAuslan FRICS
(Sept 1992)

Cornhill Property Share

Cornhill Insurance plc
32 Cornhill
London EC3V 3LJ

County Unit Trust Managers Limited

161 Cheapside
London EC2V 6EU
071-726 1000
Acquired by MIM Britannia Unit Trust Managers Limited on 28.9.87

Dunedin Fund Managers Limited

Dunedin House
25 Rauglston Terrace
Edinburgh EH4 3EX
Tel: 031-315 2500 Fax: 031-315 2222

Falcon Property Trust

(Formerly Charities Property Unit Trust)
41 Tower Hill
London EC3N 4HA
Tel: 071-480 5000 Fax: 071-702 9263
PROPERTY INVESTMENT MANAGER: Falcon's property committee

TRUSTEE: Hambros Trust Company
SIZE OF PROPERTY PORTFOLIO: £22m (1992)
DISTRIBUTION OF PORTFOLIO: Offices 59%; industrial 11%; retail 24%; agricultural 3%; minerals 3%
INVESTMENT POLICY: Mixture of retail/office/industrial (Sept 1992)

First International Property Trust
Sallmanns Management Limited
20 Regent Street
London SWIY 4PH
Tel: 071-409222 Fax: 071-930 2262

Fleming American Property Unit Trust
8 Crosby Square,
London EC3A 6AN
071-638 5858

Fleming Property Unit Trust
8 Crosby Square
London EC3A 6AN
071-638 5858

Guardian Royal Exchange Unit Managers Limited
155 Bishopsgate
London EC2M 3XY
071-628 6000

Gulliver Development Property Unit Trust
155 Bishopsgate
London EC2M 3XY
Tel: 071-628 6000 Fax: 071-214 1630
SIZE OF PROPERTY PORTFOLIO: £27.6m (Dec 1991)
PROPERTY PORTFOLIO: Offices 35.6%; shops 35%; cash and investments 29.4%
INVESTMENT POLICY: To buy and manage properties where there is refurbishment or redevelopment potential
COMMITTEE OF MANAGEMENT: Committee - D M Pickford FRICS (Chairman), C H V Collins, M P Herring, M D Reeder FCIS FCIB, E Wetherburn IPFA
INVESTMENT CONSULTANTS: Baring Houston & Saunders

Hambro Generali Fund Managers Limited
41 Tower Hill
London EC3N 4HA
071-480 5000

Hammerson Property & Investment Trust
100 Park Lane
London
W1Y 4AR
071-629 9494

Hanover Property Unit Trust
11 Devonshire Square
London EC2M 4YR
Tel: 071-626 3434 Fax: 01-621 1221
SIZE OF PROPERTY PORTFOLIO: £130m (1992)
PROPERTY PORTFOLIO: offices 38.3%; shops 35.3%; factories/warehouses 26.4%
INVESTMENT POLICY: Investment management approach is research driven and aimed at producing a balanced portfolio of commercial and industrial properties. Emphasis on buying for value and managing for performance
INVESTMENT MANAGERS/CONSULTANTS: MIM Property Services

Henderson Unit Trust Management Limited
3 Finsbury Avenue
London EC2M 2PA
071-638 5757 (BT)
071-410 4100 (Mercury)

Hill Samuel Agricultural Property Unit Trust
45 Beech Street
London EC2P 2LX
071-628 8011

Hill Samuel Property Unit Trust
45 Beech Street
London EC2P 2LX
071-638 1774

Hill Samuel Unit Trust Managers Limited
NLA Tower
12-16 Addiscombe Road
Croydon CR9 6BP
081-686 4355

Irish Pension Property Unit Trust
88 Lower Leeson Street
Dublin
010 351 3531 613499

Kleinwort Benson Property Fund
20 Fenchurch Street
London EC3P 3DB
Tel: 071-283 9846 Fax: 071-626 6318

Lazard Property Unit Trust
21 Moorfields
London EC2P 2HT
Tel: 071-588 2721 Fax: 071-638 2165
SIZE OF PROPERTY PORTFOLIO: £134.13m (1992)
PROPERTY PORTFOLIO: offices 31.6%; shops 41.4%, industrial/warehouse 23.6%; retail warehouse 3.4%
PROPERTY INVESTMENT MANAGERS: Lazard Brother & Company Limited (M J Crouch FRICS)
PROPERTY INVESTMENT CONSULTANTS: Pepper Angliss & Yarwood
NORMAL INVESTMENT POLICY: Acquisition of commercial property for pension funds and charities and subsequent management
(Sept 1992)

Legal & General Property Fund

Fitzroy House
855 Euston Road
London NW1 2AG
071-388 3211

Lilliput Property Unit Trust

155 Bishopsgate
London EC2M 3XY
Tel: 071-628 6000 Fax: 071-214 1630
SIZE OF PROPERTY PORTFOLIO: £36m (March 1992)
PROPERTY PORTFOLIO: offices 45.3%; shops 35.3%; industrials 12%; cash 7.4%
INVESTMENT POLICY: To buy and manage active management properties
COMMITTEE OF MANAGEMENT: D M Pickford FRICS (Chairman), K S Cliff IPFA, M P Herring, The Hon James Ogilvy, K J Pitcher, M D Reeder FCIS FCIB, P H Wolton MA ARICS
INVESTMENT CONSULTANTS: Baring Houston & Saunders
(Sept 1992)

Local Authorities' Mutual Investment Trust

St Alphage House
2 Fore Street
London EC2Y 5AQ
Tel: 071-588 1815 Fax: 071-588 1815
SIZE OF PROPERTY PORTFOLIO: £107m (1992)
PROPERTY PORTFOLIO: offices 43%; shops 32%; industrial/warehouses 25%
INVESTMENT POLICY: Active management of well diversified portfolio of prime investment properties involving purchasing, selling, rent reviewing to maximise performance for the benefit of unitholders
INVESTMENT MANAGER: John McAuslan FRICS
(Sept 1992)

Mercury Property Fund

33 King William Street
London EC4R 9AS
071 280 2800

MIM Britannia Unit Trust Managers Limited

11 Devonshire Square
London EC2M 4YR
071-626 3434
(Sept 1992)
MIM BRITANNIA FINANCIAL SECURITIES TRUST
FINANCIAL & PROPERTY SHARES VALUE: £21m (1988)
INVESTMENT POLICY: Long term capital and income growth
INVESTMENT MANAGER: Adrian Brown
MIM Britannia Property Shares Trust
PROPERTY SHARES VALUE: £26m (1988)
INVESTMENT POLICY: Long term capital growth
INVESTMENT MANAGER: Adrian Brown
(Jan 1991)

New Court Property Fund

PO Box 528
Five Arrows House
St Swithins Lane
London EC4N 8NR
071-280 5000
SIZE OF PROPERTY PORTFOLIO: £36m (1992)
PROPERTY PORTFOLIO: Offices 44%; Shops 35%; Industrial 21%
INVESTMENT POLICY: Addition to the existing portfolio by way of investments in the size range £1m - £3m
FUND MANAGER: T F H King FRICS
Rothschild Asset Management Limited
(Sept 1992)

North American Property Unit Trust

11 Devonshire Square
London EC2M 4YR
071 626 3646

Norwich Union Investment Management

(Formerly Norwich Union Real Estate Managers Ltd.)
Sentinel House
PO Box 432
37 Surrey Street
Norwich NR1 3PW
Tel: 0603 622200 Fax: 0603 683950
(Sept 1992)

Pan European Property Unit Trust

c/o Invecsesco MIM Management Limited
11 Devonshire Square
London EC2M 4YR
Tel: 071-626 3434 Fax: 071-621 1221
(Sept 1992)
SIZE OF PROPERTY PORTFOLIO: £95m (1989)
PROPERTY PORTFOLIO: West Germany 72.03% (retail 17.48%, offices 54.5%); Belgium 6.15% (retail 6.15%); Spain 21.82% (offices 21.82%)
INVESTMENT POLICY: The only property unit trust investing exclusively in Europe. Current policy is to purchase and manage properties to optimise performance and to target countries and cities in Europe with the best propsect of growth
CONTACT: R M Plummer FRICS
(Jan 1991)

Property Security Investment Trust (PSIT)

Fetcham Park House
Lower Road
Fetcham
Surrey KT22 9HD
Tel: 0372 376155 Fax: 0372 362338
SIZE OF PROPERTY PORTFOLIO: £234m (1992)
OTHER MAJOR (UK) BASED SUBSIDIARIES: PSIT Properties Limited; Louisville Investments; Crusabridge Investments
(Sept 1992)

Public Storage US Property Unit Trust

3 Finsbury Avenue
London EC2M 2PA
071-638 5757

Save & Prosper Group Limited

Sovereign House
16/22 Western Road
Romford
Essex RM1 3LB
Tel: 0708 66966 Fax: 0708 632555
(Sept 1992)

Schroder Exempt Property Unit Trust

36 Old Jewry
London EC2R 8BS
071 382 6000

Schroder Properties Limited

Regina House
5 Queen Street
London EC4N 1SP
071-382 6000

Scottish Mutual Assurance plc

Elphinstone House
61/69 West Regent Street
Glasgow G2 2AE
Tel: 041-248 6321 Fax: 041-353 1724
PROPERTY INVESTMENT MANAGER: David H McKean
SIZE OF PROPERTY PORTFOLIO: £1.3m (1991)
DISTRIBUTION OF PORTFOLIO: Offices 69%; Shops 26%; Industrials 5%
INVESTMENT POLICY: The fund invests mainly in office and shop properties. Up to 10% of the fund may be held in property shares. The fund does not invest in residential properties.
(Sept 1992)

T R Property Investment Trust plc

Mermaid House
2 Puddle Dock
London
EC4V 3AT
Tel: 071-236 6565 Fax: 071-634 0251
PROPERTY INVESTMENT MANAGERS: Peter Duffy/Patrick Bushnell
PROPERTY INVESTMENT CONSULTANTS: Herring Baker Harris
LOCATION OF REGIONAL OFFICES: London
SIZE OF PROPERTY PORTFOLIO: £42m (1992)
DISTRIBUTION OF PORTFOLIO: Retail 4.65%; retail warehouse 13.65%; office 26.9%; industrial warehouse 48.8%; mixed use/other 6.0%
INVESTMENT POLICY: To maintain a spread of investments by sector and geographically but to seek strong and secure income returns
MAJOR SUBSIDIARIES: Trust Union Properties Limited and New England Properties plc are wholly owned subsidiaries which own the properties
(Sept 1992)

Target Trust Managers Limited

Target House
Gatehouse Road
Aylesbury
Buckinghamshire
0296-39400

United Property Unit Trust, The

73 Brook Street
London W1Y 1YE
071-499 7191
VALUE OF PROPERTY PORTFOLIO: £72.5m (1987)
PROPERTY PORTFOLIO: offices 36.6%; shops 30.9%; industrial 13.5%; agriculture 5%; cash 14%
INVESTMENT MANAGER: Morgan Grenfell
(Jan 1991)

Windsor Property Share

Windsor Life Assurance Company Limited
Royal Albert House
Sheet Street
Windsor
Berkshire S14 1BE
0753-841786

Wyvern Property Unit Trust

1 York Place
Regents Park
London NW1 4PU
071-935 4446